Cultural Anthropology

Meghan

Neolithic Revolution

Cultural Anthropology

DANIEL G. BATES

HUNTER COLLEGE,
THE CITY UNIVERSITY OF NEW YORK

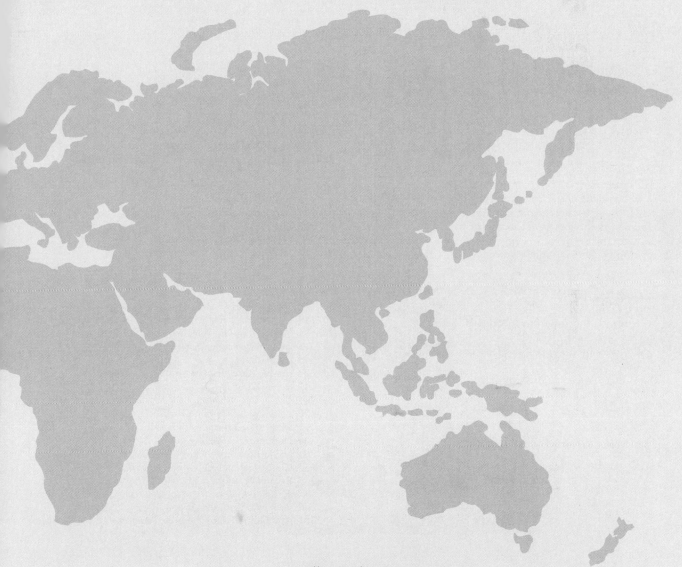

Allyn and Bacon

Boston • London • Toronto • Sydney • Tokyo • Singapore

Vice President: Susan Badger

Executive Editor: Sean W. Wakely

Consulting Editor: Sylvia Shepard

Series Editorial Assistant: Jennifer Normandin

Marketing Manager: Joyce Nilsen

Composition and Prepress Buyer: Linda Cox

Manufacturing Buyer: Megan Cochran

Cover Administrator: Linda Knowles

Photo Researcher: Laurel Anderson/Photosynthesis

Editorial-Production Service: Dustine Davidson/
The Book Company

Text Designer: Wendy LaChance/By Design

Copyright © 1996 by Allyn & Bacon
A Simon & Schuster Company
Needham Heights, Massachusetts 02194

Previously published by McGraw-Hill, Inc.

Library of Congress Cataloging-in-Publication Data

Bates, Daniel G.
    Cultural anthropology / Daniel G. Bates.
        p.   cm.
    Includes bibliographical references and index.
    ISBN 0-205-17224-5
    1. Ethnology   2. Anthropology   I. Title.
GN316.B386 1995
306--dc20   95-25344
                                 CIP

Printed in the United States of America

10 9 8 7 6 5 4 3 2 1   99 98 97 96 95

This book is dedicated to the memory of two friends whose lives
were closely caught up in the excitement of anthropology.
Fred Plog, a distinguished archaeologist;
and Pauline Herrmann, a doctoral student at City University of New York
whose premature death in 1995, shortly after beginning her fieldwork,
has robbed the discipline of a fine scholar.

Contents in Brief

Part I ▶ The Realm of Anthropology

Chapter 1   The Anthropological Perspective 2
Chapter 2   Culture and Language 32
Chapter 3   Decisions, Adaptation, and Evolution 60

Part II ▶ Adaptive Patterns

Chapter 4   Foraging 90
Chapter 5   Subsistence Agriculture 120
Chapter 6   Pastoralism 148
Chapter 7   Intensive and Industrial Agriculture 174

Part III ▶ Cultural Diversity

Chapter 8   Kinship, Marriage, and the Household 206
Chapter 9   Identity and Inequality: Gender, Ethnicity, and Nation 240
Chapter 10 Economics: Resources, Production, and Exchange 270
Chapter 11 Politics, Social Control, and Political Organization 300
Chapter 12 Religious Belief and Ritual 332
Chapter 13 Anthropology for the Twenty-First Century 360

Glossary 389
References 397
Index 415

Contents

Preface xii

Part I ▶ The Realm of Anthropology 1

Chapter 1 The Anthropological Perspective 2

The Discipline of Anthropology 5
Biological Anthropology 6
Archaeology 6
Linguistic Anthropology 6
Cultural Anthropology 7

The Anthropologist's Viewpoint 8
Holism 8
Cultural Relativism 8

Objectivity and Science in Anthropology 9
Using Anthropology: Zero Grazing to Avoid AIDS 10
Ethics in Anthropology 13

Theory in Anthropology 13
The Early Evolutionists 15
Individual Actors: A Response to Cultural Evolution 17
Functional and Structural Approaches 18
Cultural Ecology 20
Marxist Anthropology: An Alternative to Cultural Evolution 20
Cultural Materialism 21

Applying Theory: Fieldwork and Data Collection 22
Studies in the Field 22
Data and Analysis 27

Gender Issues: Becoming Invisible 28
Summary 29
Key Terms 31
Suggested Readings 31

Chapter 2 Culture and Language 32

What Is Culture? 34
Culture Gives Meaning to Reality 34
Culture Is Integrated 35
Culture Is Adaptive 35

Behavior, Biology, and Learning 37
Learning Gender Roles 40
Gender Issues: Albanian Virgins and American Berdaches 41
Learning Age Roles 42

The Roots of Language 43
Nonhuman Communication 44
The Emergence of Human Language 46

The Structure of Languages 47

Sign Language 47

Linguistic Variation and Change 48
Linguistic Borrowing and Cultural Contact 51
Lingua Franca, Pidgin, and Creole Languages 51

Sociolinguistics 52
Social Status 52

Gender Roles and Language 53
Language and Ethnicity 54
*Contemporary Issues: The Politics of Language
    in the United States* 55
Language and Nationalism 55

Summary 57
Key Terms 58
Suggested Readings 58

Chapter 3 Decisions, Adaptation, and
Evolution 60

The Human Evolutionary Legacy 62
Darwin: Evolution by Natural Selection 63
Mendel: The Genetics of Natural Selection 64
Evolution and Human Culture 64

Human Ecology 66
The Human Ecological Context 67
The Nature of Ecological Systems 69

Procurement Systems: Decisions, Adaptation, and
Food 73
The Evolution of Procurement Patterns 74
Adapting to Environmental Problems 75
*Using Anthropology: The South Turkana
    Ecosystem Project* 76
Adapting to Other Groups 79
*State of the Peoples: The Political Ecology of
    Deforestation: The Brazilian Amazon* 80

Adaptation and Cultural Evolution 81
*A Case Study in Long-Term Change: The Viking
    of the North Atlantic* 82
The Processes of Long-Term Cultural
    Change 83

Summary 86
Key Terms 87
Suggested Readings 87

Part II ▸ Adaptive Patterns 89

Chapter 4 Foraging 90
*State of the Peoples: Death of a People: Logging
    in the Penan Homeland* 93
The Organization of Energy 93
Social Organization 97
Settlement Patterns and Mobility 98
*Human Ecology: Adapting to Others: The Batak
    Foragers of the Phillipines* 100
Resilience, Stability, and Change 102
The Dobe Ju/'hoansi 103
Climate and Resources 103
Settlement Patterns 105
Social Practices and Group Composition 105
Reciprocity 106
Quality of Life 107
Diet and Nutrition 107
Demography 108
The People of the Dobe Today 109
The Inuit or Eskimo 110
The Arctic Ecosystem 111
The Seasonal Migrations 111
Demography 113
Social Relationships 113
The Impact of Modernization 114

State of the Peoples: Claiming the Land 117
Summary 118
Key Terms 118
Suggested Readings 119

Chapter 5 Subsistence Agriculture 120

The Horticultural Adaptation 122
Development 122
Energy Use and the Ecosystem 124
Horticultural Cultivation Methods 125
*Contemporary Issues: Learning about
    Monoculture from the Mountain Ok* 126
Social Organization 126

The Yanomamö 129
Farming in the Jungle 130
Village Life 132
Warfare and Violence 133
Future Prospects for the Yanomamö 136
*State of the Peoples: Are the Yanomamö
    Safe?* 137

Subsistence Plow Farming 138

The Tamang 140
The Village 141
Field, Forest, and Pasture 142
The Domestic Cycle 143

Prospects for Timling's Future 145

Summary 145
Key Terms 146
Suggested Readings 147

Chapter 6   Pastoralism 148

The Pastoral Adaptation 150
Development 150
The Organization of Energy 151
Nomadic Movement 151
Social Organization 153
*Using Anthropology: China's Cowboys of Inner
    Mongolia* 154
Wealth, Inequality, and Status 156

The Ariaal of Northern Kenya 158
The Origins of the Ariaal 158
The Ariaal Adaptation 159
The Household: Organization and Status 161
The Age Grades and Age Sets 162
Gender Roles and Power 162
Can the Ariaal Survive Development? 163
*Gender Issues: Being a Shepherdess in the
    Negev* 164

The Yörük of Turkey 165
The Market Economy 166
Social Organization 167
Adapting to a Changing Economy 168
Future Prospects 171

Summary 171
Key Terms 172
Suggested Readings 172

Chapter 7   Intensive and Industrial Agriculture 174

The Development of Intensive Agriculture 176
The Organization of Energy 178

Human Ecology: Human Labor as Energy 179
Environmental Resilience, Stability, and
    Change 181

**From Intensive Agriculture to Industrialized
Farming 182**
Population Growth 182
Intensification 183
Specialization 184
Case Study: The Shift to Sisal in Brazil 186
Centralization, Collectivism, and
    Communism 187
Case Study: A Sudanese Irrigation Project 188
Case Study: Feeding a Fifth of the World: From
    Chinese Communes to Farms 188
Expanding Cities and Migrant Workers 189
Stratification 191

Peasant Farmers in an Industrial Society 191
*State of the Peoples: China's Human
    Traffickers* 192
Sharecropping 193
Access to Land 193
Peasant Responses to Oppression and
    Change 193
Case Study: Change in the Japanese Farming
    Village of Shinohata 195

**Urbanized Rural Society: Farming in
the United States 197**
Case Study: The Development of Agribusiness in
    Wasco, California 197
Case Study: The Farmerless Farm in the San
    Joaquin Valley 199
The Family Farm 200
Case Study: Family Farmers in the Midwest: An
    Immigrant Legacy 200

Summary 202
Key Terms 203
Suggested Readings 203

Part III ▸ Cultural Diversity   205

Chapter 8   Kinship, Marriage, and the
Household 206

Kinship, and Social Organization 208
Kinship Terms and Social Behavior 208
Case Study: Yanomamö Kinship 209
The Manipulation of Kinship 210

The Classification of Kin 211
Contemporary Issues: Families We Choose 212

Descent Ideology and Descent Groups 213
Unilineal Descent Groups 213
Case Study: The Pokot of Kenya 214
Case Study: The Hopi of Northeastern
    Arizona 216

Nonunilineal Descent Groups 220

**Marriage, Remarriage, and Marital
Residence 221**
Marriage 221
Divorce and Remarriage 223
*Gender Issues: Marriage and Money
    Management* 224
Marriage as Exchange 225
*Using Anthropology: Kidnapping and
    Elopement Among the Yörük* 226
Marriage and the Division of Labor 228
Marital Rules 228

Family Households 233
Independent versus Extended Family
    Households 233

Summary 236
Key Terms 238
Suggested Readings 238

Chapter 9 **Identity and Inequality:
Gender, Ethnicity, and Nation 240**

The Social Division of Labor 242
Social Perception and Behavior 243

Gender 244
Gender Socialization 245
Case Study: Gender Socialization in Yörük
    Society 245
Gender and Work 245
*Gender Issues: Women's Movements in the
    Middle East* 246
Gender and Power 247

Race and Ethnicity 248
Race and Racism 248
Ethnicity 250
Racial and Ethnic Stratification 252
*State of the People's: One Land, Two Peoples:
    A Palestinian Village in Israel* 253
Case Study: The Memphis Garbage Strike 256

Systems and Stratification 256
Class 256
Caste–stratified Societies 259
Case Study: Caste in India 259
Slavery 262

Ethnicity, Nationalism, and Conflict 262
Nationalism and Ethnic Conflict 263
Politicized Ethnicity as a Response to the
    State 264

Case Study: What's in a Name: Bulgaria's
    Program of Rebirth 265
Ethnic Terrorism 266

Summary 267
Key Terms 269
Suggested Readings 269

Chapter 10 **Economics: Resources,
Production, and Exchange 270**

Concepts of Economic Behavior 272

Diversity in the Organization of Economies 274

Regulating Access to Resources 275
Property Rights 275
Ownership versus Use Landholding Systems 276
Private Ownership and Commercial Farming 278
Case Study: Where the Dove Calls 278
The Control of Capital Goods 280
*State of the Peoples: The Ecology of a Peasant
    Revolt* 281

Production 282
The Organization of Production 282
Productive Strategies 283
Labor, Gender, and Productivity in the
    Household 284
Case Study: The Productive Labor of Gainj
    Women 286

The Exchange of Resources 288
Mechanisms of Change 288
Case Study: **The Kula Ring** 290
The Organization of Exchange 293
Gender Issues: Money Makes Us Relatives 294

Economic Experimentation and Adaptation 294
*Human Ecology: Over the Mountains Are
    Mountains* 296

Summary 298
Key Terms 299
Suggested Readings 299

Chapter 11 **Politics, Social Control,
and Political Organization 300**

The Political Process 302
The Politics of Making Decisions 302
Access to the Political Process 303
Gender Issues: Women, Men, and Power 304
Power and Authority 306
Case Study: Varieties of Leadership Among the
    Turkmen 306

The Ecology of Political Behavior 309
Access to Resources: Cooperation and
Competition 309
Case Study: "Scramble Competition" Among the
Pathans of Pakistan 310

Evolution of Political Organization 311
Bands and Tribes 312
Chiefdoms 312
States 314

The Politics of Social Control 317
*Contemporary Issues: Responding to Oppression:
Las Madres de Plaza de Mayo* 318
Rules and Behavior 318
Informal Means of Social Control 320
Formal Means of Social Control 322
*Using Anthropology: The Politics of Time in
Ceauşescu's Romania* 323
Law and Tribes in the Twentieth Century 324

Political Relations Among Societies 326
Mechanisms of Peace 326
Armed Conflict 326

Summary 329
Key Terms 330
Suggested Readings 330

Chapter 12 **Religious Belief and
Ritual 332**

Defining Religion 334
Religion as Ideology 334
Religion and "The Sacred" 335

Belief Systems 336
Animism and Animatism 336
Theism 337
Belief Systems and Social Organization 337
*Human Ecology: Production of Protestants in
Guatemala* 338
Belief Systems and Social Boundaries 339

Ritual 340
Rites of Passage 341
Rites of Intensification 343
Gender Issues: Honoring the Dead 344
The Organization of Ritual 345

Religion and Resource Management 347
Case Study: The Maring "Plant the
Rumbim" 348

**Psychological and Sociopolitical Functions of
Religion 350**

Religion and Individual Coping 350
Social Integration 350
Reduction of Conflict 350
*Human Ecology: Religion and the Spread of
Disease* 351
Promotion of Social Control 352
Case Study: The Vodoun Church of Haiti 352
Validation of Change: Revitalization 354
Case Study: Cargo Cults 355
Case Study: Islamic Revolution 355

Summary 357
Key Terms 358
Suggested Readings 358

Chapter 13 **Anthropology for the
Twenty-First Century 360**

Beyond Industrialism 362
Organization of the Postindustrial World 363
Global Communications, Global Culture, and the
Emergence of "Cyberculture" 365
The Ecological Consequences of Post-
industrialism 366
*Using Anthropology: Imaging Resource
Depletion* 368
*State of the Peoples: The Abuse of Environmental
Rights in South Africa* 372
Case Study: The Anatomy of the SOB
Disaster 374

Medical Anthropology 377
Case Study: AIDS in Brazil 378

Developmental Anthropology 378
Case Study: The Vicos Project 379
Environmental and Ecological Factors in
Development 380
Social Ties 380
Managing Social Change 381
Impact Assessment and Evaluation 381
Case Study: Sahel Visions 382
The Ethics of Development Work 386

Summary 386
Key Terms 388
Suggested Readings 388

Glossary 389
References 397
Index 415

Preface

THE OBJECTIVE OF THIS BOOK IS TO INTRODUCE cultural anthropology to readers with little background in the subject and to present the material in a unified framework rather than as an encyclopedia of anthropological concepts and findings. Traditionally, cultural anthropology texts have treated the many topics that constitute the field as a series of loosely interrelated subjects unified by the concept of culture.

This book, like all introductory texts, uses this concept to understand unity and diversity in human social life. But the study of culture also involves the study of culture change. Change is the word that most accurately captures what is distinctive about humans. Our brief history on earth is one of unparalleled expansion, as the early representatives of our species spilled out of Africa to inhabit virtually every region of the globe. This expansion required altering human behavior in all domains to meet the demands of very different habitats: in short, the continual interplay between learned behavior we call culture and the ever-changing environments we have inhabited. The concept of culture, as used in many texts, seems to describe the relationship between culture and human behavior as a one-way street. The individual is born into a cultural milieu and conforms to its strictures, much as a newly-hired employee of IBM or GM learns and adheres to corporate rules of behavior and ways of doing business. Culture and the rules of conduct it prescribes are often presented as the only factor molding our behavior and one that

dictates how we act in many circumstances. Culture is the script, and people are a rather unimaginative cast of actors mechanically performing their assigned roles.

I do not believe that this one-sided concept of culture is adequate. A central theme of this book is that individuals are active decision makers, continually involved in creating and using their culture, however misguided their creations may sometimes be. Faced with new problems and new situations in their environment, people will often attempt to find solutions that go beyond traditional customs and cultural prescriptions. In other words, behavioral variation constantly exists within as well as between societies. Those variations that prove useful are passed on to new generations; they become part of culture. Some ways of doing things that are useful in one context, may prove otherwise in other situations; cultural innovation and transmission are not patterns of cumulative "progress," but processes of continual intergenerational experiment, "filtering," and change affecting all peoples. Every generation's ideas, technologies, social usages, and even modes of speech pass through what might be seen as a filter or screen; some, perhaps most, pass through, but not all. Generally, what becomes transmitted is what seems to work in that particular context. Processes of innovation, adoption of new ideas, and their transmission to others lie at the heart of cultural variation and are part of broader human ecological and, ultimately, evolutionary processes.

Humans are culture-bearing animals; the fact that we create and use complex and often abstract cultural artifices does not negate our biological underpinnings.

Decisions arrived at by individuals, the adaptive strategies of people and societies, and the evolutionary processes of which these are a part form the central theme of this book. The approach, then, is essentially an ecological one, using this concept in its broadest meaning. Adaptation does not mean, for example, that one can ignore what might be called the ideational or symbolic aspects of culture: the ways of behaving and believing that validate our behavior, that form our social identities, and that satisfy our aesthetic needs. The ecological perspective includes much more than simply the material aspects of life. Religious and political beliefs and practices, even kinship systems, are as much a part of human adaptation as are subsistence strategies and economic practices. I will attempt to show this throughout the text, and in so doing, show how the many topics customarily treated as basic to cultural anthropology are more than simply separate aspects of culture. Politics, economics, and religion are all closely linked together in the adaptive process.

While this book draws on a perspective rooted in the long-established tradition of anthropology as scientific inquiry, it promotes no holy grail, no simple key to unlocking the meaning of culture. What I do emphasize throughout, far more than any particular explanation or interpretation, is the fact that all humans share a common, albeit complex, heritage. Cultural diversity and plasticity are all the more interesting and amenable to study, I feel, when viewed against this unifying backdrop.

Overview of the Book

This book is a much-revised version of a popular text first published by Random House (Knopf) and later, in its third edition, by McGraw Hill. In preparing this for Allyn and Bacon, I had the opportunity to make substantial improvements in the text, reflecting the suggestions of numerous users of the earlier books as well as general developments in the discipline. Throughout, I have attempted to streamline the material and make it

more accessible to students. Since the book has been so extensively rewritten, it is worthwhile to review its present organization.

Chapter 1, in addition to introducing the discipline and basic concepts, now goes on to describe the nature of theory in anthropology, selected aspects of the history of theory, and the application of theory in research, especially in fieldwork. Methods and theory in anthropology are illustrated in case studies in many chapters, and in boxes throughout the book.

Chapter 2, Culture and Language, introduces material that was formerly in later chapters describing language, biology, and culture—thus establishing these key elements from the onset. The discussion of linguistics now is much more focused on language and culture, or sociolinguistics. The notion of gender is introduced here and developed in all subsequent chapters.

Chapter 3 offers a concise and pertinent presentation of ecological concepts and decision making and their relevance to understanding large-scale social phenomena. While the book offers a point of view rooted in the idea that human culture is part of the uniquely human apparatus for coping, it avoids the dogmatism and reductionism that often attend books tied to theoretical perspectives. What unites the often far-ranging discussion is a consistent emphasis on anthropology as a discipline concerned with the observation of reality, empiricism, and the importance of validation. This chapter, in addition to orienting students to the perspective that unifies the material that follows, now also introduces Part II.

In Part II, Adaptive Patterns, the four chapters are organized according to commonly recognized strategies of food procurement; namely, hunting and gathering or foraging, subsistence agriculture, including horticulture and subsistence plowfarming, pastoralism, and intensive agriculture and industrial farming. While this organization reflects a general evolutionary or historical scheme, it is not offered as a rigid typology or simple sequence of stages of development. It provides a closer look at the anthropological perspective in action; I use a number of case studies to illustrate how anthropologists view long-term cultural change, analyze cultural adaptation, and attempt to understand diverse aspects of social behavior. Populations whose ways of life and livelihood are as diverse as the San people of Southern Africa and the farmers of Central California are viewed similarly as people responding to, and usually coping successfully with, the problems facing them. What is emphasized are the costs and rewards of different ways of providing for necessities of life and the relationship of settlement system, mobility, and economic and political organization to other aspects of adaptation. A distinctive feature of all these chapters is that they describe not only different societies, but also a wide range of methods and techniques of studying them. This organization is intended to draw the student into interesting ethnographic material, give an insight into methodological concerns, and provide a foundation for understanding the more complex topical chapters that follow in Part III.

I have updated all of the case studies with new material and, wherever possible, attempted to place the populations in today's world. Chapter 5 presents a new case study of the Tamang of Nepal, and in Chapter 6 the Ariaal of Kenya has been added. The discussion of peasantry and intensive agriculture devotes more attention to change, including developments in China. Chapter 7 has new material on agriculture in the United States and a new case study of a Japanese farming community. All of the case studies and boxes in this section illustrate the variability and change that occurs in every subsistence system: hunters and gathers who incorporate farming and marketing, horticulturists who irrigate, and pastoralists who also farm, for instance.

Part III, Cultural Diversity, focuses on key topical areas of study in anthropology, ranging from exploring relationships of family, kinship, and marriage to the anthropology of planned change. There are frequent references to the specific procurement strategies and cases described in Part II. The chapters in this part have been extensively revised and updated. Chapter 8, Kinship, Marriage, and the Household, also treats the use of descent ideology, formerly covered in two chapters, but here updated and combined into one chapter that offers a more concise discussion. A lengthy description of kinship terminologies has been dropped.

Chapter 9, Identity and Inequality: Gender, Ethnicity, and Nation, builds directly on earlier discussions of ideology and the dynamics of social

groups and networks, in order to deal with important sources of inequality: gender, race, and ethnicity, as well as the emergence of important, larger social constructs such as nationalism. These might be seen as the negative aspects of group-level social organization—structures that create and perpetuate inequality and stratification. Chapter 10, Economics: Resources, Production, and Exchange, moves the discussion of economic behavior beyond the academic debates on this important subject matter. Chapter 11, Politics, Social Control, and Political Organization, draws on both the discussion of group-level organization and on economics to outline the dynamics of decision making, leadership, and the processes that determine "who gets what" in society. Chapter 12, Religious Belief and Ritual, devotes more attention to the importance of ideology as legitimizing secular acts, religion and politics, social change, and social control. The last chapter, Anthropology for the Twenty-First Century, examines processes of planned and unplanned change, including the events that are so rapidly transforming the world today. It also looks at the ever-increasing role played by anthropologists in development work, and includes a new case study describing an important project in West Africa and the contribution made by one anthropologist. It concludes with a timely discussion of criteria for evaluating planned change.

In this edition we have completely changed the box program. The boxes are now unified by their organization into a number of broadly defined themes: Using Anthropology examines applied issues, Gender Issues focuses on gender, Human Ecology looks at current ecologically-oriented studies—many taken from the *Human Ecology Journal*. Finally, the State of the Peoples boxes draw heavily from the *Cultural Survival Quarterly* and highlights the work being done by anthropologists to preserve the cultures of indigenous peoples around the world. While most draw on the research of anthropologists, several come from outside the discipline, which, I feel, unobtrusively indicates the linkages between anthropology and other academic fields. The anthropological research described goes well beyond what might be easily conveyed in a general discussion. For example, I use boxes to show complementary and competing interests and alignments in a Mexican village, processes of religious conversion in Guatemala, how anthropologists use their training in the battle against AIDS in the United States and Africa, and the anthropology of time in Romania.

Supplements

Allyn and Bacon/CNN Anthropology Video

In keeping with our focus on contemporary issues in anthropology, a fully integrated 120-minute video program, consisting of segments drawn from recent CNN programming from the United States and around the world, accompanies this text. These film segments address timely and important topics that illustrate key text issues or concepts. This video is divided into four general topic areas: Language; Population and the Environment; Inequality, Slavery and Ethnicity; State of the Peoples: Native Americans, and includes the following segments:

Language. "Deaf Language" demonstrates that deaf children, when exposed to their parents' signing, begin to "babble" in signs, gradually putting together meaningful signed words. "Chimp Talk" shows Sue Savage-Rumbaugh working with the pygmy chimpanzee, Kanzi.

Population and the Environment. "Zimbabwe Family Planning" demonstrates the importance of understanding the local culture in Zimbabwe when designing an effective strategy for dispensing birth control information and devices. "Population in Brazil" shows that the heart of the population problem in Brazil is unequal land distribution. With most of the agricultural land controlled by large landowners, landless peasants are forced to migrate to the Amazonian frontier or to the large cities. "Population and Energy: Lifestyles USA" uses an ecological perspective to examine the relationship of population to energy use in the United States. "Losing the Land," which focuses on land degradation by peasants around the world, provides the media view of the situation. "Mexico Rebellion" examines what has been called the "ecological" revolution in Chiapas. In this region, the peasants' lands have been appropriated by the state, disrupting their traditional subsistence pattern and leading to poverty and starvation among the Mayan Indians. "China: The Quiet Revolution" provides a commentary on the breakdown of collective agriculture in Communist China.

Inequality, Slavery, and Ethnicity. "Faces of Slavery," taken from CNN Presents, demonstrates that work situations amounting to virtual slavery still exist in the world today. In this report, CNN examines the plight of migrant workers in the United States and child labor in the Indian carpet industry.

State of the Peoples: Native Americans. "Native Americans: The Invisible People," another CNN Presents program, shows how Native Americans are recovering their culture and identity. The segments, which address various aspects of this process, provide an excellent basis for discussion of the meaning of ethnic identity.

These video segments are discussed in the *Instructor's Manual* either in the Lecture Topics or Discussion and Research Topics sections in the related chapters. Also available are selected videos from the *Faces of Culture* telecourse series. *Faces of Culture* consists of 26 integrated, 30-minute video programs that systematically cover the major topics in cultural anthropology.

Instructor's Manual/Test Bank

Written by Nancy Flowers, Hunter College, this combination manual offers a complete instructor's section and a set of test questions to accompany each text chapter. The *Test Bank* includes multiple choice, true-false, and essay questions. The *Instructor's Manual* includes, for each chapter of the text, a chapter overview, chapter objectives, lecture topics, discussion and research topics, suggested films, and a separate section explaining how the *Faces of Culture* telecourse videos can be used with this text. Recognizing the importance of film in the teaching of cultural anthropology, we have integrated film suggestions into many of the manual's suggested lecture and discussion and research topics.

Computerized Test Banks

Allyn and Bacon offers computerized test banks for both IBM (DOS and Windows) and Macintosh formats, allowing instructors the option to edit questions already in the test banks, to add their own questions, and to create multiple versions of a test. Full customer support is available.

Call-In and Fax Testing Service

The Allyn and Bacon testing center can process and send a finished test, ready for duplication, within 48 hours of request. Fax service of hard copy is available on a same-day basis.

Custom-Published Ancillaries

Allyn and Bacon can customize packages of supplements to meet instructors' specific needs. For example, an instructor may wish to add a course syllabus or additional test questions.

For more information on custom publishing or any of the supplemental materials described here, please contact your local Allyn and Bacon representative.

Acknowledgments

The first two editions of *Cultural Anthropology,* published by Knopf, were written in collaboration with Fred Plog. Under pressure of other long-standing academic commitments, Fred was not able to devote time to the third edition and, tragically, he died soon after it appeared. I wish to acknowledge his contribution here, but, more importantly, his restless intellect and often sardonic wit that made our early collaboration rewarding for me at both a personal and professional level.

It is not possible to fully recognize everyone who has been of assistance, particularly in earlier versions, but some individuals have been exceedingly generous with their time, knowledge, and expertise.

Judith Tucker worked on the project from the earliest stages to completion and made numerous constructive recommendations as to reorganization, style, and presentation. She accompanied me in the field and saw many ways in which material from our work in Bulgaria and Turkey could be relevant. She also made a major contribution to many of the boxes. Without her active assistance and genial tolerance this book would not have happened.

Sylvia Shepard, Anthropology Editor at Allyn and Bacon, had been actively and constructively involved in the revision process leading to the previous edition. Once the book came to Allyn and Bacon, her involvement in the project moved to an entirely different level; we spoke on a daily basis over a period of several months, we discussed every aspect of the new organization of the chapters and topics, and she directed me to a great deal of useful material. The book is far better for her efforts and I am deeply grateful.

Other colleagues contributed much throughout the long project; both by commenting extensively on the organization and content of this edition, and by reading drafts of chapters or partial chapters. Their often acerbic or irreverent observations frequently resulted in substantial extra work, always to the ultimate benefit of the book. Chief among them is Elliot Fratkin of Smith College who, in addition to providing material for the Ariaal study, sent me photographs for possible use. Della McMillen, of the University of Florida, was similarly uncommonly generous with her time and suggestions resulting in the case study, Sahel Visions, in Chapter 13. Francis Conant, Hunter College, graciously made available unpublished material on the Pokot. Nancy Flowers, Hunter College, provided valuable materials relating to medical anthropology and is presently preparing the instructor's manual for the text. David Gilmore, S.U.N.Y. Stony Brook, read and commented upon drafts of several chapters. Tim Bromage and John Oates, also of Hunter College, provided very helpful insights on the ever-troublesome concept of race.

This edition benefitted greatly by having been included in the American Anthropological Association's Gender in the Anthropological Curriculum Project, directed by Mary Moran and Sandra Morgan. This project paired authors with consultants with expertise in the study of gender in an effort to broaden the coverage of gender in textbooks. I was extremely fortunate to have been able to work with Rayna Rapp and Ida Susser, and feel that this edition is richer by far for their advice. Needless to say, any errors or infelicities in this area remain the responsibility of the author alone.

Academic critics and consultants, in addition to numerous reviewers, include Francis Conant, Gerald Creed, Morgan Crook, Josh DeWind, Alan Daben, Nancy Flowers, Brian Foster, David

Gilmore, Pauline Herrmann, William Irons, Greg Johnson, Robert Lawless, Louise Lennihan, Susan Lees, Paul Magnarella, Ted Macdonald, Tom Mc-Govern, Janet Midwinter, Richard Moore, Warren Morrill, Robert Netting, Michael Olien, Eugene Ogan, Tom Painter, William Parry, Burt Pasternak, Dee Raferty, Henry Rutz, Arthur Spears, Ida Susser, and Isabel Terry. I greatly appreciate their generous help.

Although not directly involved in the preparation of the manuscript, I would like to acknowledge the friendship and assistance of individuals in Bulgaria who materially aided me in a project described in Chapter 9: Haşim Akif, Mehmet Beytullah, Sabri Galip, Fevzi Ömer, Resmi Şeref, and Ognian Yanakiev.

During what turned out to be a much longer task than originally envisioned, I was assisted in numerous ways by many other people. Perhaps at the head of the list are those at Allyn and Bacon: Sylvia Shepard, Laura Pearson, and Jennifer Normandin. As noted, Sylvia guided this undertaking safely among the numerous shoals of editorial development and production. Wendy LaChance did an outstanding job of designing the book. Mary Beth Finch managed the production of this manuscript, along with George Calmenson and Dustine Davidson of The Book Company. The copyediting was provided by Sonsie Conroy. Eileen Sheerin and Ellen DeRiso provided much appreciated logistical support. Christina Mitrakos assisted ably with library research and bibliography.

Finally, I wish to acknowledge the support of family and friends during the long period of time when this project occasionally interjected itself into our lives when least opportune.

Daniel G. Bates
Hunter College, The City University of New York

Part I

The Realm of Anthropology

The three chapters in Part I introduce the main subfields of anthropology and emphasize concepts basic to cultural anthropology and to understanding the place of human society in a cultural and biological perspective. Anthropology is an exceptionally rich and varied discipline, both in terms of theoretical orientations and in terms of the ever-growing availability of data from around the world. The chapters in this section stress the underlying unity of the anthropological perspective and at the same time describe a broad range of ideas and foci.

Chapter 1 covers the rise of anthropological theory and stresses important lines of continuity as the field has developed and brings together a detailed overview of anthropological methods and a sense of what it is like to work in the field. Chapter 2 deals with the nature of culture and its place in anthropological thought, the origins of human language, and how language is used socially. Chapter 3 addresses the theme of human biological and social evolution and establishes the framework of the subsequent sections.

While not concerned with labels, the approach used is one based in human ecology or evolutionary ecology. However diverse the field may be, most anthropologists share a commitment to viewing humans holistically and, thus, to understanding human cultural unity and diversity in terms of regular processes: biological, behavioral, and cultural. By building on a clearly recognizable framework, this perspective emphasizes both the behavioral and cultural variability within societies and the crucial role of individual choice and decision making in understanding cultural change and evolution.

The Discipline of Anthropology
  Biological Anthropology
  Archaeology
  Linguistic Anthropology
  Cultural Anthropology

The Anthropologist's Viewpoint
  Holism
  Cultural Relativism
  Using Anthropology: Zero Grazing to Avoid AIDS

Objectivity and Science in Anthropology
  Ethics in Anthropology

Theory in Anthropology
  The Early Evolutionists
  Individual Actors: A Response to Cultural Evolution
  Functional and Structural Approaches
  Cultural Ecology
  Marxist Anthropology: An Alternative to Cultural Evolution
  Cultural Materialism

Applying Theory: Fieldwork and Data Collection
  Studies in the Field
  Gender Issues: Becoming Invisible
  Data and Analysis

Summary

Key Terms

Suggested Readings

Chapter 1

The Anthropological Perspective

More than any other scientific discipline, anthropology asks questions that grapple with that elusive concept, "human nature": why, for example, great imperial regimes arose in some places but not in others; why social or gender inequality is so widespread; why violence persists in a species that manifestly has the ability to see its horrible consequences.

The excitement that runs just beneath the surface of the formal discipline of anthropology arises from the dual tasks of collecting detailed data, often about very remote and isolated societies, and then fitting this array of facts into a broader philosophical framework. The ethnographer, in confronting the social practices of another society, frequently comes face to face with the question of where the outer limits of human social or cultural variability are to be located. When recently, for example, anthropologist Maria Lepowsky found that on the Vanatinai Islands, off the coast of Papua New Guinea, men and women are considered virtual equals, had she discovered a "gender-egalitarian" society, a finding which would challenge the notion that male dominance is universal (1994)? However her study comes to be evaluated, she will have broadened our view of sex-specific roles in society.

Anthropologists look at many different societies and ask many different questions in their ongoing exploration of patterns of culture—the shared beliefs, behaviors, and technology that members of all societies employ in everyday life. Although anthropologists recognize that culture is a uniquely human enterprise, they emphasize the connections between human society and the larger web of life. Only by appreciating the fact that we, *homo sapiens sapiens*, are subject to the same forces that affect all other living organisms can we come to understand those many aspects of human behavior that distinguish us from other species. And if we more fully appreciate the extraordinary diversity evident in the ways of life of the world's peoples, we may come to a better understanding of our own society.

Human beings are relative newcomers on earth, but by most criteria we are an extremely successful species—certainly the most widespread and numerous of the large animals. We are distributed throughout the world and live under the most diverse and extreme conditions. Despite the enormous variety of local problems and hazards that humans must overcome to survive, all of the world's peoples are very similar in biological makeup and physique. In comparison with many other animals we are remarkably homogeneous and even a rather dull lot, lacking plumage and other specialized survival equipment. What accounts for the success of our species, and what can we surmise about our future? Why is it that humans vary considerably in social life and customs while differing only to a small degree biologically?

While these kinds of questions about human evolution are key issues in the study of anthropology today, this concern with evolution is relatively recent. For millennia Europeans were accustomed to thinking of the world, its peoples, and all other living things as eternally fixed and unchanging. Though similarities among species were widely noted, these similarities were not thought to represent the outcome of a shared and ongoing process of change—the process we call **evolution**. Instead each species, even each distinctive human society or culture, was seen as a unique entity with its own essential or unique characteristics. No species was related to another or to anything else, except in the

seemingly obvious sense that the world existed for humans—in particular for those favored to be participants in European civilization. However, as Europeans explored more and more of the rest of the world, the customs and practices of non-European societies were systematically recorded and studied. Soon most religious thinkers, philosophers, and scientists were accustomed to thinking of the unity of humankind, and by the late eighteenth century it was widely acknowledged that European civilization might in fact have developed from what were considered to be simpler societies, such as those encountered in the New World.

While the modern discipline of anthropology is a product of this long tradition of European exploration and inquiry, this fascination with humanity's diversity is not unique to the West. The Arabs and Chinese, for instance, have for thousands of years shown a systematic interest in their own and other societies. Ibn-Khaldun, an Arab scholar and historian of the fourteenth century who was familiar with African, European, and Middle Eastern societies, proposed a general theory of social change in which simpler societies, based on ties of family and tribe, were transformed into urban-focused civilizations. Still, it was only in European centers of scholarship that the systematic study of human diversity came to flourish.

Undoubtedly the major impetus for this development was the commercial and political ties being forged between Europe and the rest of the world. But this type of study also flourished because European scholars gradually came to recognize the explanatory value of systematically organized collections of data. As early as the mid-sixteenth century, a manual was published listing various physical and cultural attributes, some three hundred in all, that travelers should record when they visited foreign lands. Very diverse materials came to be organized in terms of similarities and differences, and the idea that change was a natural and ever-occurring process was increasingly accepted. Out of this habit of thought emerged the idea that species evolve, that small but cumulative changes in a species can, over time, lead to its transformation.

By the mid-nineteenth century the idea of evolutionary change was respectable in scholarly circles, in large part as a result of the tremendous impact of Charles Darwin's famous book, *On the*

Origin of Species by Means of Natural Selection, published in 1859. In this book, Darwin stated that species are related to one another by descent, with modifications, from common ancestors. He postulated that such modifications occur primarily through differential reproduction, or the ability of some members of a species to have more surviving offspring than others. These favored individuals pass on their traits to the next generation, whereas the less favored do not do so to the same degree. Darwin called this process **natural selection** and demonstrated that it can change the characteristics of an entire species over time, or even give rise to new species.

The idea that human society also may be a product of a long sequence of ongoing change received support of a rather startling variety: the discovery of human-like fossils in association with stone tools. **Fossils** are naturally mineralized remains of organic matter—earlier forms of plant and animal life turned to stone and thus preserved—very often lying underground for thousands of years until chance discovery brings them to light. During the seventeenth and eighteenth centuries many such fossil remains of extinct plants and animals were collected and classified, and the similarities and differences between them and living species were duly noted. These discoveries (which continue to be made), along with Charles Darwin's theory of natural selection, established the idea that not only human societies but human beings themselves were the products of evolution—that is, they developed from earlier forms. Over millions of years the human body and human societies had emerged from earlier human and prehuman forms, through a combination of physical evolution (adaptive changes in biological makeup) and cultural evolution (adaptive changes in thought and behavior). The study of contemporary peoples and their social behavior is closely tied to this view of the world: the evolutionary view.

The Discipline of Anthropology

All science is an effort to describe and explain natural phenomena. The aim of anthropology (the name of the discipline is derived from the Greek *anthropos*, "man," and *logos*, "account") is to de-

scribe and explain one particular natural phenomenon: Homo sapiens, the human species. Much of what anthropologists study in their investigation of the human species concerns **culture**. Broadly defined, culture is a system of shared beliefs, values, customs, behaviors, and material objects that the members of a society use to cope with their world and with one another, and that are transmitted from generation to generation through learning. This definition includes not only patterns of behavior but also patterns of thought (shared meanings that the members of a society attach to various phenomena, natural and intellectual, including religion and ideologies), tools, pottery, houses, machines, and works of art, as well as the culturally transmitted skills and techniques used to form these. In short, culture includes almost any form of behavior that is *learned* rather than instinctive or inherited. We will leave until later the difficulties that may arise in attempts to apply this distinction.

Anthropological investigation involves comparisons of contemporary cultures and investigations of cultural and biological changes. In other words, as we shall see in subsequent chapters, anthropology takes as its object of study all human peoples, across the globe and across time, treating subjects as varied as their teeth, their diseases, their ways of getting food and shelter and rearing children, and their ideas about their place in the world. Consider the investigations of the ethnographers Teresa and John Hart (1986), who carefully determined the caloric and nutritional values of food resources in the Ituri rain forest of Zaire. Their findings indicated that the Mbuti Pygmies—hunters and gatherers in the forest—could not live independently of the farmers with whom they trade. Mark Flinn (1986), too, found some interesting facts about sexual reproduction and parent-offspring interaction when he analyzed genealogical, demographic, and economic data collected in a village in Trinidad. He discovered that men and women with the most land (the major resource) have the most offspring; that the more land a man has, the more women he is likely to have sexual relations with; and that young adults, particularly men, whose parents live in the village have more children than those who live apart from their parents. This study shows the effect of wealth and family ties on reproduction. It is this breadth of

Paleontologists study casts of hominid crania and other body parts in order to study human evolution, using material such as these displayed in an African research laboratory.

(Peggy & Yoram Kahana/Peter Arnold Inc.)

inquiry that gives anthropology its vitality. Anthropologists continually probe the essence of human existence, asking philosophical as well as pragmatic questions.

The total scope of anthropology is too vast to be mastered by any individual. For historical and practical reasons, the discipline is organized in North America in four subdisciplines: biological anthropology, archaeology, linguistic anthropology, and cultural anthropology. The differences between these areas of study, however, are less important than the dynamic way in which ideas and findings in one area influence ideas and research in the others.

Biological Anthropology

The study of the human species, past and present, as a biological phenomenon is known as **biological anthropology** (or, alternatively, physical anthropology). It is concerned with three central areas of study. The first is the reconstruction of the evolutionary history of our species—the description and explanation of the changes that caused our lineage to diverge from other primates. The second area is concerned with describing and accounting for the biological variation within and among living human populations; such investigations extend to the relationship between genetic variation and environmental or cultural factors. The third area, an important specialization within biological anthropology, is **primatology**, or the study of our primate relatives—their ecology, evolution, and social behavior.

Archaeology

Just as biological anthropologists try to reconstruct the successive stages of human physical evolution, the archaeologist tries to reconstruct the processes of human cultural evolution and the effects of those processes in different parts of the world. **Archaeology** is the study of the relationship between **material culture**—that is, the artifacts and architecture people create—and behavior. Archaeologists investigate the ways of life of earlier peoples and the processes by which their ways of life changed. While the study of early periods, usually referred to as *prehistory*, is central to archaeology, recent history is also examined. For example, historical archaeologists in the United States are often concerned with patterns of everyday life in the colonial era in North America. Marine archaeology, a growing field, similarly uses remains from shipwrecks of various periods to shed light on aspects of life for which there is scant documentation.

Linguistic Anthropology

Language is the primary medium through which culture is passed from generation to generation. To a large extent the ability to speak determined the direction our species took in its physical evolution. The major anatomical difference between modern humans and our ancestors of two and a half million years ago is that of brain size, and there is no doubt that the elaboration of language contributed to the growth of the human brain to its present proportions.

Linguist Francesca Merlin studies a hitherto unknown language group north of Mount Hagen, Papua New Guinea.

(Irven DeVore/Anthrophoto)

Linguistic anthropology (in comparison with theoretical linguistics) is distinguished by its primary concern with unwritten languages (both prehistoric and modern), with variations within languages, and with the social uses of language. Linguistic anthropologists systematically study the way a language is constructed and used: the way people combine sounds into words and words into meaningful statements. They also study the origin of language in general and the evolution of the languages people speak today. And finally, through the study of **sociolinguistics**, a more recently developed branch of linguistic anthropology, they explore the connection between language and social relations.

Cultural Anthropology

Cultural anthropology (often called social anthropology, particularly in the United Kingdom and Europe), the subject of this book, is the study both of specific contemporary human societies and of the underlying patterns of human culture. This study involves both detailed examinations of individual cultures, called **ethnography**, and the analysis and interpretation of data to discern cultural patterns, called **ethnology**.

Ethnography. Ethnography (literally, "writing about peoples") is the gathering of information on contemporary cultures through fieldwork, or first-hand study. Generally, ethnographers spend a year or more living with, observing, and interviewing the people whose culture they are trying to describe. In the course of their fieldwork they may gather data on economic processes (the way the population sustains itself materially), technology (tools and methods of using them), social organization (including ways of defining kinship, contracting marriage, and organizing families), political behavior (the formation of action groups within the society, methods of settling disputes, means of dealing with outside groups, and ways of making decisions that affect the community), and finally, the group's religious, magical, and/or scientific strategies for explaining and attempting to control the world around them. The concerns of ethnographers are as varied as culture itself. In addition to acquiring a general picture of a society, ethnographers may concentrate on a particular problem. They might go to the field to investigate the relationship between ideology, economic activities, and the favoring of female infants in Jamaica (Sargent and Harris, 1992), for example, while another might study the nature of male transvestism in modern Samoa (Mageo, 1992).

Ethnology. In their role as ethnographers, cultural anthropologists study and *describe* contemporary peoples. In their role as ethnologists, they go beyond description to *interpret* or *explain* the data collected in the field and elsewhere. Ethnology is the uncovering of general patterns and rules that govern social behavior. To formulate these rules or to identify cultural patterns, ethnologists may use ethnographic data collected by several generations of fieldworkers all over the world. If the data from a number of societies seem to suggest a general pattern—a connection between small-scale agriculture and large, extended-family households, for example—then the ethnologist will review the data from still more societies to see if this pattern holds true in general. If so, this observation may serve as the basis for generalizing about the relationship between family and household organization and technology in human society as a whole. In this way, our understanding of the way human groups organize their lives is gradually extended.

The Anthropologist's Viewpoint

All anthropologists tend to specialize, to reduce their subject matter to manageable proportions. But even when they apply themselves to specific questions, they try to retain a breadth of view. In short, what distinguishes anthropology among the social sciences is the comprehensiveness of its inquiry into the nature of humankind. This breadth of perspective, one of anthropology's distinctive features, is best demonstrated by two axioms of anthropological research: holism and cultural relativism.

Holism

Holism is the philosophical view that no complex entity can be considered to be only the sum of its parts. As a principle of anthropology, it is the assumption that any given aspect of human life is to be studied with an eye to its relation to other aspects of human life. Anthropologists attempt to understand specific problems or questions of interest within a wider context. Carol Laderman, who has worked with rural Malaysian women in an ef-

fort to understand traditional medicine and childbearing and midwife practices, writes:

> The strength of anthropology lies within a paradox. The broad philosophical and theoretical concerns of anthropology must be approached through studies of a particular people, living in a particular place and time. But in order to understand the particular, we must approach it from a generalist viewpoint. The specific nature of our inquiries cannot be allowed to limit our field of investigation. Data must be collected even in those areas which at first glance seem to impinge only peripherally upon the problem. For example, understanding a people's dietary habits requires a knowledge of their economy and ecology, as well as their religious, social and aesthetic ideologies. An analysis of childbirth practices must include an investigation into sex roles, rules of marriage and divorce, and the status and training of childbirth attendants, as well as the medical system of which these practices are a part. [Laderman, 1983, p. 1]

By taking a holistic view, the anthropologist is able to surmount some of the academic obstacles that separate, for example, the study of human biology from the study of human social behavior, or those that divide the social sciences into such discrete disciplines as sociology, psychology, history, and economics. While specialization is needed to obtain a thorough understanding of any one facet of human existence, it also has its dangers. Foremost among them is the tendency to ignore important causes or consequences of a given phenomenon that lie outside the confines of the researcher's discipline. It is this danger that anthropologists try to avoid by taking a holistic view.

Cultural Relativism

The second important principle of the anthropological perspective is **cultural relativism**—the ability to view the beliefs and customs of other peoples within the context of their culture rather than one's own. This ability does not necessarily come naturally. Our perceptions are obviously adjusted to our own cultures. So, at first sight, an African man with ritual scars on his face or a Middle Eastern woman in *purdah* (that is, with her face and body largely covered), is likely to appear strange to us.

Unfamiliar food preferences may seem revolting. When the practice in question is one that we consider a matter of morality rather than simply one of taste—as, for example, the severe female genital mutilation found in some African societies, or the infanticide practiced by the Yanomamö of Venezuela—our reactions can be far stronger. While it is comparatively easy to set aside some of our cultural biases in the interests of objectivity, there is a point where the ethnographer has to reflect on his or her own morality and its cultural sources.

Cultural self-centeredness, the tendency to judge the customs of other societies by the standards of one's own, is called **ethnocentrism**. It is by no means a phenomenon exclusive to Western societies. People in every society tend to view outsiders and their customs with suspicion and often condemnation. If we consider infanticide cruel and unnatural, those peoples who practice it may consider equally appalling our own custom of shutting old people away in homes for the aged. In fact, infanticide is most often an extreme measure taken by parents who, in times of food shortage, sacrifice a newborn infant to secure the well-being of another child.

When we can see cultural differences through the prism of cultural relativism, we can approach other cultures with empathy, understanding, and scientific objectivity. Indeed, if anthropology has any message to offer the world, it is the need for cultural relativism in an era of globalization, where communication, trade, and travel networks bring people of disparate cultures in frequent contact with one another. One consequence of this contact is the spread of infectious diseases, such as AIDS. Cultural relativism enables anthropologists to help design culturally sensitive programs for the prevention of AIDS, as we can see in the Using Anthropology box, *Zero Grazing to Avoid AIDS,* on page 10.

There is, however, a troubling dilemma inherent in cultural relativism—one that is increasingly central in discussions of universal human rights. Can we use cultural relativism to justify the violation of basic civil and human rights? Eugene Hammel has written, with respect to the bloody fighting in Bosnia and Croatia, that when a society with which one is familiar is consumed by the flames of war, the anthropologist must speak out against war

crimes, as would any moral person. These crimes, such as politically motivated rape, massacre of civilians, and torture cannot be justified even if such behavior is considered justified by those carrying it out and expected by those on the receiving end (Hammel, 1994). The dilemma is that in extending our own society's value system (for example, concepts of universal civil and human rights), we are, in fact, imposing our own moral standards on other societies.

As the impact of development threatens to destroy the cultures of indigenous peoples that have traditionally been of concern to anthropologists, more and more action-oriented anthropologists are questioning the notions that a detached, objective stance is possible and that silence on social issues equals neutrality. According to these anthropologists, failure to speak out and refusal to become involved is tantamount to support of the status quo. These anthropologists see the fieldworker's role as making resources available to the people being studied and helping them to understand possible alternatives and articulate their views. They support cultural relativism—so long as it does not become an excuse for inaction in the face of exploitation.

Objectivity and Science in Anthropology

Some anthropologists argue that, as scientists, they have an obligation to strive for the objectivity generally associated with the sciences. This position is based on the belief that it is possible to suspend one's cultural and theoretical biases in the field and to observe and report, with detachment, what one sees. Other anthropologists believe that this approach ignores one of the most basic tenets of anthropology: that every individual is a product of his or her culture. Total objectivity is thus impossible. A researcher's cultural background, academic training, and personality influence both what is perceived and what is reported. Some therefore argue that it is impossible to "go backstage," or, as Vincent Crapanzano puts it, "We were told not to ask leading questions—as if there were such a thing as a non-leading question" (quoted in Berreby, 1995, p. 46). By pretending to objectivity, it is argued, anthropologists are deceiving themselves.

Using Anthropology
Zero Grazing to Avoid AIDS

WHILE MOST DISEASES HAVE A cultural component that affects the rate of infection and those who are at risk, probably no life-threatening epidemic is more closely linked to patterns of behavior than AIDS. During the long period in which the infection is carried before the appearance of symptoms, it can be passed on through sexual contact or blood transmission. Since 1981, most adults in the United States with AIDS are homosexual or bisexual males (65 percent), homosexual or bisexual male intravenous drug users (8 percent), with the bulk of the remaining victims (about 21 percent) being heterosexual drug abusers; only 6 percent of the cases occured as a result only of heterosexual contact or blood transfusions (Curran, et al., 1988, p. 19).

But as E. Michael Gorman, an anthropologist who has worked since 1982 on AIDS-related issues in San Francisco, points out, homosexual culture simply reflected what was happening in the larger heterosexual society that had come to accept a "busy sexual lifestyle" (Gorman, 1989, p. 196ff). Anthropology, he writes, can play a role in understanding the nature of AIDS by identifying high-risk behaviors and directing preventive educational measures to alter behavior and by learning more about sexuality, particularly homosexuality. Finally, he says, in the United States a distinctive gay

lifestyle has developed in urban areas: "gay people—men and women—have taken on characteristics of certain ethnic communities," with distinctive argot and symbols, distinctive social conventions, special institutions such as churches, banks and clubs; and this offers the anthropologist a window through which to see how diseases shape cultural development. It is a means of studying the cultural environment of a disease.

But AIDS is a global problem and what may be appropriate responses in the United States may not be so elsewhere. In the United States there is a perception that AIDS is a disease of two stigmatized subcultures: male homosexuals and intravenous drug users. In Africa, which after North America has the second highest incidence of AIDS, it is often perceived to be a heterosexual disease of the urban elite. As recently as 1985, many Africans interviewed regarded AIDS as an imaginary syndrome invented by Europeans to discourage African lovers, but by 1987 most were fully aware of the fatal nature of the disease, as well as their powerlessness to prevent it.

Anthropologist Christine Obbo looks at Ugandan efforts to deal with the disease and points out where foreign examples and approaches are not useful in the Ugandan situation (Obbo, 1988, pp. 192–197). In Uganda, she

writes, people classify diseases as either "African" or "foreign" and when AIDS cases began to appear in 1982, it was dubbed a foreign illness, just one more brought by Europeans (Obbo, 1988, pp. 191–192). People called it "Slim's" because one visible symptom is rapid weight loss and its fearsome consequences soon became widely known. The fact that AIDS was associated with blood invoked strong personal and symbolic images, some of which worked against possible campaigns to educate people to alter risky behavior. Obbo identifies a number of myths that must be dispelled in order to mount effective AIDS programs in Uganda, myths not only held by foreigners about Africans, but also by African elites about country people and women (Obbo, p. 192). Some myths, she notes, are that Africans are not only physically promiscuous but also that they engage freely in sex-related discussions. While some dances and rituals refer to sex, people usually use euphemisms and exercise great care in avoiding "rude" language. Attempts to educate must be presented in an appropriate manner; one that will not give offense. Another myth is that body scarification and female circumcision is widespread and is an AIDS vector. Female circumcision is not widely practiced in Uganda, and asserting that it is a cause for the disease merely dis-

"Zero Grazing" or "Stick to Your Partner" is the theme of East African campaigns to curtail AIDS, or SIDA as it is called in French- speaking countries such as Burundi. Anthropologists have been active in these campaigns.
(The Hutchison Library)

tracts people from learning about its real causes (Obbo, p. 193). A misconception held about villagers by urban elites is that they should not be encouraged to use condoms for safe sex since they will just reuse them (Obbo, p. 193). On the contrary, Obbo writes, people are fastidious about sexual body fluids; condoms are well known to villagers but are often rejected because they mistakenly feel that penicillin injections are a cure to any sexually transmitted disease (Obbo, p. 193). A final myth discussed by Obbo is that prostitutes, including all single women in towns, are responsible for passing on the disease. This notion has led to suggestions that prostitutes should be sent back to their villages. Quite apart from stigmatizing women, this idea ignores the long period when the HIV carrier, male or female, and not just prostitutes, has no symptoms and can communicate it to others. In short, any message about AIDS will have to be translated into a cultural medium accessible to the people it is meant to reach. Hence the program called Zero Grazing—a reference to not having casual sex. The use of local idiom is essential. For example, one imported video on AIDS depicted it as a homosexual disease and in the discussions that followed people focused mostly on "the funny and strange ways of Europeans," deflecting from the grave matter at hand (Obbo, p. 192).

Breaking the chains of AIDS transmission will require rapid and widespread behavioral change. Directed social change is one of the most complex and least understood aspects of sociocultural dynamics. AIDS prevention is both personal and political. What appear to be personal or individual behaviors (and problems) are actually embedded in culturally conditioned gender roles arising out of psychological expectations and material conditions (Schoepf et al., 1988, p. 179).

Most recently, there has been a move by some anthropologists to rule out any scientific role for anthropology; some voices, indeed, renounce all science. A recent article in the *New York Times Magazine* describes Clifford Geertz as having done much to turn anthropology away from thinking of itself as an "objective science"(Berreby, 1995, pp. 44–47). Another anthropologist, Steven Tyler, goes so far as to state ". . . the postmodern world is a post-scientific world" one in which "scientific thought is now an archaic mode of consciousness" (1987, cited in Reyna, 1994). While there are many complex issues involved, they all turn on two interrelated questions. What is science? Can anthropology contribute to it?

While usually one contrasts art and science, Steven Reyna, in a provocative critique of contemporary efforts to move anthropology away from its scientific tradition, points out their similarities: "Art, among other things, is a creative, imaginative representation of experience. Science is an art. Like other art forms it is a manner of representing experience. The experience it represents is reality" (Reyna,1994, p. 556). In order to understand how reality is constituted, basic science is explanation; in order to determine how well we are explaining reality, science is validation. Science is not a quest for absolute truths or the collection of concrete facts. If it were, then anthropologists would be justified in not engaging in the endeavor—in fact this form of "science" would have little utility for anyone. Science is simply a quest for information about the world.

Anthropology can and does contribute to this quest, even if the researcher is faced with the challenge of cultural diversity. If there are doubts, one only has to look at the state of knowledge about human behavior today in comparison to forty years ago, when anthropology in Europe and America moved into the post–World War II era. The methods of anthropology—indeed, the methods of science in general—are strikingly similar to processes in nature where individuals (and the populations of which they are a part) respond to experience. Survival, cultural and otherwise, depends on successful responses to experience. Science is not concerned with what is universally true, but with what is approximately true—that is, explanations that are useful until new ones offer improvements. The methods of science are diverse but all rely on some form of validation—the encounter of explanation and experience. "If one rejects science, one rejects the art of explaining, and validating the explanation, of the experience of reality" (Reyna, 1994, p. 557).

Perhaps what is called for is a matter less of objectivity than of rigor. By using the most rigorous methods possible to evaluate their conclusions, anthropologists guarantee, if not absolute objectivity, at least comparability in the evaluation of theories and ideas. By any criteria, in the forty years following World War II, anthropology has contributed a great deal to the understanding of human behavior, origins, language, and cultural history. By any measure, anthropological scholarship meets the test of experience.

Equally controversial are questions about the relevance of topics that anthropologists choose to study. Again we find many anthropologists who believe that the pursuit of knowledge is its own justification, and that researchers should address themselves to questions that will increase our understanding of human culture over the long run. Critics of this view argue that it is immoral to place the needs of the discipline ahead of human needs, and that anthropologists should address with equal vigor the pressing social problems of their day. They add that a discipline that focuses on only theoretical issues is destined to become involuted and obsolete. A good example of this is in the use of remote sensing not only to map resources, etc., but also to promote indigenous territorial claims (see the Using Anthropology box, *Imaging Resource Depletion*, in Chapter 13).

As Michael Horowitz reports, World Bank projects where anthropologists and other social scientists are involved show a 15-percent higher rate of return of investment than comparable projects where they are not (1994). The extended case study by Della McMillan, presented in Chapter 13, shows why this occurs. Anthropologists not only accumulate factual data, they bring together experience from other areas. McMillan, in studying settlement, drew heavily on previous work by other anthropologists in Africa and Asia.

The response of anthropology to the rising incidence of AIDS is a good indication of the discipline's way of responding to a global health crisis.

Somewhat surprisingly, the initial response was minimal, reflecting both the prejudices of society toward this sexually transmitted disease and the still strong feeling in the discipline that theoretical research is of primary concern (Herdt, 1987, pp. 1–3). Complicating the issue was the initial reluctance of funding agencies to support research that was not medical. Given the fact that the impact of AIDS had been felt primarily by traditionally stigmatized and disadvantaged groups, together with the fact that cultural factors play an important role in the spread of the disease, anthropologists might have been expected to be in the forefront of AIDS research. And though they are handicapped by the funding problem, anthropologists have undertaken both theoretical research on AIDS and projects designed to deliver better health care to its victims. At the first appearance of the disease in the United States, in 1981, some anthropologists responded with proposals for relevant research. Others moved into AIDS research as it became clear that the epidemic touched upon their areas of specialization, whether medical research, social behavior, or an interest in a region hard hit by the virus. Somewhat belatedly, the American Anthropological Association (AAA) officially declared such work to have the highest priority and undertook to form a task force of experts. Today at least 200 anthropologists are working full- or part-time on AIDS-related research or projects.

Ethics in Anthropology

In 1968, in response to years of soul-searching discussion and often heated debate inflamed by the political controversies of the decade, the American Anthropological Association appointed a committee on ethics. That committee proposed a code of ethics that was eventually approved by the AAA membership.

The Principles of Professional Responsibility, as the code was titled, describes anthropologists' responsibilities to the people studied and to both home and host governments. The document states that the researcher's paramount responsibility is to the people under study. A thorough and honest explanation of the investigation, the right to remain anonymous, and fair compensation for all services are due to everyone involved. In addition, the researcher has a moral obligation to consider possible repercussions of the investigation and to communicate them to informants, making sure they understand.

The anthropologist's responsibilities to the public center on the commitment to disseminate results in a truthful and candid manner. No researcher should knowingly falsify or color any findings, or provide to sponsors, authorities, or others any information that has been withheld from the public.

As teachers, anthropologists are admonished to evaluate students solely on the basis of their intellectual abilities (not on their race, sex, or any other criterion), to alert students to ethical problems, to inform them realistically as to what will be expected of them in graduate school and what their career opportunities will be, to acknowledge all student assistance in print, and to encourage and assist students in their efforts to find secure positions and legitimate sources of research funds.

In their dealings with sponsors, anthropologists should be honest about their qualifications and research goals and should require that sponsors disclose the sources of funds and grant the researchers the right to make all ethical decisions.

Finally, the anthropologists' relationships with their own and host governments must be honest and candid. Under no circumstances should an anthropologist agree to secret research, reports, or debriefings of any kind.

There are no simple solutions for today's social scientists. Our consciousness of ethical issues has been raised; the need for each anthropologist to determine the relative merits of each case is clear. Equally clear is the need to found our ethics, approaches, and interventions on solid theoretical principles and experience.

Theory in Anthropology

The kind of problem the researcher selects depends largely on the theoretical perspective in which the individual is trained. Theories are the backbone of scientific research. A **scientific theory** is a statement that postulates ordered relationships among natural phenomena and explains some aspect of the world. The theoretical model chosen by researchers leads them to ask certain kinds of questions and helps them formulate some questions as specific hypotheses. For example, a functionalist theory of politics that stresses social stability and integration will direct a researcher to gather data on institutions that adjudicate disputes, release tension, and promote group solidarity. A Marxist theory of politics that emphasizes conflict and competition among those who control the means of production and those who supply the labor will direct a researcher to study instances of conflict reflecting class or economic divisions.

This is not to say that researchers see only what they are looking for and block out everything else. Still, perception is always selective and tends to be shaped by one's assumptions—in this case, by what one expects or hopes to find. To prevent this issue from becoming a problem, anthropologists should be careful to spell out their theoretical assumptions when they write the plans for their research and later when they report their findings. Thus their biases, if indeed they have influenced the research, are at least not hidden.

A theory is never tested directly; one tests theoretical expectations by testing specific hypotheses. A **hypothesis** is a statement about relationships that can possibly be shown to be untrue. The statement, "Cigarette smoking is bad," is not a hypothesis because it does not define "bad" or specify the relationship between smoking and anything else. It seems like a valid or logical statement, but a skeptic might well argue that the economic, social, or psychological benefits of smoking outweigh the physical harm it causes. The similar statement, "Cigarette smoking increases the risk of lung cancer," is a hypothesis because the risk of lung cancer can be measured among smokers and nonsmokers and a causal relationship between exposure to specific carcinogens in tobacco and smoking can be established. This distinction is important because unless a statement is logically falsifiable by appeal to relevant facts (or subjected to the appropriate test), it cannot enhance our knowledge of the world. If the actual results or observations are consistent with the hypothesis in a significant number of cases, the theory that generated the hypothesis is strengthened and perhaps expanded. But if the observed results of hypothesis testing repeatedly contradict theoretical expectations, the theory is eventually altered or abandoned. In short, theories survive as long as they continue to suggest useful

approaches to the phenomena that scientists are trying to explain.

A theory may be the product of decades of diligent research. Or as in the case of Charles Darwin, it may be the product of a young scientist capable of seeing through the preconceptions that block the insights of others. Every theory has its blind spots: aspects of a subject that are underemphasized or disregarded in favor of other aspects. And new theories often displace the old by redirecting attention to those neglected areas. Through this dynamic process—the constant challenging and retesting of ideas—the discipline's theoretical framework is refined and developed over time.

A variety of theories have been developed over the hundred-year history of the discipline of cultural anthropology. These reflect both traditional issues that scientists have addressed and contemporary concerns. Regardless of theoretical focus, however, virtually all anthropologists, regardless of the actual research they are pursuing, share the belief that humans are part of a larger evolutionary process; that adaptation is the driving force of evolutionary change; and that, ultimately, individual motivations, strategies for coping, and decisions determine the nature of adaptation and larger evolutionary processes.

Despite of this agreement in principle, contemporary anthropological theory is far from unified; instead, the discipline presents the student with a bewildering array of labels that signal widely divergent approaches. Rather than providing a summary of all these approaches, we will briefly introduce the two key models or positions characteristic of the field (Poggie, DeWalt, & Dressler, 1992, p. 6). One, the so-called "natural science paradigm," is the basis for the material and explanations that will be presented in this volume. The other is what might be called the "interpretive paradigm," following Milford Spiro's distinction (1992, p. 265). Terms such as "subjective," "symbolic," "relativistic," and "postmodern" are also used in conjunction with the interpretive model.

The unifying belief among anthropologists who subscribe to the natural science approach is that there are important regularities in human behavior across cultures, as well as diversity, and that these can be accounted for through empirical methods. **Empiricism** refers to the direct experiencing of the reality being described or explained. Obviously

Ethnographers collect and interpret data on every aspect of social life, including how people relate their own aspirations and points of view.
(Jeff Rotman/Peter Arnold Inc.)

there are limits to direct experience, but direct observation and measurement, implicit in the empirical approach, is central to the idea of anthropology as a scientific endeavor (see also Brown, 1991; Barth, 1994, p. 76; and Rappaport, 1993, p. 76).

The interpretive approach, strongly articulated by Clifford Geertz, argues that true objectivity is difficult to achieve. And, since each culture has to be viewed relativistically, the anthropologist should not strive to uncover general patterns of behavior but should concentrate on drawing detailed pictures on each individual culture. Lila Abu-Lughod's work with the Bedouin of Egypt is an elegant example of this approach; she has allowed women to narrate their own lives, giving first-person accounts of childhood, marriage, and social life (1993). She has thereby avoided presenting the people merely as objects of the anthropologist's imagination. While the shared humanity of the Bedouin women emerges very eloquently in their own words, there are obvious limits to this approach. It makes generalization very difficult, and it can lead to an extreme form of cultural relativism (one which might be called "cultural determinism"), by assuming that each culture is unique and unconstrained by its environment and biolog-ical processes. It tends to ignore the fact that however distinctive humans and their culture may be, human behavior, like that of all of living organisms, is mediated through the interactions of a biological entity—the individual—with a specific set of environmental factors. We will take this up in much more detail in Chapter 3, but this is the rationale for the abbreviated discussion on the development of theory that looks primarily at that work leading up to modern, empirically grounded approaches.

The Early Evolutionists

As Darwin's evolutionary perspective became established in many areas of natural science, social scientists of his day, such as Edward Tylor and Lewis Henry Morgan, also embraced at least some aspects of it. This development is not surprising, as Darwin himself was influenced by a social philosopher, Herbert Spencer, and was very much concerned with humans in an evolutionary perspective. The idea that cultural changes occur through long-term historical or evolutionary processes (**cultural evolution**) was accepted by most social scientists of the late nineteenth century, including Sigmund

Freud, Max Weber, and Émile Durkheim, extremely influential pioneers in the emerging fields of psychology, political science, and sociology.

One early issue still important to explain today concerns the following question: why, although we are all members of one species with very little genetic variation among dispersed populations, do we exhibit great cultural variation? Sir Edward Tylor, who defined the concept of culture in 1871, explicitly repudiated the idea that cultural evolution had anything to do with race or the innate superiority of any population or society. All peoples of the world, he said, shared a "psychic unity": all are equal in their innate capabilities, intelligence, motivations, and cultural potential. He invoked the concept of evolution to explain cultural diversity. Tylor held to the basic premise that cultures progress through a sequence of evolutionary stages—a pattern that we now refer to as **unilineal evolution**. The reason that societies differ from one another, he reasoned, is that they began to travel this course at different points and are traveling it at different speeds. While some (notably European societies, in this view) had already arrived at an advanced form of social organization, others were still in earlier stages of development. Tylor viewed society as being similar to a living organism, governed by its own laws of growth and thus passing inevitably from one developmental stage to another, each progressively more "mature" or advanced.

Contemporary tribal or "primitive" societies were regarded in this view as akin to "living fossils," in which the characteristic features of early stages of cultural evolution were preserved. In the wedding rituals of the Balkans, for example, symbolic expressions of hostility between the families of the bride and groom were seen as vestiges of the days when men simply kidnapped or dragged off their mates. Societies in which inheritance or political office followed the female line were viewed as evidence of an early state of matriarchy, which eventually was replaced by a more "advanced" system—patriarchy. The ethnocentrism and sexism evident in the thinking of these early theorists makes it hard today to appreciate fully the positive contributions they made.

Lewis Henry Morgan, an American contemporary of Tylor, was a lawyer who became interested in anthropology as a young man when he helped his Iroquois neighbors in central New York with their legal fight for their land. In 1851 Morgan published his impressions of the Iroquois, the first full-length field report on an American Indian tribe. Soon he gave up the practice of law to pursue his new avocation full time. Like Tylor, Morgan believed that anthropology should be relevant to contemporary societal problems at the same time that it attempted to formulate general laws. In his third major work, *Ancient Society* (1877), Morgan classified societies into three stages or levels of development: savagery, barbarism, and civilization. He divided each of the first two stages into lower, middle, and upper substages. Morgan defined his stages by the level of their technological sophistication. Each of these technological levels, Morgan claimed, was associated with specific cultural patterns or institutions—a particular kind of kinship structure, a particular type of legal system, and so forth.

Morgan was particularly interested in the evolution of the family. In the earliest stages of human development, he postulated, there was no family structure at all; men and women mated indiscriminately. Gradually human society developed a form of communal marriage, in which groups of brothers married groups of sisters—in some cases their own sisters. In the next stage, sibling unions were forbidden. People began to pair off but continued to live in large groups. Gradually, as society continued to evolve, men established the right to their own households, each with a wife, or more commonly with several wives. Only in the final stage of social evolution—civilization—did men and women become partners in monogamous marriage.

Though much of Morgan's language sounds old-fashioned and his bias toward Western society is obvious, his contribution extends beyond anthropology. Morgan has had a profound impact on modern intellectual and political history. Both Karl Marx and Friedrich Engels corresponded with Morgan and were greatly influenced by his findings, which they used in formulating their own theories regarding historical processes. Engels' book *The Origin of the Family, Private Property and the State* (1884/1972) has had a profound effect on the development of socialist thinking, and Morgan's *Ancient Society* was a major source of Engels' ideas. Thus Morgan's ideas became the basis for political ideology. Closer to our concerns here, is Morgan's finding that there was a rough fit between social organization, technology, and the organization of production.

The concept of unilineal evolution proved to be misleading. There is no neat or universal sequence to cultural change or development. Moreover, in their interest in broad features of cultural evolution, early evolutionists lost sight of the role of individuals in society and of the great range of cultural behavior that occurs within some societies. Nevertheless, they made substantial contributions to anthropology. They reaffirmed the principle, fundamental to modern anthropology, that the variations we observe among contemporary societies are due to regular cultural processes. Moreover, in speculating about developmental sequences, they inspired many archaeologists to seek concrete data that would either validate or refute their ideas.

Individual Actors: A Response to Cultural Evolution

One of the anthropologists who criticized the early cultural evolutionists was Franz Boas, who had begun his career as a physical geographer. In *The Limitations of the Comparative Method of Anthropology* (1896/1966), Boas argued that anthropologists knew far too little about preliterate peoples to construct valid theories about the origins of social life. He believed that anthropological research should focus on the relationship between individual action and custom. A great proponent of fieldwork, Boas spent years studying the Kwakiutl Indians of the American Northwest. He learned their language and dedicated much of his career to recording their beliefs and practices. His interest was not in discovering laws of general evolutionary processes but in identifying laws that explained the relationship of individual actions to consensus and custom. Boas was one of the earliest anthropologists to recognize the importance of cultural relativism. The approach Boas adopted, now called **historical particularism**, is characterized by the collection of detailed ethnographic data.

It was largely through Boas's efforts that American ethnologists came to style themselves "cultural anthropologists" and to espouse the holistic view described earlier. Boas believed strongly that individuals are the products of their cultural systems and that the concept of culture is the keystone of anthropology. Further, it was largely due to Boas

Pioneer ethnographer Franz Boas insisted upon detailed, firsthand ethnographic accounts of non-Western peoples. To this end, he immersed himself in the life and culture of the Kwakiutl Indians in British Columbia. Here Boas poses as a Kwakiutl hamatsa dancer in 1895. His meticulous attention to ethnographic detail set new standards for the field.
(The Smithsonian Institute)

that cultural relativism became an established tenet of the field.

Many of Boas's students became prominent in the rapidly developing discipline. Two, in particular, came to exemplify the field in the public eye due to the attention their work received. Ruth Benedict and Margaret Mead built directly on Boas's emphasis on culture and cultural diversity to formulate extremely influential theories—in many ways anticipating the more contemporary "interpretive" approach. One of the earliest anthropologists to suggest that each society produces its own characteristic personality was Ruth Benedict. In her widely read book, *Patterns of Culture* (1934/1959), Benedict claimed that from the grand arc of human potentialities each society unconsciously chooses a limited segment of traits to be cultural ideals, and that individuals gradually internalize these ideals. The result is a general similarity in ways of thinking and behaving—in other words, a group personality pattern.

To illustrate this process, Benedict analyzed the basic personality traits of two societies: the Kwakiutl Indians of the Pacific Northwest (the people Boas had studied) and the Zuñi Indians of the American Southwest. The Kwakiutl she depicted as an aggressive people prone to excess, constantly competing with one another for bigger and better supernatural visions, which they induced through self-torture. The Zuñi, in contrast, were portrayed as peaceful and restrained; distrustful of excesses and disruptive experiences of any kind, they always kept to the middle of the road. Benedict's ideas have been sharply criticized as unjustified stereotyping, and there is little evidence that any society is characterized by a modal or group personality. But her basic approach, the effort to characterize a group by its cultural style, continues to be of interest to anthropologists who take an interpretivist approach.

Upon completing her graduate work as a student of Boas and Benedict at Columbia University in 1925, Mead set out on her first major field trip: to study adolescents on the Polynesian island of Samoa. Because puberty was presumably rooted in the biological nature of things, the social transition from childhood to adulthood was thought to be universally stressful. But Mead believed that adolescence might not be so universally stressful after all. If behavior and values differed from culture to culture, so might the experience of adolescence.

She found, in fact, that the Samoans followed a relatively short course from childhood to adulthood. In her famous book, *Coming of Age in Samoa* (1928/1971), Mead reported these findings and stated her conclusions: "adolescence is not necessarily a time of stress and strain, but cultural conditions make it so" (1971, p. 234). In later ethnographic studies she went on to argue that sex roles and personality traits—indeed, personality in general—are not biological givens but rather extremely plastic qualities that are molded in the image of cultural ideals through childrearing practices.

Mead's work, like Benedict's, has been criticized for stereotyping and for overlooking much of the variability within the societies she studied (see Freeman, 1983; Brown, 1991). But by showing that a "fact of life" such as adolescence or masculinity can take different forms, Mead made the important point that sometimes what is taken for granted as "human nature" can be a cultural artifact.

Functional and Structural Approaches

The early British avocational and professional anthropologists collected vast amounts of data on a wide range of nonliterate societies, covering every conceivable topic from kinship, marriage, and sex-ual conduct to food, games, clothing, and houses. A picture of immense cultural diversity emerged in each area. How were these differences to be summarized? As ethnographic information became voluminous, a cross-cultural comparison of all known societies on all known traits became difficult. Anthropologists began to realize that approaches based on isolated cultural traits did not account for basic differences among societies. Patterns of behavior, they discovered, were organized—and the organization differed from group to group. Thus in order to focus on comparisons among societies, and ultimately to shed light on the reasons for cultural differences, some anthropologists began to investigate the variety of ways in which humans organize themselves. This focus, still the hallmark of British social anthropology, has had a profound impact on the field in general.

Functionalism. One major contributor to our understanding of social organization was Bronislaw Malinowski. Abandoning a career in physics and mathematics, he left Poland in 1910, studied anthropology in London, and then traveled to the Trobriand Islands in the western Pacific to do his fieldwork. Once he was there, however, World War I prevented him from returning home, and the year stretched to three years—a longer period than any other anthropologist had ever spent in the field. Malinowski became fluent in the language of the Trobrianders and immersed himself in their culture, noting in minute detail the routines of their daily life, their friendships, their fears, their ambitions, and the tones of voice they assumed in different situations. The result was one of the most thorough and vivid ethnographic studies ever done.

Malinowski's reflections on the material he collected in the Trobriand Islands led him to conclude that all the elements of a society are functional in that they serve to satisfy culturally defined needs of the people in that society. In this theory, called **functionalism,** Malinowski identified three basic types of human needs: biological needs (such as those for food and sexual activity), instrumental needs (such as those for education and the law), and integrative needs (such as the need for a common world view to facilitate communication).

To meet these needs, the society develops **institutions,** or recurrent patterns of activity, such as religion, art, a kinship system, law, and family life.

Malinowski maintained that the institutions of a society dovetail not only with the needs they fulfill but also with each other. The function of religion, for example, is to establish and reinforce "valuable mental attitudes such as reverence for tradition, harmony with environment, courage and confidence in the struggle with difficulties and at the prospect of death" (1954, p. 89). Though the Trobriand Islanders are highly skilled navigators and fishermen, for example, they perform magico-religious rituals before embarking on long ocean voyages. They do not bother with such rituals for everyday fishing expeditions, but a long voyage on the open sea in a fragile canoe is far more dangerous, and the rituals help to allay some of their apprehensions. Reduced anxiety does not mean simply a more peaceful state of mind. A crew paralyzed by fear is less likely to complete a dangerous canoe voyage than one that is confident of the protection of providence. A culture, in Malinowski's view, is an integrated network of mutually supportive institutions ultimately related to human needs.

Structural Functionalism. Like Malinowski, Alfred Reginald Radcliffe-Brown argued that various aspects of a society should be analyzed in terms of institutions and their function. In his view, however, their central function was not to satisfy individual needs but to maintain the social structure—the society's pattern of social relations and institutions. To reflect this emphasis on social structure and to distinguish his ideas from Malinowski's, Radcliffe-Brown's theory has been called **structural functionalism**.

Radcliffe-Brown borrowed from the French sociologist Émile Durkheim the notion that a society is distinct from its individual members. A society has its own internal structure of beliefs and practices, governed by norms, which mold individual behavior. According to Radcliffe-Brown, the job of anthropology is not to concentrate on individual actions but to see through these particulars to the structure governing them. And the key to that structure is the society's norms.

Thus while Malinowski focused on institutions and individual behavior as the major oranizing principle of society, Radcliffe-Brown concentrated on the norms that control behavior. In his view, all categories of social relationship in a society—the relationship between adult and child, man and woman, father-in-law and daughter-in-law, rich and poor—are regulated by such norms. Their purpose is to steer people through such relationships with a minimum of conflict. Radcliffe-Brown noted, for example, that many societies prescribe avoidance relationships between certain relatives by marriage, prohibiting them from entering the same room or speaking to one another. Other societies (including our own, to some extent) prescribe joking relationships between in-laws—superficial relationships dominated by teasing. According to Radcliffe-Brown, both norms serve the same function: to prevent conflict between potential antagonists, in the first case by keeping them alert and in the second by easing tension through laughter.

By reducing conflict in social relationships, norms perform the important function of stabilizing and perpetuating the social structure. A lawyer by training, Radcliffe-Brown appeared to think of norms as laws that people obeyed. He viewed societies as living organisms: highly ordered systems of differentiated parts, each of which contributes to the maintenance of the whole. By keeping the social "parts"—customs, practices, beliefs, relationships—working together in harmony, norms provide the structural stability that Radcliffe-Brown considered the necessary condition of existence in any society. Differences among societies depend on the way each society developed its own unique structure, its own characteristic arrangement of parts. Radcliffe-Brown believed that by uncovering the structures of a wide range of societies, anthropologists could ultimately construct a taxonomy, or comprehensive classification, of societies.

The Contributions of the Functionalist Approaches to Anthropology. Radcliffe-Brown's theories, like Malinowski's, stimulated interest in the internal dynamics of societies. And like Malinowski, Radcliffe-Brown traced the variations among societies to the means societies select to meet their basic needs—that is, to their behavioral norms and institutions. Yet neither theory explains why the cultural systems that developed out of the same basic needs vary so widely. Despite this serious shortcoming, these theories furthered anthropological study by supplying a theoretical framework for examining the internal workings of societies. Moreover, they encouraged anthropological inquiry rooted in empiricism—that is, reliance on observable and quantifiable data. Radcliffe-Brown's early view of anthropology as a scientific discipline that focuses on human society in the same way that biology focuses on other species is still held by a majority of modern practitioners (see Hughes, 1988, pp. 18–20).

In the 1950s, American anthropologists became interested once again in tracing broad patterns of cultural development. Reviving evolutionary theories, they enlarged and refined the classical evolutionist approach on the basis of new information and ideas developed in the intervening years. Like the early evolutionists, they proposed that the key to cultural diversity was evolution, but they saw cultural evolution from a new perspective—as the product of human beings' interactions with their environment. They also incorporated evidence offered by both archaeologists and ethnologists for broad regularities in the development of human culture. Moreover, the new wave of scholarship was able to analyze these broad developmental regularities without recourse to the antiquated notions of European superiority that underlay the concept of progress in earlier schemes. It had become clearer that the organizational and technological principles that nonindustrial people used in extracting resources from their environments were not simply "primitive" anachronisms but were generally practical, ingenious, and successful strategies. It was obvious, too, that sometimes these technologies were environmentally sounder than "advanced" Western practices.

One of the anthropologists who began the reconsideration of cultural evolution was Leslie White. Although White was trained in the Boasian tradition, he also greatly admired the work of the nineteenth-century evolutionists and regretted that their positive contributions had been ignored in the general rush to criticize their ethnocentrism. Like them, he believed that societies tended to develop progressively more complex forms of organization. Combining the idea that social evolution proceeded by decreasing entropy (randomness) with the theory that culture is an energy-capturing system, White (1949) sought to pinpoint the cause of cultural complexity.

White reasoned that in order to provide themselves with the basic necessities of life, human beings have to expend energy. During the early stages of human history, they used their own bodies as the major source of energy, but gradually they began to harness fire, water, wind, and other resources to do some of their work for them. Energy capture increased as people learned to fashion more and more efficient tools, to domesticate animals, to construct power-driven machines, and so on. At each step of the way, other aspects of culture evolved in response to the newly achieved level of usable energy. In other words, improvements in technology (that is, methods of energy capture) propelled the rest of culture forward. White's basic premise was that cultural development was rooted in technology, and that individual motivation and decision making were of little importance in the grand sweep of evolution. Here we see a return to the view of culture as an organism and of individuals as passive participants.

Cultural Ecology

Like White, Julian Steward was concerned with cultural evolution, but unlike White, he focused on the evolution of cultural systems through environmental adaptation. His work gave rise to an approach called **cultural ecology**. Steward's approach to cultural diversity required the simultaneous investigation of technology, culture, and the physical environment (including neighboring populations as well as climate, terrain, and natural resources). White had maintained that evolutionists should focus on human culture as a whole and identify general laws. Steward believed that this approach to discovering such laws failed precisely because it dealt with culture in the abstract rather than with the actual development of particular cultural systems. Steward (1972) called for the replacement of universal or unilineal evolutionism by another approach, **multilineal evolutionism**, which would focus on the development of individual cultures or populations without insisting that all follow the same evolutionary pattern.

Marxist Anthropology: An Alternative to Cultural Evolution

By the 1960s a large number of American scholars were interested in the internal sources of social change or disruption. By then the world had been shaken by two major wars and numerous less extensive ones; by dramatic revolutions in Russia, China, Egypt, Iraq, Indonesia, Algeria, and Cuba; and by a multitude of independence movements in Africa and elsewhere. Karl Marx's notion of dialectical materialism, which postulates that historically societies move through distinctive stages, or modes of production, seemed to have explanatory value in efforts to understand the broad sweep of historic change.

Each mode of production, Marx held, is characterized by distinctive social, economic, and political relations among members of the society. Thus, any generalization about society is meaningful only in the context of a particular mode of production. Moreover, modes of production are transformed over time in a predetermined direction. It is not surprising that there is a close resemblance between cultural evolutionist and Marxist theory; both draw on common sources in Tylor and Morgan.

The causes of this transformation lie in the internal contradictions within any given mode of production, which ultimately are resolved by progressive change. In the capitalist mode of production, the contradiction is between the interests of those who control the society's means of production (capital and technology) and the interests of those whose labor produces economic goods. The owners or controllers of production are interested in increasing their wealth by exploiting the workers. The workers are interested in improving their position, and the only way they can do so is by rebelling against those who control the means of production. In the course of history societies have passed through feudalism, Oriental despotism, capitalism, and other modes of production, each with its own combination of distinctive elements and contradictions. The idea of universal progress through a limited number of stages is very similar to Morgan's early formulation. It differs, though, in stressing internal conflict as a primary source of change.

Marxist anthropology, then, is the study of internal sources of social change, with a focus on a society's distinctive set of elements and contradictions. The main contribution of this perspective to contemporary investigations is the serious attention it directs to two critical questions: Who gets what, and how, in society? What role does inequality play in the generation of social conflict? Considerable research on these issues has been carried out in recent years, particularly in efforts to understand the relationship between underdevelopment and the activities of industrial nations. By looking for general processes that go beyond national boundaries and narrowly defined social entities (tribes, communities, ethnic groups) and examining long-term interrelationships among people who may seem to have no connection with one another, we see the truth of the commonplace observation that we occupy one world (Wolf, 1982, p. 3).

Cultural Materialism

A further elaboration of the ideas of Marx, Engels, White, and Steward constitutes a perspective sometimes called **cultural materialism**. Marvin Harris, its leading exponent (see Harris, 1988; 1993), emphasizes the material constraints on cultural adaptation. He views ideas, values, and religious beliefs as the means or products of adaptation to environmental conditions (material constraints), which include available food resources, climate, water, predators, disease, and so on. For Harris, the ideas people hold about food taboos, childrearing, and religion are best understood as having developed to further the survival of their culture in its habitat, though the people themselves are usually unaware of this function. A close variant of this approach is Magnarella's model of socio-cultural systems, which he terms "human materialism" (1993); the main difference being that Magnarella stresses the motivations of the individual actors as a dynamic force (1993, p. 14).

In some respects these approaches are similar to that of the English functionalists, who also stress the notion of society as a functioning system—each social institution playing its role in the maintenance of the structure of the whole. Harris's contribution is the notion of adaptation guided by a variety of cost-benefit calculations. Successful adaptations are those that promote a favorable balance of costs and benefits, usually from the standpoint of the society as a whole. Food taboos are a case in point. Both Islam and Judaism have dietary prohibitions against the consumption of pork (among other items). Harris has argued that this dietary law is an adaptive outcome of the fact that the raising of pigs in the arid Middle East would be an inefficient and environmentally poor use of resources (Harris, 1987). This approach has been criticized for being, among other things, unclear as to how costs and benefits are actually weighed at a societal level and even as to how anything might be shown to be mal-adaptive. Warfare, cannibalism, even female infanticide are explained in terms of large-scale utilitarian functions such as population control or protein conservation. In short, the main criticism is that it explains too little because it explains too much. Anything can be asserted to be adaptive or cost-effective in the absence of a consistent system of measurement (Vayda, 1987). Its strength is that it leads researchers to tackle basic issues of human existence and to seek out empirical data with which to test ideas.

Applying Theory: Fieldwork and Data Collection

The theories we have discussed have been built upon, refined, or abandoned over the course of a hundred years. It is this constant need for revision and testing of theories and hypotheses that propels anthropologists into the field.

Field research generates not only new theories but also new methods. For as theories are refined, they highlight new aspects of culture, stimulating the development of new techniques with which to explore them. New methods inevitably influence theory by allowing fieldworkers to uncover facts that have previously been overlooked or ignored—facts that call for modifications in current theories or, in the extreme case, explode current theories altogether.

In short, anthropological theory and method are mutually dependent. New theories produce new methods, and new methods produce new theories. Through this spiraling process, as anthropologists seek increasingly reliable means of gathering information that enable them to make increasingly accurate generalizations about human culture, the work of theory-building is carried on and our understanding of the complexities of human culture is extended.

Studies in the Field

Regardless of theoretical orientation, cultural anthropology relies heavily on the first-hand observation of human behaviors as a means of gathering data and testing hypotheses generated by theories. Most theoretical approaches are not developed in quiet corners of university libraries nor modified through laboratory experiments. They evolve through continual testing among the peoples whose ways of life they seek to explain.

Anthropologists gather data in the field partly through first-hand observation and reporting, living among the members of a group in an effort to understand their customary ways of thinking and behaving. They ask people questions and carefully record their answers. They closely examine the things the people produce: their tools, baskets, sculptures, musical instruments, weapons, jewelry, clothing, houses. Above all, they spend many hours simply watching the people's daily routines and interactions. From these activities emerge the fine-grained ethnographic descriptions that together constitute an invaluable repository of information about the breadth and variety of human culture. There is more to fieldwork than simple observation, as we shall see, but it is first-hand observation that gives anthropological reports a distinctive and vibrant quality.

Fieldwork is hard work and requires intense preparation. Today almost all anthropologists are trained at universities. Graduate programs are designed to give students a thorough grounding in anthropological literature, to make them aware of theoretical disputes and of what is already known about the cultures of a particular area, to enable them to establish a valid sample, and to formulate realistic research questions and organize and interpret the ethnographic data they collect. Just as the development of precision instruments in the natural sciences has allowed scientists to probe previously uncharted areas of nature (the surface of the moon, for example), so improved techniques of field research have enabled anthropologists to explore more systematically the many ways of human life and thus to broaden our understanding of human nature. Methodical observation and interviewing, systematic comparison, and sampling are the primary research tools of the anthropologist today.

But the process of observation is not neat and tidy. From the day the ethnographer arrives in the field to the day he or she departs, the course of research is being shaped by myriad chance encounters—often of a less than benign sort. The would-be researcher may be held up for months getting permission from local officials to visit the area targeted for investigation; lack of all-weather roads may make it impossible to visit a site during a critical period; local conflicts or strife may curtail movement from one community to another. Moreover, the data being collected are constantly affected by the researcher's own social presence. Most ethnographers gain access to a community by associating themselves with a particular family or local grouping. Such an alliance, however tenuous, invariably affects the ethnographer's relations with others in the community—sometimes favorably, but sometimes negatively. People who are on poor terms with one's hosts tend to be cool or suspicious of the guests.

Any number of unforeseen circumstances can change the direction of a project. Daniel and Ann Bradburd went to Iran in 1973 to carry out a project among nomadic pastoralists. Their objective was to model formally the process of decision making as it applied to decisions to migrate or to remain camped. They spoke with many scholars and officials familiar with various parts of the country and determined that a population called the Komanchi would be suitable, as they were sheepherders who migrated over a substantial distance during the course of the year.

Once among the Komanchi, the Bradburds soon found their initial objectives less interesting (and less manageable in practice) than other aspects of Komanchi economic and social life. Decisions to move the tents and herds turned out to be based on a few fairly obvious criteria, and, on balance, the project seemed not very likely to add much to theory regarding information processing. At the same time, unexpectedly, they found very marked differences in wealth and social position among members of a tribe they had supposed to be egalitarian. Accordingly, they shifted their focus and methods of data collection to address issues related to animal husbandry, wealth, and economic mobility—a topic on which Dan Bradburd has since published extensively. Both the original topic of research and the new one were grounded in extensive but rather different bodies of theory; their evaluation of the field situation ended up determining which was pursued (see Bradburd, 1990).

It is reasonable to ask why so much emphasis is placed on theory, method, and planning for the field when, in the end, things are likely to turn out not at all as one expected. The answer is that command of theory or theories enables researchers to be flexible and to ask significant questions no matter what conditions they encounter in the field. The researcher who has a firm theoretical focus can tai-lor work successfully to accommodate ever-changing circumstances in the field. Fieldwork usually must be preceded not only by theoretical grounding but by training in the language and history of the area chosen and in specialized techniques of sampling, computation, and analysis of data.

Today, more and more field research is problem-oriented. That is, the anthropologist focuses on one or more important theoretical issues. Nevertheless, anthropologists investigate so wide a range of problems, they must command an equally wide range of information-gathering techniques. One technique that is basic to almost every piece of field research is participant observation, used in conjunction with interviewing, and systematic collection of economic, demographic, and material culture data.

Participant Observation. The method most widely used by anthropologists to collect information in the field is **participant observation,** which begins the moment an anthropologist enters the field and continues during the entire time of residence. In practice, "participation" can range from commuting to the village or neighborhood from a home nearby to almost total immersion in community life. In general, participant observers involve themselves in the cultures they study. Malinowski, a pioneer in this approach, explains why it is essential for anthropologists to participate in the activities of the societies they investigate:

> Soon after I had established myself in [Omarakana, Trobriand Islands], I began to take part, in a way, in the village life, to look forward to the important or festive events, to take personal interest in the gossip and the developments of the village occurrences; to wake up every morning to a day presenting itself to me more or less as it does to the native. . . . As I went on my morning walk through the village, I could see intimate details of family life, of toilet, cooking, taking of meals; I could see the arrangements for the day's work, people starting on their errands, or groups of men and women busy at some manufacturing tasks. Quarrels, jokes, family scenes, events usually trivial, sometimes dramatic but always significant, formed the atmosphere of my daily life, as well as of theirs. . . .

> Also, over and over again, I committed breaches of etiquette, which the natives, familiar with me, were not slow in pointing out. I had to learn how

Participant observation, one of the main means of collecting ethnographic data, involves many hours spent in conversation. Richard Lee interviews a group of San of the Kalahari Desert.

(Irven DeVore/Anthrophoto)

to behave, and to a certain extent, I acquired "the feeling" for native good and bad manners. With this, and with the capacity of enjoying their company and sharing some of their games and amusements, I began to feel that I was indeed in touch with the natives, and this is certainly the preliminary condition for being able to carry on successful field work. [Malinowski, 1922/1961, pp. 7–8]

Participant observation, then, helps anthropologists to see cultures from the inside, to see people behaving informally and spontaneously. Furthermore, it forces fieldworkers to learn how to behave according to the natives' rules.

In taking their notes, anthropologists often use code sheets, checklists of observed attitudes and behaviors and inferred motivations for these behaviors. Such observational techniques have been used to study, for example, the relationship between personality characteristics in children and various childrearing practices (Whiting, 1963). A fieldworker might observe a child during a five-minute period and then assign a score for nurturance on the basis of the number of times the child gave food to a younger child or provided help, emotional support, guidance, or information. Similarly, the fieldworker might rate a child on aggression on the basis of the number of times the child hit, pushed, bossed, or verbally attacked other children within a five-minute span. These ratings would then form the basis of well-documented

profiles of the personality characteristics of the members of several cultures.

One very promising method of collecting behavioral data, which is largely free of cultural or observation bias, is that of **time allocation**. The anthropologist designs a schedule that records types of activities throughout the day (Gross, 1984). It is a way of sampling what people are actually doing as opposed to what they say or think they are doing. If a researcher is interested in studying father-child relationships, father-child interactions are observed and recorded at various randomly selected times during the day, thus providing insight into the frequency of various sorts of interaction.

The value of this approach is seen in the work of a research team led by Daniel Gross in central Brazil. Comparing four culturally similar Amazonian populations in different habitats and with different food resources, they found that levels of non-work activity—particularly leisure-time pursuits—were sharply curtailed where resources were least abundant (Rubin, Flowers, & Gross, 1986). All the groups worked approximately the same number of hours but individuals in the poorer habitats engaged in fewer leisure activities and encouraged their children to play games that were low in energy costs, thus conserving their strength. In other words, people were adapting to hardship by adjusting their behavior so as to husband their energy, and even that of their children.

Codebook for Time Allocation Used in Human Ecology in Central Brazil Project
1976–77
As revised 1/20/77

Var. no.	Variable description	Column no.
1	I.D. no. of household visited	1, 2
2	Day	3, 4
3	Month	5, 6
4	Year	7, 8
5	Time (use 24-hour clock)	9–12
6	Weather R – Raining	13
	S – Sunny	
	C – Cloudy	
	Note – Make note in observation column whenever it is dark at time of visit.	
7	Individual's household number	14, 15
8	Individual's ID number within household	16, 17
9	Main activity of individual (major category)	18

G – Garden labor   S – School   K – Keeping house
W – Wild product   H – Personal hygiene   D – Domestic animal care
M – Manufacture and upkeep   E – Eating   P – "Passeando" (traveling outside the village)
L – Labor for sale   R – Recreation (ceremony or sport where all involved)
C – Child care   B – Business
F – Food preparation   I – Idleness   X – Other

Figure 1–1. Field log used by Nancy Flowers.

Anthropologist Nancy Flowers has spent many years working with Amazonian populations, gathering data on topics as diverse as religious beliefs, child care, and nutrition. Here she is recording an informant's description of a religious ceremony.

(Nancy Flowers)

The advantage of combining time-allocation studies with participant observation is that researchers are able to observe commonplace events that are taken for granted and would not be noteworthy to the individuals being observed, or behaviors that individuals might not want to discuss (such as alcohol or drug use). Informants often do not remember relevant details accurately; they may also report what they think should happen, or only what they want the researcher to know. The researcher who lives among the people can check these statements against the observable facts.

Official documents (statistical and historical records) can provide valuable information. Burton Pasternak (1983, 1993), working with historical documents and government census materials, was able to document precisely the migration and settlement of Chinese farmers in Taiwan over a century ago. The statistical and historical data, together with genealogical data gathered in interviews with living residents in the villages studied, made it possible for him to reconstruct family histories and to calculate such demographic variables as family size and rates of mortality, fertility, and longevity.

Surviving in the Field. Although anthropologists arrive in the field armed with an impressive array of research techniques, they usually find their new world full of surprises from the moment they set foot in it. One of the most basic difficulties is language. While a knowledge of the native language greatly enhances the quantity and quality of data that can be gathered, it is not always possible for an anthropologist to learn that language in advance. Or there may be important dialect differences between the language learned and that which is spoken in the community ultimately chosen as the research site.

The first month or so in the field is usually spent making practical arrangements. Fieldworkers have to find a place to live and a way to obtain food and supplies. Generally, anthropologists either rent a house in the community they are studying or live with a family. Some live in a tent or trailer, in a house that local people build for them, or in a school. Others commute from a nearby town. If the researchers intend to live in a remote village, they will have to purchase in advance many of the supplies they will use.

Food can also be a problem for anthropologists who work in remote towns and villages. Eating and drinking with local people may be an excellent way to establish rapport, but it can also present difficulties. Napoleon Chagnon, who studied the Yanomamö of the Brazilian-Venezuelan border, did most of his own cooking, but found it an ordeal:

It is appalling how complicated it can be to make oatmeal in the jungle. First, I had to make two trips to the river to haul the water. Next, I had to prime my kerosene stove with alcohol and get it burning. . . . Or, I would turn the kerosene on, hoping that the element was still hot enough to vaporize the fuel, and start a small fire in my palm-thatched hut. . . . Then I had to boil the oatmeal and pick the bugs out of it. . . . Eating three meals a day was out of the question. [Chagnon, 1983, pp. 12–13]

Sometimes the sex of the anthropologist poses special problems in the field. As men and women often move in very different social circles, a male anthropologist may find it difficult to interview women, collect their personal life histories, or closely observe the portion of their social lives from which men are excluded. Conversely, women fieldworkers may have difficulty moving in male social circles or be constrained by the limits of propriety that the society imposes on female behavior. In the end such constraints can usually be overcome, though sometimes some ingenuity may be called for, as we see in the Gender Issues box, *Becoming Invisible,* on page 28.

Not all fieldwork is chancy. Although the pioneer fieldworkers and many since them have ventured into extremely remote communities, hundreds of miles from the nearest bathtub, more and more work is now being done in urbanized areas. At the same time, more and more rural communities are acquiring electricity, modern plumbing, and transportation facilities. As a result, fieldwork has become less laborious and isolated—and perhaps less romantic as well.

Data and Analysis

Ethnographic fieldwork generally involves the study of one aspect of one community, which is itself one community among many. Fieldwork is a means of collecting a sample of a much larger phenomenon. When a researcher selects a village, that choice will determine just what aspect of a larger system he or she will experience. The utility of the study is vastly enhanced if the choice is made with some knowledge of where the sample falls in the **sampling universe**—the largest entity to be described, of which the sample is a part. The sampling universe may be a village, an ethnically defined population, a region, a town, or whatever.

If one goes to a farming village, for example, one should know roughly how it compares with other such communities in the region, or in the country as a whole. In order to interpret the data correctly, the researcher must have a sense of just what kind of sample it does or does not constitute and the dimensions of the overall sampling universe. If a Nigerian anthropologist came to a rural Wisconsin community to study American family life and if he or she then returned home to generalize about the United States as a whole, the scholar may be conveying erroneous information. While the data from Wisconsin might be entirely valid for that region, they would not be accurate for generalizing about New York City. **Sampling bias**—the tendency of a sample to exclude some members of the sampling universe and overrepresent others—would preclude generalization about many American ethnic groups, about urban families, about non-English-speaking Americans, and about anything else that was excluded from the original sample (here the rural Wisconsin community). It is wise to be wary of generalizations that are based on very limited samples or that are purported to apply to a sampling universe that is not described.

Even when the community or population to be studied is relatively small, the researcher must take care that the persons who serve as informants, the times when questions are asked, the ages of the people interviewed, and the like are carefully chosen. It is never possible to get universal coverage of a topic. Knowing that the data they do collect are only a sample, most cautious researchers clearly stipulate the bounds of their samples. One cannot simply interview people on the basis of the fact that one knows them or that they are available at convenient times. The researcher considers the sorts of questions to be asked, draws up a complete list of possible informants, and then selects those who meet appropriate criteria. A potential unintentional sampling bias has to do with sex; some male researchers tend to treat sex as an unimportant variable, collecting little data on women, or ignoring them altogether (Eicher, 1988, pp. 6–10, 66–70). Many researchers have underestimated the contributions of women to the economy of the populations they studied because they focused exclusively on male activities. In some societies women are socially invisible, as we saw in the previous box, but they should never be invisible to the researcher.

An ethnographer who wants household census data for a large area will have to make a compilation of all of the households in the population and then select those to be visited. In some cases a **random sample** may be appropriate—a sample in which each individual (in this case, each household) in the population has the same chance of being selected as any other.

Gender Issues

Becoming Invisible

IN THE SUMMER OF 1974, WHILE the Kurdish uprising was at its height, the anthropologist Amal Rassam was doing fieldwork in northern Iraq. As part of her research she wanted to carry out a survey of villages belonging to different ethnic groups. Having obtained her official research permit, she hired a taxi and its driver, a villager. Her notes read:

> On Tuesday morning, Ali my driver came to the hotel to pick me up to go to the village to begin my survey. He was dressed in the traditional garb of his region, which marked him as a rural inhabitant, a qarawi, or villager. I sat at the back of the taxi and we drove off. A few miles outside the city we were stopped at a military checkpoint. The soldier ignored my driver and came around to my side of the car, put his head in the window and asked where I was going. I told him that I was on my way to the village down the road, upon which he asked to see my identification papers. Discarding my protestations and ignoring my work permit, he made us turn around and go back to the city, claiming that the road

was mined and that he could not guarantee my safety.

> On the way back, I expressed my frustration to Ali and my fears that I wouldn't be able to carry my survey through. Upon some reflection he suggested that we try again in a day or two, but this time he would put on his suit and I should wear the *abaya* (the black cloak worn by the more traditional women in Iraq). And so we did. When he came back two days later to pick me up, he was dressed like an *effendi* (an urban gentleman). As we reached the checkpoint, the soldier on duty came around this time to the window of the driver, asked to see his papers, and wanted to know where we were going. Without a direct glance my way, he waved us on, and we continued to the village (Bates & Rassam, 1983, pp. 219–220).

The first time Rassam set out, she was the one in the automobile who was socially visible: she was a woman traveling alone in Western dress and clearly a foreigner to the area. Her status was immediately recognized by the soldier, who ignored the driver and asked for her

papers. Her dress identified her as a member of an urban, educated society, and the fact that she had hired a car marked her as a person of potential significance. The soldier chose not to assume responsibility for the presence of such a person in his area.

On the second attempt, sitting next to the driver in her abaya, Rassam became publicly invisible; the soldier perceived her as belonging to the driver. Moreover, the driver, resplendent in his Western-style suit, had acquired both visibility and a certain amount of social standing. The confrontation now became one between the two men, the soldier at the bottom of the military hierarchy and the effendi representing the bourgeoisie. The woman in the car ceased to exist in any political sense. This, we might add, was one occasion when being a woman anthropologist in the Middle East was an advantage. A male anthropologist would have had to show his identification papers along with those of the driver, and on being found to be a stranger to the area would probably have been turned back.

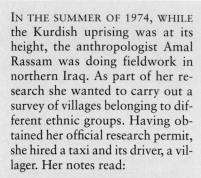

Generally the universe being investigated is sufficiently large and complex (a community, a region, a tribe) that in order to ensure a realistic sample of it, the researcher has to divide it into categories representing distinctive characteristics and then select a random sample from each category. The result is a **stratified sample**. If a sample of households in a community characterized by differences in wealth is to be meaningful, all categories of wealth have to be represented in proportion to their numbers: if 35 percent of the

population is landless, then 35 percent of the households to be visited should be landless, and so on. A researcher who did not consider variability in wealth in stratifying the sample in this community might be seriously misled if he or she chanced to visit a disproportionate number of very rich or very poor households. The researcher would similarly have to take care that female-headed households were proportionately represented, as they are likely to have distinct social or economic characteristics.

Summary

EXPLORATION, OBSERVATION, AND CURIOSITY ABOUT the diversity of the human species helped to engender the discipline of anthropology, and the scientific study and understanding of humankind have remained its dominant concerns. Anthropologists look at the human species from both cross-cultural and evolutionary points of view. For research purposes the discipline has been divided into four subdisciplines: biological anthropology, archaeology, linguistic anthropology, and cultural anthropology.

Physical anthropology, the biological branch of the discipline, is concerned with both reconstructing the physical evolution of our species and describing and accounting for the physical variations that are found among populations. Archaeology is the study of the relationship between material culture and behavior. Archaeologists explore both prehistoric and more recent societies. Linguistic anthropology is concerned primarily with unwritten languages. It is divided into three branches: descriptive linguistics is the study of the way language is constructed and used; historical linguistics is the study of the origin of language and of the evolution of the languages people speak today; sociolinguistics is the study of the connection between language and social relations. Cultural anthropology is the investigation of specific contemporary cultures (ethnography) and of the patterns that underlie human culture in its totality (ethnology).

Though anthropologists tend to specialize in one of the four subdisciplines, they maintain a holistic approach: they assume that any given aspect of human life is to be studied with an eye to its relation to other aspects of human life. Of vital importance to the holistic perspective is cultural relativism, or the ability to view the beliefs and customs of other peoples within the context of their culture rather than one's own. Although everyone is somewhat ethnocentric, judging the customs of other societies by the standards of his or her own, anthropology underscores the need to view other cultures with objectivity and empathy.

Applying the concept of culture, anthropologists make certain assumptions about the behavior, beliefs, and experiences of individuals as members of society: that the human species learns rules of behavior and is dependent on learning for survival; that learned rules of behavior and thinking supply meaning to events and the behavior of others, although each society has its own interpretations; that knowledge is transmitted via language and is to a large degree created out of symbols.

Most, but not all, anthropologists view this endeavor as part of the scientific effort to describe reality through observation. A scientific theory is a statement that postulates ordered relationships among natural phenomena. Theory provides a framework for research, directing researchers to certain kinds of questions and leading them to expect certain outcomes, against which they can check the results actually obtained. The many theories that cultural anthropologists have put forth revolve around basic questions: Why do societies differ? How do societies differ? What is the relationship between the individual and society?

Evolution explains the development of all species as the outcome of adaptation to environmental circumstances through the process of natural selection. The early cultural evolutionists applied evolutionary theory to culture. E. B. Tylor held that cultures progress through a sequence of evolutionary stages—a pattern now called *unilineal evolution*. Lewis Henry Morgan classified societies into three stages, differentiated by the level of their technological development. Impatient with such speculative theories, Franz Boas held that the proper focus of anthropologists was the relationship between individual action and custom. Boas's approach, called *historical particularism,* stresses the collection of detailed ethnographic data.

The *functionalist* school, developed by Bronislaw Malinowski, holds that all elements of a society are functional in that they serve to satisfy culturally defined needs of the individuals in that society. Every society, Malinowski held, develops *institutions*—religion, art, a kinship system, law, and family life—to meet its people's biological, instrumental, and integrative needs. A. R. Radcliffe-Brown agreed that institutions are central to an understanding of a culture, but in his view their function was to maintain the social structure rather than to meet individual needs. His focus was less on individual behavior than on the norms that control behavior. Because of his emphasis on structure, his theory is called *structural functionalism.* Though neither of these theories explains why cultural systems that developed out of the same basic needs vary so widely, they formed a valuable theoretical framework for further research and encouraged *empiricism*—reliance on observable and quantifiable data.

Both Leslie White and Julian Steward more recently advocated a return to a cultural evolutionary perspective. White's formulation viewed culture as a mechanism for harnessing increasing amounts of energy for human use, with cultural complexity developing accordingly. Steward called for the investigation of technology, culture, and the physical environment as an interactive system—an approach he termed cultural ecology. He believed that unilineal evolutionism should be replaced by multilineal evolutionism, or a focus on the development of individual cultures without insistence that all follow the same evolutionary pattern.

Karl Marx's theory that societies move through distinctive stages, or modes of production, has captured the interest of many anthropologists who seek to identify the internal sources of social disruption. Marxist anthropology focuses on a society's distinctive set of elements and contradictions in an effort to explain social change.

The approach of cultural materialism considers ideas, values, and religious beliefs to be the means or products of adaptation to environmental conditions. To Marvin Harris, an exponent of this approach, successful adaptations are those that promote a favorable balance of costs and benefits from the standpoint of the society as a whole.

Cultural anthropologists depend heavily on fieldwork, the first-hand observation of people in other societies, as their primary means of gathering data and testing hypotheses generated by theories. Most fieldwork today is problem-oriented: the anthropologist studies a given society in order to test theoretical assumptions and then concentrates on those aspects of the society that are most relevant to that theory.

The two basic techniques of data gathering in the field are participant observation and interviewing. The researcher engaged in participant observation seeks social acceptance in the culture to be observed as a means to acquire an understanding of it. This technique allows the researcher to view a culture from the inside and to observe aspects of it that interviews alone might not reveal. In order to be truly productive, the observation must be systematic; that is, the researcher should focus on a particular category of information in any given situation. Notes can be taken systematically with the use of code sheets, or checklists of observed behaviors.

Passive observation alone is not enough. In order to go beyond surface impressions and find out how the people of a society actually think, fieldworkers conduct interviews, both formal and informal. Unstructured informal interviews encourage informants to follow their own train of thought so that they will reveal what is personally important to them, but because the informants are not responding to standardized questions it is difficult to compare their responses. This problem does not arise in formal interviews, which consist of a standardized set of questions designed to elicit specific facts, attitudes, and opinions. Because the two kinds of interview provide different kinds of information, most researchers use both approaches. They also check informants' responses against their own observations to make sure the information they are getting is accurate.

While the fieldworker's primary interest is usually the behavior of the people being studied, demographic and material culture data are useful too. A census, usually in the form of a household survey, reveals the population's basic demographic characteristics. Fieldworkers also routinely map the area occupied by the community, make inventories of its material goods—tools, weapons, vehicles, and so forth—and take notes on the use of natural resources. Fieldworkers gather additional data by conducting time-allocation studies, charting genealogies, taking photographs, making films, studying official documents and folk tales, and administering psychological tests. The specific techniques that researchers rely on most heavily depend on the problem they are studying, but most fieldworkers use a variety of techniques as this strategy allows them to gather a wide range of data and also to cross-check their information.

The day-to-day experience of fieldwork involves numerous difficulties, both practical and psychological. As they strive to become part of the community, fieldworkers find that the people's capacity to accept them is limited, and so is their own ability to participate in the society and still do the research properly.

The community chosen for investigation determines the aspect of the larger system—the sampling universe—that will be described. The researcher must take care not to overgeneralize from the data collected; otherwise, the research will suffer from sampling bias (the exclusion of some members of the sampling universe and the overrepresentation of others). Sometimes a random sample is appropriate—a sample in which each individual or household has the same chance of being selected as any other. If the universe being investigated is very large and complex, a realistic sample of it may require the researcher to divide it into subgroupings and then select a random sample from each. The result is a stratified sample.

Key Terms

archaeology	hypothesis
biological (physical) anthropology	institutions
cultural anthropology	linguistic anthropology
cultural ecology	Marxist anthropology
cultural evolution	material culture
cultural materialism	multilineal evolution
cultural relativism	natural selection
culture	participant observation
empiricism	primatology
ethnocentrism	random sample
ethnography	sampling bias
ethnology	sampling universe
evolution	scientific theory
fossils	sociolinguistics
functionalism	stratified sample
historical particularism	structural function- alism
holism	time allocation
Homo sapiens sapiens	unilineal evolution

Suggested Readings

Angelino, E. (Ed.). (1995). *Annual editions: Anthropology 94/95*. Guilford, CT: Dushkin Publishing Group. A selection of articles by anthropologists focused on current topics in the study of anthropology. A good introduction to current research issues and approaches.

Applebaum, H. (Ed.). (1987). *Perspectives in cultural anthropology*. Albany: State University of New York Press. A history of anthropological theory that presents the major theoretical orientations that have influenced anthropological research and understanding.

Bernard, H. Russell. (1994). *Research methods in anthropology* 2nd ed. Thousand Oaks, CA: Sage. A thorough treatment of qualitative and quantitative approaches in ethnographic research.

Borofsky, Robert (Ed.). (1994). *Assessing cultural anthropology*. New York: McGraw Hill. A collection of essays that explore current theory and past perspectives in anthropology, stressing the diversity of thought that characterizes the field today.

Brown, Donald E. (1991). *Human universals*. New York: McGraw Hill. Explores recent findings on what appear to be universally or widely shared traits among humans of all societies. The author argues that anthropology has overemphasized the plasticity of culture and thus lost sight of what is shared cross-culturally.

Fox, Robin. (1994). *The challenge of anthropology*. New Brunswick, NJ: Transaction. Examines a wide variety of core topics in anthropology in terms of recent challenges to received wisdom.

Garbarino, M. S. (1983). *Sociocultural theory in anthropology: A short history*. Prospect Heights, IL: Waveland Press. A concise survey of the history of sociocultural theory in anthropology. A good resource with which to familiarize oneself with the major figures in the field.

Kaplan, D. & Manners, R. A. (1986). *Culture theory*. Prospect Heights, IL: Waveland Press. A survey of current anthropological theories and their origins, written at an introductory level.

Maybury-Lewis, D. (1992). *Millennium: Tribal wisdom and the modern world*. New York: Viking Press. A companion piece to the Millennium video series that deals with the ways in which Europeans have come to meet the tribal world; the problems facing tribal people today and their prospects for the future.

Podolefsky, A. & Brown, P. J. (Eds.). (1995). *Applying anthropology*. Mountain View, CA: Mayfield Publishing Co. An introductory reader that emphasizes the practical application of research methods in biological anthropology, archaeology, anthropological linguistics, and cultural anthropology. The articles are timely and interesting; they offer a view of anthropology not available in any other reader. A number of these articles are cited throughout this text.

Rigdon, S. M. (1988). *The culture facade: Art, science and politics in the work of Oscar Lewis*. Urbana and Chicago: University of Illinois Press. An examination of the evolution of Oscar Lewis's ideas and findings about the culture of poverty; offers insights into the ways in which theory develops in anthropology.

Stocking, G. W., Jr. (1987). *Victorian anthropology*. New York: Free Press. A probing look at the Victorian origins of Western European anthropological theories of human social and cultural evolution.

Wolf, E. R. (1982). *Europe and the people without history*. Berkeley: University of California Press. An analytic history of European expansion; the effects of this expansion on the native peoples of Africa, Asia, and the Americas; and how these peoples in turn affected the history of Europe.

What Is Culture?
  Culture Gives Meaning to Reality
  Culture Is Integrated
  Culture Is Adaptive

Behavior, Biology, and Learning
  Learning Gender Roles
  Gender Issues: Albanian Virgins and
  American Berdaches
  Learning Age Roles

The Roots of Language
  Nonhuman Communication
  The Emergence of Human Language

The Structure of Languages

Sign Language

Linguistic Variation and Change
  Linguistic Borrowing and Cultural
    Contact
  Lingua Franca, Pidgin, and Creole
    Languages

Sociolinguistics
  Social Status
  Gender Roles and Language
  Language and Ethnicity
  Contemporary Issues: The Politics of
  Language in the United States
  Language and Nationalism

Summary
Key Terms
Suggested Readings

Chapter 2

Culture and Language

The most distinctive single attribute of our species is that complex but elusive trait we call culture. It is complex in that it encompasses, as mentioned in Chapter 1, behaviors as diverse as tool-making, bridal costumes, funerary rites, farming, sexual practices, art—in short, anything that is based on learning and that is passed on among individuals. Culture is elusive because, while it seems easy to distinguish what is learned from what is innate (for example, how to start a fire as opposed to the emotion of fear we experience when threatened by a fire), in practice it is very difficult. This because all behaviors, learned or otherwise, have a basis in the human brain. Learning English as we grow up—as opposed to Arabic—is clearly a cultural phenomenon, but the ability to learn a language at all is a unique biological property of our species. Since culture encompasses all that we acquire through learning as we proceed through life, it can and does regularly change; after all, we do not think and behave as do our parents. Cultural behavior also varies greatly among individuals in the same society; not everyone eats broccoli or even practices the same forms of sex. Nevertheless, there are apparent limitations to cultural plasticity;

human sensory mechanisms, intelligence, emotions, reproductive systems, color recognition, and linguistic ability are universally shared. Even aspects of social life fall into very familiar patterns among very diverse cultures: notions of human beauty, the importance of family or kin ties, the importance of "reputation," the importance of religion and art are part of every human society. Thus while human culture appears as a wonderfully colorful floral arrangement, it has an underlying structure expressing our common humanity. This chapter explores some aspects of this commonality together with the nature of language itself.

Language allows us to make extraordinary use of intelligence, emotional capabilities, and even our more modest physiological endowments. Without language, our species could not simultaneously adapt to the rigors of space travel, conduct Arctic exploration, exploit the oil fields of the Arabian desert, and chart the depths of the Pacific Ocean. The ability to communicate through language underlies all aspects of culture: kinship, politics, religion, and family life, as well as science and technology. Language is the key to our ability to cope rapidly and effectively with new circumstances. It enables us to coordinate the activities of many people to achieve desired ends and allows us to codify and systematize our accumulated knowledge.

What Is Culture?

We have already stressed that culture is transmitted via our symbolic communication system that we call language. Human language has an arbitrary quality: words can change their meanings, they can be combined and modified to create new meanings, and perhaps most important of all, they can be used to represent things that are not actually present—events of the past and future, abstract qualities, and strictly mental phenomena. Language thus enables people to communicate what they would do if such-and-such happened, to organize their experiences into abstract categories (a happy occasion, for instance, or an evil omen), and to express thoughts never spoken before. Morality, religion, philosophy, literature, science, economics, technology, and numerous other areas

of human knowledge and belief—along with the ability to learn about and manipulate them—all depend on this type of higher-level communication. Cultural knowledge, then, is not only transmitted through language, it is to a large degree created out of language.

Culture Gives Meaning to Reality

Culture encompasses not only social behaviors but also ways of thinking. From our cultural training we learn what meanings to attach to the events of our world, and especially to the behavior of others, so that we can make some sense of those events and know how to respond to them. The meanings of specific actions can vary with the cultural context in which they are interpreted.

Because meaning is supplied by cultural context and because such contexts differ, people of various societies can view the world in quite different ways. For example, members of societies that speak different languages and follow different religious traditions may well make very different distinctions between the natural and the supernatural. For the Australian aborigines, certain rocks, animals, and places have souls that are very much a part of them. The sacred sites of Christianity, Islam, and Judaism have meanings for their adherents that are not shared by outsiders. The beliefs and values of a society are a cultural reality. Whether marrying more than one spouse is treated as a crime or as a preferred form of marriage depends on culturally defined rules of behavior.

Even so, we cannot regard our ability to define reality and to make rules for appropriate behavior as completely open or arbitrary. While different systems of marriage, mating, or cohabiting are practiced by societies around the world, we can easily think of variations that no society has adopted or condoned. There appear to be universal constraints on sex roles, as on other areas of human behavior, within which variation occurs (Brown, 1991). As David Gilmore points out, "All societies distinguish between male and female, providing institutionalized sex-appropriate roles for adult men and women. Most societies also hold consensual ideals—guiding or admonitory images—for adult masculinity and femininity by which individuals are judged as worthy members of their sex and are evaluated more generally as moral actors" (Gilmore, 1990, pp. 1–2).

Culture Is Integrated

The religious, political, and economic institutions of a society are shaped by common adaptive forces operating over long periods of time, and as a consequence they tend to "fit" with each other. The "fit" is often supplied by language or, at least, verbally-expressed models of the world. We use language to signify the legitimacy of a given political order or religious institution. The language used to justify equality or, on occasion, to justify a revolution is expressed symbolically in special terminology: for example, the words of the U.S. Constitution, the Bible, or the Bill of Rights. We also rely on social rules and symbols such as the shape of stop signs and the colors of traffic lights to provide order to our daily lives.

The many ways in which cultural practices are interrelated gives stability and continuity to cultural evolution; changes are incremental and often occur very slowly. We do not wake up each morning with a burning need to reconfirm the existence of institutions on which we depend or the symbols through which we interpret our reality. It is probably just because stability and continuity are so important to our survival that change and innovation are usually so conservative. It is as though humans were generally guided by the maxim, "If it ain't broke, don't fix it." Sometimes we see this tendency toward stability and continuity most dramatically when it is violated by the cataclysmic events of war or other disasters; people who are suddenly cut off from their customary practices and familiar ways of doing things experience stress not unlike what is sometimes called "culture shock"—the feeling of disorientation one may experience when thrust into an unfamiliar cultural setting. In many respects, when an individual is born into a particular society and grows up learning its language, social rules, and expectations, it is analogous to a new employee coming into a long-established corporation. The established ways of doing things is the environment in which the new employee must find his or her way; for most of the employee's career, conformity will be the rule and experimentation the exception. Nev-

ertheless, people do innovate, and, out of individual shifts in behavior, major cultural shifts or trends occur.

Culture Is Adaptive

While a given culture may largely structure people's behavior, human beings are hardly passive participants—blank slates to be gradually filled in with the wisdom of the past. We cannot ignore the fact that both cultures and circumstances are themselves creations of humans, and that people are always shaping and modifying them in various ways. The relationship between culture and the individual can be better understood, therefore, if we view culture as a set of guidelines that exists in order to be used by human beings (Leaf, 1972).

Culture is, in part, a set of codes and general rules that individuals use to interpret their environment; they adjust the rules to fit the situations in which they find themselves. Furthermore, people look not just for proper solutions but for smart solutions—solutions that may be somewhat less than strictly proper but that enable them to overcome difficulties and achieve their ends. Morris Freilich (1971) has suggested that we are all scientists of a sort, constantly gathering data to apply to decisions. We make decisions on the basis of expert authority, use experience to predict the consequences of an act, and sometimes base decisions purely on theory. Many of the data we use are part of the content of our culture, but some are acquired through experience, group interaction, or our own powers of reasoning. In this view, we are all individual actors in the culture, not stamped out by a cultural mold. Our relationship with our culture is one of dynamic interaction.

It is important to recognize the very important role that variation in behavior plays in societal change, even when that behavior is termed "deviant." Behavior that is said to be strange or outside of the established range of variation can become the basis for the survival of the group. A member of an agricultural society may be seen as strange or abnormal because he adopts a novel plant or a new system of cultivation—as for example, in the United States when a few innovative farmers in the 1980s began to farm organically (without chemical fertilizers). While considered eccentric at first, by 1995 organic farming is widespread because of changed consumer tastes and, importantly, it is often more cost-effective. In this respect, it is important to understand the powerful effect that circumstances have on the behavior of individuals and the equally powerful role that individuals can play in shaping situations and culture. How this is related to cultural adaptation will be taken up in the following chapter.

So far we have emphasized the effects of culture on the individual. Yet the behavior of individuals also affects the shared behavior of their society. By fitting cultural experience to new situations, individuals in every society experiment and arrive at innovative solutions. Sometimes these new solutions are taken up by others and become part of the larger cultural repertoire. Ways of doing things that are widely shared and passed on are usually ones that in some way facilitate the well-being of a large segment of the population, by emphasizing appropriate behavior or discouraging behavior that threatens the group in some way. Indeed, the customary patterns of behavior and thought that we inherit are nothing more than a complex of our ancestors' adaptive strategies—those that still seem to work. And by devising new solutions to fit our own circumstances, we modify those strategies before passing them on, often through the medium of language, to the next generation (Boyd & Richerson, 1985). To understand this dynamic interchange between people and their culture—that is, their systems of behavior—we must look more closely at the way individuals actually deal with behavioral practices and rules.

In any society, most people know what is appropriate to do in a given situation, but they do not always act according to a rigid formula or set rules. And when we look at the ways in which people break the rules they espouse, an interesting pattern emerges. For one thing, most of us "sin" in more or less the same way our neighbors sin; that is, we deviate in packs. A simple example of this phenomenon is seen in drivers' tendency to exceed the speed limit—just a little. When the legal limit is 55 miles per hour, most people can be found driving at 60 to 65. In fact, most of us look askance at people who obey all the rules to the letter. The rigid bureaucrat who plods through every inch of red tape, refusing to cut corners, is generally considered a deviant—an "obsessive-compulsive person-

ality." Likewise, though few Americans would openly condone lying, all would agree that in many social circumstances, telling the complete truth would be a mistake; we tell "white lies" or otherwise manipulate the facts to fit our needs.

This phenomenon appears in all societies. People everywhere establish rules for acceptable behavior and then proceed to break the rules in more or less predictable ways. The reasons for this behavior is the necessity of making received rules and values fit the circumstances of the individual. Though most people feel a need to do what is proper, and though their culture provides time-honored definitions of "proper" for them to fall back on, survival nevertheless depends on the ability to cope—to solve problems in the immediate environment and adapt to changing circumstances. Adaptation depends on smartness, not on propriety—"ingenuity, not piety, . . . resourcefulness, not goodness" (Freilich, 1971, p. 286).

People spend much of their time, then, looking for solutions to their problems. Though usually they fall back on established ways of doing things, occasionally they strike out in new directions; such words as *invention*, *discovery*, and *innovation* refer to this aspect of adapting. Once people develop a new solution, they usually begin to argue not that it is new but that it is good—not expedient but proper.

Changing gender roles in our own society is a case in point. At one time it was not considered desirable for women to work outside the home, and usually only those who had no alternative did so. In time certain kinds of work in offices, hospitals, and schools came to be viewed as quite appropriate for women, and families began to invest in the training of their daughters as secretaries, nurses, and teachers.

With the advent of World War I, industry and the civil service needed women to fill jobs left vacant by men who had gone off to war. Following the war, women not only continued to be employed in large numbers but the right of women to vote was secured. Slowly the employment of women in wider and wider sectors of the economy came to be viewed not only as legitimate but desirable by a substantial percentage of the population. In recent years the right of women to be employed in every occupation became established in law, though not necessarily in practice. Still, almost no one, however conservative, questions the political rights of women or the appropriateness of their employment in most jobs.

Once a new behavior, with its newly acquired moral value, gains enough adherents, it becomes a shared practice that is taught to the next generation as part of "the right way to do things" (Irons, 1991). In time some new solutions will be retired in favor of newer solutions. But the rule remains the same: individual ways of coping, if enough people find them useful, will become part of the system of shared behavior. Through such constant revision adaptive strategies evolve, as we will discuss in the next chapter.

Behavior, Biology, and Learning

Usually animal behavior (including of course, human behavior) is seen in terms of a basic distinction: it may be instinctive—that is, genetically controlled—or it may be learned. This is especially true when looking at human social behavior. Learned ways of behaving constitute a very large percentage of human activity, probably far outweighing instinctive behavior. We might visualize this situation by thinking of the difference between the behavior of a very young child and that of an adult in the same family. All animals have some capacity to learn, and learning is important to the survival of most species. But no other animal learns, can learn, or needs to learn as much as the human animal. In order to function as independent members of our societies, we require not only a long period of physical care but also a long period of training in how to use language, to think and behave; in other words, training in a society's system of behaviors—its culture.

A child born into Eskimo society, for instance, begins to learn behavior, language, and skills appropriate to Eskimo culture from the day of birth. The child's toilet training and feeding habits, the encouragement (or discouragement) given its first experiments in interacting socially with others, the rewards offered for correct deportment—all amount to an intensive training course in how to be a proper Eskimo. The child goes on to learn social roles specific to the appropriate sex, useful technical skills, and his or her people's religion and moral codes. This training in one's own culture is sometimes called **socialization** or **enculturation,** and what we become is greatly influenced by the persons who carry out that enculturation and the way they do it. In many societies a fairly narrow circle of people, primarily parents and kin and community elders, are responsible for the bulk of an individual's socialization. In other societies, as in our own, much of this training is provided by specialists outside the family or immediate community; we send our children to schools, churches, summer camps, and universities. To a considerable extent our behavior as men and women, our conduct as parents, our expectations, and our attitudes are shaped by this process.

Socialization is by no means uniform for all members of a society. In our own society, for example, some parents raise their children quite strictly, setting clear rules and clear punishments for violations. Others take a more permissive approach, making large allowances for experimentation and failure on the child's part. Nor are the parents the only socializing influences. Each child has a unique constellation of friends, relatives, and neighbors, and hence each learns a somewhat distinctive version of the culture. Moreover, the exact content of the socialization process varies along gender, ethnic, socioeconomic, religious, and regional lines.

For example, Yanomamö boys are encouraged by their parents to be aggressive and to display anger and rage. Their sisters are not encouraged to behave in this way, although we may assume that their capacity for anger and rage is as great as that of boys. Among the Yomut Turkmen of northeastern Iran, young men are brought up with a high regard for physical prowess and the necessity of defending one's kin and community, by force if necessary. One tribe or descent group among the Yomut, however, is considered holy, and the men do not fight. In fact, it is considered a serious religious offense to strike a member of this holy tribe or to steal their property. Boys in this group are socialized quite differently from those born into other Yomut groups, with little emphasis on fighting or self-defense.

Nevertheless, there are broad similarities in how and what the members of a single society are taught. The members of a given society tend to take

Education is more than just teaching of technical skills necessary for survival—it is part of the socialization process itself. Here a young woman learns to sew from her grandmother, and at the same time, comes to share her social and cultural values.

(Ed Kashi)

such similarities for granted (often marking them up to "human nature") and to notice only the differences. But to the outsider, individual differences in thought and behavior within a society may be less striking than the similarities. Recent research by two biologists from Israel, Eva Jalonka and Eytan Avital, suggests that some learned behavior in animals, including humans, follows the same rules as genes: parents, especially mothers, pass on behavioral traits to their children much as they do genetic ones (Angier, 1995, pp. 13–22). Thus, children learn at infancy to fancy the behavioral styles of their parents, and these modes of behavior can be passed on over generations. This, they suggest, may account for the fact that there is a decided tendency for people to favor as mates individuals who share characteristics with their parents.

This is not to say that these learned behaviors have no basis in biology; in fact, all behavior is mediated by biological processes and limitations. Our basic physiological requirements—the need for food, water, shelter, sleep, and sexual activity—underlie a good deal of our behavior. Our brains, with their elaborately encoded propensities for liking some things and avoiding others, also channel behavior in ways that are only recently being researched, as we see with the work on parental imprinting noted above. One fact seems clear: rather

than being a sharply distinct alternative to instinct, learned behavior is often guided by information inherent in the genes (see Gould & Marler, 1987, p. 74; Wright, 1994). Speech learning is a good example. "Human infants innately recognize most or all of the consonant sounds characteristic of human speech, including consonants not present in the language they normally hear" (Gould & Marler, 1987, p. 82). Learned behavior, quite apart from instinct, serves biological purposes because of the practical advantages it confers, advantages that are attested to by our success in reproducing and surviving in virtually every climatic zone on earth. Even our universally shared taste for sweets, fats, and salts, and hence the underlying basis for our dietary systems, is the result of a long evolutionary process. It has been suggested that human systems of knowledge—religion, magic, science, philosophy—are based on a uniquely human, inborn need to impose order on experience. This is not surprising, as pattern recognition (for example, seeing a dangerous situation) is a key means for processing information critical to survival.

The biological basis of human behavior, then, is important. But how we go about satisfying inborn needs and developing successful coping strategies is largely a matter of contextual learning. Whether we feed ourselves by growing yams and

In most societies today, much social learning takes place in the formal environment of the classroom. These children in a bilingual school in San Francisco are learning to read and write Chinese as well as English; they are also acquiring complex cultural skills.

(Bonnie Kamin)

hunting wild game or by herding camels and raising wheat, whether we explain a thunderstorm by attributing it to meteorological conditions or to a fight among the gods—such things are determined by what we learn as part of our enculturation. Enculturation prepares us to function as members of a given society—to speak its language, to use its symbols in abstract thought, and so forth. This ability depends in turn on genetically inherited physical traits, notably a brain of awesome complexity. But even though cultural behavior may be guided by genetically rooted limitations and propensities, it is obvious that we do not inherit genes for speaking English as opposed to Swahili, or for training as a doctor as opposed to a pilot. It is more difficult to assess the contribution of our biological heritage to the shaping of very basic aspects of social organization, sex roles, aggression, and family, but clearly there are limits to the range of variation found in different societies. People everywhere construct their social worlds using the idiom of family and kinship and recognize the same range of emotions in much the same way.

While people share certain biological traits that account for some of the broad similarities in human behavior, there are biological causes for certain behavioral differences among individuals in the same population. On the individual level, a person's build, health, and stamina affect ability to perform certain kinds of activities. Prenatal stress or malnutrition during the first years of life, for example, prevent full development of the brain and in extreme cases may cause mental retardation. Even with an excellent diet, some people are simply not strong enough to work as stevedores or professional athletes, just as some lack the manual dexterity to assemble minute transistors or to perform intricate passages on the piano. Physiology sets upper limits on individual capabilities that training cannot always overcome.

We are beginning to learn more about the biological bases of certain kinds of behavior. As people have known for centuries, such drugs as alcohol and marijuana can significantly alter behavior by altering body chemistry. By the same token, many scientists now suspect that some behavioral states as well as behavioral disorders may have a biochemical basis. It has been discovered, for example, that when some people are severely depressed, their nerve cells do not fire as quickly as usual. The severe psychosis called schizophrenia has been shown to have a genetic basis. It has also been found that deficiencies of the B-complex vitamins can have significant effects on the nervous system, causing confused thought processes, severe anxiety, and exhaustion. Many scientists now believe that the emotional basis for male-female bonding may have a chemical component (Fisher, 1987). Even the amount of sugar in the blood can affect behavior: blood sugar level is an important factor in some manifestations of aggression.

Study after study has shown that men are more prone to physical violence than women, whether it is evidenced in warfare in a tribal society or in the crime rate in an industrial one. In a study of bullying behavior in the Norwegian school system, Dr. Dan Olweus, professor of psychology at the University of Bergen, found that of 568,000 schoolchildren, 41,000, or over 7 percent, bully others regularly. The majority of the bullies were boys, and the tendency increased with age in boys but declined in girls.

While socialization factors cannot be excluded, one hormonal cause seems to be implicated also: the blood level of testosterone, the male sex hormone, is linked to aggression in both sexes, and males are more likely to have elevated levels of the hormone. In a smaller study of teenage boys, Dr.

Olweus found a close link between testosterone levels and intolerance of frustration and response to provocation (cited in Konner, 1988). When Dr. June Reinisch, director of the Kinsey Institute, studied twenty-five boys and girls who had been prenatally exposed to an artificial hormone similar to testosterone, she found that they were more aggressive than their same-sex siblings (cited in Konner, 1988). A parallel example in the case of females is the nurturing behavior that results from the enhanced levels of the hormone prolactin, generated when women nurse (Trevathan, 1987). In short, biological factors affect individual behavior in ways of which most of us are only superficially aware.

Learning Gender Roles

There is no society that does not recognize, encourage, and even demand behavioral differences between the sexes. *Gender* refers to the behaviors associated with the distinct sexes, and it is this behavior that varies from culture to culture. Parents in all societies begin to train their children at an early age in the social behavior, or gender roles, considered appropriate to their biological sex. Gender identity is one's feeling of being male or female. Gender identity and gender roles usually develop in tandem (Frayser, 1985). Gender roles tend to be defined by the society and establish the kind of behavior that is appropriate and inappropriate for a male and a female. Children are socialized also to respond favorably to what are perceived as the social tasks or jobs appropriate to their gender. The Hopi, for example, traditionally gave a little girl a doll to reward good behavior; when she is especially well-behaved, they say glowingly that she will grow up to be a fine cook. Boys were rewarded with arrows and praised with hints that they are destined to become swift runners. Similarly, boys in Los Peloteros, the Puerto Rican shantytown described by Helen Safa, were allowed to run free after school; much like their fathers, they generally turned up at home only for meals. Girls, in contrast, were expected to stay at home and help their mothers with the cooking, cleaning, and care of younger children (Safa, 1974).

But gender constructions, however obvious they may appear, are not uniform across all soci-

A number of North American societies recognized cross-gender females as a distinct and respected gender classification.

(The National Anthropological Archives/Smithsonian Institute)

eties, as we see from the examples in the Gender Issues box, *Albanian Virgins and American* Berdaches. A *berdache*, in some Native American cultures, is a male who assumes a female social identity. Also, in some Native American societies biological females could take on masculine gender identity; they have been referred to as "cross-gender females" (Blackwood, 1984) and as "Amazons" (Williams, 1986, p. 234), after the legendary Greek female warriors. The Spanish explorer Pedro de Magalhaes de Gandávo gave this name to

Gender Issues

Albanian Virgins and American *Berdaches*

NOT ALL GENDER ROLES ARE neatly defined as simply male or female. In traditional Northern Albanian society women occupied a relatively low social position and the norm for daughters was to marry young and to men selected by their parents. However, under certain circumstances they had an option: they could take an oath of perpetual virginity and elect to live as males, carrying arms, and pursuing occupations normally forbidden to women; outsiders referred to them as "Albanian virgins" (Durham, 1987).

Several North American Indian societies recognized and respected at least one clearly defined alternative gender: the *berdache*, or bio-logical male who does not conform to a society's normative expectations for masculine behavior. It had been thought that the status of berdache had died out among Indian groups, but Walter Williams (1986) demonstrated otherwise when he reported his extensive research among contemporary berdaches in the United States and Mexico. Europeans who encountered the berdache tradition in earlier centuries ridiculed it and tried to suppress the custom. Berdaches were men who opted out of masculine gender identity; they declined the roles of warrior, husband, and hunter and assumed a distinct identity. They were regarded as a special group, and sometimes were honored as healers, shamans, and seers. Some were asexual; some married and lived as the wives of other men. Most tribes did not regard it as proper for two berdaches to have sex with each other (Williams, 1986, p. 93); to do so was seen as incest. The identity of "masculine," as opposed to "feminine," was viewed as a character that one assumed independent of biological sex. Thus a man who lived with a berdache retained his masculine identity through his general deportment in society: he asserted his masculinity, performed appropriate tasks, and undertook the role of husband and provider.

the great river in Brazil after he encountered the Tupinamba in 1576. He wrote:

> There are some Indian women who determine to remain chaste; these have no commerce with men in any manner, nor would they consent to it even if refusal meant death. They give up all the duties of women and imitate men, and follow men's pursuits as if they were not women. They wear their hair cut in the same way as the men, and go to war with bows and arrows and pursue game, always in company with men; each has a woman to serve her, to whom she says she is married, and they treat each other and speak with each other as man and wife. [in Williams, 1986, p. 233]

Evelyn Blackwood (1984) writes that some thirty-four North American Indian societies recognized cross-gender females as a distinct and respected gender classification. The roles and status of cross-gender females, like those of berdaches, vary from society to society, but they were re-spected as a special instance of gender identity. Clearly the notion of gender has to be taken as culturally malleable, not something that is everywhere the same and unchanging. It is less clear whether our various cultures represent only a symbolic veneer masking a common bedrock of sexual thinking (Gilmore, 1990, p. 2).

Thomas Gregor, who has conducted cross-cultural studies of sexuality, believes that while gender ideals vary from culture to culture, underlying the variations are intriguing similarities in sexual stereotyping (Gregor, 1985, p. 200). Cultures may be more alike than different in this regard. David Gilmore (1990), in investigating what lies behind the notion of masculinity, found that widely separated and otherwise unrelated people had very similar notions as to what masculinity should be and how a man achieved it. In fact, "achieve" was the word Gilmore found best suited to express a man's attainment of masculine gender identity: men almost everywhere have to demonstrate masculinity by passing tests, performing certain tasks, and undergoing various forms of initiation. Gilmore shows impressive regularities in what seems to define masculinity in a wide variety of cultures: arduous tests of strength, risk-taking, and demonstrations of bravery and resistance to pain.

While it is important to look for possible cross-cultural regularities that may shed light on the elusive subject of human nature, we have to avoid thinking that biology is destiny. This point was made most forcibly by Margaret Mead, and while a number of her specific findings have been challenged, the general point remains sound. She found (or thought she had) that adolescence in Samoa was almost wholly lacking in the trauma that characterized growing up in American and European society. Young people there, she reported, were encouraged to engage in premarital sex, and were attached not exclusively to their individual parents but to a large, less authoritarian cluster of individuals that included kin and nonkin alike. Rape, sexual jealousy, and adolescent violence were virtually unheard of—a result, in her view, of the permissive and relaxed Samoan approach to child rearing. Thus, she claimed, Samoan social relations proved that human nature does not of necessity involve a tension-ridden puberty. Since then Mead's studies have been at the center of much debate, including allegations that her observations were, quite simply, wrong.

Derek Freeman, an Australian anthropologist, has raised the question of the reliability of Mead's early studies. His challenge, published in 1983 (just after her death), has led to a vigorous round of charges and countercharges. He found that during the period of her fieldwork rape was at least as common in Samoa as in the industrialized nations, as was other adolescent male criminal behavior. He found, too, that contrary to Mead's observations, premarital sex was much frowned upon, that violence arising from sexual jealousy was common, and that children were, and still are, vigorously supervised and punished by their natural parents. Freeman concludes that human nature is the same everywhere and so are human passions. In short, his picture of Samoa is directly at odds with Mead's.

Most scholars familiar with the issues agree that Mead overstated her case by ignoring both the considerable variability within the societies she studied and the contrasting evidence that others have seen in her case studies (Feinberg, 1988; Brown, 1991). Most seem to agree that she underestimated the incidence of aggressive behavior among the Samoans but that she is generally correct in her reporting of Samoan sexuality (Scheper-Hughes, 1979).

One ethnographer, Allen Abramson (1987), who worked very close to Mead's original field site, suggests that both Mead and Freeman are at least partially correct but that they are looking at rather different aspects of Samoan culture. Abramson found that sexual contact was indeed common before marriage, but that the young people's parents disapproved. As Mead worked with adolescent girls, often spending hours in their company with no other adults present, she may have uncovered a reality that eluded Freeman, who concentrated his attention on senior men—who would have been unlikely to admit that such "deviant" behavior was widespread. The consensus is that Mead's general proposition is valid: that gender roles are variable and that individuals can be—and often are—socialized and enculturated to quite different sex-specific behaviors in different societies. At the same time, men and women do differ biologically; what socialization can do is either minimize or exaggerate such differences (Konner, 1988). In fact, Margaret Mead often emphasized her belief that sex-role variability is constrained by physiology—a point often overlooked by her admirers and detractors alike (Brown, 1991).

While gender roles are grounded in biological distinctions, there is nothing biological in the gender-based allocation of economic, social, and political rights and responsibilities. As we see in the United States today, our view of gender, including that of people who do not conform to our societal ideal (such as homosexuals), is continually subject to change. Human society has few roles that cannot be filled by both males and females. The most important exceptions are those related directly or indirectly to childbearing and child rearing.

Learning Age Roles

Societies also teach us age roles, and as we are constantly getting older, at each stage of our lives we have to learn the types of behavior—the privileges and obligations—appropriate to our years. Our own culture makes rather vague distinctions among infants, children, and adolescents and among young, middle-aged, and elderly adults. Different degrees of responsibility and self-reliance are expected of people in the various categories, but we are not greatly shocked when people act older or younger than their years. In most of the cultures that anthropologists have studied, such relative indifference to age roles would be unthinkable. Many societies treat aging as a passage through very distinctive states, not as movement along a chronological continuum.

Many African societies, in particular, have developed elaborate systems of age roles. Every Ariaal male (see Chapter 6) with the other males of his generation, belongs to an age class (or **age set**) whose membership remains fixed throughout his life. We recognize a similar grouping in our own society when we identify ourselves as members of the class of 1995, for instance. Also among the Ariaal from infancy to old age, each class of males moves through a series of five clearly defined and named **age grades**. The class occupies that grade—and the well-defined set of social roles that goes with it—for a period of years and then is initiated into the next higher grade. Just how long members of a junior grade must wait before moving on is a matter of some contention. With each advancement comes increased status and responsibility, which may threaten the status of older men. The group occupying the final age grade, for example, is expected to exercise major military and governmental responsibilities. Thus at each stage of the cycle, the society instructs its members on the roles appropriate to their grade, and in some measure the members become what the role dictates.

The matter of age roles illustrates an important point about socialization: it does not end with childhood. We learn more new information in childhood than in adulthood. Nevertheless, even as adults we are constantly stepping out of old roles and into new ones—from housewife to worker, from married to single and perhaps to married again, from parent of dependent children to parent of independent adults, from middle-aged person to old person, from employee to retiree, from spouse to widow or widower. With each role change comes a shift in behavioral expectations, and to some degree in values as well. Thus the individual is affected by, and reacting to, the processes of social-

ization from birth to death. This is often formally recognized by society with special rituals or celebrations, sometimes referred to as **rites of passage.**

One of the most effective means of formally inducting an individual into a new role is participation in a communal or public rite of passage. Among the Ariaal each move from grade to grade is celebrated with feasting and the sacrifice of animals. Such rites as the Jewish bar and bat mitzvah and the Catholic confirmation give the person a sense of identification with his or her new role; a notion that its privileges and obligations are not mere abstractions but are to be translated into action. Rites of passage are important signals to the larger community that an individual has changed roles, and such rites are powerful evidence of our common humanity and the role language plays in shaping it.

The Roots of Language

Presumably human language began as a **call** (or gesture) **system**, but language as we recognize it differs from such systems in several ways. Animal calls, probably because they are in large part genetically determined, are rigidly stereotyped; the call is always the same in form and meaning. Moreover, animal call systems are closed; that is, elements of one call cannot be combined with elements of another to produce a new message. The calls are unique, limited in number, and mutually exclusive.

Human language is open—the number of messages that can be conveyed is infinite. Indeed, with language people can, and continually do, create entirely new messages—sentences that have never before been spoken—whereas call systems can generally convey only a very few simple meanings: danger, hostility, sexual excitement, the availability of food, and so on. As Bertrand Russell put it, "No matter how eloquently a dog may bark, he cannot tell you that his parents were poor but honest" (cited in Fromkin & Rodman, 1988, p. 346). Human language can be used to communicate a vast range of meanings, from subtle philosophical abstractions to complex technical information to delicate shades of feeling. This flexibility is made possible by the arbitrariness of human language. Unlike animal calls, the sounds of a language have no fixed meaning. Instead, meaning emerges from the way sounds are combined into words and words are arranged to make sentences, in accordance with a complex set of rules (grammar).

Another distinctive feature of human language is that it is stimulus-free. That is, a linguistic utterance need not be evoked by an immediate situation. We do not have to turn a corner and come upon a tiger in order to say the word "tiger" or talk about "danger." We can discuss things that are not present—things experienced in the past, things that may happen in the future, even things that are not true or not real, such as unicorns and utopias. Little of this sort of communication appears to be possible in call systems, which lack the dimensions of time and possibility. While animals have been observed to send false signals, generally the use of call systems for deception is limited. It has been said, with some justice, that hominids became truly human when they became capable of telling a lie.

Nonhuman Communication

One way to appreciate the uniqueness of human language is to contrast it with nonhuman systems of communication. All animals seem to have means of transmitting messages to one another. Seagulls cry when predators appear. Honeybees, by means of intricate dances, tell one another where food is to be found. By releasing scents, dogs indicate their readiness to mate. Even amoebae appear to transmit rudimentary messages to one another, by emitting small amounts of carbon dioxide. Though we associate human language with speech, sounds are not a necessary aspect of language; people who cannot hear or speak can acquire and use language. Conversely, when a parrot imitates human utterances, it is not using language the way a human does. Language uses sounds, but what distinguishes it from other communication systems is not simply vocalization.

Because human language is fundamentally different from the communications of animals, and because children seem to learn language almost automatically, many scholars believe that linguistic ability must somehow be built into the human brain. Other scientists have challenged this position, claiming that nonhuman species—especially the apes—have an undeveloped capacity for language. The most recent view is that both positions are valid up to a point. Human language does involve structures in the brain that other primates lack; at the same time, apes, in particular, have unexpected linguistic ability—but short of true language. In primates the pharynx (a tunnel of muscle connecting the back of the mouth to the larynx, crucial to the production of speech) is smaller in relation to body size and is shaped differently than in humans. As a consequence, the earliest experiments that sought to teach chimpanzees spoken language were not successful. To get around the vocal-tract problem and test intellectual capacity, two psychologists, Alan and Beatrice Gardner (1969), decided to teach their test chimp, Washoe, American Sign Language (ASL).

In four years Washoe not only learned to use 130 signs, but, more important, she showed that she could manipulate them creatively. Having learned the signal "more" to persuade the Gardners to resume a pillow fight, she spontaneously used the same signal when she wanted a second helping at dinner. Furthermore, whereas chimpanzee calls are never combined, Washoe spontaneously combined hand signals to make new words. Not knowing the signal for duck, for instance, she dubbed it "water bird."

One of the most successful of the later experiments involved a gorilla named Koko. At age four she was able to use 251 different signs in a single hour. After five years of training in ASL, she scored between 80 and 90 (the equivalent of a five-year-old child) on an IQ test for nonreading children. Like Washoe, Koko could combine words creatively to name new objects. She was also particularly adept at expressing her feelings. Whenever Penny Patterson, her trainer, arrived late at Koko's trailer, the gorilla would sign "sad." On other mornings, when asked how she felt, she would report herself "happy" or sign "I feel good." This was the first clear instance of emotional self-awareness on the part of a nonhuman primate.

There have also been experiments using, not sign language, but lexigrams—symbols that represent common objects, verbs and moods. Starting in the late 1970s, Sue Savage Rumbaugh trained two chimps, Sherman and Austin, to use a keyboard to produce lexigrams (Rumbaugh & Lewis, 1994). When they had become fairly fluent, she constructed an experiment that entailed Sherman and

Researchers have gained valuable knowledge about the nature of language by studying chimps and other animals. Researcher Sue Savage-Rumbaugh taught her chimp, Kanzi, to communicate using a special keyboard.

(Photo courtesy of CNN)

Austin having to cooperate to perform various tasks. She found that they spontaneously used the lexigrams to learn from and communicate with each other. Even more interesting is the case of Kanzi, a young pygmy chimpanzee, who surprised the psychologists when he revealed that he had learned to use the keyboard to produce lexigrams entirely on his own by watching his adoptive mother.

It would be incorrect, however, to conclude that these animals use language in the human sense. First, the languages that the test apes learned were in part iconic—the symbols imitated the things they stood for. There is a geometrical relationship between some of the signs and the things they represent. The ASL sign for book, for example, is two palms pressed together, then opened, much like the geometrics of opening a book. Thus, we still do not know whether apes have the intel-

lectual capacity to handle a totally arbitrary language such as our own. Second, there is still some doubt as to whether the test apes put together sentences spontaneously or simply by rote, although the lexigram experiments with Sherman, Austin, and Kanzi seem to indicate that the chimpanzees were not merely responding to cues from researchers without really understanding the meaning. Third, even if ape language differs from human language only in degree, the distance separating them is vast. The suggestions of subtle reasoning in the apes' verbalizations are quite intriguing, but they are also quite rare. Finally, teaching language to an ape requires immense effort under highly artificial conditions, whereas human children learn it naturally, without training. Apes may share with us certain faculties necessary for language, but it is clear that these faculties have remained relatively undeveloped in their line.

The Emergence of Human Language

Because sounds leave no trace, researchers investigating the origins of language have to depend on indirect evidence: studies of the way children acquire language, comparisons of human and nonhuman vocalizations, guesses as to what kinds of brains and vocal tracts might have accompanied fossil skulls, and of course cultural evidence of the way our early ancestors lived.

The cultural evidence seems to indicate that language began to evolve as early as four million years ago (Schick & Toth, 1993). It was probably around that period that our early ancestors made a crucial change in their way of procuring food, from individual foraging for vegetable foods to regular eating of meat and vegetables on a communal basis. The new pattern required cooperation and the coordination of hunting and gathering activities, for which at least an advanced call or gesturing system seems to have been required. The cultural evidence, in the form of stone tools, suggests a very early date for the first rudimentary language skills (Schick & Toth, 1993). The flakes made by these early hominids are far more sophisticated than anything a chimpanzee can make when taught by trainers to do so. Most importantly, the earliest stone tools indicate, by how they were struck in constructing them, that their makers were preferentially right-handed—suggesting that their brains were already lateralized as are modern humans (and unlike other primates).

To speak, the early humans had to have more than just the need to communicate. Speech requires physical mechanisms as well, such as certain structures in the brain. These structures allow us to associate incoming auditory messages with remembered messages from other sensory pathways—especially with the memory of the words that we will need to voice our thoughts. They also enable us to signal the muscles of the vocal apparatus to make the movements necessary to produce the appropriate sounds. Current research indicates that these operations are carried out mainly by three specific parts of the brain, all located in the cerebral cortex, the thick rind of gray matter that constitutes the outer layer of the brain.

The cerebellum of the human brain, a fist-sized structure just above the brain stem at the back of the head, is a recent development; it expanded rapidly and quite late in hominid history and is distinct from that of other primates. Around the time of the transition to food sharing and meat eating, the early human brain was less than half the size of ours and its cerebral cortex was smaller still, but still larger than modern nonhuman primates. Thus, while it seems unlikely that the language-producing structures of the cortex were fully developed at this time, it is a fair assumption that the conversion from call system to language had begun about four million years ago.

By about 100,000 years ago, when the Neanderthals lived in Europe and the Middle East, the cerebral cortex had reached approximately its present size. Presumably these people had the mental equipment necessary for a complex language. Without doubt, the cultural evidence (sophisticated tool manufacturing and deliberate burial of their dead), suggests abstract reasoning and well-developed modes of communication. Still, until recently it was thought that Neanderthals may have lacked the physiological equipment necessary for fully human speech.

In addition to the cerebral cortex, as we noted in the discussion of language in other primates, the pharynx is crucial to the production of speech. Until very recently, it was thought that the pharynx developed to the size and shape necessary to produce intelligible sounds only after the Neanderthal period. However, a Neanderthal skeleton excavated in Israel in 1989 with the small bones of the larynx intact appears to have had the physiological capability for human speech. Still, it is possible that truly fluent language is only a very recent achievement in the history of our species.

The use of language is undoubtedly responsible for the development of human culture. Groups whose members communicated effectively with one another hunted more successfully, gathered more efficiently, made more sophisticated tools, built stronger shelters, found more suitable locations for habitation, and argued and resolved their differences without necessarily coming to blows. This later point is important because complex social behavior associated with group living and cooperation entails individuals reconciling their immediate self-interest with their long-term prospects. Language greatly facilitates this, as individuals can negotiate long-lasting relationships of mutual trust and assistance that last beyond any given event. The concomitant growth of language and culture in turn created strong selective pressures for more complex brains, which made possible the development of yet more elaborate language and culture. There arose, in other words, a feedback cycle: language, culture, and the brain evolved together, each stimulating and reinforcing the development of the others.

The Structure of Languages

The study of language requires some knowledge of language structure and of the way that structure varies from one language to another. Let us now look at the components of language: the sounds, the way sounds are grouped into words, and the way words are combined to form sentences or utterances. In combination, these elements make up the formal structure of a language—what linguists call a grammar.

Any person who has tried to communicate in a foreign country with the help of only a bilingual pocket dictionary can tell you that languages vary in subtle and complex ways. The differences are more than just a matter of vocabulary; every language has its unique repertoire of sounds. Further, every language has words for which other languages have no exact equivalents. Finally, every language has its peculiar structure. One cannot take an English sentence, translate all the words into Turkish, and expect the result to make sense to a Turkish speaker. The rules for proper word order, among other things, differ significantly in the two languages. For example, the English sentence "I saw a dog yesterday," is, in Turkish, "Dün bir köpek gördüm" ("Yesterday a dog I saw"). Further, the pronoun "I" is contained in the Turkish verb form.

Thus, in order to understand a language, we must first understand its rules: the sounds that it recognizes and the way it organizes sounds into words and words into meaningful statements. To discover these rules for English or French, we might begin by looking at a grammar book, where we could read how to form verb tenses and so forth. Yet many languages have verb tenses and other structures which, unlike French, differ greatly from ours; moreover, many have not been formally studied and described. Therefore, in order to speak a particular language and to compare languages, linguists have had to develop a special set of descriptive categories, applicable to all known languages, as well as a special alphabet for transcribing the full range of sounds used in human languages.

Linguists describe the structure of any particular language by studying three central areas: (1) its **phonology**, or sound system; (2) its **morphology**, or the system by which its speech units are combined to form meaningful words; and (3) its **syntax,** or the arrangement of words into meaningful utterances. Language is thus describable in accordance with rules, most of them followed unconsciously by the native speaker, which bring these three elements together. Linguists usually use **grammar** to describe the combinations of these three divisions. Our ability to learn through language and to use language creatively depends on this intuitive understanding of grammar. If, instead of learning grammatical rules, people learned only a vast collection of specific sentences, they would be unable to understand any statement unless they had already heard it and knew what it meant and remembered it. But by applying grammatical rules, people can readily understand statements they have never heard before, and they can continually make statements that no one has ever made before.

Sign Language

We take for granted that normal language involves oral communication, and tend to assume that nonverbal communication systems such as computer languages are somehow artificial or incomplete. This is not the case, as is clear from what is known about sign languages, dramatically illustrated in the following account:

> When I was a small child I used to play with the girl next door. She didn't understand anything I tried to tell her, but it didn't matter. We played together all the time, using simple gestures to communicate. I thought something was wrong with her, but I adapted easily to her limitation.
>
> One day when I was about four, I went inside her house. As I stood there, her mother came downstairs. Nothing happened between her and the girl

that I could see. Then I saw her mother point at the doll house in the hallway. The girl ran and moved the doll house back into her room, as if she had just been told to do so. I was astounded. I knew it was different, something different. I knew that they had communicated, in a form I couldn't see. But how? I asked my mother about what I had seen. "They are called 'hearing'," she explained. "They don't sign. They are hearing. They are different. We are Deaf. We sign."

I asked if the family next door are the only ones, the only hearing people. My mother shook her head. "No," she signed, "it is us that are alone." I was very surprised. I naturally assumed everyone was like me. [Sam Supalla, quoted in Perlmutter, 1986]

Linguists and laypeople alike have been slow to recognize the fact that human languages are of two kinds—signed and oral—and sign languages are still generally left out of surveys of the world's languages. It is not even clear how many sign languages exist, since their boundaries do not coincide with those of oral languages. It is reasonable to assume that sign languages, like oral languages, have existed throughout human history, and, while little is known about the genetic affiliations of sign languages, it is clear that they are not the same as coterritorial oral languages. For example, while American Sign Language (ASL) is not related to British Sign Language, it is related to French Sign Language, which in turn is related to a number of other European sign languages, including Irish, Swedish, Latvian, Dutch, Swiss, Austrian, and Russian (see Figure 2–1). While ASL is used throughout the United States, in Germany a number of distinct sign languages are in use (Perlmutter, 1986).

There has recently been much discussion in the United States concerning the recognition of ASL as an academically acceptable language. Despite the fact that the number of postsecondary ASL courses has increased phenomenally over the last ten years, and that they are often among the most popular, only a handful of colleges and universities permit ASL to be used in fulfillment of undergraduate or graduate requirements for a second language (Wilcox & Wilbers, 1987).

According to Wilcox and Wilbers, much of the debate about ASL's status as a language stems from the widespread confusion of speech with language. Speech, like writing or signing, is merely an external form of language. Research has demonstrated that sign languages such as ASL are natural and complete languages, with an expressive range that is indistinguishable from that of any oral language. ASL is *not* a form of English; it has a distinct grammatical structure, which must be mastered by nonnative speakers in the same way as that of any oral language, and its acquisition as a first language follows essentially the same pattern as that of oral languages. There is also evidence that the system of manual gestures used in ASL has a structure similar to that of the phonological system of an oral language (Wilcox & Wilbers, 1987).

Linguistic Variation and Change

It is estimated that about 5,000 languages are spoken in the world today. However, as Suzanne Romaine (1984) points out, any such estimate is complicated by the problems inherent in defining terms such as *language* and *dialect*. "The very concept of discrete languages is probably a European cultural artifact fostered by processes such as nationalism, literacy and standardization. Any attempt to count distinct languages will be an artifact of classificatory procedures rather than a reflection of communicative practices" (Romaine, 1994).

The tendency toward linguistic variation appears to be the key to the development of distinct languages. Within geographical regions one can find linguistic variation among speakers of the same basic language living in separate communities, although they often tend to be slight and develop gradually. These are usually called **dialects.** Just how slight and gradually developed they may be was illustrated by Gillian Sankoff's study of language differences in a string of New Guinean villages. Sankoff (1972) proceeded from village to village, telling the people of each village a story in the dialect of the preceding village. In every case the story was easily understood. Indeed, the people often understood the story in dialects three and four villages removed. The villages at opposite ends of the line did not understand each other's language, but at no point along the line could one draw a boundary between two separate languages.

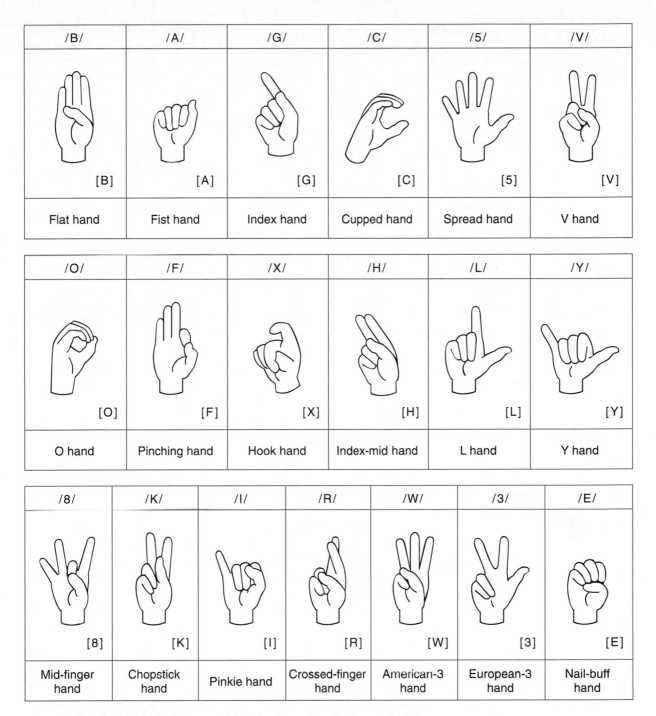

Figure 2–1. The hand configurations for American Sign Language (ASL) "primes," the signs that correspond to sounds of spoken language.

(From Fromkin and Rodman 1988: 385)

It should be noted that social factors are as important as linguistic criteria for deciding what counts as a language or a dialect. For example, the dividing line between the languages we call Swedish, Norwegian, and Danish is linguistically arbitrary (their grammar is very similar, and there are generally only minor differences in vocabulary and pronunciation) but politically and culturally relevant. As Max Weinreich states, "a language is a dialect with an army and a navy" (in Romaine, 1994).

As long as people speaking different dialects remain in contact with one another, reciprocal influence and the need to communicate will prevent the two dialects from drifting very far apart, as is the case with American English and British English. If groups speaking different dialects become isolated from one another, however, the dialects will diverge over time, eventually evolving into distinct languages.

This is what happened when geographical groups speaking different dialects of Latin became culturally isolated from one another during the early stages of the Christian era. Eventually these dialects became separate languages: French, Spanish, Italian, and Portuguese. English and German evolved in the same way. Both are descended from an ancestral Proto-Germanic tongue spoken 1,500 years ago.

There are several ways to trace the development of various languages from their common ancestral language. First, we can look for regular correspondences between the sounds of two languages. We find, for example, that many words that begin with /t/ in English correspond to words beginning with /z/ in German: *to* and *zu*, *ten* and *zehn*, *tame* and *zahm*. Likewise, an initial /d/ in English often corresponds to an initial /t/ in German, as in *daughter* and *tochter*, *day* and *tag*. Both vocabularies include many **cognates**—words so similar from one language to the next as to suggest that they are both variants of a single ancestral prototype. (All the German-English pairs enumerated are cognates.) Numerous other correspondences suggest that German and English are modern variants of an older Proto-Germanic tongue. Similar comparisons indicate that this same ancestral language also gave rise to modern Swedish, Dutch, Icelandic, Flemish, and other northern European languages.

We have no written records to prove that Proto-Germanic existed or to show how the modern languages of northern Europe developed from Proto-Germanic dialects, but we can reconstruct the process by tracing certain regular patterns of sound change backward through time. Indeed, by going back still further we can reconstruct the development of Proto-Germanic from an even earlier language.

During the early nineteenth century, Jakob Grimm—who later, with his brother Wilhelm, developed his linguistic interest while compiling fairy tales from various parts of the world—noted that regular phonemic changes took place from one language to another over the centuries. He found, for example, that the Sanskrit word *brata* ("brother") became *phrater* in Greek, *frater* in Latin, *broder* in Old English, and *bratu* in Slavonic. Similarly, Sanskrit *ad-mi* ("eat") became Greek *edomai*, Latin *edo*, Old English *etan*, and Slavonic *jadetu*. Numerous regularities of this type suggest that all these languages are related. Linguists now classify them as members of the same language family, Indo-European. All are descended from a single original Proto-Indo-European tongue, a language probably much like Sanskrit (see Figure 2–2).

By analyzing the vocabulary of various Indo-European languages, anthropologists have tried to reconstruct a picture of this early speech community's culture. This is done largely through the study of cognates. For example, cognates for "snow" appear in so many modern Indo-European languages that it was undoubtedly part of the original proto-vocabulary. It is probably safe to assume, then, that the Proto-Indo-European community did not originate in a snowless southern area such as India (Bloomfield, 1965). Likewise, since cognates for "milk," "yoke," and "wheel" are fairly widespread, it is assumed that this speech community had domesticated cattle and used wagons.

By similar comparative studies, anthropologists have discovered a good deal about the movements and historical relationships of various cultural communities. We know, for example, that the Semitic languages—of which Hebrew is one—originated in the Arabian Peninsula. At some point, probably as early as 2500 B.C., the Semitic speakers began to extend their influence over wider areas of the Middle East. Subsequently, there developed local dialects and eventually distinct languages. Today, more than 200 million people speak Arabic, a Semitic language. Joseph Greenberg (1993) has recently startled linguists with a new classification of North American Indian languages into three families, as opposed to the several hundred previously supposed, a controversial finding that would suggest that the continent was settled in three distinct waves of migration from Asia via the Bering Straits.

Linguistic Borrowing and Cultural Contact

Much linguistic change occurs when speech communities learn to adapt to one another. People use language to communicate, after all, and when their communication is hindered by current usage or the lack of important vocabulary elements, they may adapt their language by borrowing terms from another group. Such borrowing rarely affects grammar, the most conservative aspect of language. But vocabulary rapidly crosses language frontiers. Consider the menu for an American breakfast: A typical meal might begin with juice or fruit—perhaps grapefruit (a compound of two French words first joined on American soil), melon (of Greek origin via French), or cantaloupe (named after a town in Italy). Or the meal might begin with an orange, derived from the Arabic naranj. After juice or fruit, the American breakfast usually consists of cereal (derived from Ceres, the Roman goddess of agriculture) or bacon (French) and eggs (Old Norse), with toast (French), butter (Latin), and marmalade (Portuguese). The beverage may be coffee (Arabic), tea (Chinese via Malayan Dutch), or cocoa (Nahauatl via Mexican Spanish) (Farb, 1974, pp. 296–297). All of these words reflect a history of trade and transport of food products across national and linguistic boundaries.

Borrowed words are seldom adopted wholesale. Pronunciation is usually changed in accordance with the native sound system and patterns of stress, tone, and nasalization. For example, American pronunciation of *petits fours* and *chaise longue* bears little resemblance to their pronunciation in the original French.

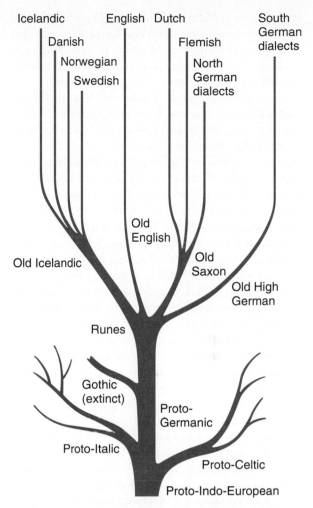

Figure 2–2. All germanic languages evolved from a single original Proto-Indo-European tongue—a language probably similar to Sanskrit.

Lingua Franca, Pidgin, and Creole Languages

As cultures began exploring other cultures and establishing trading relations, new languages developed to facilitate this trade. In medieval times a trade language evolved in the Mediterranean region consisting of Italian grammatical structure mixed with Arabic, French, and Spanish vocabulary, and was called **lingua franca**, or "the language of the Franks." The term is now generalized to mean any language used as a common tongue by people who do not speak one another's native tongue. A contemporary lingua franca is English as it is spoken in India and Pakistan. Here individuals who may speak one of several hundred languages as their first tongue use English to communicate. Yiddish, derived from German, has served a similar role among the Jews of Eastern Europe.

A contrasting form of language that facilitates cultural contact is **pidgin**, a language based on a simplified grammar and lexicon taken from one or more fully developed languages. For example, Melanesian Pidgin English, or Tok Pisin, has about 1,500 words, 80 percent of which are taken from English. It is used widely in Papua New Guinea. Though simplified, pidgin is governed by rules for verbs and word order. When the Duke of Edinburgh, in a speech to the English Speaking Union Conference in Ottawa, observed that he was "referred to in that splendid language [Tok Pisin] as 'Fella belong Mrs. Queen'," he was right that Tok Pisin is a language, but wrong in his designation. He would be called "man bilong kwin." In Tok Pisin *fella* can be used only as a suffix and has a number of grammatical functions, for example to mark adjectives and numerals, as in *tufela blakfela pik*, "two black pigs," and to mark the second person plural form of "you," as in *yufela i no ken go*, "you (plural) cannot go" (Romaine, 1994).

Pidgin languages sprang up along the coasts of Africa, China, and the New World during European colonization. In some places pidgin languages have become the native language, a process called "creolization." A **creole** language is a pidgin that has evolved into a fully developed language with a complete array of grammatical distinctions and a large vocabulary. Some linguists suggest that Proto-Germanic developed about 1000 B.C. out of a pidgin used by the Germanic tribes of the Baltic region. If this supposition is correct, then English, Dutch, and German all originated in a former pidgin language (Fromkin & Rodman, 1988, p. 263).

Sociolinguistics

We have seen that speech communities adapt their languages to new situations and new needs. In much the same way, individuals adapt their language to different social situations. The study of this phenomenon, the interrelationship of social variables and language, is called **sociolinguistics**. As sociolinguists have discovered, it is not only geographical separation that causes the same language to be spoken in a variety of ways. The formality of the speakers' relationship and their situation, status, sex roles, and even age are expressed in distinctive linguistic behavior. On hearing language, individuals continually seek out clues to the status and intentions of the speaker, and in speaking, deliberately or not, send out information regarding themselves to the listener. All of these messages are exchanged in addition to the nominal content of the utterances spoken. Within any society, the choice of expressions, vocabulary, dialect, or even language reflects social status, education, geography, and the way the speaker wishes to be viewed by others.

Social Status

Another domain of sociolinguistics is that of the context in which speech occurs. Depending on who is addressing her, a woman may be Professor Johnson, Ms. Johnson, Elizabeth, Beth, Mommy, Ma'am, or Darling. These terms are by no means interchangeable, for each carries a distinctive social connotation. Professor Johnson's husband would be unlikely to greet her as Professor Johnson, and a student would not address her as "Hey, Beth." By the same token, her husband and her friends will feel freer than her students in their choice of words and tone of conversation when they speak to her.

Indeed, it is quite common for a language to use the same signals both for status differences and for formality of relationship, even though the two are not always congruent. In America, for example, there are two main forms of address: title plus last name (Professor Johnson, Mr. Jones) and first name alone. This system tries to do two things at once: to signal the degree of intimacy and to signal the relative status between the speaker and the person being addressed. This system can create problems. For example, if a younger colleague joins the faculty at Professor Johnson's college, he may have trouble appropriately addressing her at first. If, in view of the fact that she is older and that they barely know each other, he calls her Professor Johnson, he is incorrectly suggesting that her social status is higher than his. But if he uses "Elizabeth,"

Men and women differ in many, often subtle ways in their use of language. In the American workplace, women are often expected to be less assertive than their male counterparts.

(Peter Menzel/Stock, Boston Inc.)

he is suggesting that they are friends, which they are not.

Of course, social status also has a profound effect on a person's language in general, regardless of whom he or she is addressing. In complex societies, where status differences are marked and where formal education increases these differences, the rich and the poor, the educated and the uneducated speak what amount to separate dialects, with considerable variation in vocabulary, grammar, and pronunciation. Until recently, most New Yorkers, like other residents of other major Eastern cities, did not pronounce /r/ following a vowel when it preceded a consonant or fell at the end of a word. The word *bartender,* for example, was (and still often is) pronounced something like *batenda.* Since World War II, however, it has become more prestigious to pronounce the /r/, a mark of upper-middle-class speech.

It is possible that historical changes in language often evolve through people's efforts to climb this linguistic social ladder. A number of sociolinguists have noted that people tend to imitate the speech of social groups that they admire or aspire to join.

Tribal peoples in eastern Burma are quite likely to learn Shan, a dialect of Thai spoken by members of a higher social class. But Shans rarely bother to learn any tribal languages. Sometimes both tribal peoples and Shans learn Burmese, the language spoken by the most politically influential group. Few Burmese, however, learn Shan, and fewer still learn the tribal languages (Leach, 1954).

Gender Roles and Language

Gender distinctions, as culturally defined, also structure the use of language. For example, many years ago it was noted that young women when interviewed, pronounced the -g twice as often as the boys in words such as *talking, going, seeing,* and so forth. In the United States, females may try to speak more "properly" than males. A variety of polite expletives, such as "my goodness" and "dear me," along with the intensifiers "so" and "such" ("It was such a delightful party!"), are often characteristic of female speech, though this usage seems to be disappearing. One reason is that gender roles are rapidly changing and such usages are associated with patterns of submissiveness. It is interesting that not only does vocabulary vary by sex, but so do patterns of conversing. It has been found that American men interrupt women in conversation far more frequently than women interrupt men and that most topics of conversation are introduced by male speakers. In the American workplace, female speech patterns often reflect job-related subordination through hesitancy and indirectness, features also heard in the speech of male subordinates when speaking to their superiors. The difference often is that when a woman overcomes her diffidence she may receive an epithet like "bitch" (Tannen, 1994).

Male-female linguistic differences are even more marked in many non-European languages, although propriety may fall on either side of the sexual barrier. Among the Yakinankarate of Madagascar, for example, men strive for diplomacy in speech. They are discreet, hide their feelings, and avoid open confrontations. This is the avowed ideal form of speech behavior. This ideal, however, applies only to men. Women have to express their emotions directly and bluntly. Whenever direct confrontations are unavoidable, the men incite the women to handle the unpleasantness on their behalf; women are also expected to do the haggling in the marketplace and to reprimand children (Farb, 1974).

Language and Ethnicity

One striking phenomenon within such complex societies as nation-states is seen in the distinctive ways in which ethnic and other socially distinct groups use the national language. Communities emphasize their uniqueness by developing a **speech community** or dialect. This variety of language diverges from the national language in vocabulary, pronunciation, and even grammar. One language form—the dialect of the dominant social or political group—is usually considered standard. In contemporary society, the mass media (radio, television, and newspapers) promote the standard language. Network newscasters generally do not use ethnic dialects unless they are attempting to be humorous.

Regionally or ethnically localized dialects often have social and political significance. Black English, a dialect of some African Americans, is perpetuated because it promotes a sense of shared communal identity. Most speakers can move between the use of Black English at home or in the neighborhood and a variant of standard English at work. Often such dialects are regarded by people who do not speak them as "substandard," but this is an ethnocentric (better, linguacentric) perspective. After all, everyone speaks some dialect or other; the denigration of some dialects simply reflects the social ascendancy of the group whose dialect is considered standard. Sometimes the use of a dialect may have negative repercussions, particularly when the dialect is not prestigious or is politically charged. Americans who speak a southern dialect in the Northeast may find themselves stereotyped as rural, unsophisticated, or worse. The same social stigma may be experienced by a Yankee in a small southern town. Still, dialects persist because of their association with a wider set of cultural values and community identity.

Quite apart from dialects, several languages may be spoken in one country; indeed, this is the case in the majority of countries. In the United States, Spanish is the most widely used language apart from English. In New York City, there are bilingual elementary and high school programs in Spanish, Chinese, Haitian, Creole, Russian, Korean, Arabic, Vietnamese, Polish, Bengali, French, Urdu, and Albanian. In 1994, 84,517 students were enrolled in these bilingual programs, which offer instruction in English as a second language, native language arts instruction, social studies, science, and math using both the native language and English. A further 63,014 students are enrolled in programs that teach English as a second language but do not use the students' native language (Board of Education of the City of New York, Division of Bilingual Education, 1993–1994).

Whether bilingualism should be encouraged is a controversial political issue as we see in the Contemporary Issues box, *The Politics of Language in the United States* (page 55). During 1987, thirty-seven states considered amendments to their constitutions making English the official language; in thirteen states, the amendments passed. In 1988 these thirteen were joined by Texas, Florida, Arizona, and Colorado. Although in many cases the

---

Contemporary Issues
The Politics of Language in the United States

PRESENTLY IN THE UNITED STATES there are two diametrically opposed political movements focused on language. One involves the efforts of many educators, usually in urban areas with many recent immigrant families, to establish bilingual or multilingual secondary school programs. Opposed to this are quite vocal proponents of laws or ballot initiatives that establish English as the official language of government and education. While the latter groups are rarely explicit, their usual motivation is to limit the use of Spanish for official or instructional purposes. In 1994, for example, New Jersey passed a law making a knowledge of English a requirement for obtaining a driver's license. The effectiveness of bilingual education, while a legitimate concern, is not the real issue. Rather, it is to preserve the dominance of one segment of a diverse population.

The history of German in the United States illustrates this nicely, as B. J. Craige (1988) shows us. In 1790, German speakers comprised 8.7 percent of the population. During the nineteenth century, the German-speaking population continued to increase; between 1830 and 1890 five million Germans settled in the United States. During this period, in order to encourage German support for the new public school system, some public schools in Wisconsin and the rural areas of the Midwest were run entirely in German. However, during World War I, in many states it became a crime to teach in German or even to speak German on the street, on the telephone, or in church; there were even public burnings of German books. By 1921, some 18,000 people had been charged under these laws.

Between 1915 and 1932 the number of students of German had declined by 98 percent, even though in 1923 the Supreme Court had struck down statutes in over twenty states that made English the official language and prohibited the use of other languages in the classroom. While in 1910, 83 percent of all high school students studied foreign languages, by 1948 this had declined to 22 percent, and today the figure is fewer than 18 percent (Zentella, 1988).

As with German in the past, the English-only movement directed at Spanish speakers is aimed at minimizing apparent cultural diversity and threats to the status quo. As Zentella, a bilingual linguist, sums up her impressions, "Americans are looking around and not liking what they see. Home doesn't feel like home anymore. There are too many different people, with different races and faces, different foods and music, different ideas and ways of doing things; and too many don't speak English" (1988, p. 39).

---

final word still lies with the courts, we see here the political importance of language.

Language and Nationalism

Nationalists in many countries, notably France and Germany, have often equated the use of foreign vocabulary with unwanted foreign influence, even though historically no language evolved in isolation and there are no "pure" languages. In modern Turkey, not only is standard Turkish regularly reviewed for "foreign loan" words (which are replaced by newly minted Turkish ones), but the use of any language other than standard Turkish in the media or in public institutions is forbidden (with a few exceptions, such as the use of English in some schools). Kurdish, spoken by at least 4 million people, is suppressed because the government is fighting a separatist Kurdish political movement, the Kurdish Liberation Movement. The paradox is that the main reason that this violent organization has any popular support is precisely because of years of linguistic and cultural suppression. For the Kurdish-speaking population, its language is a badge of individual cultural identity.

Language is a crucial element in forming individual and group identity. In Bulgaria, the former Communist government attempted to suppress the use of Turkish by over a million of its Moslem minority. Here religious and other leaders meet to demand recognition of their linguistic and religious rights.
(Fevzi Omer)

In Bulgaria prior to the collapse of the Communist regime in 1990, there was a determined effort by the government to eradicate all evidence of Bulgaria's Moslem minorities—about 10 percent of the national population. Accordingly, not only were Islamic symbols and practices outlawed, but individuals were forced to abandon their birth names and assume Slavic ones; fines and prison sentences were imposed on those who were discovered speaking Turkish. From the official point of view, minorities did not exist (see Bates, 1994). But as one would expect, these heavy-handed efforts backfired, just as they have elsewhere. The beleaguered minorities not only organized political resistance, forming an underground movement, they responded by reviving interest in their language and religion. In short, language suddenly became of prime importance in minority self-identity.

In the case of groups that are struggling for or have recently achieved political independence, such efforts to differentiate one's language from that of outsiders may be extreme, taking the form of what

has been called linguistic nationalism. Consider the case of Hebrew. For centuries this language was barely used by the Jews outside their religious ceremonies. Today it is spoken daily by most of the citizens of Israel. As many Jews had some knowledge of Hebrew and it had great symbolic significance, it was the logical choice for the national language of Israel, with its population of immigrants from all over the world. However, the return to this ancient language was also a powerful symbol reinforcing Israelis' claim to their newly created homeland. Likewise, in Ireland and Wales efforts are being made to revive Gaelic and Welsh, which all but died out under English influence. In India and Burma special commissions have been set up to create native substitutes for the English terms that crept into the languages during the period of colonial rule.

To many observers these efforts to breathe new life into languages that have been threatened or replaced for political reasons seem historically naïve, yet the theory behind them is sound. As we saw earlier in this chapter, language mirrors, reinforces, and arguably even molds a culture. If a people's language is replaced by that of another people, their culture is replaced as well. Language, then, is a great deal more than a symbol of a group's culture. To a large extent, it reinforces the group's identity—its particular ways of thinking and behaving.

Summary

ALL PEOPLE ARE BORN WITH CERTAIN BIOLOGICAL traits that account in part for broad similarities in human behavior. Biology also affects us on an individual level by setting limits—through our health, stamina, and body build, for instance—that cannot be overcome. In addition, biological factors affect certain kinds of individual behavior.

Through social learning, members of a society develop their own ways of behaving or perceiving, which differ from the ways of other societies. Social learning occurs primarily through socialization, the process by which the social group and the family, through formal training and unconscious modeling, pass on skills, knowledge, values, attitudes, and behavior to the next generation. Channels of socialization include childrearing, education, gender- and age-role learning, and rites of passage.

Role learning—adapting to a set of behavioral expectations appropriate to one's position—is an important part of education. While roles channel a person in certain prescribed directions, each individual interprets a given role in a somewhat distinctive way. Both gender roles and age roles are affected by socialization. The form and intensity of the set of distinguishable characteristics associated with each sex—a social construct referred to as gender—vary from society to society. Many societies treat aging as a passage through distinctive states rather than as movement along a continuum.

One of the most effective expressions of socialization is the rite of passage, which marks the induction of a person into a newer, more responsible role. School graduations, weddings, confirmations, and bar and bat mitzvahs are all rites of passage. Neverthess, both the individual's specific circumstances and his or her ability to manipulate the cultural environment are vital elements in the determination of human behavior. The relationship between the individual and her or his culture is one of dynamic interaction.

While all animals apparently communicate through call systems—repertoires of sounds, each of which is produced in response to a specific situation—humans are the only animals that use language. Human language presumably began as a call system. Language differs from animal call systems in that it is open—the number of messages that can be conveyed is infinite. This flexibility is made possible by the arbitrariness of human language—sounds have no fixed meaning—and the fact that it is stimulus-free: an utterance need not be evoked by an immediate situation. Training apes to use limited sign language has convinced some researchers that their linguistic ability differs from ours only in degree; however, while apes may share with us certain faculties that are necessary for language, it is clear that these faculties have remained relatively undeveloped in their line.

Researchers can only speculate on the origins of language. Cultural evidence suggests a very early date for the first language skills; the physical evidence suggests a later date for the full development of language. It seems likely that the change to language from call systems began about four million years ago and proceeded only gradually. It is believed that human language developed through the blending of calls to produce new calls with more complex meanings. This transition is largely responsible for the development of human culture. Language, culture, and the brain evolved together, each stimulating and reinforcing the others.

Languages vary in subtle and complex ways. Grammar—the formal structure of a language—consists of phonology, morphology, and syntax. To study and compare languages, linguists have developed an alphabet and a special set of descriptive characteristics applicable to all known languages. Moreover, linguists now know that signed, as opposed to oral, languages have existed throughout human history and are as fully developed as any spoken language. American Sign Language (ASL) is not related to

British Sign Language, but it is related to French Sign Language.

Linguistic diversity may evolve as the result of certain internal processes in a language—changes in sounds, grammatical structures, word order, and meaning. The tendency toward linguistic variation may be a key to the development of distinct languages. Within geographical regions, linguistic differences tend to be gradual; distinct languages apparently evolved when groups speaking different dialects became isolated from one another. Through comparative studies, linguists have determined regularities among those languages they classify as the Indo-European family. Many words in those languages are cognates—so similar as to suggest that these languages are descended from a single Proto-Indo-European tongue. Similar comparative studies of language have revealed information about the movements and historical relationships of various early cultural communities.

Language also reflects culture, in that people choose to respond to stimuli that are important to them. But according to some observers, culture is molded by language; different ways of speaking create different ways of thinking. This statement is not definitive because of the simultaneous evolution of language and culture, and evidence for the structuring of social processes by linguistic characteristics is weak. Linguistic change is also brought about by elements borrowed from other speech communities.

Sociolinguistics is the study of interrelationships of social variables and language. Ethnic and other socially distinct groups emphasize their uniqueness by developing a speech community or dialect, which diverges from the national language in vocabulary, pronunciation, and grammar. Other groups may develop a community identity, making an effort to distinguish themselves from outsiders by their speech. The context of a situation—its formality or informality and the relationship between the speakers—is a factor in the choice of terms of address and of words or even languages. Social status influences a person's use of language; it is possible that historical changes in pronunciation may occur because of attempts to climb the linguistic social ladder. Gender roles also affect linguistic variables.

The accumulation of random variations in a language accounts for linguistic change. So do the accommodations a people must make to their social and physical environment. In this way, language and culture are interrelated.

People who do not speak one another's language but are in regular contact with one another often adopt a lingua franca, another language that all understand although it is the native tongue of none of them. Another form of language that facilitates cultural contact is pidgin, based on a simplified grammar and vocabulary taken from one or more fully developed languages. If a pidgin language becomes a fully developed language in its own right, it is called a creole language.

Key Terms

age grade	morphology
age set	phonology
call system	pidgin
cognates	rites of passage
creole	socialization
dialect	sociolinguistics
enculturation	speech community
grammar	syntax
lingua franca	

Suggested Readings

Fromkin, Victoria & Rodman, Robert (1988). *An introduction to language* (4th ed.). New York: Holt, Rinehart & Winston. An introduction to the study of linguistics directed toward students from many disciplines. This latest edition reflects the newest developments in linguistic theory and related fields.

Giglioli, Pier P. (Ed.). (1986). *Language and social context.* Harmondsworth, England: Penguin Books. A selection of readings that discuss the varied aspects of the social organization of speech.

Gilmore, David D. (1990). *Manhood in the making: Cultural concepts of masculinity.* New Haven: Yale University Press. Addresses the question of what does it mean to "be a man" in different cultures around the world. The author treats manhood as a status achieved through culturally approved stressful, competitive tests.

Gumperz, J. & Hymes, D. (1964). The ethnography of communication. *American Anthropologist*, 67(6), part 2 (special issue). Essays in this volume describe language behavior in specific communicative contexts.

Labov, William (1972). *Sociolinguistic patterns.* Philadelphia: University of Pennsylvania Press. A stimulating and important book on sociolinguistics that details the author's work on contemporary U.S. language uses, especially Black English.

Leibowitz, Lila (1978). *Females, males, families: A biosocial approach.* North Scituate, MA: Duxbury Press. A wide-ranging look from an evolutionary and cross-cultural perspective at the prehistory, development, and diversity of the human family.

Lincoln, Bruce (1991). *Emerging from the chrysalis: Rituals of women's initiation*. New York: Oxford University Press. The author examines women's initiation rituals much as does David Gilmore male rituals. Unlike male rituals, female initiation rituals do not involve a change in hierarchical status but rather a sanctification of a generally subservient status.

Pinker, S. (1994). *The language instinct: How the mind creates language*. New York: HarperCollins. This is an excellent book for the nonspecialist who needs some familiarity with the fundamentals of contemporary linguistic theory.

Trudgill, Peter (1983). *Sociolinguistics: An introduction to language and society*. Harmondsworth, England: Penguin Books. A synthesis of contemporary sociolinguistic research with a special emphasis on the varieties of spoken English as well as several related pidgins and creoles.

Wardhaugh, Ronald (1986). *An introduction to sociolinguistics*. New York: Basil Blackwell Ltd. A sound, basic coverage of most of the topics concerning the relationship between language and society, drawing on a wide variety of sources.

The Human Evolutionary Legacy
Darwin: Evolution by Natural Selection
Mendel: The Genetics of Natural
    Selection
Evolution and Human Culture

Human Ecology
The Human Ecological Context
The Nature of Ecological Systems

**Procurement Systems: Decisions,
Adaptation, and Food**
The Evolution of Procurement Patterns
Adapting to Environmental Problems
*Using Anthropology: The South
Turkana Ecosystem Project*
Adapting to Other Groups
*State of the Peoples: The Political
Ecology of Deforestation: The
Brazilian Amazon*

Adaptation and Cultural Evolution
A Case Study in Long-Term Change:
    The Vikings of the North Atlantic
The Processes of Long-Term Cultural
    Change

Summary

Key Terms

Suggested Readings

Chapter 3

Decisions, Adaptation, and Evolution

The Dobe !Kung, or Ju/'hoansi as they are increasingly called, a subgroup of the San people of the Republic of Botswana in southwest Africa, live in a dry, sandy plain at the edge of the Kalahari Desert, where dependable agriculture is impossible and where food and water resources are constantly fluctuating. However, until about ten years ago, the Dobe !Kung lived by hunting game and gathering wild plant foods, the most ancient of all human subsistence strategies and one that has allowed them to exist rather comfortably in their habitat. This fact in itself merits investigation.

In an ongoing effort to put together a complete picture of a hunting-and-gathering way of life, many researchers have been involved in a project spanning two decades that examines every aspect of the Dobe !Kung existence.

First, one must study the group's relationship to its environment and the effect of this relationship on population and social organization. How, precisely, do the !Kung respond to seasonal variability in the supply of game, wild plants, and drinking water? How do they spend their time and expend energy? How does the necessity to move regularly affect their birth and death rates? How does their commitment to hunting and gathering affect the way they organize their domestic groups?

Second, the health and nutrition of the !Kung must be examined. How hard do they have to work to keep themselves alive and healthy? What is the incidence of nutritional deficiency and of stress-related disorders?

Third, one must look at child development among the !Kung. How is the experience of growing up in a hunting-and-gathering society different from that of growing up in an agricultural or industrial society? Do these children reach the development milestones—walking, talking, and so forth—more quickly or more slowly than children in other cultures? What impact does the hunting-and-gathering way of life have on sex-role development?

Finally, the cognitive world of the Dobe !Kung requires exploration. How do they perceive themselves in relation to other peoples? What forces do they see behind nature? How do they perceive their resources? What constitutes their medical knowledge? How, in sum, do they see the world and their place in it?

The thread that unites these diverse questions is the assumption that they can be best answered by viewing the people as ever-evolving populations, themselves part of larger environmental systems. What the !Kung do for a living, their beliefs, and their family organization can all be seen as closely interrelated and can be understood in terms of their adaptation to their environment. **Evolutionary ecology** is the theoretical orientation that emphasizes the problem-solving significance of culture and behavior, from procurement systems to kinship systems to political and religious life. In this chapter we will explore the rationale for this perspective in greater detail, building on our discussion of evolution and cultural ecology in the first chapters. We will discuss what is meant by adaptation, the role of variation and decision making in adaptation, and finally we will place evolutionary processes affecting humans in an ecological context.

The Human Evolutionary Legacy

It is easy to overlook the fact that evolution is an ongoing process. Our species and all of its constituent populations are continually being shaped by evolutionary forces. While most often we speak of natural selection as the major force acting on the genetic compositions of populations, any force that causes the genetic composition of a population to change is an evolutionary force. Interbreeding, or gene flow, is a major source of both unity and change in human populations. Our species is a quite recent product; we are also highly mobile and local populations continually interbreed. As a result, we are relatively homogeneous in terms of genetic material. In fact, most anthropologists feel it is inappropriate, or at best difficult, to speak of different races (Rensberger, 1989).

C. Loring Brace has studied skeletal remains from Japan. His results indicate that the present population of Japan is the product of the interbreeding of two genetically distinct groups: the Ainu, which he says are the original inhabitants of the islands, and the Yayoi, who migrated from Korea and China only slightly more than 2,000 years ago. He further claims his evidence shows that the famed Samurai warrior class descended from the people of northern Hokkaido (the Ainu), that Japanese royalty and nobility intermarried with them, and that other Japanese were primarily descended from the Yayoi (Brace, 1989). This view almost completely reverses traditional Japanese thinking about their heritage, in which the Ainu are considered to have no role. Today they in fact suffer from social discrimination. Whether Brace's theories turn out to be true or not, the point is that we have to be wary about considering any population as a fixed entity. We will return to this issue in Chapter 9.

In January 1988, the popular media ran a series of major stories on what was widely described as "The Search for Eve" (see Tierney et al., 1988). The report that focused national attention was by Rebecca Cann, a biological anthropologist. Her work was based on new techniques of studying the origins, unity, and diversity of our species that do not rely on the examination of fossils or bones, but rather on the cell tissues of infants. By collecting and analyzing mitochondrial DNA from placentas of babies born throughout Asia, Africa, Europe, and the Americas, Cann and her coworkers appeared to have established that about 200,000 years ago all present-day Homo sapiens shared a female ancestress who lived in Africa (Cann, 1988, pp. 127–143).

Since the publication of her original findings, some aspects of the dating techniques have been questioned as well as the implications that modern humans simply replaced existing hominids throughout the world, rather than interbreeding. The notion of a single, recent origin for our immediate ancestral line has long been the subject of controversy. A recent origin would imply that many earlier hominids, such as the widespread Neanderthals found in different parts of the Old World, did not directly contribute to our family line. Although the idea of our ultimate African origins is now well-established, it is unclear whether our modern species evolved only there and subsequently spread, or whether our species emerged more or less separately in different parts of the Old World, coexisting in places with our close relatives, the Neanderthals (see Stringer & Brauer, 1994; Frayer et al., 1994, for opposing interpretations). Regardless of the outcome of this debate, it must be kept in mind those features that we often use to describe different peoples of the world—skin color, eye color and shape, stature, and hair—are all the products of very recent and minor adaptations—adaptations that are continually changing every population.

Stephen Jay Gould, speaking of these recent research developments, says, "It makes us realize that all humans, despite differences in external appearance, are really members of a single entity that's had a very recent origin in one place. There is a kind of biological brotherhood that's much more profound than we had ever realized" (Gould, quoted in Tierney et al., 1988). The major differences we see between human beings are the products of behavioral or cultural adaptation. As Lewis Binford (1989) writes,

> Our species had arrived—not as a result of gradual, progressive processes but explosively in a relatively short period of time. Many of us currently speculate that this was the result of the invention of language, our peculiar mode of symbolic communication that makes possible our mode of reasoning and in turn our behavioral flexibility. [p. 30]

Humans are bound to the rest of nature by evolutionary history—that is, by descent from common ancestors. Our species is kin to every other living thing on earth—not just in a metaphorical or sentimental sense but in a strict biological sense, as two cousins are related by virtue of having the same grandparents. Of course, we are related more closely to some species than to others. Chimpanzees are much closer kin to us than are monkeys, not to mention nonprimates. Varying degrees of kinship are reflected in varying degrees of anatomical and behavioral similarity. Ultimately, however, all living things, ourselves included, are descended from the same forebears: minute organisms that lived billions of years ago in a world we would not recognize.

How, from such beginnings, did we and all the other species of the earth come to be what we are? The answer to this question did not become clear until the early twentieth century. In the eighteenth and early nineteenth centuries, some scientists recognized that species could change over time as organisms adapted to their environments. But they could not visualize how or why such changes occurred. Indeed, most of them did not believe that such changes could actually create new species. Natural processes might produce new "races," or strains within a species, but only God could create a new species. It was not until 1859, when Charles Darwin (1809–1882) published his treatise, *On the Origin of Species by Means of Natural Selection*, that the major mechanism of evolution was finally described in a way that accounted both for change within species and for the emergence of new species without divine intervention.

Darwin: Evolution by Natural Selection

Darwin was convinced that new species arose not through acts of divine intervention but rather through a blind and mechanical process. He understood that all species of plants and animals tend to produce more offspring than the environment can support and that this results in intense competition for living space, resources, and mates. Only a favored few survive long enough to reproduce. Darwin noted also that individual members of a species differ from one another physically. In a given population of animals, for example, some may have thicker fur or longer limbs than others. These variations are adaptive if they enhance the animal's chances of survival and, more important, if they enhance its chances of producing offspring that survive to reproduce themselves. Needless to say, this process depends on the nature of the demands placed on the organism by its environment and by the changes that environment is undergoing.

(Thick fur, for example, could mean a longer life in an increasingly cold environment, whereas it might be a handicap in an increasingly warm one.) Those individuals whose peculiarities give them a competitive edge in their particular environment produce more offspring, and those offspring inherit their parents' peculiarities, so they in turn survive longer and produce more offspring. Thus with each generation the better-adapted members of a population increase in number at the expense of less well-adapted individuals. In the process, the species as a whole changes.

This is the mechanism that Darwin called "natural selection." It served to explain not only gradual changes within a species but also the appearance of new species. For as different populations of a species adapted to different environments, they eventually diverged until the differences in their anatomy or behavior became so great that they could no longer interbreed. In other words, they became separate species. According to Darwin, this process—adaptation to environmental circumstances—accounted for the great variety of species observable in nature. Speciation is not, in fact, quite as simple a phenomenon as is described here. Many species are "ring species," which means that adjacent populations can interbreed but nonadjacent ones cannot. Also, in studying populations of the past, it is not always possible to determine whether or not separate but fairly similar populations could have interbred. The concept of species, however, remains useful as a standard despite empirical problems in applying it.

Mendel: The Genetics of Natural Selection

A major weakness of Darwin's theory was that he could not explain how favored characteristics were inherited—and such a systematic explanation was needed, for the prevailing belief was that each individual inherited a blend of its parents' characteristics. If this belief were true, advantageous variations would be lost by dilution with less advantageous traits long before natural selection could act on them. It was an obscure Austrian monk named Gregor Mendel (1822–1884) who discovered the hereditary basis of natural selection.

In the garden of his monastery, located in what is now Czechoslovakia, Mendel spent years cross-breeding strains of peas and other plants in an effort to find out how traits were transmitted from one generation to the next. He discovered that biological inheritance was not an irreversible blending of parental traits. Rather, individual units of hereditary information, later called "genes," were passed from parent to offspring as discrete particles according to certain regular patterns. In one individual a gene's effect might be blended with the effects of other genes, or even suppressed altogether. But the gene itself remained unchanged, ready to be passed on to the next generation, where it might express itself and thus be available for natural selection.

Mendel's work attracted no attention in the scientific community until both he and Darwin were dead. It was rediscovered in the early 1900s, but its relevance to evolution was not fully appreciated until the next generation. By that time, other apparent discrepancies in Darwin's theory had been resolved and it was finally accepted that the human species, along with every other species, is a product of evolution. Today evolutionary theory is at the very heart of all research in the biological and natural sciences. With the recent breakthroughs in modern genetics, population biology, and biochemistry, the utility of the "evolutionary synthesis"—as it is now called—is established beyond doubt.

Evolution and Human Culture

While agreeing with the premise that humans have to be understood as products of a long evolutionary heritage, cultural anthropologists have generally emphasized the importance of learning and cultural plasticity relatively unconstrained by biological factors (apart from obvious physiological requirements). In the 1980s, however, this position has been challenged by new theoretical perspectives on evolution that have emerged from the natural and social sciences—in particular from the areas of neurobiology, population genetics, ethology, and psychology. The main contention is that genetically controlled biological processes are responsible for shaping a good deal more of social behavior than is generally acknowledged. The arguments are often controversial. As they have focused much attention on the relationship of biology and culture, we will look at them in some detail.

In the last twenty years, new approaches to the study of social or cultural behavior, called variously human behavioral biology, human ethology, evolutionary ecology, and sociobiology, have been propounded (see Cronk, 1991, pp. 25–53, for a review). They share the view, brought most dramatically to popular attention by E. O. Wilson in 1975, that Darwinian models of natural selection apply to aspects of human culture and social behavior as well as to animal social behavior. Researchers found a significant percentage of social behavior in nonhuman animals to be under the direct or indirect influence of genes, and they argued that such behavior has adaptive significance (Dyson-Hudson & Little, 1983; Chagnon & Irons, 1979). Types of behavior in question included mate selection, parenting, social relations among kin, food sharing and strategies for procuring it, and mutual assistance and reciprocity. Genetic influence does not imply that a specific gene (or genes) controls a particular behavioral complex (say, the love of a parent for its offspring), nor does it imply determinism, as is sometimes charged. Behavior, where genes are concerned, is best seen as an "open program" whereby a trait is shaped by the interactions of genes and environmental influences; thus, an organism continually tracks environmental changes, a process Irons refers to as "adaptive plasticity" (Chagnon & Irons, 1979, p. 250).

The animal whose mating, defensive, and food-procurement behaviors work best within its given environment is the animal most likely to survive, reproduce, and rear its offspring to maturity. Organisms have a genetically based propensity to respond to various environmental circumstances in ways that are appropriate—that is, in ways that promote or facilitate individual reproductive success. Some aspects of this approach are well-established and not subject to controversy. Certainly genetically conditioned aspects of animal social behavior are the result of and continually influenced by the forces of natural selection. Much social behavior involves cooperation among close kin (sharing much genetic material), as this approach would predict. The genes that control behaviors that contribute to reproductive success are preferentially transmitted through generations, whereas genes that facilitate less adaptive behavior gradually disappear. So well-established is this basic premise that virtually all behavioral research

with primates and other social species takes it as a given.

Should this line of reasoning apply only to nonhuman animals? A variety of studies point to the value of the evolutionary model for an understanding of broad patterns of human behavior: the importance of kinship and family and male-female reproductive strategies. The usual argument for exempting the human species from this line of reasoning is that once humans developed culture (and the behavioral flexibility that accompanies it), they parted ways with the other animals (see Gould, 1986). Our social behavior came to be based primarily on learning, and our ability to learn can produce behavioral changes much more rapidly than natural selection can ever affect them via specific genetic codes. Our behavioral repertoire has been passed down to us through our culture rather than through our genes. The behaviors that have survived have been of value less to individuals than to groups, for culture is, in this view, the property of groups.

Even granting these points, those who employ the evolutionary model argue that while culture is transmitted by learning, what is inherited is a built-in propensity to learn and pass on some cultural rules and beliefs at the expense of others. In other words, we learn what we are conditioned by instinct to learn (see Gould & Marler, 1987). There is no simple resolution to this disagreement. We cannot doubt that lines of continuity run through the behavior of all animals. This line of reasoning has produced a wealth of useful studies (see Cronk, 1991; Smith & Winterhalter, 1992). For example, William G. Irons proposed that in most societies, what is considered "cultural success" (prestige, power, respect), consists of accomplishing things that make biological success probable (1979, p. 258). He tested this on data from the Yomut Turkmen of Iran and found that the wealthier, culturally more successful half of the population had more surviving children. This has been followed up by numerous studies of other populations with results that seem to confirm his hypothesis. Still, there may be other ways to interpret these findings, ways that do not require the assumption that behavior is generally directed to reproductive success (Cronk, 1991, p. 29). Whatever the results of particular studies, we cannot doubt that human capacity for culture adds a unique dimension to

Social prestige, wealth, and reproduction can be closely related in traditional societies. Among the Turkmen, wealthy men have numerous children. Here, a well-off rural family sponsors a feast with wrestling competitions to celebrate a son's circumcision ceremony.

(Daniel Bates)

human social life. Much of what anthropologists are interested in explaining is not directly addressed by this model; for example, the nature and persistence of inequality, the role of value systems and ideology in social life, and the evolution of contemporary political systems. Nevertheless, any serious inquiry into human behavior will have to consider the complex ways in which cultural and biological processes intersect (Brown, 1991; Fox, 1994). Social scientists in such diverse fields as political science, economics, and psychology increasingly draw on evolutionary theory (see Dennett, 1995; Wright, 1994, for examples).

Human Ecology

In the social and biological sciences there are a number of themes and interests that bridge disciplines and bring new, often unsuspected, insights to light. Ecology is one example and the only somewhat less broad subfield, **human ecology**, is another. Human ecology links the disciplines of anthropology, biology, geography, demography, economics—to name just a few. Ecologists, whether concerned with humans or other species,

are interested in three very broad questions. One, how does the environment affect the organism? Two, how does the organism affect its environment? And, three, how does an organism affect other organisms in the environments in which it lives? The quest for answers to these questions encompasses almost everything ecologists do. What distinguishes human ecology from ecology is not so much the larger questions, but the species that is of prime interest: human beings.

Without ignoring the complexity of the issues involved, it is possible to design strategies for research that are at once empirical and consistent with biological models used in studying behavior in general (Smith & Winterhalter, 1992, pp. 4–5). As the term suggests, human ecology combines two approaches: an interest in those features that are unique (or at least distinctive) attributes of humans, and the science of ecology, including evolutionary theory, on which it is ulimately based.

Human ecology is distinctive not only because of its focus on our species, but also for theoretical reasons. Ecological models designed to study the interactions of other species are often inadequate to fully accommodate our own. Humans hold an unusual position in nature and their special, if not unique, attributes pose problems for modeling local interactions.

As we have noted earlier, humans rely upon and are dramatically affected by our symbolic interpretations and representations of ourselves and other things (White, 1949). Symbols guide the ways that we interact with the organic and inorganic elements of our environments by making the environment intelligible in ways specific to our cultures—say, by representing what is good to eat and what is not, who may eat what and when and how. Of major importance to humans is the way that we distinguish group differences symbolically, creating cultural diversity among ourselves. This cultural diversity is often an important element of our social environment, affecting the ways we interact with one another and other elements of our environments.

Our propensity to engage in exchanges of goods and services and information among individuals and groups in widely separated territories has the effect of vastly extending the range of our resources and of our impacts upon them. It is rare today for a local population to rely entirely on localized resources, or to be uninfluenced by adjacent or even distant populations.

Ecology is "the study of the relations between organisms and the totality of the physical and biological factors affecting them or influenced by them" (Pianka, 1974, p. 3). In other words, **ecology** is the study of the interplay between organisms (or the populations to which they belong) and their environment. Implicit in this definition is the connection between ecology and evolutionary theory. As we said earlier, evolution operates primarily through the mechanism of natural selection. That is, certain characteristics become more and more common within a population because within the context of that population's environment these characteristics give individuals an edge in the competition for survival and reproduction. So a crucial factor in the evolutionary process is an ecological factor—the fit between organisms and their environment.

The Human Ecological Context

Humans, along with every other form of life, are a part of a single **ecosystem**—the cycle of matter and energy that includes all organic things and links them to the inorganic. All organisms depend on energy and on matter. Most of the energy and matter that animals use are not taken directly from the sun and the earth. Rather, these are produced by other organisms and cycled among species through feeding—"eat and be eaten" is the rule for all. Humans breathe the oxygen emitted by plants, and plants take in carbon dioxide emitted by humans and millions of other species of animals. Such relationships, taken together, constitute a vast network of individuals exchanging the energy, nutrients, and chemicals necessary to life; humans and bacteria alike are involved in the same process.

The usefulness of the ecosystem concept is, first, that it can be applied to any environment. Second, and more important, the ecosystem concept allows us to describe humans in dynamic interaction with one another, with other species, and with the physical environment. We can chart and quantify the flow of energy and nutrients and specify the interactions critical for the maintenance of any local population. Thus the ecosystem concept gives us a way of describing how human populations influence and are influenced by their surroundings (Moran, 1990).

There is usually considerable order and continuity in natural ecosystems. This is not surprising since, over time, the millions of component species of any ecosystem have come to mutually limit one another as they feed, reproduce, and die. The fact that ecosystems appear to persist through time does not mean, however, that they are static. While most ecosystems are viewed as being in equilibrium or near-equilibrium, in fact relations among the component populations are continually changing. One ecologist, C. S. Holling (1973), employs two concepts to describe continuity and change in ecosystems: resilience and stability.

Resilience is a measure of the degree of change a system can undergo while still maintaining its basic elements or relationships. **Stability** is a measure of the speed with which a system returns to equilibrium after absorbing disturbances. Systems with high resilience but low stability may undergo continual and profound changes but still continue to exist as a system; that is, their constituent parts persist together even though they take a very long time to return to their initial states. Systems with high stability but low resilience, on the other hand, may show little change when suffering some disturbances, but then collapse suddenly.

The Exxon Valdez *Alaskan oil spill was cleaned up within two years; what is not known is the long-term consequences of this and other sources of marine pollution.*
(Vanessa Vick/Photo Researchers Inc.)

These concepts have considerable relevance for our study of ecosystems. We often assume that if an ecosystem appears to be in equilibrium or is very stable that it is likely to persist unchanged. As pointed out, this is often not the case. A highly stable system, such as the Arctic terrestrial ecosystem, may in fact be very close to the threshold at which it could collapse. The most resilient ecosystems, are resilient only to a point—beyond which they collapse. We should bear this in mind when we feel that we are having no serious impact on our ecosystems simply because we see little evidence of immediate changes. For example, the seas around us may appear little changed despite the oil and other wastes dumped into them. Thus, they would seem to be quite stable. Yet each new addition of oil or wastes requires the organisms and microorganisms of the sea to respond in some way, and there are limits to their capacities to continue to do so. The resilience of marine ecosystems is limited, even if the threshold for change is obscured by the appearance of stability.

Anthropologist William Abruzzi (1993) applies ecological models developed from plant and ani-mal research to account for how members of an American religious movement, the Mormons, came to colonize the arid and seemingly inhospitable Little Colorado River Basin in northeastern Arizona. He makes good use of the concepts of stability and resilience as they apply to ecological systems. While his main focus is on environmental variables such as rainfall, floods, and other hazards to farm life, he shows that settlement is closely linked to the nature of the larger organization—the church. Settlers agreed to come to this then-remote region because of their beliefs, their faith in church leadership, and because they feared persecution; they were able to do so because the church hierarchy made resources available (in particular, what was needed to tide settlements over during droughts or other disasters).

The settlers were farmers who, in the late nineteenth century, attempted to settle three distinct ecological zones or habitats: the river basin itself, where dams could be built for irrigation; the middle slopes above the rivers, where runoff water was available; and the upper slopes. As it turned out, the middle slope settlements were the most sucessful over the long term—they had the resiliency to survive most threats to farming. The upper communities found rainfall too unpredictable and died out; the lower-level communities achieved a high level of production through damming rivers but this was often punctuated by disasters, as flooding destroyed dams, which then had to be rebuilt. The middle range of settlements were able to construct water storage facilities enabling them to survive both droughts and floods. None of the colonizing would have been possible without the strong, centralized authority of the church. Members paid tithes and contributed skills that enabled the central organization to assist communities in need.

The Nature of Ecological Systems

The structure of ecological systems—the flow of energy and nutrients—puts fundamental constraints on the way of life of any human population. Applying the ecosystem model to specific human populations, we can address two major questions. First, what is the population's place in its particular ecological system—that is, what are its relationships with the rest of the living world? Second, how are particular behaviors characteristic of this population related to its place in the ecosystem?

Humans hold a rather unusual position in their ecosystems. First, we occupy a remarkable diversity of such systems. This fact becomes strikingly evident when we look at the habitats and the niches that our species occupies. The **habitat** of a species is the area where it lives—its surroundings. Its **niche** is its "way of making a living," as defined by what it eats, what eats it, and how it reproduces and rears its young. Most animals are limited to a few habitats and a relatively narrow niche. By contrast, we occupy an exceptionally broad niche (think of the great variety of foods eaten by human beings and the many ways in which they are produced), and we live in an extremely wide range of habitats. Indeed, there are very few habitats, from deserts to Arctic ice sheets to tropical rain forests, where human beings have not found a way to thrive.

Second, once humans enter an ecosystem, they tend to become its dominant species. We strongly affect the life chances and reproductive rates of the other populations. While we are affected by other species, especially by those that threaten our well-being (such as malaria-bearing mosquitoes), our influence on them is far greater than theirs on us.

Our dominance is due to the sophistication of our tools. (We will see the effects of our toolmaking ability throughout Part II, where we will examine the various strategies human societies use to provide food for their members.) Some other species use tools, but no other species has developed them to the extent we have, and no other species depends on tools for its survival as we do. Our technological expertise has allowed us to transform a vast variety of materials—including some rather unlikely ones, such as fossil fuels—into sources of usable energy. It has also enabled us to be creative in our use of the resources we share with other animals. To use the energy stored in a tree, for example, other animals must drink its sap, seek shelter in it, or eat its leaves and branches. Humans not only eat parts of the tree, but cut it down and use the wood to build houses and furniture. We also use its energy in the form of fire to warm those houses and cook our food. Likewise, we can use the energy stored in animals' muscles, not only by eating them, as other animals do, but also by harnessing them to plows and by putting bits in their mouths and riding them. When a plant or animal is not suited to our needs, we can alter it through selective breeding to make it more useful to us. The use of tools has enabled us to create artificial environments, such as farms and cities, in which we maintain very high human population densities by greatly increasing the inflow and outflow of energy, materials, and information.

Human-dominated ecosystems are considerably less resilient than other ecosystems because they can be maintained only by constant expenditure of human energy and ingenuity. Cities depend on surrounding ecosystems for their food, water, and other necessities. In fact, inhabitants of cities tend to organize the countryside around them since they control the capital, markets, and transportation systems on which the rural farming sector depends. Cities also produce large quantities of waste products that the surrounding ecosystem must absorb.

When urban ecosystems become large or numerous, the balance between the cities and the food-producing areas that sustain them may break down. In any event, these ecological arrangements depend on massive and costly inputs of energy. With our recent dependence on fossil fuel for energy, the stability of today's urban systems may be severely limited—not only by future fuel shortages, but by problems of waste disposal.

Despite all of our technological advances, we are still as deeply enmeshed in our ecosystems as any other group of organisms. Indeed, anthropologists interpret human customs in part as accommodations to the physical environment. What distinguishes humans from other species in their relation to environmental problems is the rapidity with which we respond through learning. Different human societies may develop wholly different ways of life as they adjust to their environment. Moreover, they can change rapidly as circumstances require. Thus human adaptation has a unique flexibility. We can most usefully study the nature of this adaptive process by combining ideas from evolution and ecology.

Adaptation. While evolutionary research is diachronic (that is, through time) by definition, ecological research tends to be synchronic (that is, primarily concerned with the present). However, both focus on ultimately the same phenomenon: adaptation. **Adaptation** is the process whereby organisms or populations of organisms that live together in a defined environment make biological and/or behavioral adjustments that increase their chances for survival and reproduction. An evolutionary study may trace adaptation backward through time in an attempt to understand major causes of change within a given species as an outcome of natural selection and other evolutionary forces. Ecological studies, in contrast, tend to focus on the present and to look at the outcome of the adaptational process by analyzing the totality of relationships among organisms in a given environment. Evolutionary-ecological research unites these two approaches by studying living organisms within the context of their total environment to discover how their evolved characteristics and strategies for survival contribute to their success within that environment; in other words, how they have adapted.

Still, culture, or aspects of it, has an identity quite distinct from behaviors that are directly acted upon by such evolutionary forces as natural selection. In fact traits adopted and favored by groups or cultures may, for a while at least, work at cross-purposes with individual strategies for adaptive success. People enthusiastically embrace beliefs and adopt behavioral traits that apparently have little immediate relevance, either to their own well-being or to that of a larger collectivity such as a group or a community.

Sometimes extreme examples are more useful illustrations than are commonplace ones where costs and benefits are obvious. Consider societies that have stressful initiation rites, including in some instances severe genital mutilation. It is hard to understand just how such practices, with the attendant risk of death or injury, can benefit the individual (or his or her parents), except in the important context of social relations. Traditional practices of female circumcision and female infibulation (sewing the vagina closed), found in the Sudan and East Africa, and male subincision (cutting open the penis and the urethra), found among the Australian aborigines, hardly promote the well-being or reproductive success of the individuals who suffer through them, except as they contribute to the initiates' social acceptability. They also may benefit other members of the society at the initiates' expense. For example, female circumcision aids male control of female sexuality and reproduction, and male subincision enhances older men's control of younger men (Irons, 1995). Such practices appear to be related to the nature of the society itself—the way it forms its cultural identity, defines concepts of sexuality and social maturity, and effects social control.

Many of our beliefs and ideas about the world are passed on through social learning even when they do not appear to have immediate utility for the individual. Many anthropologists argue for a "dual inheritance" perspective, from which cultural transmission and change are seen as working simultaneously with a parallel process of natural selection (Boyd & Richerson, 1985; Durham, 1991). This means that we should not expect humans to operate within the narrow constraint of immediately perceived costs and benefits, but rather to respond to and solve problems using a wide range of cultural tools. Further, culturally transmitted ways of doing things need to be shown to be adaptive—not simply assumed to be so. Any realistic approach to understanding human cultural behavior has to allow for a great deal of indeterminancy, even though ultimately all behavior has implications for the success of the individuals involved.

We have seen that evolution is a process of cumulative change, which is itself the outcome, in large measure, of the responses of organisms to their ever-changing environments (adaptation). Adaptation can be an elusive concept because it involves processes that seem to operate on several different levels at once. Furthermore, adaptation can only be observed over long periods.

However, we do know that the long-term processes of adaptation are dependent on the ability of organisms to appropriately resolve problems they face on a daily basis. Thus, the concept also encompasses all of the responses and behaviors of the organism that affect its immediate survival, even though these may have no immediate implications for natural selection. Like many other species, humans adapt by learning new ways of doing things. The swelling human population is testimony to just how rapidly we can adjust our systems of food production and other technologies. Our ability to learn rapidly and to communicate learning is, in large measure, due to our ability to use language. As we saw in Chapter 2, our capacity for language is undoubtedly closely related to the manner in which the hominid cerebral cortex evolved very early in our family history. Once our brain developed beyond a certain threshold, making symbolic communication possible, our evolutionary course was altered. As Chomsky (in Brown, 1991) put it, we learn language as easily as we grow pubic hair! This ability has enabled us to develop technologies that allow us to occupy most areas of the earth—something no other large animal can do. In the long run, of course, these technologies may also prove to be maladaptive; we may be a species with a relatively short history.

Adaptation involves changes of all sorts that continually affect the relationship of the organism to its environment. It results in changes that can never be ideal, as the environment is itself constantly changing. No adaptation or response is a perfect or final solution; each carries with it certain costs and hazards. Adaptation is always opportunistic because organisms, ourselves included, take advantage whatever resources are available to them at a particular time (including available genetic and cultural materials), often with little regard for future consequences.

Rituals such as circumcision must be understood in terms of the particular cultural environment of which they are a part. For the young Masai male, the year of circumcision, the most important in his life, marks his emergence into manhood.
(George Rodger/Magnum)

The opportunistic nature of adaptation is amply illustrated by the multitude of uses to which the front and rear limbs have been put in related sea and land mammals—for example, cows and whales, which share a common ancestor. For a culturally based example, industrialized societies began to use oil as a fuel at the beginning of the twentieth century in an initially very limited way. This adaptation soon solved the problem of furnishing an effective, cheap fuel to power modern machinery. Its use was opportunistic in the sense that the oil was there to be tapped and our technology happened to have developed to the point that allowed us to make use of it. In adapting to oil fuel, we made numerous commitments that have altered the structure of our society: We rely on food produced by heavy equipment; we grow crops dependent on fertilizers and pesticides derived from the petrochemical industry; we use rapid transport, cheap electricity, and productive systems too numerous to mention. All these activities are fueled by oil. In recent years, the environment has been changing in unexpected ways. We are faced with declining reserves of oil, with the toxic consequences of a highly developed industrial society, and perhaps with long-term changes in the atmosphere—all consequences of heavy oil use. It is also certain that whatever other energy sources we turn to next will be imperfect solutions and will generate a host of new and unforeseen difficulties as well. Adaptation is at once the solution to a particular problem and the source of unanticipated changes and new problems.

Decisions, Variation, and the Environment. Variation, whether biological or behavioral, is the key to the process of adaptation. One of the main contributions of recent studies of animal behavior is the recognition that among animals of all sorts, systems of mating, male-female differences, feeding habits, food sharing, social interaction, and the like can be understood as the outcome of behaviors that start as individual strategies. Groups are never homogeneous; all contain individuals who respond somewhat differently to the problems at hand. Seen in this light, patterns of behavior become increasingly interesting. As human culture is elaborated, new solutions that seem to work can be rapidly added to the repertoire of knowledge that is passed on. The acceptance of innovations depends to a great extent on the fact that customary ways of acting are always subject to variation. Individuals constantly make decisions in every society, and decision making gives rise to behavioral variation. There are enough conflicting versions of proper behavior in every society to create some ambiguity, thus allowing for the introduction and acceptance of innovation.

To understand the nature of human decision making or problem solving, we have to consider the environment in which it takes place. We are all too prone to treat the environment as a fixed landscape or static fact, and so fail to consider the nature of variation in all environments. Environ-

ments are complex and forever changing. The environment of any individual or population consists of all external factors that effect it in any way—not only the obvious features of the habitat (the place where the population lives), but the presence of organisms that transmit disease, competitors, shelter, and climate. It also includes the cultural setting in which the individual must operate. In a society in which male initiation rites are important, for example, this social fact is part of the individual's environment. The environment also includes the demographic structure of the population; often, the most important feature of an individual's environment is the presence of other members of the same population among whom an individual will find both allies and competitors.

Finally, environments are dynamic. One ecologist, Lawrence S. Slobodkin (1968), has argued that four patterns of change underlie the dynamics of all environments: the degree of novelty (how new), frequency (how often), magnitude (how much), and duration (how long) of environmental events of all sorts. The organism with the best chance of success is not necessarily the one most perfectly adapted to its environment at any particular point, but rather the one that maintains its ability to respond to the environment in flexible ways. Generally speaking, the most successful response is the one that involves the minimum sacrifice of flexibility. In other words, choices among alternatives should be made to minimize risk, not simply to attempt to make large gains. This seems to be the case with humans, in that people are generally conservative in their behavior and hesitant to change ways of doing things that appear to work.

In general, behavior is fairly predictable and conventional; people tend to arrive at similar decisions under similar circumstances. Were it not so, group life would be impossible. People regularly make major decisions regarding such basic issues of subsistence as whether to plant one crop or another or whether to migrate to new pastures or not; they also make day-to-day decisions such as with whom to socialize or to whom to send a greeting card. The structure of human societies provides the context for and information concerning choices among alternatives. At the same time, human society is itself the outcome of this process. As Frederik Barth (1981) has put it:

Social life [is] generated by actors who go about their activity by pursuing their interests fitfully, often thoughtlessly, and generally conventionally. Yet they are concerned about the outcomes of their efforts in so far as these affect themselves. In this concern their judgments are based on values which serve to organize choice and action by providing standards to compare different alternatives and outcomes, both prospectively and retrospectively. When doing so, people tend to maximize the amounts of value they obtain by pursuing benefits and avoiding losses and drawbacks inasmuch as they see a way to do so. [p. 102]

Human social organization is a product of the decisions made by individuals; most of these decisions concern the trivia of everyday life, but cumulatively they direct the course of adaptation. Thus decisions, adaptation, and evolution go hand in hand.

Procurement Systems: Decisions, Adaptation, and Food

Of all the problems people face, securing adequate food is the most fundamental. When ecologists note that "you are what you eat," they mean that the source and variety of foods used by any population, human or otherwise, is critical to its maintenance. While a vast array of adaptive patterns can be found throughout the world, if we concentrate on the central issue of the way a population procures and distributes its food, we will note common strategies.

The behavioral strategies that a particular group uses or has available to secure foodstuffs can be termed its **food-procurement system**. Within these general patterns, the available strategies are so numerous that no two systems are exactly alike. In fact, it is rare to find two individuals within a society practicing precisely the same strategy. However, there are some important generalizations that can be made about food-procurement behavior that will help to explain the nature of adaptation in this context. Five major patterns of food procurement have been identified:

1. **Foraging** (or hunting and gathering): collecting wild vegetable foods, hunting game, and fishing.

2. **Subsistence agriculture:** a simple form of agriculture (sometimes called horticulture or extensive agriculture) based on working small plots of land with perhaps some use of draft an-

Food procurement is fundamental to all populations. Humans today rely on intensive agriculture for most food and today's populations could not be sustained without the highly industrialized techniques utilized by this American farmer. The agricultural decisions of individuals have implications for the availability and prices of food products in distant countries.

(John Running/Stock, Boston Inc.)

imals, plows, or irrigation. In contrast to foragers, subsistence farmers produce food by managing domesticated plants and animals.

3. **Pastoralism:** an economy based on herding. Pastoralists maintain herds of animals and use their products and by-products (milk, curds, whey, butterfat, meat, blood, hides, bones), both to maintain themselves directly and to exchange with other populations.

4. **Intensive agriculture:** a form of agriculture that involves the use of draft animals or tractors, plows, and often some form of irrigation. Intensive agriculture produces far greater yields per acre of land with less human labor than can be obtained by subsistence agriculture. Intensive agriculture is often highly specialized, with farmers relying on one or two main crops.

5. **Industrial agriculture:** food production and manufacturing through the use of machines powered largely by fossil fuels, including modern commercial fishing and marine farming.

The Evolution of Procurement Patterns

As we have stressed, the crucial selective pressures giving rise to the divergence of the human line from that of the apes probably entailed brain-related behavioral changes—the gradual development of a greater commitment to group life and cooperation and language use. The Australopiths, from which the earliest humans evolved, probably ate meat only occasionally; their main food resources were the plants of the East African savanna, which they ate as soon as they found them. From what we can guess, one or a few populations of Australopiths, while still relying heavily on vegetable foods, began to supplement their diet with a regular intake of meat that they procured by hunting and scavenging. Furthermore, they probably began sharing their food more extensively; they brought both the vegetables and meat they found to be divided among the whole group. In time, this change in food procurement, along with associated behavioral changes, produced the unique anatomical features on which the human lineage was founded. One of the behavioral changes was an increased emphasis on learning, as exemplified by the development of tool use. The anatomical changes included increased brain size and decreased tooth size.

Foraging, or hunting and gathering, has itself changed greatly since the time of the Australopiths, some 4 million years ago. However, in one form or another it continued to be the universal human food-procurement strategy until relatively recently. Over the centuries, it was gradually perfected. People learned to make containers and digging sticks to help them in gathering, and they developed improved weapons—spears, spear throwers, and eventually the bow and arrow—to increase their efficiency as hunters. By 40,000 years ago, different local populations had also learned to be highly specialized in terms of procuring specific kinds of game and plant resources in very different habitats. As early as 20,000 years ago, European hunters and gatherers (and probably others as well) were using textiles and basketry, indicating a high degree of technological sophistication (Soffer, Vandiver, & Klima, 1995).

From specialized hunting and gathering, with skills adapted to the exploitation of particular plant and animal species, it is a relatively short step to systematic planting and herding. Although we do not know precisely how or why, we do know that about 12,000 years ago societies in various parts of the world began experimenting with the domestication of plants and animals. However, another 3,000 or 4,000 years passed between the first appearance of agriculture and its widespread use. Not until 5,000 years ago, in the Near East, are we able to find signs of irrigation and the beginnings of intensive agriculture. (In this period, too, specialized pastoralism probably became important.) Over the next 2,000 years, agricultural practices became more efficient and productive in some areas. Large-scale irrigation works were constructed in Mesopotamia and Egypt, making it possible to support larger and larger populations in limited areas.

Finally, as recently as the nineteenth century, certain Western societies developed a new pattern, industrial agriculture, whereby machines began to do some of the work of farming, animal husbandry, manufacturing, and other subsistence activities. As a result of the Industrial Revolution, the family farm was first transformed into a highly mechanized and capital-intensive operation and more recently is being replaced by agribusiness.

Because procurement systems are so varied, most societies do not fall tidily into one or another food-procurement pattern. When we refer to foragers, subsistence farmers, pastoralists, agriculturists, and industrial societies, we are merely pointing out a cultural emphasis on the use of particular food-procurement methods. The specific procurement systems that people use involve varying strategies and varied degrees of reliance on the same strategy. People typically combine several methods. In most societies, for example, subsistence farming is supplemented by hunting and collecting wild foods. In others, horticulture (subsistence farming without the use of plows) is practiced alongside plow farming: the former in steep and rocky areas, the latter in flatter areas where plowing is possible. Pastoralism is generally found in conjunction with other procurement strategies—in some cases with hunting and gathering, in other cases with small-scale horticulture. And, needless to say, many agriculturists raise animals not only for transportation but also as sources of protein, wool, and hides.

Adapting to Environmental Problems

The assumption that a given food-procurement system is an adaptation to a certain type of environment still does not explain very much. It is certainly true that the characteristics of environmental zones of different sorts—grasslands, deserts, tropical forests, temperate forests, the Arctic, and the subarctic—place limits on the kind of life that can be sustained in them. One does not farm in the Arctic, nor does one herd animals in a tropical rain forest. Yet these broad environmental factors account for only a small portion of the variation we see in procurement systems. They do not tell us why inhabitants of similar regions—indeed, of the same region—often practice widely different procurement strategies, or why inhabitants of different regions sometimes practice remarkably similar strategies.

In order to understand how and why specific procurement systems develop, we must consider them as responses less to broad environmental characteristics than to specific environmental problems in local areas. Some common problems faced by local populations are fluctuations over time and space in quantity, quality, and availability of resources, and the activities of other human groups in competition for those same resources.

Adapting to Available Resources. Every local environment or habitat has a limited potential for supporting any of the forms of life within it. This demographic potential is called the environment's **carrying capacity**—the point at or below which a population tends to stabilize. The most obvious limiting factors may be the availability of food or water. Others include disease, temperature, and even the regularity and predictability of critical resources. It really doesn't matter so much that a food source is available during the year, for example, if the people who rely on it cannot predict with accuracy when it is going to be available. The best way to determine carrying capacity is to observe the demographic characteristics of the population: its rates of birth, death, and migration. Anthropologists may also estimate an environment's potential carrying capacity for a particular population by computing the minimum amount of water and of vegetable and animal matter available on a regular basis for human consumption. A long-term project in East Africa is illustrative of some of the issues involved in such research, as we see in the Using Anthropology box, *The South Turkana Ecosystem Project*, pages 76–77.

It is estimated that the ecosystem of the Kalahari Desert, for example, can indefinitely support about 40 humans per 100 square miles, if they live as the indigenous inhabitants did and if the technology and requirements of the population remain constant (Lee, 1968). Here a major limiting factor (a key factor) is water. Water holes in the Kalahari may be as much as 100 miles apart, and the average water hole can support only about 30 people in years when the rainfall is normal (fewer during periods of drought). Thus Kalahari residents, of necessity, live in small groups broadly scattered over a large territory. Regions in which food is scarce or the supply fluctuates greatly show a similar population pattern. In areas where food and water supplies are more abundant, larger populations may be sustained in permanent sedentary communities.

The carrying capacity of an area is affected not only by the total amount of food available but also by the availability and distribution of essential

Using Anthropology

The South Turkana Ecosystem Project

THE SOUTH TURKANA ECOSYSTEM Project is a collaborative effort of scientists from universities in Kenya and the United States, with research interests as diverse as human genetics, demography, rangeland management, plant ecology, nutrition, and ethnology. About half of the scientists are anthropologists, many affiliated with the State University of New York at Binghamton.

The lands of the Turkana are subject to extremes of temperature; daytime highs average 87 to 100°F (35–37°C) and highly erratic rainfall that varies from 5.8 to 19.5 inches (150–500 millimeters) a year. This low and variable rainfall, combined with intense solar radiation flux, results in a short growing season; farming is limited. Most of the Turkana people of northwestern Kenya, a population of 150,000 to 200,000 distributed among a series of tribes and subtribes, exploit this region by "nomadic movements of their polygynous family settlements and the five species of livestock that they herd—camels, zebu cattle, goats, sheep, and donkeys. Home settlements will move, on the average, one or more times each month" (Little, 1988, p. 697). The Turkana live almost entirely on the products of their animals, and starvation is a constant specter.

As part of the project, one study conducted by rangeland ecology specialists and ethnographers (Coughenour et al., 1985) addresses a key issue in the study of pastoral adaptations to extremely arid lands: how do these people maintain enough animals to sustain themselves without degrading their habitat? Using detailed measurements of energy expenditures, the researchers were able to map plant-animal-human food pathways. They not only studied animal requirements, but also measured ground cover and the diets of a sample of nomadic households. They found that the Turkana derived 92 percent of their food energy from animal products (meat, milk, and blood) and from maize meal, sugar, and other foods that they acquired by bartering animal products. Though their animals produce less milk and meat than American and Australian breeds, they are more resistant to disease, heat, and drought-related stress.

The Turkana can maintain an adequate diet and keep a critical reserve to face unexpected losses without degrading their rangelands because of two factors: (1) the number of animals they can keep is limited by the availability of water holes, and (2) they manage a mix of five species, each with its unique productive qualities. When milk from the cow fails, they turn to their camels; when meat is needed, they can kill small animals such as sheep or goats.

---

dietary items such as protein, vitamins, and minerals. In other words, the nutritional quality of resources is as critical as their quantity. To avoid chronic malnutrition, humans must somehow adjust to the variations in nutritional value among available foods. While some physiological adjustment is evident among human populations in areas of diverse resources, generally people solve the problem through restrictive dietary practices and in the way they prepare their foods.

A final factor affecting carrying capacity is the human ability to recognize resources. Even the determination of what plants and animals are edible varies considerably among cultures. Goosefoot and lambsquarter, two plants that we consider weeds, were important sources of both seeds and greens among many Native American groups. These and many other plants and animals that we do not now consider edible are staples (and even delicacies) in other societies. Many resources identified as usable in one culture are ignored in others.

As these examples illustrate, an environment's human carrying capacity is not a simple product of local resources. We cannot simply say that a given environment can support x number of human beings per square mile. The number varies with the

Cattle that do not produce milk provide blood, which is nutritionally rich. The livestock is often scrawny by European standards, but if the rains bring a bumper crop of vegetation, the animals put on weight rapidly and their fertility rate goes up.

Another study sheds light on the role of blood as human food in such a system (Dyson-Hudson & Dyson-Hudson, 1982). Turkana cows yield only one-tenth the milk of well-fed American Holsteins, but their blood is a more efficient source of energy than meat (which involves much waste and of course requires the slaughter of the animals). Twenty-one pints (9.9 liters) of blood are taken from each thousand-pound steer every four to six months; lesser amounts are taken from breeding stock and smaller animals. The use of blood in the Turkana's diet greatly enhances the herd's productivity, particularly because it can supplement the diet during the season when cows are not producing milk.

Among the people themselves, Paul Leslie and Peggy Fry (1989) found extreme seasonality in births, with more than half falling between March and June. The rate of conception, then, is highest during the early dry season (July through September), when the food supply has been at its peak for some time. The Turkana claim not to time their children's birth (as some African populations do) and attribute the seasonality of births to the separation of spouses during the pastoral cycle, high temperatures that inhibit coitus, and other factors. Whatever the reason, the human population closely tracks the environmental fluctuations.

In yet another study, three researchers (Little, Galvin, & Leslie, 1988) examined the Turkana's health in an effort to determine the effects of a diet as high in fat as theirs, based as it is on milk, blood, and meat. Blood pressure is lower among all age groups than in a comparable American population, cardiovascular disease is rare, and general nutritional status is good, though the eye infections common to the area are prevalent. One of the researchers, Kathleen Galvin (1988), used project data to explore variation in the Turkana's nutritional status from season to season and according to food availability. She found that the nutritional status of a population at risk may be evaluated by means of dietary, ecological, and anthropometric measures of body fat and robustness: mid-arm circumference and skin-fold thickness. She cautions against reliance on any one measure, particularly when little body fat is normally present in the population. Her findings, like those of the other participants in the project, have a significance far beyond the Turkana ecosystem.

These plus other completed and ongoing studies of the Turkana Ecosystem Project not only contribute to a much fuller understanding of the Turkana people and their ecosystems, but they also have a wider significance for pastoral, ecological, and medical research.

nature of the procurement system practiced in the area. Also, as we will see in later chapters, carrying capacity depends on the organization of the society and on the exchange of food and tools among populations.

Adapting to Fluctuations in Resources. Populations must adjust not only to the quantity and quality of available resources but also to fluctuations in their availability. Over a five-year period, say, an area may produce an average of 100 kilograms (about 221 pounds) of corn per year, but if production drops to 50 kilograms (about 110 pounds) one year, the people must adjust or risk starvation.

The Shoshone Indians who lived in North America's Great Basin before the coming of the Europeans provide a good historical example of adjustment to fluctuations in resources. Because of extreme variation in rainfall in this region, the Shoshone were never able to predict with any certainty where or how much plant and animal food would be available from one year to the next. A spot that was highly productive one year might offer little food the next. The Shoshone adapted to these environmental uncertainties by relying on a

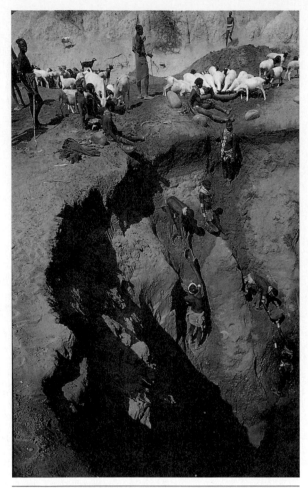

A low water supply may limit the number of people an environment can support. In Ethiopia's arid Omo Valley, residents search for water by digging under a dry riverbed.

(George Gerster/Comstock)

would plan to arrive together in time for the harvest and would separate again after the resources had been collected (Steward, 1953).

People who live by cultivating crops or raising animals generally have a more stable food supply than those who depend on wild resources alone. But these groups are also affected by seasonal and yearly fluctuations and must adjust to them. Since population is more concentrated in these groups than among hunter-gatherers, the effects of food shortages may be even more devastating to them. The Ariaal of western Kenya depend on agricultural produce for the bulk of their caloric intake. However, droughts and fluctuations in rainfall can result in crop failure, in which case the Ariaal can fall back on their cattle and goat herds for their food supply. Thus their cattle may be seen as a means of storing energy as much as a means of producing it.

Another example involves an ancient American people that farmed in an extremely unpredictable climate. The Anasazi Pueblo Indians relied on a diverse set of agricultural strategies in order to minimize risk of crop failure in an area of high aridity. One strategy used in the fourteenth and fifteenth centuries was to engage in what is called "pebble mulching"; that is, deliberately adding small pebbles to the soil of their gardens. This served to conserve soil moisture, reduce erosion and to extend the growing season (Lightfoot, 1993, p. 116).

Consumers in our society rarely experience sudden short-term fluctuations in resources, since we depend on the products of a huge area serviced by an efficient transportation system. A wide variety of fruits, vegetables, grains, meats, and dairy products are available to us throughout the year. This steadiness of supply is due to our technology; producers have means of storing and transporting food in such a way as to cover shortages, and our technology enables us to minimize some fluctuations in resources (although often at considerable cost).

When a rancher's pasturelands go dry, the rancher feeds his cattle by hauling forage and water to them with tractors and trucks rather than by moving the animals. Similarly, a farmer can bring water to his crops through irrigation, control insects with chemical sprays, and spread fertilizer to add nutrients to the soil of a depleted

wide variety of resources and pursuing a highly mobile way of life, changing their location and residence patterns according to the kind and quantity of resources available. During most of the year a Shoshone family traveled alone or with one or two related families, gathering roots and seeds and hunting small animals. Periodically, however, when rabbits or antelope became unusually plentiful, several families might band together temporarily for a collective hunt. And when isolated families heard reports that a resource such as pine nuts seemed promising in a particular locality, they

field. The farmer can even grow crops in the dead of winter by constructing hothouses. But these techniques have costs that are passed on to the consumer. Modern agriculture depends on machine technology and is thus subsidized by the large-scale use of fossil fuel in the form of gasoline and diesel oil.

Despite the apparent advantages of modern agricultural techniques, we should not make the mistake of assuming that industrialized societies are somehow better at minimizing uncertainty in food production than technologically simpler ones. Perhaps the greatest paradox of recent human adaptation is that responses aimed at stabilizing and increasing food production are in many cases having the opposite effect. That is, they are creating a new and more serious threat to the stability of the procurement system. In order to diminish the threat of drought or irregular rainfall, for example, a community may increase its dependence on irrigation agriculture, only to discover that the increased irrigation has elevated the salt content of the soil to the point where it can no longer support crops.

Thus, while people in technologically advanced societies may accomplish impressive feats of environmental engineering, they must still remain sensitive to the environment in which they live. Ultimately the success of a group's adaptation to its resources depends not only on its ingenuity in manipulating its ecological system, but also on its care in maintaining that system. As a consequence, the internal distribution of resources among people through social interaction is as important as are the resources on which they depend.

Adapting to Other Groups

The type and distribution of basic resources are only one aspect of an environment. Human populations make up another and no less basic aspect. Every society must adjust to the presence and activities of neighboring peoples, just as surely as it must adjust to variations in local resources. The study of this adaptive process is important enough to constitute an entire approach in human ecology. This approach, called *political ecology*, is the study of how people struggle to gain access to, maintain control of, and utilize natural resources in the face of competing interests.

Humans engage in many exchanges with people outside their own group. They also compete with one another for access to resources. If we step back from the study of societies as individual entities, we see a vast, ever-changing social mosaic, with each local population occupying its place in the larger picture. Of all large animals, we have the widest range of local patterns of behavior, each an adaptation to the challenge of making a living in local environmental circumstances.

When different groups occupy different niches in the same habitat, or when they occupy different habitats in the same region, they may come to rely heavily on one another for trade, each group benefiting from the products of the other groups' economies. In the Ituri Forest of northeastern Zaire, two populations have a long history of trade: the Efe foragers, who supplied game and forest products such as honey; and the Lese farmers, who traded their crops, and, more recently, manufactured goods, for the products supplied by the foragers (Wilkie & Curran, 1993, pp. 389–417).

It is not inevitable that groups occupying the same environment will learn to coexist peacefully through niche specialization. In Zaire, the Efe have become dependent upon the Lese, and hence in a subservient position (Wilkie & Curran, 1993, pp. 389–417). In other places, one group may be driven out or absorbed by a larger or technologically more advanced group. This is what happened when European settlers moved into regions occupied by Native American groups, and what is presently underway in the Amazon River Basin. In Brazil, landless farmers are pouring into the Amazon, establishing small farm sites and generally threatening the position of indigenous peoples.

The niche occupied by a human group that has developed a distinctive adaptive pattern is very different from the niches of other animals in the same environment. An animal species' commitment to its niche is much more binding than a human group's commitment to an adaptive strategy. Humans can decide to change their diet and food-procurement strategies in a very short time, and will do so if they have to. Thus if pastoralists' grazing lands dry up, they may quite suddenly begin to compete with neighboring agriculturists for arable lands, and what was once peaceful coexistence will become open hostility. Adaptation to other human

State of the Peoples

The Political Ecology of Deforestation: The Brazilian Amazon

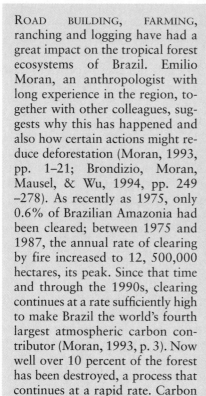

ROAD BUILDING, FARMING, ranching and logging have had a great impact on the tropical forest ecosystems of Brazil. Emilio Moran, an anthropologist with long experience in the region, together with other colleagues, suggests why this has happened and also how certain actions might reduce deforestation (Moran, 1993, pp. 1–21; Brondizio, Moran, Mausel, & Wu, 1994, pp. 249 –278). As recently as 1975, only 0.6% of Brazilian Amazonia had been cleared; between 1975 and 1987, the annual rate of clearing by fire increased to 12, 500,000 hectares, its peak. Since that time and through the 1990s, clearing continues at a rate sufficiently high to make Brazil the world's fourth largest atmospheric carbon contributor (Moran, 1993, p. 3). Now well over 10 percent of the forest has been destroyed, a process that continues at a rapid rate. Carbon is being released through forest fires at a far faster rate than it is being fixed or captured by grow-

ing vegetation. Thus, the vast Amazonian Basin is in a state of human-induced disequilibrium. Tropical rainforests cover only 11 percent of the earth's surface but contain 41 percent of the earth's terrestrial biomass and over 50 percent of its species (in Moran, 1993). It is not clear at what point the process of deforestation will exhaust the resilience of the Amazonian forests' ability to regenerate, but there is agreement that this may be relatively soon (ibid).

The causes of deforestation in Brazil are essentially political. It began with the policy of road-building in 1958 and expanded greatly with the ongoing extension of the TransAmazon Highway. Increases in cattle ranching, farming, mining (which uses charcoal as fuel), and, to a lesser extent, logging have also contributed to the problem. The political nature of the situation lies with Brazilian government policy, with the influence of powerful military figures, and with existing tax laws and reg-

ulations. The government, beginning with the building of the new capital, Brasilia, and more recently with highway contruction, has taken the position that the vast Amazon Basin has to be both developed and integrated with the rest of the nation. Underlying this policy is the belief that more land must be brought under cultivation: over 70 percent of Brazilian farmers are landless and 84 percent of farmland is owned by 4.5 percent of the population (in Moran, 1993, p. 17).

Unfortunately, the Amazon does not lend itself to the sort of agriculture most newly arrived farmers are familiar with. The military views the Amazon in terms of national sovereignty, and thus regard any criticism of how it is being transformed as a threat to Brazil's integrity; tax and land use laws give a substantial incentive to those who "improve" land—by cutting the forest down, for example. Thus a landless farmer might settle along a highway, get inex-

groups, then, is a shifting, dynamic process, as is adaptation to any environmental condition.

Almost everywhere there is an additional element involved in the equation of intergroup adaptation: the power employed by the state to regulate how local populations use resources. For most local populations, be they foragers, peasant farmers, or pastoralists, access to resources (and even their relations with neighboring groups) is controlled by the distant but powerful force of state-level politi-

cal institutions. Thus, whether or not indigenous peoples of the Amazon will retain their lands is very much dependent on the support they receive for their cause by the Brazilian Federal Government, as we see in the State of the Peoples box, *The Political Ecology of Deforestation: The Brazilian Amazon*, above. Similarly, in Iran, how, when, and by what route the nomadic Qashqai tribe might move between summer and winter pastures, as well as the tribe's relations with sedentary populations depend

pensive title to a number of hectares, burn it clear, and, after making a minimal effort to plant crops, sell the "improved" land at a substantial profit. Speculators and ranchers do likewise.

Since the root causes for Amazonian deforestation are political, it makes little sense to simply recommend that this huge region be placed off-limits to road building, mining, and farming. What Moran and his colleagues suggest is politically feasible: environmentalists should not view the vast region as having a uniform set of problems—rather each area within the Amazon has to be treated separately. In some areas, it is ranching which should be more closely regulated, with, they suggest, tax benefits for leaving forest uncleared; in other areas, taxes should be collected on capital gains from selling improved land, thus limiting land speculation. More importantly, methods of farming that maintain the Amazon forest cover already exist, are as economically rewarding as mechanized methods, and involve skills that can be easily transfered (Brondizio et al., 1994). A major means of "farming" the wetter portions

Kayapo boys prepare for a ceremony. Ceremonial life and the world of symbols are intrinsic to every society and are important means by which individuals assume their cultural identity.

(The Hutchison Library)

of the forest is through palm oil extraction and diversified garden-farming or horticulture (see Chapter 7)—which does not involve massive clearing, and, when pursued by nonmechanized methods, does not have a major impact on the forest ecosystem.

Further, Moran and his colleagues demonstrate how a space-age technology allows anthropologists and other earth scientists to follow environmental events over a broad area: satellite-based remote sensing imagery has allowed them to closely compare the effects of ranching, farming, and diversified garden-agriculture on vegetation and forest regrowth.

on political relations with the representatives of the government (see Beck, 1991). This will be elaborated upon in subsequent chapters.

Adaptation and Cultural Evolution

Observations from many sources indicate some recurring long-term processes of systemic change that cumulatively have transformed human society and that continue to do so. These patterns of general evolution—the patterns of behavior or organization that can be observed in a group or population—are the products of short-term adaptations, and none is universal. One way to see the long-term consequences of specific adaptations is to go back in time: archaeological data offer us an insight into the processes of long-term change. They also caution us not to predict long-term success or failure on the basis of short-term perspectives.

A Case Study in Long-Term Change: The Vikings in the North Atlantic

The history of Viking exploration and settlements in the North Atlantic provides one example of an accumulation of short-term adaptations that result in an ultimately dramatic long-term change. Thomas McGovern and other archaeologists who specialize in Norse or Viking history have attempted to unravel the checkered history of Norse settlement in the North Atlantic (McGovern, 1980; McGovern et al., 1988). Numerous islands were settled between A.D. 790 and 1000, including the Shetland and Faroe islands, Iceland, and Greenland, and very likely the east coast of North America as well. The colonies had rather different histories, and the westernmost ones, Iceland and Greenland, mark the outer limits of significant Viking settlement. The once thriving settlements of Greenland (which failed by 1500) and Iceland (which suffered a significant decline in population after several centuries) offer some insights into the processes of long-term adaptation.

The Viking settlers brought with them an established food-procurement system: they raised cattle and sheep, fished, and, where possible, cultivated wheat or barley. They also came equipped with a social and political hierarchy that separated the free from the slaves and encompassed quite rigid distinctions among servants, tenants, landowners, and chiefs. By law, every free landowning farmer or household had to be associated with a particular chief. Each tenant—a family that was contracted to run a farmstead for a specified period—was bound to a landowning householder. The entire colony was run by an elite comprising chiefs and, in the later periods, the Norwegian king's appointees and church dignitaries. The early colonial period was quite successful; most of the settlers were free, and they established independent holdings on which to raise sheep and cattle wherever they found sufficient pasturage. The settlers were quick to incorporate the rich marine life into their diets. The population of Greenland's settlements grew, as did that of Iceland; the two together reached some 60,000.

With success, however, came the gradual transformation of the Viking colonies. In the beginning, each settlement was relatively autonomous and the predominant form of homestead was that of a free family working pastures and lands that they owned and on which they paid taxes. Though slaves were brought over initially, no more were imported and the labor that nonfamily members performed was provided by servants and tenants. As time passed and settlements grew, churches were erected and homesteads spread to the outer limits of pasturage in this severe environment.

Gradual social and political changes had profound effects. First, the number of tenant farmers increased in relation to freeholders as many freeholders had to sell their lands to pay the taxes levied. Thus land became much more subject to indirect management. The people who worked the land were under pressure to produce as much hay or to raise as many sheep and cattle as possible, with little thought to possible long-term effects. Evidence of overgrazing and soil erosion is abundant. Second, what were formerly petty chiefs became powerful leaders, controlling considerable land and often warring with rivals. By the mid-thirteenth century a few families had come to control most of the land. In short, land use became intensified. Socially, the society was more stratified; specialized priests, warriors, smiths, and urban craftworkers proliferated; and decision making became more centralized as power accrued to the chiefs and bishops.

In 1262–1264, Greenland and Iceland came under the direct control of the Norwegian state and most land was now controlled by church and crown. The church sent bishops to rule and encouraged the building of monumental structures quite disproportionate to the size and resources of the colonies. Taxes and tithes were collected, administered, and forwarded to the state by foreign-born appointees. The colonies were closely integrated into a growing North European economic system. But economic integration did not bring prosperity to most of the people of the colonies, and ultimately it had dire consequences. Environmental degradation through soil erosion and depletion of marine resources caused hardship. Much of the pasturage became barren rock, and by 1500 the colony on Greenland had become extinct, unable to cope with the demands of its top-heavy administration, a depleted resource base, and the harsh climate. Greenland was once more left to its North Ameri-

In the ninth century B.P., *Viking political and economic influence stretched from southern Russia through Scandanavia and the British Isles to North America. Ultimately Viking or Norse settlements from Greenland westward failed completely, and those in Iceland were greatly diminished.*

(Werner Forman Archives)

can inhabitants—the Eskimos, whose time-proven adaptations the Vikings chose to ignore or dismiss. By 1600, 94 percent of Iceland's people were reduced to tenant farming and the population declined sharply. This colony survived, but prosperity returned only in this century when Iceland reorganized itself as an independent and locally self-sufficient society (see also McGovern et al., 1994).

Processes of Long-Term Cultural Change

With this case study in mind, we can review some very general processes involved in long-term cultural change.

Intensification. The per-capita energy requirements of the simplest human cultures are very small when compared with those needed by the most complex societies. As a society increases in complexity, more and more of its energy budget must go to maintaining institutions—churches (as in our Viking example), universities, banking systems, stock markets, etc. (Tainter, 1988, p. 91). A key element in the increasing complexity of the infrastructure is the **intensification** of food production. This process of intensification involves increasing the product derived from a unit of land or labor.

Most societies that rely on hunting and gathering obtain less food from a unit of land than do societies that rely on intensive agriculture. In the latter, increasing numbers of people rely on a constant amount of land to produce increasing amounts of food. Again, we have seen this dynamic at work in the Viking settlements. Quite apart from land-use intensification, ever more nonfood energy is harvested and consumed on a per-capita basis.

Presently, the world's population stands at 5,500,000,000, double what it was 30 years ago. At the moment, thanks to agricultural intensification using fertilizers and new seeds, food production has roughly kept pace and some economists feel that it will continue to do so. At the 1994 Cairo Conference on Population and Development, this was a matter of considerable debate. However, one thing can be agreed upon: there are no reliable guides as to how long growth in food production can be sustained. Moreover, high levels of productivity entail high costs in energy use and waste removal.

Specialization. A process parallel to intensification involved in long-term change is **specialization**, the increasingly limited range of productive activities in which a single individual is likely to be engaged. As specialization increases, the average person is engaged in a smaller and smaller percentage of the entire set of activities carried out in a society. Industrial society (or postindustrial society) is simply the latest point reached in a process that is as old as human culture. As individuals have become increasingly specialized, societies have tended to be characterized by increasing **differentiation**; that is, organization in separate units for various activities and purposes. Hunter-gatherer societies contain no more than a few dozen distinct occupations, while industrial societies may have over a million . Overspecialization, however, is a problem of some concern. How, for example, can a region whose agriculture has been devoted to one or two cash commodity crops such as coffee, cocoa, or tea, adapt to declining prices on the world market?

Centralization. A third evolutionary process has been **centralization**, the concentration of political and economic decisions in the hands of a few individuals or institutions. This process has been related to the growth of political, economic, and social differentiation. A strong centralized power is useful, even necessary in efforts to orchestrate diverse activities and interests—not to mention efforts to defend extant resources and possibly to acquire those of neighboring populations (Lees, 1994).

The development of political centralization probably began not long after the **Neolithic Revolution**—the changeover from hunting and gathering wild food to domesticating plants and animals. With food production, populations became larger and denser and sustained themselves through increasing economic specialization. All of this required the growth of more centralized institutions to process information, manage more complex distributive and productive systems, and maintain public order in the face of conflicting interests. As a consequence, today almost all of the world's peoples now live within the political structures of highly centralized states. However, as the history of the Viking settlements show, centralization can have dire consequences when those making the decisions—levying taxes and tithes in this case—cannot perceive the long-term consequences.

Another example is in the former Soviet Union, which is today facing an ecological disaster of al-

most unparalleled magnitude. The Aral Sea, in 1960 the fourth largest lake in the world, is drying up so rapidly that in 1994 it was half its original size. One scientist predicted that by the end of the century it will be nothing more than a vast briny swamp, (Micklin, 1988, pp. 1170–1173). Water that formerly fed the Aral has been diverted to complex and distant irrigation schemes, some more than 1,300 kilometers away. The water that does flow into the Aral from surrounding agricultural schemes is contaminated by chemical fertilizers and pesticides. Gone is the rich fishing industry, and communities once located on the lake's shores are being stranded as the shoreline recedes. The rapidly diminishing surface area of the lake is already resulting in hotter, drier summer temperatures and lower winter temperatures in the surrounding regions. These temperature changes and the falling water table have disrupted oasis farming in the region and contributed to the desertification of the area.

The main culprit in this case and in many others is an abstraction: a highly centralized system of planning and decision making with inadequate ability to anticipate long-term costs. Of course we know that abstractions have no influence over environmental events: the decisions are made and carried out by myriad individuals united in a bureaucratic hierarchy, each concerned with such mundane matters as career advancement, job security, and day-to-day survival. Adhering to productivity goals, limiting one's liability and responsibility for mistakes, and demonstrating bureaucratic achievement in extending the scope of one's authority are critical to the success of individuals in bureaucracies. In this context, local information and early warning signs that might signal impending environmental or social problems are easily ignored.

Stratification. Another trend in the long-term evolution of cultures is **stratification**—the division of a society into groups that have varying degrees of access to resources and power. In complex societies, entire groups may have very little or no access to decision-making processes and little access to the resources of the larger society. As we have seen, the Viking settlements in Greenland and Iceland eventually collapsed because the tenant farmers were excluded from the decision-making process and were forced by the church and the crown to over-exploit the land.

In no society do all people enjoy equal prestige or equal ability to participate in all social and economic activities. Even within the simple foraging society of the San people of Africa, some men acquire the title of "headman" and are accorded great respect. Among the Tiwi, another foraging group located in Australia, inequality, in terms of status, may affect a male's chances of marrying. Older men use accumulated social credits and status to acquire a large number of wives, creating a shortage of mates for the younger men.

While inequality of this sort may entail great hardship for some members of a society, it is not the same as socioeconomic stratification, that can lead to a situation in which entire segments of a population are disadvantaged in comparison with other members of the same society. This disadvantaged position, which is largely passed from generation to generation, engenders systematic constraint or exploitation by other segments of the population over a substantial period of time. In this sense, the groupings formed in stratified societies perpetuate inequality, and such inequality has little to do with the personal strengths or weaknesses of individuals.

Settlement Nucleation. In almost every part of the world, stratification and centralization have been associated with **nucleation**, the tendency of populations to cluster in settlements of increasing size and density. Cities are an exclusively characteristic of state-organized societies and arose comparatively recently in human history; at most, 7,000 years ago. Without question, the world's population is increasingly focused or dependent on cities, although we might well see shifts away from this as some productive systems and communication networks depend less upon concentrations of workers. Still, the overall trend is toward larger and larger urban "mega-regions," always at the expense of agricultural land. Istanbul's population in 1964 was aproximately 750,000; in 1994 it is over 12 million people—far outstripping its ability to provide its population with basic services such as water and sanitation. Similar instances of hyper-growth can be found on every continent: Cairo, Be-

jing, Lagos, New Delhi, and Mexico City, to name a few.

These trends are not, of course, inevitable. New developments in technology, especially in areas related to communication and production, may alter things dramatically. Nor are these general, long-term evolutionary trends independent in a causal sense. First, important systemic relationships link them. Second, changes in each may be responses to similar environmental changes. Intensification and specialization, for example, may both serve to extract more resources from a deteriorating environment through the reorganization of work. Centralization may accomplish the same end through increased efficiency in the flow of resources or information concerning their availability. Also, we have to make a clear distinction between trends or processes that can be seen in individual populations or social systems and those that appear to extend to societies around the globe. Any particular society may as easily be in the process of decentralizing or deintensifying land use as centralizing and intensifying it. The Viking settlements are again a case in point: after several centuries of political and economic centralization, the trend was reversed rather dramatically.

Joseph Tainter, in reviewing the circumstances under which a number of complex societies collapsed, concludes that often the decline of any particular complex society or civilization can be seen as a predictable outcome of the same processes that earlier had led to its rise (1988). He examines, in considerable detail, the collapse of the Western Roman Empire, the Mayas, and the Chaco Canyon society of northwestern New Mexico. Even though each instance is unique in terms of levels of complexity achieved, environment, and details of decline, they all can be seen as illustrative of the same general principle: declining marginal returns on investment in complexity (1988, pp. 187–192). That is to say, after a point, each society was investing more in maintaining its essential institutions (temples, cities, the military, etc.) than it was able to benefit from them. Investing in complexity, like any other investment strategy, can reach a point of diminishing returns; after this point is reached, sociopolitical organizations constantly encounter problems that require increased investment simply to maintain the status quo.

"Once a complex society enters the stage of declining marginal returns, collapse becomes a mathematical likelihood, requiring little more than sufficient passage of time to make probable an insurmountable calamity" (1988, p. 145).

Put in terms of our earlier discussion of stability and resilience, we can say that a complex society may reach a stage where it achieves stability at the expense of resilience. Though it is true that if we consider all societies over the course of human existence as a whole, cultural evolution has tended to proceed from the simple to the complex, it is a mistake to believe that all societies pass smoothly or uniformly in this direction. And it is also a mistake to equate increasing complexity with progress or with improved adaptation.

Summary

EVOLUTIONARY ECOLOGY IS A THEORETICAL ORIENTATION that emphasizes the adaptive significance of culture and behavior, from procurement systems to kinship systems to political and religious life. There are two aspects to this orientation: evolutionary theory and ecology, the study of the interplay between organisms and their environment.

Anthropologists are concerned with the ways in which individuals and groups adapt to their ecological environments. In its simplest sense, adaptation refers to the ways organisms make adjustments that facilitate their survival (and hence reproductive success), which determines their genetic contributions to future generations. The success or failure of adaptive responses can only be measured over the long term, and the evolutionary consequences of any observed behavior are unpredictable. We, like many other species, adapt by learning new ways of doing things. No adaptation or response can be seen as a perfect solution; each carries with it certain costs and hazards. Also, any adaptation is opportunistic in that it makes use of whatever is already at hand.

Variation, whether biological or behavioral, is the key to the process of adaptation. The recognition of variability draws attention to the process of selection among choices, the process of decision making. To understand the nature of human decision making or problem solving, we have to consider the environment in which it takes place. Environments are dynamic. One ecologist, Lawrence Slobodkin (1968), has argued that four patterns of change underlie the dynamics of all environments: changes in the novelty, frequency, magnitude, and duration of environmental events of all sorts. The organism with the best chance of success is not necessarily the one most perfectly adapted to its environment, but rather the one that maintains its ability to respond to the environment in a wide variety of ways—to be flexible.

A multitude of strategies for coping with different environmental problems are practiced in any human population. Nevertheless, behavior is usually fairly predictable and conventional. People guide their decisions according to expectations about consequences. To predict the course of future behavior or the way a population may respond to some novel event, anthropologists have to work with certain assumptions about human decisions or choices. Larger patterns or processes are simply the expressions of myriad individual acts and beliefs. Assumptions of rationality and individual self-interest are obviously too simple and too narrow to account for the entire range of cultural behavior. Despite their limitations, however, such assumptions are useful in that they allow us to form expectations of behavior with which actual behavior can be compared.

Anthropologists may use the concept of an ecosystem—the flow of energy and nutrients among the numerous species of plants and animals in a particular setting—to describe how human populations influence and are influenced by their surroundings. The matter (or nutrients) that flows through these elements is cyclical (that is, the same matter is constantly reused), while the energy is constantly resupplied by the sun. The area where a species lives is called its habitat. While an animal species' commitment to its niche (its adaptive strategy in the larger scheme) is relatively binding, the human species is distinctive in its capacity to alter its adaptive strategy and accommodate itself to many niches. However, humans are still subject to the rules established by the flow of matter and energy. We depend, as do all living things, on other species and must adjust our numbers and activities to our environment and available resources.

An ecosystem may be in equilibrium—all of its components in balance—or it may not be, and thus be changing. The properties that allow an ecosystem to adjust to change are resilience (its ability to undergo change while still maintaining its basic elements or relationships) and stability (its ability to return to equilibrium after disturbances). All ecosystems are limited in their capacity for change; it is often human activities that place the greatest strain on natural ecosystems. Each local environment also has a limited potential for supporting any of the life forms in it. The point at or below which a population tends to stabilize is called its carrying capacity.

Specific human food-procurement systems develop in response to both general environmental characteristics and environmental variables in the local area. These variables include the quantity and quality of available resources, fluctuations in the availability of resources, and the number of other groups competing for the same resources. A population's long-term success in adjusting to its resources may depend on its ability to maintain its ecological system; in this respect, simple societies can be as successful as technologically advanced societies.

A vast array of adaptive strategies are employed throughout the world, but within that wide range are certain common patterns. Among food-procurement strategies, for example, there are five basic patterns: foraging or hunting and gathering, subsistence agriculture, pastoralism, intensive agriculture, and industrial agriculture.

Over the long term, we see a number of interrelated trends in cultural change or evolution. As societies increase in population size and complexity, their energy budgets must allocate a larger share to maintain infrastructure; to maintain larger populations, food production is intensified; society becomes increasingly differentiated in terms of tasks performed and activities engaged in; production in general becomes more specialized; political and economic power becomes more centralized; settlements become larger and denser; and, socially, populations show increased stratification (division into groups that have unequal access to resources and power). At the same time, as with the Vikings in the North Atlantic, complex societies may break up with political and demographic collapse.

Key Terms

adaptation	intensification
carrying capacity	intensive agriculture
centralization	Neolithic Revolution
differentiation	niche
ecology	nucleation
ecosystem	pastoralism
evolutionary ecology	resilience
food-procurement system	specialization
foraging	stability
habitat	stratification
human ecology	subsistence agriculture
industrial agriculture	

Suggested Readings

Abruzzi, William S. (1993). *Dam that river! Ecology and Mormon settlement in the Little Colorado River Basin*. Lanham, MD: University Press of America. See pp. 68-69: a rich account using ecological models of Mormon settlement in the nineteenth century.

Boyd, R. & Richerson, P. J. (1985). *Culture and the Evolutionary Process*. Chicago: University of Chicago Press. Discusses the ways psychological, sociological, and cultural factors combine to change societies. The authors also develop models to analyze how biology and culture interact under the influence of evolutionary processes to produce the diversity we see in human cultures.

Campbell, B. (1994). *Human ecology: The story of our place in nature from prehistory to the present*. Hawthorne, NY: Aldine. This book is intended as a supplementary text for social science courses dealing with our current ecological crisis. It uses the study of human prehistory as a means to understand our present evolutionary and ecological situation.

Cultural Survival, Inc. (1994). *State of the peoples: A global human rights report on societies in danger*. Boston: Beacon Press. A selection of papers by both cultural anthropologists and others that describe the urgent threats facing distinctive societies around the world as they adapt to a rapidly changing world.

Moran, E. F. (1982). *Human adaptability*. Boulder, CO: Westview Press. A review of principles of adaptation as well as an introduction to ecological concepts and methodology. Although somewhat dated, the book is the best general review of the topic for anthropologists. The volume is particularly useful for its case-study approach to human adaptation in different environmental contexts.

Moran, E. F. (Ed.). (1990). *The ecosystem approach in anthropology*. Ann Arbor: University of Michigan Press. A reassessment of the utility of the ecosystem concept and the current relevance of this ecological approach to anthropological explanation.

Smith, Eric Alden & Winterhalter, Bruce (Eds.). (1992). *Evolutionary ecology and human behavior*. New York: Aldine. An excellent discussion of the general principles of evolutionary ecology, together with very interesting illustrative case studies.

Part II

Adaptive Patterns

The four chapters in Part II build directly on the ideas developed in Part I. Each chapter is concerned, at least in part, with adaptive strategies: how the members of a specific population cope with food procurement, the demands of their habitat, relations with other populations, and important aspects of domestic and community organization. Specifically, the chapters deal with hunting and gathering, horticulture, pastoralism, and intensive agriculture and industrial society. While the chapters are organized in what has come to be regarded as an evolutionary framework, each exemplifies a facet of the ongoing processes of adaptation that apply equally to every population.

Detailed ethnographic case studies in each chapter illustrate the various adaptive strategies and demonstrate how ethnographic data are used and are collected. While each case offers its own unique insight, several shared themes run through them all: internal variation and sources for change, environmental costs and consequences of different activities, and the larger environmental, social, and political implications of the activities described. The ethnographic materials highlight both the important lines of continuity that run through them and the differences between individual cases. The discussions of the cases put them in a global context and emphasize how, through the actions and decisions of individuals, change is a continuous process. Labels such as "pastoralist," "peasant," or "farmer" are no more than convenient titles that encompass much variability.

State of the Peoples: Death of a People: Logging in the Penan Homeland

The Organization of Energy

Social Organization

Settlement Patterns and Mobility
Human Ecology: Adapting to Others: The Batak Foragers of the Philippines

Resilience, Stability, and Change

The Dobe Ju/'hoansi
Climate and Resources
Settlement Patterns
Social Practices and Group Composition
Reciprocity
Quality of Life
Diet and Nutrition
Demography
The People of the Dobe Today

The Inuit or Eskimo
The Arctic Ecosystem
The Seasonal Migrations
Demography
Social Relationships
The Impact of Modernization
State of the Peoples: Claiming the Land

Summary

Key Terms

Suggested Readings

Chapter 4

Foraging

Humans and their immediate hominid ancestors have lived on the earth for more than four million years, and for more than 99 percent of that time they grew no food. They lived by hunting animals and gathering the plants that grew wild in their habitats. This adaptation is usually called foraging or hunting and gathering. This complex form of subsistence requires careful scheduling for collecting many (often hundreds) species of plants and hunting game; detailed environmental knowledge; and sophistication in storing, processing, and preparing food items. Further, in many instances it involves active management of resources by such techniques as water diversion, building weirs or dams constructed out of branches, and selective burning of grasslands or forests (see Gottesfeld, 1994).

Between 30,000 and 40,000 years ago anatomically modern humans appear in the archaeological record in sites across Europe, Asia, and Africa, and, soon thereafter, in North and South America. While there are many theories as to how modern Homo sapiens ultimately replaced the closely related species of Neanderthals, all seem to agree that it occurred because of major-cultural breakthroughs in subsistence technology critical to foraging (Jolly & White, 1995; Fagan, 1992). The modern hominids, as evidenced from their camps, kill sites (where game was killed or butchered), and from remains of stone tools, developed a hitherto unknown sophistication in hunting and gathering involving the cooperation of many individuals, probably from different groups or bands. They made specialized tools consisting of different parts (such as spear throwers); bladed instruments using wood, antlers, and ivory; they created sturdier housing and clothing; and they produced art—as shown so strikingly in the cave paintings of France and Spain. At this time, we also find the first evidence for long distance trade as a means of providing tool-making materials to groups whose environments did not supply them. This could have also facilitated the development of a collective body of knowledge among hundreds of local groups over wide areas. At the same time, there is striking evidence for cultural diversity: in Africa, for example, there were at least eight different traditions of tool making among early humans.

Today, foraging as a primary subsistence strategy is relatively rare and becoming rarer, not just because local people are quick to adopt new technologies but also because the lands available to sustain people in this endeavor are being encroached upon by outsiders. A review of the approximately 860 historically known hunter-gatherer societies tabulated in the Ethnographic Atlas found that only 179 survived into recent times (Ember, 1978, p. 440). Of those 179, far fewer remain today and none are unaffected by close relations with the products of industrialism and market economies. In fact, existing foragers are threatened on every continent where they still attempt to follow their traditional adaptation, as we see in the State of the Peoples box, *Death of a People: Logging in the Penan Homeland* on page 93.

Anthropologists, in describing any society in which they are not actually working at the time they are writing, often employ the convention known as the **ethnographic present**. The term indicates that the information being presented applies to the time when the data were collected; it doesn't necessarily describe the way the people in question may be living at the time the report is read. All of the peoples we discuss should be understood with this fact in mind, for lifestyles and technologies can change radically from one year to the next.

In this chapter we will look at two examples of foraging or hunting-and-gathering groups. The first are the people mentioned in Chapter 3: the Dobe Ju/'hoansi or !Kung (also sometimes called the Basarwa), who lived, when the first studies were carried out, by gathering nuts, vegetables, fruits and by hunting wild animals on a semiarid plain in southwestern Africa. In their case, the term "foraging" is certainly appropriate; while they made economic use of hundreds of species, the bulk of their diet was supplied by plants. The second case is a composite portrait of the people whom outsiders usually refer to as the Inuit or "Eskimo"; that is, the indigenous populations of the circumpolar regions of arctic Alaska and northeastern Canada. Many of these peoples still support themselves primarily by hunting and fishing (using modern technology to do so), but also increasingly by performing wage labor in the oil fields.

In certain respects, the lives of these modern hunter-gatherers, until quite recently at least, probably paralleled the lives of early prehistoric humans. This is one of the reasons they are of such great interest to anthropologists and also are the source of some controversy (Wilmsen, 1989a, 1989b; Lee, 1993; Burch & Ellanna, 1994). The study of recent or contemporary foragers may help us to understand why and how some aspects of human culture developed as they did, but it is important to bear in mind that the hunter-gatherers of today are not "throwbacks" or "living fossils." As Wilmsen and others have stressed, every modern population has a long and varied history regardless of whether written records exist, and cannot be seen as direct evidence of how earlier populations might have lived (1989). On the contrary, they are twentieth-century people with twentieth-century problems. As Eder (1988) has pointed out in the case of the Batak in the Philippines, hunter-gatherers are quick to incorporate new technologies into their subsistence systems. They deal with governments that have jurisdiction over them and with neighbors whose cultures may be quite different from their own. All hunter-gatherers have been drawn into exchanges with other groups: doing occasional wage labor for nearby agriculturists and

State of the Peoples

Death of a People:
Logging in the Penan Homeland

AT THE BEGINNING OF THE CENTURY, Wade Davis writes, over 100,000 nomadic hunter-gathers roamed the forests of Sarawak, Malaysia, on Borneo, the world's third largest island; now only 7,600 remain: the Penan people (Davis, 1993, p. 24). Eighty percent of Borneo is covered by a dense equatorial rain forest—one of the oldest living terrestrial ecosystems, and central to the life of the Penan. In many respects, the Penan resemble the Mbuti pygmies of Zaire in that they depend on the forest for food and they revere it as an intricate living thing. "Identifying psychologically and cosmologically with the rain forest and depending upon it for diet and technology, the Penan are skilled naturalists, with sophisticated interpretations of biological rela-

tionships" (p. 25). A partial list of their plant lore shows that they recognize over one hundred fruit trees, fifty medicinal plants, and eighteen sources of poison or toxins (used in hunting and fishing). Unfortunately, their way of life is threatened.

Throughout their territory, the sounds of chain saws and logging tractors pierce the air as logging concessions, granted by the Government of Sarawak, fell trees in the Penan's rainforest home. The assault is not new; between 1963 and 1985, 30 percent of the forests of Sarawak were logged, while another 60 percent have been given in concessions. Where do these ancient trees end up? For the most part, they are shipped to Japan, where they are transformed into cement molds, disposable contain-

ers, and shipping flats. Granting concessions has, in effect, created a class of instant millionaires among members of the Sarawak State Assembly (pp. 26–27). In 1987, the Penan and their neighbors, the Dyaks, responded by organizing resistance. They held meetings, rallies, and ultimately placed barricades on logging roads, bringing operations to a temporary halt. Despite international protests, the government retaliated and made arrests. In 1988, the blockades went up again, as they did in 1990. Even though a state task force recommended that the Dyak-Penan region be respected as biosphere reserve, this has not been acted upon. Ultimately the fate of the Penan will rest with world opinion; the prognosis is not good.

pastoralists, buying from and selling to traders from industrialized societies, and even at times receiving welfare from their governments.

Modern foragers are people for whom some version of this ancient subsistence strategy is still effective in their particular environments. The fact that most hunter-gatherers throughout history lived in areas far more hospitable than those they inhabit today implies that food sources were more abundant and reliable, nutrition better, and population densities higher than we see today among foragers. As we examine some of the methods of food procurement used by hunter-gatherers, their systems of kinship, residence patterns, and other cultural traits, we will see that these behaviors constitute solutions to the problems of making a living in their particular habitats.

The Organization of Energy

Hunters and gatherers subsist primarily on wild plants and animals. Unlike agriculture, the hunting-and-gathering economy does not involve direct or intensive intervention to regulate the growth and reproduction of the life forms on which people depend. Thus the diet of hunter-gatherers is more strictly determined by habitat than that of other groups. In fact, abundant wild resources are available in any American city, but not in quantities sufficient to sustain a population of any great size.

As local environments vary, so do the dietary staples of their inhabitants. Peoples who live in areas where plant life is more abundant or reliable than game depend primarily on vegetable foods—nuts, fruits, and the like. Such is the case, for

Figure 4–1. !Kung territory

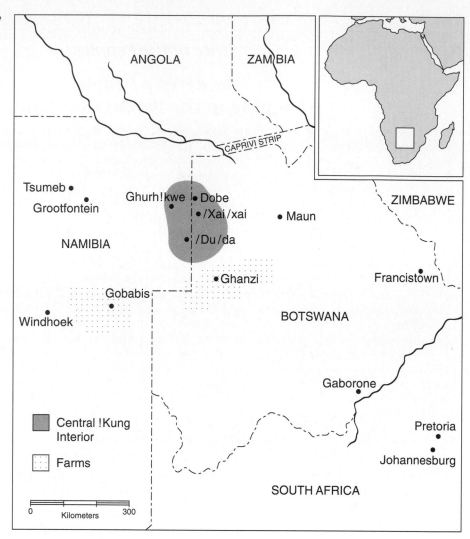

example, with the Dobe dwellers of the Kalahari. The Eskimo, by contrast, rely much more heavily on meat and fish, for plant life is scarce in the Arctic. Whatever its emphasis, however, the diet of hunter-gatherers tends to be highly diversified, since it must be responsive to seasonal and annual fluctuations in resources. Scott Cane, writing about the foragers of the Central Desert region of Australia, describes several hundred species ranging from tiny plants and insects to large animals that the people incorporate into their seasonal diets, as well as the elaborate efforts made to secure adequate water and nourishment during the dry months (1987).

This is not to say that foragers do not manage their resource bases. In both North and South America, indigenous foragers use fire to burn forest cover on a regular basis in order to promote the growth of vegetation supporting favored game animals (Lewis & Ferguson, 1988) or favored root tubers or berries (Gottesfeld, 1994). Coincidentally, this periodic burning may be instrumental in promoting the long-term health of the forest as well, since it prevents the buildup of undergrowth that can cause dangerous fires or harbor disease.

Most, if not all, foraging peoples engage in varying degrees of exchange with other societies. The Mbuti Pygmies of Zaire, although often described as self-sufficient hunters, sell antelope and other game to visiting traders and buy the agricultural products and manufactured foods of their

Table 4–1 Edible Seeds

Scientific Name	Aboriginal Name	Habitat	Relative Importance
Acacia acradenia	Wilbud	Sandplains	Minor
Acacia adsurgens	Nganamarra	Sandplains	Moderate
Acacia ancistrocarpa	Wadayurru	Sandplains	Moderate
Acacia aneura	Mandja	Flood, Laterite plains	Moderate
Acacia coriacea	Gunandru	Deep sandplains	Major
Acacia holosericea	Gilgidi	Adjacent water	Major
Acacia ligulata	Wadarrga	Sandplains	Moderate
Acacia monticola	Birrbin	Sandplains	Moderate
Acacia stipuligera	Djibrin	Deep sand, dune flanks	Major
Acacia tenuissima	Minyinggurra	Sandplains	Moderate
Acacia tumida	Ngadurrdi	Sandplains	Moderate
Brachiaria miliiformis	Balgurrba	Adjacent water	Minor
Bulbostylis barbata	Lyillyil	Adjacent water	Minor
Capparis loranthifolia	Yidaringgi	Flood plains	Minor
Chenopodium inflatum	Garndubungba	Clayey sand	Minor
Chenopodium rhodin-ostachyum	Galbarri	Clayey sand	Major
Cyperus iria	Yanmid	Adjacent water	Moderate
Dactyloctenium radulans	Burrandjarri	Adjacent water	Moderate
Daspalidium rarium	Yulumburru	Rocky ground	Minor
Diplachine fusca	Miarr Miarr	Floodplains	Minor
Echinochloa colunum	Dudjurnba	Adjacent water	Moderate
Eragrostis eriopoda	Wangganyu	Sandplains, near water	Moderate
Eragrostis laniflora	Burrindjurru	Deep sand	Minor
Eragrostis tenellula	Marradjirralba	Various	Moderate
Eucalyptus camaldulensis	Yabulin	Creeks	Minor
Eucalyptus microtheca	Dindjil	Adjacent water	Moderate
Eucalyptus odontocarpa	Warilyu	Deep sand	Moderate
Eucalyptus pachyphylla	Djibuburru	Deep sand	Moderate
Fimbristylis oxystachya	Lugarra	Sandplains	Major
Hedyotis pterospora	Yurrundju yurrundju	Sandplains	Minor
Panicum australiense	Yidagadji	Sandplains	Major
Panicum cymbiforme	Gumbulyu	Deep sand	Major
Panicum decompositum	Willinggiri	Flood plains	Minor
Portulaca filifolia	Bulyulari	Sandy ground	Moderate
Portulaca oleracea	Wayali	Sandy ground	Moderate
Scirpus dissachanthus	Gunamarradju	Adjacent water	Moderate
Sida sp. A (unnamed)	Dadji dadju	Sand dunes	Minor
Stylobasium spathulatum	Nirdu	Sandplains	Major
Tecticornia verrucosa	Mangil	Claypans	Minor
Triodia basedowii	Nyanmi	Sandplains	Minor
Triodia longiceps	Lanu lanu	Rocky ground	Minor
Triodia pungens	Djinal	Sandplains	Minor

Bantu and Sudanic neighbors (Milton, 1985). It is extremely doubtful that they could have survived otherwise (Hart & Hart, 1986). The Dobe people also trade with and work for the Bantu farmers (Wilmsen, 1989a, 1989b). The Eskimo hunt not only for their subsistence needs, but also to enable them to trade for the numerous products of industrial society on which they have come to depend—snowmobiles, kerosene, rifles, canned goods, even televisions and motor vehicles (see, for example, Feit, 1994, pp. 421–440).

One of the reasons anthropologists find hunter-gatherers especially fascinating is that these people show us how humans can live on a low-energy budget. A **low-energy budget** is an adaptive strategy by which a minimum of energy is used to extract sufficient resources from the environment for survival. We humans are distinctively adept at extracting energy from the environment, but we also expend great amounts of energy in doing so. A single sack of potatoes, for example, represents a considerable investment of energy: in manufacturing the fertilizers and pesticides that were used on the potatoes; on powering the machines that planted, fertilized, sprayed, and harvested the crop; in packing and transporting the harvest; and so on. In comparison with other animals, humans—especially in industrialized societies—live on a high-energy budget. Foragers are the dramatic exception to this rule.

In general, the primary source of energy that hunter-gatherers expend in food procurement is that contained in their own muscles. While they may invest energy in building shelters, traps, and even boats or weirs, relatively little effort is directed into the construction of a complicated infrastructure of food procurement—cleared fields, irrigation systems, or fuel-burning machines. As a result, hunter-gatherers spend much less energy to support a single unit of population than do other peoples. And since they generally support themselves rather well in terms of nutrition, leisure time, and general physical well-being, their system must be regarded as remarkably efficient.

They are efficient, too, in preserving their resource bases. Because of their low expenditure of energy and because they tend to exploit a wide variety of foods, hunter-gatherers place relatively limited demands on any one of their resources. At the same time, their way of life seems to limit their pop-

ulation growth; their numbers tend to remain proportionate to those of the animal and plant species on which they depend. The combined result of this adaptive strategy—low-energy needs, a wide resource base, controlled population—is that foragers interfere relatively little with other components of their ecosystems. Because humans are the most versatile predators in their habitats, they do affect the populations of the species on which they feed. However, their ecosystems appear to be in relative equilibrium and their resource bases may remain unthreatened, at least in comparison with those of other economic systems. This "conservationist" approach is largely inadvertent and easily altered by new technologies that have been introduced during periods of rapid population growth.

One such rapid expansion of population accompanied the development of agriculture in most parts of the world. With this development, many foragers became pastoralists or horticulturists, relying on domesticated plants and animals for their subsistence. Later, as new agricultural techniques (such as irrigation and plowing with livestock) were introduced, horticulturists turned to intensive farming, which led to further growth in human populations. While the populations in some societies have stabilized, most are still experiencing population growth as new technologies are introduced. The resultant demand for ever more food encourages people to increase their efforts to produce reliable harvests.

Thus people come to reshape their environments—digging canals, planting crops, eliminating insects—and in the process they are locked into a struggle to maintain themselves at the expense of the equilibrium of the ecosystem. Of course, hunter-gatherers are also quite capable of over-exploiting their resources. The Miskito Indians of Nicaragua came close to wiping out the local turtle population. Though turtles are their primary source of protein, they were lured by cash payments from turtle-packing companies to hunt the sea animals to the verge of extinction. Fortunately, the nine-year war with the Sandinistas interrupted the commercial fishing operations and the sea turtle population has recovered. Now the Miskito are actively trying to gain rights to their sea territories so they can again use traditional means to manage this resource. No longer partners in the commercial fishing operation, Miskito communities are now fighting to pre-

Hauling a green turtle (chelonia mydas) *on board off the Miskito Coast, Nicaragua. Commercial hunting has greatly reduced this once-abundant species.*
(Bill Curtsinger)

serve their valuable resource (Nietschmann, 1995). Likewise, when the native North Americans suddenly found themselves in contact with a European market for beaver skins in the eighteenth century, they hunted nearly to extinction an animal on which they had depended for centuries. In both cases, we see essentially the same process: once people who have been exploiting a resource for a limited market (themselves) are tied in to an unlimited market, the attraction of short-term gains often leads to the depletion of the resource.

As these examples suggest, those hunting-and-gathering peoples who have preserved their resource bases have not necessarily done so because they embraced a conservationist ethic, although some may do so (Gottesfeld, 1995). Nor can it be safely claimed that they deliberately limit their population in order to adjust it to their resources. It appears, rather, that several interrelated factors

have operated to maintain these peoples in balance with their resources. These factors include limitations imposed by their storage technology, the absence of a wider market for the food produced, the lack of fossil fuels, and other environmental conditions that constrain population growth. As we examine the Dobe !Kung and the Eskimo, we will see how people in two societies make a living and how various cultural practices contribute to their adaptation to harsh environments.

Social Organization

No one type of social organization inevitably issues from any food-procurement strategy, including foraging. The way foragers organize themselves politically and socially varies widely. However, since the environments of most recent and contemporary foragers tend to be the less-desirable habitats with relatively sparse and highly variable resources, the groups occupying these environments share certain broadly defined attributes of social organization.

Foragers typically live in small groups; camps of closely related families. The size of the camps, and of the society as a whole, is limited by the local supply of natural resources. Unlike agricultural societies, hunter-gatherers cannot easily increase food production to accommodate an increase in population. Their population levels reflect the availability of food during the worst season of the year, since for the most part they lack the technology for bulk food storage. When food (or even water) cannot be stored, the season in which the least food is available limits population, no matter how abundant food may be in other seasons. And since their lands today are marginal, their population densities are generally low. This, of course, was not true for many earlier populations where abundant and predictable food sources permitted large, settled concentrations of population such as on the northwest coast of North America.

A critical factor in the adaptation of modern foragers is the rule of **reciprocity**—that is, the systematic sharing of food and other goods. Food procurement is generally viewed as a family or household enterprise, and the tasks that it involves may be divided along sexual lines. While early studies identified men as hunters and women as gatherers, recent research has revealed that this division of labor is not universal. For example, among the Ache of Paraguay, men do considerable gathering along with the women (Hill et al., 1984), while in the Philippines, Agta women do a significant amount of hunting (Estioko-Griffin & Griffin, 1981). Regardless of this variation in gender roles, the individuals who do the hunting and gathering generally share their food with the entire local group. Rarely does anyone go hungry if others have adequate food, and no one has to work all day every day. Likewise, tools, ornaments, and other material possessions pass from hand to hand in an endless round of gift giving and gift taking so that inequalities of wealth are minimal.

Some members of a hunting-gathering band will have more influence than others and men tend to have more influence than women, but it is rare for anyone to have institutionalized power—that is, an office authorizing one person to make decisions for others. Decision-making power is spread fairly broadly among all the families in the group. Those who disagree are likely to simply move away.

Systems of social control in foraging groups also tend to be informal. Order is maintained on a day-to-day, consensual basis rather than through adherence to codified laws enforced by an administrative hierarchy. Codes of conduct and their enforcement are integral parts of the group's traditions, myths, and religious ideology. Both the definition of crime and the appropriate punishment reflect the consensus within the group at any given time. Some Eskimo, for example, had "dueling songs" to resolve all disputes except those involving murder (Hoebel, 1954). The two disputants, with their families serving as choruses, perform songs to express their side of the story and to vent their anger, and the winner is chosen by the applause of those attending the song duel. No decision is made as to who is right or wrong in terms of a body of law existing apart from public opinion. The most important thing is that the parties feel that the complaint has been raised and laid to rest; they then can resume normal social relations.

In extreme cases, individuals who repeatedly violate rules and social expectations in foraging societies may be ostracized by the group. But most commonly, the dispute is between two parties and if it cannot be resolved, the disputants and their families simply move apart.

This type of social organization, characterized by great fluidity, flexibility, and equality, is by no means inherent in the hunting-and-gathering way of life. When food resources are regularly available in relative abundance, foraging can support a highly structured cultural system accompanied by high population density. We know from archaeological evidence in the Old and New Worlds that some foraging societies of the past (much like fishing communities today) had large year-round settlements numbering several hundred members, with considerable inequality of status and wealth (Price, 1981; Hayden, 1994). Indeed, various groups of Native American hunter-gatherers lived in permanent villages, had chiefs and hierarchies of other officials, and observed rankings of wealth and power—all predicated on a complex division of labor that involved castes and slavery. They traded with other groups, conducted warfare, incorporated captives into their labor force, and so forth. In such complex foraging societies, competition among individual and groups was intense and, as Hayden suggests, very closely related to the fact that certain resources were abundant, concentrated, and capable of being stored or transformed into political power and prestige. In short, they very much resembled advanced agricultural societies.

Settlement Patterns and Mobility

A major concern of anthropologists who study human-environmental interaction, is the manner in which people distribute themselves over the landscape. What is the nature of the settlements they occupy? How frequently, if at all, do they move? How are such decisions affected by the variability of resources from place to place and from time to time? Forager groups today tend to be nomadic. Their seasonal migrations on their home ranges are adjusted to the availability of resources in different places at different times. Once again, the limits of storage and transport technology are important. Most foragers deal with variability in resources by moving people to the food rather than by moving food to the people.

Often the camps of related families form larger groupings, called **bands,** within a territory. The

Kwakiutl dancer and leader Charlie George of Blunder Harbor, B.C. in 1950. Coastal waters rich in marine life supported a large population of village-dwelling hunter gatherers before the arrival of European settlers.

(William Heick)

members of a band may come together at one or another of these camps for ceremonies, or the band may simply be an aggregation of people who regularly intermarry. The bands are strikingly flexible in their composition, expanding and contracting in response to fluctuations in resources. When certain resources are scattered, the members of the bands also scatter. Later, when game converges in one area or when large permanent water holes offer the only available water, camping groups come together again to exploit these resources jointly. Social habits also play a part in the flexibility of the bands. Groups are continually re-forming as families visit or entertain their kin, move away from bands with which they do not get along, or move into bands that are short on people or long on resources and fellowship. Generally, foragers exhibit a territorial system of land use; that is, they identify a particular tract of resources as belonging to a particular local group with outsiders having limited access (Gottesfeld, 1994).

The main source of variability in this is the degree to which usage is exclusive and the willingness of the putative owners to defend their territory by force.

While most contemporary foragers make use of mobility to track seasonal food sources, more sedentary patterns can be found. The Kwakiutl of the American northwest coast, the Chumash of Southern California, the Ainu of Japan, and the Andaman Islanders of India are foraging groups whose members lived in large, sedentary villages. In such cases, the key factor seems to be the availability of large quantities of stable and storable resources. Especially important are environments containing great quantities of fish and shellfish, which are often fairly concentrated, predictable, and abundant. Also, as we see in the Human Ecology box, *Adapting to Others: The Batak Foragers of the Philippines* (pages 100–102), one should not be too quick to generalize about the relationship of sedentism to foraging or farming.

Human Ecology

Adapting to Others:
The Batak Foragers of the Philippines

IT HAS BEEN GENERALLY ASSUMED that as hunting and gathering societies take up farming, they are almost immediately incorporated into the wide society and that they make a sharp transition from mobility to a sedentary lifestyle. In other words, as hunters and gatherers become more integrated with (and often dependent upon) the wider social system, it is assumed that they settle down.

James Eder, who conducted research among the Batak of the Philippines, a tropical forest foraging people, extends this line of reasoning. He postulates that the nature and direction of the changes a hunter-gatherer society undergoes as it becomes increasingly connected to the wider society are to some extent determined by its own cultural characteristics (Eder, 1988). Using historical accounts, interviews with the oldest Batak, and comparative observations of other hunter-gatherer societies, he has examined how Batak hunting and gathering practices have altered over the past hundred years as they incorporated other practices into their subsistence system. He also found that the Batak are becoming more, not less, mobile as they become more integrated in the wider society.

The Batak inhabit the mountains of central Palawan Island and are distributed in eight groups, each associated with a particular river valley. The number of households in each group range from three to twenty-four, and the groups are located between 3 and 10 km upstream from coastal Filipino villages. Like other contemporary hunter-gatherer societies, the Batak no longer rely exclusively on hunting and gathering for subsistence, although foraging still provides them with about half their basic needs. They are still able to provide for their subsistence exclusively by hunting and gathering for extended periods of time, even a year or more, as they did during World War II and during an unsuccessful government attempt to relocate them in 1970 (Eder, 1988, p. 38). Nevertheless, trade, horticulture, and wage labor are also part of their current economy. In fact, trade and horticulture are probably not at all new to the Batak, but wage labor emerged more recently, with the arrival of the first lowland settlers during the latter half of the nineteenth century. As the Batak became more involved with the settlers, their desire for lowland foods and manufactured goods increased and patron-client relationships rapidly evolved, tying individual Batak to individual settlers. An even more recent development has come in the form of foreign tourists, who have discovered the Batak, and now provide them with a minor source of income as guides.

Another change wrought by the arrival of settlers was in the Batak settlement pattern. When root crops were still the mainstay of Batak horticulture, periodic visits to swidden fields (partially cleared areas in the forest) were part of a pattern of year-around residence in temporary forest camps. However, today the Batak plant their swidden fields exclusively with upland rice, and during the agricultural season it is from their field houses that they make periodic foraging trips to the forest.

A further change in settlement pattern dates from the early twentieth century, when government officials encouraged the Batak to come down out of the mountains and settle permanently on the coast. In 1930, five of these coastal settlements were declared to be reservations exclusively for Batak use. The legal disposition of the land was never clear, and in any event the settlements were too small to provide the Batak with adequate subsistence. Thus, although the Batak did build houses on the reservations, they never occupied them full-time. In fact, by the 1950s the reservations were overrun with non-Batak settlers and the Batak, in a pattern of movement that still continues, began relocating their settlement sites further up their respective river valleys, leaving themselves relatively isolated but conveniently situated for access both to the lowland areas and the forests (Eder, 1988, p. 40).

Eder uses seven criteria against which to measure changes in Batak hunting and gathering practices: seasonality, encampment duration (mobility), encampment size, resource utilization, division of labor, hunting technology and length of workday.

Seasonality. Eder's data showed that forest camps were used more frequently during the first six months of the year (when the weather is dry and not suitable for agricultural pursuits) than the latter six months (which are mainly rainy and swidden-oriented). Since the Batak do most of their hunting and gathering from forest camps, his data suggest a marked seasonality in contemporary foraging. Although he concedes that this may always have been the case, his own view is that it is a more recent development: the tropical monsoon forest in which the Batak live has a distinct dry season that would promote growth of edible plants; in addition, the Batak themselves maintain that they once lived off the land and state that in any season at least a few of the eight species of wild tubers they utilize are available (1988, p. 44).

Encampment Duration. According to Eder's informants, in the past forest camps would be occupied for periods of up to three to four weeks. Today, the occupation periods are considerably shorter, usually a matter of two to seven days. The reason for this is that individuals now must balance the demands of hunting and gathering against those of cultivation and participation in the market economy. Occupation periods are now shorter, and forest camps are left, not for other camps, but to return to swiddens and settlement houses. Although the encampment duration is short, the Batak spend 40 percent of their time in camps of one sort or another—indicating that they now have a greater rate of residential mobility (Eder, 1988, p. 45). However, the shorter duration of encampments makes travel to and from camps more costly in terms of energy—energy expended over several days rather than weeks. The Batak also do not make their camps as far away from the settlements and from one another as they did in the past, and thus resources are more quickly depleted in regularly visited areas. The energy costs of round-trip travel to camps are further increased because today the Batak bring along a lot more baggage: pots and pans, flashlights, radios, and so on (1988, p. 53).

Encampment Size. Eder found that it was rare today for more than seven households to camp together, whereas in the past thirty to forty households would commonly join forces. In part this is due to demographic changes—there are simply fewer Batak today. However, more significantly, Eder traces the change to the same scheduling conflicts that affect encampment duration. Each household has a different swidden location, the timing of their agricultural cycle differs, each has a different set of ties to lowlanders. "Not everyone, in effect, can get away to the forest at the same time" (1988, p. 46).

Resource Utilization. Eder offers two explanations of why the Batak today utilize a much narrower range of plant and animal resources than in the past. First, wild resources are seasonally available and cannot be utilized if their availability coincides with the planting or harvesting season. Second, not only are the Batak aware that the lowlanders consider them "primitive" because of the forest foods they use, they also regularly obtain many lowland foods (sugar, coffee, etc.), which may have changed their preferences for traditional foods (1988, p. 48).

Division of Labor. Eder found that there have been subtle changes in the division of labor as a consequence of certain foraging activities being discontinued, the depletion of game, and the fact that from August to October the women harvest the rice fields while only the men occupy forest camps. This latter development has had the consequence that today, over the period of a year, husbands sleep separately nearly 10 percent of the time—a new phenomenon among the Batak (1988, p. 49).

Hunting Technology. Traditionally, the Batak hunted with blowguns. However, the use of blowguns ceased after World War II and now the chief weapons are spears, used in conjunction with hunting dogs, bows and arrows, and homemade guns.

Length of Work Day. Although he has no time allocation data from the past with which to compare his own observations, Eder concludes that contemporary Batak work longer hours. He bases his conclusions on the fact that at least some foraging now is for trade as well as subsistence and that the women are now involved in making articles for use in agriculture, such as harvesting baskets and rice-drying mats.

Eder concludes from his study that despite the fact that the overall returns of hunting and gathering for the Batak today ought to be higher than in the past—fewer Batak forage in the same location,

(Continues)

Human Ecology

Adapting to Others:
The Batak Foragers of the Philippines (continued)

and they stay for shorter periods of time—they are, in fact, lower. Because the Batak are now engaging in a range of economic activities, none will be as remunerative as they would be if pursued full-time. Not only has Batak hunting and gathering ceased to be as successful as it once was, Batak horticulture, because it is pursued only part-time, also does not create the returns that, for instance, the lowlanders' farms do. On the other hand, they are sucessfully maintaining themselves and have been quick to incorporate new technologies into their subsistence system.

In the light of recent findings, including Eder's, it is necessary to reexamine many anthropological theories regarding the relationship of hunting and gathering societies to the wider social systems into which they are becoming integrated. One should not assume that change is a simple process whereby traditional hunter-gathers are absorbed or quickly overwhelmed by contact with farming populations. Also, one need not assume that increased participation in agriculture is inevitably associated with increased sedentism and decreased mobility. People are resourceful and innovative; hunters and gathers no less than others.

Resilience, Stability, and Change

Of all the adaptive patterns, that of foragers interfered the least with the resilience of their ecosystems. While interaction and exchange occur, ties of dependency between families (and especially between groups) are minimal. These people adjust to the environment by making use of any local resource that is abundant. At the opposite extreme are societies such as our own, that use a vast array of chemical and mechanical strategies to control the environment irrespective of changing conditions.

The viability of the hunter-gatherer strategy is based on the limited degree to which environmental problems are transmitted from one group to another. Some groups succeed; some fail. Yet this is the food procurement strategy that humans employed as they became the dominant species on earth. It is interesting to note one circumstance in which this form of adaptation came into direct competition with a technologically more advanced system of procurement. As we saw in Chapter 3, the Vikings of Norway settled Greenland in the tenth century and maintained colonies whose economy was based on farming, seal hunting, and fishing. They did not, however, adopt the patterns of

hunting used by the indigenous Eskimo, whom they feared and despised. The Viking practices were not well-adapted to the environment in Greenland and the settlers were unable to secure food in sufficient abundance to support themselves. Eventually, the colonies died out, leaving Greenland once again the exclusive domain of the Eskimo (McGovern, 1980; McGovern et al., 1988).

The superiority of the indigenous hunter-gatherer adaptations to the European technology introduced into Greenland is not an isolated instance. In 1846, Sir John Franklin and his entire expedition (two ships, 200 men) starved to death in the heart of Netsilik Eskimo territory, presumably because they could or would not use Eskimo food-procurement techniques (Cyriax, 1939). The Burke and Wills expedition of 1861 attempted to cross Australia from south to north and return; all but one explorer starved to death as they refused to forage and or accept assistance from the Aborigines until it was too late (Moorehead, 1963).

Let us now examine two foraging populations that illustrate the points we have been stressing. Keep in mind, though, the warning regarding the rapid changes that such peoples everywhere are undergoing. The two societies we will explore are those of the Dobe Ju/'hoansi, or !Kung, of southwest Africa and the Inuit (or, as they are still commonly referred to, the Eskimo) of Alaska and northeast Canada.

The Dobe Ju/'hoansi

The Ju/'hoansi are one of five culturally related groups of southern african who are known collectively as the San. The San are something of a historical mystery.[1] An educated guess is that they once occupied most of southern Africa but were eventually displaced by successive waves of Bantu and European invaders. Those who were not killed or absorbed into the invaders' populations were gradually forced back into the arid wastes of the Kalahari Desert and its surrounding areas in Botswana, Namibia, and Angola. Most of the estimated 50,000 San who still live in and around the Kalahari are slowly being absorbed by the surrounding agricultural, industrial, and pastoral communities although they still maintain their distinct cultural identity.

The several hundred Ju/'hoansi San who live in the Dobe area, on the northern edge of the Kalahari, are an exception. Although the Dobe Ju/'hoansi have been in contact with Bantu and Europeans since the 1920s, share water holes with Bantu pastoralists, and sometimes work for them, the majority (over 70 percent) were almost self-sufficient hunters and gatherers at the time they were first studied by contemporary anthropologists. Since their way of life has changed dramatically, our description will begin with how they once lived and conclude with their present situation. In the mid-1960s, when Richard B. Lee lived with them, they had no interest in agriculture, herd animals, or firearms. They neither paid taxes to nor received services (except for smallpox vaccinations) from the government of Botswana. They traded with neighboring Bantu pastoralists but worked for them only occasionally. Thus, although the Dobe Ju/'hoansi are not isolated, until recently they were largely independent—mainly because they occupy territory that no one else wants.

Until 1992 they were in the middle of an international power struggle among white-ruled South Africa, Angola, and now Namibia, a newly independent state. As a consequence, the Ju/'hoansi's traditional freedom of movement was severely curtailed beginning in the early 1970s. Parts of their territory are still divided by a massive chain-link fence. Many Ju/'hoansi were employed by the South African army as scouts, and all, willingly or not, are involved in the processes that are transforming this once remote land. Their situation is changing rapidly, and in all likelihood the life we describe will soon be transformed beyond recognition. As Richard Lee has remarked, those working with the Ju/'hoansi in the 1980s and 1990s find it hard to visualize the society that he found and described in 1965, and thus came to conclude that he had misinterpreted what he had witnessed (1993). We will refer to both early and recent accounts, beginning with an account of their way of life when Lee first encountered them.

Climate and Resources

The Dobe area is an inhospitable environment for humans, a fact that has protected the Ju/'hoansi from invasion and assimilation, if not from contact. Dobe is a transition zone between the Kalahari Desert to the south and the lusher regions, inhabited mainly by agriculturists and pastoralists, to the north. It consists of semiarid savanna with a scattering of trees and grasslands and very few permanent water holes. The temperature ranges from below freezing on winter nights to 37°C (100°F) in the shade during the summer. Even more variable than the temperature is the rainfall. For six months of the year, the area is completely dry; during the other six months, there are heavy rains. Furthermore, rainfall varies considerably from year to year. In 1967–1968, for example, rainfall in the area was 250 percent greater than it had been in 1963–1964 (Yellen & Lee, 1976). Such variation in rainfall, along with the sandiness of the soil, makes agriculture impossible. Nor is the area an

[1] Until recently, they were known as Bushmen, a name given to them by the Dutch who settled in South Africa in the seventeenth century. Africanists, however, now prefer the term San, which means "original settlers" in the Cape Hottentot dialect. The population described here was often referred to as the !Kung; Richard Lee, who has worked with them since 1962, advocates referring to them as they prefer to call themselves—which is the Dobe Ju/'hoansi (pronounced "doebay zhutwasi"). To confuse matters further, the preferred usage of the Botswana government is Basarwa.

Table 4–2 The Harvard Kalahari Research Group

Name	Affiliation	Research Interests
Megan Biesele	Nyae Nyae Development Found., Namibia	folklore, ecology, development
Alison Brooks	George Washington University	prehistory, anthropological theory
Nicholas Blurton Jones	UCLA	ethology, evolutionary ecology
Irven DeVore	Harvard University	ecology, evolutionary theory
Nancy DeVore	Harvard University, Anthrophoto	photography
Patricia Draper	Penn State University	child behavior, aging, evolutionary ecology
John Hansen	Witwatersrand University, Johannesburg, S.A.	pediatrics
Henry Harpending	Penn State University	demography, physical anthropology, Ju, Herero
Nancy Howell	University of Toronto	demography, evolutionary ecology
Richard Katz	Saskatchewan Federated Indian Colleges, Saskatoon, Sask.	ritual, healing, change
Melvin Konner	Emory University	infancy, evolutionary theory
Richard Lee	University of Toronto	ecology, social organization, history, anth. of development
Marjorie Shostak	Emory University	life history, gender studies
Stewart Truswell	Sydney University, Australia	medicine, health and nutrition
John Yellen	National Science Foundation, Washington, D.C.	ethno-archaeology, prehistory

ideal hunting ground; because the vegetation is scattered, it cannot support large migratory herds.[2]

Nevertheless, the Ju/'hoansi manage a livelihood in this habitat, in part because they exploit such a wide variety of resources. Despite the extremes of climate, Dobe supports about 500 species of plants and animals. Of these resources, the Dobe Ju/'hoansi use about 150 plants and about 100 animals and they eat approximately 100 species of plants and 50 animals (Yellen & Lee, 1976). They gather wild nuts (chiefly from mongongo trees), berries, melons, and other fruits; dig for roots and tubers; collect honey in season; and hunt everything from warthogs, kudu, and leopard tortoise (three favorites) to springhare, guinea fowl, and rock pythons. The larger animals, such as the antelope and kudu, are shot down with poisoned arrows. The Ju/'hoansi hunt the smaller animals with dogs or trap them in ingenious snares. Very young animals, inept at running, are sometimes simply chased and snatched up. Although the Dobe Ju/'hoansi definitely prefer some of these foods to others, their versatility in using a wide

[2] In the mid-1960s their population was 466—379 permanent residents and 87 seasonal visitors (Lee, 1968, p. 30). In this discussion we will rely heavily on the preliminary work of Richard B. Lee and Irven Devore, along with the more recent writings of the rest of their Harvard team, many of which are collected in *Kalahari Hunter-Gatherers* (1976), edited by Lee and Devore. We also use Lee's monograph, "The Dobe Ju/'hoansi" (1993) and Wilmsen's 1989a book.

range of resources ensures that they are seldom without something to eat.

Most of their other needs are also easily supplied by the resources of the area. Their huts are constructed of branches and grass found throughout the area. Ostrich eggshells, also readily available, make ideal water containers. A wooden digging stick, whittled in an hour, lasts several months. A bow, arrows, and a quiver, which take several days to make, last years. The people's few luxuries—ostrich eggshell necklaces, thumb pianos, intricately carved pipes, and children's toys—are likewise made from materials readily at hand. Indeed, there is only one important resource that the Dobe Ju/'hoansi traditionally obtain through exchange with other groups: iron for making tools. But even in this case they exercise a certain independence: they collect scraps of metal from the Botswana Veterinary Station fences to make arrowheads.

Limited in their needs and resourceful in filling them, the Dobe Ju/'hoansi have little difficulty obtaining food and raw materials. The scarcity of water is the major problem, and it is this factor that in large part makes the Dobe Ju/'hoansi a nomadic people.

Settlement Patterns

As rainfall determines the availability of water in the Kalahari, it also determines the people's settlement patterns. During the dry season, from June through September, the Ju/'hoansi congregate in relatively large camps of about twenty to forty people around the large permanent water holes, the only available sources of water (Yellen & Lee, 1976). In this period, the people rely primarily on roots and tubers found within a day's walk (about a six-mile radius) of their camps. The cool, clear weather makes for good tracking and hunting, and small groups of women periodically hike to the mongongo forests to collect nuts. By August, however, many of the preferred local foods have been eaten up and rising temperatures make hunting and long gathering treks hard and uncomfortable. At this time, the Ju/'hoansi turn to less desirable foods—gums and the larger, bitter-tasting roots and melons that they passed up a month or two earlier.

But this period of austerity does not last long. In October the rains begin, filling the hollow trees

and the standing pools in the upcountry with fresh water and transforming the parched landscape into a lush green, thick with new plant and animal life. This is the season of plenty. The Ju/'hoansi now separate into groups of perhaps two or four families and scatter over the land to take advantage of the new crop of fruits, melons, berries, and leafy greens and the new generations of birds and animals that follow the rains. For seven to eight months the small groups move from camp to camp, staying an average of about three days in each spot and returning periodically to the permanent water hole. This pattern continues through April, when the pools of water begin to dry up. In May the wandering upcountry groups return to the permanent water hole to set up new camps, and the cycle begins again (Yellen & Lee, 1976).

The Dobe Ju/'hoansi, then, are an extremely mobile people. Accordingly, their goods are the kind that can be moved easily or left behind. Even houses fall into this category. When a group sets up camp, in a matter of two or three hours each woman constructs a small hut (perhaps 1.5 meters—about 5 feet—in both height and diameter) for her own nuclear family. The huts are arranged in a circle around an open space where the camp activity takes place. Very little goes on in the huts. Indeed, it is unusual to find anyone inside a hut, except perhaps a person who is taking a nap or seeking shelter from a storm (Draper, 1976). A hut serves simply as a storehouse and as a marker, a sign of a family's residence in the camp. When the camp is broken up, the huts, representing little investment of time, energy, or material, are abandoned. Each member of the Ju/'hoansi tribe can pack all of his or her possessions into a pair of leather carrying sacks and be ready to move in a few minutes (Lee, 1993, p. 43).

Social Practices and Group Composition

The Dobe Ju/'hoansi are very gregarious people; they spend about a third of their time visiting other camps and another third entertaining guests. (The size of the camp Lee studied on his first trip varied from twenty-three to forty persons in a single month.) This tradition of conviviality, along with fluctuations in the availability of resources, keeps the Ju/'hoansi on the move. The two factors should

The !Kung are extremely mobile. They construct huts in two or three hours and can abandon them in minutes.

(M. Shostak/Anthrophoto)

not be thought of as independent. In fact, the habit of visiting is probably an adaptation to the necessity of adjusting the populations of camps to local resources. It also facilitates exchanges of information about game and other matters of concern to the dispersed local groups. Both Lorna Marshall (1961, 1965) and Richard Lee (1993) describe the constant babble of voices at night in Ju/'hoansi camps, when residents and visitors exchange notes on rainfall and water holes, ripening vegetables and fruits, and animal tracks in what amounts to a debriefing.

Ju/'hoansi social customs provide not only for short-term visits but also for much lengthier stays. When a couple marries, for example, the husband moves to the wife's camp for an indefinite period of **bride service**—payment for his bride in the form of labor—and he may well bring his parents or a sibling with him. Usually he stays with his wife's people until the birth of their third child (about ten years). At that point he may return to the group into which he was born (perhaps taking some of his wife's kin along), or stay where he is, or move to a camp where one of his brothers is doing bride service or where his wife's siblings have settled. Bride service may also have evolved as a way for parents to keep their brides, who can be as young as nine or ten, at home for a longer period of time (Lee, 1993, p. 66). Since people are marrying later today, this service is also changing.

Such shifts are not limited to bride-service graduates. Any Ju/'hoansi family may leave their group and move into another group where they have kin. Kinship is interpreted very broadly. The Ju/'hoansi recognize ties among all individuals who share the same name, and address all of that person's relatives by kinship terms. Because the number of names used among the Ju/'hoansi is limited, a person is quite likely to find a name-mate in camps where he or she has no relatives and be welcomed there too. Thus the Ju/'hoansi have considerable freedom of choice with regard to residence. Lee (1968) estimates that every year about a third of the population makes a shift in group affiliation.

These changes in group composition, like the rounds of brief visits, help the Ju/'hoansi to tailor the populations of their camps to local resources. At the same time, the flexibility of the group helps to prevent quarrels from turning into serious fights, which are carefully avoided. The Ju/'hoansi are keenly aware that they all possess poisoned arrows and that fights have been known to end in killing. To avoid such an outcome, families that cannot get along together simply separate—one or both of them moving to another group.

Reciprocity

The Ju/'hoansi have a saying, "Only lions eat alone." One of the characteristics that distinguish human beings from other animals, they are saying, is sharing and exchange. Though all humans share periodically, the Ju/'hoansi system of distributing goods is characterized by continuous giving and receiving of gifts. Reciprocity, or *hxaro,* is the basis of their economy and much of their social life as well (Lee, 1993). Hxaro is practiced daily as adults hunt and gather over a wide area. Working individually or in pairs, they find a variety of foods that they share with the entire camp.

It is easy to over-romanticize the altruism of this system. The appropriate distribution of food is a common cause of quarreling among the Ju/'hoansi. The way the day's take is divided depends on a variety of factors. In some cases, as when someone has brought in a large animal, the distribution is rather formalized. The owner (the person who owns the fatal arrow, whether or not he actually killed the animal) divides the meat into portions according to the size of the hunting party. The recipients then cut up their shares and distribute them among their relatives and friends, who in turn give pieces to their relatives, and so forth, until everyone has eaten.

The size and distribution of shares of meat are matters of individual discretion, but the Ju/'hoansi take care to meet their families' needs and to repay past generosity. Smaller animals and vegetables are distributed more informally. A family may invite someone standing nearby to sit at their fire, send children to neighbors with gifts of raw or cooked vegetables, or take fatty bits of meat and nuts with them on a visit. Thus each family's dinner is a combination of the food its members collected and the food they are given. The exchange of food constitutes an effective system that permits each family to store up good will and obligation against times of need.

The various artifacts used or enjoyed in daily life circulate in a similar manner. When a person receives an arrow or a dance rattle as a gift, he keeps it for a few months then passes it on to someone else with the expectation of receiving a gift of more or less equal value in the future. As with food, the giver expects no immediate return, nor is there any systematic way to calculate the relative worth of gifts or to guarantee that the other person will reciprocate in kind. The Ju/'hoansi consider bargaining and direct exchange undignified, and although they trade with the Bantu, they never

trade among themselves. Food sharing and gift giving are based on norms of reciprocity that are understood and accepted by all Ju/'hoansi; as they put it, "we do not trade with things, we trade with people" (Lee, 1993, p. 104).

Quality of Life

We have briefly described the Dobe Ju/'hoansi's way of life. Before Lee and his colleagues began their study of these people, it was widely assumed that the Dobe Ju/'hoansi (indeed, all foragers) waged a constant struggle for survival, battling hunger and poor nutrition from day to day. After all, the Ju/'hoansi live in an area where game is scarce, their weapons are unsophisticated, and they have no way of storing their food. On the surface, they seem to lead a precarious, hand-to-mouth existence. Yet as Lee established through his painstaking research in the 1960s, the appearance bears little relation to the reality. In comparison with some other groups, the Dobe Ju/'hoansi lead secure and easy lives (Lee & Devore, 1968; Lee, 1969, 1993).

Diet and Nutrition

From July 6 through August 2, 1964, Lee kept a diary of subsistence activities at an average dry-season camp. (Remember that this is a period of relative scarcity.) Each day he recorded the number of people in camp, the number that went out to hunt or gather, and the hours each spent acquiring food. He weighed all the animals the hunters brought back to camp during this period and all the bags of nuts and other foods that the women acquired in the course of each day's foraging. He even counted the number of mongongo nuts the Ju/'hoansi cracked and consumed in an hour. By dividing the population of the camp in a given week into the total amount of meat and vegetable foods acquired and then into the total number of hours devoted to their preparation, Lee was able to calculate the Ju/'hoansi work week and daily consumption of food. The results were surprising.

Lee found that the vegetable foods the women gather account for the bulk of the Ju/'hoansi diet by weight; the meat that the men bring in amounts to only 20 to 25 percent. Meat, then, is a delicacy for the Ju/'hoansi, not a staple. The reason is obvious: a man who spends four hours hunting may kill one animal (this is the average), whereas a woman who goes out to gather vegetable foods always finds something for her family to eat, even if it is not an especially choice item. Lee estimates that gathering is 2.4 times as productive as hunting in the Dobe area. One man-hour of hunting brings in approximately 800 calories; one woman-hour of gathering, approximately 2,000 calories. Thus the success of the hunt is not the critical variable in survival as it was once thought to be. It is vegetable foods, not meats, that form the basis of the Ju/'hoansi diet—and it is the women, not the men, who are the chief breadwinners in Ju/'hoansi society.

Drought-resistant mongongo nuts are the Ju/'hoansi staple, making up 50 percent of the vegetable diet. The average daily consumption (about 300 nuts) provides an individual with 1,260 calories and 56 grams of protein—the equivalent of 2.5 pounds of rice or 9 ounces of lean meat. In addition, everyone in the camp Lee studied ate an average of about 9 ounces of meat per day. Together mongongo nuts and meat gave each person 2,140 calories and 92.1 grams of protein per day—well over the U.S. recommended daily allowance (1,975 calories and 60 grams of protein) for small, active people such as the Ju/'hoansi.

Not only do the Ju/'hoansi eat well, they do so with little effort. By counting the numbers of hours each person devoted to acquiring food during the twenty-eight-day period, Lee discovered that by Western standards the Ju/'hoansi invest relatively little energy in the quest for food. Typically a man will spend five or six days hunting, then take a week or two off to rest, visit, and arrange the all-night dances that the Ju/'hoansi hold two or three times a week. Furthermore, it is not at all unusual for a man to decide his luck has run out temporarily and take a month's vacation. The women also have considerable leisure. In one day a woman collects enough food to feed her family for three days. Household chores take between one and three hours. Plenty of free time is left to rest, visit, and entertain. Lee calculated that the average Dobe Ju/'hoansi adult spends only six hours a day acquiring food, two and a half days a week—a total of fifteen hours a week.

Demography

The work week figures are all the more surprising when one considers Ju/'hoansi demography. It was once thought that few people in such societies lived beyond what we consider middle age. This assumption, too, has proved to be unfounded—at least for the Dobe Ju/'hoansi. Lee found that 10 percent of the Dobe residents were over sixty years old. These old people do not participate directly in food procurement. Neither do the young, who constitute another 30 percent of the population. Unlike other African foragers, Ju/'hoansi children do not actively contribute to subsistence activities; they are kept in camp or with their mothers until adolescence (Jones et al., 1994, pp. 189–215); a fact that puts a greater strain on those who actively provision the family. (Ju/'hoansi do not expect young people to work regularly until they marry, usually between ages fifteen and twenty for women, twenty and twenty-five for men.) Thus, 40 percent of the population are dependents who live on the food that the young and middle-aged adults bring in. Such a proportion of nonproducers is surprisingly high, resembling that in agricultural communities.

At first glance these figures may suggest that if the Dobe Ju/'hoansi worked harder, they could support a much larger population. This is not the case, however, for while the people as a whole could certainly spend, say, twice as many hours collecting food, the Dobe environment could not produce twice as much food for them to collect or twice as much water for them to drink.

This observation brings us to a factor that seems to be crucial to the Dobe Ju/'hoansi's way of life: the control of population growth. The well-being of any group, human or otherwise, depends in large part on the ratio of population to resources. For hunter-gatherers this ratio is especially critical, since, unlike agriculturists, they cannot increase their resources.

The Dobe Ju/'hoansi are particularly interesting in this regard, for their fertility is unusually low. On the average, Ju/'hoansi women do not become pregnant again until four years after the birth of the previous child. The Ju/'hoansi do not have a long postpartum taboo (that is, prescribed abstinence from sexual intercourse after childbirth), nor do they use chemical or mechanical birth control devices. The women of Dobe attribute their low fertility to "the stinginess of their god, who loves children and tries to keep them all to himself in heaven" (Howell, 1976, p. 147). Prolonged breast feeding is probably a factor. Because they have no soft foods on which to wean infants, Ju/'hoansi mothers nurse their babies for at least three years, until the child is able to digest the tough foods of the Ju/'hoansi diet (Draper, 1976). Breast feeding is not a guaranteed birth control technique, but it does inhibit ovulation to some degree. Nancy Howell has suggested that gonorrhea, probably introduced through contact with Bantu and Europeans, may have reduced the fertility of some Ju/'hoansi women. Of course, infant mortality, including occasional infanticide, is also a factor in the wide spacing of Ju/'hoansi siblings. Twenty percent of infants die in their first year (Howell, 1976).

This factor of controlled population, along with other factors that we have discussed (high mobility, flexibility of group membership, reciprocity, and a low energy budget) allows the Ju/'hoansi to strike a balance with their environment. This is not to suggest that the foraging life does not have its own hazards and limitations. Climatic and other disturbances can cause hunger, even starvation. By keeping their numbers and their energy needs low and by operating on the principle of flow—flow of groups over the land, flow of people between groups, flow of resources among people—they are able to fit their needs to what their habitat has to offer from day to day. As a result, they live a relatively easy life; they eat well, work only in their middle years, and have time to rest and play. They are also well-prepared for hardship. In times of shortage, Bantu pastoralists fare worse than the Ju/'hoansi, and Bantu women turn to foraging with the Ju/'hoansi to feed their families. Though the Dobe Ju/'hoansi may not qualify as "the original affluent society," as Marshall Sahlins has termed the early hunter-gatherers, their adaptive pattern is still remarkable in that it yields them such a stable and comfortable existence within such an austere habitat.

The People of the Dobe Today

In 1963, three-quarters of the Dobe area people had been relying on hunting and gathering and there was a virtual absence of institutions associated with the state and a market economy: stores,

Traditional diet in the Dobe area relied heavily on nuts, roots, and grass seeds gathered by women.
(M. Shostak/Anthrophoto)

schools, clinics, feeding stations, drilled wells, or air strips. In 1967, the first trading post opened near the region (although the Ju/'hoansi had no money) and also a fence was erected that cut them off from their nearest neighbors, the Nyae Nyae. Since foraging was greatly restricted by the fence and since the government offered assistance in starting cattle herds, many began to build semipermanent mud-walled houses near cattle kraals (enclosures). Many, too, became dependent on government feeding programs, a problem made worse by the game laws of the 1980s that limited their rights to hunt. Even the shape of the village changed, reflecting a changed social order (Lee, 1993, p. 156). Instead of houses drawn up in a

Today, the people of Dobe increasingly live in permanent government-built settlements and work in agriculture or for wages. This man has used his wages to buy a car.

(N. M. Namisea))

circle, the new ones are all in a line and focused on their private property: the herds. While formerly their diets had made them a population with remarkably low levels of serum cholesterol and a general absence of heart disease, this has changed (pp. 156–157). Their present diet is dominated by refined carbohydrates, together with heavy tobacco and alcohol consumption. Many men were induced to sign up with the South African Army during its long war in Angola, dramatically increasing the cash in circulation. The film, *N!ai: The Story of a !Kung Woman,* documents the militarization and alcohol-induced brawling that characterizes some settlements.

Namibian independence from South Africa in 1990 has brought its own changes, some good and some bad. On the negative side, the people of the Kalahari have become relatively poor and are a weakly represented minority in their own lands. Positively, the new government is recognizing their rights to control their own traditional lands and to restrict outsiders from setting up commercial ranches at will, although elements of this have yet to be worked out (Lee, 1993, pp. 164–165).

Not all has changed; when Richard Lee and others returned, they found familiar faces and people caring for each other and sharing in the manner they recalled from the 1960s. Moreover, the people have retained their dignity and cultural self-identity. Lee attributes this to what he calls their

"communal mode of production" and egalitarian spirit (1993, p. 174). This has enabled them to persist in the face of integration into the contemporary market economy. People still take care of one another and, while eager to accumulate consumer goods, they take care to do so within limits. Care for the elders and the infirm is seen as natural—their entitlement—and not a burden. There are lessons for us here, he concludes.

The Inuit or Eskimo

Until quite recently the Eskimo peoples[3] who lived on the vast, treeless plains (or tundra) and along the changing coastlines of the Arctic were isolated from the rest of the world by their formidable environment. Like the Dobe Ju/'hoansi, they occupied land that no one else wanted and so for centuries they remained self-sufficient hunters and gatherers, relatively uninfluenced by the agricul-

[3] Our discussion will be based primarily on Asem Balikci's now classic study (1970, 1989) of the Netsilik Eskimo of northeastern Canada and Ernest Burch's study of the Inupiat in northwestern Canada (1970, 1994) with reference also to William B. Kemp's study (1971) among the Baffin Island Eskimo and a recent summary and synthesis by William Sturtevant and David Damas (1984). Keep in mind that the various groups we describe are widely separated and that among the Eskimo there are many variations in language, custom, and ways of making a living.

tural and industrial societies that grew up to the south of them in the more fertile regions of the North American continent. The Inuit Eskimo language family, dialects of which are spoken by the dispersed people we will be describing, is distributed over a vast area, from Northwest Alaska and Canada to the coasts of eastern Greenland and Labrador. For this reason we shall refer to them as Inuit (Burch, 1994).

Since the beginning of this century the isolation of the Inuit has slowly broken down. Money has become an important factor in their relationship with their environment. While most Inuit groups are fully settled today, some are still hunter-gatherers and in some ways resemble the Dobe Ju/'hoansi. At the same time, because of cultural changes resulting from their buying and selling in the world market and because of their residence in the United States and Canada—not to mention their unique habitat—they provide an interesting contrast to the Ju/'hoansi.

The Arctic Ecosystem

If the Dobe seems an inhospitable environment, the Arctic circumpolar region of North America seems almost uninhabitable. Throughout much of the region, from October through July, the waters are locked in ice while the land lies frozen and almost bare of plant and animal life. During this period (the local population's fall, winter, and spring), the Arctic animals, with the exception of seals and walruses, either migrate south or hibernate. By midwinter the ice is six to seven feet thick. Temperatures during the eighteen-hour Arctic nights may drop from a mean of −16°C (−30°F) to −27°C (−50°F). Forty-mile-an-hour winds with gusts up to seventy miles an hour are common. In the Hudson Strait area, forty-five-foot tides build walls of broken ice along the coast, making navigation extremely hazardous.

In most years, the freeze continues into late July. Then this land on top of the world enjoys a brief summer. Temperatures rise above freezing, and daylight lasts as long as twenty-two hours. Lichens, mosses, shrubs, and tufted grasses sprout on the tundra, attracting a variety of wildlife: herds of caribou, musk oxen, polar bears, foxes, rabbits, and migratory birds. Seals and walruses bask in the sun; whales may appear; large schools of salmon run downriver to the sea in July or thereabouts, returning to inland lakes in August. But this Arctic summer lasts a short six to twelve weeks. The sea begins to ice over in late September, and the long freeze begins once again.

Foraging in this environment is quite different from living off wild foods in the Dobe area. Except for the summer berries, there are no vegetables, edible roots, or fruits in the Arctic; the long, dark winters, incessant winds, poor soil, and short growing season discourage plant life. The Inuit's subsistence strategy is centered on animal life—on hunting, fishing, and, to a lesser extent, trapping and gathering of duck eggs, clams, and the like. And whereas the availability of water largely determines the migrations of the Dobe Ju/'hoansi, it is the availability of animals and fish that structures the Inuit's patterns of movement.

The Seasonal Migrations

Like the Dobe Ju/'hoansi, most circumpolar populations are to some degree nomadic people, changing the sizes and locations of their camps as their resources change with the seasons. The pattern of these migrations is essentially the same as with the Ju/'hoansi: dispersal in small groups in the season of plenty, concentration in large groups in the time of scarcity. Again employing the ethnographic present, we will examine the pattern of livelihood and social life of one population, the Netsilik Eskimo, and then turn our attention westward to their distant relatives in Alaska.

In the summer, when food is abundant, the Hudson Bay Netsilik Eskimo traditionally form small groups of twenty to thirty people consisting of one or more extended families, and move inland to take advantage of fish runs and caribou migrations. Each August, for example, the Netsilik carry their belongings up the waterways to the stone weirs (circular dams) they have built to trap schools of salmon. Some of the fish are eaten raw, on the spot; the rest are dried and stored for the winter.

Toward the end of the month the group packs up once again and moves farther inland to await the coming of the caribou. Depending on the terrain, the Netsilik may construct knife-lined pits in

Most Eskimos have turned to modern, high-powered rifles, but they complain that these weapons have destroyed the mutual trust between animals and humans.

(Gordon Wittsie/Peter Arnold Inc.)

the caribou's paths (which are well-known to the Inuit) or stalk them with guns, much as in earlier days when they hunted with bows and arrows. Another common technique is to stampede the animals into a trap. Howling in imitation of wolves, a few men drive the herd into a narrow valley where hunters lie concealed, or into a river where the hunters wait in kayaks. Caribou provide not only meat but also another crucial resource: skins for clothing. In 1970, Balikci estimated that a family of four needs about thirty skins to see them through each winter. In October and November the Netsilik live primarily on food stored during the caribou hunts, supplemented by occasional

fresh fish and musk ox. The most important activity in this period is making winter clothing, a job that is performed by the women.

In December, the scattered Netsilik come together once again in their winter camps along the bays and straits, where fifty, sixty, or as many as one hundred people join forces to hunt the major cold-season resource: seals. Although some seals migrate south for the winter, others remain in the Arctic, digging breathing holes up through the sea ice. (Seals need air every fifteen to twenty minutes and dig several holes.) Hunting seals in midwinter involves hours of silent, motionless waiting at the breathing holes, harpoon in hand. For much of the winter, seals plus an occasional fox are the only sources of fresh food.

In May or June, when the ice begins to melt, the Netsilik move to tents on solid ground. Hunting seals is easier and more productive in these months, for the animals often come out of the water. By July the ice starts to crack and seal hunting becomes dangerous, so the Netsilik camps divide once again into smaller groups for their annual inland treks (Balikci, 1989, chap. 2).

The Inuit's seasonal round is similar to that of the Dobe Ju/'hoansi, but there are important differences between the patterns of the two groups. For one thing, the Inuit, unlike the Ju/'hoansi, can store food. When fish are running and game is abundant, they collect as much as they can and smoke or store the surplus in stone or ice caches. However, the cold also requires the Inuit to work on a higher energy budget than the Ju/'hoansi. In such a climate, simply to stay alive (to say nothing of hunting) requires a relatively high-calorie diet. Furthermore, the Inuit have to invest a good deal of energy in the task of protecting their bodies from the cold: building shelters (traditionally igloos in the winter and skin tents in the summer), making clothing (multilayered garments, boots, and mittens), and heating their shelters (with seal-oil lamps or kerosene stoves). And they have to feed their sled dogs, a vital component of their traditional nomadic way of life.

These activities require not only considerable energy but an accumulation of material goods. While the Ju/'hoansi travel light, the Inuit, with their dogsleds and snowmobiles, motorboats, tools, rifles, clothing, lamps, and stockpiles of food, have a good deal to carry around. Further-more, their tents and igloos, unlike the Ju/'hoansi's disposable huts, take time to build and cannot be lightly abandoned. Hence, even during the summer season, the Inuit change camps much less often than the Ju/'hoansi.

Demography

From what we can gather from early explorers' and ethnographers' accounts, this way of life did not enable the Inuit to support sizable numbers of dependents, or at least not in bad years. Old and sick individuals who could not keep up with the group were occasionally left behind to manage for themselves—in other words, to die (Balikci, 1970). Furthermore, the unequal sex ratio in some Inuit groups at the turn of the century suggests that they also limited the number of the dependent young through female infanticide (see Freeman, 1971; Balikci, 1970, 1989).

In some cases, population controls were probably quite deliberate attempts at family planning. The threat of hunger is a recurring theme in Inuit conversation, even in communities where the evidence indicates that hunting accidents have caused many more deaths over the years than hunger (Kemp, 1971)—and one way to stave off hunger is to limit the number of nonproducers to ensure that at least some children survive. The archaeological record does contain evidence of some large and formal villages that were exceptions to this pattern, but they appear to have been short-lived.

The ratio of population to food resources may become a more realistic worry in the near future, for Inuit populations are rapidly increasing. With improved health care supplied by the United States and Canadian governments, the mortality rate has declined steadily in recent years. At the same time, their fertility rate has increased. In the Inuit community of Wainwright, Alaska, for example, the average woman gives birth to nine or ten live children in the course of her reproductive years. The average Dobe Ju/'hoansi woman, on the other hand, has five. As a result, the population of this group is growing at a rate of 3 percent a year (Milan, 1970), six times the 0.5 percent rate of the Dobe Ju/'hoansi. Other groups are expanding at similar rates, putting a strain on their ecosystems.

Social Relationships

The Inuit, like most other hunter-gatherers, have extensive networks of kin, but the most important social unit is the extended family. This is considered to be the "real family." Jean Briggs notes in her study of the Uktu in Hudson Bay (neighbors of the Netsilik), "Whenever possible, it is with their 'real family' that the people live, work, travel, and share whatever they have. Moreover, it is only with their 'real family' that they appear to feel completely comfortable and safe" (1970, p. 39). These extended families are organized into larger kin groups that generally camp and work together. Like the Dobe Ju/'hoansi, however, Inuit families have considerable latitude in choosing the people with whom they will camp. It is common for everyone in an Inuit society to be considered kin to everyone else—if not by blood, then by marriage, adoption, or shared names (a practice that we have already seen among the Ju/'hoansi). These extensive ties allow families to shift about on short-term and long-term visits and thus enable the Inuit to adjust the makeup of their groups according to the availability of resources and personal preference, especially in the scattered inland camps during the summer and fall.

In their personal relationships, the Inuit place great value on restraint. Demonstrations of emotion are frowned upon. Briggs (1970) noted that Uktu husbands and wives and their older children never kiss, embrace, or even touch one another in front of anyone else. Even more unwelcome is a show of negative feelings, especially anger. To these Inuit, the ideal personality traits are shyness, patience, generosity, and an even temper.

It is no surprise that many local populations traditionally had no formal group leadership. Though a man with a reputation for wisdom or expertise in hunting may come to have some influence in decision making, anyone who tries unabashedly to impose his will on others is regarded with deep suspicion. Likewise, the Inuit have no formal code for dealing with people who violate social norms. Stingy or bad-tempered individuals are not directly criticized or punished; rather, the others will try to soothe or tease them out of their folly. If this strategy does not work, the offender is simply avoided. The worst punishment that Inuit societies can inflict is ostracism, a very serious threat in harsh Arctic conditions.

The Impact of Modernization

After Balikci's investigation, William Kemp (1971) made a careful study of energy use in one of the last all-Inuit communities on Baffin Island, to the north of Netsilik territory. The value of his observations lie in his documentation of the effects of new technology on energy use. These were changes that have transformed all Inuit communities, including the Pella Bay community studied by Balikci.

The village Kemp studied consisted of four households whose total population varied from twenty-six to twenty-nine over the period of the study. Three of the families lived in wood-frame tents covered with skins and old mailbags that the people had sewn together and insulated with a layer of dry shrubs. These tents were heated by traditional seal-oil lamps. The fourth family lived in a prefabricated wood house supplied by the government and heated by a kerosene stove.

This house was not the village's only sign of industrial technology. Among them, the villagers owned two snowmobiles, a large motorized whaling boat, and a twenty-two-foot freight canoe with an outboard motor, along with several large sledges and thirty-four sled dogs. In 1971 hunting was still the most important subsistence activity, but they were also hunting with rifles as well as harpoons. The younger men spent only part of their time hunting; they also mined soapstone and carved it into statuettes for export, and some of the young men left the village periodically to work for wages at government construction sites. In one year, village members earned $3,500 from carvings, $1,360 from animal skins, $1,225 in wages, and $670 in government subsidies.

Energy Flow among the Baffin Islanders. Kemp's 1971 analysis of energy flow in this small community was similar to Lee's study of the Dobe Ju/'hoansi's subsistence practices and standard of living. But Kemp had to take into account the use of fuel as well as muscle power, the hours spent working for wages as well as foraging, and the acquisition of store-bought as well as wild foods. To calculate the energy flow, he reduced both the num-

ber of hours individuals spent at various activities and the various foods they acquired and consumed to the common denominator of kilocalories (thousands of calories). This procedure enabled him to analyze in considerable detail the sources of energy, the routes along which it flowed, and the uses to which it was put.

Kemp calculated that over the fifty-four weeks during which he kept records of village activities, the Inuit expended some 12.8 million kilocalories of human energy in hunting, mining, and carving; working for wages; taking care of household chores; traveling; and visiting. In addition, they used 885 gallons of gasoline, 615 gallons of kerosene, and 10,900 rounds of ammunition. During the same period they acquired 12.8 million kilocalories in wild food for human consumption (plus 7.5 million kilocalories in food for the dogs) and 7.5 million kilocalories in store-bought food. Thus important sources of energy lie outside the local economy, and indeed the Inuit are as dependent on industry and fossil fuels as is the rest of North America's population. They may spend more time and energy in hunting, but such activities as wage labor and soapstone carving force them to depend on critical inputs of imported energy.

When observed, the Inuit ate well. Game—primarily seal but also whale, caribou, and other animals—remains their dietary staple, accounting for 85 percent of their food. In Pella Bay, the villagers have given up seal hunting and rely mostly on caribou, which has a better taste, and does not involve traveling far from the settlement. The Baffin Island villagers rarely bought canned meat and vegetables, though they did purchase sugar, powdered milk, quantities of flour and lard for bannock (a pan-baked bread), and small amounts of such delicacies as peanut butter and honey. Kemp estimates that this combination of wild and store-bought food provides each adult with 3,000 calories a day. The Inuit's calorie intake, then, is about 50 percent higher than that of the Dobe Ju/'hoansi. Their protein intake, accounting for 44 percent of their calories, is also quite high—a reflection of their heavy dependence on game. Of their remaining foodstuffs, 33 percent are in the form of carbohydrates and 23 percent in fat. Such a diet fortifies them for the exertions of Arctic life. Kemp noted, however, that when the men of one household abandoned hunting for a month to work for wages and the family ate only store-bought food, 62 percent of their diet consisted of carbohydrates and only 9 percent of protein—an unhealthy balance. Such a diet resembles that of the poor in North American cities, who rely heavily on factory-prepared snack foods.

Changes in Settlement Patterns and Hunting Techniques. The products of industrialization—motorized vehicles, high-powered weapons, store-bought foods—have affected the relationship between the Inuit and their environment throughout the circumpolar region. Almost everywhere the people have become sedentary, living in year-around villages or towns. Settling in towns has meant that Inuit children can attend schools near their homes; going to high school no longer means that a student has to move to a distant boarding school (Burch, 1994). Snowmobiles and boats enable hunters to travel to their hunting grounds in a relatively short time, so it is no longer necessary for the whole village to pack up and move. Store-bought food provides the insurance against hunger that was once provided by seasonal moves to exploit a wide variety of game. However, caribou is still an important food item among the Inuit (Burch, 1994), and it is easily hunted with new high-powered rifles.

While many Inuit value the introduction of the rifles, some complain that it has destroyed the mutual trust between humans and animals (Kemp, 1971). Seals are wary of the rumbling motors and rifle reports; only young animals can be coaxed within shooting range. Also, when guns were first introduced in the late nineteenth century they led to the near-extinction of native caribou herds. Today, however, caribou have been reintroduced and are now regulated by the U.S. government (Burch, 1994).

The Inuit point out that rifles are not necessarily better than their old weapons. In the spring, for example, seals fast, losing their winter layer of fat; when melting snow reduces the salinity of the water, the animals are less buoyant. Unless an animal that has been killed by a rifle is immediately secured with a harpoon, it will sink—a fact that renders long-range weapons useless. Kemp notes that in one thirty-hour session of continuous hunt-

An Inuit woman shopping in a supermarket in Baffin Island, Canada. Even though all now purchase most of their food from shops, hunting remains culturally and nutritionally important.
(Kevin Fleming/Woodfin Camp & Associates)

ing, the Inuit killed thirteen seals but retrieved only five.

Kemp observed that, in the fall, the hunt yielded enough food to last through the winter, so the villagers were able to spend more time visiting than hunting in February, March, and April. Although they might have used this time to collect extra skins for trading (and perhaps dangerously reduce the seal population in the process), they chose to travel instead. Whether this choice was based on conservationist concerns is debatable. The people may have been conscious of the need to preserve the supply of wild game. They may also have decided that the returns on hunting were simply less than those gained from the time spent on craft production, wage labor, or even than the rewards of visiting friends and relatives. Practices that limit hunting—visiting days, the soapstone industry, even the custom of observing Sundays as a day of leisure—help the Inuit maintain a balance between their needs and their resources.

Adaptation is not simply a matter of the direct interplay between technology and the environment. Rifles and snowmobiles do not inevitably spell ecological disaster, for social customs intervene between technology and the uses to which it is put. The need to earn money through carving

The contemporary Inuit settlement of Igaluit, Baffin Island, Canada. Recent changes in Canadian law that gives native peoples control over their resources has transformed Inuit society in recent years. (Bryan & Cherry Alexander)

takes young men away from the hunt. And the same snowmobiles that enable them to kill more sea mammals give them the option to forgo hunting and visit distant kin when they have enough to eat.

Surviving in the Modern World. The Inuit ethic of sharing is evident in the way the Pella Bay Inuit adapted to the introduction of the mission store. As the Inuit became more and more integrated into the wider market economy, the original store was replaced by a cooperative store, owned and managed by the Inuit to serve the community. This proved to be a successful operation, not only addressing the needs of those who wanted to buy and sell goods, but also providing an interface between the community and the government, negotiating for government contracts and the like. The co-op became "the principal economic integrator of the community and the mediating agency between the community, the government and the Euro-Canadian economic system in all matters of commerce and economic enterprise" (Balicki, 1989, p. 253).

While modernization has transformed the lives of the Inuit, they have managed to retain elements of their traditional culture. Despite the physical distance that now exists between members of a kin group, they maintain ties through telephones and CB radios. In the Inupiat territory, in northwestern Alaska, where 74 percent of the population is Inuit, the Inuit language remains in use and is taught in schools, and traditional food is still preferred by most. In the State of the Peoples box, *Claiming the Land* (p. 117), we see how the Inuit continue to change and how they have begun to fight for the rights to their land.

In September, 1988, the Canadian government passed legislation giving the Inuit and other native peoples of the Canadian northern territories formal title to their extensive and potentially resource-laden lands. The economic and social future of the Inuit appears to be far brighter than that of other contemporary hunters and gatherers.

State of the Peoples

Claiming the Land

IN ALASKA, THERE HAS BEEN A profound transformation in the economies and ways of life of indigenous peoples in the course of the Cold War and in the aftermath of oil exploration. During the long period of rivalry with the former U.S.S.R, the U.S. government considered Inupiat territory on the Beaufort Sea to be a front-line area. While building bases offered a certain amount of employment, traditional patterns of hunting and fishing were disrupted by the appropriation of 4,500 acres (as an air base) and all of Barter Island—causing forced relocations (Chance, 1990, p. 141). Later, following several years of planning in which the Inupiat were not invited to participate, the Atomic Energy Commission, with the support of the Alaskan state government, announced a plan to detonate one or more atomic weapons in Inupiat territory in order to create an artificial harbor (Chance, 1990, pp. 140–143). This occasioned such local outrage that people organized in opposition, thus for the

first time creating a united Inupiat political organization devoted to securing their aboriginal land rights—a movement that came to cooperate with other Native American political action committees (Chance, 1990, pp. 140–143). Soon they were able to defeat the proposed harbor project and, more importantly, set in motion a political mechanism—the Alaska Federation of Natives—for dealing with nonindigenous forces—namely, the state and federal bureaucracies, oil companies, and business interests. This organization was soon to become a significant political voice.

After years of litigation, Inupiat and other Alaskan populations have received substantial allocations of land as well as a percentage of oil and gas royalties. While welcome to many, it is, for others scant compensation for what they have lost: their autonomy. Oil wealth has transformed life; the village of Katovik where Norman Chance had lived in 1958 now has modern housing, a new school

with an indoor pool, government offices, and shops (1990, pp. 200–201). While subsistence and nutrition are still based on fishing and hunting, the Inupiat use three-wheelers and snowmobiles to check their nets and take game. While the older generation retain the old skills, the younger, educated members of the community do not have the self-reliance of their parents. They are, however, being educated in modern facilities, they travel widely, and they are finding employment in the larger U.S. economy. This, in turn, has given them a new perspective on their personal needs—one that is much like that shared throughout the American population. The dilemma facing the Inupiat—indeed, all of us—is how these new needs can be satisfied in the face of unequal distribution of wealth and without even greater environmental risks being taken (Chance, 1990, p. 218).

Summary

THE FORAGING ADAPTIVE PATTERN, WHICH HAS been dominant for much of human existence, is illustrated in this chapter by the Dobe Ju/'hoansi of the Kalahari Desert and the Inuit of northeastern Canada.

Foraging peoples traditionally have been self-sufficient but they are becoming less so as they become less isolated from the dominant societies around them. Unlike societies that cultivate their food resources, hunter-gatherers eat what nature provides and diversify their diet to accommodate fluctuations in resources. Survival necessitates an adaptive pattern that balances resources, the group's technology, and its social organization.

Foragers typically live in small, flexible groups that can scatter when natural resources become scarce and converge when resources again become plentiful. Some hunter-gatherers move regularly from campsite to campsite as resources become available in various locations; others occupy a permanent settlement from which they move to temporary camps to exploit seasonally available resources. Their kinship system creates ties over large areas, so that people can move in and out of groups as resources fluctuate. Reciprocity—the sharing of food and other goods—also allows hunter-gatherers to adapt to fluctuations in resources. Their systems of decision making and social control tend to be informal.

One reason for the success of hunter-gatherers is their low energy budget. They invest relatively little energy in the quest for food resources and obtain substantial returns. Their traditional adaptive strategy of low energy needs, a wide resource base, and a controlled population results in minimum interference with their ecosystem. Hunter-gatherers risk wiping out their resources when they attempt to exploit them for an unlimited world market.

The Ju/'hoansi San occupy the Dobe area on the northern edge of the Kalahari Desert. They are able to satisfy their needs and live comfortably in this inhospitable region by exploiting a wide variety of resources. Seasonal migrations are necessary because of fluctuations in the availability of water. The nomadic Ju/'hoansi possess only goods that can be moved easily or left behind. Social practices contribute to the mobility of the Ju/'hoansi and the flexibility of their groups. The Ju/'hoansi enjoy visiting kin in other camps, and bride service can take families to other groups for indefinite periods. Flexibility in group composition helps tailor population size to local resources and also helps to reduce friction among group members.

Although meat (hunted by men) is a prized resource, vegetables and fruits (gathered chiefly by women) are the staples of the Ju/'hoansi diet. The quality of the Ju/'hoansi's life is apparently quite high; their diet is nutritionally sound and procured with relatively little expenditure of energy, and they enjoy a great deal of leisure time. A low birth rate is crucial to the Ju/'hoansi adaptive pattern.

The Inuit have traditionally depended on a seasonal quest for animals to provide food, clothing, tools, and fuel. Contact with the world market, however, has eroded the isolation and self-sufficiency of the Inuit.

The Arctic environment dictates the adaptive patterns of the Netsilik of northeastern Canada and the Baffin Island Inuit. These people change the sizes and locations of their camps as their resources change with the seasons. In the summer they disperse to take advantage of abundant food, and in the winter they come together to hunt seals. Unlike the Ju/'hoansi, they are able to store food for the long winters but their climate forces them to adopt a higher energy budget than that of the Ju/'hoansi and to accumulate material goods (such as heavy clothing, snowmobiles, lamps, and rifles) that reduce their mobility. In the past the Inuit have kept their population level in harmony with their food resources, but now their population is rapidly increasing, with a resultant strain on their ecosystem.

Extensive kinship ties allow the Inuit, like the Ju/'hoansi, to move easily in and out of groups, but the most important social unit is the extended family. The Inuit frown on shows of emotion or of negative feelings. They have no formalized leadership or code of social control.

A study of the Baffin Island Inuit revealed that their intake of energy is high and their output low. They hunt seal, caribou, and other animals, and catch fish in weirs (circular dams) they have built of stone. Their natural resources are supplemented by store-bought food, particularly the ingredients to make bannock (unleavened bread baked in a shallow pan) and such items as snowmobiles and kerosene stoves.

Industrialization is changing the life of all Inuit. Seasonal migrations are no longer necessary, as they can quickly travel to their hunting grounds by snowmobile, and store-bought food provides insurance against hunger. The introduction of high-powered weapons almost led to the destruction of the Inuit's traditional resource base, but the U.S. government intervened and the caribou herds have returned. Today most Inuit live in villages with most of the amenities of contemporary North American life. Still, they retain their languages, social identities, and many traditional food preferences.

The Inupiat of Alaska illustrate some of the problems contemporary U.S. native peoples face as well as how they have organized to take at least some political control over their own destinies.

Key Terms

bands	low-energy budget
bride service	reciprocity
ethnographic present	

Suggested Readings

Bailey, R. C. (1991). The behavioral ecology of Efe Pygmy men in the Ituri forest, Zaire. *UMMA Anthropological Papers, 86*. Ann Arbor: Museum of Anthropology, University of Michigan. A detailed volume of Efe foraging activity with a focus on time allocation and hunting returns, using a socioecological approach.

Biccheiri, M. G. (Ed.). (1988). *Hunters and gatherers today: A socioeconomic study of eleven such cultures in the twentieth century*. Prospect Heights, IL: Waveland Press. Historical reconstructions and ethnographies provide a general perspective on the adaptations of hunters and gatherers.

Burbank, V. K. (1994). *Fighting women: Anger & aggression in aboriginal Australia*. Berkeley: University of California Press. Contemporary and controversial, this book focuses on the aggressive behavior of Aboriginal women in Australia and offers an interesting perpective on domestic violence.

Burch, Ernest S. Jr. & Ellanna, Linda J. (Eds.). (1994). *Key issues in hunter-gatherer research*. Oxford: Berg. A collection of recent articles based on research among contemporary hunter-gatherers, with an introduction and concluding sections dealing with the general state of such research and its prospects.

Chance, N. A. (1990). *The Inupiat and arctic Alaska: An ethnography of development*. Fort Worth: Holt, Rinehart & Winston. A detailed account of how one population has coped with a changing political environment and sucessfull gained control of much of their traditional lands.

Howell, N. (1979). *Demography of the Dobe Ju/'hoansi.* New York: Academic Press. A thorough analysis of two years of demographic fieldwork with the Dobe Ju/'hoansi that uses stable population theory for its perspective on the functioning of this group.

Lee, R. B. (1993). *The Dobe Ju/'hoansi*. Fort Worth: Harcourt Brace College Publishers. A broadly oriented case study on the hunter-gatherer way of life of the Ju/'hoansi of the Kalahari Desert, exploring topics such as subsistence techniques, kinship, religion, and environment.

Peterson, N. & Matsuyama, T. (Eds.). (1991). Cash commoditization and changing foragers. *Senri Ethnological Studies 30*. Tadeo Umesao, gen. ed. Osaka: National Museum of Ethnology. A collection of eleven essays that address the effects of cash and commoditization processes on recent foraging societies on four continents.

Schrire, C. (Ed.). (1984). *Past and present in hunter-gatherer studies*. Orlando, FL: Academic Press. This collection of papers attempts to understand both the past behavior and current ways of life of hunter-gatherers by focusing on the history of their interactions with other peoples.

Siskind, J. (1973). *To hunt in the morning*. New York: Oxford University Press. An intimate account of fieldwork among the Sharanahua Indians of the Amazon jungle. It is especially interesting for its emphasis on the way modernization is affecting this population.

Sturtevant, W. C. (Ed.). (1984). *Handbook of North American Indians*, vol. 5, Arctic. Washington, D.C.: Smithsonian Institution. Part of an encyclopedic summary of the information available about the prehistory, history, and cultures of the aboriginal peoples of North America in archaeological and ethnographic accounts. The organization of these volumes is by geographical area. Volume 5 deals with the special problems of the regions and populations that together form the Arctic habitat zone.

Turnbull, C. (1961). *The forest people*. New York: Simon & Schuster. An intimate view of the Mbuti Pygmies of equatorial Africa that explores the relationships of the people to the forest and to their horticultural neighbors.

Wilmsen, E. N. (Ed.). (1989). *We are here: Politics of aboriginal land tenure*. Berkeley: University of California Press. An anthropological investigation that explores the issues of aboriginal relations to land and territory.

Winterhalder, B. & Smith, E. A. (Eds.). (1981). *Hunter-gatherer foraging strategies*. Chicago: University of Chicago Press. A collection of ethnographic and archaeological analyses that apply optimal foraging theory.

The Horticultural Adaptation
    Development
    Energy Use and the Ecosystem
    Horticultural Cultivation Methods
    Contemporary Issues: Learning
    about Monoculture from the
    Mountain Ok
    Social Organization

The Yanomamö
    Farming in the Jungle
    Village Life
    Warfare and Violence
    Future Prospects for the Yanamamö
    State of the Peoples: Are the
    Yanomamö Safe?

Subsistence Plow Farming

The Tamang
    The Village
    Field, Forest, and Pasture
    The Domestic Cycle
    Prospects for Timling's Future

Summary

Key Terms

Suggested Readings

Chapter 5

Subsistence Agriculture

In Zimbabwe, a man and his sons burn trees and brush to open a circular field on which they will plant millet; in Brazil, a woman pushes seed yams into the soil of her irregularly shaped garden; in Peru, a family works together to place stones to form a terrace that they will plow in order to plant corn. These mundane, everyday acts, taken cumulatively, sustain many of the earth's some 5.5 billion people. This chapter will look at societies that practice agriculture relying primarily on localized inputs: human labor, locally made tools, and, if used at all, animals for traction (plowing, pumping, and transport). Such forms of agriculture are often termed *subsistence agriculture;* production, even if traded, sold, or bartered, is primarily aimed at household provisioning rather than investment.

Food production, however simple or complex in terms of technology, is the very foundation of contemporary human existence. Foraging, as we have seen, involves the collection of naturally occurring food resources in a given habitat with relatively little intervention or management. Agriculture involves the domestication and management of edible species that characteristically cannot survive or reproduce without human assistance. We have no direct evidence that people who lived in prehistoric times consciously or unconsciously tried to influence the reproductive cycles of the species on which they depended, but since they were intelligent, experiments certainly occurred. Over the ages, however, as people and animals and plants interacted, selective pressures changed the reproductive success of the animals and plants favored by humans.

These changes need not have resulted from a conscious manipulation of a species by the people who used it. Such changes could have come about as inadvertent by-products of the way people were altering their environment—being selective in the killing of members of a particular population, for example, or harvesting grain in such a way as to change the genetic makeup of seeds by selectively retaining some and discarding others. Such selective pressures eventually led to **domestication**, the process by which people began trying to control the reproductive rates of animals and plants by ordering the environment to favor their survival—protecting them from pests, predators, and competitors, for instance, and supplying them with water and nutrients. Ultimately these efforts led to agriculture, one of the most significant achievements of the human species.

The development of agriculture irrevocably affected the course of human cultural history. The full impact of these changes can be seen in the societies that practice intensive agriculture (discussed in Chapter 7), the most productive and technologically sophisticated form of food production. But the contrast from the hunting-and-gathering adaptation can be seen clearly even in societies that practice a modest and comparatively simple form of agriculture: horticulture.

Horticulture, meaning "garden cultivation," is almost always accompanied by some reliance on hunting, fishing, and collecting wild plants. However, unlike hunter-gatherers, horticulturists depend primarily on domesticated foods, especially plants; and unlike intensive or industrialized agriculturists, they raise these plants in small plots using relatively simple methods and tools. Agricultural techniques, along with other forms of behavior, vary widely from group to group. Yet the shared procurement strategy—production of food crops primarily for personal consumption—creates certain broad similarities in settlement patterns, so-

cial organization, and interactions among groups. First, we will examine how the strategy developed and its general features. Then we will focus on two specific groups of farmers: the Yanomamö of Venezuela and Brazil, who live in a tropical rain forest; and the Himalayan Tamang of Nepal, who have adapted to a high-mountain habitat by means of plow agriculture combined with animal husbandry. Although these cases represent very different technologies, they share the fact that human labor is the main input, they can produce themselves all or most of the tools they need for farming, and their households are highly self-sufficient.

The Horticultural Adaptation

Development

By approximately 12,000 years ago a number of local populations in the upland areas of Mesopotamia in the Middle East had started to grow crops, and by 10,000 years ago most of the people of the Middle East had come to rely very heavily on wild cereals: wheat and barley (Fagan, 1992, p. 290ff). This development was closely paralleled in Asia and Africa as well. By about 9,000 years ago, there were signs that people had begun to plant and harvest crops and to domesticate various animal species. This shift in adaptive pattern is of great interest to anthropologists and because it ultimately set in motion greater changes in social life and technology than had occurred over the preceding millennia.

While the earliest evidence of cultivation and herding appears in the Middle East, where wheat and barley were the first staple crops, horticulture also appeared early in China and Southeast Asia. Surprisingly, millet, not rice, was the primary crop in early Chinese cultivation. The origin of rice, one of the world's most important crops, is still poorly understood. While our knowledge of the domestication process in Africa is incomplete, there is evidence for the cultivation of sorghum, millet, and a variety of other plants that dates back some 4,000 years. In Mesoamerica and South America, cultivation appeared thousands of years later than in the Old World. Corn, beans, and squash were the important crops cultivated in higher-altitude areas; manioc was grown in coastal zones.

Egyptian tomb fresco dating from about 3500 B.P. showing a man and his wife plowing and sowing; in the lower panel are various types of fruit trees. Egyptian farmers in a very early period developed plow technology and sophisticated systems of water control which transformed subsistence farming into the basis for sustaining large urban populations.

(Robert Frerck/Odyssey Productions)

Some archaeologists have suggested that agricultural experiments began when humans noticed plants growing from seeds in their garbage dumps. There is evidence that hunter-gatherers were well aware of the relationship between plants and seeds, and it is possible that horticulture began with tending useful herbs. The interesting question is why hunter-gatherers would give up a stable existence for one that requires substantially more work.

However one judges the record, it is clear that people came to exercise more control over their environment. Ultimately, they chose more productive resources, stored seeds, selected from among the seeds those most likely to generate productive plants, and altered the conditions under which the plants were growing by removing weeds and supplying additional water.

Despite many regional differences, the common thread underlying the development and spread of agriculture is that it accomplished population growth or, at least, pressure on resources, and the instability that accompanied it. The most common

early strategy for solving the problem of food procurement was to move to a new location, but as population levels became high in relation to available resources this alternative became less possible and more settled patterns of existence resulted. This new pattern of sedentism probably upset the balance between human groups and the resources on which they depended. When mortality, fertility limitations, or migration were not sufficient to keep a population within acceptable limits, some groups began to manipulate the natural availability of resources (by planting, etc.). This strategy made it possible to sustain a larger number of people without depleting their resources. As these groups grew and spread, other groups imitated their practices. Because they could increase the carrying capacity of their environment in ways in which hunter-gatherers could not, horticulturists became more predominant.

It is important to emphasize that the initial expansion of horticulture did not occur because it was a universally superior adaptation to hunting and gathering. People often had to work harder. Analyses of skeletal material from the time periods suggest that overall health decreased and disease and malnutrition increased. But the increased productivity and reliability of the food supply provided the basis for further population growth, a cycle that has continued to the present. Both depend on the elaboration of methods of cultivation.

Energy Use and the Ecosystem

The objective of any form of agriculture is to increase the amount of predictable or reliable energy that a given unit of land can yield for human use. Although horticulturists usually extract far fewer food calories or other products per acre than do plow farmers (let alone modern, intensive farmers), they also expend less labor than intensive agriculturists. They use neither their land nor their labor to the fullest. Simply producing enough to feed the family takes much less work than people are capable of doing, so that many of the able-bodied (such as adolescents) may not have to work at all while those who do work may do so intermittently and spend more time hunting or in other activities. That is not to say that horticulturists are lazy. They may simply have more options as to how to use their time. A comparison of four populations in the Brazilian Amazon finds that while all hunt to acquire needed protein, those who live in the best horticultural areas hunt the most. Meat is a desired luxury and the men can afford the time to seek it (Werner et al., 1979, pp. 303–315). Horticulturists have time left over after the minimum required subsistence tasks to devote to elaborate food preparation, ceremonies, and luxury items beyond their basic needs.

In general, the lower the energy demands a human group makes on its environment, the less the group alters that environment. Clifford Geertz, in an early and very influential discussion of the subject, has argued that swidden farmers in the tropical lowlands do not so much alter their ecosystems as create "a canny imitation" of it (1969, p. 6). Their ecosystem contains a remarkable diversity of living things packed in a small area—that is, the ecosystem is generalized rather than specialized. Although tropical soil is often thin, it can support this dense variety because the nutrients are rapidly recycled rather than being locked up in deep soil.

The dense canopy of trees prevents this layer of rich organic soil from being washed away by rain or baked hard by the sun.

The plots of the swidden farmers copy these qualities of the tropical forest. Unlike the specialized fields of most intensive agriculturists—all rice or all tomatoes—the swidden plot contains a jumble of crops, from roots and tubers to fruit trees and palms, flourishing primarily in a bed of ash. Like the trees of the uncultivated forest, the domesticated trees of the swidden plot form a cover that filters sun and rain, thus protecting the soil from erosion or parching and at the same time reducing the encroachment of undergrowth. And within a few years this plot reverts back to forest.

Horticulture differs from intensive agriculture in several ways. First is the relatively simple technology associated with this type of farming. Only small and often scattered plots of land are cultivated at one time, and they are usually worked without the help of plows or animal traction, to say nothing of machines. The only tools used are simple hand tools: knives, axes, digging sticks, and hoes. In other words, horticulturists, like hunter-gatherers, still rely mainly on the energy stored in their own muscles in order to procure their food.

Second, in comparison with intensive agriculture, horticulture provides a relatively low yield per acre of land; for this reason, it is frequently categorized as **extensive agriculture**. For every unit of energy produced, horticultural methods require much more land than intensive agricultural techniques. The amount of energy horticulturists extract from the land is enough to sustain them, but they generally do not produce large food surpluses for the purpose of trade. While trade is often of concern to horticulturists, usually it is for the acquisition of items produced by another population. Exceptions occur when horticulturists are in close contact with hunter-gatherer groups, from whom they may acquire animal products. The Mbuti Pygmies of northeastern Zaire, for example, are a hunting people that supply their Bantu-speaking horticultural neighbors with meat and honey from the forest (Peacock, 1984, p. 15).

Third, in general, horticulture allows for household self-sufficiency. Each group, and in most cases each household, is capable of producing most of the food it needs. Most important production decisions are made at the household level. Horticulturists need not depend on other groups for food because they cultivate a wide variety of crops with an exceedingly modest technology. This orientation toward self-sufficiency is one of the reasons that the production of horticultural societies remains low.

Horticultural Cultivation Methods

Most contemporary horticulturists occupy marginal territories: either tropical regions, where soil is thin; or arid regions, where the water supply is a constant problem. In this respect, they resemble hunter-gatherers. They often have been excluded by competing groups from better-favored lands where intensive agriculture is possible. In such circumstances, they cope with the challenge of agriculture in several ways. They may concentrate on crops that make few demands on the soil. They may plant next to rivers or in areas that flood in the rainy season. They may plant in several locations so that if one field fails, another may still feed them, or they may shift their fields regularly to avoid depleting the soil. Many horticulturists use several of these techniques. The last, however, which in its present form is called **slash-and-burn agriculture,** or **swidden agriculture,** is the most common.

Slash-and-burn Agriculture. Slash-and-burn agriculture is a method of farming in which fields are cleared, the trees and brush are burned so that the soil is fertilized by the ash, and the fields are then planted. Each field is used for perhaps two or three years, then it is left to regenerate for about ten years while the farmer moves on to other fields. Swidden agriculture was practiced in Europe until the beginning of the Christian era and in North America until about the seventeenth century. (Indeed, it has been suggested that one reason for the success of the European colonists in North America was that they imitated the slash-and-burn techniques of the Native Americans.)

Unfortunately, all too often traditional horticultural plots are being consolidated into open-field farms and ranches in environments unsuited to such enterprises. The Amazon rain forest is being burned and bulldozed at an ever-increasing rate to make way for ranches and open-field farms (Posey, 1984, pp. 95–96), whereas horticulturists

such as the Yanomamö (whom we will meet shortly) have managed to exploit the rain forests without harming the environment. With more intensive land use in the same areas, the thin soil rapidly erodes.

The slash-and-burn technique demands a fine sensitivity to the environment. Swidden farmers must know exactly when to move their fields and when to replant a fallow field. They must also make rather precise calculations as to when to burn—on a day when there is enough wind to fan the fire but not enough to spread it to the rest of the forest. Horticulturists in general (swidden and otherwise) know an enormous amount about their environment, including minute details about different kinds of soil, about the demands of different kinds of plants, and about the topography and microclimate of their habitats. This knowledge is the secret of their survival.

Polyculture. The mix of crops, or **polyculture,** can vary considerably among swidden cultivators even in the same general region, as studies in the Amazon have shown (Flowers et al., 1982, pp. 203–217). Earlier studies have emphasized the diversity of crops and the apparent helter-skelter aspect of horticulture—a complex mix of plants and trees that is as ecologically diversified as the forest itself. Recent work shows that very often the people rely on one or two main crops but intersperse them with useful trees; the planting is not done in a random or unplanned fashion, but is carefully patterned so that as the garden ages different crops become available in turn (see Flowers et al., 1982; Beckerman, 1983; Boster, 1983). Thus even the return to fallow is carefully regulated, each stage providing some product to the cultivators.

All agricultural systems, at least temporarily, simplify specific portions of their natural ecosystems. It is also claimed that fertility is sustained by the complementary characteristics of different plants: the nutrient enriching tendencies of some balancing the nutrient robbing tendencies of others.

Polyculture (the planting of more than one crop in a field) has long been considered the key to ecological stability and sustainable, reliable yields in traditional horticulture; while monoculture, as practiced in intensive systems of agriculture, has often been linked to major disasters such as the Irish potato famine of the 1840s and even the Sahelian

Contemporary Issues

Learning about Monoculture from the Mountain Ok

POLYCULTURE (THE PLANTING OF more than one crop in a field) has long been considered the key to ecological stability and sustainable, reliable yields in traditional horticulture. Monoculture, as practiced in intensive systems of agriculture, has often been linked to major disasters such as the Sahelian famines of the 1980s. Unfortunately, monoculture is usually the easiest way to increase yields—something that is desperately needed in many countries. For years, many researchers have argued that polyculture is more "natural" than monoculture, in that the mix of different species in a field parallels the diversity of the forest and thus the mix provides a great resistance to diseases that might threaten a single species. The issue is an important one, as securing a reliable, locally-produced food supply is the only thing that can stand between survival and starvation for many millions of people living in tropical areas.

A number of researchers are now suggesting that the issue is not simply the contrast between monoculture and polyculture. From research on one population, we learn that it is possible to intensify horticultural systems through a form of monoculture without sacrificing reliability. In a study of the Mountain Ok of central New Guinea, George Morren and David Hyndman found that a sustainable and low-risk *Colocasia* taro monoculture has persisted there until the present day (1987). Taro is a starchy edible root crop common in the Pacific. They argue that these taro monocultures exhibit many ecological and systemic properties commonly attributed to polycultures.

The Mountain Ok, numbering 28,000 and speaking eight closely related languages, inhabit an extensive region (20,000 km^2 or 12,500 mi^2) of central New Guinea, which can be roughly divided into highland, mid-altitude, and lowland. Although they exhibit considerable sociocultural variability, which is partly a reflection of environmental diversity, Morren and Hyndman found a common cultural pattern throughout the area that gave it a clear identity.

The Mountain Ok appear to have access to the same range of agricultural technology regardless of region. They practice forms of slash-and-burn agriculture, show a cultural preference for *Colocasia* taro, practice extensive swine production, use minimal tillage, have short croppings and long fallows.

However, Morren and Hyndman found that local swidden gardens are clearly differentiated according to crop composition. For the high-altitude dwellers, the sweet potato is the staple and they keep taro gardens separate from

---

famines of the 1980s. One of the chief criticisms of monoculture, and one that is associated in particular with the use of modern hybrid varieties of crops, is the loss of biological variability. Unfortunately, monoculture is usually the easiest way to increase yields—something that is desperately needed in many countries. For years, many researchers have argued that polyculture is more natural than monoculture in that the mix of different species in a field parallels the diversity of the forest and thus acquires a great resistance to diseases that might threaten a single species. Recently researchers (Boster, 1983; Hames, 1983) have concluded that these same effects can be achieved in monocultures by interplanting different varieties of the same species. (See the Contemporary Issues box, *Learning about monoculture from the Mountain Ok*, pages 126–127.)

Social Organization

Horticultural or extensive farming societies, however varied, tend to share a number of very general characteristics when compared with low-energy budget foragers. One is **sedentism**, the practice of establishing a permanent, year-round settlement. Whereas hunter-gatherers invest time and energy in moving from place to place to find food, farmers invest their energy in increasing food production in one place: their fields.

sweet potato gardens. On the other hand, the mid-altitude peoples plant only taro gardens, and these monocultures are, the researchers find, highly flexible and low-risk.

The Mountain Ok of the mid-altitude range are able to practice a conservative form of swidden cultivation because generally population densities are low and land is extensive. Their use of flat or gently sloping land reduces the risk of erosion; they clear secondary rather than primary forest (and can thus take advantage of greater soil fertility); and they make small gardens with large forest margins between gardens, so that the fields are better shielded from pests and successional fallows are enhanced. Rather than totally clearing a field, they stunt the trees by scorching or ringing and often plant in undisturbed forest litter (which also improves fallows). By not completing clearing until the crop is established, they ensure that young plants are protected, moisture is retained, and erosion avoided. They harvest only once a year, saving vital nutrients for trees; and, by leaving the gardens a minimum of twelve years fallow, they allow for the restoration of essential nutrients.

All agricultural systems, at least temporarily, simplify specific portions of their natural ecosystems (p. 306). Recently, the view that disturbances (agricultural or otherwise) play an important role in sustaining and even increasing diversity of natural species in tropical forests has begun to supplant the older view that monoculture is a major departure from natural complexity. Tropical forests are a patchwork of areas, varying in size, in which single species predominate. From this perspective, a swidden field is simply a large patch.

Polyculture is advocated because the use of many different varieties of plants is seen as minimizing the risk of pests and disease. However, these same effects can be achieved in monocultures by interplanting different varieties of the same species. Morren and Hyndman note that the Mountain Ok do indeed plant a very large number of different varieties of the staple taro crop—some groups recognize over 100 different cultivars—and new varieties are constantly being introduced through diffusion or by discovery and trial (p. 308).

As Morren and Hyndman illustrate in their study of the Mountain Ok, using the three criteria of ecosystem simplification, biological variability, and vulnerability of the food supply, the taro monocultures they describe exhibit all the advantages often regarded as characterizing polyculture. Nonetheless, they warn that monoculture should not be regarded as an exclusive category. Rather, specific cases must be placed in the broader context of the surrounding ecosystem. It is possible to practice monoculture and reap its productive rewards while not sacrificing flexibility if there is access to other food sources at the same time, fields are widely spaced and retain forest borders to shield plants from pests, and many variants of the same species are interplanted to decrease the risk of disease.

Population density is also generally higher. In a group that is not on the move constantly, infants, old people, and sick people have a better chance of surviving. The fertility rate may go up, for when men are no longer called away to the hunt, they spend more time with their wives (Binford, 1968). Similarly, storage, which equalizes the distribution of resources through the year, is easier in a permanent settlement. Sedentary groups, then, tend to have higher population densities than nomadic or semi-nomadic groups.

Both these conditions—sedentism and increasing population density—tend to result in a more complex society. Agriculture is a group effort, involving considerable cooperation in clearing fields, planting, harvesting, and storage of crops. The crops and fields have to be protected from predators, including the threat of theft by others. At the same time, since agriculturalists invest time and energy in the land, organization is required to regulate access to the land and to resolve disputes that inevitably accompany life in a large residential grouping. Finally, a group that contains many people, interacting on a permanent basis, needs to order the relationships of the group members: to determine who owes loyalty to whom, who can marry whom, who must give in to whom in a quarrel, and so forth. Hunter-gatherers have fewer such problems. They can work individually, they own the land collectively, and when disputes arise, they can simply pack up their belongings and move. The horticultural life presents more social challenges, that must be met through a more complex social structure. Horticulturists, for example, frequently consider land to be the property of the group. However, individual households have exclusive access to the crops they produce on a given plot. Though farmers, too, may move when disputes break out, once they have invested in a plot, it is harder to do so.

Relations Within the Community. The basic unit of a society heavily dependent on farming is the household, a small group of people closely related by marriage and kinship who work together to produce food, share in its consumption, and cooperate on a day-to-day basis. Thus it is a unit of production and consumption analogous in many ways to a small family firm in our society. These family-based households, as we have mentioned, are relatively self-sufficient since their gardens or fields allow them to produce almost everything they need. Nevertheless, they cannot afford to be completely independent of one another, for agriculture creates vulnerability. Once a family has invested its energy in a plot of land, crop failure or a raid by another group can wipe out its livelihood in one stroke. Therefore, as insurance, households must make alliances and integrate themselves into a larger social unit: the community. They achieve integration primarily through kinship ties and participation in community-wide religious or political groupings. In some respects, collective land ownership by kin groups or small, closely knit communities is rein-

In the American Midwest, friends and family help with a post-and-beam barn raising. While this specific activity is rare today, cooperative efforts are central to the success of the family farm and farming communities.
(Ben Barnhart/Offshoot Stock)

forced in the horticultural communities of the tropical lowlands by the practice of having long fallow periods. These long periods during which families cease to cultivate their plots to allow the forest to regenerate do not encourage individuals to assert exclusive control over any given plot. Also, in most circumstances, the fact of collective ownership limits incentives for long-term investments in the agricultural infrastructure such as constructing terraces or systems to control the flow of water.

Kinship is often (though not invariably) the basis for recognition of individual rights to the use of land. Kinship is almost always the basis of extensive gift exchanges that establish reciprocal ties and obligations throughout the community. By regularly sharing surplus produce among friends and kin, horticultural families ensure that they will not be stranded if they fall on hard times. Indeed, it might be said that gift exchange is the horticulturist's way of storing food or ensuring future assistance, just as among hunter-gatherers.

After kinship, the second integrating force is political organization. While differences in wealth are usually slight or nonexistent in most horticultural groups, there are differences in power. Farming communities tend to have better-defined leadership roles than do hunter-gatherers, although the authority of the leaders varies from group to group. As we shall see, the headman in a Yanomamö village is simply a man with influence; he has no formal office and no right to coerce others. Whatever the allotment of power, the headman serves to integrate the horticultural community by helping families to settle their quarrels, arrange their marriages, and so forth; and by leading them in feasts, religious rituals, and raids.

Relations Between Communities. As social organization within communities becomes more structured, so do relations between communities— whether friendly (as in the case of exchange) or hostile (as in the case of conflict). Both of the groups we will be describing engage in some trade. The Yanomamö acquire metal tools from neighbors, government officials, and missionaries. Their involvement in trade is expanding each year as they are increasingly drawn into the national economies of Venezuela and Brazil. Historically, the Tamang

of Nepal traded salt and some food crops to obtain a narrow range of items they could not produce themselves; today, they are far more closely integrated into the Nepalese market economy—in large part due to improved transportation that links them to the capital (Fricke, 1994).

Yet self-sufficiency is still the rule among extensive agricultural communities, and much of their intergroup exchange is a form of gift giving rather than impersonal commercial trade. A Yanomamö man gives a man in another village a dog; some months later, the second man gives the first a bow. Neither party necessarily depends on what the other gives: both can acquire dogs in their own villages and make their own bows. What they do need is each other's support, either in warfare or in obtaining a wife. Thus just as gifts passed within groups serve to foster good will, so gifts passed between groups help to create and cement alliances; exchange is as much a social as an economic transaction. Arranging marriages with other groups is the ultimate expression of solidarity among the Yanomamö and many other tribal agriculturists.

In sum, social organization among farmers is decidedly different from that of most hunter-gatherers. Hunter-gatherers form small, relatively amorphous groups whose resources and members flow back and forth in such a way as to blur boundaries between subunits. The nuclear family remains intact, but it is not a distinct economic unit; the economic unit is the band as a whole. A farming society, by contrast, is a complex structure made up of well-defined and largely self-sufficient households within relatively stable and self-sufficient communities. These communities in turn are likely to have relatively formalized relationships with one another, often mediated by a system of kinship-based groups, each with its own territory and insignia.

The Yanomamö

Napoleon Chagnon, who has worked periodically among the Yanomamö for twenty-five years (for a cumulative period of field research adding up to more than sixty months), believes them to be one of the largest unacculturated tribes in South America, numbering about 20,000 members (1992). When Chagnon arrived among the Yanomamö people in

*Figure 5–1 Yanomamö
territory.*

1964, missionaries had already established posts in two villages, but many of the Yanomamö knew of the outside world only indirectly from the metal axes and pots they obtained through trade. Today interaction with outsiders in missionary settlements and through work for ranchers and government agents has brought the Yanomamö into far greater contact with the external world. There are now few Yanomamö who have never seen a non-Yanomamö. Thus this case study is first presented in the ethnographic present (as the Yanomamö appeared when anthropologists first began to work with them) and updated to show them today.[1] It is also worth repeating what we noted in Chapter 1, that Napoleon Chagnon, the anthropologist who pioneered research among the Yanomamö, is the center of some controversy as he has implicated the

work of missionaries in causing heightened mortality among the Yanomamö from disease and from mission-introduced shotguns.

Farming in the Jungle

The Yanomamö live in villages of 40 to 250 inhabitants (the average is 70 to 80), widely scattered through the dense tropical jungle in southern Venezuela and northern Brazil. For the most part, the land is low and flat, with occasional rolling hills and mountain ridges. It is crossed by sluggish, muddy rivers that become rushing torrents in the rainy season. Palms and hardwoods create a dense canopy over a tangle of vines and shrubs. The rain pours down two or three times a day, increasing in intensity between May and August. The humidity rarely drops below 80 percent, intensifying what to us would be uncomfortable year-round temperatures of 26° to 32°C (80° to 96°F).

---

[1] The material on the Yanomamö, unless otherwise noted, is from Chagnon's updated book, *Yanomamö, the last days of Eden,* San Diego, CA: Harcourt Brace Jovanovich, 1992.

A Yanomamö man uses a hoe to cultivate his garden plot in a clearing in the Brazilian jungle.
(Robert Harding Picture Library)

This habitat provides the Yanomamö with a variety of wild foods. They collect palm fruits, nuts, and seed pods in season; devour honey when they can find it; snack on grubs, a variety of caterpillars, and roasted spiders. They fish by a rather ingenious method known among many nonindustrialized groups: they dam a stream, pour a drug in the water, wait for the stunned fish to float to the surface, and then scoop them into baskets. They hunt monkeys, wild turkeys, wild pigs, armadillos, anteaters, and other species with bows and poisoned arrows. A survey of their hunting practices and game brought into the villages indicates that their intake of protein is approximately 75 grams per person per day, well above the 30 to 50 grams necessary to support an adult (Chagnon & Hames, 1979).

Wild foods alone are not abundant enough to support the Yanomamö at their present population level. Fruits and tubers are seasonal. Animals are small, many are nocturnal, and most live singly, so that they are difficult to hunt (Good, 1995, pp. 59–60). Chagnon notes that although on one occasion he and a group of Yanomamö hunters killed enough game to feed an entire village for one day,

on another occasion five days of searching did not yield enough meat to feed even the hunters (1992). Moreover, the Yanomamö's technology does not allow them to exploit the rivers as they might. Their bark canoes are too awkward to navigate upstream, and so fragile that they are generally abandoned after one trip downstream.

Even though they hunt from necessity since they do not raise animals, they tend to engage in hunting much more than is required from a nutritional perspective; they go on hunting treks because they enjoy doing so (Good, 1995, pp. 59–63). Even though it is the men who actually hunt, it is not unusual for the entire community to set off on a month-long trek to the coolest portion of the untouched forest. Also, meat is the only item that is shared village-wide and is therefore of great social importance; sharing creates important bonds among families, and not to share can be disruptive of normal relations (Good, 1995, p. 61).

Thus the Yanomamö depend mostly on their gardens, which provide 85 percent of their calorie intake. The most important crops are plantains and bananas (which together make up 52 percent of their diet in calories); manioc, a root crop used to make flour for cassava bread; sweet potatoes, taro, and maguey; and peach palm trees. Less important crops are maize, avocados, squash, cashews, and papayas. The Yanomamö also cultivate cane for arrow shafts; cotton for hammocks, belts, and cords; hallucinogenic drugs; and a variety of "magical" plants. One of these plants (cultivated by men) makes women sexually receptive, another (cultivated by women) calms male tempers, and others cause miscarriages and similar calamities in enemy villages. Finally, every Yanomamö garden has a sizable crop of tobacco, which is highly prized and is chewed by men, women, and children.

Like other Indians of the South American jungles, the Yanomamö practice slash-and-burn agriculture. To clear land for a garden, they first cut away the undergrowth and small trees with steel axes obtained from missionaries and through trade (or from anthropologists). They let the cut vegetation dry in the sun, then burn it off on a day when the wind is right. This task done, they set about felling the large trees, which they leave in the fields to mark boundaries between individual family plots and to chop for firewood when the need arises. The most difficult part of planting a new garden is carrying cuttings from plantain trees in the old garden to the new site. This is an arduous job, for a single cutting can weigh up to 10 pounds (4.5 kg). Planting other crops involves little more than making a hole with a digging stick and depositing seeds or small cuttings. Gardens are individually owned while they are being tended, and each man plants a variety of crops on his land.

Newly established gardens produce in spaced cycles. Thus, at the beginning there are alternating periods of scarcity and plenty. Then, after two or three years, the gardens mature, and overlapping plant cycles produce a constant supply of food (Chagnon, 1983, pp. 71, 74–79; Meggars, 1971, pp. 19–20).

The Yanomamö do most of the heavy work of clearing the land during the rainy season, when swamps and swollen rivers make it impossible to engage in visiting, feasting, or fighting with other villages. Once established, a garden takes only a few hours a day to maintain. Men, women, and children leave for their plots at dawn and return to the village around 10:30 A.M. (if the men have decided not to hunt that day). The women also gather firewood and supervise the children playing nearby. No one works during the midday heat. Sometimes a man will return to the garden around 4:00 P.M. and work until sundown. Most men, however, spend the afternoon in the village, resting or taking drugs, while the women go out to collect more firewood and haul water.

Cleared land in a tropical forest will not support crops indefinitely. Once a garden has been cultivated continuously for two or three years, the farmer gradually begins to shift it. Every year he abandons more land at one end of the plot and clears more land at the other end, transplanting crops to the new addition. The garden "moves" in this way for about eight years, after which time the weeding problem becomes insurmountable and the soil unproductive. The plot is then abandoned and an entirely new site is cleared. Left fallow, the old plot recovers its natural forest covering in about ten years. It should be noted that the Yanomamö are somewhat unusual in their swiddening. Most horticulturists use their plots for longer periods and carefully supervise the long fallow period, going back regularly to harvest wild fruits and other resources as they appear (Denevan et al., 1984, p. 346).

Village Life

The Yanomamö live near their gardens in circular villages they call **shabono**. Each man builds a shelter of poles and vines for himself, his wife or wives, and their children. These homes are arranged around a central courtyard, and the spaces between them are thatched to form a continuous roof with an open space over the courtyard. The shabono, then, is roughly doughnut-shaped. For safety, most Yanomamö groups also construct a high pole fence around the shabono, with a single opening that can be barricaded at night.

What authority there is in the village rests in the person of the **headman**, an individual who has proved his superiority in combat, diplomacy, hunting, or some other skill. Headmen have no official right to order others around; they lead only to the extent that people respect or fear them. Kaobawä, the headman of the village in which Chagnon lived in 1964–1965, is probably typical. Kaobawä had demonstrated his fierceness in numerous raids and quarrels. He also enjoyed a large natural following: five adult brothers and several brothers-in-law, who were under obligation to him for the sisters he had given them in marriage. Having established his superiority, he simply led by example. People came to him of their own accord for advice, which he dispensed with an air of quiet authority.

Most members of a village are related to one another, either by blood or by marriage. Kinship among the Yanomamö is reckoned by **patrilineal descent**; that is, it is traced through the male line. Both men and women belong to their father's lineage. Typically, a village consists of two patrilineages whose members have intermarried over several generations. Within a single lineage, all males of the same generation call one another "brother," and all females call one another "sister." For a man, however, the really important ties are not with his "brothers" but with the men of the lineage from which he can acquire a wife. Wives cannot be chosen according to fancy. Yanomamö marriage rules specify that a man must choose a woman from a lineage other than his own. In practice, his choice is narrowed to a small group of women in the village's one (or two) other lineages.

Neither the composition nor the location of a Yanomamö village is permanent. Villages move every few years. Sometimes the group relocates for the purpose of acquiring fresh lands, but as a rule there is plenty of land to cultivate in the immediate vicinity for villages are widely separated. As with many other horticulturists, a growing shortage of firewood is an important reason for movement. However, the Yanomamö also move because hostilities make it impossible for them to stay where they are. Sometimes internal feuds divide a village into two factions, which then go their separate ways. More commonly, a village moves because warfare with other villages has escalated to such a degree that the only way to survive is to flee. Kaobawä's group, for example, had made sixteen major moves in seventy-five years. One move was motivated by the need for fresh land, one by a desire to acquire steel tools from a group of foreigners newly arrived downstream, and the remaining fourteen by either bloodshed within the group or warfare with neighboring villages (Chagnon, 1983, pp. 174–177).

Warfare and Violence

Violence, in fact, is a salient feature of Yanomamö social life; internal hostilities are exceeded only by external hostilities. Intervillage duels, raids, ambushes, and kidnappings are almost daily fare. Why is there so much conflict? According to Chagnon, the reason that is given by the Yanomamö is women (Chagnon, 1992; Horgan, 1988, pp. 17–18). Other observers have alternative interpretations. Some feel that while the Yanomamö may explain their actions in terms of conflict over women, there are other, underlying causes. Brian Ferguson views Yanomamö conflict, internal as well intergroup, as arising out of the impact of external forces, notably the governments of Venezuela and Brazil, which have altered tribal territories and destablized social relations among populations far from centers of power (1995a, l995b). We will consider these interpretations as well as Chagnon's.

Unbalanced Sex Ratio. The only forms of family planning the Yanomamö practice are a long **postpartum taboo**—a woman may not have sexual intercourse while she is pregnant or while she is nursing a child—and infanticide. If, despite the taboo, a woman does become pregnant while she is still nursing her last child—a practice that itself de-

creases the likelihood of pregnancy—she will kill the new baby rather than deprive the older child of milk. A woman is also likely to kill her first baby if it is a girl, for her husband of course wants a son, and displeased Yanomamö husbands can be brutal, even murderous. The practice of selective female infanticide creates a sexual imbalance among the Yanomamö. The boys of a given village invariably outnumber the girls, sometimes by as much as 30 percent (Chagnon, 1992). The fact that older, more powerful men usually take second and third wives makes the shortage of women a particular problem for the younger men. Chagnon has reported that men who have been successful in raiding and who are known to have killed enemies are far more likely than other men to have two or more wives, further exacerbating the situation (Horgan, 1988, pp. 17–18).

The unbalanced sex ratio increases conflicts within and between villages. Competition for the limited number of women eligible as brides under the marriage rules turns biological and classificatory brothers into potential enemies. Suppose there are ten young men in a lineage, only seven young women eligible for them to marry, and older men take two of these girls as brides. The men grow up knowing that only five of them will be able to marry within the village. Somehow they must outshine or disgrace the competition, and this necessity tends to undermine whatever solidarity might develop among them as brothers. (A young Yanomamö may seek a bride in another village, but most are reluctant to do so because they would have to undertake years of bride service.)

In addition, the shortage of women increases the temptation to commit adultery—a temptation to which married men succumb as readily as bachelors, especially during the four years or so when their wives are taboo. If a man succeeds in seducing another man's wife and is caught, the husband will retaliate with all the ferocity he can muster. Club fights over women are the major cause of villages splitting up. After they split, hostility between the two groups tends to continue on its own momentum, each group taking turns avenging wrongs inflicted by the other group.

Warfare between totally separate villages follows the same pattern. Fights over women may precipitate the conflict, or one village may suspect that its crops are being pilfered by a neighboring

Horticultural societies are not entirely peaceable. In fact, violence is a salient feature of Yanomamö social life. These Yanomamö are preparing to depart on a raid.

(Napoleon Chagnon/Anthrophoto)

village. If a child falls sick, the illness will be blamed on sorcery emanating from another village. (The Yanomamö may invoke evil demons to steal the souls of children in enemy villages.) Whatever the original causes, contests over women are usually part of the ensuing hostilities. Typically a raiding party will kill one or two men and abduct any women they can lay their hands on. This raid precipitates a counterraid to avenge the murders and recapture the women. The retaliatory raid in turn triggers another, and so on.

Eventually the members of one village will be put to flight. Abandoning their gardens and homes, they take refuge in another village until they can plant new gardens. This arrangement, while necessary for the group's survival, further exacerbates

the woman-shortage problem, for the hosts are almost certain to take advantage of their guests' weakened position to demand temporary or permanent access to their women.

Thus the Yanomamö, according to Chagnon's accounts, are locked into a vicious cycle. The more the men fight over women, the more eager they are to have sons who will help in the fighting, the more female infants they kill, the fewer women there are, and the more they fight. Moreover, the men encourage their sons to be suspicious, hot-tempered, and quick to take violent action against the slightest offense. Teasing fathers often provoke small sons to hit them and then reward the boys with laughter and approving comments on how fierce they are becoming. By raising their sons in this way, the

Yanomamö perpetuate hostilities in the effort to defend against them.

Environmental Factors. Chagnon's explanation for Yanomamö warfare is not without its critics. Most observers agree with his data indicating a high frequency of fighting and high mortality associated with it, and most agree that warfare of the sort reported is (or was) widespread among Amazonian groups. But Marvin Harris and others have argued that the importance of women has been overstressed and that environmental factors are directly or indirectly implicated. Harris (1974, pp. 276–279) and Daniel Gross (1975) state that underlying the frequency of warfare is a shortage of game and other sources of protein. Although the Yanomamö grow more than enough produce to fill their stomachs and have miles of virgin forest to clear for new gardens, the foods they cultivate do not provide large amounts of protein. To meet these protein requirements, they must hunt and fish. Harris suggests that at some point the Yanomamö began to intensify their agricultural activities and that their population level rose accordingly. As the population grew, they killed increasingly larger numbers of wild animals, thus depleting their game resources. Today, Harris argues, there is not enough protein to go around and what the Yanomamö are fighting over, albeit unwittingly, is hunting territory.

Gross traces not only warfare but also several other aspects of Yanomamö culture to the scarcity of protein. Above all, the settlement pattern—the establishment of small, widely-dispersed villages separated from other villages by a no-man's-land and abandoned every few years—is, according to Gross, a strategy for preventing the overexploitation of game in any one area. Likewise, infanticide and a long postpartum taboo lower the protein demand by keeping the population in check. The hypothesis that Yanomamö warfare—the most striking aspect of this tribe's culture—may be an adaptation to protein limitations is intriguing, but so far it has not been substantiated by any reports of protein deficiency among the Yanomamö. One study has found some signs of infant malnutrition but also evidence that children who survive childhood mature into healthy adults (Holmes, 1985). Although warfare may indeed serve to preserve

hunting territories, it does not appear that this is the immediate or conscious objective of the combatants (Chagnon & Hames, 1979; Chagnon, 1992). Such different observations, while difficult to resolve, provide new and innovative directions for research.

Political Alliances. In this hostile social environment, the Yanomamö devote considerable time and resources to cultivating alliances with neighbors. Overtures begin cautiously, with parties of visitors bearing gifts. The gifts are not free, however; the takers are obliged to reciprocate at some point in the future with gifts of equal or greater value. If visiting goes well, specialization in craft production may begin: one village may rather suddenly abandon the making of pots and the other the manufacture of arrow points, so that they become dependent on each other. These contrived shortages express growing trust; all Yanomamö have the resources and skills to make everything they require.

After a period of trading, one group takes the next step toward alliance by holding a feast for the other group. They harvest and cook great quantities of food, amass goods for exchange, and prepare elaborate costumes and dances. Because giving or attending a feast implies a higher level of commitment, the occasion must be handled with caution and diplomacy. The dances and songs are essentially displays of strength. Each side tries to impress the other with the fact that it does not really need allies and probably never will.

Almost invariably, disputes break out and the toughest men of the two villages challenge one another to contests of physical strength: chest-pounding duels, in which two antagonists take turns socking each other squarely on the chest; and side-slapping duels, in which the contestants take turns hitting each other on the flanks. The object is to stay in the game until your opponent withdraws or is knocked unconscious. If tempers get hot, these fights can escalate into club fights, full-scale brawls in which the men of each village beat one another over the head with eight-foot poles.

An occasional club fight leads to full-scale violence, destroying the alliance altogether. Usually, however, these carefully graded levels of hostility allow the Yanomamö to vent their ever-present aggression, display their fierceness, and still finish the feast on a friendly note. If all goes well, the fighting ends in a draw and gifts are exchanged. The guests depart peacefully, the hosts can expect to be invited to a return feast, and each group assumes it can count on the other for refuge and food in times of trouble.

The final step is an exchange of brides between the two groups. This step is not taken unless the villages are convinced of each other's good intentions or unless one is so weak it has no choice. Villages that exchange women usually can expect support in their raids and skirmishes with other Yanomamö. But even alliances based on marriage ties are tenuous; no village honors a commitment when it sees some advantage in breaking it.

In sum, the Yanomamö are great fighters and poor allies. Consequently, their social world is one of chronic suspicion and hostility. The human costs are high. Warfare accounts for at least 30 percent of all male deaths; approximately two-thirds of people aged forty or older have lost at least one close biological relative: a parent, sibling, or child (Chagnon, 1992, p. 239). This figure seems startling, but it is comparable to those of New Guinea tribes and of Native American societies that feuded regularly.

The problem, as Brian Ferguson points out, is not so much whether or not the Yanomamö fight, but whether this is a long-established feature of their way of life (1995b). No one, including, of course, Chagnon, argues that the Yanomamö are the "living embodiment of a violent evolutionary heritage" (Ferguson, l995a, p. 62). But the interpretation of their level of conflict depends on the extent to which this is caused by forces outside their immediate habitat, which is the view argued by Ferguson (1995a and 1995b). While it is obvious, as we shall see shortly, that the Yanomamö are greatly affected by contemporary developments in Venezuela and Brazil, what is not so plain is how deeply they have been affected by outside events over the last 300 years.

Outside influences began when the colonists arrived in the early seventeenth century and began raiding for slaves; the ensuing conflicts wiped out a number of societies in the Yanomamö region and destabilized others. Most important, apart from direct contact, was the competition among groups that developed as trade goods were introduced. This competition often was played out in warfare

(Ferguson, 1995a). Rather than a pristine example of tribal warfare, Ferguson suggests, "The Yanomamö case shows the extraordinary reach and transforming effects a centrally governed society or state (here the states of Venezuela and Brazil) may have, extending way beyond its last outpost" (1995a, p. 63).

Future Prospects for the Yanomamö

The Yanomamö at the end of the twentieth century are in a much more precarious position than at any time in their history. Generally, anthropologists describe what happens when two cultures impinge on each other as **acculturation**, which leads to changes in both cultures. In particular, the politically or technologically dominant society exerts the greatest impact. This process is transforming all the Indian tribes of the Amazon rain forest, and resembles what was experienced by native populations throughout North and South America in the early days of European colonization. They have been abruptly brought into contact with a technologically advanced and alien cultural system. However, the case of the Yanomamö is so extreme that Chagnon refers to it as "catastrophic change" (1992, p. 243).

When Napoleon Chagnon arrived in 1964, the villages closest to European settlements had seen only a handful of whites and those of the interior none at all. Trade goods had been reaching them, passed on through intermediate groups, but no extended contact had occurred between the Yanomamö and the outside world. Since the period of first contact, roads have been built to provide access to the Amazon region. With the completion of the first road, change has occurred rapidly and often against a backdrop of misery and misfortune.

The arrival of the roads brought an immediate adaptive response. The Indians nearest the road ranged themselves alongside it to beg and barter for shorts, shirts, food—doubtless it seemed like an easier way to make a living than their traditional horticulture and hunting. Some went to work on farms and sawmills; for twenty or thirty days' work, they received a little money (not more than $2 or $3) and some cigarettes and used clothes. They tried to emulate the ways of the Brazilians

State of the Peoples

Are the Yanomamö Safe?

ANTHROPOLOGIST LINDA RABBEN argues that while Brazil has taken a big step by demarcating Yanomamö territory, it is unclear how the boundaries of their reserve will be protected and by whom (1993). As recently as 1991, the governor of Amazonas threatened to send state police with machine guns to shoot agents attempting to demarcate indigenous territory in his state; in 1993 the federal government admitted that 11,000 prospectors had reentered Yanomamö territory and it appears unable or unwilling to expel them. Still, demarcation seems to be the only possibility for preserving indigenous peoples and their resources. Other Brazilian populations such as the Kayapo are lobbying to have their lands effectively protected, enlisting foreign assistance where possible. Prince Charles of Great Britain and the rock star Sting have lobbied for them, and in 1993 the perimeter of their lands was physically marked using funds raised largely by such foreign help.

But marking boundaries alone cannot protect indigenous peoples. Many in Brazil cannot understand why groups such as the Yanomamö should be protected while millions of small farmers have no land and 100 million city dwellers live in dire poverty (Rabben, 1993, p. 14). Thus, the pressures on their territories are increasing, not decreasing. Many local politicians see foreign efforts to help native peoples as threats to sovereignty and economic development. The situation is further complicated by dispute and controversy among those who would assist them. Chagnon, who has spent his entire career with the Yanomamö, has been accused of overstressing their warfare and aggressive male behavior—thereby indirectly encouraging outsiders to view them negatively. Recently, Jacques Lizot went so far as to suggest that depictions of Yanomamö warfare actually incite intruding gold miners to massacre them (Lizot, 1994). Chagnon, who has been an advocate of Yanomamö rights throughout his career, responds by pointing out that Brazilian gold miners are unlikely to have read any of his scientific publications, and furthermore, they are hostile to all indigenous groups who stand between them and gold (Chagnon, 1995, pp. 187–189). Chagnon has been attacked also in letters sent by Lizot and Salesian church officials to academic leaders accusing him of promoting "racist" theories—a notion that is not supported by a reading of his numerous publications (see Wolf, 1994). Salesian missions operate among the Yanomamö ostensibly to help them as well as to convert them, but according to Chagnon and others, the shotguns given to converts are used against their neighbors and thus add to Yanomamö mortality rates. While it is entirely appropriate to disagree with a scholar's findings and interpretations, it is unfortunate where it interferes with the advocacy that endangered populations such as the Yanomamö so badly need.

While demarcation is a necessary step, Rabben argues, indigenous groups need the active support of public opinion to obtain control over their resources. This has to occur at local, regional, national, and international levels. There also has to be international monitoring. At the moment, miners are largely undeterred by federal police and the government has been able to do little to prevent malaria and other contact diseases from causing high mortality of indigenous populations. Unfortunately, we must conclude that the Yanomamö are not yet safe.

(*civilizados*) and not to appear to be *indios bravos* (wild Indians).

The "roadside" Yanomamö came to differ from the unacculturated villagers of the interior. They adopted Brazilian haircuts, took up smoking cigarettes, bought canned foods and candy, and added lots of salt to their food. In fact, their traditional diet was superior to that of the average Brazilian farmer; with contact, their diet declined in terms of calories earned per unit of labor expended. But because they wanted to appear like the Brazilians and to interact more with them, they adopted as many Brazilian practices as they could. Not only did they adopt such utilitarian items as aluminum pots and pans, steel axes, shotguns, and other tools that facilitated subsistence activities, they also came to depend on large numbers of consumer items that tied them ever more closely to their Brazilian suppliers. As John Saffirio and Raymond Hammer write (1983), it is doubtful that they would have embraced this alien culture so wholeheartedly if they had understood that in so doing they were losing their political autonomy and entering Brazilian society at the very bottom of the social and economic hierarchy.

Along with contact have come diseases to which the Yanomamö have no immunity. They have been decimated repeatedly by epidemics; one disastrous influenza epidemic in 1973 killed a quarter of the population in the villages sampled (Chagnon & Melancon, 1983, p. 59). These scourges have had a severe impact on the traditional social organization; ritual specialists have died before passing on their knowledge and skills, kin groups have been broken up and forcibly resettled, and leaders have succumbed to these new diseases.

While the Yanomamö's territory has been exploited for 20 years by lumbermen cutting down their rainforest, the most serious assault came in 1985 with the discovery of gold in the Amazon. This discovery, which coincided with the completion of the Perimetral Norte highway that cut through the heart of the Yanomamö territory, precipitated a gold rush into the Amazon. Since 1985, over 50,000 miners have invaded Yanomamö territory (Gorman, 1994). Once again, epidemics took an almost instant toll: villages studied soon after the road was constructed had lost between 30 and 51 percent of their populations (Chagnon, 1992). The mining operations have further ravaged the fragile environment, damming rivers and polluting water. Even though the land rights of the Yanomamö were protected in the Brazilian constitution, the government made no effort to enforce those rights.

However, the plight of the Yanomamö did not receive international attention until four Indian men were killed when they wandered into an illegal mining village. Ironically, the public outcry that resulted was not in response to the killing, but in response to action taken by then-President Sarney. He ordered all journalists, missionaries, anthropologists, medical workers, and international workers out of the territory and embarked on a plan to reduce the Yanomamö territory from 37,000 square miles to 12,000. This announcement led to a four-year battle for the preservation of the Yanomamö land rights fought by international rights organizations as well as Brazil's own Indian protection agency. Finally, in November, 1991, the new president, Collor, authorized the official demarcation of 36,000 square miles of Yanomamö territory, providing $2.7 million to physically and legally implement this demarcation. Soon after, a demarcation order was also issued for the Kayapo (Rabben, 1993).

Despite these gains, the future of the Yanomamö is still in question. Miners continue to operate illegally in their territory, and there are reports of continuing violent confrontations between the Indians and the miners. In 1993, Chagnon was part of a team that investigated a massacre of Yanomamö women and children. According to Chagnon, this was in retaliation for earlier killings of miners by the Yanomamö. Apparently, some Yanomamö men had shot two Brazilian miners after they had killed five Yanomamö men near an illegal mining site (Chagnon, 1993).

As we can see in the State of the Peoples box, *Are the Yanomamö Safe?* (page 138), the authorization for the demarcation of indigenous territories does not necessarily guarantee the preservation of the Yanomamö.

Subsistence Plow Farming

The subsistence plow farming techniques used by the Tamang of Nepal (discussed in the following section) are technologically different from what we have described as horticulture. However, the broad outlines of the domestic economy are similar: egalitarian, independent households as primary units of production and consumption. Depending on the nature of the terrain, fields are usually small and irregularly shaped and inputs are generally limited to what the household can supply itself: labor for planting, weeding, and harvesting, animal traction, natural fertilizers, and sometimes water. Generally speaking, such farming using animals involves a significantly shorter fallow period than does most swiddening. At most, fields are left fallow for a single year.

Using animal traction for plowing and cultivating vastly increases the productive capacity of farmers.

(Betty Press/Woodfin Camp & Associates)

A higher annual production per acre means that the land can support larger communities. However, as with the horticulturists, production is organized to fulfill the subsistence needs of the household rather than to produce a marketable surplus that could, in turn, be reinvested. The main differences have to do with the utilization of livestock, the exploitation of a number of distinct microenvironments within the region, and relations with the outside world. None of these differences, it should be stressed, is absolute.

The fact that households make significant use of large domesticated animals for food and traction creates an increased demand for household labor to manage them, so the households of such farmers tend to be large. The family must also have access to land for grazing and housing its cattle, oxen, or other domestic animals. This usually means that they are simultaneously exploiting a

number of distinct ecological zones: fields specific to whatever crops may be planted, orchards for arboreal produce, grazing areas, and places in which fodder is collected for the months when animals cannot be pastured. This gives the household both additional sources of food and a means of storing surplus production: on the hoof.

While most horticulturists today are integrated into market economies in some manner, it is safe to say that all plow farmers are. Not only are they participants in the market system, their production sustains a larger political system in which they are dependent players. They are the "peasantry." Despite the fact that they operate within a larger market economy, they can also be viewed as subsistence farmers because they produce primarily for family subsistence rather than for profits to be reinvested (Wolf, 1966). Much of their produce may be sold, but the profits accrue to middlemen and urban elites, not to the peasants. For them, farming is a way of life and a means of sustaining a household within a community.

It is, then, much more than simply a strategy for making money. Such farmers, often materially poor, closely identify with their villages and way of life. The term "peasant" subsumes a great diversity in standards of living, even within one country. The common element is a farming household whose efforts are directed to maintenance and subsistence—not reinvestment of capital for profits. In most cases, peasant families are dominated by holders of power outside the local community. In tsarist Russia before 1889, for instance, a peasant household was bound to a landed estate; to leave without permission was to risk death or imprisonment. The peasants of Western Europe acquired full civil liberties only in the nineteenth century, and often their standard of living, however simple, set them apart from the poor people of the cities. Still, their form of farming permitted little accumulation of capital or material wealth.

In Latin America, India, and the Middle East, many peasants gain access to land through some form of sharecropping—that is, they work land owned by others in exchange for a share of the yield. Sharecropping is one means of getting land to farm; there are others. The way people control the lands they farm is a major determinant of the degree of political freedom they enjoy, and usually of their material well-being.

Farmers who control their own land and tools, such as the Yanomamö and the Tamang, decide for themselves how hard they will work and dispose of their produce as they choose. Usually, peasants do not have this freedom. Their access to land, equipment, and capital—even the allocation of their own labor—is regulated by people more powerful than they. Even the local agriculturists who own their own land, elect their own leaders, and control their own labor are heavily dependent on an administrative and commercial network. In one way or another, the middlemen who link the farm with distant markets, the rulers, governors, and tax collectors—even the merchants in faraway cities or on local estates—determine how and what the peasants produce and what they earn for these products (Wolf, 1966).

The Tamang

In June, 1981, Thomas Fricke, armed with a Fulbright grant, an ability to speak Nepali, and a set of questionnaires, arrived in the Himalayan village of Timling after a week's walk through Tamang country. [2] While fully aware of the larger nation of which they were a part, few men in Timling (and even fewer women) had been to the capital of the nation, Kathmandu. Although they were relatively poor and isolated, the people of Timling were warmly receptive to Fricke's presence. He quickly settled into the top floor of a rented house, made it known that people were welcome to drop in for tea and a cigarette, and, more importantly, established an informal clinic from which he dispensed aspirin and treated minor wounds. Soon people came to take his presence for granted and he could turn to his main objectives: the study of population dynamics and the domestic economy in a small farming community.

Within weeks of his arrival, he began making a careful map of the village, giving each house a number for use later to ensure that his data did not exclude the poorer ones. Soon thereafter, he began the arduous task of visiting each of the 132 households and collecting detailed data on marriages, kinship, age and gender of all members, as well as economic data. In the final stages of research, again using his list of households, he selected some thirty households as a special sample in which more detailed questioning would occur. Even though much of his research, like that of Chagnon among the Yanomamö, was highly structured and quantitative, the personal was never far removed:

> The anthropologist, crouching near a peasant's cooking fire and sharing corn beer, lives in a world of imposing immediacy. In a village of a hundred or so households, those events that are swallowed up by the grand scale of an urban or national context take on an enlarged, often passionate significance. One night there is laughter and joking with a father-to-be about the paternity of his child. Another day there is the intrusion of sudden death

---

[2] The following discussion, unless otherwise noted, is based on Thomas Fricke's *Himalayan households: Tamang demography and domestic processes*, originally published in 1986, but significantly revised in 1994.

when a hunter loses his footing on a rain-soaked trail. The anthropologist observes, or hears about, these happenings as they occur and gives them a kind of permanency by writing them down. [p. 7]

The Tamang people, including the inhabitants of Timling, are a widely-dispersed population of Tibetan origin living in Nepal. Their numerous villages stretch in a broad arc north and eastward from Kathmandu, the national capital. Those who live near the capital are more integrated into Nepal's national life and culture than are those to the east and north, such the people of Timling. The Temang practice a form of Buddhism that closely resembles that of their more famous neighbors, the Sherpa, who are well-known internationally as mountaineers and guides. The village of Timling is only fifty miles from Kathmandu, but to reach it the traveler has to take a five-hour bus ride, followed by a four- or five-day trek, depending on the season. Until the eighteenth century, the region of Timling was a small, independent chiefdom; one among many. Even though now, administratively, it holds a marginal and dependent status within the kingdom, it is somewhat misleading to characterize Timling as a typical peasant society. Unlike many peasants, the people maintain control over their own lands and variation in wealth among households is not great.

The Tamang as a whole are organized into patrilineal clans or lineages called *rui*. As is the case with the Yanomamö, the Tamang practice exogamy; that is, marriage must be outside the clan. In some parts of the country, the clans of the Tamang are ranked hierarchically so that wealth, social standing, and political influence is distributed unequally. This is not true in Timling, whose people are, writes Fricke "an extraordinarily egalitarian group, with no institutionalized basis for distinguishing among the status of clans" (p. 32).

The Village

The 132 households are laid out in four neighborhoods, or *tol*, each associated with a dominant clan (although others will be present as well) and each with its open-air meeting place. Sons build their homes on land they inherit from their fathers; thus, they may add to the size of a neighborhood. Most

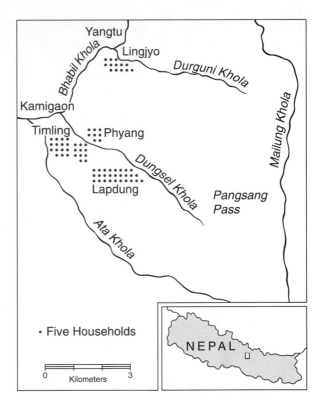

Figure 5–2. Timling and its daughter villages.

houses are of two-story construction and built with stone and timber, with wood or slate roofs. In one neighborhood, the homes of clan members display large stone phalluses under the eaves that are supposed to ward off ghosts and other malevolent beings. The upper stories are used primarily for storage, with the family living quarters downstairs where the symbolically important cooking hearth is located. The hearth is emblematic of the household as an independent unit. The fire from the open hearth fills the houses with smoke, but the overall effect is a warm, dry haven in the colder months or during the monsoon rains.

Timling is, by any standard, a fairly dangerous and dirty place. During the monsoon rains, the central paths of the village turn into running streams. Since these paths are also the repository of human waste, the drinking water frequently becomes contaminated during monsoons. On the often treacherous trails, the risk of accidents is high given the slippery rocks and sheer drops of hundreds of feet. On the positive side, the village is too high to be af-

Tamang family—husband, wife and one of their children—threshing millet during harvest season in Timling, Nepal.

(Courtesy of Tom Fricke, The University of Michigan)

flicted with malaria-bearing mosquitos, and leeches, fleas, and lice are limited seasonally by the winter cold and summer dry seasons (p. 114).

Religious practices incorporate both Buddhist beliefs and shamanistic practices (to be elaborated upon in Chapter 12). The two sorts of religious specialists reflect this mix; about half are *lamas* trained in the Buddhist tradition and capable of conducting elaborate rituals on a calendar that is coordinated with the agricultural cycle, and the others are *bompos* (**shamans**) who appease forest deities that bring illness to villagers and their herds. A shaman is an individual who has unique skills in curing, divination, or witchcraft, usually involving the ability to communicate with the world of spirits (see Chapter 12). Parents regularly bring in *bompos* to heal their sick children with all-night rituals involving spirit possession and the sacrifice of chickens and goats. The *lamas* carry out death rituals or funerals, cleanse the village periodically by casting out evil spirits (a task that involves the entire community working together for three days), and annually bless the fields.

Political organization is focused on the clans and neighborhoods. Technically, the village is part of a national system of administration; in practice, most decisions of communal interest are made within the clans via meetings and a council of elders. Disputes are resolved locally, usually by informal sanctions and fines, and violent conflict is rare (unlike the Yanomamö).

Field, Forest, and Pasture

Timling's agro-pastoral economy is directed toward the subsistence needs of its people and, until recently, has been largely (but never entirely) self-sufficient. Until 1956 they traded locally mined salt with Tibet; today, they trade for small amounts of grain and manufactured commodities in a market town some four days' walk to the south—part of a gradual but steady shift to a cash economy. As with any population, we have to think of their present adaptation as part of a long historical process that is ongoing. In previous periods, the ancestors of the present population had exploited the lowlands, using classic horticultural techniques. Gradually, as a result of pressure on resources and declining low-land forest area suited to swiddening, they increased their reliance on animal husbandry. Today, plow farming is the principal strategy of food production, supplemented by pastoralism or animal husbandry.

The main characteristic of mountainous regions is that relatively short distances involve great changes in altitude, thus offering a wide variety of ecological zones for potential exploitation. Timling's territory contains three large, vertical zones based on how people use the altitude-related climate differences: cultivated areas, forests, and pasture lands. The best cultivable land is the lowest (of that to which they have access), from 5,300 to about 6,000 feet. This lies below the critical snow-line (the village itself is frozen hard through much of the winter), and is intercropped with millet and maize. Somewhat higher fields, from 6,000 to 7,000 feet are planted in maize, potatoes, millet, and barley in an alternating cycle. The poorest arable land, up to 8,500 feet, is used for potatoes and wheat in a three-year cycle, including a one-year fallow period. All in all, the 132 households farm approximately 418 acres (or .65 acre per person). This modest amount of land, when combined with animal production, supplies enough food to sustain a household. The typical breakdown of crops in terms of land is 26 percent planted in maize, 16 percent in millet, 15 percent in wheat, 29 percent in barley, and 15 percent in potatoes (p. 68).

Communal grazing is available to some degree in all three zones, but most grazing land lies in the high pastures above 12,000 feet. The seven square miles are grazed by herds of sheep and goats, including some from other villages, from May until mid-September (p. 65). In order to save labor, all of the village's sheep and goats (about five or six per household) are combined into three herds. In addition to sheep and goats, most families maintain cattle or oxen for plowing, and, in a few cases, water buffalo for milk. Over half of what a family has invested in animals (in the sense of capital) is devoted to cattle, which are used primarily for traction; sheep and goats are used for food and wool. Most families produce their own sturdy clothing from wool—essential in this harsh environment.

Work in Timling is a matter of survival. Each household can be thought of as an independent economic unit defined by the need to provide food for the hearth (p. 73). All households are involved in agricultural, pastoral, and maintenance efforts in a cycle determined by the requirements of the different crops and animals. The principal sources of food are the crops, even though men regard herding, which they do almost exclusively, as preferable to the arduous tasks of plowing, seeding, weeding, harvesting—and even guarding the plots from monkeys and bears that would forage on them. In all, it appears that the people of Timling have to work almost twice as hard during the year as do the Yanomamö; even household maintenance requires great effort. The mountain environment requires substantial structures for housing. To build a house, the Tamang must go to the forest, cut logs, float them downstream, and then laboriously drag them up the hillside and fashion them into boards. The Tamang must also work hard to gather firewood, since a single family will burn about 154 person-loads of firewood each year. Water has to be fetched. The family makes its own tools, storage baskets, and clothing. In this cold environment, each person requires two outfittings of heavy clothes. In all, a typical home requires 185 ten-hour person-days per year of hard work just to perform general maintenance, even though cooking itself is a fairly simple procedure. Daily meals usually consist simply of flour and water cooked as a thick gruel, perhaps accompanied by boiled nettles or potatoes. Meat is eaten only occasionally, when sacrificed in rituals or when an animal falls to its death, as they sometimes do on the steep trails.

The Domestic Cycle

Given the nature of agriculture and private ownership of fields and cattle, the **domestic cycle**, or how households are formed and organized and how they develop is very important. If one simply looks at Timling's households at a point in time, as Thomas Fricke did in his initial study, almost 70 percent were nuclear in composition—that is, a married couple and their unmarried children.[3] But, as he

---

[3] The people of Timling accept polygyny but it is now rare. The most common cases occur when men from the village move to India to work, often establishing second marriages there.

A Tamang man and his cow. The man is wearing typical highland clothing except for his shirt, which was purchased at a bazaar five days walk from Timling.

(Courtesy of Tom Fricke, The University of Michigan)

notes, this is misleading, as each family unit is transformed over time. Children are born, grow up and marry, and deaths occur. The rule is that daughters, when they marry, leave their natal home and move to their husband's, where they reside with his parents, single siblings, and possibly married brothers. This is called, by anthropologists, **patrilocal residence**. A more mature household will often contain at least two married couples of two generations and their children—referred to as an **extended family household**. Even though most households go through this phase in their development, only a few (about 5 percent) are extended at any given time. The reason is that soon after the oldest son marries, the next son begins thinking along similar lines. Once the second son does marry, the eldest son, his wife, and children are likely to move out to build their own house, set up their own hearth, and tend their own plots—thus beginning their own domestic cycle within a new nuclear household.

A son inherits his share of lands and animals at this point, usually prior to his father's death. The rule is for the youngest son to marry and continue to live in his parents' house until their deaths, when he will inherit the remaining property. This mother/father/youngest son unit is termed a **stem family**; about 25 percent of Timling's households were of this sort. The composition of the household is of vital importance to its members' quality of life; the sudden death of a young adult can dramatically affect the ability of the family to adequately provision itself. Generally, mature households have a more favorable ratio of workers to consumers, which reduces the effort devoted to sustaining daily consumption and which may allow for the purchase of additional land or the opening of new fields—all of which can be used to support new households when married sons leave.

Sexuality and Marriage. Marriage is a vital transition event, far surpassing such earlier celebrations as those marking the maturation of the child: a girl's first menses, and a boy's *chewar* (first hair cutting). Marriage marks the move to adulthood and ties households together in a web of mutually supportive relationships. Marriages can be arranged by parents or simply entered into by a couple choosing to live together without ritual or money changing hands. When money or wealth is exchanged, it is given by the husband's family and relatives to the girl's father and then passed on to the bride as a form of inheritance: she will have no further claim on her parents' property. Sexual activity begins at puberty and is not viewed with disapproval. Unmarried couples find their ways into the forest and young girls bring their lovers home at night, although trying to keep their amorous activities secret in a crowded communal room is a virtual impossibility.

Clearly, attitudes in Timling toward sex, and especially female sexuality, are drastically different from those of the Yanomamö, where men regularly fight over women and adultery is considered a serious offense. In Timling, if an unmarried woman has a child she simply names the father. If he is a single man he may or may not marry her, and if he is already married he is asked to help support the child. A male child will inherit from his father even if his father and mother never marry and he is reared in his mother's household. In any event, by age twenty most women are married and either beginning their own households or residing patrilocally as part of their husband's natal household. Children of unwed parents are not stigmatized. The main concern is to establish paternity for reasons of clan membership and inheritance. Clan membership is socially crucial, since one is the member of one's father's clan and to marry within the clan is forbidden. The people of Timling do not practice any form of contraception; on the contrary, they promote fertility. While the birthrate is not among the world's highest, probably for reasons of health and because of spousal separation when men go to work abroad, a woman can typically expect to have five or six children. For the time being, at least, children are seen as a source of future household wealth and security, not as dependents who must be supported and among whom land must be divided.

Prospects for Timling's Future

When Thomas Fricke concluded his first fieldwork, he was mildly pessimistic regarding Timling's future. Judging from the experience of other Himalayan communities, he feared that as they continued to be drawn into Nepal's national economy and as the population continued to grow, standards of living would decline and an increasingly uneven distribution of wealth would ensue. Children would no longer be a source of family se-

curity but simply mouths to feed from a declining resource base. The villagers themselves were optimistic, thinking that the then-approaching road that would link them to markets would enable them to sell fruit and find better employment. In his most recent visits, Fricke found both views to be true. The village has changed greatly; in some ways for the better, and in other respects not. Now there is an active government-run school and children are receiving a formal education; a clinic has opened and health and hygiene have improved. By 1992, most of the villagers had converted, at least nominally, to Christianity; the effects of this transition on traditional attitudes and values are yet to be seen. Now many people are living and working outside the village; some have second homes in the capital. Younger men are finding employment as trekkers—working with parties of tourists who come to hike in the spectacular mountains. The economy has become monetarized at the expense of the previous era's system of reciprocity, and some villagers have clearly improved their standards of living. Others, particularly older people, feel that they are being neglected in their old age as their sons and daughters go abroad to work or settle elsewhere where resources are more abundant. Just as with the Yanomamö, willingly or not, they are becoming active players in an increasingly interconnected world with perhaps the first harbinger of change being the sudden visit by an anthropologist.

Summary

FARMING SOCIETIES DEPEND ON DOMESTICATED foods, especially plants; that is, people try to control the reproduction rates of their food resources by ordering the environment in such a way as to favor their survival. Human labor and simple tools are the primary means of working the land, and extensive farmers do not produce consistently large surpluses for others' consumption. Their subsistence economies make both the group and the individual household largely self-sufficient and independent. Yet trade with neighboring groups is an important

feature of their survival strategy and is integrated with their agricultural activities, as are some hunting and gathering activities.

Since contemporary horticultural societies generally occupy marginal territories and do not use major technological aids, they have developed a variety of techniques to exploit their environment. The most common technique is slash-and-burn (or swidden) agriculture. Trees and undergrowth are cut and burned to form a layer of fertilizing ash. Several varieties of plants are cultivated for several years, then the area is left to lie fallow and new land is cleared. The success of swidden agriculture, and of horticulture in general, depends on an intimate knowledge of the environment.

Subsistence farmers can support more people per unit of land area than can hunters and gatherers, but in comparison with other agriculturists they operate on a low energy budget. They do not have to use their resources or labor to the fullest in order to subsist.

Among the social conditions that normally accompany a dependence on agriculture are increased sedentism—the practice of establishing a permanent, year-round settlement—and increased population density. These conditions tend to increase social complexity and interdependence.

The household is the basic unit in horticultural societies; the integration of families into a community is achieved primarily through kinship ties and political organization. Kinship networks are often the basis for both recognition of individual rights to the use of land and extensive gift exchange throughout the community.

Relations with other communities may be peaceable or warlike, or somewhere in between. Trade, alliances, and intermarriage foster peaceful relations; while competition for resources, raids, and exploitation provide excuses for war.

The two farming societies discussed in this chapter are the Yanomamö of Venezuela and Brazil and the Tamang of Nepal. As the two peoples inhabit different environments, their adaptations have taken very different forms.

The Yanomamö hunt and gather, in addition to practicing swidden agriculture in their dense tropical jungle. Authority in their villages rests with the headman, who leads by example rather than by institutionalized power. Kinship is reckoned by patrilineal descent (through the male line), and a typical village consists of two lineages that have intermarried. Strict marriage rules specify that a man choose a wife outside his lineage.

Villages normally move every few years, mostly because of internal feuds or warfare with other villages. The Yanomamö social world is one of chronic suspicion and hostility. Political alliances are cautiously negotiated by the exchange of gifts, followed by trading, feasting, and exchange of brides, but even alliances based on marriage ties are tenuous.

Some anthropologists attribute the hostile social environment to a shortage of sources of protein. Marvin Harris believes that Yanomamö warfare is concerned—unwittingly—with hunting territory, and Daniel Gross holds that the settlement pattern—widely dispersed mobile villages—is a strategy for preventing the overexploitation of game in any one area. Yet Napoleon Chagnon, who has studied the Yanomamö longer and more intensively than anyone else, finds no evidence of protein deficiency among them. Chagnon attributes their bellicosity to intense competition for women, caused by their practice of female infanticide and the custom of powerful men to take more than one wife.

The peaceful village of Timling could not be in stronger contrast to the Yanomamö way of life. They have a relatively relaxed attitude toward sex, prize peaceful relations with others, and engage in no warfare. Their mountain environment is in sharp contrast as well; they exploit a variety of vertical climate zones, some of which they plow and plant in wheat, corn, potatoes, and millet; others of which they use for animal production and foraging for firewood and building supplies. Whereas the Yanomamö, until very recently, were relatively cut off from people living in state- or urban-based political systems, the people of Timling, however independent, have long been in close contact with Tibet and Nepal—as well India and Bhutan, where men have long gone to work. Their religion, while containing unique elements, is part of a much larger, literate tradition of Buhddism. Both the Yanomamö and the people of Timling face uncertain futures—the Yanomamö because their lands are being encroached upon by farmers and miners and because of alien diseases introduced by foreigners. The people of Timling do not face such direct threats to their survival, but are at risk of losing their independence and self-sufficiency as they are drawn into a national culture and its market economy.

Key Terms

acculturation	polyculture
domestication	postpartum taboo
domestic cycle	sedentism
extended family household	shabono
	shaman
extensive agriculture	slash-and-burn (swidden) agriculture
headman	
horticulture	stem family
patrilineal descent	subsistence agriculture
patrilocal residence	

Suggested Readings

Chagnon, N. A. (1992). *Yanomamö: The last days of Eden*. San Diego: Harcourt Brace Jovanovich, Inc. A distinguished albeit controversial anthropologist reviews his work among the Yanomamö, answering those who have criticized his analyses in the past while stressing the problems the Yanomamö face today.

Damas, D. (1994). *Bountiful island: A study of land tenure on a Micronesian atoll*. Ontario: Wilfrid Laurier University Press. This book examines the land tenure system in an atoll society and its relationship to population densities and land ownership.

Grinker, R. R. (1994). *Houses in the rainforest: Ethnicity and inequality among farmers and foragers in central Africa*. Berkeley: University of California Press. A groundbreaking ethnograhic study of a farmer-forager society in Northeast Zaire and its complex social relations.

Lepowsky, M. (1994). *Fruit of the motherland: Gender in an egalitarian society*. New York: Columbia University Press. An ethnography of the Vanatinai of New Guinea that contradicts the ideology of universal male dominance by exploring gender roles, ideology, and power.

Sahlins, M. (1968). *Tribesmen*. Englewood Cliffs, NJ: Prentice-Hall. A now-classic discussion of the economic arrangements, social structure, and ideologies of tribal societies, most of which are horticulturists.

Vayda, A. P. (Ed.). (1968). *Peoples and cultures of the Pacific*. New York: Natural History Press. The societies of the Pacific islands number some four million people, and historically much of this population has engaged in horticulture. This collection of twenty-four articles is an excellent introduction to the many peoples of the Pacific.

Werner, D. (1984). *Amazon journey: An anthropologist's year among Brazil's Mekranoti Indians*. New York: Simon & Schuster. An informal and sympathetic portrayal of modern anthropological field data collection and analysis among horticulturists in the rapidly changing Amazon.

Whiteley, P. M. (1988). *Deliberate acts: Changing Hopi culture through the Oraibi Split*. Tucson: University of Arizona Press. A detailed portrait of the history and social organization of a Hopi village that focuses on social change over a hundred-year period.

The Pastoral Adaptation
  Development
  The Organization of Energy
  Nomadic Movement
  Social Organization
  *Using Anthropology: China's Cowboys
  of Inner Mongolia*
  Wealth, Inequality, and Status

The Ariaal of Northern Kenya
  The Origins of the Ariaal
  The Ariaal Adaptation
  The Household: Organization
    and Status
  The Age Grades and Age Sets
  Gender Roles and Power
  *Gender Issues: Being a Shepherdess in
  the Negev*
  Can the Ariaal Survive Development?

The Yörük of Turkey
  The Market Economy
  Social Organization
  Adapting to a Changing Economy
  Future Prospects

Summary
Key Terms
Suggested Readings

Chapter 6

Pastoralism

Pastoralism, as we saw with the Tamang, is *animal husbandry*—the breeding, care, and use of herd animals such as sheep, goats, camels, cattle, horses, llamas, reindeer, and yaks. When animal husbandry is pursued as a primary adaptation, it is a highly specialized strategy of land use that in certain respects resembles hunting and gathering. In terms of productivity, however, it is more comparable to intensive farming. Like most hunter-gatherer groups, pastoralists use lands whose vegetation they only minimally manage: they graze their animals on wild grasses, shrubs, and sometimes fallow crop lands. Like agricultural populations, pastoralists invest time and energy in the management of productive resources—their livestock.

Most pastoralists are nomadic, moving their herds from pasture to pasture on a seasonal schedule within a well-defined territory. The degree of mobility varies from group to group, and even from year to year within a group, depending on such environmental factors as rainfall, vegetation, and the availability of water holes. Economic and political constraints also affect the pattern of nomads' movements. Pastoralists must deal with the demands of other groups—even governments—in order to gain access to pastures and to the markets where they can exchange animals and animal products for clothing, tools, weapons, and food.

The extent of **specialized pastoralism**, the adaptive strategy of primary reliance on animal husbandry, varies with environmental and market conditions. Few groups rely exclusively on their herds for day-to-day subsistence. To do so would entail heavy risks in two respects. In order to keep their animals alive, pastoralists have to adjust to the vagaries of the environment: cold, lack of water, lack of pasturage, and so forth. At the same time, they must coexist with other groups with whom they may be in competition. Given these complications, it is no surprise that when the environment permits, pastoralists tend to pursue a more generalized subsistence strategy, raising at least some crops along with their animals (Barfield, 1993; Berleant-Schiller & Shanklin, 1983).

In fact, most pastoralists, no matter how specialized, subsist more on grains than on animal products. The camel-herding Bedouin of Arabia greatly prize their independence but are now, and always have been, linked by numerous economic and social ties to the larger, sedentary society. Even before the coming of trucks, camps in Arabia were regularly visited by merchants laden with wares to trade for camels. The merchants would set up shop in distinctive white tents (in contrast to the black tents of the nomads) and it was a breach of the codes regulating warfare to rob or harm these visitors, so important were they to the well-being of the pastoral community. Today, of course, most Bedouin households have trucks or jeeps and can drive to the nearest town to shop.

Before we take a close look at two pastoral societies, let us see how pastoralism developed and what its social consequences are for groups that pursue it.

The Pastoral Adaptation

Development

The archaeological record indicates that mixed farming based on a combination of domesticated plants and animals preceded specialized pastoralism (Redman, 1978). Mixed farming was a multi-faceted strategy that provided a hedge against droughts, crop failures, diseases, and other natural calamities. For farmers, livestock not only provided valuable material (skins for clothing and shelter) and food products, but the animals themselves were a means of storing food against future use: a freezer on the hoof. At the same time, if the animals died, the crops were there. Diversification provided both the alternatives and the reserves necessary to survive fluctuations in the food supply. Such diversification is still common in many parts of Africa, Europe, and the Middle East, particularly in mountain villages.

Despite the many advantages of diversification, changes in agricultural practices, especially the development of canal irrigation and intensive agriculture, created the preconditions for specialized pastoralism. Increased productivity based on canal irrigation made possible population growth and the expansion of settlements, with a consequent increase in land devoted to intensive farming and a decrease in land available for animals. It also stimulated interregional trade. Grazing areas were pushed farther from the settlement region into territory where forage was not so lush. To get adequate food and water for their herds, animal owners had to expend more labor and travel greater and greater distances. Furthermore, the animals were more vulnerable to predators and especially to raiders. Thus, care of the animals began to drain energies away from agriculture. At the same time, agriculture became more time-consuming, for farmers now had to clear, tend, and repair the canals in addition to working the fields. The increased demand of each of these strategies may well have led to a divergence, with certain households specializing in increasingly intensive agriculture and others concentrating on animal husbandry or pastoralism.

In some cases, plow farmers may have attempted to move into intensive agriculture but failed in their attempts to utilize canal irrigation. Extensive irrigation may cause the **water table** (that is, the level of water under the earth) to drop, so that wells and canals run dry. Or the water may so increase the salinity of the soil that crops begin to fail. Canals also fail in areas of inadequate stream flow. Other agriculturists who had always struggled to raise crops in marginal areas had incentives to concentrate their attention on animal husbandry. Eventually the differences in strategies between the farming and herding groups led to spatial and cultural differentiation as well, creating distinct groups of pastoralists and agriculturists.

Pastoralism, then, may have developed hand in hand with intensive agriculture. Whatever the reasons for its development, pastoralism is a strategy predicated on agricultural surplus and on regular interaction between herders and farmers. Pastoralism may be an alternative to agriculture, but it is almost never independent of it.

The Organization of Energy

Like horticulture, pastoralism is more productive than hunting and gathering. Hunters do not try to increase the numbers of animals or use the products of living animals. They may, as we have noted, hunt in a conservative fashion in an effort not to eliminate their prey altogether, but they do not practice animal management. Pastoralists do invest labor in breeding and caring for their animals, and so increase their reproduction and survival rates. Tim Ingold notes that apart from reindeer herders, pastoralists are usually concerned with the production of milk, hair, blood, or wool, and with traction—using animals as vehicles or sources of work energy (1980, p. 87). Meat production is almost incidental with one or two notable exceptions. By investing human labor in the production of milk rather than meat, the herder gains a greater net return: the animal need not be killed to be useful. In fact, successful herders can generally increase their holdings at a faster rate than farmers, for as the animals reproduce, the offspring can be incorporated into their herds. Of course, this advantage is partially offset by the precarious nature of herding in most areas: animals are susceptible to disease, drought, and theft, any of which can reduce a rich household to poverty overnight.

Full-time pastoralism may be less efficient than farming in areas where cultivation is possible. People can produce approximately ten times as much food, measured in calories yielded per acre of land, by raising grains instead of livestock. But in areas where agriculture is risky or impossible, pastoralism is a useful strategy for converting forage—sources of energy that humans cannot use directly—into milk, blood, and meat. These foods are stored in the form of animals until the people

need them either to eat or to trade for agricultural foods, clothing, and other items they cannot otherwise obtain. Furthermore, the fact that animals can move themselves permits herders to move the production system to the resources.

By using a strategy of simultaneously exploiting more than one environment, pastoralists have found a relatively efficient way of extracting energy from an environment not suited to agriculture. For example, the herds of most East African pastoralists are mixed, and include not only zebu (oxen distinguished by a hump, much like a camel's) but also large numbers of goats, sometimes sheep, donkeys, and, in very dry areas, camels. The importance of the mixed herd lies in the fact that each species has its own feeding preferences so that not one but several environments are exploited. However, since pastoralism produces much less food energy per acre of land than agriculture, specialized pastoralists necessarily have low population densities.

Nomadic Movement

In nonindustrial societies, **sedentary pastoralism**, or animal husbandry that does not involve mobility (ranching, say, or dairy farming) is relatively rare. The practice more generally followed is **nomadic pastoralism**, the adaptive strategy of moving the herds that are one's livelihood from pasture to pasture as the seasons and circumstances require. Land that is rich enough to support a herd indefinitely in one location will yield far more output if it is given over primarily to crops. By taking advantage of the mobility of herd animals and their own ability to group and regroup, however, pastoralists can adapt to marginal areas by moving as conditions dictate. Mobility is the key that unlocks widely dispersed resources and allows a population to gain a living from an environment that could not sustain a settled community.

While the main reason for pastoralist migrations is to secure adequate grazing on a year-round basis, this is not the only reason. William Irons (1975) has pointed out that the Turkmen pastoralists of northern Iran move to maintain their political and cultural independence, as well as to seek grazing lands. In the past, they also frequently raided non-Turkmen sedentary populations and caravans. If they were pursued by a more powerful force, they could simply disperse with their animals into inaccessible areas. Though they were "pacified" by the Iranian government in the early twentieth century, they have managed until recently to retain considerable control over their own affairs. They did so by using the one skill they had developed far beyond the abilities of other populations: moving.

Today, even within the boundaries of contemporary state bureaucratic systems, mobility often allows nomadic pastoralists to maintain greater political autonomy than settled communities enjoy. With continuing political uncertainty in Iran, both nomadic and settled Turkmen are reasserting their claim to a separate identity, and the nomadic groups are apparently the more successful in their efforts. In other countries, nomads may be able to avoid onerous civic duties such as military conscription and taxation.

The economic strategies of individual households within a given population of pastoralists often vary considerably. Such variations are sketched very clearly in the ever-changing composition of the camp group and in individual decisions on migration. Some groups among the Turkman of Iran, for example, may move frequently one year and be largely sedentary the next. Regular patterns often underlie this variability. In Turkey, Yörük households with many animals may move early in the spring to pastures in the mountains, braving cold weather to get to the first grasses. Others with smaller flocks may feel they cannot afford the risk of losing even a few animals to the cold, and so move later in the season. In general, though, the variability of movement patterns is due to the variation in types of herds, quality of grazing lands, climate, and availability of water. An area of rich pasture land and mild climate does not require as many moves as one dominated by poorer-quality pastures (Barfield, 1993).

There are two basic systems of nomadic movement, despite much variation. One pattern, plains or **horizontal migration,** is characterized by regular movement over a large area in search of forage, a necessary strategy where no particular area is capable of sustaining a herd for a long period of time. The Bedouin of the Arabian Peninsula exemplify this form of nomadism; members of Bedouin tribal groups are dispersed over hundreds of square miles as they make use of the scant vegetation of an extremely arid region. Although they gather in larger encampments around seasonal water holes, the density of population is strikingly low. This pattern has been widespread throughout the cattle- and goat-keeping portions of Africa, the deserts and steppes of Central Asia and the Middle East, and, in later times, the plains of North and South America.

The second pattern is that of seasonal movement of livestock between upland and lowland pastures, or **transhumance.** This form of nomadism has been found throughout the mountainous zones of the Middle East, parts of Eastern Europe, Switzerland, Central Asia, and, in later times, North and South America. Transhumant nomads often camp together for extended periods of time in two major grazing areas: summer pastures in the mountains and winter pastures in the valleys. During the migrations between seasonal encampments the roads and trails are crowded with people and animals on the move.

Despite the fact that most pastoral populations adopt a nomadic lifestyle, we often see individual families giving up herding altogether for other pursuits. This is what families in the Middle East tend to do when they have accumulated enough wealth to invest in a more secure form of capital, such as land or a shop, or when their herds have become so small that they can no longer support the household. In many regions, settlement, followed by a return to herding, is a regular process (Salzman, 1980). On the other hand, agricultural households may shift to herding if they consider it advantageous to do so. Thus most of the people described as pastoralists have strong cultural ties in sedentary communities and usually have relatives there as well. The Bedouin of the Negev in Israel, for example, have been largely forced to settle for political reasons but still keep as many animals as they can manage.

However we may think of nomadic pastoralists, we should not fall into the trap of perceiving them as inflexibly committed to a single way of life. Nomadism is a strategy, a means of making specialized animal husbandry work. A group can be more or less nomadic depending on conditions. People can organize themselves into sizable groups and stay together for extended periods when they gain advantages from that strategy, but they will work separately when that approach is more productive. Although we often speak of "group cohesiveness," "corporateness," and "economic strati-

Camels have declining economic importance in Arabia, but are still vitally important livestock in East Africa and the Sahel, where water is a scarce resource. Here Ethiopian herders water their herds.
(Woodfin Camp & Associates)

fication" as characteristics of a society, we should not lose sight of their ultimate origins in individual behavioral motivation. What we see as patterns of social organization are the outcomes of the strategies individuals adopt as they cope with their problems and evaluate their opportunities.

Social Organization

There is no single form of social organization that is peculiar to nomadic pastoralists; such adaptations occur in varied environmental, political, and cultural contexts. The social life of Lapp reindeer herders may closely resemble that of neighboring Finnish communities. The Bedouin of Arabia may be culturally similar to tribal villagers in Iraq. Still, most researchers who have studied or worked with nomadic pastoral societies see certain aspects of social organization related either to the necessity (or capacity) for mobility or to the requirements of the animals they tend.

Virtually all nomadic pastoralists are organized in tribes, sociopolitical communities whose members are bound by ties of kinship—most commonly by presumed descent from one or more common ancestors. Such groupings can easily encompass many thousands of individuals through the expedient of recognizing subgroups defined by degree of kinship: clans, lineages, or even large family clusters. Such groupings (which will be more precisely characterized in Chapter 8) do not depend on a definition of community that rests mainly on residence in a territory or locality; a member of one's tribe is a relative.

A member of the cattle-keeping Nuer tribe in Sudan, described by E. E. Evans-Pritchard (1940), is a Nuer wherever he or she may happen to be. Every Nuer is also a member by birthright of one of a series of "segments" or genealogical parts of the tribe, each having a distinctive name, not unlike a family name in our own society. Each segment of the Nuer tribal system is supposed to assist the others largely in accordance with the closeness of the presumed relationship between them. This segmentary lineage system, widespread in Africa and the Middle East, provides a highly flexible means of adapting group size to the resources at hand. Groups come together or split up along lines of kinship. Though not all or even most tribal societies are pastoralists, most nomadic pastoralists are organized in tribes of one sort or another.

Camp Groups and Household Organization. Individuals and households in herding societies frequently change their patterns of movement and the groups with which they camp. They move in response to changing economic and political conditions and also to new social circumstances. Individual households camp with people with whom they enjoy good relations, and such people are most often kin. There appear to be strong constraints on the number of households that can

Using Anthropology

China's Cowboys of Inner Mongolia

WE CAN OFTEN LEARN A GREAT deal about social organization by looking at how people cope with change. One instance is described in a recent study by Burton Pasternak and Janet Salaff of Han Chinese living in Inner Mongolia and following a pastoral mode of production (1993). Their work shows how ecology and technology create diversity in China, despite strong pressures from the state and cultural institutions for uniformity. Working with Chinese colleagues, Pasternak and Salaff studied four communities over a number of years. The Han are Chinese immigrant farmers who, beginning in the late 1940s, left traditional riceland farming, crossed the Great Wall, and began farming and herding in the grasslands of Mongolia.[1] They came seeking a better life but found a setting where the indigenous people were hostile, the climate precarious, and the land difficult. Only those who were prepared to alter their behavior were to succeed on China's famed—and feared—northwestern frontier. We will look primarily at those who chose pastoralism as their new economy.

The Han people, whether they speak Mandarin or some other dialect, have a common history and culture; in short, a style of life that the researchers call the "Chinese Way." The Chinese Way, in addition to representing common values and beliefs about family and identity, also represented a particular division of labor, organization of households, and gender roles. However successful the Han have been over the centuries in adapting to China proper, primarily through intensive farming techniques allowing them to squeeze ever more food out of severely limited land (see Chapter 7), the Great Wall always seemed to mark the limits of where the Han could live in the Chinese Way: it marked the end of civilization for them.

Inner Mongolia is a natural laboratory in which to study how ecology shapes social organization. The seasons are extreme, with very cold winters and cool and short summers. Most of the region was stripped of forest cover in the nineteenth century and now erosion threatens farmlands and pastures alike. In 1990, the population was 80 percent Han, with the indigenous Mongolians a distinct and often resentful minority in one of China's poorest regions. Fieldwork was difficult for the anthropologists, who found a fine brown dust in everything they ate; water was either so scarce as to make bathing impossible or so plentiful as to turn the dirt road to a sea of mud. Even privacy was a serious problem; there were no latrines on unobstruced plains often lacking even rocks or trees.

While some Han adapted to the new region through farming, other Han populations adopted pastoralism—a strategy unfamiliar to them. In this, they came to resemble their Mongol neighbors in important ways while still maintaining their Han identity and language. Mongols and Han herders remain separate subcommunities and rarely intermarry. When Han first took up herding, they focused mainly on dairying, as they were more familiar with

readily coordinate their activities in an egalitarian society that lacks strong leadership roles. Two observers have noted considerable uniformity in the average size of nomadic camps or migratory groups—usually in the range of 100 to 300 persons (Tapper, 1979, p. 81; Johnson, 1983, p. 176).

When Gregory Johnson examined a large number of nomadic societies whose people lived together by choice rather than by coercion, he found that a camp group comprised on average six households or clusters of very closely related households, such as father-son groupings (1983, p. 183). If conflict were to occur in the camp group, often the easiest solution was for the antagonists simply to move apart. In many respects the shifting composition of nomadic camping-and-herding groups resembles the camps of nomadic hunter-gatherers. People use mobility to minimize conflict and to associate with those they find congenial.

In most pastoral societies it is possible to speak of the **co-resident household**, a grouping whose members often dwell in tents as a basic economic

cattle from their past experience as settled villagers. This meant that they could remain largely sedentary, with their cattle kept near their homes. They supplemented this activity with fishing and cutting and selling hay. Neither strategy was used much by the traditional Mongols, who ranged far afield with herds of sheep and other animals. In time the Han began to shift to sheepherding, even though it required much more male labor and meant either moving their dwelling or having the men absent for long periods. Sheep have to be moved regularly and require close supervision and guarding, as the pastures are distant from the main settlements. The Han began to experiment with sheep because, despite the costs and risks, the payoff in wool, meat, and milk production was greater than with cattle alone. With time, they came to emulate the Mongols in other respects; some adopted Mongol traditions and became yurt-dwellers in distant pastures, making tent-like homes out of felt covering a framework of wood and wicker, consuming mutton and beef instead of pork, using strong alcoholic beverages, and drinking strong tea mixed with milk.

The Han shepherds have become the new nomads, or what Pasternak and Salaff call China's new cowboys. But it is the requirements of sheep herding, not cultural assimilation, that have encouraged similarities with Mongol social organization and ways of life. This is reflected in the division of labor, age at first marriage, fertility, and family age/size composition. Sheep herding requires high levels of continual labor for supervision and herd management, and animals are kept on distant and regularly changing pasture sites. Since the minimum size of a herd that can be profitably managed is nearly 200 animals, this represents a major capital investment, as well as one that is highly vulnerable to disease and predation.

While women and children may help out in managing the animals, the pastoralists feel that only grown men can adequately care for the flocks in distant and sometimes dangerous pastures. As a result, there is a sharper division of labor by sex: Han women usually stay home tending to the family's cattle and gardens, while men work hard in the pastures, where, in addition to shepherding, they cut hay and bring drinking water home in heavily laden carts requiring great physical strength to manage. In short (and unlike other nomadic populations elsewhere), the labor of women and children is apparently of relatively less importance.

The Mongols, likewise, place a high value on male labor and regard women's work as a distinct sphere of activity that men do not enter. Since male labor is more remunerative, young girls are more apt than boys to be able to go to school; but unlike farmers (since female labor was less in demand), the sons of pastoral households married at a later age and lived more often in smaller, neolocal domestic units. Han pastoralists average nearly 4.5 people per household as opposed to farmers who average 5.0. Farmers usually try to keep a large household together after one or more son marries; the pastoralists (like the Mongols) usually start new, independent households. Farmers, too, have higher fertility than herders; reflecting, the researchers argue, the higher value placed on child labor.

[1]This box is based entirely on the work of Pasternak and Salaff (1993) and Pasternak's summary of this in *Portraits of Culture*, 1994, Ember, M., Ember, C., & Levinson, D. Englewood Cliffs, NJ: Prentice Hall.

unit and coordinate their herding and other productive activities. In a society in which groups move frequently and the composition of larger groupings changes regularly, the household takes on added social significance—particularly, Ingold contends (1980, pp. 188–189), when market relations engender competition. The household, like the camping group of which it is a part, must respond to changing economic circumstances—sometimes by an increase in size, sometimes by dispersal into smaller households. One study in China's remote northwest frontier, profiled in the Using Anthropology box, *China's Cowboys of Inner Mongolia*, above, gives us an insight into the ways in which pastoral production can shape household organization.

Hierarchical Tribal Organization. While pastoralists' camp groups may resemble the fluid camps of hunter-gatherers, most such societies have a more complex sociopolitical organization that unites the constituent households and camping groups in tribes. Some nomadic tribes, such as the Bedouin of Arabia and the Mongols of Central Asia, have strong leaders. Undoubtedly, the existence of such roles reflects the fact that these peoples were in close contact, even regular conflict, with agricultural communities and lived within the boundaries of nation-states. The Qashqa'i of Iran, for example, have an elaborate hierarchy of leaders, each part of a fairly well-defined chain of command (Beck, 1986, 1991).

A hierarchical tribal organization often has highly specified membership criteria (as by patrilineal or matrilineal descent) and is composed of well-defined subgroups. Such an organization allows for more than just communication across great distances. It is a means of coordinating large-scale migrations, gaining access to grazing land, holding and defending territory, and even on occasion gaining control over sedentary farming populations.

A study by Arun Agrawal of nomadic shepherds, the Raikas of Western India, show how this works. The Raikas are the largest group of nomadic pastoralists in India, migrating from settlements in Rajistan and Gujarat with flocks of sheep for more than two-thirds of the year. Generally shepherds move to a new camp location almost every day; there are several hundred thousand shepherds on the move. Their mobile camps—*dang*—have as many as eighteen herds (or up to 7,000 animals) and over one hundred men, women, and children. "Daily movements of fifty to one hundred human beings and their animals demand critical collective decisions" (Agrawal, 1993, p. 263). They achieve this by delegating decision making to three groups in each tent.

The first is the *nambardar*, who is the senior leader because of his wide experience, wealth, and contacts with leaders of other camps. He spends his time scouting possible routes and visiting other camps. The second leader, the *kamdar*, makes decisions while the *nambardar* is out of camp and participates in the council of five elders, made up of men representing a broad spectrum of Raikas' interests. The third level of decision making is the *mukhiya*, a man who is the leader of the individual herders in the camp and who intimately knows the needs and characteristics of the herds. The leaders are chosen on the basis of experience, age, wealth, and kin relationships. The *nambardar* makes most decisions about migration, marketing, camp-wide

shearing, and camp-wide management; he is the best informed about the possible routes and camp sites. The *kamdar* serves to manage internal relations in the camp during the *nambardar's* frequent absence and to coordinate with the council of elders—thus maintaining a check on the *nambardar's* authority. Finally, decisions having to do with herding, labor, and when to bring the animals home rest with the *mukhiya*, who best knows flock management (Agrawal, 1993, p. 270).

Wealth, Inequality, and Status

In many traditional pastoral societies, livestock constitutes the sole form of economic wealth. Rights to animals are held by individual households and are passed down from father to son. Because some may inherit more than others or may have more success in managing their herds, the number and quality of the herds vary from household to household. However, everyone is subject to loss of livestock through disease, theft, drought, or just bad luck—a wealthy household may be reduced to poverty in one season. Thus, in many pastoral societies where there is no market for livestock, periods of wealth and poverty are temporary and tend not to create permanent disparities in economic status.

However, it is probably safe to say that distinctions of wealth are more evident among pastoral populations than among the horticulturists we discussed in Chapter 5. Among the Komanchi sheep herders of Iran, for example, Daniel Bradburd (1990) found not only great disparities of wealth among households, but also systematic exploitation of poorer households by wealthy ones. Such disparities are reflected in marriage arrangements and in many other areas of social life; the poorer households have a limited opportunity to improve their lot (Bradburd, 1990). This case may be extreme, but economic differentiation among households is common. Among the Ariaal of Kenya, to be discussed shortly, drought tends to kill off a larger percentage of the wealthy herders' animals since they are not cared for as carefully as the animals of small stockowners (Fratkin & Roth, 1994). But since the rich have more animals, particularly drought-resistant camels, they survive periods of drought with far less risk of being impoverished and forced to settle permanently in one location.

The Social and Symbolic Value of Livestock. In addition to the fact that livestock are central to the pastoral economy, they also have considerable social and symbolic value. For example, some Bedouin tribes keep small herds of pure white camels; others maintain special racing camels. Today, as most camels are being replaced by trucks, their continuing value resides in their significance as a cultural symbol marking their identification with the past and with familial honor (Barfield, 1993, p. 89).

Among the horse-riding pastoralists of Central Asia, horses are prized far beyond their utilitarian value. In fact, sheep and goats have much more value in subsistence terms. However, while horses were never the primary focus of these people, they endowed their riders with the speed to facilitate communication and cooperation and the mobility and power to triumph in battles. Thus they symbolize military and political power.

In East Africa, cattle have a paramount and pervasive symbolic value. Melville Herskovits (1924) long ago identified this focus on cattle as the "East African cattle complex": a socioeconomic system in which cattle represent social, not economic, wealth. They were exchanged as part of marriage ceremonies, ritually slaughtered at other ceremonial events, given as gifts, and prized for their beauty. According to Herskovits, the possession of large herds was such an important status symbol that cattle were neither traded nor used as a regular source of food. This symbolic explanation was used to account for an excessive number of cattle in a culture that did little trading.

However, further research has revealed that, while cattle are clearly central to the social life of these herders, they also have an economic function. First, the cows' main contribution to the subsistence economy is milk, which is the primary pastoral product. Since the cattle that can survive in the harsh environment of East Africa aren't very productive, large herds are necessary to satisfy subsistence needs. Also, although eating beef except on ritual occasions was forbidden, these ritual sacrifices occured often enough to suggest that beef was a signficant source of food. Keeping great numbers of cattle was also part of a subsistence strategy that divided and dispersed herds over a wide area as a kind of insurance against loss of all one's cattle in one place to raiders from a neighboring group or to disease.

A Yomut Turkmen elder on his prized horse. Horses were formerly an important key to Turkmen military prowess, as well as a source of prestige.
(Daniel Bates)

We shall consider two groups of pastoralists, each with a distinctive adaptive pattern. The first group, the Ariaal of northern Kenya in East Africa, are among the African tribes for whom cattle are economically and culturally important. Yet they also keep camels as well as sheep and goats—whose products they consume or trade for grain, tea, and sugar. Even though they are pastoralists, they eat meat only occasionally. Milk, blood, and a porridge made of sorghum and other grains form the basis of a diet won from a harsh and unpredictable environment.

The second group, the Yörük of Turkey, raise their herds for the purpose of exchange with other groups. Traditionally the Yörük cultivated no crops, preferring to use the income from their stock to buy grain and other foodstuffs from the agriculturists of their region. Nor did they have permanent settlements; they moved regularly and on a tight schedule in order to get adequate pasturage. Economic factors have caused them to change their pattern somewhat in recent years, however, and the majority now live in towns and villages.

Elliot Fratkin with his field assistants Patrick Sunewan and Larian Alia-yaro. Fratkin, in keeping with the general ethno-graphic approach to field-work, has spent many months living with the people about whom he reports.

(Elliot Fratkin)

The Ariaal of Northern Kenya

In 1974, Elliot Fratkin stopped his unreliable mo-torcycle in the dusty market town of Marsabit, un-able to continue to Ethiopia, where he had planned to carry out fieldwork among pastoralists: the bor-der was closed because of a coup against Haile Se-lassie (Fratkin, 1991, p. 4).[1] Sitting dejectedly in a bar and considering the problem of what to do next, he was approached by a young man who in-vited him out to a settlement ten kilometers to the south to see a dance. He accepted, and thus he be-gan a study of the Ariaal that has continued until today. The dance that he witnessed was not a tourist show; over 300 warriors were in the middle of a ritual lasting several days that was held to min-imize the disharmony caused by the recent killing of one of their leaders (1991, p. 5). He remained two years; he returned in 1985 for more work and again in 1990, 1992, and 1994. Thus, Fratkin has been able to see how Ariaal society has changed: how they have coped with the many intrusions into their earlier way of life, and, in particular, how the development projects that were meant to assist them actually worked out. Well-intentioned efforts at relieving famine and drought often have had un-intended, negative consequences.

[1] The following account of the Ariaal is based on Elliot Fratkin's 1991 book, *Surviving drought and development: Ariaal pas-toralists of Northern Kenya*, unless otherwise noted.

The Ariaal probably number some 7,000 per-sons living in Kenya's most arid and least densely populated district; other pastoral populations nearby include the closely related Samburu (70,000) and the Rendille (15,000), and the more distantly related Maasai (350,000) who live to the south.

The Origins of the Ariaal

While ethnic identities often seem fixed and time-less, it is important to keep in mind that social identity is always being transformed with the pas-sage of time: new formations arise and others dis-appear. The Ariaal are a good example of this process. Today, they strongly stress their unique identity and the ways in which they differ from their neighbors. Still, there is good evidence that this identity has its historical origins in groups of refugees from the Samburu, Rendille, and possibly Maasai groups who came together as a result of in-tertribal warfare and drought. Over the years they coalesced as a distinctive population with its own approach to pastoralism. The last quarter of the nineteenth century was a turbulent era for pas-toralists in Kenya. Not only was there a prolonged period of drought, but a number of epidemics dev-astated many herds. It was in this context that war-fare broke out as pastoralists raided each other's herds, particularly among Maasai groups. Impov-erished groups of Samburu, whose herds were rav-ished by rinderpest, fled to Rendille territory where

Figure 6–1. Territory of the Ariaal, Samburu, Rendille, and Pokot.

they formed mixed Samburu/Rendille communities subsisting on camels and sheep and goats.

They were, by necessity, confined to fringe areas that neither the main elements of the Samburu nor the Rendille exploited. However, as is often the case with the impoverished or socially marginal groups, they soon came to prosper by adopting practices from each population and developing their own distinctive pastoral strategy. They made careful use of a wide range of resources—raising camels as well as cattle and small stock, strategically deploying labor, and maintained close relations with their more populous neighbors. The Ariaal speak Samburu (a Nilotic language related to Maasai) and most are also fluent in Rendille (an Afro-Asiatic language related to Somali); they in-

termarry with both; and they share some religious and social customs with each (but in their own unique mix).

The Ariaal Adaptation

What really distinguishes the Ariaal, apart from their own assertions of identity, is their approach to animal husbandry. They have adapted to the plains and slopes around Mt. Marsabit and the Ndoto Mountains—an ecologically marginal region that they successfully exploit by using a highly diversified system of husbandry based on large inputs of household labor (Fratkin, 1991, p. 16). Unlike the Samburu (whose economy is based on raising cattle and small stock) and the Rendille (who raise camels and small stock), the Ariaal utilize all three types of animals, thus using a broader spectrum of resources and affording greater economic security.

The complexity of the terrain and the variety of resource potentials it offers provide the key to their subsistence strategy. The Ariaal live in a semi-desert environment with low and variable rainfall, and marked seasonality; they ". . . use their domesticated animals to convert patchy and seasonal vegetative resources into a constant supply of food in the form of milk, meat, blood, and a surplus with which to trade for grains, tea, and sugar" (p. 39). Water is clearly the factor that determines much of the Ariaal's herding activity and patterns of movement. The Ariaal have almost 10,000 square kilometers in which to herd, but this region is among the most arid in Kenya. The highlands receive an average of less than 500mm (20 inches) of rainfall per year and the lowlands average 250 mm. The rainfall is erratic and irregular, so that one cannot predict its occurrence or intensity (p. 39). However, most rainfall occurs in two seasons: the "long rains" between March and May, and the "short rains" in October and November. The periods between the two rainy seasons are called, very appropriately, the "long hunger" and the "short hunger" (p. 39).

During the wet season, provided the rains come as hoped, the Ariaal can utilize surface water in temporary flood plains, in pools, and in transient rivers. During the dry seasons, they must rely on hand-dug wells around the base of the mountains as well as a limited number of mechanized wells (pp. 39–42). They cannot, however, live or camp too near the water sources or their herds will destroy the vegetation.

The key to survival is herd diversity and mobility. Herd diversity allows a family to use different pastures and ensures against loss due to epidemics (p. 37); mobility is an effective adaptation to their arid environment, where rapid deterioration of vegetation for grazing requires regular herd movement. Moreover, vegetation is only rich in nutrients during the limited growing season.

Diversity in Livestock. Ariaal herds generally consist of cattle, camels, and small stock such as sheep and goats. Cattle, which are grass-eaters and require water every two days, need to be kept in the highlands. Desert-adapted camels can go for days without water and eat leaves and shrub stems that do well when grasses are in decline. Sheep and goats do well in the desert, but must be kept near water sources to meet their need for water every two days. Because of these different requirements, the animals are divided into **domestic herds**, which are kept near the settlements, and **camp herds**, which are taken great distances in search of grazing and water. The domestic herd usually contains stock that produces milk (cattle and camels), a few male camels and donkeys for transport, and some sheep and goats for meat and trade. The camp herd will contain the balance of the non-milking animals.

In this harsh environment, a high rate of livestock mortality is a constant problem. In some years, the Ariaal may lose half their animals. The Ariaal have adapted, as have many East African pastoralists, by keeping a large number of diverse livestock. This is in contrast to many herders in better-endowed regions, who generally prefer to concentrate on few species and to maintain their number at a lower level so that each animal is well fed. The Ariaal prefer female animals due to their reproductive and milk-producing capabilities. After a drought, females can replenish the diminished herd. Females also can supply the Ariaal with milk, which constitutes about 70 percent of the diet in the wet season. The balance of their diet is supplied by meat, purchased grains, and occasionally blood tapped from living animals.

Camels are the primary milk producers, particularly during the dry months when they continue to produce (unlike cattle, sheep, or goats). Unfortunately, they are very slow to reproduce and up to one-third of their offspring may die. Like many East African herders, the Ariaal keep the East African breed of zebu cattle, which have a back hump to enable the animal to store calories in the form of fat. They cannot survive in the lowlands, and their milk production (in this very arid environment) is half that of camels. Still, they reproduce at least twice as fast as camels. One important function of cattle is to serve as exchange goods, particularly for wives, and as ritual sacrifices at weddings, etc. Cattle also are a major source of cash when sold to purchase store-bought maize meal—ground corn meal, which is a crucial food item when milk is scarce.

The value of small stock cannot be underestimated in the household economy; some households have as many as 300 goats and sheep. Poor households tend to have proportionately more small stock. Camels and cattle, which are considered prestige items, are slow to reproduce and are expensive to buy. The Ariaal tend to prefer goats to sheep, since they do better in the intense heat, but both animals reproduce rapidly and are easily sold or traded if the family needs cash. They are also a ready source of meat.

Seasonal Movements. Ariaal herding camps, in their search for graze and browse, disperse over a large area, particularly in the dry months of the year (October through February or March). In the driest months, the household breaks up into two quite different units. In one, the **domestic settlement,** the younger cattle, along with a few camels and goats and sheep, are maintained by older married men, women, and adolescent children of both sexes. Since the domestic herds have to be given water every two or three days, these settlements are often near trading centers and permanent sources of water.

The second unit, the **stock camp,** keeps the mature nonlactating cattle, camels, and some small stock far out on the plains or up in the Ndeto Mountains. The stock camp is staffed by young unmarried men, members of the warrior age grade (discussed on page 162), and older boys, who are faced with the dangerous and exhausting task of tending the camp herd. The herd must be continually moved over long distances during the day and guarded at night against human and other predators. The stock camp's personnel and their livestock may be drawn from as few as one or two households or as many as a dozen or so if a number of households lack sufficient labor of their own.

The cattle in the dry-season stock camps are mature animals strong enough to withstand the rigors of being herded to distant grazing areas and to require watering only every three days or so. Camels are usually herded separately in the desert plains. The fact that camels and goats browse on leaves and branches not only widens the resource base to include shrub land, but very likely also keeps the thornbush from spreading at the expense of grass. In many of the drier parts of East Africa,

thorn shrubs and trees of the genus Acacia are dominant over the grasses; by keeping the acacias in check, the browsing activities of goats help make possible the grazing activities of cattle (Conant, 1982).

The consumption of blood drawn from living cattle and other livestock is common in East Africa. Among the Ariaal, blood is regularly taken from all livestock. Men and older boys are responsible for bleeding cattle by shooting a blocked arrow into the jugular vein; the blood is then caught in containers. In the settlement camps, blood is usually mixed with milk, since women are not supposed to drink pure blood; the pure blood is consumed largely by the warriors in the stock camps, where there is little milk. Up to four liters may be drawn from a mature camel or oxen every three to four weeks.

The remote camps place the herders at some risk from raids by neighboring groups, who, much like the Ariaal themselves, are always searching for grazing and water resources in a region where both are diminishing. The neighbors of the Ariaal who might be in competition include the Turkana and the Boran. The Samburu and the Rendille are traditional allies, and their frequent sharing of water and grass resources is facilitated by gift-giving and marriage exchanges. It is when the dry season is prolonged that the risk of conflict or the weakening of established ties is greatest.

The Household: Organization and Status

The economy and social life is rooted in the household. Fratkin puts it this way: "An Ariaal household can be defined as the smallest domestic group with its own livestock and which makes decisions over allocation of labor and livestock capital. Daily life and social interaction are focused on the household and the settlement in which it is located" (1991, p. 57). The settlement consists of independent households who, whether temporarily or not, live together; usually, the settlements are composed of patrilineally related men and their families.

Households are typically headed by a married male stock owner and include his wife or co-wives, children, and occasionally a dependent mother-in-law or married daughter who has not yet joined her husband's village. Each married woman is responsible for building and maintaining her own house; consequently, an individual household may consist of three or four houses including two co-wives, a widowed mother, or a poor affine (in-law) and their children. While household maintenance takes some time, most settlement life revolves around animal care. Just as in the distant herding camps, animal care in the community involves a great deal of cooperation in watering and grazing the animals.

From one season to the next, each household can drastically alter its herding strategy and change herding partners. A large household (one with several wives and married sons) may split up into smaller units, which then scatter over thousands of square miles of rangeland. Ties of kinship are obviously more difficult to maintain and manipulate among pastoralists than they are in the more densely populated and far more stable farming areas. In such circumstances, people tend to establish extra-descent group ties through the device of **age grades**. An age grade consists of people of the same sex and approximately the same age who share a set of duties and privileges.

Just as with the Tamang of Tingling there is a great deal of variation among households due to the domestic cycle. Among the Ariaal this is amplified by variability in inherited wealth, with some men gaining larger herds than they can manage with their labor while others may not have enough to support themselves and be forced to work for other households in order to buy animals and build up their own herds.

The Age Grades and Age Sets

The Ariaal age-grade and age-set systems, like those of many other East African peoples, are highly complex institutions with multiple functions. These systems are widespread throughout East Africa and are particularly prominent among such pastoral groups as the Ariaal, Rendille, Samburu, Turkana, and Pokot. Among the Ariaal, the age grades serve primarily to organize labor and structure politics. Men pass through different age grades as members of named cohorts or **age sets** that are formed every fourteen years.

Males are divided into boys, warriors, and elders; females into young girls, adolescent girls, and circumcised (by clitoridectomy) married women.

Each age grade has its distinct insignia and rules about what it can and cannot wear, what foods it may consume, and with whom it may associate. Each grade is also associated with particular rights, duties, and obligations. Age grades determine the formal political structure and the system is based on the primacy of elder males over younger males and men over women. Elders are the heads of households and function as the leaders of the tribe.

The warriors are responsible for herding, and spend approximately fourteen years as herdsmen caring for animals in the stock camps. They grow their hair into long red-dyed plaits and may not eat food that has been even seen by women. When young men between the ages of eleven and twelve are initiated into the warrior grade together, they will mark this by being circumcised as a group and given a group name that they will use for life, and which will, even subsequent to the death of the last member, be used to identify historical periods.

Adolescent girls are responsible for tending the small stock near the settlements, and are forbidden to associate with any married men—even their own fathers. When they move into the "married woman" stage, they become dependent members of their husband's household and lineage. Adolescent boys and married elders may milk camels, but women and warriors may not. These and many other ritual prohibitions, rights, and duties sort society into specific work groups.

The Ariaal rise through the age grades with a specific cohort of their contemporaries that is seperately named and that stays together for life. Progression through the age grades is automatic, and it is assumed that each member of an age grade will be able to perform the age-appropriate role. The age grades through which age sets pass are effective ways to organize labor. Age sets also provide the basis for exchanges and alliances that cut across the boundaries of patrilineal clans and lineages. Men, for example, form close friendships with age set mates and exchange gifts of cattle and small stock; they may even take up residence in a settlement belonging to another clan by using the age set connection.

Gender Roles and Power

Clearly, social and economic roles are allocated according to gender as well as age among the Ariaal.

The division of labor starts very early and lasts until death. By age two or three, girls and boys are encouraged to participate in symbolic activities that quickly become gender-specific tasks. Girls play at such chores as gathering sticks for fuel, carrying water, milking, and gathering food. Boys play at tending livestock, hunting, making spears and bows and arrows, and being warriors. By the time they reach age four or five, their play has become work. The small amount of water children can carry and the help they can give in managing livestock soon become measurable contributions to a household's energy budget. The children soon add the care of younger children to their tasks. While women are responsible for their own infants, almost all child care is in the hands of slightly older children and of some elderly men and women.

Ariaal women and girls commonly milk all of the domestic cattle, sheep, and goats. Women supervise or carry out gathering the firewood, the grass for thatching, and the thornbush needed to build and repair houses and fences. They haul water to the homestead, while men dig the step wells. Among the Ariaal, the men, exclusively, tend camels, as well as all animals sent to distant pastures. This is not always the case in pastoral societies, as we see in the Gender Issues box, *Being a Shepherdess in the Negev*, page 164. Men are also responsible for butchering livestock. While the Ariaal cut the throats of goats, cattle are often killed with spears in the context of a ritual.

Women play critical roles in economic life; indeed, their labor and reproduction is essential to the household's well-being and the social standing of its male head. This is reflected in both the idealization and practice of polygyny. More than half the households contain co-wives. At marriage, a woman's father is given a customary "bride-wealth" payment (see Chapter 8) of eight cattle. Shortly thereafter she joins her husband, who is of another lineage and thus another settlement. If her husband dies, she will still live with her husband's lineage, and may well bear children fathered by his younger brother (this is called levirate fatherhood; see Chapter 8). It is very hard for a woman to return to her natal settlement should she wish to divorce or move after a husband's death; her family would have to return the cattle they had received.

Ariaal women are virtually powerless in the formal political arena. They may not participate in

Ariaal woman milking her goat. As with many East African people, small animals are predominately the concern of women.

(Elliot Fratkin)

public discussion, where decisions affecting the group are usually taken consensually by elder males. They also have very little economic power. While her husband will "give" her a herd of milking stock to tend, she may not sell or dispose of them. She does control the house itself, since she builds and repairs it. All animals are male owned; all food, in principle at least, is controlled by her father or husband. She will not inherit either from her father or husband. All livestock passes to the male children. Thus the work a young man does for his elders is eventually paid for in the form of gifts or inheritances. Women, on the other hand, receive no compensation for their labor.

Can the Ariaal Survive Development?

Until quite recently, the Ariaal lived in a situation of benign neglect as far as the outside world was concerned. Ariaal pastoralism traditionally was dependent on the local ecosystem, constrained by the availability of water and the range of environments that could be exploited by mixed herds of goats, cattle, and camels. They had close relationships with the Rendille and Samburu, with whom they

Gender Issues

Being a Shepherdess in the Negev

BEDOUIN ANTHROPOLOGIST AREF Abu-Rabia describes contemporary Bedouin pastoralism in great detail (1994). The Bedouin of the Negev today pasture their flocks of sheep in the general vicinity of their homes, although in the past they were much more mobile. Generally herding is seen as the work of men and boys, but because so many of them are employed in construction work, even young girls are involved in shepherding. In fact, women have come to feel that girls are better at caring for the sheep than are men or boys; after all, in her traditional role a girl already was milking the ewes and devoted to the flock (p. 62). Women are the first to rise in the morning and the last to go to bed; girls are taught to take ad-vantage of being with the flocks to collect firewood, to spin wool and goat hair, and to embroider. Since two or more girls watch the herd together, this is an opportunity to practice the art of trilling—a distinctive form of singing for which Bedouin women are well known. "The bond of the Bedouin woman to the flock is expressed in the following song:

'Oh, happy am I, the shepherdess, giving utterance to my freedom. My destiny and that of the flock are bound together.' "[1994, p. 62]

But there is a difference in male herding and the activities of young girls. Because of strict codes of family honor, young women cannot risk being in the company of unrelated males. As a consequence, they have to watch the flocks in the vicinity of the house, where they can be watched in turn by their relatives. Usually younger women go into the fields in pairs, and, while the flock is in the pasture, they sit on top of a hill so that they can be seen from a distance. This watch is maintained because female seclusion is basic to their sense of family honor—a belief shared by both sexes. "Men and women constantly discuss the subject, and so heighten awareness of the women's honour" (Abu-Rabia, 1994, p. 60). While restricting the activities of women, the notion of family honor does not hinder their productive roles in the domestic economy. They are central to it.

---

intermarried, traded, and sometimes competed. Until Kenya attained independence from Great Britain in 1967 the Ariaal were fairly self-sufficient, trading with neighbors when necessary. Responses to external events were relatively rare. But since independence, such external factors as government-provided health and education services, famine relief, and the construction of wells and roads have forced basic changes in their way of life, especially among those living near administrative centers and missions. Many missions have opened schools with the explicit aim of separating children from their traditional religious beliefs (and hence their native culture). Missions and national and international agencies have all intervened in ways that threaten the delicate balancing act that has so long enabled the Ariaal to survive drought and epidemics.

Since the Kenyan government opened the region to foreign missionaries in the 1970s, dozens of Christian mission stations have been opened. The government and the missionaries, despite very different ideologies, share the view that pastoralism is a primitive, backward way of life and that people should be settled in towns (Fratkin, 1991, p. 77). While the missionaries wish to make converts, the government's policy is based on the notion that pastoralism is incompatible with a modern society and maintaining tight control over its citizens. Whatever the goals, moving pastoralists to towns is problematic in an arid region that cannot support an agricultural subsistence pattern.

One means by which the pastoralists are brought into larger settlements is through food subsidies or handouts. This is a practice used to gain converts in many parts of the world by many different religions. The insidious aspect of this approach is that people quickly incorporate the cheap or free food into their domestic economy, soon becoming dependent and losing their traditional self-sufficiency. As a result, many Ariaal families are camping near mission stations. Often households split, with one wife and her children living near town and the second wife staying with the husband in the traditional settlement.

Paradoxically, a further problem involves efforts to promote conservation. Many people automatically blame nomadic pastoralists for overgrazing and the spread of desertification. In fact, the Ariaal system of production prior to the settlement of communities near the missions and administrative centers was entirely conservationist in effect. Animals were moved regularly to follow the major peaks in vegetative production; they were not kept on declining pastures or browses, as to do so would be counterproductive. However, the handouts and restrictions on land use have led to overgrazing of land near mission and government-created towns.

Elliot Fratkin, while pessimistic about the future of the Ariaal people's traditional economy, does see hope in their natural resilience and ability to respond to changing circumstances. He has some practical suggestions which, if adopted, could improve their chances as Kenya continues to develop a modern infrastructure.

1. Development planners need to appreciate the sophistication of adaptive systems, which, like those of the Ariaal, have developed over long periods of time.

2. Planners should concentrate on assisting animal production through veterinary services and pest control, rather than trying to curtail production to reduce herd size.

3. Grazing restrictions should be lifted, since they interfere with herd dispersal, the ecologically and economically sound practice of grazing many herds over a wide area.

4. The market economy would be enhanced by improvements in transportation, auction facilities, and information, and by deregulating animal prices.

Lugi Lengesen, Elliot Fratkin's close friend among the Ariaal, sums up his prospects for the future. "This is not good land to grow corn or raise gardens. That is something people in the south know how to do very well. But we Ariaal know how to grow our cattle and camels, we know this land because it is our farm. Give us veterinary medicines for our animals, medicine for our infants, schools to educate our children in livestock and health, and markets and transportation to sell our animals. Then places like Korr can become beautiful."

The Yörük of Turkey

The Yörük are transhumant sheepherders who move their flocks back and forth between two grazing zones in southeastern Turkey. In winter, they camp on low plains on what is geographically an extension of the Syrian steppe. In spring, when the weather warms, they move the herds inland some 100 kilometers (62 miles) to craggy, mountainous summer pasturelands. Traditionally, the Yörük kept camels to transport their belongings during migrations; their economy was based on the sale of sheep and sheep products (Bates, 1973). Today the nomadic Yörük use trucks and tractor-drawn wagons to move their flocks and possessions. The Yörük's sheep, unlike the Ariaal's stock, serve almost exclusively as the capital basis for market production. Although the nomadic Yörük do eat some of their animal products—milk, butter, cheese, and yogurt—for the most part these products, along with wool and male lambs, are sold. And with the money they receive the Yörük buy their necessities—chiefly the agricultural products that constitute most of their diet.

This, then, is not a subsistence economy. The Yörük are completely dependent on a market economy not only to sell their animal products and buy their food but also to rent the lands on which they graze their sheep. They actively use the market system to increase their holdings in livestock, to accumulate cash to buy consumer goods, and even to acquire land or urban houses. As a result, even relatively small fluctuations in market prices can bankrupt a household—or make it rich.

When wealth and poverty were relatively temporary conditions, and when each household expected to increase its herds over time, the society was relatively egalitarian. By and large, no one family or elite group held substantial economic or political power over others. This is the situation among many herding peoples, since the volatility

Figure 6–2. Yörük territory

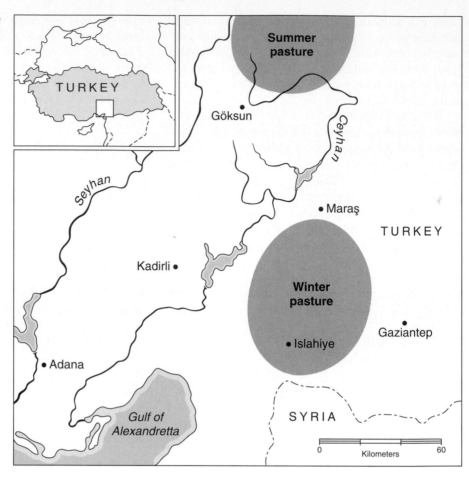

of animal capital works against the long-term perpetuation of rule by a special class within their society. Today, the situation among the Yörük is changing. Poverty is no longer a temporary condition among herders, and the group of well-to-do merchant families who have emerged in recent years may well constitute a distinctly privileged group.

The Market Economy

The market economy is part of the Yörük way of life. All transactions are made on the basis of established market values, even when goods and services are bartered. If a Yörük family trades wool for tobacco, for example, the exchange is made according to the relative market value of each item. Supply and demand within a particular area can al-

ter the values, of course, but such variations only restructure market prices to fit local conditions. The vast majority of transactions, however, involve cash or promissory notes. Often a herd owner will contract to supply animals or milk at a future date, accepting an advance payment in cash. Fluctuations in the market prices of animal products, of the foods the Yörük buy, and of the land they rent become significant problems to which they must continually respond.

While the Yörük are dependent on the market, they are just as dependent on other groups: the condition of the crops grown by those other groups, their needs, and the value they place on their own and the Yörük's goods. For the Yörük, the presence of other groups constitutes an all-important environmental variable that shapes their economic decisions at every turn.

In spring, the Yörük move their animals and camps to high-mountain pastures. Today this move is usually made by trucks carrying both sheep and herders.

(Daniel Bates)

Probably the most significant feature of such interactions is the Yörük's reliance on other groups for pastureland. Unlike the Ariaal, for example, the Yörük do not own or even have traditional claims to the pastures they use; they must rent them. In some cases they also have to pay for access to lands along the migration route, although not when they move the animals by truck. Thus, although the outer limit of their migration schedule is established largely by climate and topography, political and social factors help determine the actual schedule. When Yörük herd owners want to move their animals, they must take into account the wishes of the people who own the land that the animals must cross. This land is predominantly agricultural. The pastoralists would prefer to keep the animals longer in the lowland plains, but herd movement too late in the season would cause extensive crop damage. They would prefer to return to the plains earlier in the fall, if they did not have to wait for the harvest.

As one might expect, disputes often develop between pastoralists and agriculturalists over crop damages. In recent years, the Turkish government has intervened to regulate the herd migrations and to see that all claims for crop damage are satisfied. Without governmental regulation, some agricultural lands would probably have to be abandoned because damage would be too frequent and too costly. This was a common problem in the past. Each annual migration, then, is a complex strategy determined by the availability of grass, planting or harvest schedules, and the restrictions set by the government.

Social Organization

As with the Ariaal, the composition of Yörük camp groups changes regularly. As many as twenty households or as few as two may camp together; larger clusters generally gather in the summer pasture areas. Although in some pastoral societies (such as the Ariaal) the labor of herding is pooled among members of a camp group, the Yörük household is, in effect, a self-contained producing unit: it relies almost exclusively on its own labor. The rental of pasturelands is an important function of the larger camp group. Though the families that make up the camp do not generally pool their labor, they do pool money to rent their grazing lands jointly.

The composition of a camp group depends on several factors, but not on the same kind of rigid rules that govern Ariaal camp groups. Kinship is one such factor. The Yörük place great emphasis on patrilineage, and often families that camp together are patrilineally related. Some households, however, camp with people more closely related to the wife than to the husband. Sometimes this arrangement simply reflects the woman's wish to be with her sisters or brothers for a season or two. Or it may be a way for the family to secure better grazing than they could get by cooperating with the husband's patrilineal relatives. In other cases, family quarrels may be the determing factor. Thus, while kinship to some degree determines the camp membership, sentiment and economic strategy keep such communities flexible.

Adapting to a Changing Economy

In recent years the Yörük have had to face a variety of new situations. One major problem is inflation, which has affected the entire country. Although rental fees for pastures have gone up rapidly, so have the prices of animal products. This development has resulted in a significant transformation of Yörük society. Generally speaking, small animal husbandry has enabled them to cope with a changing economy better than most other groups. At the same time, new developments in mechanized transport and in the opening of new markets in the oil-rich Arab world have created new possibilities for some Yörük.

New Strategies. The Yörük today actually practice three adaptive strategies: nomadic pastoralism, sedentary agriculture, and trade or shopkeeping in town. The nomads have developed a very specialized adaptation, engaging in animal husbandry and trading in animals and animal products. At the same time, entire villages of settled Yörük now engage in agriculture, shopkeeping, and commerce. The ability of the Yörük to adapt to their changing environment is evident by looking at some of their activities. Some, for example, operate mobile dairies and follow the herders, buying their milk and converting it to cheese for urban markets. During the Iran-Iraq war in the 1980s, those that owned trucks transported goods to the war-torn countries. Today, some Yörük have become brokers buying large numbers of animals and shipping them to distant markets in Arab lands, where meat is in great demand. Very frequently entrepreneurs engage in several of these activities simultaneously, sometimes coordinating their ventures in town and only sometimes camping in tents.

One point must be stressed. Yörük society, like most others, is changing rapidly, and the challenge to the ethnographer is to describe a way of life without implying that what is observed is a timeless pattern. Daniel Bates first went to southeastern Turkey in 1968, but few of his initial economic observations still hold today. Culturally, too, the

Yörük are changing. In 1968, patterns of male-female interactions, recreation, and socializing were very different. Now even pastoral households have access to television sets, refrigerators, and other modern appliances. They usually keep them in village or town dwellings, where they spend part of each year and where children of school age live while attending school.

While the nomadic herders and the new class of businessmen and farmers are economically distinct, they differ little in cultural identity and there is no antipathy between them. After all, they are all Yörük. Some of the strategies are actually complementary: the town-based businessmen often depend on the herders for their trade, while the herders depend on the small businessmen for the credit they need in order to go on herding in a volatile market economy. The different strategies are also interrelated in that families move from one to another as circumstances warrant. Many people who were settled in a town when Bates revisited the area in 1978 were once again living in tents in 1983. While they had liked town life, they decided they could make more money raising livestock than selling shoes. Today, wealth or access to capital determines whether a household herds or settles down to other endeavors.

In 1978, and later in 1983, Bates found that the herders who were using trucks to transport their animals between pastures no longer migrated as a group. Herding had become a form of ranching, where the "ranch" consists of many pastures used sequentially, as sheep are trucked among them. The contemporary Yörük household stays behind in a town or village, leaving herding to the menfolk or hired shepherds. In fact, by 1983 some herders were making so much money from animal export that they could afford to rent wheat fields and turn them into pastures, and thus could spend most of the year in one place.

Far fewer families were being supported by pastoralism in 1983, and those few were the better-off members of the society. The majority of households that had been nomadic in 1968–1970 had settled in villages and towns as laborers and tenant farmers, unable to continue making their living in the traditional way because of the rising costs of pasture and feed. Some were living precariously; those who had invested what they had in a shop or some other business had prospered.

The adaptation of the Yörük, then, is a matter not simply of accommodating to the physical environment but of finding a niche in a larger social system. To understand even their pastoral economy, we must take into account who owns what. Likewise, it is impossible to discuss the specialization of nomadic pastoralism among the Yörük without reference to other specializations within the larger society on which the Yörük depend for trade. Thus, the effective environment of the Yörük has a political and social dimension as well as a physical and biological one.

Increasing Stratification. Wealth is no longer spread evenly among the Yörük. The new economic system has transformed a generally egalitarian society to one that is decidedly stratified. The poorer herders, those with just enough animals to make herding viable, are often in debt and seldom have the ready cash they need to rent pastureland, pay for winter grains, or, more recently, hire truck transport. To pay debts accumulated during the winter, they are forced to shear their sheep at the beginning of spring. But early shearing leaves them at a disadvantage in the migration to high pastures: they must wait longer before leaving, as shorn sheep are vulnerable to disease in snow and extreme cold. When they finally do leave, they may travel over lands already grazed by sheep belong-

ing to wealthier herd owners who could afford to forgo an early shearing. The poor grazing leaves the last flocks tired and hungry by the time they reach summer pasture. The sheep of the poorer herd owners are more likely to die during migration than those of the wealthier ones. The affluent herders not only have healthier sheep, but they are also able to transport animals to choice but distant grazing areas.

Even after selling their spring wool, many Yörük herders do not usually have the cash necessary to rent summer pasture. Needing an additional source of income or credit, many supplement their income by selling milk to the mobile dairy tents that follow the flocks. Many of these dairies are owned by the wealthier herders, who have established dairies and have bought stores and land in an attempt to diversify. Just as there is a limit below which a flock is not economically viable, there is an upper limit as well. Huge numbers of animals require a large deployment of labor, so the wealthy can only increase their wealth through diversification once their herds reach an optimal size.

The dairies are rather sizable enterprises with a ready supply of capital that enables them not only to buy the herders' milk but to purchase it in advance. Such milk futures are purchased at a relatively low price, but they give the poorer herders the money they need for pasture rental. Once the

In the late 1960s entrepreneurs established mobile dairies that follow the herds, collecting milk and processing it into cheese for urban markets.
(Daniel Bates)

In the 1960s, traditional Yörük marriage customs began to change, reflecting changes in the larger Turkish culture. The two couples here reflect this in their attire and lifestyles.
(Daniel Bates)

dairymen have the milk, they process it into cheese and sell it for a substantial profit in urban markets. Thus, the dairies allow the herders to fend off bankruptcy at the same time that they yield high profits to the dairymen.

It is easy to see that such a system encourages **economic stratification**, the creation of increasingly fixed classes of rich and poor. In the past, the Yörük had no such permanent economic groups. As long as the people remained herders, they could expect to go from rags to riches and back again several times in the course of their lives, because animals are such a volatile form of capital. But once the temporarily wealthy began to invest their wealth in more fixed forms of capital such as farms, shops, and dairies, their wealth ceased to be temporary, and indeed, it began to increase. The increase in wealth enabled them to settle down. The traditional way of life—nomadic, egalitarian—is slowly giving way to a more complex, stratified pattern with a variety of strategies feeding into one another and reinforcing economic differences.

Future Prospects

In many respects the Yörük are prospering in the rapidly developing domestic economy of modern Turkey, since animal production is a profitable endeavor. Few families still live in the traditional tent—at least not throughout the year. They now live in town, and the children are attending schools. However, many of the young among the Yörük are abandoning the pastoral lifestyle and moving to Ankara, the capital, or to Istanbul, which is now swollen to over 12 million people. Some have migrated, legally or not, to Europe or the United States in order to secure a better future.

The reasons why the Yörük would leave a region in which their main subsistence strategy seems to be working very well are quite simple. With over two-thirds of the population below the age of twenty, the local economy cannot absorb all of them into the work force. Education and access to information about the rest of the world gives rise to demands for a standard of living and consumer items that cannot be met through local wage employment. Finally, pastoralism is now a highly specialized and capitalized mode of production, and is engaged in by fewer and fewer households, each managing larger and larger herds.

Summary

PASTORALISTS ENGAGE IN ANIMAL HUSBANDRY: the breeding, care, and use of herd animals such as sheep, goats, camels, cattle, horses, reindeer, or yaks. Most pastoralists in nonindustrial societies are nomadic. Both the mobility of pastoralists and the degree to which they rely on animal husbandry varies with environmental, social, and economic conditions. Few pastoralist groups rely exclusively on their herds; they tend to pursue a more generalized subsistence strategy.

Nomads follow two basic patterns: horizontal migration, characterized by regular movement over a large area in search of fodder; and transhumance, or seasonal movement between upland and lowland pastures.

Specialized pastoralism, or exclusive reliance on animal husbandry, may have developed from a farming/herding pattern. Changes in agricultural practices, such as the use of canal irrigation, may have pushed grazing lands farther from settlements. The consequent increased demands of both herding and agriculture may have led some families to specialize in agriculture and others to choose herding exclusively. The divergence of strategies may have been encouraged by the failure of irrigation for some groups. Extensive irrigation may cause the water table (the level of water under the earth) to fall, or it may increase the salinity of the soil until crops no longer thrive.

While pastoralism is a relatively efficient means of extracting energy from a harsh environment, it produces less energy per acre of land than agriculture, and population densities are correspondingly low. Pastoralism is an alternative to agriculture, but it is almost never independent of it. If pastoralists don't raise vegetable foods, they acquire them through trade.

In nonindustrial societies, sedentary pastoralism, or animal husbandry that does not involve mobility, is generally rare. The usual pattern is nomadic pastoralism—the practice of moving one's herds from pasture to pasture as the seasons and circumstances require. The main reason that pastoralists migrate is to secure adequate grazing land in a marginal environment. However, migration may also be a means to maintain political autonomy or even to control settled groups. The composition of local groupings in pastoral societies often shifts as nomadic camping units move, break apart, and come together with other units.

Virtually all pastoral populations are organized in tribes, communities of people who claim kinship, usually by descent from one or more common ancestors. Tribal organization provides for positions of leadership and allows for coordination of social and economic activities.

The basic economic unit is the household. Households may move frequently one year and be largely sedentary the next. One household may herd alone, while others may temporarily combine forces. Families may shift between agriculture and herding, or they may give up herding for other pursuits such as shopkeeping.

The Ariaal of Kenya maintain a subsistence economy through a balanced and diversified strategy of keeping cattle, camels, and small stock (sheep and goats). The Ariaal display many aspects of the East African cattle complex, a socioeconomic system in which cattle represent social status as well as wealth. The cattle play a significant symbolic role in social ties, obligations, and rituals. The traditional bridewealth is eight head of cattle given to the father of the bride-to-be.

The basic unit of social organization is the household. A household consists of one or more houses belonging to the wife or wives of the male head of household. Households are located in settlements usually belonging to one patrilineal clan, a large group whose common descent is traced through the paternal line. The Ariaal marry out of their natal clans and, to some extent, intermarry with the neighboring Rendille and Samburu. The groom's family gives bridewealth to the bride's family to compensate them for the loss of their daughter's services. The labor of women and girls is crucial to the functioning of households. Men tend the camels, as well as manage the family's livestock on distant grazing and browse lands.

The Ariaal are organized in age grades, each grade consisting of people of approximately the same age and sex, who share a set of duties, prohibitions, symbols, and privileges. Most important, age grades structure the organization of labor. Young men of the warrior grade, for example, will spend approximately fourteen years as herdsmen caring for the animals in the stock camps, which are distant from the households main settlement residence. After completing their duties, the same named set of men will all become elders.

While the Ariaal have survived drought and famine because of their ability to simultaneously exploit a number of species of livestock and different microenvironments in their 14,000 sq. km. range, they may not be able to withstand development. Northern Kenya has seen a great deal of missionary and governmental activity aimed at settling the pastoralists and, for rather different reasons, changing the Ariaal way of life. What is happening to the pastoralists (as with other such populations in East Africa) is that they are becoming dependent on food subsidies and handouts; their traditional grazing areas are restricted and their herds are limited in size.

The Yörük of southeastern Turkey traditionally have been nomadic pastoralists who move their sheep between summer and winter pastures. The Yörük are dependent on a market economy to sell their animal products, buy their food, and rent the lands on which they graze their sheep. The activities of the Yörük are shaped not only by climate and topography, but also by political and social factors; the strategy of their migrations is determined by the availability of grass, village planting or harvest schedules, and the restrictions on migration set by the government.

Yörük social organization is flexible. The composition of a camp group may be determined by kinship, sentiment, or economic strategy. Each family within the camp group is a self-sufficient producing unit, although the camp group does rent pastureland jointly.

In recent years the nature of animal husbandry has changed. The rents charged for pastureland have risen, but new opportunities have also opened up. Now many Yörük avail themselves of truck transport and sell animals in Arab countries. As a result, they now practice diverse and complementary strategies: sedentary agriculture, trade, brokerage, and shopkeeping, as well as pastoralism. Until recently, wealth determined whether a household herded or settled down. The rich herders tended to diversify into trading or farming, while the poor struggled to keep their herds. While some of the poorest herders of earlier years have become rich in today's market, this economic system has created increasingly fixed classes of rich and poor for the first time in Yörük society.

Key Terms

age grade	forage
age set	horizontal migration
animal husbandry	nomadic pastoralism
camp herds	sedentary pastoralism
cattle complex	specialized pastoralism
co-resident household	stock camp
domestic herds	transhumance
domestic settlement	water table
economic stratification	

Suggested Readings

Abu-Lughod, L. (1988). *Veiled sentiments: Honor and poetry in a Bedouin society*. Berkeley and Los Angeles: University of California Press. A person-centered ethnography of a community of Bedouins in the western desert of Egypt that focuses on the oral lyric poetry that is used by women and young men in this once nomadic but still pastoral society.

Beck, L. (1992). *Nomad: A year In the life of a Qashqa'i tribesman in Iran*. New Haven, CT: Yale University Press. This political ethnography of elites is a historical and anthropological account of the Turkic-speaking Qashqa'i. The Qashqa'i are a predominantly pastoral nomadic people, but they have highly developed sociopolitical institutions, including a ruling elite that has participated in national and international politics.

Black-Michaud, J. (1986). *Sheep and land: The economics of power in a tribal society*. Cambridge: Cambridge University Press. An examination of the Luristan region of western Iran and the ways in which different populations relate to each other through exchanges between sedentary agricultural and nomadic pastoral populations.

Bradburd, D. (1990). *Kin, class & conflict among Komachi pastoralists*. Washington D.C. and London: Smithsonian Institution Press.

Ekvall, R. B. (1968). *Fields on the hoof: The nexus of Tibetan nomadic pastoralism*. Prospect Heights, IL: Waveland Press. A clearly written case study of pastoralism in a region that is poorly understood ethnographically.

Fratkin, E. (1991). *Surviving drought and development: Ariaal pastoralists of Northern Kenya*. Boulder: Westview Press. Focusing on drought and famine, this ethnography gives us a lucid narrative of the Ariaal and their ability to persist in being pastoralists despite enivornmental and political pressures to settle.

Galaty, J. G. & Bonte, P. (Eds.). (1991). *Herders, warriors and traders: Pastoralism in Africa*. Boulder, CO: Westview Press. A collection of articles on pastoralism in East and West Africa.

Goldstein, M. C. & Beall, C. M. (1994). *World of Mongolia's nomads*. Berkeley: University of California Press. This study looks at a community of Mongolian herders and their adaptation to a market economy since the Soviet bloc breakup.

Janzen, J. (1986). *Nomads in the sultanate of Oman: Tradition and development in Dhofar*. Boulder, CO: Westview Press. A comprehensive and insightful analysis of the traditional living conditions and economic circumstances of the nomadic-peasant population of Dhofar and the rapid changes to which they have been subjected.

Khazanov, A. M. (1984). *Nomads and the outside world*. Cambridge: Cambridge University Press. A good discussion of the many ways in which nomadic pastoralists are integrated into states and empires. The author is a specialist in Central Asia, but deals with pastoralism in general.

Pelto, P. J. (1973). *The snowmobile revolution: Technology and social change in the arctic*. Menlo Park, CA: Benjamin. A study of how the Skolt Lapps of Finland incorporated the snowmobile into their traditional economy, which was focused on reindeer herding.

The Development of Intensive Agriculture
  The Organization of Energy
  *Human Ecology: Human Labor
  as Energy*
  Environmental Resilience, Stability,
    and Change

**From Intensive Agriculture to
Industrialized Farming**
  Population Growth
  Intensification
  Specialization
  Case Study: The Shift to Sisal in Brazil
  Centralization, Collectivization, and
    Communism
  *Case Study: A Sudanese Irrigation
  Project*
  *Case Study: Feeding a Fifth of the
  World: from Chinese Communes
  to Farms*
  Expanding Cities and Migrant Workers
  *State of the Peoples: China's Human
  Traffickers*
  Stratification

Peasant Farmers in an Industrial Society
  Sharecropping
  Access to Land
  Peasant Responses to Oppression
    and Change
  *Case Study: Change in the Japanese
  Farming Village of Shinohata*

**Urbanized Rural Society: Farming in
the United States**
  *Case Study: The Development of
  Agribusiness in Wasco, California*
  *Case Study: The Farmerless Farm in
  the San Joaquin Valley*
  The Family Farm
  *Case Study: Family Farmers in the
  Midwest: An Immigrant Legacy*

Summary
Key Terms
Suggested Readings

Chapter 7

Intensive and Industrial Agriculture

If one were to observe the heartland of the Middle East from an earth-orbiting satellite, most striking would be the sharp contrast between the great expanses of desert and the lush green of cultivated areas. One can stand with one foot in a wheat field and the other in the desert. The Middle East, where agriculture began some 10,000 years ago, is the home of some 200 million people, most of them supported by the crops produced on less than 10 percent of the land by a land-use strategy referred to here as intensive agriculture. Agricultural production is vastly increased through such technological innovations as irrigation, chemical and organic fertilizers, mechanization, and fossil fuel powered equipment.

The impact of intensive land use is evident in Egypt. For example, in 1995, 98 percent of Egypt's population was concentrated on less than 4 percent of its territory; an average of 1,200 to 1,400 people occupied every square kilometer of arable land. Today Egypt has to import large quantities of foodstuffs from other regions of the world. The irony is that both great productivity and accelerating social and economic hardship all too often march hand in hand. In Roman times, Egypt was a major source of grain for the Mediterranean world; as an ancient historian, Ibn Batuta, said, "when famine strikes Egypt (whose lands have been irrigated longer than those of any other area), the world itself cannot feed her people."

Similar patterns of recurring famine and rural hardship are found in other regions where civilizations arose with the development of intensive farming. China, for example, where 1.2 billion people are supported by the production from 11 percent of its land area, has a long history of chronic famine and mass starvation—particularly among the people who themselves produce the food that sustains the country. The present government apparently has reduced the possibility of famine in the near future, but even with increased production and improved food distribution, the threat of hunger is real. As China's population continues to grow, the country has not only more people to feed but less land with which to do it. Urban centers are spreading and the fertility of the soil is diminishing: land is being lost at a faster rate than it can be reclaimed (Smil, 1984, 1994). China has lost about one-third of its crop lands in the last 40 years; percapita farmland availability was reduced by 10 percent in the 1990s and a further 15 percent will be lost by the year 2035 (Smil, 1994, p. 8). Even as the country strains to produce ever more food, the very fact of intensification has caused worsening erosion and soil degradation (Tyler, 1994, p. 8).

India and Bangladesh experience similar pressure on their land; Indonesia, once the most productive region of southeast Asia, is seeing its people's well-being decline. To arrest such a decline, governments often encourage even greater efforts in agriculture, including the destruction of tropical rain forests, to support people forced out of other areas. In Africa south of the Sahara, where population-driven land-use intensification (along with long periods of drought) have often led to devastating environmental problems such as spreading desertification, the spectre of mass starvation looms (Stevens, 1994, p. 10). Nevertheless, within each of these areas we find numerous striking instances of human resourcefulness in the face of environmental problems. This chapter deals with the rise of intensive agriculture and its social corollaries: urbanism, social stratification, and the emergence of a class of peasant farmers. We also discuss the emergence and consequences of industrial farming, which now sustains most of the world's 5.7 billion people (Cowell, 1994, p. 10).

The Development of Intensive Agriculture

The interrelated processes of agricultural intensification and ever-rising requirements for food in combination with declining resources are seen throughout the world. Anthropologists and scientists in other fields have long been concerned with the origins of intensive farming and early civilization, with the social and economic structure of rural society, and with the strategies that have enabled diverse populations to adapt to environmental and other problems. In Chapter 3 we said that intensification involved increasing the yields from labor or land; this implies that there are at least two routes to intensification, and actually many more, due to the complex ways in which land and labor are interrelated. Usually, the perspective of most American or European economists is to concentrate on the former: agricultural history is usually described in terms of progress in labor-saving technology—the plow, seed drills, cultivators, threshers, and the like—because the economies of the Western World experienced labor shortages over much of their histories (Boserup, 1981, p. 99; Bray, 1994, p. 3). This, of course, not only may increase food production by allowing the same labor force to cultivate more land, but also may free up labor for other endeavors. Thus Australia, Canada, and the United States produce massive amounts of food with a relatively small rural labor force.

But production can also be intensified by increasing the productivity of land without reducing the labor requirements; that is, expanding production using an existing labor force or even a larger one (Bray, 1994). This can be important, for example, where there are few alternative sources for employment, as is often the case in densely populated developing countries. Irrigation and the introduction of new crop strains are well-known examples of this form of intensification. Water control may allow for multiple harvests of a particular crop; new plant strains may also increase productivity without new capital inputs needed to reduce labor requirements. At least one anthropologist, Francesca Bray, argues that from this perspective traditional Asian rice-based farming using high labor inputs is not a case of "arrested development" when compared to Western agriculture, but is a solution to the problem of sustaining large populations with adequate nutrition (1994). We will return to intensification and its consequences later.

One of the most ancient (and still important) ways land productivity can be increased is through water management. So diverse are the ways in which moisture can be controlled, it is somewhat misleading to refer to them all as "irrigation." Simply adding pebbles to fields, as did the ancient Pueblo dwellers of North America, can enhance the field's ability to retain moisture (Lightfoot, 1994). In this sense, irrigation, or at least "moisture control," is as early as agriculture itself. Archaeological evidence in the Middle East indicates that simple systems of water control predate the rise of large agrarian states with their concomitantly dense populations. Populations near rivers or marshes would simply capture or divert annual flood waters or runoff from rains. Irrigation refers to actually transporting the water to the field and then managing its direct application and subsequent drainage (drainage is important in order to maintain a salt-free soil base).

The earliest known large-scale system of irrigation in Egypt appears with the emergence of one government throughout that land in 5100 B.C. (Fagan, 1992, p. 352). We know that even fairly complicated irrigation systems can be managed by local farmers, although the potential for interfamilial or intercommunity conflict is substantial. People who share a common water resource may have very different interests in its use. As a consequence, we see a widespread pattern of large-scale irrigation systems coming to be run by special managers, with a corresponding lessening of control by households or even by local communities. Centralized decision making facilitates mobilizing large work forces, allocating water, conflict resolution, and storage of surpluses.

In the emerging prehistoric states of Mesopotamia, this managerial role was first assumed by religious leaders and only later by secular rulers (Fagan, 1992). It is interesting to note that the earliest large-scale irrigation systems in the southwest United States were managed by the Mormon Church (Abruzzi, 1993), as we described in Chapter 3. To make water control feasible, it required the centralized control of a committed bureaucracy willing to use resources to sustain building and rebuilding dams and canals beyond the ability of local communities.

The main impetus for irrigation, in most places, is simply the need to have water available in areas where rainfall is unpredictable—not necessarily a wish to increase the average yield of a unit of land. But with the advent of irrigation, slight differences in the productivity of different pieces of land became greatly magnified. Those fields that lent themselves to irrigation—fields that were close to the water source or that drained well—produced far more than those less suited to irrigation.

Other routes to intensification include learning to breed strains of grains or other crops that mature more rapidly and bear more edible products. Rice, for example, was transformed into a substantially more productive grain staple through selective breeding by farmers in ancient China (Bray, 1994). Animal traction used to plow and cultivate fields developed very early in the Middle East and Far East (but not in the New World); a pair of oxen, it is calculated, produces over ten times the horsepower of a human being, and, when relative costs are considered, is half as expensive as human power when used in tilling a field (Giampietro, Bukkins, & Pimentel, 1993, p. 230). Crop rotation and fertilizers, too, are means of intensifying yields. Arboriculture, as practiced in the Pacific, can be the basis for intensive production, as early travelers found when they first encountered the densely populated islands of Polynesia (Kirch, 1994). Here, carefully tended breadfruit trees provided a high yield in a form that could be stored in large, underground stone-lined pits.

Where and when there was agricultural intensification, human societies tended to increase in numbers and in social and technological complexity. When farming produced more food than the farmers themselves could eat, segments of the population came to specialize in crafts such as the making of tools, pots, and the like, which they then traded for food they had not produced themselves. The division of labor within society thus became more complex, with even spatially distant groups becoming mutually dependent.

Simple horticultural societies, such as the Yanomamö of Chapter 5, have remained politically autonomous until now and can be studied as distinct societies with distinct cultures. Intensive farming communities, on the other hand, are closely interdependent and must be studied as part of a larger agrarian society. Given the fact that much of their organization is tied to distant cities and national administrative offices, they cannot be understood outside the context of the larger political and economic system of which they are a part. Thus, as intensive agriculture developed, the land fed not only the farming households and the craftworkers but other emerging classes of nonproducers: religious leaders, politicians, administrators. Increasingly the economic demands of urban populations and the political power of their elites came to exercise a profound influence on the life of rural peoples, although the country folk often sought means to avoid the power of the state. Town and country came to be part of an integrated system, though the results of increased productivity were not shared equally by all sectors of the economy. As agrarian societies evolved into large-scale states, as in the ancient Middle East, some communities inevitably prospered and grew; those far from the major markets, religious institutions, and other developments of the urban centers languished. In Mesoamerica, for example, regional or "core" centers such as in the Valley of Oaxaca, developed great urban complexes while peripheral zones, linked to the centers by trade or tribute, were relatively underdeveloped (Feinman & Nichols, 1992). Such regional differentiation may be the basis for significant social and cultural variability within a society, and is reflected in the subsequent development of industrialized societies.

The first cities in the Middle East (and, until recently, many African, European, and Asian cities) were little more than administrative and trading centers, established to serve the surrounding countryside that provided them with food. The priests, military leaders, and artisans who were not serving the governing elite were serving the farmers. Only after about the fifteenth century (with a few exceptions) do we see a change: the rise of cities not as agricultural trade centers and administrative centers but as manufacturing centers. The production of goods in great volume went hand in hand with the spread of trade and invention. Improved armaments and navigational equipment on sailing ships gave Europeans access to all the world's seas.

European cities grew, fueled at first by the power of water, wind, and human and animal muscle, and later by fossil fuel.

The Organization of Energy

Howard Odum (1971, 1992) was one of the first ecologists to observe that the structure and function of animal, plant, and human social systems are understood at least to some extent by the way they acquire, channel, and expend the energy necessary for their maintenance. Anthropologist Leslie White was one of the first to recognize the importance of the role of energy in cultural evolution (as we saw in Chapter 3). What we often call the Industrial Age, White (1949) has called the Fuel Age.

Societies vary greatly in their energy budgets and in how energy is organized. Mechanized use of nonhuman energy sources—fossil fuel or hydroelectric power, for example—distinguish the technologically advanced societies. In the United States, about 230,000 kilocalories of energy are expended per capita; in Burundi, Central Africa, 24,000 are expended (Giampietro et al., 1993, p. 239). Moreover, only 10 percent of the country's "total time" (the population $\times$ 24 $\times$ 365) is allocated to work; in Burundi, 25 percent of the nation's total time is needed; in short, they work twice as hard to extract a fraction of the usable energy that the U.S. worker does (p. 239). Where human labor constitutes the main power supply there is little spare energy to devote to anything other than maintaining current infrastructure, reproduction, and food procurement. Thus, intensification, which we have defined earlier as the process of increasing yields through an increase in energy expenditure, is best achieved when that increase is accomplished with nonhuman energy sources. As we can see from the Human Ecology box, *Human Labor as Energy* (page 179) human labor is extremely costly; exclusive reliance on it impedes development.

In the final analysis, it is energy that distinguishes intensive agriculture—both energy invested in crop production and energy extracted from the land. The exact point at which horticulture becomes intensive farming is not always clear, but one can recognize the consequences of the shift even without employing economic criteria. Rarely can large numbers of people maintain themselves in stable year-around communities without intensive

ECONOMISTS DEFINE HUMAN labor productivity as the monetary value of what is produced (dollar value added per hour of work) by a unit of human labor. This definition, however, does not work well in thinking of labor in nonmonetarized societies or in developing societies with a significant subsistence economy. Also, it is hard to compare a monetarized economy with a partially monetarized one. Energy is an alternative measure of productivity, one that offers new insights into the changing role of human labor in relation to technological development. Giampietro, Bukkens, and Pimentel (1993) have created a sophisticated model based on this principle, which is described in a simplified manner below.

Assessing the productivity of labor requires two measurements: what has been acheived energetically, and what energy has been expended to gain it. A simple model illustrates this. If we compare the horsepower (HP) efficiency of human power (0.1 HP), a pair of oxen (1.2 HP), a 6-HP tractor, and a 50-HP tractor in tilling a one hectare field, applied human power is twice as effective as that of the pair of oxen and over four times as effective as the tractors (that is, effective in the amount of work performed per horsepower). However, if we calculate the gross energy requirements (metabolic and fuel inputs, shelter, construction costs or—for living components—reproductive costs, etc.), this is reversed: human power is 3.45 times more expensive than the tractors, and twice as expensive than the oxen.

The indirect costs of human power are very high: people have to have food, clothing, and shelter whether or not they are actually working. Furthermore, it takes time and energy inputs to "produce" a worker. Eighty percent of the metabolic expenditure for a human worker is outside the workplace. A related issue is time constraints. Productivity has to consider how the power level affects the time to complete a task. While one person may be able to harvest a crop that requires 700 labor days, this is clearly not feasible; more reasonable would be seven farmers working 100 days or 100 workers working one week. Thus, human power, while very efficient in terms of the work that can be accomplished by a unit of horsepower, is both low in absolute levels and costly.

Any system can be seen as having energy *sources* and energy *converters* that generate power or useful work. In preindustrial or partially industrialized societies, energy sources are largely in standing biomass: the trees, plants, and animals available to support humans and that can be converted into useful work to support the population and its material culture, through human labor. This may be supplemented by animal traction, but even so, the available power is limited. In the United States in the 1850s, 91 percent of energy expended came from standing biomass; today only 4 percent does. The balance comes from fossil fuels, converted into useful work by machinery. Industrial societies are more limited by energy sources; nonindustrial societies by the low rate at which energy can be converted through human labor only partially amplified by animals and machinery.

The implications for development are serious. The addition of one bullock for every ten villagers in India would have have the effect of doubling the power level per capita in that country, but it would still remain more than a thousand times less than the per-capita power level in the United States. Preindustrial societies respond to the energy limitation by scheduling agricultural activities to be as constant as possible throughout the year—avoiding periods of peak demand. Thus, traditional farmers often make use of a mix of crops and livestock, each with different labor demands. In industrial agriculture, this is not necessary, since labor is not the main means of converting energy—machines are.

The notion of humans living directly from the fruits of their own labor assisted by the family's horses or oxen may be romantic, but mechanical conversion of energy is vastly more productive and is required to raise standards of living. Unfortunately, rapid conversion of the standing biomass in preindustrial societies into energy would facilitate more useful work, but it would devastate the environment—as we see when forests are clear cut. This is, in fact, what is happening in many countries. In the Sahel and the Sudan, the World Bank forecasts that by 2000, in a rural population of 40 million, 19 million will run out of wood while 3.7 million will be severely short of food (in Giampietro et al., 1993, p. 252). On the other hand, should a region undergo rapid industrialization of agriculture, people will be displaced as their labor is less needed on the farm, contributing to rural-urban migration and subsequent urban poverty.

food production, and nowhere do we see urban centers without a hinterland containing highly productive farms. The vast energy surpluses that flow from the countryside to the city result from the investment of energy in agriculture. The increase in the energy invested can come from many sources: from animals yoked to plows, from human labor spent in terracing land or digging wells, or from farm machinery powered by fossil fuels.

Investment of energy in order to gain an even greater return in energy is characteristic of intensive agriculture and is expressed in the management of fields and paddies. A crucial factor in the evolution of intensive agriculture was the advent of plow cultivation and fertilization, which allowed farmers to reduce the length of **fallow time**—the time that must be allowed between crops for the soil to rest and regenerate its organic and chemical content. The fallow period is critical to a high level of food production over the long term. When other factors—availability of water, type of soil, and the like—are equal, sustained agricultural yields vary with the length of the fallow period. The shifting agriculture practiced by the Yanomamö is a long-fallow system requiring as long as ten to twenty years of fallow time for each field.

In intensive agriculture, the fallow period can be reduced to the point where the land can undergo nearly continuous cultivation, and, in some areas, can produce multiple crops each season. This approach requires developed technology, large inputs of human labor, and an investment in other forms of energy. Fields have to be prepared (often specially laid out for irrigation); plow animals must be cared for; tractors fueled and maintained; water collected, distributed, and controlled; fertilizers or other nutrients spread on the fields, and crops carefully tended throughout the growing period. The result is a vastly increased amount of food per unit of land.

Both land and farmers work harder under intensive agriculture, and the result is a great increase in the production not only of food but of such crops as cotton and flax. It may sometimes appear that the possibilities of intensification seem almost limitless. Even with modern techniques, however, only 11 percent of the earth's land area is suited to intensive farming and the potential for intensification is limited. A point is always reached at which increased investment of labor or capital is not matched by productive gains; we will return to this point later. Further, intensification may lead

Chinese farmers are masters at the science of intensive agriculture, combining skilled labor, water control, and fertilizers to reap rich harvests.
(Reuters News)

to soil loss if nutrients are not maintained; erosion may accompany mechanized cultivation, and irrigation may result in waterlogged or salinized soils—this occurs when too much water is applied or where drainage is inadequate to prevent salts building up in the soil. Worldwatch reports that 60 million hectares (150 million acres) of cropland worldwide has been damaged by salinization and waterlogging. India, which has the most irrigated land of any country, has damaged about one-third of its croplands and abandoned seven million hectares because of salinization. Paradoxically, the United States, which pioneered industrialized farming, also leads the world in soil loss due to erosion; 69 million acres are eroding at rates that diminish productivity (Cunningham & Saigo, 1995, p. 229)

Environmental Resilience, Stability, and Change

Intensive agriculture is accompanied by a massive reshaping of the landscape—a process that is ever accelerating. In swidden horticulture, the forest is partially cut or burned and allowed to grow back. Intensive agriculture entails laboriously clearing fields, building terraces, and excavating drainage ditches, ponds, and canals. These tasks completed, the work has just begun. The new agricultural environment must be maintained through constant effort. Although intensive agriculture allows humans more control over their environment, it can be as much a problem as a solution. By creating elaborate waterworks or clearing hillsides for terraces, a farming population may indeed protect its yields or even increase food production. But as agriculture becomes more complex and specialized, it becomes more vulnerable to disruption. Irrigation canals may silt up, fields may become unproductive as natural salts become concentrated in the soil, topsoil may erode—the list is long. These calamities accompany intensification as surely as the increased yields. A farmer who plants the same crop year after year to obtain the maximum yield is increasing the risk of total crop failure from soil depletion or disease.

The problem is not simply a lack of planning or a tendency of individual farmers to take this year's yield more seriously than environmental consequences a decade or a generation from now. In response to market demands or government inducements to produce more food, entire regions may be threatened by depletion or erosion of the soil or by its contamination by chemical residues. These problems arise in all major agricultural nations. Stability and continuity require investments in the infrastructure that are not immediately reflected in crop yields: soils protected from erosion, drainage maintained, crops rotated, and soils allowed to regenerate. If such investments are not made, the stability of the productive system is threatened.

So even as intensive agriculture solves some problems, it creates new ones. Irrigation has left such concentrations of minerals in the soil of California's Imperial Valley that productivity is leveling off and threatens to decline, and there is virtually no way to divert the contaminated water from the fields and downstream communities. Irrigation is often associated with environmental problems of this sort. Paradoxically, one response is to intensify production further by expanding the area under irrigation, building larger dams, digging deeper wells, using expensive chemicals to remove the salt, and using more water. Again, such efforts may solve the problem in the short run only to create more serious problems in the long run, such as causing the water table in the area to drop or further increasing the salinity of the soil. Consequently, cultivators have to work harder just to maintain the same level of productivity.

Intensive agriculturalists clearly do not free themselves from environmental constraints. On the contrary, they seem to labor under many more constraints than people whose technologies are less sophisticated. Intensive agriculturalists rearrange their ecosystems and must make tremendous efforts simply to support the artificial balance they have created. Intensification increases vulnerability. It opens up new possibilities for mishaps and magnifies the cost of mistakes. It widens the area and numbers of people who are affected, too, should a major problem occur. This is not to say that intensive agricultural systems inevitably fail or result in severe environmental problems. We have evidence of continuous, environmentally stable agriculture practiced in many parts of the world for thousands of years. And while the development of industrial methods is not a necessary consequence of intensive agriculture, certainly today's population levels require agroindustrial techniques.

From Intensive Agriculture to Industrialized Farming

In Europe, particularly in England, France, and Germany in the early nineteenth century, steam and internal combustion engines were harnessed to machines both for manufacturing and for transport. Just as with the rest of society, industrialism has transformed farming and farm society, but it can still be seen as a series of adaptive responses much like those we have already examined in other subsistence systems. It is a way of coping with challenges and resolving specific problems. As in all other instances of behavioral adaptation, the very act of coping creates the potential for negative as well as positive effects. The success or failure of industrial adaptations to human problems can be seen only in terms of long-range survival. What we call industrialism is a major societal commitment that has been underway for some 250 years. Not all the consequences are clearly understood even now. Further complicating the picture is the fact that industrialism is not an adaptation to a single local set of constraints or problems, and so the costs and benefits vary widely. Can we truly say that unemployed steelworkers of Ohio are benefiting from the system to the same degree as computer specialists in California's Silicon Valley? Are the unemployed young farmers of eastern Turkey, where the soils and rugged terrain limit mechanized farming, benefiting to the same extent that their western counterparts are when they use tractors and combines, or export fruit and vegetables raised in heated greenhouses? Unfortunately one of the consequences of intensive agriculture and industrial development is an increase in disparities among individuals occupying different positions within the economy. It also has had a profound and ongoing effect on the world's population.

Population Growth

The industrial age ushered in a whole host of social changes. First, and perhaps most obvious, population increased rapidly. Europe's population grew from 100 to 187 million between 1650 and 1800, then leaped to 400 million in the nineteenth-century coal age—an increase of 260 percent (White, 1949, p. 384). Today the world's population is doubling every thirty-five years (Cowell, 1994, p. 10). Birth rates are significantly higher in the Third World than in industrial nations today, while death rates are declining; the result is explosive population growth. The Central American nation of El Salvador, the most densely populated country in the Western Hemisphere, has more than 670 people per square mile, or 5.6 million people packed into an area smaller than New Hampshire. The world's highest fertility rate is found in one of its poorest countries, Rwanda, with eight children per woman. India's population is growing at a rate of 18 million a year (Cowell, 1994, p. 10). In the industrialized nations, on the other hand, the rate of population growth has leveled off and even declined in some cases.

The changes that are occurring in human populations around the world are part of what demographers call the great **demographic transition**: a rapid increase in a society's population with the onset of industrialization, followed by a leveling off of the growth rate (Ehrlich & Ehrlich, 1972, pp. 18–20). Until approximately 200 years ago, the world's population stayed remarkably constant. Then, with urbanism and industrialization, it started to grow rapidly and continues to grow as more and more countries become industrialized (see Figure 7–1). The point at which it will again stabilize is still distant. Every country appears to follow roughly the same trajectory as it develops: a spurt of rapid growth followed by a slowing of the rate of increase. The economically advanced nations may have zero growth rates, as the existing population simply maintains itself. The reasons for rapid explosion followed by a declining rate of population growth are exceedingly complex. The initial spurt of growth may be caused by a declining death rate attributable to improved health care in combination with high fertility. One factor that encourages high fertility is the value of child labor.

Peasants in largely rural El Salvador say that "every child is born with his bread under his arm"; not surprisingly, the birth rate in that country is over 45 per thousand of population—more than double that of the United States. More and more families come to depend on the sale of labor to meet their needs, and very often the income they derive in this way buys less food than they could produce directly. The mechanization and commercialization of agriculture precludes that option for

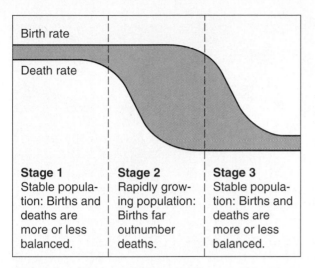

Figure 7–1. Demographic transition

Even though water shortages are often seen as limiting food production, over-watering is often a more serious problem because of the dangers of ruining the soil through salinity.

(J. Gazdar/Woodfin Camp & Associates)

most families. Rural people who have migrated to the cities simply do not earn enough to get by unless their children work as well. Children can help in the fields, work in the factories, peddle or produce crafts, scavenge, and otherwise bring in needed income. Given high rates of infant and childhood mortality, the more children a couple has, the more likely some will survive to take care of them when they are too old to support themselves. In countries that have no publicly supported health or welfare programs, these are vital considerations.

The reasons for a decline in the rate of growth following economic development are equally complex. It appears that the decline in the usefulness of child labor together with a rise in the costs of education are often important factors in the decision to limit family size. Changes in the work force are important, too, as women who work outside the home find it difficult to care for many children. Burton Pasternak and Wang Ching (1985) found that Chinese women who worked in factories tended to stop breast-feeding their infants in favor of buying prepared foods for them. This change is not necessarily a positive one in terms of the health of the child, but it does free the mother to work. It also shows the impact of women's employment on decisions to limit family size.

Unfortunately, many developing countries in which fertility remains very high for a considerable time after mortality has dropped find that their population levels are so high that the standard of living cannot be raised. All that can be said for certain is that present rates of growth cannot long continue: if they did, in 700 years there would be one person for every square foot of earth! One of the important decisions taken by the 1994 United Nations Conference on Population in Cairo was to emphasize the role of education and, in particular, education for women in encouraging decisions for smaller families.

Intensification

Increasing population demands an increase in food production through intensification, and during the Industrial Revolution this process proceeded at an incredibly rapid pace. In fact, one of the first areas in which factory production made itself felt was the farm. Steel plows, threshers, combines, reapers,

European farmers are extremely productive, although farm sizes are much smaller than in North America. Government subsidies serve to maintain the small farms in the face of competition with foreign producers.

(George Bates)

and mowers developed in the nineteenth century were followed by the gasoline tractor early in the twentieth.

Mechanization. Much of the energy involved in industrialism is channeled through machines rather than through animals and humans. However, **mechanization**—the replacement of human and animal labor by mechanical devices, enabling humans to vastly increase the amount of product derived from one unit of land and labor—began long before the industrial age. Sails have been used to power ships for millennia. Mechanical devices of increasing size and complexity have been developed over the centuries for a variety of purposes: waging war, forging metals, constructing monumental buildings, grinding grain, making cloth. It is quite astonishing to note how far mechanization had proceeded even during what are sometimes called the Dark Ages. Outside of Paris in the sixteenth century, an ingenious system of hydraulic pumps drew water from the Seine for manufacturing purposes. However, it was only with the invention of the steam engine (and later the diesel and internal combustion engines) that populations were able to harness the concentrated solar energy stored in the fossil remains of organic matter (coal, oil, and gas). With these sources of energy, people

throughout the world have vastly increased the scale of intensive agriculture, enabling humans to harness more energy per capita, as explained in the Human Ecology box (page 179).

Despite the ingenuity of these machines, it was not until the relatively recent development of sophisticated metallurgical techniques and power transmission systems that a breakthrough was achieved in the amount of power that could effectively be delivered. Such machinery has transformed our idea of work. Labor is increasingly devoted to the management and maintenance of machinery, rather than to the products the machines make. The whole field of robotics is a case in point. Specialists in programming and maintaining industrial robots are now key personnel in heavy, light, and service industries.

New sources of energy and the technology to harness them laid the groundwork for expansion of agricultural production on a scale never witnessed before. However, farmers in industrial societies often invest more energy in fertilizer and gasoline for their tractors than they harvest in calories of food energy, even with high-yield grains. Moreover, large quantities of energy are diverted to non-food-producing activities. Thus an industrial society is significantly less efficient than nonindustrial societies in the sense that it requires more energy to support a unit of population—but it is this pattern of high consumption that produces high standards of living.

Nonmechanized Approaches to Intensification. Another means of intensifying yields is by developing new crops and new strains of established ones. Francesca Bray documents how, over the centuries, Asian farmers developed new varieties of rice, increasing productivity and shortening the growing season (1994). The U.N.'s Food and Agriculture Organization (FAO) predicts that 64 countries will be unable to feed their peoples by the year 2025 (Cunningham & Saigo, 1995, p. 204). The main hope is that new crops and strains will produce ever more food, since croplands are limited.

Following World War II, a number of foundations and governments began research on ways to increase yields of cereal crops, mainly rice, corn, and wheat. The results have ushered in what is called the **Green Revolution**; new strains have tripled or quadrupled yields per hectare. Without these new varieties, there would be even more widespread hunger in the world, but the so-called "miracle crops" are really "high responders" rather than high yielders (Cunningham & Saigo, 1995, p. 105). They respond more efficiently to increases in fertilizers and water, and have higher yields in optimum conditions; they often do poorly in bad years. Thus the benefits of the Green Revolution tend to accrue to the richer farmers who can afford to buy the seeds, fertilizers, and water.

Fish farming, sometimes called the **Blue Revolution**, has the potential for contributing as much to human sustenance as the Green Revolution. In just the past decade, fish farming has grown immensely. Worldwide, some ninety species of finfish and shellfish are grown commercially. Over one-half the trout and salmon consumed in the United States is farmed; in many Asian countries, two-thirds of the protein needs of subsistence farmers is provided from domestic fish ponds. Shrimp farming is the most rapidly growing productive sector in South America and Southeast Asia. While fish farming has emerged as a major export industry, it is not without its environmental costs. A salmon farm typically holds 75,000 salmon; they produce organic waste equivalent to a town of 20,000 people. In South America and Southeast Asia, millions of hectares of mangrove swamps have been cleared for shrimp farming, endangering many species of wildlife (Cunningham & Saigo, 1995, p. 209).

Specialization

Some key components of the industrial era are as important for their cognitive as for their technological effects. The development of precise instruments for measuring time was critical to most sophisticated technologies and processes. At the same time, the gears that drove elaborate mechanical clocks were pivotal elements in the directing of human attention to a mechanical view of the world, which in turn became a key to the physical knowledge on which industry is based. The view of the world as a machine underlies the concept of the assembly line, which depends on quality (or, more accurately, precision). Specialization in high-volume production depends on the availability of interchangeable parts, which requires a level of precision that did not develop in a significant way until the early nineteenth century (initially in the weapons industry). Centralization is also required because industry standards must be developed to facilitate the use of interchangeable parts. Even on the assembly line, tasks are broken down into simple components. This division of labor permits the employment of unskilled labor, the worker becoming one more component in the productive process.

Workers often come to see little of themselves in their product. Their labor is used impersonally and they respond in kind. Perhaps belatedly, industrial employers are realizing that this is not necessarily the most efficient way to organize production in a high-technology society. General Motors recently built a new facility at which teams of workers have responsibility for producing entire cars. Increasing amounts of knitwear are being manufactured in New England homes, reviving a cottage industry that had almost died out by the end of the nineteenth century.

Along with the specialization of tasks, spatial specialization continues to intensify in industrial as well as postindustrial societies. Regions, cities, and even neighborhoods become associated with particular products, while agricultural districts come to depend on a limited array of crops. In fact, the bulk of the world's population is sustained by three crops: rice, wheat, and maize (corn) (Cunningham & Saigo, 1995, p. 215). This is in sharp contrast to the self-sufficiency that marked local adaptations in earlier eras where local populations relied on local and very diverse food sources. The city's workplaces or factories come to be highly specialized. Each produces only a limited range of products, but often they are of exceptionally high volume and quality.

Today we can see this specialization on a global scale. The increasing congruence of the world's cultures is a direct product of industrialization. Advanced transportation and communication systems, along with international migration, have brought peoples once isolated into contact with other societies. Above all, geographical barriers have been broken down by the economic forces of an international market system. Products are manufactured on one continent from the raw materials of another and sold on still another. The decisions made by Iowa wheat farmers affect the price of bread in India; the cost of oil in the Persian Gulf helps determine the cost of corn in the United States. In essence, the world's people are coming to live and produce under increasingly similar economic conditions.

When agriculture becomes specialized, farmers tend to view their work as a business, emphasizing cash flow and yield per unit of capital invested. Contemporary farmers in America, Europe, and the Third World concentrate on producing cash crops while buying food for themselves in the marketplace. In most countries it is the exception rather than the norm for a rural household to rely directly on what it produces for food, shelter, and clothing. As we have seen, in Turkey nomadic herders now sell their milk and wool, and use the cash to buy margarine, flour, and factory-made clothing. Agricultural specialization allows for a broader participation in a market economy. This generally provides access to a wider range of goods and services, but it also has some negative consequences. Reliance on cash crops increases the risk of failure. Moreover, this risk increases as intensified agriculture moves toward industrialism. Now many of the world's most important cash crops are not only volatile in price, but inedible. A farm family cannot eat the cotton it cannot sell.

Agriculture has become specialized in another fashion that some feel can be dangerous over the long term. As the Green Revolution has succeeded, the number of crop varieties has dramatically decreased. A few so-called "miracle varieties" have replaced several hundred types of wheat in the Middle East; the same is true of corn in the Americas. A hint of what might happen is the U.S. corn leaf blight of 1970, in which nearly all the hybrid (bioengineered, high-yield) corn was threatened (Cunningham & Saigo, 1995). The lack of genetic diversity makes crop failure on a massive scale possible.

Social relations also change with increasing specialization because households no longer operate as an integrated, self-sufficient unit. When agribusiness supplants traditional farming, the farm family is increasingly removed from the family network on which it once relied not only for social interaction but for labor and loans. In places of urban employment, kin groups become removed from production or redistribution: people rely less on family members than on fellow employees or associates. Social class, professional affiliation, ethnicity, and union membership take on functions of mutual responsibility and support formerly restricted to relatives. This is not to say that kinship is unimportant, but its functions change.

CASE STUDY:

The Shift to Sisal in Brazil

A CLASSIC EXAMPLE OF THE DANGERS OF SPECIALization in agriculture was investigated by the anthropologist Daniel Gross and the nutritionist Barbara Underwood (1971) in the *sertao*, an arid region of northeastern Brazil. The *sertao* has always been a place of hardship and uncertainty. Historically, its people relied on cattle raising and subsistence farming. However, the years of self-sufficiency were regularly punctuated by disastrous droughts, with resultant starvation and mass exoduses from the region. In the 1950s, many subsistence farmers thought they could see an end to the cycle of uncertainty. A new drought-resistant crop, sisal, was beginning to be harvested for export. Sisal takes four years to mature and produces a tough fiber used to make twine. The extraction of the fiber from the leaves, a process known as decorting, is a long and arduous task requiring heavy machinery.

The first sisal plantations were owned by wealthy landholders. Soon smallholders came to abandon subsistence crops in the hope of sharing in the ever-rising profits from sisal. While waiting for the sisal to mature, they worked as laborers on the plantations of others. Unfortunately, by the time their own sisal had matured, the market price had fallen, leaving them with little or nothing to show for their investments. At the same time, even harvesting the sisal was costly; the smallholders had to rent decorting machines. Once planted, sisal is extremely hard to eradicate, and many formerly self-sufficient farmers were forced to remain as day laborers on the large plantations.

Another aspect of this shift to wage labor concerns nutrition. Gross and Underwood (1971) measured the calories the laborers expended while they worked on the sisal plantations and the amount of food they could buy with their wages. They found that many workers could not afford to buy enough food to meet their own needs and those of their families. Forty-five percent of the children of sisal workers were significantly undernourished.

In contrast to the hopes raised by the shift to a cash crop, the result was a poverty more severe than the small farmers had originally experienced. Moreover, their poverty was compounded by their new dependence on the people who owned the large farms and controlled the machinery. This is the reason that rural people in many countries leave the countryside, even though the city offers them little but the squalor of an urban slum. ❱

Centralization, Collectivization, and Communism

As we saw in the case of the Vikings in Chapter 3, cultural evolution generally involves centralization, as growing populations and social complexity require that central authorities coordinate diverse ac-

tivities and interests. This process, which had been going on for centuries in Europe and elsewhere, continued during the Industrial Revolution as intensification and industrialism took hold around the world. One of the early signs of political centralization is the emergence of state institutions. More recently, centralization has moved beyond state boundaries, and is now evident in the formation of large regional confederations, in the U.N., and other global organizations. Economic centralization occurs as economies become closely interdependent, and a small number of institutions such as major stock, bond, and commodity markets determine the prices of items produced and consumed around the world. Centralization is also at work when key regions emerge as highly developed, economic cores, and create (or at least dominate) distant, less developed, peripheries. Within countries, centralizing tendencies can be seen in the agricultural sector.

The twentieth century has produced an extreme form of centralization, what Wolf calls the **administrative system** or **commune,** in which land is owned and managed by the state (1966). In most communist countries such as China (until 1980) and the former Soviet Union, collective and state farms were the basis of most agricultural production. Peasants on a state-owned farm work under the direction of government agricultural experts, who set production quotas and determine how labor will be allocated. Collective farmers may escape the extreme poverty and social degradation that often characterize peasant life under the other forms of land control, but as their labor and income are at the disposal of a bureaucratic ruling class, they are still peasants in the economic and political sense of the term. Variants of this arrangement are seen in the large state-run farm projects in some parts of Africa and Latin America.

Collectivization has seemed attractive to many governments for several reasons, not all of them laudatory. The main argument in favor of collectivization is that large agricultural enterprises gain from economies of scale; that is, expensive equipment can be shared, large fields tilled and irrigated efficiently, and labor pooled. In developing countries, particularly, it often seems easier to provide schools, clinics, and marketing facilities to large concentrations of people than to dispersed hamlets and villages. Another reason for collectivization is one not often openly argued: it is one means of controlling rural people and ensuring a level of agricultural production adequate to meet the objectives of the ruling elite. Two examples illustrate some of the positive and negative aspects of modern collective farms.

CASE STUDY:

A Sudanese Irrigation Project

THE GIANT RAHAD IRRIGATION PROJECT IN SUDAN, established in 1973 to harness the waters of the Blue Nile for cotton production, regulates the lives of some 100,000 people in forty-six villages. Each farm family is regarded as a tenant and is given up to twenty-two acres to farm, according to an administrative plan governing all decisions in regard to crops, crop rotation, and animal production. Tenants receive housing, schools, and other community services. The project maintains strict authority in most areas of community life: it recruits and evicts tenants, provides all services and agricultural inputs, and processes and markets the cotton produced. It monitors each household's use of its lands, imposes sanctions it considers appropriate, and determines the profits the household is to receive (USAID, 1982, pp. 4–6).

The Rahad Project has made some important positive contributions to the national economy of the Sudan and it has offered a substantial improvement in the quality of life of many tenants by providing better access to schools and clinics. Still, most aspects of the economy are regulated—often to the detriment of the individual farmer, who is called upon to produce cotton needed for Sudan's foreign markets rather than crops that would be more useful or profitable locally. Farmers see the most immediate return from their individual garden plots and from raising livestock, endeavors the authorities try to restrict. The immense scale of the project has caused some difficulties in management, and decisions are sometimes made that are almost impossible for farmers to implement if they are to survive. Most seem to cope by manipulating the rules, by raising more foodstuffs for private sale, and by adding to their herds of goats and cat-

tle. However, they then run the risk of punishment or eviction. ◗

CASE STUDY:

Feeding a Fifth of the World: From Chinese Communes to Farms

CHINA HAS RADICALLY TRANSFORMED ITS LAND tenure and rural society in this century—not just once, but several times. Following the success of the Communist Revolution in 1949, the traditional patrimonial estates were abolished and family private holdings were restricted in size, with much property being redistributed to the landless. Very rapidly this arrangement gave way to collectivization on the Soviet model, and by the early 1950s all farming was organized around collective farms or communes. At first these communes were relatively small and often consisted of closely related families, but soon the government ordered them consolidated into far larger entities, with all planning and administration carried out centrally. In 1956, for example, the government forced cooperatives to purchase over a million double-wheel, double-blade plows, even though they were virtually worthless in paddy cultivation. Authorities even dictated a specific planting density for rice, regardless of local conditions (Lardy, 1985, p. 38; Cunningham & Saigo, 1995, p. 203). By 1960 the government eliminated almost all aspects of rural entrepreneurship and private trading, closely controlled the prices of all produce, and set rigid quotas for grain production. The most consistent aspect of agricultural policy was the underpricing of rural products so as to support a large urban population.

Because central planning was unresponsive to local conditions and prices were low, production of critical food crops dropped drastically while the authorities continued to set high production quotas in an effort to feed the teeming cities. It has been estimated that between 1959 and 1961, food shortages and rural economic dislocations resulted in the deaths of 10 to 60 million Chinese, possibly the worst famine in the history of the world (Cunningham & Saigo, 1995, p. 203)! Most of these deaths occurred in the countryside, where 80 percent of China's people still live. Agriculture im-

Collectivization in China initially produced positive results but ended in near-collapse when the government created oversized farming collectives, managed centrally. Now almost all agriculture has returned to private ownership.

(H. Topping/Photo Researchers Inc.)

proved somewhat after 1961 but then stagnated until 1978, when the post-Mao government decided to return to decentralized, family-run farming. In the subsequent four years the proportion of people earning less than 100 yuan a year (the rural poverty line) fell from 30 to 3 percent—an achievement hailed around the world. China is now number one in both rice and wheat production (p. 203). Production is 50 percent higher than in the best of the commune years; China now has less than 3 percent of its population underfed, compared to 10 percent in the United Sates (p. 203). Yet some Chinese communes had prospered during the years of collectivization, particularly those that were small,

that enlisted members who trusted one another, and that offered greater rewards for shared labor than members could reap alone. When farming was returned to the private sector, many, but not all, profited (Parish, 1985). But since private farming requires less labor than the inefficient communes, this has led to unemployment on a scale not seen since World War II (Kwong, 1994). ▶

Expanding Cities and Migrant Workers

The process of devaluing agricultural products and labor in relation to other commodities, along with the mechanization of agriculture, serves to push people off the land and set up population movements both within and between nations. The migration of Europeans to North America, closely paralleling the spread of industrialization through Europe, reached a peak at the beginning of the twentieth century. More than 52 million people, or a fifth of Europe's population, migrated overseas between 1840 and 1930. By and large, the immigrants were displaced from farming by mechanization, monoculture, and other changes. They came to America believing that U.S. factories offered opportunities for wage labor.

Today, small-scale agriculturists displaced by large-scale industrialized agriculture are leaving the land at an alarming rate. Some settle in towns, where they work as unskilled laborers when there is work to be had. Some settle in large urban centers. Still others become migrant laborers. Northern Europe is dotted with temporary settlements of Turkish, Greek, and Spanish laborers who travel north every year for a few months of labor in the factories or fields and then return home. Many more migrants establish long-term residence in large cities. The organization of this mobile labor force varies considerably, as does the profitability of the arrangement for the laborers.

The Turks—nearly a million and a half of them—who labor as "guest workers" in the factories of northern Europe generally receive the same wages as native workers and are able to return to Turkey with substantial savings. But at the same time, they are the first to be fired in times of recession and they suffer considerable social isolation

Much of the hand labor on industrial farms all over the world is carried out by poorly-paid migrant farm workers who follow the harvest seasons in search of employment.

(Christina Taccone/Offshoot Photo)

and discrimination. Migrant workers in the United States, most of them Mexicans or Central Americans, are seldom able to earn a living that is considered adequate by North American standards or to save enough to allow them to upgrade their salable skills. Throughout the year they move from harvest to harvest, staying in crowded and often squalid migrant camps. Most such camps are under the direction of crew leaders, who make the arrangements between the farmers and the laborers and provide the trucks to transport the laborers from place to place. Laborers are heavily dependent on their crew leader. When work is delayed, as it often is, they must borrow from him to buy their food. And often it is the leader who sells them their food—at an inflated price.

The rural landless have options other than settling in industrial farming communities or joining the migrant labor force. The overwhelming majority have chosen to try their luck in the cities. Since the Industrial Revolution, population has moved in a steady stream from the countryside to the city. In many nations now becoming industrialized, the stream has become a flood as unskilled rural people pour into the cities. In most countries, one or two cities become the targets for the majority of the migrants, and these cities swell beyond their capacity to provide employment or social services. In the Arabic-speaking countries of the Middle East,

only 30 percent of the population were urban in 1962, but today more than half are. The population of Cairo, for example, increased from 3 million in 1947 to over 12 million in 1994. Mexico City, now the world's largest city with more than 20 million inhabitants, is experiencing massive problems: the world's worst air pollution, frequent breakdowns in public transportation and other services, and high rates of infant mortality. Like similar cities around the world, much of Mexico City's growth is due to an influx of rural dwellers. As elsewhere, these recent migrants form an extremely disadvantaged and socially distinct segment of the population, with a high rate of unemployment, a high rate of crime, and substandard housing. In some respects these poor city dwellers are fortunate. A U.N. study indicates that more than 12 million people around the world live in refugee camps and many more live on the brink of starvation—displaced not just by a changing global economy but by the brutal facts of war, famine, and political oppression. The FAO estimates that 15 to 20 million people (mostly children) die of malnutrition each year (Cunningham & Saigo, 1995, p. 212).

Today rural people are pouring into cities all over the world for similar reasons. Others have adapted to changing patterns of food production by becoming migrant farm laborers. (Of course, migration is not limited to rural populations. The true nomads of industrial society are middle-class, white-collar workers who move from job to job or from city to city in the same job.) The European Community sees this migration from the land as a threat to its future ability to feed itself, not to mention maintaining its traditional rural/urban settlement patterns. Consequently countries in the European Community provide massive subsidies to farms, which allows them to continue to compete with North American agribusiness. Peter Kwong, a New York anthropologist, describes the sometime tragic human face attached to the global phenomenon of economic migration, which usually involves poor, rural dwellers who wish for a better life, in the State of the Peoples box, *China's Human Traffickers* (page 192).

Stratification

With the development of intensive agriculture, the difference in productivity between richer and poorer lands was multiplied, creating and amplifying regional disparities. Similar processes of regional or national differentiation continued as societies industrialized, with more extensive effects. Today we can still see this stratification occurring on a global level, as regions with access to cheap energy and sources of capital, labor, and appropriate raw materials develop rapidly while adjacent areas suddenly appear underdeveloped by comparison. Within countries, the people who control land and capital can reap far greater rewards than those who have only their labor to sell, so that great social and economic disparities are apparent.

This is cruelly evident in India, which is the world's third largest producer of staple crops. Over 300 million of India's citizens are undernourished, or about 40 percent of all malnourished people in the world (Cunningham & Saigo, 1995). Nevertheless, India exported 24 million metric tons of grain in 1986, primarily to feed livestock in Europe and the Near East. The wage value of labor is so low that people often cannot support themselves. This, in turn, is partially due to the fact that commodity prices for the crops and products most commonly exported from less-developed countries have been falling relative to imported manufactured goods; a ton of rice in 1950 would purchase twice what a ton of rice would in 1985.

Peasant Farmers
in an Industrial Society

The application of industrial technology to farming, while undoubtedly necessary to feed the world's burgeoning population, has wrought profound changes in almost every country. One of the most profound has been the emergence of a peasant class. Peasants, as we discussed in Chapter 5, are farmers who lack control over the means of their production: the land and other resources, the capital they need to grow their crops, and the labor they contribute to the process. The state directly or indirectly shapes their lives, since the national institutions are controlled largely by the town-dwelling literate classes. Money and energy left over from their labors are regularly siphoned off in the form of land and equipment rentals and taxes. In the past they were subject in many countries to a sort of tax to be paid with their labor for the state, called **corvée**—that is, unpaid forced labor on public projects such as road construction.

When tractors and other equipment are introduced, the richer farmer is usually the one to benefit. New technology always entails risks. Large farms offer their owners the security that enables them to assume the risks entailed by the adoption of innovations, such as new high-yield seeds. As we saw in earlier chapters, rural people have responded in diverse ways but rarely have avoided being drawn into new markets and a near total dependency on distant sources of energy.

Drawing on the experiences of a number of countries, it has been commonplace to assume that the effects of industrialization on rural farming communities follow a fairly predictable course: peasant handicraft production will be replaced by factory goods, peasants will purchase in the marketplace much of what they used to produce at home (thus becoming dependent on money), farm production will be focused on cash crops rather than on food for consumption, and wage labor will largely replace reciprocity and family-organized farming. The social consequences are usually assumed to be negative: poor farmers are unable to compete in a fully monetarized economy and lose their lands; small farms and plots are consolidated into larger units that are run as businesses using hired laborers (usually those who have lost their

State of the Peoples

China's Human Traffickers

"MR. ZHENG FROM WENZHOU, China, may be unlucky to have been one of the passengers on the ill-fated Golden Venture, which rammed the shore of Queens more than a year ago. He is however, the envy of his fellow inmates at the Metropolitan Detention Center in Lower Manhattan, because his wife comes to see him every day during visiting hours" (Kwong, 1994, p. 422). Mrs. Zheng had arrived illegally in the United States three years earlier, and soon came to realize that it was not what she had hoped for. Working at low wages she was under the unbearable pressure to pay off the $30,000 debt she owed her "snakehead," the smuggler who got her in. Accordingly, she advised her husband not to come, but he misinterpreted her advice to mean that she was leaving him. Placing their four-year-old daughter with his parents, he began his journey to the United States. His oddysey began when he took a bus to the Burmese border. Then he went on foot through the jungle to Thailand, where, for $17,000, he boarded the ship that took him first to Singapore, then Mauritius, and finally to Kenya. He waited there for six months before embarking on the Golden Venture with 300 other Chinese would-be immigrants.

Mrs. Zheng has been fighting for her husband's release but it is not easy. She speaks no English, works eleven hours a day as a seamstress in Manhattan, and then travels back to her apartment in Queens, which she shares with five other "snake people"—undocumented workers from Wenzhou. Even then she works several hours at night assembling garments—trying to scrape together the money she owes her snakehead.

Peter Kwong and two American journalists decided to visit the district of Wenzhou, 200 miles south of Shanghai to see for themselves why people were leaving. Their first stop was the Zheng family home, where they showed his tearful mother a video they had made of him in jail. She could not understand why an honest person was being held in jail when all he wanted was to work. When they explained that once media attention died down, Mr. Zheng would likely be released and sent back to China, his mother broke down completely and cried that if he returned, she would commit suicide. The family, like others, had borrowed huge sums at high rates of interest to pay for his journey in the expectation that he would find work; now they were borrowing more just to pay off the interest. If he returned, they would have no way to repay the money and would be at the mercy of the snakeheads.

About forty of the Golden Venture's passengers were from Wenzhou; surprisingly, most were Christians. Mrs. Peng's only daughter is languishing in a Louisiana prison; Mr. Sung, a former low-level Communist official, has four family members in jail in the United States. He said, "We are simply trying to make a better life for ourselves by going to America." He went on to state that while market reforms have improved conditions in the countryside, as evidenced by the numerous small factories that have sprung up, the benefits have not lasted. Further, since Communist officials have monopolized the most lucrative businesses, they have benefitted the most from privatization.

The country, too, is increasingly polarized, with rural people from the interior moving southward in search of work in the coastal provinces. In an unregulated labor market, factories (including foreign-owned ones such as Reebok) pay low wages and expect long hours. Wages are low because there are some 50 million people in search of work. While the reforms have brought great increases in farm production, they have also led to a chain reaction of "inflation, congestions, depressed wages, high unemployment and social disorder to cities in the infant stages of industrial development" (Kwong, 1994, p. 423). This leads people to turn to the snakeheads, however expensive and risky it may be. "In some cases the snakeheads simply make the debtors their virtual slaves. During the day, the victims work at restaurants that have been linked to organized crime. At night, after they are brought back to prisonlike dorms, they hand over all their money and are locked up until the next day" (Kwong, 1994, p. 425).

own lands); and, as the scale of agriculture increases, more and more work is provided by migrant farm workers—the poorest of the poor. This, in fact, has occurred in many places, but it is not an inevitable scenario.

The loss of distinction between rural and urban households is another consequence of the transition to market dependency. This homogenizing effect is particularly evident when market dependency is coupled with industrial forms of transport and communication. Widely separated households end up eating, dressing, entertaining, and in general living very much the same way. Farm families in this country share most of the expectations and values of urbanites of the same cultural backgrounds. Even their daily diets are very similar. We can see this same process at work on a global level as cultural and ethnic distinctions fade, with resultant worldwide similarities within class lines. Robert Murphy sees "little doubt that by the year 2000 there will no longer be primitive societies" (1986, p. 16). Eskimos use jeeps and snowmobiles, and watch the same TV shows as people in Florida and Brazil. Across continents, people are drawn into one global system; styles of life reflect this convergence.

Sharecropping

Traditionally, **sharecropping** was a very exploitative farming arrangement in which farmers worked the land owned by others for a share of the yield (Wells, 1987). Sharecropping reached its peak in the United States during the Great Depression of the 1930s, when more than 25 percent of American farms were operated on this basis. The arrangement had advantages and disadvantages. It did ensure the landless of access to farmland, even when market conditions left them so poor that they were unable to rent land for cash. At the same time, it yielded far greater profits to landowners than they could realize from rents. Sharecroppers were invariably among the poorest of the poor. These days, however, with the price of land high and rising, many family and corporate farms have returned to sharecropping of a sort: they invest in equipment rather than in more land, use it to farm land belonging to someone else, and pay the landowner in a share of the crop. These sharecroppers are among the more successful farmers in their communities.

In some cases, Miriam Wells (1987) reports, migrant workers become sharecroppers. When crops require a great deal of skill and much labor to raise, it can make sense for the landowner to give the farmworkers a share in the proceeds. California is once more a case in point. Strawberry production has shifted to sharecropping in recent years, with much of the work being done by the same Chicanos who were formerly migrant laborers. By and large, the workers have benefited from this arrangement, as they are their own bosses and share in the profits produced by their labor. Though few have yet moved from sharecropper to farm owner, many are hopeful.

Access to Land

One way to understand the factors common to the structures of contemporary farming is to determine how people gain access to land. Very often the material circumstances of peasant households and the degree of exploitation depend on the way the land is controlled, which in turn depends on the political configuration of the larger society. The private property form of landholding most prevalent today is associated with profound societal changes stemming from the rise of capitalism and industrialism in eighteenth-century Europe and the beginning of colonial empires. Land came to be viewed not as the hereditary privilege and responsibility of a local lord or ruler but as a commodity like any other—the private property of individual owners. Land became another form of capital, with rents or the sale of crops providing the return to the owner. Wherever European colonialism reached, this form of land tenure was encouraged (Wolf, 1982). When land became a commodity, it was relatively easy to encourage increased production and the settlement of Europeans in the new colonies such as those in Africa and the Americas; this system of ownership encouraged landowners to reinvest rents in their lands and to modernize their farm technology.

Peasant Responses to Oppression and Change

Although the lot of peasant cultivators varies widely, it is rarely enviable; "peasants of all times and all places are structured inferiors" (Dalton,

1972, p. 406). Wherever a peasantry exists, it represents a politically dependent and often oppressed segment of the society. Some observers say that peasants have been beaten down too long to be able to change their circumstances; generations of oppression have turned them into passive drudges, resigned to the injustices of their position and indifferent to political events outside the confines of their villages. Others argue that peasants' passivity is a rational, conservative response: poor farmers or peasants simply cannot afford to take risks.

Still, we see that all over the world peasants have effected drastic changes in the way they live. In communities throughout southern Asia, for example, small tractors are used to till the paddies, entrepreneurs start up rice mills, and people almost everywhere are raising crops and animals they never raised before. Rural change is highly visible in China, where peasant farmers are now encouraged to reap the benefits of agricultural entrepreneurship. The Russian Republic is at last taking the same approach, but very slowly. One problem faced by Russia is that after several generations of collective farming, people have become accustomed to having agricultural decisions made for them and to the security of salaries rather than uncertain profits.

Anthropologists report that most peasant farmers are far from passive and are quick to seize an opportunity. A study by an American anthropologist working with an Egyptian colleague documents a long history of entrepreneurial activity in a Nile Delta village, with effects that varied over time. In the early part of the century, rural entrepreneurs invested their profits in the accumulation of land and the community benefited little from their activities. With the enactment of strict laws limiting land ownership in Egypt, entrepreneurs started to invest in other endeavors that stimulated the village economy. One entrepreneur began to raise chickens for sale in Cairo. He built incubators, sheds, and cages, and he purchased feed and equipment suited to a modest initial probe of the market. Soon his business was prospering and expanding. His success motivated others in the village to follow his example. Today raising chickens has become a major village industry (Saunders & Mehenna, 1986, pp. 84–85).

Not all farming families can solve their immediate economic problems by adopting new agricul-
tural techniques. Often the prosperity of one village household depletes the resources of a less fortunate one. One very common response is to pack up and move, just as thousands of Oklahoma farmers did during the great Dust Bowl era of the 1930s. Tens of thousands of Brazilian farm families are attempting to settle in the Amazon region, and even more turn to the cities in the hope of betterment. We may deplore the social and environmental consequences of pioneer settlements in the rain forest and of the proliferation of urban slums, but we must recognize the tenacity of people who are doing their best in a world that does not always serve them well.

Peasants do periodically mobilize themselves into armed opposition. Indeed, history has witnessed a series of exceedingly bloody peasant revolts, in which centuries of accumulated resentment, masked by seeming docility, burst forth in massive waves of violence. England in the fourteenth century and Germany in the fifteenth and sixteenth centuries were shaken by peasant uprisings. In more recent times, the Algerian, Mexican, Russian, Chinese, and Cuban revolutionaries owed much of their success to peasant uprisings that furthered their aims. The irony is that today, these aging regimes are facing their own internal crises, including rural rebellions. In Algeria, Islamic fundamentalists are waging a battle rooted, in part, in the poverty-stricken countryside; in 1995, Indians in Chiapas, Mexico rose in rebellion against the government and demanded that they be given land.

As Eric Wolf (1966) points out, peasant uprisings are usually motivated by a drive not just for practical social change, but for utopian justice and equality. Such hopes may serve to unite the peasants, but not to organize them. The organization and leadership are usually provided by politically sophisticated outsiders. When a government is strong, the usual outcome of a peasant revolt is the death of many peasants and the return of the others to their fields. (An awareness of this likelihood has no doubt served to limit the number of peasant uprisings.) When, on the other hand, the government is already weakened, especially by war, then it may in fact fall if a strong leader manages to rally the peasants to his cause. This was the case in China, where Mao Zedong's revolution was furthered by the devastation of China's long war with Japan. Even when peasant revolts succeed, their success rarely brings complete equality since urban elites often replace the earlier or traditional elite. In China, as we have just seen, even the newly installed Communist government continued policies that disadvantaged people in the countryside, particularly peasants. While the system of land control is usually changed and poverty may be alleviated, a sizable class of rural producers remains in a subordinate social and political position, so there is still a peasant class.

In the remainder of this chapter we will first see how farmers in a Japanese community cope with mechanization and industrialism, and then we will turn to the United States to observe how the American family farm has changed and see the effects of the farmerless farm in the San Joaquin Valley in California.

CASE STUDY:

Change in the Japanese Farming Village of Shinohata

IN 1993, BRITISH DEVELOPMENT RESEARCHER Ronald Dore returned to the tiny, remote village of Shinohata where he had lived in the 1950s and about which he had written in the 1970s (Dore, 1994). The village is situated in the mountains, twenty-five miles from the modern city of Sano, which is located in the wide, industrialized Sano Plains. Formerly it was a five-hour walk from the last train stop. Today, Shinohata is a mere eight-minute taxi ride or a couple of stops on an express electric commuter train from Sano. No longer isolated, it is as much a commuter neighborhood as a community—although many wish it to remain a community. When Dore returned to Shinohata in 1993, about the only sight he could recognize from his old photos were the mountains and the majestic white peak of the one volcano. The village, and the lives of its inhabitants, had in the course of a short generation been radically transformed. For the better, he asked himself, or . . . ?

While there are differences in wealth, these are far less apparent than prior to land reform in 1945, when many had no land at all. Now every child has access to an education and a career. As a develop-

ment expert, Dore is led to speculate about what can be learned from Shinohata's experience. In Japan, the current approach to development stresses poverty-focused planning, or aiding the very poor. In reality Japan's wealth, and Shinohata's prosperity, did not come from efforts to improve the plight of the poor; they were a by-product of years of massive industrialization and individual sacrifice in which the poor contributed, predictably, the most. Is this a model for other countries? Probably not, he concludes, as people today are no longer prepared to wait to see improvements in their lives. Capital accumulation made Japan's present prosperity, but few other developing countries have the ability to defer consumption in order to achieve it.

In 1955 when Dore first settled in the community, the economy was entirely focused, as it had been for centuries, on the agricultural round: backbreaking hand preparation of the rice ponds, mulberry and silk-worm production, and tending household gardens. Ten years prior to his arrival, immediately after the war, a land reform act had redistributed much of the land in Shinohata to those who had previously worked for absentee landlords. Now most people owned two to six acres, with no one owning more than twelve. Thus the village was a community of owner-farmers who believed themselves well off, particularly the few households whose sons held salaried jobs outside the community. While new rice strains had increased yields, the labor involved was largely unchanged. The rice fields had to be prepared with a fine, perfectly level "tilth" or bed for planting made by cutting and chopping grass collected elsewhere and mixing it into the soil, hand transplanting, constant regulation of the water level, and maintaining earthen walls around the field. At the end of the season, the farmer was left with twelve or so bales of rice.

Between rice harvests, wheat and barley and mulberry leaves were grown on the dry fields. Women of the household fed the mulberry leaves to silk worms, turning their cocoons into silk. In 1958 only 17 of the 60 households sold over $550 worth of produce on the commercial market, and about one-third of their profit went to buy fertilizers. Their tools were simple: an ox, plow, harrow, and simple cart, along with a hand-pushed rotary tiller. Most of the energy that went into farming

Rural houses in Japan, as in Europe and North America, increasingly resemble urban houses; lifestyles and consumer patterns are also converging.
(J. Holmes/Panos Pictures, London)

was human, fueled by meals that consisted of large quantities of rice, soya beans, and fresh vegetables in summer, and pickled ones in winter (p. 63). The first motor scooter, sold by Dore, came in 1956; one electric line served the village's needs and piped water had just arrived at individual homes.

By the 1970s, the village was electrified; every house had telephone and electricity lines along with a proliferation of appliances. Most households had motor vehicles, and the roads and sidewalks were paved. Many of the homes also had undergone two major phases of home investment. The first was to build indoor plumbing and to modernize the household's bath—a central domestic institution then, as now. The second involved remodeling the entire house with formal porches, glass windows and doors, hardwood floors, tile and formica kitchens, and often a Western-style living room with parquet flooring, plastic-wood wall panelling, sofas, and arm chairs. No longer does the visitor simply slide an entrance panel aside and shout, "excuse me"; there is a formal door on hinges, a brass nameplate, and a bell to ring. People no longer live in a microcosm where everybody is expected to know everyone else. Even the new toilets have refinements: they are called "Western-style" but they are rarely found outside of Japan. They have electrically heated seats and a little bowl built into the top of the cistern or tank in which one can wash one's hands. The family oxen disappeared in the 1960s when most of the livestock was sold off and everyone purchased multipurpose motorized tillers. In the 1970s when cheap American grain became available as feed, cattle were reintroduced. However, they never leave their feeding sheds until they are fat enough to sell. Beef prices are the highest in the world in Japan, and little or none is imported.

Even though they are now modernized, the villagers have not acquired the modern "cult of the natural," Dore writes. They have little nostalgia for the time when each house carried its night soil to cisterns for storage and later application on the fields, or for the flies and mosquitos that the women used to swat away from the food while the men ate. In 1955, the village shop was a social as well as redistributive center; people would shop and gossip. It is gone, as is the visiting vegetable seller. Everyone shops in large markets in town and stores produce in deep freezes and refrigerators. Gardening used to be largely a utilitarian endeavor, although some homes had modest decorative rock gardens with carp ponds. Now many have decorative gardens, usually reflecting how much an urban designer was paid to set it up (prices begin at $2,000).

Most of the family's food is purchased; only four households now make their own soya sauce, once a major and prized household product. Many still engage in farming of a sort, and it is profitable since Japan offers heavy subsidies for those who raise rice. The fields are now leveled and prepared mechanically; each plot is banked with expensive cement blocks, and some are even left to grow weeds under a government agricultural subsidy plan. Weeds are no longer mulched, but fertilizers are employed instead. The seedlings are planted by an ingenious machine that plucks them from a container and plants them in finger-deep, perfectly aligned holes. Threshing, too, is mechanized. Only a few elderly ladies persist in the labor-intensive business of silk worm production. Agriculture alone no longer sustains modern Shinohata standards of living. Every family has members working in industry, commerce, or for the government. Many outsiders have moved in, either as second-home dwellers or as commuters.

The road from Sano City, nowadays crowded with vehicles, winds through the plains and up into the hills that are now sites on which Tokyo residents build second homes and where vacationers stay in lodges with exotic names such as "Monte Carlo" and "Motel Arizona." The hungry can stop at a friendly *duraivin* (drive-in); shops along the road out of town have automatically opening glass doors—a feature that in most industrialized countries is restricted to major buildings.

Socially, the community has changed as well. By 1993, the days of large communal outings to shrines or resorts was over; the fire department no longer takes the day off for a fishing and drinking party. Indeed, there are few activities that bring everyone together. Politics is a consuming issue, as the village has always made skillful use of subsidies and grants provided by the government. The villagers have no longer to work together to repair the roads or to build each other's homes. Even religious activities, which used to be occasions of near-mandatory attendance (and male drinking sessions), no longer attract more than the diehards. Most excuse themselves and hurry home to television. Reaching Shinohata on his last visit, Dore was confronted by the newly renovated village hall, renamed "Multi-Purpose Center."

Are the people of Shinohata really better off with lives focused on jobs, TV, and commuting schedules? One person answered Ronald Dore in 1993, " . . . you used to say none of this 'where are the snows of yesteryear' business. None of this green nostalgia for a warmer, unpolluted, nonpolluting, natural human past. All of the changes in Shinohata are for the better. That's what you used to say. But what about now? Are you still of the same mind?" ◗

Urbanized Rural Society: Farming in the United States

Over 90 percent of American farms are family operated (contrary to the perception of many), although there are far greater differences among them than there were a generation or two ago. Farms of 3,000 acres that gross more than $500,000 a year account for only 2 percent of the total, but produce 35 percent of the output; the top 5 percent account for more than half the output (Feder, 1994, p. 1). The majority of American farmers have significant off-farm income; it is the larger ones that adopt new technology, often working directly under contract with food processors such as Frito-Lay or McDonalds. The modern American farmer has to be as much a financial and marketing expert as anything else. We will examine the development of American farming with case material from California and the Midwest.

CASE STUDY:

The Development of Agribusiness in Wasco, California

AMERICAN ANTHROPOLOGISTS WERE SOMEWHAT slow to recognize the importance of studying farming communities in their own society. In the early 1940s, however, Walter Goldschmidt (1978) undertook a now classic study of Wasco, California, a town of 7,000 to 8,000 people, most of them involved in various aspects of industrialized commercial agriculture. By living in the town, participating in local organizations, conducting interviews, and examining official records and historical documents, Goldschmidt was able to trace the radical transformation that the town had undergone in the previous few decades. More recently the study of rural America has become a major focus of research, and not surprisingly, much of it has been directed to California (see Chibnik, 1987).

Until the first decade of this century, the land on which Wasco's farms now sit was desert, and the main activity in the area was sheep herding. Wasco itself consisted of one store, one hotel, and

Agricultural land is disappearing in most parts of the world as urban and industrial centers spread, such as this one north of Los Angeles.

(David Parker/Photo Researchers Inc.)

a handful of saloons frequented by ranch hands and an occasional homesteader. Then in 1907 a developer persuaded the corporation that owned the entire Wasco area to sell part of its holdings and began to advertise for homesteaders, promising to provide the necessary irrigation. The sales pitch worked (the land was bought quickly), but the irrigation system did not. In all probability, the farmers would have abandoned Wasco to the sheep if a power company had not brought in a line, enabling the settlers to install electric pumps. This was the beginning of the industrialization of Wasco.

For small farmers, as most of the original settlers were, an electric pump is a major investment. In order to recoup that investment, the farmers turned to cash crops, specializing in potatoes, cotton, sugar beets, lemons, or grapes. Both the profits and the settlement grew. In some years the payoff for commercial farming was spectacular. In 1936—a Depression year—one farmer was ru-

mored to have made over $1 million from his potato crop.

Such booms encouraged Wasco's farmers to expand. Some of them rented land on which to grow profitable but soil-depleting crops for a year or two. (Once the soil was exhausted, the owner would revitalize it by planting alfalfa and then rent it again.) This strategy of expansion required the planter to hire large numbers of workers and to make substantial investments in tractors and other motorized equipment. Other Wasco farmers used their profits to expand in other areas. Having made a large investment, a farmer would look for ways to maintain a steady flow of produce and income. He might, for example, buy the fruits of another landowner's trees and hire his own laborers to pick them. Or better still, he might purchase more land. In this way, the average size of landholding increased from about 20 acres when the homesteaders first moved in, to about 100 acres at the time of Goldschmidt's study—a 500-percent increase in about thirty years.

In no time Wasco was attracting outside corporations—first the utility companies, then a national bank, oil companies, and chain supermarkets. These developments changed the social landscape. The representatives of the state and national government agencies and of corporations (whose loyalties lay outside Wasco) tended to become leaders within the town. Even farmers with relatively small holdings began to see themselves as entrepreneurs rather than as tillers of the soil. One informant told Goldschmidt, "There is one thing I want you to put in your book. Farming in this country is a business, it's not a way of life" (1978, p. 22).

Wasco began to attract large numbers of unskilled laborers who could find work in the town and dream of buying a place of their own one day. First Mexicans (Chicanos), then (after World War I) blacks, and in the 1930s refugees from Oklahoma, Arkansas, and other drought-stricken states poured into the town. They were markedly poorer than the Wasco farmers, who did not consider them their racial, cultural, or social equals. The social contact between the two groups was very limited. At the time of the study, the Mexicans, the blacks, and to a lesser extent the Oklahomans lived in their own separate communities with their own stores and churches. They were outsiders in every sense, and that was just what Wasco's commercial farmers needed: "a large number of laborers, unused to achieving the social values of the dominant group, and satisfied with a few of the luxuries of modern society" (1978, p. 62). In its urban orientation, its commercial production and consumption, and its economic gap between owners and laborers, Wasco might as well have been an industrial center. Above all, in its social structure—the impersonal, purely economic relationship between the landowners and the laborers—the town showed its urban-industrial face. To see how Wasco continues to change, we turn to a more recent California study. ◗

CASE STUDY:

The Farmerless Farm in the San Joaquin Valley

MARK KRAMER DESCRIBES THE SUBSEQUENT phase in the transformation of California agriculture: the farmerless farm (1987, pp. 197–278). It is tomato harvest time in the San Joaquin Valley, 3:00 A.M., and 105,708,000 ripe tomatoes lie ready for picking—altogether, some 766 absolutely flat acres of irrigated cropland. Out of the darkness rumble giant tractor-drawn machines resembling moon landers—two stories high, with ladders, catwalks, and conveyors fastened all over and carrying fourteen workers each. As they lumber down the long rows, they continually ingest whole tomato plants while spewing out the rear a steady stream of stems and rejects. Fourteen workers sit facing a conveyor belt in the harvester, sorting the marketable tomatoes from the discards.

It is a giant harvest carried out almost without people; only a few years ago more than 600 workers were needed to harvest a crop that 100 manage today. There are no farmers involved in this operation: only corporation executives, managers, foremen, and laborers. The word "farmer" has virtually disappeared; in this operation, one refers to "growers" and "pickers." Managers take courses in psychology to help them determine appropriate incentives to offer tractor drivers for covering the

most ground (if speed is too great, they may damage equipment; if they go too slowly, productivity falls). Managers similarly calculate pickers' productivity very precisely and regulate it by varying the speed of the conveyor belts and by minimizing the time spent turning the machines around at the ends of rows, when the workers are prone to get off for a smoke. Right now, Kramer reports one manager as saying, the industry is moving to a new-model harvester that will do the job of fourteen men with only two. The other twelve can move on to other employment if they can find it.

Tomato consumption closely reflects the changing eating habits of American society; these days, each of us eats 50.5 pounds of tomatoes every year, whereas in 1920 consumption was 18.1 pounds. This change is accounted for by the fact that far more of our food is prepared somewhere other than in the home kitchen. This development has produced a demand for prepared sauces and flavorings, such as catsup and tomato paste. The increased productivity required to meet demand has resulted in dramatic genetic changes in the tomatoes we eat.

Processors of tomatoes demanded a product that is firmer; growers needed standardization of sizes and an oblong shape to counter the tomatoes' tendency to roll off the conveyors; engineers required tomatoes with thick skins to withstand handling; and large corporate growers needed more tonnage per acre and better resistance to disease. The result is the modern American tomato: everything but flavor. "As geneticists selectively bred for these characteristics, they lost control of others. They bred for thick skins, less acidity, more uniform ripening, oblongness, leafiness, and high yield—and they could not also select for flavor" (Kramer, 1987, p. 213). Even the chemists made their contribution: a substance called ethylene (which is also produced naturally by the plants) is sprayed on fields of almost ripe tomatoes in order to induce redness. Quite like the transformation of the tomato itself, the ownership of the farms that grow them has been altered. As one might expect in view of the massive inputs of capital needed to raise the new breed of tomatoes, most are raised on corporate spreads. The one Kramer describes consisted of more than 27,000 acres and was owned by several general partners, including a major insurance corporation, an oil company, and a news-

Mechanization of agriculture may cost far more in terms of energy invested in farm equipment and fertilizers than is yielded in food energy. Giant tractors are used throughout North America and other industrialized countries to prepare the fields and to harvest crops.

(John Colwell/Grant Heilman Collection)

paper; and thousands of limited partners, most of them doctors and lawyers who invested in the operation for its tax benefits. There is little room under these conditions for the small farmer—or so it would seem. ❱

The Family Farm

Even in food production there are limits to the efficiency of large farms: they require middle-level managers and get less out of individual workers than do smaller, family-managed operations. Large, corporately managed farms can make large-scale mistakes. Kramer reported that one worker in California sprayed a huge area with the wrong insecticide, and some managers' heavy investment in unsuitable crops resulted in big losses. In fact, the large farm Kramer describes subsequently sold off half its holdings as unprofitable. Under some conditions, a smaller farm can be more efficient than a huge one, but it still will be highly capitalized and employ modern equipment, up-to-date accounting methods, and trained management. Most suc-

cessful farmers in the United States are college graduates.

Many observers report a revival of the family farm in North America, but one with a new face (Gladwin & Butler, 1982; Salamon, 1992). The family-run farm now often involves a new division of labor, with the wife assuming primary responsibility for farming operations, often of a specialized nature, while the husband holds down a salaried job and helps out when he can. This is clearly the pattern in the Midwest on smaller farms, but on large spreads of over 500 acres the family manages today much as before: with its own labor and skills.

CASE STUDY:

Family Farmers in the Midwest: The Immigrant Legacy

SONYA SALAMON HAS SPENT MANY YEARS studying Midwestern farming communities and families (1992). Most of her research concerns seven farming communities in Illinois where she has been carrying out research for over a decade. Land and family are her main interests, since families cannot farm without land. Yet this resource has to be acquired and passed on in order for the community (if, indeed, it is one) to have continuity. Family land, then, is a cultural patrimony and land tenure and farm management and inheritance shape the personalities of rural communities. About half of the communities she studied were of German descent, coming from both the Protestant and Catholic regions of Germany; the other half, which she calls "Yankees," are of largely Protestant backgrounds and came to the Midwest from New England and the British Isles. One unexpected finding of her research is that far from being homogeneous after so many years, there is a definite mosaic effect in the rural American settlement pattern—and one which is changing with time.

These two groups are only part of the ethnic diversity of region; Michigan, for example, has many farmers of Polish, Dutch, and Finnish descent but the processes of community formation seem remarkably similar. In the mid-nineteenth century, with the coming of the railways, the Midwest saw development unparalleled in American history. Within fifty years, the Midwest was transformed from forests and prairies into densely settled and intensively farmed agricultural lands. Towns and villages shot up seemingly overnight, populated by immigrant Europeans. There were many reasons for them to emigrate, including inheritance rules in Europe that encouraged farm fragmentation and rural poverty. The newly established railroads provided easy access to the Midwest and land grant acts by Congress made it easy, if not free, for settlers to acquire land. Even the railroads offered inducements for migrants to settle. This was not, of course, altruism—just good business. With farming came the need to transport produce to markets and industrial products to the farms.

While all immigrants faced similar challenges, different ethnic groups responded to these in different ways. Those Salamon calls Yankees came from predominately English backgrounds. While unlikely to have been landowners at home, they tended to approach farming much as in the home country. Land was viewed as a commodity, which, if possible, should be worked for profit using hired help or tenant farmers. Children of owners were not so much induced to stay at home but rather to strike out and find new farmsteads for themselves. This set the basis for settlement; successful farmers set their sons up with farms in distant regions, not necessarily next door. Absentee ownership was also common, and, in general, these farmers were not known for their "stewardship of the soil"— looking instead to profit rather than sustainability. The Yankees had the advantage of being part of the linguistic and political majority and could move rather easily. The German settlers came from different regions of Germany, spoke different dialects of German, and belonged to different churches. They shared, however, a common origin in tightly knit peasant communities that they intended to replicate in their new country. Some of the newcomers were able to acquire land; some simply worked for Yankee farmers as tenants. But even as tenants, their objective was to save enough to acquire land near other German-speaking members of their local church. Initially, the Midwest was predominantly Yankee, with much land in Illinois held in huge spreads of over 10,000 acres used mostly for livestock production. As settlement progressed, the absentee owners often took advantage of rising land prices to sell out. Usually they sold to their German tenants or neighbors. Thus, with time, the German component in the settlement pattern grew until today it is the dominant one.

Salamon distinguished two divergent strategies that shaped settlement and community patterns and continue to do so. One strategy, which she terms the "yeoman" approach, is more characteristic of the German population.[1] The other is the "entrepreneur" approach more characteristic of the Yankees.

The yeoman sees land as a sacred trust and farming as a means of membership in a community. There is a relative hierarchy in the family, since whoever owns land has power and seniority in management decisions. The yeoman's goals are to own as much land as feasible without undue debt or risk, maximize kin involvement, and avoid anything that would alienate the land from the family.

In contrast the entrepreneur views land as a commodity and farming as a business. There is a weaker family hierarchy, as farming is not necessarily

---

[1]By "German" is meant those with German surnames indicating German descent; they may no longer speak German, but they do identify themselves as such in national censuses.

thought to be the logical thing for an heir to do. The entrepreneur does not always favor ownership over renting land; renting land allows the entrepreneur to expand and utilize capital better. For this reason, their farms are larger, more capital-intensive, and more in debt.

In recent decades the approaches have necessarily drawn closer together; almost all farms are heavily capitalized, few are free of debt, and all must be as skillful in marketing as in crop production. What is clear from Salamon's research is that

the family is very much part of the family farm in America, perhaps even more than ever. Since farm sizes have increased so much in recent years, something of the older prairie feeling has returned to farm life. Houses are now farther apart and families rely on church and community get-togethers to see friends and neighbors. Of course, this is mediated by the use of mobile phones and CB radios, and everyone follows local and national events in the media. ❿

Summary

INTENSIVE AGRICULTURE IS DISTINGUISHED FROM horticulture by both an increased investment in energy and increased productivity per unit of land. The additional energy may come from a variety of sources, including animals yoked to plows, fossil fuels for farm machinery, fertilizers, and human muscles. Methods of intensification include irrigation canals, terracing, crop rotation, and selective breeding of crops and livestock. Through these techniques, the output of cultivated fields is increased, more fields can be cultivated, and fallow periods can be decreased or eliminated. While both the land and the farmer work harder under intensive agriculture, the result is much higher production.

Intensive agriculture substantially reshapes the environment. By constructing irrigation systems to overcome the problem of insufficient rainfall, for instance, farmers may create new, complex problems that become increasingly difficult to solve. The more people alter their ecosystems, the more labor and organizational effort are required to maintain their bases of production.

The social consequences of intensification are far-reaching. The development of irrigation is associated with the emergence of cities and territorial states, with accompanying social changes: higher population densities, economic stratification, increased trade, the appearance of craft specialists, and the development of hierarchical civil and religious organizations. The need for centralized authority to make decisions, variations in the productivity of land in the region, and a surplus of food all contributed to the rise of cities and states. Farming communities that were at one time autonomous were absorbed by the states, and the

farmers (or peasants) lost control over the social and economic system and the means of production. Peasants are agriculturists (usually villagers) who do not control the land, capital, and labor on which they depend; further, they are often subject to corvée, unpaid labor to build and maintain roads and bridges. In some parts of the world peasants gain access to land by sharecropping, or working land owned by others in exchange for a share of the yield.

Corporate ownership of land and resources, which typifies horticultural land use systems, is generally giving way to private ownership. Under private ownership, land is regarded as the private property of the individual owner. In the early twentieth century, a new form of land tenure arose and became widespread. Under the administrative system, formerly prevalent in all communist countries, the state owns the land and can control much of the peasant's labor and income. The administrative form of land control has had a mixed record. Collective farming led to the near-collapse of food production in China and was largely abandoned there as public policy. Some collective enterprises do prosper, particularly those that are small, that offer participants some advantage, and that produce items that farmers could not produce by their individual efforts.

Under exceptional circumstances, peasant farmers may find their situation intolerable and rise in revolt. In this century they have supported revolutions in Algeria, Mexico, Russia, China, and Cuba. Even when such uprisings are successful, the farmers often remain disadvantaged in relation to the urban population.

Industrialism is characterized by a highly developed factory system of production based on the harnessing of vastly increased amounts of energy, on specialization, and on mechanization—the replacement of human and animal labor by mechanical devices. The rise of industrial society has provoked dramatic changes in our physical and social environments. The more energy industrial societies extract, the more they require for their survival.

Industrialism has numerous social consequences. Human populations are increasing more rapidly than ever before, with consequent pressures on natural resources. Industrialization brings a demographic transition: the population increases rapidly and persistently before the growth rate finally levels off. Massive migrations both between and within nations have occurred as people have left rural communities for the cities in the hope of industrial jobs. Increasing specialization of labor and concentration of wealth have resulted in new kinds of social relations and organizations. Differentiation between classes has increased, while differentiation based on cultural and ethnic distinctions within classes has declined. The economy brought about by industrialism has transcended geographical barriers. This chapter focuses on the industrialization of agriculture, the adaptations that people have made to this phenomenon, and the impact of technology and multinational corporations.

One example of the problems inherent in industrialized agriculture is sisal culture in Brazil. A group of small farmers in Brazil, hoping to share in the prosperity of the large landowners, abandoned their subsistence crops to plant sisal for export. By the time their crops matured, the price of sisal had dropped and they were forced to work as laborers on the large plantations to survive. Vast numbers of such displaced farmers all over the world finally seek a better life in the cities, where they slowly adapt to an urban and industrial society.

This chapter pays special attention to two cases of intensive farming: a Japanese village, Shinohata, whose families are rapidly being absorbed into that country's growing industrial sector; and California's industrialized farming system.

In Shinohata, farmers are rapidly adopting new technology such as chemical fertilizers, motor tillers, and power sprayers. Many younger people are leaving the village to work in factories, leading to a decrease in household size. But even though farm size has increased and town and country have been integrated, some of the expected negative results have not appeared. The household remains the basic unit of production and consumption, wealth has not become concentrated, and those who do move to the city remain in close contact with their rural families. In short, industrialization has, on balance, been beneficial to most,

in contrast to the uneven situation in many other countries. This is because Japan's rapidly growing economy can absorb those who do not make it on the farm.

In the experience of Wasco, California, we see the urbanization of a rural community by mechanization—the transformation of farming as a livelihood to farming for profit, the change in social reference from the local community to that of the wider world, and the breakdown in social relations from close personal ties to relatively impersonal ones. In the San Joaquin Valley, large corporations run giant farms without farmers, relying on managers and foremen to supervise crews of migrant laborers. The family farm is still the dominant form of farming in the United States, even though a commercially successful operation now involves over a thousand acres of land. In the Midwest, there is still a definite ethnic texture to the settlement pattern, with, in Illinois, families of German descent now predominant.

Key Terms

administrative system	fallow time
Blue Revolution	Green Revolution
commune	mechanization
corvée	peasants
demographic transition	sharecropping

Suggested Readings

Bentley, J. W. (1992). *Today there is no misery: The ethnography of farming in northwest Portugal*. Tucson and London: University of Arizona Press. A thorough study of the agricultural system of northwest Portugal with an optimistic view of peasant farming.

Bray, F. (1994). *The rice economies: Technology and development in Asian societies*. Berkeley: University of California Press. This book extensively describes the history and techniques of rice cultivation.

Dore, R. (1994). *Shinohata: A portrait of a Japanese village*. Berkeley: University of California Press. A lucid and detailed account of a Japanese village over the past twenty years, including methods of rice cultivation as well as what it means to live in this village.

Durrenberger, E. P. & Tannenbaum, N. (1990). Analytical perspectives on Shan agriculture and village economics. *Monograph Series, 37*. New Haven, CT: Yale University Southeast Asia Studies. This volume discusses and analyzes the economics of Shan agriculture and farmer decision making.

Freeman, J. M. (1977). *Scarcity and opportunity in an Indian village*. Menlo Park, CA: Cummings Publishing.

A study of a small village in India that has experienced an ever-widening gap between the privileged high castes and the less privileged lower castes. The economic basis of this gap seems to be that the higher castes have benefited from the growth of a nearby city, while members of the lower castes have little opportunity to improve their lot through urban contacts.

Kirch, V. P. (1994). *The wet and the dry: Irrigation and agricultural intensification in Polynesia*. Chicago: University of Chicago Press. A fine-grained review of intensive agriculture in a region that is often overlooked.

Pasternak, Burton. (1983). *Guests in the dragon: Social demography of a Chinese district, 1895–1946*. New York: Columbia University Press. An analysis of the relationship between domestic institutions and demographic behavior in one Hakka district of Taiwan that details the different choices among the possible forms of marriage and the implications these choices have for rates of adoption, mortality, and fertility.

Salamon, S. (1992). *Prairie patrimony: Family, farming and community in the midwest*. Chapel Hill: University of North Carolina Press. An excellent account of family farming in the Midwest.

Scott, James C. (1976). *The moral economy of the peasant*. New Haven, CT: Yale University Press. A study of peasant politics and rebellion that focuses on the critical problem of a secure subsistence as the explanation for the technical, social, and moral arrangements of these societies.

Part III

Cultural Diversity

Part III explores in greater detail many of the ideas introduced in Part II. The topics are basic to understanding the anthropological perspective in action. Each chapter shares a number of common themes: focus on individual behavior, variability within society, and coping with problems arising from the environment and from within and outside one's own society.

Our treatment of social life begins in Chapter 8 with a discussion of kinship, marriage, and family—key building blocks for social formations of a larger scale. The role of descent ideologies is introduced; the political implications are handled in Chapter 11. Chapter 9 devotes significant attention to the often contradictory and misused notions of gender, race, and ethnicity—particularly in terms of systematic inequality and its perpetuation. The treatment of economic and political organization in Chapters 10 and 11 extends the discussion of the basic organization of social groups. The discussion of religion in Chapter 12 makes use of concepts introduced in our discussion of economics and political life.

Throughout these chapters, there is a concern for the ideational aspects of culture: the human need to commemorate, to ceremonialize, is universal. Rituals range from the sacred to the mundane; they may be public or private, personal or political. We all tend to organize the routines of our daily lives into private, personal, and sometimes idiosyncratic ceremonies.

The last chapter focuses on the important issues of social change, planned or unplanned; the way in which anthropologists can contribute to understanding processes of change; and the ethics of development or applied anthropology.

Kinship and Social Organization
  Kinship Terms and Social Behavior
  Case Study: Yanomamö Kinship
  The Manipulation of Kinship
  The Classification of Kin
  Contemporary Issues: Families
  We Choose

Descent Ideology and Descent Groups
  Unilineal Descent Groups
  Case Study: The Pokot of Kenya
  Case Study: The Hopi of Notheastern
  Arizona
  Nonunilineal Descent Groups

Marriage, Remarriage, and Marital Residence
  Marriage
  Gender Issues: Marriage and Money
  Management
  Divorce and Remarriage
  Marriage as Exchange
  Using Anthropology: Kidnapping
  and Elopement Among the Yörük A
  Problem Reconsidered
  Marriage and the Division of Labor
  Marital Rules

Family Households
  Independent versus Extended Family
    Households

Summary
Key Terms
Suggested Readings

Chapter 8

Kinship, Marriage, and the Household

The importance of kin ties to the dynamics of social relations is hard to overestimate. One Scottish folk rhyme expresses it nicely:

Adam Smith
Was disowned by all his kith
But he was supported through thick and thin
By all his kin

"Kith" are neighbors and close friends, who in this rhyme were fickle in their loyalties. Steadfast, however, stood the kin. The same attitude toward kin is reflected in an old Arabic saying, which also shows how even relatives who are on bad terms with one another may close ranks against outsiders:

I against my brother; my brother and I against my cousins; I, my brother, and my cousins against the outsider.

The single most important aspect of human adaptation, as we have stressed earlier, is the ability to respond to problems in a flexible, creative fashion. Our ability to work in cooperation with others in large social groupings and coordinate the activities of many people to achieve particular purposes—to live, work, even to fight and compete as members of a social group—is a vital part of human adaptation. One important aspect of human adaptation consists of people's perceptions of their relatives, their ways of organizing themselves in kin groups, marrying, establishing households, and using ties of kinship and other relationships to accomplish their ends.

Kinship is a basis for social organization we share with all social species, including other primates. This chapter deals with the basic ideologies, or models, of kin-based social organization. "Ideologies" here refers simply to the fact that our ideas of family, ancestry, descent, and relatedness or kinship are cultural constructs—mentally carried images—much like our religions and other beliefs. It is best to think in terms of ideologies because ideas of family and kinship, although they exhibit some regularity across cultural boundaries, also vary greatly. So we will begin with a general discussion of kinship and proceed to the ways in which kinship ties are created and used socially. While we describe some simplified analytic models, human behavior is so varied that no single model can encompass all practices, even within one society.

Kinship and Social Organization

One way to look at a system of kinship is to see it as a model of statuses and reciprocal roles (see Chapter 2). The model used by one society may differ from the model used by another, so that the first may give prominence to statuses that the second does not emphasize or even ignores. As we shall see, many cultures recognize one's mother's brother as a very special uncle and use a special word to specify him. This status does not exist for most English speakers, who use the word "uncle" to describe all the brothers of both parents. In most societies, kinship is the basis for social relations that link people across generations, and hence provide major channels for the transmission of knowledge through time. This includes not just technical knowledge but the more basic social knowledge of such things as what a person is, what a role is, what a status is, what a relation is, and what an obligation is. By the same token, kinship is usually the first system of social roles to which a person is introduced; the major, and sometimes the only, sys-

tem of roles applied to an individual from birth and unchanging throughout life. As Napoleon Chagnon (1983) puts it, "kinship is the heart of social structure."

Studies of **kinship**—the way people define and classify their kin and the way these classifications relate to social behavior and social organization—are a fundamental part of anthropology. Anthropologists have come to realize in the course of their research that kinship is important even in extremely complex industrial societies: most of us live with and carry on our most intense and enduring relationships with people related to us either by blood or by marriage. The new familial arrangements that are coming into being in the United States today because of the high incidence of divorce and remarriage are very interesting. Children of one or more previous marriages may live together with children of their common parent's current marriage. They may end up with large numbers of half-siblings or step-siblings, and even a substantial number of people who behave toward them as grandparents. Even so, kinship roles are universal organizers of behavior and hence are universal keys to the structure of society.

Kinship Terms and Social Behavior

Anthropologists are interested in the way people of different cultures classify their kin because people tend to structure their behavior in accordance with the way they perceive themselves in relation to others. Kinship terminology, after all, is part of a language system. A person whose kin terminology automatically separates father's kin from mother's kin is not likely to regard (and treat) his or her relatives the same way as one whose kin terminology lacks such distinctions. The Hopi of Arizona, who employ kinship terminology that anthropologists label "Crow," distinguish father's sister from mother's sister. A Hopi man has especially close and intimate relations with his kya'a (father's sister), and the relationship lasts throughout her life (Whiteley, 1985, p. 360). In fact, this relationship may be more meaningful than relations among members of the same matrilineage (the Hopi have matrilineal clans and lineages).

Classification systems tell us how people organize their perceptions of those relatives whom they view as belonging to the same category and toward

Three generations of women in a Yörük family. The daughter-in-law, on the left, is also a first cousin to her mother-in-law.
(Daniel Bates)

whom they are expected to behave in a certain manner, and how they assign separate terms to relatives whom they perceive as excluded from that category and toward whom they are expected to behave somewhat differently. Of course, kinship terms cannot predict behavior with absolute accuracy. For one thing, no two people interpret kinship roles, or any other roles, in precisely the same way; as long as certain guidelines are observed, the rules can be adjusted to suit the people involved. Thus, though we may try to remember both of our grandmothers' birthdays, we may visit one twice as often as the other simply because we enjoy her company more. Also, though kin terms may group people into one category, distinctions within that category exist. For example, we may lump together mother's brother and mother's sister's husband under the single term "uncle," but most of us, if we needed a loan, would probably turn to the uncle who was a "blood relative" before we approached the one who was related to us only by marriage (unless we know the latter to be far more wealthy or generous).

The terminology, then, both assigns and reflects important social roles. The following brief example illustrates this principle. In looking at it, we should keep in mind that it is presented from the perspective of a man in that society; women view some of the same kin relationships in quite a different fashion.

CASE STUDY:

Yanomamö Kinship

AS WE HAVE SEEN, THE YANOMAMÖ ARE A group of South American Indians who live in an environment marked by violence. Regular warfare between villages creates a need to establish allies; at the same time, men have difficulties in obtaining wives, because of the practice of female infanticide, which creates a shortage of women and thus encourages warfare. So to the Yanomamö two things are especially important: finding a wife and finding allies.

Underlying these two preoccupations, and reinforced by them, is a network of well-defined kin relationships. Membership in Yanomamö named kin groups is inherited through the male line; both males and females belong to the kin group, or lineage, of their father. The kin group to which a person belongs is particularly important in regard to marriage, for men and women are required to marry specific types of cousins in a kin group other than their own. This prescription often leads young men of different kin groups to exchange sisters. When the same two kin groups continue to exchange women for generations, strong bonds are created between them. Such alliances are extremely important in time of war.

The terms by which the Yanomamö refer to many of their relatives reflect these marriage rules and the alliances they create. Within a particular generation, all the members of a kin group refer to one another as "brother" and "sister," a reflection of the prohibition of marriage between them. At the same time, a man refers to all his marriageable female relatives in other named kin groups (relatives that we would call "cousins") as "wife"—whether or not he in fact marries them. Similarly, the same man refers to the brothers of all of his "wives" as "brothers-in-law," indicating their close potential ties through marriage. Among brothers, as we saw in Chapter 5, relationships are often tense, for they are competing for the same wives. Relationships among brothers-in-law, on the other hand, are often quite friendly, since these men have much to gain—wives and wartime alliances—from one another.

Among the Yanomamö, kinship categories are critical to the establishment of patterns of social interaction. A person's status in most social situations can be described, in large part, by a single kin term. Chagnon describes the case of an orphaned adolescent boy who came to live in the village where Chagnon was conducting his fieldwork. The boy had no real relatives in the village, but he attempted to define his own place in society by calling the headman of one of the kin groups "father." This tactic established a basis for developing and manipulating his ties to others in the village.

Kinship classification systems, however, reveal only the structure of social relationships; they do not reveal people's actual behavior. If a Yanomamö calls one man "brother" and another "brother-in-law," the terms tell us that he regards himself as playing two different roles vis-à-vis these two men. But it does not tell us what those roles actually are. To find out, the ethnographer must examine the society through observation and interviews. Once the

ethnographer learns what the reciprocal roles of brothers and brothers-in-law involve, he or she can predict and interpret with some accuracy any male Yanomamö's behavior toward any man to whom he refers by one of these terms. ▶

The Manipulation of Kinship

In adapting the general rules of kinship to the specific requirements of daily life, people manipulate not only kinship roles; they may also manipulate kinship terms. The terms we have discussed so far are **terms of reference**, the terms by which people refer to their kin when they speak about them in the third person. Most kinship studies are concerned primarily with terms of reference, for such terms reflect most consistently the society's system for classifying kin. However, the language of kinship also includes **terms of address**, the terms people use when they address their kin directly. Terms of address are particularly interesting because they are the ones that people are likely to manipulate to suit their needs in various situations. These are the terms used in direct, face-to-face speech and may be deliberately at variance with terms of reference.

A commonly observed social strategy is to use a kinship term with absolutely no genealogical justification in order to invoke a desired role relationship. During the Black Power movement of the 1960s, for example, many blacks adopted the practice of calling one another "brother" and "sister" in order to stress their group solidarity. For precisely the same reason, feminists sometimes refer to unrelated women as their sisters. This ad hoc manufacturing of kin relationships for political reasons has been observed in nonindustrial societies as well, despite the fact that they sometimes seem to interpret kinship more strictly than we. Claude Lévi-Strauss (1943) has reported on a population of Brazilian Indians that included members of two tribes that did not speak the same language. The men of the two merged groups called each other "brother-in-law," a term they had previously applied only to the brothers of all eligible brides in their own separate groups. This manipulation of kinship terminology helped to promote peaceful relations in a situation of potential conflict.

The Classification of Kin

When we study kinship it is crucial to keep in mind how the people of a society classify kin, rather than how kin might be categorized on a biological basis. The manner in which biologically based relationships are sorted and grouped has more to do with values, beliefs, and economic practices than with biology. The classification of kin or the system of words used to describe relationships is a cultural and linguistic phenomenon as well as a social fact central to the operation of any society.

A Yanomamö man, for example, uses the same word for his brother and for his father's brother's son; and a man has almost the same expectations of his father's brother's sons as of his biological brothers. They fight the same battles, marry into the same group of women, and interact in reciprocal ways. In much the same way English speakers call quite diverse relatives "cousin," and while we have few specific expectations in regard to our cousins, the term makes it clear that we do not distinguish much between those on our father's side and those on our mother's side. So when we study a community or population it is not enough to determine how people are related to one another biologically; one must also determine how the people themselves define these relationships. The key to such definitions is the society's linguistic system for classifying kin.

People in every society have a diverse cast of relatives. First and often of primary importance are those who are related to us by birth—our **consanguineal kin**. One's brothers and sisters, one's father and mother, his and her brothers and sisters and their children, one's grandparents and their brothers and sisters are some, but by no means all, of one's consanguineal kin. One's **affinal kin** are the people related to one through marriage—one's spouse and all of his or her relatives, as well as the spouses of one's own consanguineal kin.

Consanguineal and affinal relatives are usually our most important kin, but the list does not stop there. In many societies, including our own, families may adopt otherwise unrelated individuals, who then acquire the rights and obligations of kinship and are socially recognized as members of the family. In addition, people use consanguinity as a model to create relations, such as godparents, compadres, "blood brothers," and old family friends whom children call "aunt" and "uncle." These people are sometimes called **fictive kin**, although the relationship may be as intense as that between consanguineal kin.

In the Middle East, people recognize "milk" brothers and sisters: children who have been nursed, however briefly, by the same woman. Some women who are close friends briefly nurse each other's child just to forge such a bond between their children. In the United States, children who are biologically unrelated may be reared together as siblings, most often when people with children remarry after divorce or widowhood. In some ways the notion of fictive kin is a contradiction because in the broadest sense, most kinship terms are fictive in that they are cultural rather than purely biological categories.

Jenny White, in studying the ways in which poor women in Istanbul work in the garment industry, found that most transaction took place between individuals who used the terminology of kinship (little sister, big brother, uncle, etc.) to stress reciprocity (White, 1994). Women did not feel that they were employed, but rather that by taking in sewing for pay, they were simply helping their families. Using the idiom of fictive kinship in speaking with employers helped to change the relationship into a quasi-personal one. The main distinction between fictive and other kin types is that the terms of fictive kinship are imposed arbitrarily. In the final analysis, families and kinship are what people make them out to be, as we see in the Contemporary Issues box, *Families We Choose* (page 212).

Every language distinguishes categories of relatives in a systematic manner. Anthropologists refer to the terms that systematically designate these distinctions as kin terminology. In no society do people refer to each and every one of their many relatives by a separate term. Instead, they group some relatives in a single category and refer to them all by one kin term: brother, sister, aunt, uncle, grandmother, grandfather, and so on. All systems of kinship terminology are to some extent classificatory; they vary widely, however, in the number of distinct relationships named and in how they are organized.

All societies use a limited number of criteria for classifying kin, though not necessarily the same

Contemporary Issues
Families We Choose

IN THE UNITED STATES, KATH Weston (1991) finds, there is an expanding interpretation of the concept of family—one that includes lesbian and gay couples. This is obviously a highly politicized issue, as protracted court fights indicate, not to mention the often vitriolic political discourse on the subject. Nevertheless, sanctioned or not, approved of or not, gay and lesbian couples dispute the old saying, "You can pick your friends, but you can't pick your relatives"(p. 2). Through her research, Kath Weston has concluded that gay families cannot be understood apart from the families in which the men and women have grown up. There is no standard-

ized "gay family," nor is the gay family an alternative family. It is, instead, a reflection of the ever-changing ideas of American kinship and family.

Like most heterosexuals, homosexual informants insisted that family members are people who "are there for you"; people you can count on (p. 113). For middle-class Americans of all backgrounds this is the main thing that delineates family from friends—family members are willing to provide material support, often without immediate thought of self-interest. Individuals come to regard themselves as family at some point where, going beyond sharing cooking, cleaning up, and shop-

ping, they offer material and emotional support in all domains of activity.

This does not mean that gay and lesbian families view themselves as "alternative" households; quite emphatically, most also look to and depend on the affection and support of biological kin. A very large percentage desire to have and rear children. What patterns of gay family life show is the extent to which all family life is more than simply blood and contract; that kinship is also grounded in that elusive quality we call love. Examined closely, all families rest on strong bonds of affection.

---

criteria. Most distinguish among relatives on the basis of sex, using different terms for male and female kin. We refer to our female parent as "mother" our male parent as "father"; we also distinguish brothers and sisters, aunts and uncles. Many societies also distinguish the mother's side of the family (**matrilateral**) from the father's side (**patrilateral**). This is extremely important among peoples (such as the Yanomamö) who inherit their membership in a named kin group exclusively through either the mother or the father. In such societies some distinction must be made between, for example, mother's brother and father's brother (both of whom English speakers call "uncle"): one belongs to ego's kin group—and therefore has certain rights and obligations in relation to ego—while the other does not. (**Ego** is the term conventionally used to indicate the individual who is the point of reference in a kinship relationship; that is, the speaker, who with no justification but tradition is always assumed to be male.)

Most systems of kinship also use different kin terms to distinguish between generations. English speakers have separate terms for grandmother, mother, daughter, and granddaughter. In addition, the majority of societies (including our own) make some distinction between **lineal relatives** (direct ascendants and descendants) and **collateral relatives** (people to whom one is related through a connecting person). An uncle who is related to ego through one of ego's parents is a collateral relative. Some societies, however (not including our own), go one step further and use separate terms for collateral relatives connected to ego through a female and those connected through a male. A distinction between mother's brother and father's brother is frequently found. So is the use of separate terms for **cross cousins** (mother's brothers' children and father's sisters' children) and **parallel cousins** (mother's sisters' children and father's brothers' children)—as among the Yörük of Turkey and the Yanomamö.

In summary, to understand the behavior of individuals in a particular society one has to understand the kinship system both as a framework for behavioral norms and as a linguistic model. Also, an attenuated aspect of kinship—the idea of descent from a common ancestor—can serve to define social groups or categories of people. Descent can be the basis for inheritance as well as for responsibilities and obligations. And, as we shall see shortly, kinship serves the important function of structuring at least one vital area of human behavior: whom one may and may not marry.

Descent Ideology and Descent Groups

Kinship systems do more than mold social behavior and establish a pattern of statuses and roles. They can also sort the members of a society into groups—collections of people who interact on a fairly regular basis and who have a sense of common identity. The most significant of such kin-based groups is the **descent group**, a group of consanguineal kin united by presumed lineal descent from a common ancestor. The primary importance of descent as a form of kinship reckoning is that it can be the basis for unambiguous membership in a group; it may further structure property rights and political obligations. According to the legal systems of most countries of the Middle East, for example, it is assumed that a child is primarily identified with its father—hence, he almost always assumes custody following divorce. This principle is usually described as descent ideology, as the biological facts of ancestry are less important than social constructions; at the same time, most descent ideologies emphasize only one of many means of calculating descent from a given ancestor. Genealogies and ideas of descent and ancestry are every bit as ideological as kinship terminologies.

In societies with a strong descent ideology, the descent group's sense of collective identity is based not solely on a presumption of common biological ancestry but on a whole set of beliefs, myths, and symbols that have considerable religious and social significance. Of course, much more than ideology holds any group together; as we shall see, members of descent groups provide one another with many essential services. Yet the descent ideology serves both to reinforce group solidarity and offer justification for what in other respects are highly pragmatic relationships.

Minimally, a descent group of any size or level of inclusiveness must have some recognized function in the larger society. It may be as important as owning resources the society needs or as simple as supplying individual identity. Though one cannot predict a patrilineal descent ideology on the basis of the technology a society employs or of its level of political integration, patrilineal descent is the most common form found throughout the world. Still, one can say that it is more likely to be found in some contexts than in others; for example, most (but not all) nomadic pastoral societies are patrilineal (Pasternak, 1976, pp. 112–113).

Descent groups fall into two general categories: **unilineal descent groups**, in which descent is traced through one parental line only, and **nonunilineal descent groups**, in which descent may be traced through either parent or through both. The ideological basis of descent groups is perhaps most obvious in societies with unilineal descent.

Unilineal Descent Groups

Membership in a unilineal descent group is inherited through either the paternal or the maternal line, as the society dictates. Such groups are known as patrilineal and matrilineal descent groups, respectively, and are often divided into more specialized segments such as clan and lineage (of which we will speak shortly). The point to bear in mind is that descent ideology alone does not constitute a descent group; it defines a category of people who are qualified to become members.

Patrilineal Descent. Under **patrilineal descent** ideology, all children are members of the descent group or groups of which their father is a member (see Figure 8–1). If a man is a member of a particular group or has specific social rights attributable to descent, his children share this membership or set of rights. This does not mean they are less attached to their mothers than to their fathers. A mother simply does not pass on her descent-group membership or social rights to her children in such a society.

The female member of the society who marries out of her kin group (as generally she must) cannot

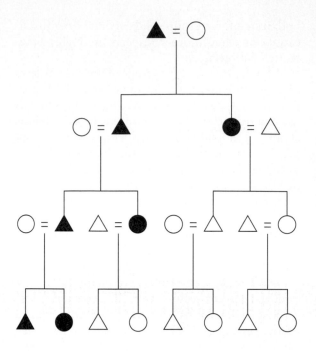

Figure 8–1. Patrilineal descent

provide new members for her lineage in the suc-
ceeding generation; her children are members of
her husband's lineage, not her own. The significance of this arrangement for the role of women
varies. While the role of Yanomamö women in politics is extremely subordinate to that of men, in
some African patrilineal societies, such as the Tal-
lensi of West Africa, women play a more central
role in politics.

It should be kept in mind that however strongly
a population expresses an ideology of patrilineal
descent, ties of kinship among and through women
are likely to be extremely important in practice:
they will affect where one lives, whom one relies
on, and many other aspects of domestic life. Further, the patrilineal structure of a society is no measure of relative contribution of men and women to
the economy, although it may mean that womens'
contributions are under-esteemed. In rural Turkey
some say that "women are the enemy of the
spoon" meaning that they do not contribute to the
household's income (Moghadam, 1993, p. 100).
Nothing could be further from the truth; women
are a major part of the labor force in both rural
and urban sectors, but their contribution is often

over-looked (White, 1994). We will return to this
problem when we look at household organization
later in this chapter.

CASE STUDY:

The Pokot of Kenya

THE POKOT OF KENYA NUMBER SOME 200,000
persons, and follow the patrilineal principle of descent. The Pokot exploit a complex terrain, which,
in the variety of settings it offers, reflects much
wider areas of East Africa. Thus, within West
Pokot District alone there is a range in elevations
from over 11,000 feet down to barely 2,000,
which the Pokot exploit through cattle herding
and farming (much like the Ariaal, discussed in
Chapter 6).

The basic unit of Pokot social organization is
the neighborhood, referred to as the *korok* (Conant, 1963). In social terms the korok consists of a
number of households (sometimes as many as one
hundred but more commonly about fifty), physically spaced well apart from each other and with
each household located in farming areas surrounded by fields under cultivation or in fallow. In
herding areas, the households are surrounded by
corrals (*kraal*) for the livestock and separated from
each other by stretches of bush and shrubland. A
major difference between the koroks in farming
and herding areas is that among farmers, membership in a korok is a long-term affair sometimes
spanning many generations. Among herders, the
korok is a kaleidoscope of shifting membership, often limited to a single season and rarely completely
duplicated from one season to the next.

The korok in both farming and herding areas is
regulated by a council made up of the heads of the
resident households. Even though the head of a
household may be a woman, the representatives
sent to the council are always men. The neighborhood council meets when anyone wants it to and
has a defined gathering place. The council reaches
its decisions by consensus. When no one is willing
to argue a point any further, if someone attempts
to do so, the standard response is for members of
the council to turn and face away from the speaker.
Members of the council, who nominate one of

A Pokot man and his wives and children in northwest Kenya.
(George Rodger/Magnum)

their number as *kirwokiin* or "big talker," have broad powers to recruit labor, levy fines, and mediate disputes.

Marriage among both farmers and herders is more a matter of contract between households than a "love match" between individuals. The contract involves what is known as **bridewealth;** that is, the family of the groom agrees to turn over to the family of the bride an agreed number of cattle. The transaction is almost always made by installment, one at the beginning of the marriage, one at the birth of a first child, and the last at the birth of a second. Among Pokot, a marriage is a process that begins with betrothal and is only considered complete when a second child is walking and talking and the first is still alive. Since infant mortality among traditional Pokot could be as high as 30 percent or 40 percent and the mortality of women in their reproductive years may have been as much as 5 percent, it is evident that transaction of the bridewealth by installments is a safeguard against a possible failure of the new household unit to mature and grow. ❿

Matrilineal Descent. Under **matrilineal descent,** all children are members (or at least eligible to be members) of their mother's group (see Figure 8–2). Again, this is not to say that children in societies with matrilineal descent ideology are less attached to their father than to their mother. A father is simply not a member of the same descent group as his children. Matrilineal descent ideology is far less common than patrilineal ideology, for reasons that are unclear.

Though one might suspect that women would have more political power than men in matrilineal descent groups, this is not necessarily—or even often—the case. The titular head of a western Pueblo matrilineal descent group was its oldest woman. As such, she was accorded much respect and deference. But the person who took charge of the group's religious objects and directed its rituals was that woman's oldest brother. Indeed, women were barred from participating in certain rituals. When, as with the Pueblo, matrilineality is combined with **matrilocality** (residence of a married couple in the wife's natal household), women may achieve higher status and more authority than they

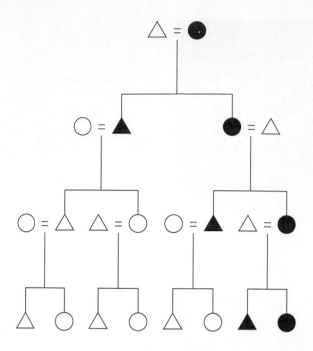

Figure 8–2. Matrilineal descent

can in patrilineal and patrilocally constituted communities.

A fairly similar pattern can be observed in most societies with matrilineal descent ideologies. In theory, while the descent group is defined by descent in the female line, in practice actual descent groups are headed by a woman's male siblings and/or her sons. Though the society, in keeping with the matrilineal descent ideology, may well prescribe that married couples establish residence in the wife's village and near the wife's natal home, men who marry within the village can also remain near the home where they were raised. This arrangement keeps a man near males of his kin group and facilitates strong male participation in public affairs.

CASE STUDY:

The Hopi of Northeastern Arizona

THE HOPI OF THE WESTERN PUEBLO AREA ARE A Native American population in which matrilineality is an important part of their social organization

and is central to an individual's social identity. The Hopi are divided into a number of named, matrilineal clans, which in turn are grouped in twos or threes to form nine named supra-clans. The Native American peoples who are often referred to collectively as "Pueblo" have been beset for several centuries by competing populations: Spaniards, other Indian tribes, and Northern European settlers, all of whom the Hopi were active in resisting (see Rushforth & Upham, 1993). The Hopi are one such population.[1]

The Hopi are the cultural and biological descendants of hunter-gatherers who migrated to the American Southwest over 10,000 years ago. The ancestors of today's Pueblos were skilled basketmakers, weavers, potters, and above all, architects. They are famed (and named) for their pueblos— "apartment buildings" three and four stories high, containing honeycombs of interconnected rooms, some of which open onto protected inner courtyards, where *kivas*, round ceremonial chambers, were sunk into the pavement. One such village or town has been designated in 1995 by the United Nations as a "world heritage cultural site" since it is the place in the Americas occupied continuously for the longest time.

The typical western Pueblo village contains members of the main clans. The clan itself is divided into lineages that control the land. Their membership was determined by matrilineal descent, with men farming land belonging to their wives. It used to be the case that extended families were the norm as daughters usually stayed in their mothers' households for life. Sons moved to their brides' households, but they continued to regard their mothers' houses as home and returned to them regularly to participate in rituals. Within each of these extended families, the women and girls tended the group's vegetables; prepared the meals; hauled the water; made the baskets, pottery, and clothing; and cared for the children. Within such a family, both the senior woman and her brother were important sources of leadership and authority. Now families more often reside in nuclear households but they still maintain close contact among lineage members. Each small lineage or ex-

---

[1] The now-classic study of the Hopi is Fred Eggan's 1950 study; recent important books include Peter Whiteley (1988) and Scott Rushforth and Steadman Upham (1993).

San Ildefonso Pueblo Hopi indians preparing for the Corn Dance.
(John Running/Stock, Boston, Inc.)

tended family is relatively autonomous with respect to domestic and agricultural responsibilities.

This does not mean, however, that families are independent of one another. On the contrary, they are bound together into higher-level social units of equal, if not greater, significance. These are the clans, organizations of matrilineally related families. Most important, religious societies are the property of the clan. The eldest woman of the clan is recognized as its ceremonial head and her household is its religious center. Different clans own the different rituals and ritual paraphernalia associated with a particular *katchina*—Hopi spirits symbolized by dancers wearing distinctive and quite beautiful costumes. However, membership in societies is drawn from the community at large, regardless of clan affiliation. Individuals choose to join one society or another because they feel a calling or are dedicated to it; for everyone except the clan head, participation is voluntary. This cross-cutting of clan boundaries within the societies has the important function of creating ties between members of different clans. In this way, nearly all members of a pueblo are related—if not by clan membership, then by society membership. This helps to prevent villages from dividing along clan lines under normal conditions.

Religion is central to the lives of the western Pueblo—a fact that is possibly related to the quality of their environment. Constantly plagued by the uncertainty of the rains, and therefore of their livelihood, they turn to the supernatural to explain and influence nature. Efforts to bring the divine forces over to their side are largely the responsibility of the katchina societies (Dozier, 1970). In the katchina ceremonies, masked dancers assume the roles of the supernatural beings who are petitioned to favor the crops. Although the Hopi traditionally invested considerable time, energy, and faith in religion, society leaders did not exercise control over other aspects of people's lives. They were religious leaders, not chiefs. When they met periodically, they confined their deliberations to ceremonial matters. The earlier western Pueblo had no formal political leaders and no formal means of social control (laws, judges, or trials); now they have elected leaders and formal courts. Gossip and ridicule—institutionalized in the so-called "clown cult," which mocked deviants—kept most people in line. The weakness of large-scale political integration and the strength of the clans were probably responses to a highly variable and unpredictable resource base. If times grew hard, a clan could simply break off from the village to seek its fortune elsewhere. Since government, religion, property, and community affairs were already organized around this social unit, the clan provided the ready-made core of a new village. ◗

Organization of Unilineal Descent Groups. Unilineal descent groups follow certain basic patterns, whether the ideology involved happens to be matrilineal or patrilineal. Generally speaking, anthropologists categorize such groups according to their inclusiveness, from lineages through clans.

A **lineage** is a unilineal descent group composed of people who trace their genealogies through specified links to a common ancestor. Depending on whether descent is traced through the maternal or paternal line, such groups are called matrilineages or patrilineages. Some societies have hierarchies of lineages; individuals belong to smaller minor lineages as well as more inclusive larger lineages. The larger, more encompassing lineage is likely to be defined by descent from a more distant ancestor.

The Tiv of Nigeria, for example, are organized into **segmentary lineages**, descent groups in which minimal lineages are segments of minor lineages, minor lineages are segments of major lineages, and so on, with the result that all of the more than 800,000 Tiv regard themselves as related in a single genealogical hierarchy (Bohannan, 1965). Segmentary lineage systems may develop when tribes expand into territory already occupied by another group, as did the Nuer of Sudan in the nineteenth century (Kelly, 1985).

The segmentary system enables a particular lineage segment to enlist the aid of progressively larger and larger groups of related segments when its territory is threatened. Of course, the entire tribe rarely functions as a completely integrated whole, but the system does provide the basis for broad military alliances that endure as long as they are needed to ward off attack or defend newly acquired territory. The segmentary lineage system also serves to regulate the relations between the various segments. When conflicts erupt between minimal segments, for example, other minimal segments take the side of the party to whom they are most closely related. One segment joins another until minor and even higher-order segments are pitted against each other.

Kin groups may extend beyond the limits of known ancestry. Some societies have descent groups whose members believe themselves to be descended from a common ancestor and therefore have a sense of collective identity, even though they are unable to reconstruct exact genealogical connections. These are the groups known as **clans**, as we saw with the Hopi. They are called matriclans or patriclans, depending on which parent determines ego's affiliation. In many societies, a matriclan or patriclan will be named after a plant or animal, called a **totem** (from the Ojibwa Indian word *ototeman*, meaning "relative"). To clan members the totem generally holds some special significance, usually related to the group's mythical ancestry. If little else, such symbols help to make a clan's sense of collective identity and unity more concrete.

Often clans appear to derive from lineages that became too large or too dispersed to keep track of their genealogies. Others may be formed when two or more lineages join forces (perhaps after a famine or invasion has reduced their populations) and invent a common ancestor to cement their union. The details of clan formation can only be guessed from the myths that commonly surround them. In some societies, several clans band together and extend the rights of kinship to one another yet retain distinct identities for some purposes. An entire society can be organized into two large descent groups, or moieties. Some moieties are not based on kinship. The Miwok Indians of California, for example, are divided into two moieties, one called Land, the other Water.

When groups of related lineages and clans share a common name and identity, they are often referred to as a **tribe**. The word is used in several ways in anthropological literature. In its most general meaning, a tribe is a culturally distinct population that uses various principles of kinship and descent, a shared language, and a common history to define its political limits. In the literature on Africa, very large populations are sometimes referred to as "tribes," whereas in other regions of the world similar entities would be called "nations" or "ethnic groups." We are concerned here with a much more specific and restricted sense of the term. The tribe is a decentralized descent- and kinship-based grouping in which a number of subgroups are loosely linked to one another. Leadership is informal and constituent subgroups form cooperative alliances, but these can easily shift or break up. There is no centralized system of authority, decision making, or social control, but the potential exists to unite a large number of local groups for common defense or warfare. The internal organization of the tribe is similar in principle to that of the lineage or clan. Just how the lineages are expressed and maintained varies from society to society. One system is for two or more groups, clans, or lineages to see themselves as related, even though each group generally will act autonomously in managing its affairs. However, the sense of common identity can be called into play for defense.

The Functions of Unilineal Descent Groups. No kin group in any society is formed simply because people perceive themselves to be related to one another through descent. For a group to exist at all, its members must have shared interests that give them a reason to join forces and view themselves as a collective entity. The anthropologist E. R. Leach has explained:

> Kin groups do not exist as things in themselves without regard to the rights and interests which center in them. Membership of such a group is not established by genealogy alone. Properly speaking, two individuals can only be said to be of the same kinship group when they share some common interest—economic, legal, political, religious, as the case may be—and justify that sharing by reference to kinship ideology. The anthropological question that then arises is to discover these common interests. [Leach, 1982, p. 66]

Some anthropologists have argued that the common interests that usually underlie unilineal descent groups are economic: such groups develop when some permanent resource, such as land, requires allocation (Barth, 1981, p. 57). The Hopi, whom we have just described, are a good example of this. Hunting-and-gathering bands, whose ecological adaptation requires mobility and dispersal across large areas of varied landscape, seldom have lineages and clans. However, with the development of cultivation and the changes that accompany it—a sedentary way of life, increased population density, and exclusive ties to specific territories—we find unilineal descent groups proliferating, presumably to protect access to resources.

A related factor in the formation of unilineal descent groups may have been warfare. After all, property does not have to be protected until someone else wants it. In a sample of a large number of societies, fighting between communities or between larger territorial groups was found to be common in 94 percent of those with a unilineal descent system (Ember, Ember, & Pasternak, 1974). There appears to be a causal association between unilineality and warfare, although the precise linkages are complex.

Intergroup fighting may favor customs and institutions that provide affiliation with clearly defined groups of people who can be relied upon in time of need. In societies with a high level of political development, such affiliation may be provided by membership in a centralized political unit. But when political development is not so advanced, unilineal descent may constitute an especially fitting response to the challenge of competing groups (Pasternak, 1976, pp. 107–108). Unilineal descent groups are not, however, incompatible with state forms of political organization. In some regions of the Middle East, where state-dominated societies have been in existence longer than anywhere else in the world, tribes or unilineal descent groups are important as a means of promoting local groups' autonomy in the face of powerful governments, with their tax collectors and administrators.

Whatever the common interests that prompt the development of unilineal descent groups, it is clear that such groups serve many important functions for their members. The regulation of marriage is one such function, as we saw in our discussion of the Yanomamö. In societies with unilineal descent ideologies, lineages and clans are often (but not always) exogamous—that is, marriage within one's own descent group is strictly forbidden. By forcing its members to look to other groups for marital and sexual partners, the kin group presumably saves itself a good deal of internal discord. Perhaps more important, rules of exogamy create ties of alliance and cooperation between kin groups—ties that can be invaluable when resources are scarce and warfare is common.

Another extremely important function of unilineal descent groups is the regulation of land use. In patrilineal and matrilineal societies, it is often the descent group, rather than individuals or the village as a whole, that owns the land, allocating plots to its members for their use. By virtue of affiliation with a descent group, individuals have rights to the land on which they plant their crops or graze their animals. The descent group may also control other essential resources, such as water, and may have collective ownership of the tools that its members use to make their living. This arrangement is often called "corporate" ownership.

In addition to regulating marriage and allocating resources, unilineal descent groups provide mutual aid and support to their members. People who belong to the same descent group are bound together by a code of reciprocal rights and obligations. The strength of this bond varies with the closeness of the kinship ties. Mutual obligations between the members of the same lineage, for example, are usually quite strongly felt; those between members of the same clan somewhat less so; and the members of the same tribe are often so distantly related and so widely dispersed that they may feel virtually no obligation toward one another.

The mutual aid and support provided by unilineal descent groups cover both political and economic activities. In some unilineal societies, the entire lineage is held accountable for the actions of individual members if they infringe on the rights of members of other lineages. If a person murders a member of another lineage, for example, vengeance may justifiably be inflicted on any of the slayer's kin. By the same token, individuals can depend on their kin to help them exact justice for wrongs committed by members of other descent groups. In some societies, people also have the right to expect food from members of their descent group when their own crops fail. In this case, unilineal descent groups serve to redistribute wealth in the absence of such mechanisms as welfare systems and unemployment insurance.

Nonunilineal Descent Groups

Many of the societies that early anthropologists encountered had strongly unilineal descent ideologies, which led them to expect that most other societies in the world also had unilineal descent groups. The one large and obvious exception to unilineal rule—European and American society—was explained as the result of industrialism. In complex industrial societies, individuals could obtain help from many different sources: employers,

friends, government agencies, clinics, and so on. Therefore, they did not have to align themselves with a strictly defined kin group.

This assumption proved to be false. Eventually anthropologists encountered many nonindustrial societies in which descent ideology was less strongly enforced, more ambiguous, or used less extensively as the basis of group formation than in unilineal societies. These peoples were not only nonindustrial; they were often hunter-gatherers with exceedingly simple technologies. This discovery laid to rest the notion that nonunilineal descent was an idiosyncrasy of complex societies.

Nonunilineal descent groups are classified by anthropologists into two basic types, ambilineal and bilateral.

Ambilineal Descent. In societies with an **ambilineal descent** ideology, a person affiliates with kin groups on the basis of ties traced through either the paternal or the maternal line. In some ambilineal societies, a person is expected at some point to choose among the various kin groups to which he or she is in some way lineally related. In other ambilineal societies, a person is free to move from one descent group to another, as long as he or she affiliates with only one group at a time. And in still others, a person may affiliate, for whatever different purposes, with as many groups as he or she claims ties to.

Ambilineal descent systems, then, have more flexibility than do unilineal systems; they leave more room for individual choice concerning kin-group affiliation. This is fairly common in the Pacific. On the Gilbert Islands, for example, membership in a landholding ambilineal descent group is open to all individuals who can trace their descent to the person who originally owned the land. If one descent group becomes overcrowded, people will affiliate themselves with another that is short of heirs. As a result, the distribution of people in the various land owning groups is invariably guided by population pressure. Such flexibility may be quite useful, but it is achieved at the cost of clear-cut loyalties.

The same is true of ambilineal societies in general: as a rule, the looser the membership rules of the descent group, the less cohesive it is and the less impact it has on its members' day-to-day lives. In ambilineal societies in which the individual must choose a single descent group to affiliate with permanently, the functions served by descent groups are often similar to those in unilineal societies: collective ownership of land and other productive resources, regulation of marriage through rules of exogamy, provision of mutual aid and support. But when ambilineal descent permits people to have multiple or temporary descent-group affiliations, the functions of the descent groups tend to be fewer and less critical.

Bilateral Descent. With **bilateral descent**, the system that we use in our own society, individuals define themselves as being at the center of a group of kin composed more or less equally of their mothers' and fathers' relatives of all kinds—grandparents, aunts and uncles, great aunts and great uncles, cousins and second cousins, nieces and nephews, and of course the nuclear family.

The resulting collection of bilateral kin, called the **kindred**, is significantly different from the descent groups we have discussed so far. Indeed, a kindred is not a group at all in the true sense of the word, for most of its members do not perceive themselves as having a collective identity. Nor is there any reason why they should, since each member of a given kindred has a different kindred from everyone else (except siblings). Ego's kindred, for example, is not the same as his parents' kindreds, for his own combines relatives from both of theirs. And ego's kindred has only half its members in common with his cousin's kindred. A kindred, then, is not technically a group but a network, a set of interlocking social relations as seen by the ego to whom they are all related. This is why anthropologists refer to a kindred as being ego-oriented rather than ancestor-oriented. While descent groups consist of people who have a real or fictive ancestor (along with all the members of their group) in common, kindreds consist of people who have a relative (ego) in common.

A kindred, then, exists only in relation to one person. Furthermore, it changes through time. When we are children, our kindred consists of contemporaries and older kin; as we grow and bear children and as our older kin die, the membership of our kindred shifts to contemporaries and younger kin. And when we die, our kindred ceases to have any meaning—unlike descent groups, which are self-renewing.

Because of its personal, changeable, and temporary character, the kindred is ordinarily less powerful than the unilineal descent group. While it may still regulate marriage rules, it generally provides fewer essential services for its members. In our own society, kindred may be called on for help, but they are usually assembled only for ceremonial occasions: when ego is christened, married, or buried. This type of loosely organized network is particularly well suited to a society that places a premium on personal independence and mobility, of which our own is a prime example.

In some societies with bilateral concepts of descent, groups are more clearly structured and lend themselves to corporate enterprises. Among the nomadic reindeer-herding Saami (Lapps) of northern Scandinavia, for example, residential kin groups are formed on the basis of bilateral descent, with sibling ties forming the core of such groupings (Hultkrantz, 1994, p. 354). Usually a group of brothers with their wives and children will band together, with other consanguineal kin attaching themselves to the sibling core. Although an individual may belong to several bands during his lifetime, each affiliation will be based on bilaterally reckoned genealogical links.

Marriage, Remarriage, and Marital Residence

Of course the terminology and beliefs associated with kinship and descent are only one dimension of the way people conceptualize their relationships with others. Another dimension is seen in the various ways people choose spouses and establish families and households. Such choices are influenced by socially prescribed rules, but not to the exclusion of other factors. In almost every society marriage is the institutionalized means by which new families are created and existing ones expanded, and family organization forms a basis for most domestic groups (households).

Marriage

Marriage is not easy to define; however, it usually provides a legal contractual basis for the sharing of property, economic responsibility, sex, and obligations toward children born as a result of the union.

Laplander marriage party going to a wedding.
(Jim Martin/Offshoot Stock)

There are, nevertheless, variations for which this definition is inadequate. In the United States, people debate whether homosexual couples should be permitted to marry and have legal standing comparable to that of heterosexual couples. In 1989 Denmark allowed homosexuals to register partnerships, in effect, allowing them to marry but without the right to adopt or gain joint custody of a child. In 1994 New York City allowed same-sex couples to register their relationships officially, making them eligible for some benefits allowed to married city residents.

The financial rights and responsibilities of men and women in legal marriages are also rapidly being redefined. In Europe and the United States many couples are choosing, too, to ignore church or state-endorsed marriages and simply live together, but in every other respect to behave as a married couple. The colloquial term "significant other" is sometimes used socially to refer to a coresident sexual partner to whom one is not married. It avoids any implication as to the gender of the partner or the legal status of the relationship. But almost all societies have some form of marriage, in that special recognition is given to a sex-

ual and economic union between two or more people that legitimizes their offspring and establishes reciprocal rights and obligations among them.

Marriage almost everywhere involves some form of reciprocal economic obligations. In the past in American society, wives were expected to provide domestic services; husbands gave financial support. This arrangement has changed, but the notion that husbands and wives have different spheres of responsibility in marriage is still prevalent. Unless they arrange otherwise, a couple's private wealth and future earnings become joint property upon marriage. We see this in the Gender Issues box, *Marriage and Money Management*, on page 224. In addition, a husband and wife are jointly responsible for supporting and raising the children they have together, whether or not they remain married.

Marriage, as legally and socially defined, varies around the world, though everywhere it is bound up in notions of mutual rights to sex and responsibilities toward and rights over children. Even in the matter of intended permanence, marriage customs vary. In Iran, members of the Shi'a faith can enter into a special form of marriage in which they stip-

Yörük men at a wedding feast. Women and girls will eat once the men are fed. Occasions such as these may last for several days and provide an opportunity to form or renew social networks.
(Daniel Bates)

ulate how long their marriage contracts are to remain in force. What is considered appropriate sexual conduct is also culturally variable. We tend to view sexual relations as appropriately restricted to a monogamous couple. In many societies, a man may be married to more than one wife at a time, and in a few others a woman may have more than one husband at a time.

Among the Nayar of Kerala, in India, until the practice was forbidden by British authorities, marriage did not prohibit a woman from having a sexual relationship with any suitor of an appropriate caste status; her ritual husband had no more claim to her sexual favors than any other qualified man. In fact, the term *group marriage* has been used, rightly or wrongly, to describe the practice whereby Nayar women took multiple "visiting husbands" and men similarly visited multiple women. While the Nayar no longer follow this custom, it is possible that the traditional emphasis on women's prerogatives underlies the higher status that women enjoy in Kerala than in the rest of India. Women here marry later, have fewer children, have high rates of literacy, and enjoy superior health (Weisman, 1988).

The economic rights and obligations that accompany marriage also vary. A Trobriand husband is expected to help support his sisters but is only partially responsible for the support of his wife and children. A Nayar husband is not expected to provide any financial support for his ritual wife and her children at all. In fact, he may never even see his wife again after their wedding; the marriage is significant primarily as a political statement indicating relations among groups. Hopi women find it relatively easy to divorce their husbands and, traditionally at least, have done so quite frequently; their children, like corn, their main crop, were seen as their property (Whiteley, 1985). Of course, the converse is also found; under Islamic law, women inherit only half of the property that would fall to a comparable male heir and in rural areas often do not inherit land at all. And upon divorce, women have no claim to their children or to any property that came to the couple from the husband's family.

Marriage is not a prerequisite for the legitimacy of children in all societies, as we saw with the Temang. A Nuer man in southern Sudan can legitimize the child of an unwed mother by making a specified payment. Nor are parents everywhere responsible for the care and teaching of their children. In Israeli kibbutzim, children may live apart from their parents in nurseries and dormitories. Although parents have a special relationship with their own children, the entire community assumes substantial responsibility for their upbringing.

Divorce and Remarriage

In Samuel Johnson's famous words, "remarriage is the triumph of hope over experience." However marriage is defined, divorce or dissolution of marriage by formal or informal means is a worldwide phenomenon. While the norm may be marital monogamy, many individuals marry more than once.

In traditional Navajo society most people marry and divorce four or five times, and do not marry with the expectation of remaining together for life. Among the Kipsigis of Africa, when a wealthy man has enough children (particularly sons) to manage his farm, he may marry again, move to his new bride's home, and begin the family cycle again, maintaining what amounts to visiting relationships with his other wives. The Ariaal,

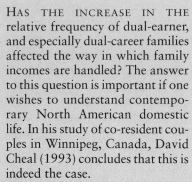

Marriage and Money Management

HAS THE INCREASE IN THE relative frequency of dual-earner, and especially dual-career families affected the way in which family incomes are handled? The answer to this question is important if one wishes to understand contemporary North American domestic life. In his study of co-resident couples in Winnipeg, Canada, David Cheal (1993) concludes that this is indeed the case.

In Canada in the 1960s, the dominant husband-wife family type was the breadwinner/homemaker family, where the husband was employed and the wife kept house (61 percent in 1967), whereas only 34 percent were dual-earner families (that is, both spouses were in the labor force). By the 1980s, this situation was reversed: in 1986 dual-earner families comprised 62 percent of husband-wife families, and the relative frequency of breadwinner/homemaker families had fallen to 27 percent.

By the early 1950s, a system of companionate marriage, which assumes a natural identity of interests between husband and wife, was well established among upper- and middle-class Canadians. Such a system is based on an ideal of family democracy, including joint decision making by husband and wife. However, in practice, the division of labor between the husband as earner and the wife as homemaker meant that the husband could exercise greater control over the money he earned. In a 1956 study of an affluent upper-middle-class suburb, it was found that husbands were assumed to have a greater interest in, and facility for, handling large sums of money, while wives handled smaller sums used to purchase things for the day-to-day comfort and convenience of the household.

In 1988, Cheal conducted interviews with 226 people in Winnipeg living in husband-wife families; for the purposes of his research, Cheal defines husband-wife families as "heterosexual couples who are either married and currently living together or unmarried and cohabiting" (pp. 201–202). These couples were divided on the basis of their employment practices into three types: contemporary breadwinner/homemaker families (where the husband is employed and the wife keeps house for her husband and children); provider/coprovider families (where the husband is in regular employment and the wife is one of Canada's approximately 25 percent of employed women who work part-time); and dual-career families (both partners are equally involved in occupational employment as a lifetime activity) (p. 202).

Cheal found that provider/coprovider and dual-career families combined constitute 60 percent of preretirement husband-wife families, and that dual-career families comprise 69 percent of dual-earner families and 42 percent of all husband-wife families in Winnipeg. All types appear to maintain a high level of matrimonial property egalitarianism, with 95 percent of home-owning dual-career families, 90 percent of provider/co-provider families, and 87 percent of breadwinner/homemaker families owning their home jointly. All couples stated an overwhelming preference for regarding individual earnings as family income, but how are these family incomes handled in practice? "Family income" can mean two things: individuals keep full control over their earnings, but aim to spend all or part of the money on contributing to the family's well-being; or it can mean that managing money is regarded as a shared responsibility subject to joint decision making.

Cheal reports that approximately three-quarters of dual-career families report sharing control over their incomes, whereas in breadwinner/homemaker and provider/co-provider families there is a higher level of personal control over individual income.

Wives who make a substantial monetary contribution to the maintenance of the household are more likely to negotiate reciprocal control over income and joint ownership of property, presumably because of their greater bargaining power. As a result, husbands in dual-career families have a lesser degree of personal control over their earnings by comparison with husbands in breadwinner/homemaker . . . and in provider/co-provider families. [pp. 209–210]

Cheal concludes that these findings suggest that as wives' employment status improves, families' financial arrangements are being reconstructed in ways that serve to maintain and even strengthen joint management, while at the same time providing a greater degree of autonomous spending power for women. "The net result of these changes is greater economic egalitarianism in marriage" (p. 210).

described earlier, do likewise, but few men wish to go through the formality of divorce, perhaps because of the ramifications of attempts to retrieve the bridewealth they paid the first wife, which they would need for a formal union with a second (Fratkin, 1991).

Can any pattern be found in the data on marriage stability in various cultures? Helene Fisher (1987) thinks so; she finds some basic regularities in both marriage and divorce. In a sample of fifty-eight societies at all levels of technology, she identifies three "divorce peaks," or life stages in which couples are most likely to divorce. The couples most susceptible to divorce are those who have been married for four years; next most susceptible are couples between the ages of twenty-five and twenty-nine; and finally, couples with no children or one dependent child who have been married more than four years.

These times of peak divorce are interrelated, and arise, she asserts, from both the reproductive process and psychochemical processes. Four years of strong bonding between the sexes is, she claims, the product of our evolutionary history. It is the period of time needed to have an infant and to bring it to a point where the combined forces of both parents are not critical to its survival. The main impetus for divorce or separation comes after four years of marriage, when the couple feels less strongly attached to each other. She terms it the "four-year itch," and she attributes it (as do others) to brain physiology: chemical processes in the brain foster an intense attachment or infatuation that can last no longer than two years, after which different brain chemicals (the endorphins) set the basis for strong attachment but without the sexual excitement and intensity of infatuation. A United Nations sample of fifty-eight countries indicates that 48 percent of divorces occur within seven years of marriage, most clustering around the four-year peak.

This is not to say that no significant economic or social factors are involved. Even if the peaks for divorce seem to be regular, the rates of divorce vary widely. Again Fisher suggests that rates of divorce are lower where men and women are economically dependent on each other, as in intensive agricultural societies. Thus, with industrialization and the increasing economic autonomy of men and women, divorce rates rise. In the United States, recent studies show, the chances are about 50 percent

that a woman born in 1970 will have one marriage end in divorce and 15 percent that she will have two marriages ending in divorce (Chira, 1995, p. 42). Even so, about half to one-third of American marriages last for life (Bird & Melville, 1994).

Despite its variations from one society to another and the possibility of divorce, the institution of marriage is nearly universal. United Nations records for countries that conduct censuses show that an average of 93 percent of women and 92 percent of men will marry (cited in Fisher, 1987, p. 26). One explanation is that marriage functions as a useful social and economic contract—bonding not just a man and a woman, but social groups as well. It is a means of binding family to family and kin group to kin group. Another reason for the prevalence of marriage is that it serves as a means of organizing economic sharing and cooperation.

Marriage as Exchange

When a man or woman marries, he or she acquires not only a spouse but also a new set of parents, brothers- and sisters-in-law, and other affinal relatives. Exchange is the most basic way of establishing a bond between individuals and groups. Quite apart from what is exchanged, the act of exchange itself creates a precondition for further social interaction. In many societies, marriage is the most important form of exchange. It is usually women who are the key figures in exchange marriages, in part because of the high value placed on a woman's labor and reproductive capacity. Very often women are seen to symbolize the wholeness of a group, be it family, clan, or tribe. Thus often it may be the case that the woman's role as sister is what is critical in forming ties among groups—a pattern seen both in the Trobriands and in the days of European royal marriage-based alliances (see Weiner, 1992). Marriage represents either a union of the bride's group with the groom's or occasionally the submission of one to the other. The latter situation is seen when men of a dominant group take wives from people whom they would not permit their own women to marry. The Yörük of southeastern Turkey will arrange marriages with non-Yörük women, but even though they live in multi-ethnic communities, they will not give their own women to outsiders. Among Bedouin tribes, the giving of a daughter in marriage may resolve a blood feud: the family that gives its woman placates the other.

Using Anthropology

Kidnapping and Elopement Among the Yörük:
A Problem Reconsidered

PEOPLE DO NOT ALWAYS WANT TO do what is expected of them. Departures from social norms often occur in the relatively minor decisions we make in the course of our everyday routines, but they may also affect major life decisions—for example, marriage. People often marry in ways that not only displease their families, but even flaunt established norms and conventions. When this author first went to study the Yörük of Turkey in 1968, I knew from Turkish newspaper accounts that marriage conventions, not to mention the law, were sometimes violated. The topic offered, it seemed, a clear example of a discrepancy between real and ideal behavior: newspapers frequently contained lurid stories of women being abducted, raped, and forced to marry against their will.

I decided to inquire about such kidnapping, as the locals termed it. My Yörük informants (see Chapter 6) at first were adamant: such disgraceful behavior occurred only among others. As it turned out, a few nights after having learned this, a young woman was ab-

ducted from the family with which I was living, and after the initial excitement settled, I learned that such disgraces were quite common—the source of both local amusement, but unfortunately also some violence.

Briefly, what I learned (or thought I had learned at the time) changed with subsequent trips back, most recently in 1991. Yörük society is patrilineal, strongly emphasizing first-cousin marriage, especially father's brother's daughter (or son). The result of this preference is that most members of any patrilineal group are closely related by numerous ties. The Yörük consider marriage a serious matter, and parents take great care to arrange suitable matches for their children. Given this emphasis on arranged marriages, I was surprised to discover the number of marriages that were the result of elopement and "bride theft" (*kaçırma*). Bride theft means that the prospective husband kidnaps a woman and rapes her—an act that, in a society that places a premium on virginity, greatly diminishes her

prospects for marriage and increases the chances that she will agree to stay with her abductor. Elopement, also called *kaçırma*, refers to the couple's joint decision to run away together—ignoring parental rights. The Yörük frown intensely on both of these procedures. When they occur, the result is extreme shame and outrage, particularly on the part of the girl's family. Yet such acts result in 23 percent of all Yörük marriages. What accounts for this high proportion?

In addressing this question, I first concluded that, in part, kaçırma provides a means for the expression of individual choice in an otherwise highly structured system. That a boy and girl may love each other, for instance, traditionally plays little or no role in the arrangement of a marriage. Furthermore, because it is through marriage that adult status is gained, kaçırma allows young men to hasten their entry into mature society by bypassing the normal procedure of marrying in birth order and only after the substantially high bride price has been

In some societies, families create alliances by exchanging daughters directly. Among the Tiv of Nigeria, a man may exchange one of his sisters for the sister of another man, binding their families together. But such direct exchange of women is relatively rare. More commonly, a man pays the family from which he takes a daughter in marriage (**bridewealth** or **bride price**) or works for them

(**bride service**); the payment helps the family replace the daughter with a wife for one of their sons. This indirect exchange of women is found throughout the world (recall the discussion of bridewealth among the Ariaal of Kenya in Chapter 6). Regardless of the specific rules governing marriage arrangements, actual practice may vary dramatically from the norm, as we see in the Using An-

raised (which could take several years).

Kaçırma marriages, taken as a group, involved higher than average bride price payments. But even though some were very high indeed, some involved little or no payment. It appeared that wealthy families whose sons committed kaçırma were obliged to pay very high bride price sums in order to avoid legal action or prolonged hostility. Poor families, however, often paid very little or nothing at all. Once the act has been committed, there is not much the girl's family can do to collect if the boy's family has little money. In this way, kaçırma can also be seen as equalizing the burden of high bride prices for people of differing wealth.

I concluded that kaçırma, although vigorously disavowed and discouraged as deviant behavior, plays a significant—and in some cases even predictable—role in Yörük social interactions. It seemed that elopement, because it tended to involve marriage among a wider circle of people, served to broaden and diversify kinship networks. I also assumed that this aspect of their marriage system had been in existence for a long time and was one that would likely carry on. Subsequent inquiries have proved this wrong and suggest that it might be best to be wary of tidy explanations of social phenomena. While it may be true that decisions (such as those to elope or not) may have social consequences that are unanticipated by the actors (such as giving people a wider network of kin) this is not a sufficient explanation.

On return trips I found that the prevalence of kaçırma was declining, until by 1984 none had occurred in a year. Moreover, I found that the time-honored custom of bride price, which had so preoccupied the people in 1968, had dwindled to a mere symbolic payment, and by 1991 was almost completely reversed. Instead of large sums of cash paid by the groom's family to the father of the bride, they gave money directly to the bride and her father was expected to contribute as well. In short, the arrangements came much more to focus on the couple and establishing their household (still patrilocal, however) than on kin and lineage.

Why did the Yörük engage in kidnapping and elopement? Some of the original answers still hold, but considering this as a normal feature of society I had ignored not only the possibility that it could suddenly cease, but also that it had an origin. Recently, looking over some old data, I noticed that there was a fairly narrow age spread among women who had been kidnapped; they were only a subset of all married women, and this group had reached its maximum numbers about ten years before the study. Further analysis confirmed this. It seems that kidnapping as a frequent occurrence began around the end of World War II, increased during the 1950s and 1960s, and by the early 1970s started to decline as a marriage option. Many, if not most social preferences and practices—even deviant ones—are like that. In the Yörük case, one might speculate that kidnapping and elopement roughly tracked the rapidly changing economic and political environment. Following World War II, many traditional grazing areas, sources of prestige, and sources of income were declining at the same time the Yörük were increasingly drawn into an all-cash market economy. Many, of course, found new opportunities and some flourished as meat and wool prices went up. Others did not do so well and became indebted. All of these occurrences could have worked to disrupt normal marriage arrangements, but there was an additional factor at work. Bride price, which had formerly been expressed in terms of a few animals, became monetarized and then was subject to rapid inflation.

thropology box, *Kidnapping and Elopement Among the Yörük*, above.

The reverse custom, paying the groom's family a **dowry** to take a daughter, was common in medieval Europe, and exists today in parts of Eastern Europe and particularly in India. In India, the practice has occasioned a great outcry as police have reported many incidents in which poor men have murdered their wives in order to remarry and collect a second dowry.

Bride price payments and bride service are most common in societies where a woman leaves her family to live with her husband's kin and the children she bears become members of his patrilineal kin group. In effect, the husband is compensating his wife's family for the loss of her economic services and reproductive capacity. (When the couple remain in the vicinity of both kin groups and the husband's and wife's families have equal rights to the assistance of the couple and their children, reciprocal gift exchange is more common.) Bride payments and gift exchanges help to ensure that neither the couple nor their families will take the marriage lightly. Perhaps more important is the fact that when potentially hostile groups intermarry over several generations, they establish a lasting bond. As each group has vested interests in the other in terms of past, present, and future offspring, they have established a basis in kinship for cooperation and communication.

Two social customs, the **levirate** and the **sororate**, exemplify the widely held conception of marriage as an exchange between kin groups. These social customs extend the marriage contract beyond the death of a spouse. Under the levirate, a man has both the right to marry his dead brother's widow (or to demand bride payment from another husband she chooses) and the obligation to provide for her. The woman is seen as having an obligation to produce or rear heirs for her husband's family even if he is dead. Under the sororate, a widower has the right to marry one of his deceased wife's sisters, and her kin are obliged to provide him with a new wife. In American society, where one is not expected to marry one's deceased spouse's brother or sister, individuals often assume at least some continuing responsibility toward the family into which they marry.

Marriage and the Division of Labor

Many anthropologists have suggested that one reason marriage is so widespread lies in its economic advantages, quite apart from childrearing. Marriage unites two economically complementary people, a man and a woman. Among the Dobe San people, as we have seen, women spend many hours gathering vegetable products for the family and camp, while men range far afield in the hunt. Though the women may produce more calories of food energy than the men, their roles are basically complementary.

Men can perform some physical tasks more easily than women, which, in a preindustrial economy, can be a significant factor in organizing work routine (Giampietro, Bukkens, & Pimentel, 1993, p. 256). Also, they usually have greater freedom of movement, as they are not burdened by a nursing infant on their back. Because women bear children and usually assume primary responsibility for their care, women supervise more aspects of housekeeping and other work that does not interfere with child care. Such responsibilities and the attendant division of labor are not static; they have changed through history. Carol Ember, surveying the data from a large number of horticultural and intensive agricultural societies, finds that as agriculture intensifies, women not only continue to work hard in food production, but take on added duties mainly associated with the preparation of foods that require more labor (Ember, 1983, p. 290).

Particular divisions of labor within the household are, of course, by no means inevitable, and today traditional systems are rapidly changing. Even if a couple does not allocate tasks along customary lines, they can still share the burden of work in some way, thus reaping the benefits of collaborative labor. Marriage serves as a convenient way to institutionalize such economic cooperation.

Actually, the economic alliance in a marriage is more complex than a balancing of strengths and talents between wife and husband. In many societies, labor is scarce; a greater number of family members means more potential sources of labor. The economic strategies of husband and wife frequently shift as children are born, grow up, and then either leave the family unit or bring spouses into it.

Given the importance of marriage in the creation of bonds between kin groups, promotion of economic cooperation, and provision for the care and education of children, the arrangement is not taken lightly in any society. In fact, all societies have both explicit rules and implicit norms defining who is an appropriate spouse, how many people one should marry, and where a newly married couple should settle.

Marital Rules

Marriage rules are generally not inflexible, but they are often backed by strong social pressure. The rules establish regularities in the way people marry, and the resultant organization of marriages and marital ties can be viewed as a coherent system.

The rules also serve to strengthen the potential for alliances and other bonds between groups. Perhaps the most significant marriage rules, at least in regard to the possible range of choices open to an individual, are those prescribing whom a person should and should not marry.

Whom Should One Not Marry? In virtually every society, sexual relations (and, by extension, marriage) between parents and children and brothers and sisters are forbidden or "taboo." The exceptions to the **incest taboo** are few. For religious and political reasons, the ancient Egyptians, the Incas, and the aboriginal Hawaiians required brothers and sisters of royal families to marry—a practice forbidden to other members of society. While the incest taboo is universal, the inclusion of first cousins among prohibited mates is not. Some societies ban cousin marriage, some tolerate it, and some even favor this form as a cultural ideal. And while incestuous relationships are disapproved of, they can be fairly common in practice. Many explanations have been proposed for this universal taboo on incest.

One explanation, popular at the turn of the century, is that people have no desire to mate with members of their own family (Westermarck, 1889/1922). Familiarity leads to sexual disinterest: long-term close associations simply discourage eroticism. This view is supported by both observation and by psychological and biological theory. Marriages between people born and raised together at an Israeli kibbutz are extremely rare. In fact, one study of 2,769 second-generation kibbutz marriages found not one intrakibbutz marriage (Shepher, 1983). On the other hand, records from ancient Rome indicate that brother-sister marriages among the farming class were quite common (Leach, 1982).

An explanation of the incest taboo favored by another early anthropologist, E. B. Tylor (1871), focuses on its sociocultural functions. In brief, the taboo prevents social isolation by ensuring that individuals participate in social units beyond the family in which they were raised. More recent alliance theories are related to Tylor's. They stress the positive consequences of "marrying out" to create interfamily alliances that enhance social cohesion.

Freud was also much interested in the taboo, and he speculated that it reflects the need to control a subconscious desire for incestuous sex. Certainly an instinctive recoil from sex with close relatives could be the mechanism by which this form of mating is avoided. However logical this position may seem, it is difficult to see why an instinctive taboo is needed to achieve such utilitarian social ends.

Still another theory, similar to Tylor's, centers on the social consequences of role disruption caused by incest (Malinowski, 1927). The complex relationships that would ensue when men, for example, in addition to being husbands, were acting as both parents and lovers to their children within the same household at the same time would probably have proven disastrous among early hunting-and-gathering groups in which cooperation was necessary for survival. On a large scale, the role confusion would have disrupted the transmission of culture through socialization.

Seymour Parker (1976) concludes that incest avoidance is "wired in" to humans and other vertebrates as a result of two factors. First, it evolved as an instinctive behavior through selective advantages that derived from outbreeding as opposed to the ill effects of inbreeding: individuals who avoided mating with close kin had more surviving offspring. Second, it developed as an adaptive behavior as groups learned the survival advantages of exploration and connection with a large social network. From Parker's point of view, the incest taboo is an example of "the complementary relationship of culture and biology." This perspective seems confirmed by growing evidence from behavioral studies with animals as well as with humans. Even a slight risk of genetic damage would be very deleterious to a species that reproduces slowly and whose adult members have a large investment in their offspring (Shepher, 1983, pp. 150–200).

Whom Should One Marry? Beyond the incest taboo, societies have a variety of rules that specify who is considered acceptable as a marriage partner. The **exogamy** rule defines the group out of which the individual should marry. Where rules of exogamy apply to members of a village, men must seek their wives (and women their husbands) in other communities. More commonly, however, these rules apply to some or all of a person's kin. Because cultures classify kin in a variety of ways, rules of exogamy take many forms. In societies that do not have a concept of unilineal descent, such as our own, rules of exogamy generally apply to most of a person's consanguineal relatives. Americans generally avoid marriage between first cousins. Traditionally the Chinese carried exogamy to the extreme, forbidding marriage between individuals who had the same last name on the theory that they might be related, however distantly.

In some societies with a concept of unilineal descent, rules of exogamy may apply to all members of a lineage. Thus in some patrilineal societies, individuals may be permitted to marry first cousins on their mother's side of the family but not on their father's. The prohibition usually forbids unions with all the people one calls brother or sister. Many societies forbid marriages between members of a clan or lineage, but lineage exogamy, while prevalent, is not universal. In the Caucasus, most populations insist that while one should marry within the ethnic group or population, no detectable degree of kinship should exist between spouses. In Bulgaria, ethnic Turks feel this way as well and, as a consequence, most families in this minority population have an exceedingly wide network of kinship ties outside their own villages (Bates, 1995).

The choice of a mate may alternatively be regulated by rules of **endogamy**, which prescribe the outer limits of acceptable marriage. Many Middle Eastern and North African peoples practice endogamy within a very narrowly defined kin group. First-cousin marriages are common. In such a marriage, of course, both the husband and wife may belong to the same descent group and usually knew each other as children. Indeed, in some Middle Eastern groups a man has a recognized right to marry his father's brother's daughter (his parallel cousin) and must be consulted and compensated amply if she marries another man (Bates & Rassam, 1983).

Although we may not always think of it as such, endogamy is practiced in our own society. In fact, most Americans marry a person who grew up within a few miles of their own family's residence. Marriages across socioeconomic, religious, national origin, and racial lines are in a distinct minority—in part because our society is structured in such a way that we have more frequent social contacts with people whose backgrounds are similar to our own, and in part because parents and others pressure young adults to marry within their groups. In complex societies such as our own, ethnicity often sets the outer limits to an acceptable marriage.

Of course, such norms as exogamy and endogamy are not always consistently followed within a society. Many mitigating factors may cause individuals to depart from recognized marriage norms. One of the most powerful factors is proximity—the nearness of potential mates. Even on the tiny island of Tikopia in the South Pacific (two miles by three miles), people are far more likely to find marriage partners in the same or neighboring villages than further afield. One study (Adams & Kasakoff, 1976) found that propinquity ranked as high as clan considerations or any other factor in determining the choice of a mate.

Although many societies do not sanction first-cousin marriages, people in approximately one-third of the world's societies allow or prefer marriage of certain selected cousins. Let us suppose a young man belongs to an exogamous partrilineage. Marriage with any cousin on his father's side of the family would be considered incest if the kinship terminology labels members of ego's descent group in his own generation brother and sister. Nor could he marry any of his parallel cousins on his mother's side of the family; he probably refers to those women as sister as well. But he could marry a cross cousin on his mother's side of the family. Moreover, marriage with his mother's brother's daughter might have certain advantages. It would allow him to formalize affectionate ties he has developed with his mother's family and strengthen his ties to a family he knows and trusts. Also it would reinforce interfamily ties established in the preceding generation by his mother and father.

In matrilineal societies, marriage with one's father's sister's daughter serves the same purposes. Thus anthropologists generally believe that exchange and alliance are among the important functions served by cousin marriages and the cultural preferences that structure them.

How Many Should One Marry? Just as societies have rules regulating who an individual may or may not marry, so they also have rules regulating how many spouses an individual may have. Historically, most societies have not followed the rule of **monogamy**, which restricts marriage to only one man and one woman at a time. Instead, they allow, or even prefer, some form of **polygamy,** or plural marriage. Many groups that prescribe monogamy consider it acceptable for a man to maintain one or more mistresses and their children in separate households—if he is reasonably discreet. In our own society, **serial monogamy** (divorcing and then remarrying, perhaps many times) is becoming an acceptable alternative to lifelong marriage to one partner.

There are actually two basic forms of polygamy: **polygyny** (marriage between one man and two or more women at the same time) and **polyandry** (marriage between one woman and two or more men at the same time).

Polygyny was, for high-status males, the preferred form of marriage among the ancient Hebrews, in premodern China, and in traditional India. It is permitted in much of Africa, the Middle East (the Koran permits a man four wives), and Asia. In most polygynous societies, only a few wealthy and powerful older men actually have more than one wife. After all, since there are usually approximately the same number of males and females in a population, widespread polygyny within a society would require some men to remain single, at least during part of their adult lives. It is no accident that polygyny is closely associated with male competition and is thus a prerogative of the senior men. From a male perspective, women are an economic asset. Women not only perform a significant amount of work themselves, they also bear sons to support a man in his political struggles and daughters who can someday be exchanged in forging alliances and for bride payments. Thus multiple wives can be a source of wealth, power, and social status. Patricia Johnson found that the number of women in a household was a major factor in determining its wealth: the women were vital to agricultural success, particularly in growing cash crops (Johnson, 1988).

Conflict among co-wives, a potential problem when the wives reside together or not far apart, is usually mitigated by an established domestic hierarchy. The senior wife nearly always enjoys superior status and authority over younger wives. She, not the husband, assigns the other women's work. Sometimes wives encourage and even help their husband to obtain new wives, but as Lila Abu-Lughod shows graphically in her narratives of Bedouin women of Egypt, the husband's taking a

second wife is usually a sad occasion for the first (1993). However brave a face a woman may put on, when her husband decides to take a second (and usually younger) wife, she often feels personally wounded and embittered.

Polygyny, it seems, is closely associated with sociopolitical systems that enforce male authority and gender inequality. Serial monogamy might be seen in the same light. Robert Wright, in a review of evolutionary psychology, reports on the functional similarities between polygyny and serial monogamy, particularly as practiced by high-status males (1994). Men in North America generally marry younger women; should they divorce, as many do, they usually remarry, again to younger women. The outcome of this pattern of marriage and remarriage is that men may occupy the best reproductive years of life of more than one woman, often leaving her to rear their children alone; Wright calls this the "Johnny Carson syndrome."

Polyandry is much rarer than polygyny, and is found as a widely recognized form of marriage in only a few societies. The Toda of India and the Tibetans, for example, traditionally allowed a woman to marry a set of brothers (fraternal polyandry), who shared her bed on an agreed-upon schedule and who jointly undertook responsibility for support of her children. In the Pacific, Marquesan men thought it advantageous to marry a woman who had several unrelated lovers and make them subsidiary husbands, because co-husbands would then act as allies. Polyandry as a lesser or poorly regarded form of marriage may be more widespread. The Dobe !Kung, for example, tolerate such marriage. Under certain conditions, polyandry may be advantageous for all concerned. If the ratio of males to females is seriously unbalanced, polyandry equalizes a man's chance to find a mate. If resources are scarce, it can also be a means by which limited land is shared by brothers, who otherwise would have to divide it up. On the other hand, it may not be favored by men under most circumstances because it reduces the number of offspring an individual man can produce (Hiatt, 1980). This practice can still be useful when resources are scarce, as in Tibet, where much of the arable land traditionally was controlled by a multitude of monasteries. If brothers marry one woman and have only one set of children, and the sons continue to practice polyandry, their land (not large enough to support several families) passes intact from generation to generation.

Nancy Levine, who worked for many years among ethnic Tibetans in northwest Nepal, has written the most detailed account of life in a polyandrous community. The Nyinba villages she studied were unusual in that fraternal polyandry was the norm. "Every man who has brothers—with the rarest exceptions—marries polyandrously, and virtually all the brothers remain intact, fraternally polyandrous marriages throughout their lives" (Levine, 1988, p. 3).

As Levine had expected, the presence of more males than females in polyandrous marriages has important consequences for household organization and the domestic economy. The Nyinba are a tightly bounded and closed society in their marital and social arrangements. Land in their mountainous region is limited and villagers have little possibility of acquiring any by means other than inheritance. Marriage in general is highly endogamous by category of wealth as well as by the narrow limits of the community. Households resist the partition or splitting up of domicile and land whenever possible. Against this backdrop, the members of the society see polyandry as a logical means of preserving resources intact. Sexual jealousy among men who share a wife is not prominent, although difficulties are most likely to break out when the brothers are not full brothers.

Polygyny is far less common but is permitted in the same communities that permit polyandry. This might come about when a man marries the sister of his present wife. In many respects this is a male-focused domestic arrangement, as the household and its resources are passed on in the male line. Even in regard to child care and consequently child mortality, boys are favored (Levine, 1988, p. 75). Men in a fraternal household frequently engage in trade or craft activities, leaving the farming and domestic work to the women, as we saw with the Temang, where men would often be absent for years working or engaging in trade in India while their wives would maintain the household in Nepal.

Marital Residence Rules. All societies have norms governing where newly married couples will live. Our own norm is called **neolocal residence** ("neo" meaning "new"): a married couple usually establishes their own household apart from both the husband's and the wife's kin. This residence rule is comparatively rare. In many other societies, married couples move in with the kin of one spouse or the other, joining an established household.

Patrilocal residence—residence of a married couple with or near the husband's kin—is the preferred arrangement in most patrilineal societies, as we saw with the Yörük and the Pokot. The couple may build their own dwelling in the compound or village of the husband's father or of another senior male of his kin group, or the bride may just move into her husband's father's house. But in all cases, they are residentially in the husband's kin group and are subject to its authority. Even so, there is always room for maneuver and deviation from the rules.

Matrilocal residence—residence of a married couple with or near the wife's kin—is also quite common, as we saw in the earlier Hopi example. Matrilocal residence is usually found in matrilineal societies that favor marriage to someone in the same village (village endogamy), so most male members of the matrilineage remain in their natal neighborhood. In some matrilineal societies, however, sons move to their mother's brother's community and set up households there. This pattern—residence of a married couple with or near a brother of the husband's mother who is a senior member of his matrilineage—is known as **avunculocal residence.**

The Suku of Zaire (Kopytoff, 1977) combine matrilineal descent with patrilocal residence—a situation that anthropologists once assumed was unstable. Members of a lineage are dispersed within an area that extends as far as thirty kilometers (twenty miles) and both men and women live with or near the man's father or brothers. But each kin group also has a ceremonial "anchor village," the matrilineage center, to which kin-group members return frequently for ceremonies and rituals. Because members of a matrilineage are in regular communication with one another, the combination of matrilineality and patrilocality has been stable.

In a fifth pattern, **bilocal residence**, a married couple regularly alternate their residence between the household or vicinity of the wife's kin and that of the husband's kin. Rather similar is **ambilocality**, a pattern in which the couple reside with or near the kin of either husband or wife, as they choose.

The preference for patrilocal over matrilocal residence (or vice versa) is a subject of much debate. For some time anthropologists have associated patrilocal residence with hunting, the herding of large animals, and complex agriculture—all of which require cooperative male labor. Matrilocal residence was thought to be adaptive for horticultural societies, where subsistence depends largely on female labor, but cross-cultural data do not support this view (Ember & Ember, 1971). Although most matrilocal societies practice horticulture, more than half of all patrilocal societies are also horticultural. The data, Ember and Ember suggest, show that where warfare among subgroups or neighboring communities of a single society is common, residence is patrilocal. If the family has to be on the lookout for attack, it makes sense to keep sons close to home. Patrilocality ensures that men are closely associated with the communities they are called upon to defend.

Family Households

Ties of kinship and marriage are basic to human social organization, and the most fundamental group in most, if not all, societies is the **household**: the domestic residential group, whose members live together in intimate contact, rear children, share the proceeds of labor and other resources held in common, and in general cooperate on a day-to-day basis (Blanton, 1994, p. 5). While households as residential and cooperative groups need not be formed on the basis of kinship and marriage, most of them are. We will therefore refer here to the family household. The household often functions as a small corporation, regulating consumption and production, commonly owning property, and holding defined rights in society.

We already have seen how marriage customs can vary. Since it is through marriage that family-focused households are formed, it is not surprising that variations in these customs can affect people's ideas about acceptable or preferred forms of domestic groupings. In essence, definitions of the family household vary from society to society in accordance with the way people conceptualize two relationships.

First, there is the **conjugal relationship**, that between spouses. In most but not all societies, the

The government of India, as in many countries, tries to promote smaller family size. This poster at a bus stop stresses the ideal of a two-child family.
(George Bates)

conjugal bond is basic to the structure of the family household. The conjugal relationship may, as we have seen, be monogamous, polygynous, or polyandrous.

The second relationship, the maternal and paternal ties, are those of descent between mother and child and between father and child. The maternal relationship, no matter how it is conceptualized, is universally recognized; the paternal relationship may not be, although such cases are relatively rare. The Nayar of India, mentioned earlier, are one of the few societies in which the definition of the household excludes both the conjugal bond and the father-child relationship. The Nayar family is (or was traditionally) based solely on the bond between a mother and her children; it is therefore called a **matrifocal family household**. This term is sometimes employed in our society to describe a household that comprises a single mother and her children. Thus numerous variants of the household are possible, each depending on the relationships included in the definition and on the way those relationships are conceptualized or stressed.

Independent versus Extended Family Households

One axis of variation based on the conjugal and descent relationships is the number of generations of married adults who live together in a household. The **independent family household** is a single-family unit (be the marriage relationship monogamous, polygynous, or polyandrous) that resides by itself, apart from relatives or adults of other generations. The independent family household formed by a monogamous union, the most common type in the United States, is often referred to as the **nuclear family household.** Far more common in other parts of the world, as an ideal at least, is some variant of the **extended family household,** a multiple-family unit incorporating adults of two or more generations.

The composition of a household in every society, regardless of the type that is culturally prized, changes regularly with the processes of birth, marriage, aging, and death. Thus any family household may best be described in terms of a **domestic cycle;** that is, according to the series of demographic events that it undergoes over time. An elderly couple whose children have left home form a rather different household from that of a newly married couple who have not yet had children. Individuals are likely to reside in a variety of household arrangements in the course of their lives, each depending on their age, the number of spouses they or their siblings have (whether serially or simultaneously), the health of their parents, and other factors. Thus it is difficult to assign one household type to an entire society or even to a local community, even if one form or another is clearly the cultural preference. Thus even in a society that stresses the importance of the extended household, the majority of people may actually be residing in independent or nuclear households. Also, regardless of the actual domestic living arrangements, households may form larger, closely cooperating units—functionally speaking, they could be called "super-households."

Richard Wilk has carried out research over many years on economic change and social life among the Kekchi of Belize (1991). The Kekchi are Mayan-speaking tropical farmers who vary greatly among themselves in terms of agricultural methods. Over a number of years he has collected data on some 38,000 individuals. Generally, it has been assumed that the move toward intensive agriculture is paralleled by a decline in the size of the co-resident family—as, for example, we see in the United States. In Africa, a similar process has been described for the Kofyar farmers of Nigeria (Stone et al., 1994). But what Wilk found was that one has to go beyond typologies that separate households into simple categories. Among the Kekchi, the household is a loosely defined unit and the activities that define it change as conditions change. If one looks at the most progressive farmers among the Kekchi and if one looks at actual patterns of shared labor and economic cooperation, the functionally defined household is significantly larger than those among the more traditional swidden farmer. This is because clusters of households in cash-cropping villages cooperate in production so that they can accumulate capital faster with which to purchase herbicides and fertilizers and perhaps even trucks (Wilk, 1991). In the final analysis, households are the products of ongoing negotiations among and decisions by individuals.

Each domestic arrangement has its advantages and disadvantages, and the advantages and disadvantages will vary in accordance with ego's position and gender. For example, the extended household in a patrilocal society may be less advantageous to a young bride than to her mother-in-law. The chief benefits of the single family household unit are mobility, privacy, and independence. But the costs of independence may be high. The independent family household is relatively vulnerable to labor problems arising from illness, care of children, and other potential demands for more time and energy than its few adults can muster. Moreover, in times of crisis or conflict, smaller households may find it hard to compete for economic resources against larger and thus politically stronger households. It is not accidental that nuclear households are both favored and very common where the larger political system assumes much of the burden of security, health care, and education.

The extended family household provides economic benefits (through the sharing of expenses and labor), defense, social security (illness or death do not leave individuals stranded), and companionship. And extended families are flexible: the members of the family can divide into teams to perform different kinds of work simultaneously and share what they produce. But there are disadvantages, too: friction between parents and adult children and among adult siblings; domination by elders, who achieve positions of leadership on the

Several generations of men in an influential Pakistani family near Lahore.

(George Bates)

basis of age rather than ability; and lack of privacy (Nimkoff & Middleton, 1960).

Extended family households usually center on either the paternal or maternal descent relationship as expressed in rules of marital residence. A patrilineal extended household consists of a man and his wife or wives, his unmarried daughters, his sons, and their wives and children. In the small towns and villages of Turkey, a bride commonly moves into her husband's father's household. The couple may have their own room but the bride shares cooking chores with the other women of the household and the family members eat together and share resources. Even if adults work for wages outside the household, they are expected to pool their money for household use, largely as the head of the household determines. The groom's father is the recognized head of the household and his wife exercises authority over the younger women and gives them daily work assignments. This arrangement is quite common throughout Eastern Europe, the Middle East, and the Mediterranean area, though for demographic reasons it is unlikely ever to be the predominant mode of household organization.

Despite the Yörük stated preference for extended family households, for example, only 30 percent of the households are so constituted. One outcome of this preference is that closely related men tend to remain in close proximity to one another while women, if they are not close relatives, come to the neighborhood from elsewhere. Even if a man does not actually co-reside with his married brother or with his parents, he usually tries to settle as close to them as possible. Thus the household can be seen as a mirror of the larger community—a fact that has been noted in many cultures.

A matrilineal extended household consists of a woman and her husband or husbands, her unmarried sons, her daughters, and their husbands and children. The Pueblo matrilineal extended family, for example, placed great emphasis on the mother-daughter bond. The oldest woman headed the household, while husbands (as well as sons to some extent) occupied peripheral positions, and the children were viewed as belonging to the women (Whiteley, 1985, p. 370).

In Bulgaria, among the Turkish minority, a strong emphasis is still placed on patrilineal extended households, but the situation is changing (Bates, 1994). It used to be the fact that men regarded living with their wife's parents as intolerable, as it would imply that they were in a subordinate social and economic position. Now this form of residence is becoming increasingly common. All rural-dwelling Turkish families share the feeling that large households are preferable—perhaps because of the uncertain political and economic environment in which they live. But some households find themselves without marriageable sons, only daughters. Such a household may now insist that the son-in-law reside with them. This practice is no longer viewed as disgraceful for the groom, as it is recognized as a legitimate interest because families now have fewer children than before. Also, in the modern economy the son-in-law does not work for the father-in-law, but will more likely have a salaried job.

A complex extended household, formed through polygyny or polyandry or through the decision of married siblings to live together is often termed a **joint family household**. It is common for a husband of multiple wives to establish a separate dwelling for each wife, or at least to provide separate domiciles within a family compound or building. In the most common form of joint family household, married brothers live together, with the senior brother assuming a position of leadership. One advantage of this arrangement is that resources need not be divided. The disadvantage, much commented upon, is that interpersonal conflict frequently leads to the dissolution of the household, especially when the wives of the younger brothers, determined to protect the inter-

ests of their children, come to resent the leadership of the senior brother and his family.

Anthropologists have looked at a variety of social and economic relationships in an attempt to explain why the extended or joint family household is so commonly idealized and why in some societies (such as ours) the independent family arrangement is preferred. They have found that extended families are prevalent in agricultural societies, while independent families are more frequently associated with industrial or hunting-and-gathering modes of subsistence. Over 80 percent of the world's hunters and gatherers spend most of the year in independent family groups. Extended families, on the other hand, can exist in societies that offer an abundant food supply, property ownership, and a settled lifestyle. These observations do nothing to negate the possibility of great variability within communities, and, in particular, during the domestic cycle. This statistical association has been basic to the traditional explanation for the dominance of one or the other type of family structure in a particular society.

Summary

THE FOUR FOCUSES OF THIS CHAPTER ARE KINSHIP— the most crucial factor in social organization—descent, marriage, and the family household. Social organization may be seen as a network of reciprocal roles, each organizing in a predictable way the behavior of the individual who occupies it. In all societies, but especially in small-scale societies, important roles are defined by kinship: relatedness by marriage or by descent from common ancestors. Since kinship roles are universal organizers of behavior, they are universal keys to social structure.

In most societies kinship is the major system of social relations that links people across generations, hence providing major channels for the transmission of social and technical knowledge through time. Kinship must be understood in the terms the people themselves use to categorize kin, both when they speak about them (terms of reference) and when they speak to them directly (terms of address). Although kinship terms use a biological idiom—"father," "mother," "sister"—they are cultural and linguistic

creations. Hence they vary in accordance with the society's values, beliefs, and ways of making a living.

Kinship is the basis for the formation of important social groups, the largest of which are descent groups. Underlying a descent group is not just common ancestry but a whole set of beliefs, myths, and symbols—a descent ideology—that reinforces group solidarity. A descent group is either unilineal or nonunilineal. Unilineal descent groups are those in which membership is traced through one line only, either the father's (patrilineal descent group) or the mother's (matrilineal descent group). In nonunilineal descent groups, descent may be traced through either parent or through both. Unilineal groups are generally categorized according to their inclusiveness. Members of a lineage trace their genealogies through specified links to a common ancestor—female links to a female ancestor in a matrilineage, male links to a male ancestor in a patrilineage. Members of clans, whether matriclans or patriclans, believe themselves to be descended from a common ancestor but are unable to trace the exact genealogical connections. Many clans are named for a totem, a plant or animal to which they claim a special relationship. Moieties are even more inclusive categories, often comprising several clans or half of a local community. When related lineages and clans have a common name and identity, they become a tribe. Tribes are formed of segmentary lineages, each lineage encompassed by a larger lineage, which is a segment of a still larger lineage, and so on until all members are related in a single genealogical hierarchy. For a unilineal kin group to exist, its members must recognize some shared set of interests that give them reason to join forces; that reason may be economic or related to the need for protection. Whatever the common set of interests, it is clear that unilineal descent groups serve many important functions for their members, including the regulation of marriage and land use and the provision of mutual aid and support.

Anthropologists classify nonunilineal descent groups into two basic types: ambilineal and bilateral. In societies with an ambilineal descent ideology, a person affiliates with kin groups on the basis of ties traced through either the paternal or the maternal line. Bilateral descent ideologies define individuals as being at the center of a group of kin composed more or less equally of their mothers' and fathers' relatives of all kinds. It is a mistake to assume that all societies with the same descent ideology have identical systems of behavior with regard to kinship. Descent ideologies are regularly manipulated and may change with time.

Social rules are only one among many important factors a person will consider in a given situation. The family is a social construct based for the most part on ties of kinship. The term may refer to the co-residing domestic group or household, or to a broad network of relatives by birth and marriage; thus, its form varies considerably from society to society. It is also necessary to distinguish between social norms of family organization, other family units, and the actual living arrangements people make. A household is a minimal residential unit, but it is not necessarily a family, just as not all families are households.

Marriage is a contractual basis for the sharing of property, economic responsibility, sexual access, and the responsibilities of parenthood. But marriage is culturally variable in terms of permanence, sexual privileges, and economic rights and obligations. Moreover, legitimacy of children is not dependent on marriage in all societies. Marriage binds families and kin groups together. The act of exchange inherent in marriage creates a precondition for further social interaction. In some societies, interfamily alliances are

created by the direct exchange of daughters. Dowry may be paid by the bride's family to the groom's. Usually, however, marriage entails a bride price or bride service, which is paid or rendered by the prospective husband to the kin of his wife. This custom is most common in patrilineal societies, where women leave their families to live with their husband's kin. A lasting bond is thus formed between the groups, which tends to alleviate any potential conflict. Some societies extend the marriage contract beyond the death of a spouse. Under the levirate, a man has the right to marry his brother's widow and the obligation to provide for her. Under the sororate, a widower has the right to marry a sister of his dead wife, or her kin are obliged to provide him with a new wife.

All societies have explicit rules and implicit norms concerning marriage and residence. Virtually every society maintains the incest taboo, which prohibits sexual relations—and therefore marriage—between brothers and sisters or between parents and children. Most also enforce rules of exogamy, which require people to marry outside a particular group. These rules take various forms, depending on the kin classification within the society.

Many strongly exogamous societies forbid marriage between members of a clan or even of a lineage. In other societies, rules of endogamy apply, requiring a person to marry within a defined group. This form of marriage guarantees that one will marry and live within a circle of fairly close relatives. Cousin marriages are sometimes preferred or even prescribed. Such marriages enhance exchange and alliance with other kin groups.

Societies also enforce rules governing the number of people one may marry. Our society prohibits marriage with more than one person at a time (monogamy), but permits divorce and remarriage (serial monogamy). Most societies practice (at least ideally) some form of polygamy. The two basic forms of plural marriage are polygyny (marriage between one man and two or more women) and polyandry (marriage between one woman and two or more men). Tibetans traditionally practiced fraternal polyandry, under which a woman married two or more brothers.

Rules dictate where a married couple must establish residence. Norms in our society call for a newly-married couple to establish neolocal residence, apart from both the husband's and the wife's kin. Other societies prefer patrilocal residence, in which case the married couple lives with or near the husband's kin. Other alternatives are matrilocal, avunculocal, bilocal, and ambilocal residence. It has been suggested that residence rules reflect defense as well as economic considerations: where warfare is common, it is advantageous for those who fight together also to live together.

Perhaps the most basic group is the co-residing domestic group, or household. Usually, but not always, the household is based on ties of kinship. Members of such family households share food, labor, and material resources. Inasmuch as marriage customs affect the composition of the family household, the conjugal relationship is basic to its structure. Male and female roles in the household are affected by the society's emphasis on descent relationships. The matrifocal family household is based solely or primarily on the bond between the mother and her children. A single-family unit that resides apart from relatives of an older generation is an independent family household. When the union is monogamous, it is usually called a nuclear family household. The extended family household, which includes adults of two or more generations, is widely found as a cultural ideal, particularly (but not exclusively) in farming societies. An extended household formed through the decision of married siblings to live together with their spouses and children is usually termed a joint family household.

Because of the series of demographic events that make up the domestic cycle, individuals are likely to reside in a variety of household arrangements in the course of their lives, whatever the cultural ideal. Each domestic arrangement has advantages and disadvantages. Extended families tend to be prevalent in agricultural societies; independent families are more common in industrial and hunting-and-gathering societies.

Key Terms

affinal kin	domestic cycle
ambilineal descent	dowry
ambilocality	ego
avunculocal residence	endogamy
bilateral descent	exogamy
bilocal residence	extended family household
bride price	
bride service	fictive kin
bridewealth	household
clan	incest taboo
collateral relatives	independent family household
conjugal relationship	
consanguineal kin	joint family household
cross cousins	kindred
descent group	kinship

levirate	patrilateral
lineage	patrilineal descent
lineal relatives	patrilocal residence
matrifocal family household	polyandry
	polygamy
matrilateral	polygyny
matrilineal descent	segmentary lineage
matrilocality	serial monogamy
matrilocal residence	sororate
monogamy	terms of address
neolocal residence	terms of reference
nonunilineal descent	totem
nuclear family household	tribe
	unilineal descent
parallel cousins	

Suggested Readings

Blanton, R. E. (1994). *Houses and households: A comparative study*. New York: Plenum Press. This volume makes a substantial contribution to the study of households by taking a cross-cultural approach to the understanding of variation in households and household behavior through aspects such as use of space, architecture, and gender relations.

Ember, M. & Ember, C. R. (1983). *Marriage, family, and kinship*. New Haven, CT: HRAF Press. A collection of previously published essays by the authors that examine, in a cross-cultural perspective, variations in family and household, the incest taboo, postmarital residence, and related topics.

Fricke, T. (1994). *Himalayan households: Tamang demography and domestic processes*. New York: Columbia University Press. A comprehensive study of the household structure and organization of the Tamang of Nepal, while they are on the verge of major socioeconomic changes.

Gorkin, M. (1991). *Days of honey, days of onion: The story of a Palestinian family in Israel*. Berkeley: University of California Press. An intimate account of a Palestinian Arab family living in Israel.

Lebra-Sugiyama, T. (1992). *Japanese social organization*. Honolulu: University of Hawaii Press. A collection of works that deal with the elusive features of Japanese social organization.

Levine, N. E. (1988). *The dynamics of polyandry: Kinship, domesticity, and population on the Tibetan border*. Chicago: University of Chicago Press. A rare ethnographic account of life in polyandrous households. The author has carried out intensive fieldwork in Nepal among villagers of Tibetan ancestry who practice fraternal polyandry.

Modell, J. S. (1994). *Kinship with strangers*. Berkeley: University of California Press. An insightful perspective on adoption that challenges the traditional conception of kinship.

Netting, R. McC., Wilk, R. R., & Arnould, E. J. (Eds.). (1984). *Households: Comparative and historical studies of the domestic group*. Berkeley: University of California Press. The editors introduce issues of methodology and theory in the study of household organization; the individual essays describe a wide range of current research.

Schneider, D. M. (1980). *American kinship* (2nd ed.). Chicago: University of Chicago Press. A now-classic account of kinship as a system of symbols and meanings, rather than just a network of functionally interrelated roles. A clear and concise introduction to kinship in American society.

Stacey, Judith. (1991). *Brave new families: Stories of domestic upheaval in late twentieth century America*. New York: Basic Books. This study deals with contemporary American life and explores how the traditional nuclear family has been replaced by various new relationships not previously defined.

Weston, K. (1991). *Families we choose: Lesbians, gays, kinship*. New York: Columbia University Press. This book gives insight into the gay and lesbian experience with a focus on the reconfiguration of kinship.

The Social Division of Labor
Social Perception and Behavior

Gender
Gender Socialization
Case Study: Gender Socialization in Yörük Society
Gender and Work
Gender and Power
Gender Issues: Women's Movements in the Middle East

Race and Ethnicity
Race and Racism
Ethnicity
State of the Peoples: One Land, Two Peoples: A Palestinian Village in Israel
Racial and Ethnic Stratification
Case Study: The Memphis Garbage Strike

Systems of Stratification
Class
Caste-stratified Societies
Case Study: Caste in India
Slavery

Ethnicity, Nationalism, and Conflict
Nationalism and Ethnic Conflict
Politicized Ethnicity as a Response to the State
Case Study: What's in a Name: Bulgaria's Program of Rebirth
Ethnic Terrorism

Summary
Key Terms
Suggested Readings

Chapter 9

Identity and Inequality: Gender, Ethnicity, and Nation

I n the previous chapters, we have largely focused discussion on human ingenuity in solving problems (adaptation) and have discussed population-wide social processes, as well as some basic concepts we can use to discuss societal integration. At this point, however, it should be obvious that societies are far from homogeneous; the remaining five chapters will explore this internal diversity as well as establish certain broadly shared commonalities.

In this chapter, we will explore the ways in which social identity is constructed, manipulated, and, all too often, used to divide and even oppress as much as to unite people. In some respects it seems counter-intuitive to say that social identity at all levels, from individual to nation-state, is "constructed"; are we not, after all, born as males or females, do we not grow up as members of families and social groupings that exist in very concrete manifestations? A Yanomamö child does not "invent" Yanomamö culture or a particular Yanomamö tribe, any more than the child of Jewish parents invents Judaism.

Nevertheless, we do construct our identities and, by extension, those of even large social groupings through conscious and unconscious choices among numerous alternatives. We do this in our behavior, expectations, and perceptions of others. Even if we take our gender identity for granted, how we come to identify a particular constellation of behavioral traits and values with proper male or female roles is intensely personal and varies among individuals within families as well as within larger populations. While the cultural environment into which we are born provides most of the materials with which social identity is built, individuals can and do make significant choices, the collective outcomes of which include new religions, political movements, tribes, ethnic groups, and nations. The 100,000-member Aum Shinrikyo religious group, which gained notoriety in the March 1995 Tokyo subway gas attack, was founded in 1987 and all of its adult adherents were born and raised in households professing other faiths. We will never know what went on in the minds of those who abandoned the beliefs of their families, and often their families as well, but the outcome of their decisions is clear: a new religion has appeared.

The Social Division of Labor

Some dimensions of personal identity are undoubtedly rooted in the psychological makeup of the individual; others have more general antecedents. It is the latter we will concentrate on here, and, in particular, those that tend to create structures dividing or separating individuals within society into groups or social strata.

All societies are formed by the integration of smaller groups or subsets of the whole, whether the smaller entities are households, lineages, political parties, labor unions, or other units. The great nineteenth-century French sociologist Émile Durkheim (1964) referred to this process as the **social division of labor**. The division of labor within a society is essentially the social organization of the work force. Social and economic processes are always compartmentalized and often specialized, with each segment or grouping occupying its own position within the whole. Durkheim identified two contrasting modes of integration in human society with respect to the division of labor, a distinction that still is useful.

One form of society is built up of similar parts; for example, societies in which all of the social units are comparable—households, lineages, or other descent groups. Take the pastoral Ariaal of Kenya, for example. Every member of the society (of the same sex and age category) belongs to the same sorts of social groups as does every other member, each household does much the same productive work as the others, and most people (of a particular age-sex category) possess the same skills. This form of organization exhibits what Durkheim termed **mechanical solidarity**, exemplified by a number of the populations described earlier, and refers to the fact that social integration is based on a shared "sense of belonging" to the society. These shared strong moral sentiments are reinforced in rituals stressing common ancestry, origin myths, and in specific social customs (such as the age grades among the Ariaal) that tie different households and different segments of society together even though there is little economic specialization. Durkheim referred to these sentiments as "collective conscience" because people almost automatically feel that they belong together. It is interesting that the thirteenth-century Arab philosopher-sociologist Ibn Khaldun identified an almost identical concept, 'asabiye or "group feeling," the strength of which he saw as critical for the maintenance of organized society.

The second form of social organization is more complex: society is built up from dissimilar, economically specialized social groupings. This becomes most pronounced with the advent of industrialization. No individual can participate in all the social groupings, but each participates in at least some. Durkheim characterized this sort of society as exhibiting **organic solidarity** because it resembles the structure of a living organism, constructed from numerous but specialized parts, each with a separate function. What unites the differentiated parts is interdependence, not emotional ties. Complex societies are almost always structured so that some of the social groupings have preferential access to resources, prestige, and political power. In short, they are stratified. Since interdependence also goes hand-in-hand with persistent inequality, societal integration often involves varying degrees of coercion and political control. While this distinction is a guide to looking at social and economic complexity, it is not by any means absolute;

Despite advances in gender equality, many sex stereotypes persist. Here men and women participate in the same endeavor, but as part of sex-segregated groups.

(Ellis Herwig/Stock, Boston Inc.)

industrial societies impose codes of behavioral conformity every bit as strong as in tribal communities, and the actual organization of production in horticultural and hunting-and-gathering societies is far more complicated than Durkheim imagined. However, his observations provide an effective framework for understanding how and why people use sources of personal and group identity and how these affect the integration of large-scale social systems.

Social Perception and Behavior

The way we view and classify people greatly influences the way we behave toward them and the way we expect them to behave. Thus, it is useful to focus on the way people in a given society categorize one another if we are to understand that society's organization and patterns of interaction. Such a focus can also help us to understand social cleavages and, ultimately, the differences in access to resources and power among members of the society.

A **social category** is composed of all the people who share certain culturally identified characteristics. For example, people classify others on the basis of certain perceived social characteristics that serve to set apart segments of society, as we saw in our earlier discussion of kinship. We are also using a system of categories when we refer to people according to their age, sex (or, more accurately, gen-

der), and family status, not to mention such categories as social class, race, and ethnicity.

All of us belong to social groups whose members interact on a regular basis and have a sense of collective identity. This sense of collective identity, usually a vital part of social organization, is based on criteria that can range from age, sex, family, and kinship through more abstract categories such as shared religion, ethnicity, and political views. From household to nation, these identities and claims are reflected in a pervasive "we-they" dichotomy. Societies at all levels of technology place a heavy emphasis on their uniqueness vis-à-vis outsiders. Band and tribal societies may have special insignia for clans or lineages, and the integrity of the whole is expressed in dress, dance, and ritual. Xenophobia (the fear of foreigners) is a global phenomenon. The Yanomamö, like many other tribal peoples, have elaborate myths that place them at the center of humanity, not unlike the creation myths of the Old Testament.

Even very small aggregates of people tend to arrange themselves in groups set apart in collective identity from the rest for some purposes. In more complex situations, people participate in a wide variety of named groupings. Any resident of a North American city who has a job is likely to be a member of a union; most belong to a church, mosque, or temple congregation; some are affiliated with a political party. Men and women may socialize in separate spheres and have distinctive social networks. Moreover, viewed as residential or neighborhood populations, there will be clear concentrations of people of different ethnic identities or nationalities—in particular where African Americans, Hispanic, East Europeans, and Asians are concerned.

State-organized polities have formally demarcated frontiers, emblems of citizenship, and myriad signs of common membership in a social and political system. But nationalism or patriotism, the ideological glue of most modern states, boil down to sentiments not particularly distinct from those employed at the family or tribal levels. The overarching social and political structure of the state encompasses any number of smaller social and political groups, each announcing its own uniqueness, involving religious affiliation, ethnicity, social club, or even family. Within any society, the nature and activities of constituent groups are basic to the organization of the larger population. Ethnicity in state societies, for example, can become a major means of distinguishing local populations or segments, even though all may participate in the same larger social order.

Sometimes, as we shall see, notions of ethnicity become a rationale for oppression or exploitation, as with racial segregation or discrimination in the United States. Racism, as we usually term the use of ethnic criteria to restrict social or economic activities, is a case in point. Apart from ethnicity, it is impossible to ignore the fact that people often do not participate equally in society, a fact so widespread as to amount to a human universal (Brown, 1991).

Gender

It is impossible to understand any society in the absence of gender as a category of analysis; at the same time, gender itself requires a cultural and historical context (Susser, 1989, p. 343). Although gender is a universal source of individual identity and a pervasive means by which access to resources and political power is structured, generalization in the absence of specific historical or cultural experience is risky. The gender experiences of people vary with historical processes, as reflected in religion, cultural conventions, access to resources, and education—not to mention the fact that within a complex society gender experience varies with ethnicity, class, and region.

Because gender roles are so intensely socialized and so personal, it is difficult to separate the present from the possible. It is no accident that until recently anthropologists (like other observers of society) largely ignored intercultural variation in gender roles; they simply took it for granted as a biological given that men and women belonged to different spheres of activity and the female domain was domestic while the male domain was everything else: productive, political, ceremonial, and military. Not only was great variability in gender roles overlooked, but so was the fact that even apparent similarities in gender relationships could have very diverse roots. In the West, traditional male power and authority has been largely based in property rights and control of wealth; the classic patriarchy, in Roman law, gave the male head of house final title to almost all property and control over his children (to the exclusion of his wives). Among the Yanomamö, male dominance seems to rest, in part, on the threat of physical violence. Among other Amazonian peoples (the Mundurucu, for example), male social and political precedence rests on their ability to dominate religious and ceremonial life through control of rituals and ritual objects (Murphy & Murphy, 1985).

Anthropologists have become aware of the shortcomings of ignoring gender, in part because of the recent transformation of their own societies. European and American society has changed radically since 1950. In the United States, female public-sector employment has grown rapidly, but with most hired in low-paying, temporary, and part-time jobs; since 1980, women with children under six have become the most rapidly increasing sector of the work force (Susser, 1986, pp. 343–344). Moreover, there has been a transformation in American family life: only 27 percent of the households in the United States are now constituted as "nuclear" (the supposed norm), and female-headed households continue to rise in numbers throughout the population. Further, the availability of contraception, abortion, and reproductive technology in the late twentieth century has changed established gender roles and has led people to rethink parenthood, sexuality, and cultural expectations of gender. How do processes such as migration, employment, childcare, and access to resources generally affect gender roles? What is of particular interest here is how gender is related to **gender hierarchies**. Gender hierarchies result from gender-specific differential access to resources and the political process, and are widespread but not inevitable. There are three interrelated areas that are of primary concern in analyzing gender: gender socialization, gender and work, and gender and power (Susser, 1986, p. 344).

Gender Socialization

Gender socialization of children begins immediately after birth and generates systematic inequality between the sexes. It is largely in the process of socialization that individuals form their notions of what gender identity means in terms of appropriate or expected and acceptable behavior.

Girls are often taught at an early age to defer to their brothers and to accept roles that emphasize child care and home-focused activities. This little Yörük girl is already caring for her infant brother.
(Daniel Bates)

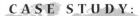

CASE STUDY:

Gender Socialization in Yörük Society

IN YÖRÜK SOCIETY, THE BIRTH OF A BOY IS often celebrated with the sacrifice of an animal and a feast; the birth of a daughter is hardly announced at all. Socialization immediately establishes the very different social worlds the sexes are expected to occupy. The daughter, rarely fussed over, is taught at a very young age to care for her younger siblings, if she has any; to help in collecting firewood and cleaning; and, as her skills develop, to sew and weave. The essence of the training is summed up in the expression, "The sun never shines on a sleeping bride." In order to become a desirable bride, a girl is expected to show her willingness to work from before dawn to after dusk; she watches her mother and older sisters make much fuss over her brothers and other growing male adolescents.

The socialization of a Yörük boy means he is both the center of a great deal of maternal and sisterly attention, and also subject to a great deal of teasing in the form of "Be a man! Be strong! Be brave!" A boy's economic contributions do not begin until he is old enough to attend to the family herds, a task rarely given to girls since they must be kept where their outdoor activities can be continually supervised. He will routinely accompany his father and older brothers on trips to the market (a rare treat for his sisters), and when he finally marries, his wife will join him in the household while his sisters, upon marriage, move out. He will inherit his share of the family's herds; his sisters will not, even though by law they have equal rights. The girls will have been conditioned to accept this as natural; after all, their own husbands will inherit and look after them. Should they be widowed or divorced, their brothers will be their final security. While attitudes and practices vary and change over time, the irony is that the women themselves have the biggest role in socializing their children into gender expectations that seemingly do not benefit their daughters. ❱

Gender and Work

Secondly, the organization of work in society is critical for understanding gender. Labor is often valued differently for men and for women, with the work done by women often seen as private or domestic (rather than productive) and hence undervalued. Further, even restricting access to nonproductive

Gender Issues

Women's Movements in the Middle East

ECONOMIC DEVELOPMENT, INcreased educational opportunities, mass communications, and legal reforms throughout the Middle East have produced a class of women whose very existence challenges traditional assumptions about the patriarchal organization of society. Educated, middle-class women are at the center of this change, as activists, as beneficiaries, and sometimes as losers. The expansion of women's movements throughout the region has often been a response to fundamentalist Islamist movements, which tend to be especially critical of Western influences on gender relations and seek to reimpose traditional behaviors for women, relegating them to a secondary role within society.

In Algeria, there were two crucial points that focused the activities of feminist groups: in the 1980s, when the government was reforming Algerian family law to conform to Islamic precepts; and in the early 1990s, when the Front Islamique du Salut (FIS) was gaining political support for a program introducing Shari'a (Islamic law) and hijab (dress codes for women, ostensibly to free them from the prying eyes of men). Algerian fem-

inists continue to be very active, although there is a significant divide, both ideologically and culturally, between Islamist and non-Islamist women. The latter group, mostly older university-educated women from the first post-independence generation of intellectuals, are critical of past government practice, which subsumed the question of gender relations under more general issues of liberation and nationbuilding. Doria Cherifati-Merabtine, herself part of this group, observes that these women "have learned, at their expense, that no change is possible if the outlook on woman and her place within society does not evolve" (quoted in Moghadan, 1993, p. 251).

The fact that Tunisia grants women a wider range of rights than do other Arab countries is often attributed to the policies of its first president, Habib Bourguiba. However, even in the early twentieth century, Taher El Haddad, a male feminist leader, was advocating emancipation for women and condemning the veil, polygamy, sex segregation, divorce law, and unequal access to education. El Haddad's book, *Our Women in the Shari'a and in Society*, was

banned, but his ideas persisted and were finally incorporated into the personal status code of 1956, which abolished polygamy, forced marriage, and unilateral repudiation; and established civil marriage, divorce, and child custody rights for women. However, Tunisian feminists emphasize the gap between legislation and practice; they also "point out that women are still unequal in inheritance and that the law prohibits the marriage of a Muslim woman to a non-Muslim man while allowing a Muslim man to marry a Christian or Jewish woman" (Moghadan, 1993, p. 252).

During the 1980s, the Taher El Haddad Club became a center for discussion of social problems and women's rights; there are several other groups still active, including the Women's Commission of the General Union of Tunisian Workers, the Tunisian Association of Women Democrats, and the National Union of Tunisian Women. "In North Africa a series of books has been published under the editorial supervision of Fatima Mernissi that focuses on women and the law. . . . Several films and videos have been produced. . . .

sectors such as religious ritual and ceremonial leadership differentiates between the sexes. In most cases, it is women who play a secondary role in ritual and public ceremony. While there are exceptions, when examined more closely it becomes clear that women appearing in prominent ritual, ceremonial, and even political roles are often regarded as honorary men for that purpose. (However, see

the Gender Issues box, *Women's Movements in the Middle East,* above.) Using gender to create different domains of activity usually contributes to stratification. While gender considerations obviously affect access to resources and contribute to inequality, gender usually has to be viewed along with other sources of identity used to compartmentalize and divide society.

[and] a directory of women's rights activists and scholars in Algeria, Morocco, and Tunisia, as well as a bibliography on women's studies" (Moghadan, 1993, pp. 52–53).

In Egypt, the women's liberation movement has been in place since the early twentieth century. In the 1980s, a group of professional women produced a booklet in Arabic, *The Legal Rights of the Egyptian Woman in Theory and Practice*, with an entire chapter devoted to the Egyptian personal status code and instructions on how women could write protective conditions into their marriage contracts. There are currently a number of activist feminist groups. One, the New Woman Group, defined its position in 1990: "The New Woman Group is a progressive and democratic feminist group of women who believe that while Egyptian and Arab women share with men the hardships brought about by backwardness, dependence and economic crisis, they have to carry a double burden and suffer from a variety of forms of subordination, oppression and suppression arising specifically from their position as women" (Moghadan, 1993, p. 253).

The women's movement in Turkey was begun by educated and professional women, who were beneficiaries of the reforms of Kemal Ataturk during the 1930s.

Today there are three main factions to the women's movement: Islamist, Kemalist, and new-wave feminism. Islamist and non-Islamist groups both oppose the commercial exploitation of women's sexuality, but they are divided over veiling and the introduction of Islamic legal codes. Kemalist feminists continue to associate feminist issues with other political agendas such as nationalism or socialism, and are puzzled by the new-wave emphasis on questions of sexuality and home life. The new-wave activists see the Kemalist emphasis on secularism and capitalism as ignoring the fact that women from different economic backgrounds had differential access to services, such as education and employment opportunities.

Valentine Moghadan (1993) posits several reasons as to why women should join Islamist movements despite the fact that Islam relegates them to a secondary position in society and in the home. Perhaps it is one way of defying the West, perhaps it is due to financial and moral support coming from such countries as Saudi Arabia and Iran, perhaps it is a redefinition of an old identity, perhaps it is defiance of state control of religion. "The answer may be all of the above and more. Many of the women who have embraced the Is-

lamic way of life are becoming more and more active" (p. 255).

Moghadan also finds interesting the effect of these women's activism on the Islamic movements themselves. "An unintended outcome of their participation in Islamist movements is that Islamist women become more participatory, more political, and more demanding of the men within their own movements. . . . [I]n Iran, Islamist women are asserting their right to criticize gender discrimination. . . . Such women are not only more open to change but more willing to engage in dialogue with persons outside their movements" (1993, p. 255). Moghadam quotes Turkish academic Suna Kili: "[Islam] has to rethink its values and role and has to learn to be open to dialogue. It needs to reform itself and to define its role in a modern society. . . . Developments in recent years have amply demonstrated that Islamic women are becoming more and more aware of this responsibility. It is perhaps because these women have more to gain from such a renaissance than men" (from Kili, 1991).

Material for this box is taken from Valentine M. Moghadan, 1993. *Modernizing Women: Gender and Social Change in the Middle East*. Boulder and London: Lynne Rienner Publishers.

Gender and Power

The third area of concern is closely related to socialization and the organization of the work force: that is, gender, power, and access to the political process (see Chapter 11). Even family life can be seen as political, in that individuals are contending for resources. Moreover, social control operates quite dif-

ferently on men and women in many instances. In societies where notions of family honor are important in local politics or public life, this may be linked to male control over female sexuality and, by extension, many aspects of female public behavior. Thus, it might be thought threatening to family honor for female members of the family to be seen with nonfamily males. This puts serious constraints on female

Police restrain an African-American woman on the ground during a racial protest march in Birmingham, Alabama in 1963.

(AP/Wide World Photos)

behavior, sometimes so as to make it difficult for a woman to accept employment outside the home.

Outside the household, gender can be seen as an aspect of stratification, particularly, as we shall see shortly, when taken in conjunction with race, ethnicity, and class. Women from different ethnic groups in the United States, for example, experience very different rates of poverty, childbearing options, and involvement in community mobilization. Class inequality can be greatly amplified by gender expectations regarding housework and childrearing for poor women.

However gender is understood, it has to be kept in mind that gender relations can and do change; in the final analysis, gender is shaped in society by the activities, beliefs, and values of both men and women. Women are not simply passive respondents, as the Gender Issues box, *Women's Movements in the Middle East* (pages 246–247) indicates. This region has been long associated in Western eyes with sexual segregation and male dominance; while aspects of this view are sometimes valid, it is also true that here, as elsewhere, gender expectations are changing.

Race and Ethnicity

People almost universally identify themselves and others according to their *perceived* roots or shared history. The word "perceived" cannot be overemphasized: perceptions are what establishes such closely related ascriptions as race and ethnicity; here, social reality is simply what people believe. Race, in particular, is a troublesome concept because in everyday usage it carries two contradictory meanings: biological ancestry and social identity. Even the use of race as a biological concept is sometimes confusing. We tend to conceptualize biological races as having clear boundaries; they do not. We tend to conceptualize biological races as fixed categories; they are not.

Race and Racism

Even though the biological view of race is very different from the socially constructed concept, these are often confused, sometimes with very misleading results. Jonathan Marks, a physical anthropologist, was struck by an inconsistency he spotted in the *New York Times* (1994, p. 32). Lani Guinier, a prominent law professor, was described in a photo caption as being "half-black" while in the article she identified herself as "black." The inconsistency, he felt, was trivial but illustrative of a problem in American use of racial categories to refer to presumed biological and cultural heredity. To describe Professor Guinier as "half-black" is a statement (technically in error) of her biological ancestry, since one of her parents is black. When she describes herself as black, she is affirming a cultural category according to which one can be white or black, but not both.

A **biological race** is a population sharing a distinctive genetic makeup derived from a common gene pool; that is, a biological subgrouping of a species. Usually, biological race is used to refer to a population in a particular geographical area or ecological zone. The means for categorizing such as race is in terms of its phenotypic characteristics. A **phenotype** is simply the material or observable manifestations of the expressed parts of genetic makeup, or **genotype**. Skin color, eye color, hair form, etc., are phenotypes, and while they are obviously affected by immediate environmental factors, they do reflect genotypic variation. For example, Sub-Saharan African, Northern European, Mediterranean, South Asian, and Native American are well-established examples of regionally or geographically defined distinctive human subgroupings. This seems straightforward, and does roughly correspond to some situations in which we would, in everyday speech, use the term "race." It is actually quite complicated.

The first complication with the attribution of biological race, especially to humans, is that boundaries that separate regionally distributed races are almost always indistinct. This is because the most observable traits one might use to categorize individuals (skin color, body shape, eye color) simply vary in degree across populations, much as does rainfall and temperature across a continent. The distribution of most traits tends to be clinal; that is, changing along a gradient. Few early travellers even bothered to comment on it. As Loring Brace put it, "The concept of [human] race didn't exist until the invention of ocean-going transport," which enabled travellers to wind up on different continents without traversing the lands in between. When one travels, as did Marco Polo,

overland to China at 25 miles a day, it is hard to racially categorize the peoples encountered as there are no clear borders (Brace, in Shreeve, 1994, p. 60). There are always population movements and intermarriages that work to minimize differences between adjacent populations.

Most genetic variation within a species is not apparent except at the molecular level—hence, of little use in everyday classification. After all, we cannot look at someone and say he or she is "blood group A+ race," or a carrier for the sickle-cell gene (which confers resistance to malaria). The frequencies of genes in animal populations vary over their geographic ranges, thus giving rise to subpopulations or races, but usually in a way that does not yield sharp or easily observable boundaries. Since every individual differs genetically from all others, what constitutes a biological race is sometimes arbitrary. That is to say, it is defined according to the problem or issue one is interested in studying. Thus, one could legitimately divide the world up into races based on the presence or absence of any gene; the sickle-cell gene, for example, would place Yemenites, Greeks, New Guineans, Thais, and Dinka in one "race" (Diamond, 1994, p. 84). Using the lactase enzyme gene, which allows some adults to digest raw milk, would group Arabians, Northern Europeans, and West Africans as one "race," with the "lactase-negative" grouping including most other Africans, East Asians, American Indians, and Southern Europeans. There are no "pure" races, nor could there be. Biological race is strictly based on genetic differences, always of a minor nature, within the species. Since our species is of relatively recent origins, and because of population movements and interbreeding, the amount of variation between human populations is small relative to that within populations.

This is not to say that biological race cannot be usefully studied. For example, DNA studies have compared Native American, European, African, and Asian samples in order to reconstruct ancient population movements. Luigi Cavalli-Sforza and coworkers have used DNA sequencing to track large-scale, intercontinental migrations, including three distinct waves of migration from Asia into the Americas, beginning 30,000 years ago (Cavalli-Sforza & Piazza, 1994). The distribution of the far-flung sickle-cell trait has given new insight into how evolutionary change through natural selection is part of human adaptation. In fact, most genetic variability within the species is due to natural selection and sexual selection (which results from those with preferred attributes surviving and having more mating opportunities). But given the arbitrary nature of the biological classification of race, it is of little practical use as a means of classification. If the term were not so widely employed, most social scientists would simply cease to use it.

Another major source of confusion or, worse, invidious conclusions, is the erroneous attribution of social or cultural attributes to racial categories. Where race is used to describe groups that have cultural or social attributes in addition to presumed biological heritage in common, we might term this usage "social race," and it is this usage that most social scientists discourage. In this usage, what appear to be (or are even imagined to be) distinctive biological features (skin color, for example) are confounded with social or cultural features (language, dress, religion, distinctive behaviors, ways of life, etc.). This is the confusion noted by Jonathan Marks, where the same individual was described at once as "half-black" and "black." Even the U.S. government, not to mention many other institutions in that country, unwittingly encourages this confusion.

When we read in a Census Bureau report that in 1991 " . . . 32 percent of the black population, in comparison with 11 percent of the white, lived in households whose incomes were below the poverty line; that is having a cash income of under $13,400 for a family of four . . . " we are learning about a deplorable social inequity—not about attributes of biological race (Farley, 1993, p. 197). The Office of Management and Budget (OMB), which collects statistics for the government, categorizes Americans as "black, white, American Indian, Eskimo, Aleut, Asian, or Pacific Islander (and 'other')"; now the OMB is considering adding slots for the 2000 census for native Hawaiians and Middle Easterners (Shreeve, 1994, p. 58).

For sheer confusion and inconsistency, it is hard to match the system of racial or social categories used by City University of New York in which individuals (job applicants) are described as "black, white, Hispanic, Asian-Pacific Islander, American Indian, or Italian-American" (C.U.N.Y. Faculty Data Form). It is not surprising that 30 percent of individuals surveyed in two consecutive years in a recent study changed their racial self-ascription (Shreeve, 1994, p. 60). These systems confuse labels that imply biological differences with those of a clearly cultural nature.

In fact, the U.S. population is genetically very heterogeneous since it has been strongly shaped by immigration of people from all over the world within a relatively short period of time. Racial categories such as white, black, African American, Hispanic, etc., do not refer to biological groupings; after all, most African-Americans, for example, carry a significant portion of their genes (over 20 percent on average) from white ancestors (Shreeve, 1994, p. 59). Whites, in turn, have received their genes from very diverse ancestral gene pools. Hispanic refers to Spanish-speakers of diverse origins in the New World, but excludes those born in Spain. What appear to be phenotypic or physical indicators of distinctive ancestry are, in practice, simply clues to social identity—and often incorrect ones. Race in this sense is a social construction, one that has to be understood in the context of specific cultures (Spears, 1991, p. 17). The term "race" is used very differently in Brazil, for example, than in the United States. In Brazil, some 300 or 400 racial groups are recognized in everyday language; in the United States, three or four racial categories are commonly employed (Harris, 1988, p. 100).

This sort of confusion is ultimately the basis for **racism**, which has been characterized as acting on the belief that "races are biologically unequal in terms of their ability to acquire culture" (Spears, 1991, p. 18); or, more broadly, behaving as though races have unique behavioral propensities—prone to crime, industrious, lazy, intelligent, slow-witted, hot-blooded, and the like. As we shall see later, use of racist appellations can be part of ideologies that maintain social and economic inequality—even slavery.

Ethnicity

A more useful way of describing social identity is in terms of ethnicity, since this term, in current usage, has no biological connotations. In fact, references to racial equality or racial discrimination are usually references to ethnicity. **Ethnicity** refers to a social or group identity that the individual ascribes to himself or herself and that is also accepted by others. Ethnicity is a basis for categories that are rooted in socially perceived differences in origin, language, and/or religion. In many respects, ethnicity resembles descent ideology: it stresses one's origins or descent as part of one's social identity and is usually ascribed at birth. Any society is the product of a long and varied historical process. People, whether literate or not, are conscious of this process, and often an awareness of the group's past serves to validate the present. Historical themes are used to inspire group loyalty, patriotism, or loyalty to an organization such as an army or a religious body.

The Yörük of Turkey, whose pastoral way of life was described in Chapter 6, take pride in their Central Asian ancestry and the fact that they are among the first Turkish peoples to have settled in the region. While such an awareness of the past is a source of unity, it also emphasizes that which sets one segment of the population apart from others. Within our society, Native Americans, African-Americans, Chicanos, Jews, Puerto Ricans, Chinese-Americans, Japanese-Americans, Irish-Americans, Italian-Americans, and Polish-Americans are significant ethnic categories. Each group has a sense of a unique identity, derived from a sense of a common history that other groups do not share.

The ethnic categories in any state-organized society can be numerous and varied. Accra, the capital of Ghana, for example, encompasses more than eighty ethnic groups. A study of 423 residents in eleven apartment buildings on a single street in Accra revealed twenty-three distinct ethnic groups and fourteen first languages (Sanjek, 1977). Roger Sanjek found a good deal of interaction among these ethnic groups, including intermarriage and widespread multilingualism. In one especially complex household, he found representatives of three ethnic groups who regularly spoke seven languages. When asked to identify the "tribes" living in Accra, each of the local subjects who were sampled listed between one and fifty-five ethnic terms; the mean number was ten. Thus, Sanjek concluded, the residents of Accra are typically aware of the ethnic diversity, but there is no agreement on the number of distinct ethnic groups that are represented in their neighborhood.

Because ethnic categories are culturally defined, they can be manipulated and changed. The definition of an individual's ethnicity can change with his or her situation. In one situation, for example, we

Laplanders, like other ethnic groups, use distinctive clothing to help emphasize their identity.
(Sisse Brimberg/Woodfin Camp and Associates)

might identify ourselves by emphasizing the national origin of one of our many ancestors, and if the situation changes, we might choose another of a different origin. In fact, as we saw with the Ariaal, ethnic identity is regularly reformulated or reinvented.

A striking example of changing ethnic identity associated with economic change can be seen in the now-classic case of the Fur of the Sudan. These are hoe-agriculture people, but some of them are abandoning their separate identity to become part of the Arabic-speaking, nomadic, cattle-herding society known as the Baggara. (Oddly enough, this process has come about not because people were being pushed off the land and into a nomadic group, but because they had accumulated wealth to invest and traditional Fur society provides no outlet for it.) But the Fur cannot simply leave the land and take up herding without sacrificing an important part of their ethnic identity. As the Norwegian anthropologist Frederik Barth explains it, each subsistence strategy entails a whole style of life, which is subsumed under the ethnic label Fur or Baggara (Barth, 1969, p. 26). A Fur who herds cattle becomes a Baggara.

Many ethnic classifications largely define social roles. Members of some ethnic minorities, for example, are usually traders, sometimes to the exclusion of the native majority. The Chinese in Southeast Asia and the Asians in East Africa are two prominent examples. Brian Foster has examined the same phenomenon in Thailand, where the Mons are the traders. Originally from Burma, this group is similar to the Thai people in most ways except language. But the Mons who are traders are less likely to be assimilated into the larger society than Mons who are not traders. Foster hypothesized that the ethnic distinctions between the Mons and the Thais served an important function. "Ethnic differences set off commercial people from the society around them in such a way as to (1) minimize the stress inherent in market transactions, and (2) free the merchants from the social constraints of an anticommercial peasant society that would otherwise strangle commercial enterprise" (Foster, 1974, p. 5). Traditional Thai society stressed generosity, lack of profit in dealings with others, and extreme civility to avoid conflict and competition. So long as villages were self-sufficient, these values proved viable. But as the possibilities for extensive outside trade developed, Thais faced the choice of either forgoing trade or flouting social expectations—a serious conflict. Only an outsider could violate the social rules without endangering the stability of society.

However, when ethnic differences are expressed in economic deprivation or monopoly of a resource, acrimonious relations are often the result. Relations between members of different ethnic groupings within a nation-state are frequently characterized by conflict. This is especially true where land is at issue and where different groups base their claims to its as part of their ancestral patrimony, as we see in the State of the Peoples box, *One Land, Two Peoples: A Palestinian Village in Israel* (pages 253–255).

Even societies that pride themselves on democratic access to political power, such as the United States and Great Britain, are not immune to ethnic conflict, which is often exacerbated by real or perceived injustice. In 1985 Great Britain was rocked by violent confrontations between native Britons and ethnic Asian immigrants. In Germany, 1.4 million Turkish "guest workers" are viewed with some misgivings, and since 1990 there have been an increasing number of violent assaults on Turkish homes and places of business. In both Britain

and Germany, extremists among the native population came to feel that the foreigners were benefiting unfairly. In Germany, the strains of reunification, which has caused widespread unemployment, have contributed to the problem. The Turkish-speaking population's response has probably been unhelpful, although quite predictable. They have turned further inward, and now more than ever resist assimilation. Northern Ireland, until late 1994, has been the scene of conflict between Protestants and Catholics, with the latter having had a history of economic and political disadvantage. Southeast Asia seethes with constant hostility between the indigenous populations and communities of Chinese and Indian nationals involved in trade and commerce. Most of the world's some 44 million refugees, people forced from their chosen place of residence, are displaced because of ethnic conflict (Lewis, 1993, p. 6).

At the same time, ethnic distinctions, like social distinctions based on age and gender, may be the basis for the formation of special action groups. In the United States, members of ethnic minorities have joined in a large number of formal organizations to enhance their status and combat discrimination by the dominant society. The same process of ethnic-group formation can be seen in other societies as well. The Ibo of Nigeria, who have migrated from the tribal territory to the cities, have formed tribal associations to assist newcomers, sponsor events that preserve Ibo culture, start businesses, educate children, and exert political pressure. In many respects, the very idea of ethnic identity is an important means by which people adapt to the realities of life in complex societies. By stressing a special identity and a separate heritage, thus emphasizing the "we-they" distinction, they create conditions that favor concerted and forceful action.

Racial and Ethnic Stratification

A common feature of polyethnic societies is the use of ethnic categories to restrict access to resources or full participation in political decision making. This process of stratification leads to entire segments of a population becoming disadvantaged in comparison with other members of the same society. Moreover, this disadvantaged position is largely passed on to their children. They come to

State of the Peoples

One Land, Two People:
A Palestinian Village in Israel

THERE ARE SOME 700,000 PALES-tinian Arabs living in Israel today, comprising 16 percent of the pop-ulation. With rare exceptions they are neither actively involved in the *intifada,* nor members of the Pales-tine Liberation Organization (PLO). In 1982, Michael Gorkin, a Jewish-American clinical psy-chologist, decided to learn for him-self what life was like for a Pales-tinian Arab family in Israel. Between December 1988 and Sep-tember 1990, he spent one to three days a week with a family in the Palestinian village of Kufr Qara, located in the center of Israel and one of the approximately 110 all-Arab villages and towns in the country.

The family of Abu Ahmad com-prises three generations: Abu Ah-mad (70 years old), his wife Umm Ahmad (63 years old), their nine living children, and their 26 grand-children. Both Abu Ahmad and Umm Ahmad are descendants of the original clan that founded Kufr Qara in the 1700s and both have spent all their lives in the village, apart from an eleven-month pe-riod during the war of 1947–49 when they were forced to flee. They are peasants—*fellaheen.* All of their children, and of course their grandchildren, have grown up in the period since the estab-lishment of Israel. Gorkin presents their story in the form of vignettes from daily life or recollections and historical flashbacks told to him by family members or their friends, and wherever possible, in their own words. Here we shall look at the family's life under the military

government from 1949 until 1966. The war, known to the Jews as the War of Liberation and to the Arabs as the Disaster (Il Nakba), estab-lished the State of Israel and led to the destruction of approximately 370 Palestinian villages and towns and created between 600,000 and 760,000 Palestinian refugees. The western portion of the territory that had been earmarked for a Palestinian state in the partition recommendation was absorbed into the new state of Israel; the eastern portion was annexed by Jordan (Gorkin, 1993, p. 103).

The Palestinians remaining in Is-rael, virtually all *fellaheen* or poor urban workers, were nominally considered equal citizens (called Is-raeli Arabs). "But in fact they were subject to considerable discrimina-tion. The vast majority of them, some 80 percent, found themselves living under a military govern-ment" (Gorkin, 1993, p. 123), and subject to laws controlling their movements, their work, and their property. The period of military rule was especially difficult for the inhabitants of Kufr Qara. Some 75 percent of the village's 24,000 *dunams* (6,000 acres) were confis-cated, so many villagers had to give up farming and seek work outside the village. However, special travel permits were required to go more than two kilometers outside the vil-lage, and in the early years these permits were difficult to obtain. Also, because of its proximity to the Jordanian border, the villages in the area were subjected to a nightly curfew.

During this time Abu Ahmad's

family grew from three children to ten. For the first five years of mili-tary rule, he managed to find work outside the village. Because he had played a pivotal role during the war, he also emerged as one of the village leaders, so that by the time he was 40 years old he was head of his clan and a member of the vil-lage council. "It is from this dual perspective, as father and village leader, that Abu Ahmad views the post-war military government pe-riod—a seventeen-year span which left its indelible mark on him, on Kufr Qara, and ultimately on all 700,000 Palestinians living in Is-rael today" (Gorkin, 1993, pp. 124–125).

The war had been a terrible time for our people. Kufr Qara had been emptied and we were scat-tered like leaves all over the area. We lived like refugees for eleven months. . . . When we finally did return, in April 1949, and the Jews let us go to our well and get water, I felt that our nightmare was over. Soon, I thought, life would go back to the way it was before the war. We would live with our Jewish neighbors as we did before the war—with respect and dignity. We would return to farming our lands and life again would be good. . . . It wasn't long before I could see that it would-n't be that way. In May 1949— May 22 to be exact—the army came to Kufr Qara and to all the villages in the area, and the mili-tary government took over. . . . We could live in the village, they said, but we would not be free to go about when and where we wanted. . . . At night, we were un-der a curfew—at first from 8.00

(continues)

State of the Peoples

One Land, Two People (continued)

P.M. to 5.00 A.M. and later from 10.00 P.M. to 4.00 A.M. In the first few years it was strictly enforced. Later they eased up. In the daytime, we were unable to leave the area of the village without special travel permits. . . . We could not go south of the main village area, or to the west, where almost all our fields were. All this was considered a "closed area."

. . . Things were so difficult in those early years of the military government that some people in the area decided to leave and go to Jordan. My uncle in Ar'ara, the man my family had stayed with during the war, was one of these. And he was not alone. Hundreds, maybe thousands, of people from villages just to the east of us went over the border to Jordan. . . . These people had spent the war in their own villages under the Iraqi army. They didn't know what it was like to be refugees. In Kufr Qara, because we had been refugees during the war, we knew what it was like. So, even though the situation was very bad, our people didn't leave. We stayed on. We were determined not to become refugees again.

For my family these years were also extremely hard, but not as hard as they were for others. That was because of my Jewish friend, Moti. He helped us. He remained loyal to the agreement that we had made with each other before the war. Just as I had promised to protect him and his family if we won, so he had promised to protect me and my family if they won. And he did. . . . It was Moti who arranged for Kufr Qara to be given the status of a refugee village, which en-

abled us to receive supplies from the Red Cross. That alone saved many people here. And to me personally he was very helpful. He made it possible for me to have a travel permit right from the beginning, when they were almost impossible to get. (Gorkin, 1993, pp. 125–135)

Thanks to Moti, Abu Ahmad was able to obtain a concession to sell fertilizer to the Jewish settlements, so that he was able to support his family. However, after a few months, being unwilling to collaborate with the military, he lost the concession. Again Moti helped out by arranging for Abu Ahmad to get a job as a guard in a temporary camp for immigrants being built a kilometer or so to the west of the village. "During the period the camp was being built and for a few months after the new immigrants came, I did guard duty there. I made good money, enough to help my brother, Ibrahim, get married, and to pay for an eye operation for my mother so she didn't go blind" (Gorkin, 1993, pp. 125–135). However, this job too came to an end after about a year, when one of the immigrants, a Jew from Iraq, complained that he should have the job, "not an Arab." For a few months, able to pass himself off as a Jew named Eli since he speaks Hebrew, he made three lirot a day working in construction in Tel Aviv (Arabs made half as much), but he was unhappy at the deception and disliked being away from his family all week. So he went back to Kufr Qara and worked as a day laborer on nearby Jewish settlements for a few years.

Abu Ahmad continues:

After five years of working outside the village, I finally was able to go back to farming here. Not on *my* land—all that was confiscated—but on land that I was given as compensation. It happened like this. During those five years, the Jews had closed off almost all the farmland of the village and didn't let us go there [Article 125 of the Defense (Emergency) Regulations]. And according to this law they passed, [Emergency Regulations (Cultivation of Waste Lands) Ordinance 5709–1949] because the land wasn't in use, they were able to confiscate it and then give it away. . . . Our family's fifty-seven and a half *dunams* were given to Kfar Glickson and to a new kibbutz, Regavim. In 1954, the Jews offered compensation for the land they confiscated, either money or some other land instead. The money they offered was only a fraction of the land's value, and the land they compensated us with—no more than thirty *dunams* per individual family—was the worst farmland in the village. They had taken the best.

Some people in the village refused to take compensation—especially those with large holdings . . . they held out, hoping that someday soon the Jews would be defeated by the Arab armies, and they'd get all their land back. Or, in some cases, they really were just hoping that by holding out, the Jews might give them a better deal. Me, I could see the Jews were here for the foreseeable future, and I figured the deal they were offering right then, even if it wasn't fair, probably was the best we were going to get. . . . Anyway, when they offered my family and my brother's family together some fifty-seven and a half *dunams* of sloping, rocky land—in exchange for our fifty-seven and a half good *dunams*—I saw no point in waiting. I went to the men in the village whose families had owned the land and I said, "This is what the Jews have offered me. Is it your intention to come to terms with them and take back the land?" They said no. "In that case," I told them, "we are going to accept the offer." There were some hard feelings at first, but less than you might think. All of us were in a terrible situation. Hardly anyone got his own fields back. People understood that it was a question of survival and there wasn't much anyone could do about it. (Gorkin, 1993, pp. 125–135)

After six months of hard work, helped by his wife and oldest daughters, Abu Ahmad had turned the rocky fields into usable farmland. He then formed a cooperative with forty other farmers from his own and related clans, and they were able to raise sufficient money to get themselves hooked into the national water system so that they could irrigate their fields. Although travel permits were still required,

they were now issued for periods of six months rather than 15 days, and the farmers were able to take their produce and sell it in the Jewish markets in Tel Aviv and Haifa. "So all in all, life was easier for us—many of us. But for many others, who had lost their lands and got only money in return, or nothing at all, life remained hard. . . . Some of them even wound up working as farm laborers on their own lands, which belonged now to the Jewish settlements" (Gorkin, 1993, pp. 125–135).

During the final years of military government, there were no curfews and travel permits were easier to come by. "But we still had a feeling of being isolated—cut off not from other Palestinians in Israel but from Palestinians and all Arabs outside Israel. It was illegal to get newspapers from Arab countries and many books were banned. It was also illegal to listen to any Arab radio station except the Voice of Israel in Arabic. People did . . . I did. But to do so was to break the law of *my* country." Military rule ended in 1966. Abu Ahmad concludes, " . . . I know there are Jews of goodwill here. It was Moti, after all, who

helped save my village and my family. . . . For this I will always be grateful. But Moti, and people like him, were not able to prevent a lot of things that happened to us during those years. And anyone who lived through il Nakba, and the military government that came after it, learned one thing for sure—as Arabs in Israel, we have reason to be afraid. I am sad to say this, but it is the truth."

Gorkin concludes his book with an acknowledgment of just how much his experiences with Abu Ahmad and his family influenced him. "My contact with the family and the village remains to this day an important part of my life in Israel. . . . I still believe in the need for a Jewish state, but as a result of my experience in the village, I have come to believe just as strongly in the right of a Palestinian Arab state to exist. I am also more aware than ever of the discrimination against Arabs in Israel, and feel more fervently than before the need to eradicate it. . . . Today in Israel/Palestine any political position is difficult to bear" (Gorkin, 1993, afterword).

---

be not only disadvantaged but systematically constrained or exploited by other segments of the population over a substantial period of time. In this sense, the groupings formed in stratified societies perpetuate inequality, and such inequality has little to do with the personal strengths or weaknesses of individuals. This process can be seen most clearly when members of the dominant group in a society discriminate against other ethnic groups. In this country until quite recently, African-Americans and members of other ethnic groups such as Chinese were routinely refused housing in white neighborhoods, enrollment in white schools, and access

to many hotels, restaurants, and other public accommodations. Such restrictions, expressed in terms of ethnic separateness, often serve to maintain preferential access to resources for some members of society at the expense of others.

Also, rapid changes in the social or political structure of a society may cause disadvantaged segments of the society to realize that they have little to lose by organizing to resist exploitation that earlier they took for granted. As Thomas Collins found in his study of the Memphis garbage strike of 1965 (in Cole, 1988, pp. 360–369), African-American workers who had long accepted discrimination in pay and working conditions were suddenly galvanized into resistance. Far from passive, they organized unions and struck when circumstances were suitable.

CASE STUDY:

The Memphis Garbage Strike

TRADITIONALLY, MEMPHIS HAD BEEN THE FIRST stop for rural southern blacks on their way to Chicago and other cities of the North. Most of the migrants came from areas of high unemployment, had little money and minimal education, and consequently were willing to accept any job they could get in Memphis. Those who grew dissatisfied moved north rather than fight to improve conditions. The employment available consisted mainly of menial service jobs, since Memphis was a commercial rather than an industrial city. Garbage collection was one option for blacks, though the pay was only $1.30 an hour at the beginning of the 1960s and job security was nil.

By 1963 union organizing had begun, but Memphis had a long history of crushing municipal workers' unions and it took the garbage workers' union five years to become powerful enough to sustain a strike. In those years, cutbacks in pay and in equipment maintenance created more reasons for dissatisfaction. At the same time, the black middle class had become frustrated by the slow pace of desegregation, and their frustration grew when a hard-line white mayor was elected in 1967. Thus, when the sanitation workers walked off the job over a blatant incident of racial discrimination in February 1968, they had a militant union and a unified black community behind them. Despite intimidation, scab labor, and the use of outright force against them, the workers held out. When the assassination of Dr. Martin Luther King, Jr., focused national attention on the strike, the city had no choice but to capitulate. The Memphis garbage strike marked a major turning point in the history of the civil rights movement.

Collins (1974) concludes that a combination of circumstances contributed to this success. The recent migrants were able to cushion their vulnerability as outsiders by maintaining close supportive ties within their own communities and by organizing groups to press their interests. Moreover, op-

Memphis sanitation worker glances at a litter basket filled to overflowing. About 200 workers marched in downtown Memphis on February 26, 1968, protesting the city's refusal to bargain with a sanitation workers union. The Memphis strike was a turning point in the civil rights movement in the United States.

(UPI/Bettman Archives)

portunities for blacks in the North were decreasing, and as more migrants stayed in Memphis, the motivation to press for change increased. Finally, the workers' success depended a great deal on the support of the black community, particularly of the black middle class. ▶

Systems of Stratification

Class

Although not so contested as the concept of race, the use of the term "class" in the social sciences is the source of controversy and not a little confusion. Class quite simply refers to individuals within a population who share certain characteristics, most particularly with respect to access to prestige, power, and resources. Given that in most complex societies, there are clear lines of inequality, the term is readily applicable to describe such differences. Thus, with respect to both ancient and modern China, one can speak of the ruling class, the military, the peasantry, and so on.

The problem and controversy arises when the concept is applied analytically to explain the persistence of inequality and stratification. We know that there are extremes of poverty and wealth in China; what concerns the anthropologist, among others, is to explain the origins and perpetuation of these extremes. Class as an explanatory tool tends to posit systematic stratification as a result of individuals "reproducing" their place in society in the lives of their children. That is, classes replicate systematic inequality as the children of the disadvantaged stay disadvantaged and those of the advantaged retain their parents' advantages.

The concept of class thus leads one to ask, "How is favored access to prestige, power, and resources maintained across generations? How do people perceive their position in society? How are efforts for advancement thwarted or assisted by the institutions in place in society?" Marxist anthropologists, who stress the importance of class, look at how in a class system many seemingly unrelated aspects of society come together to perpetuate inequality. The fact that industrial workers are paid less than managers might thus be explained as the effort of a managerial class to perpetuate itself. Others might rather explain this inequality as the outcome of competitive forces in the marketplace or the political arena. Wages are seen as simply the market value of an individual's skills. Here we will treat two of the primary forms of class stratification that have implications for systematic inequality.

Social Class. Most modern state societies, including our own, can be viewed as stratified to some degree along lines of social and economic class. The term **social class** is used to describe people who have generally similar educational histories, job opportunities, and social standing. The term often implies some consciousness of membership in a distinctive social group that is ranked in relation to others and is replicated over generations. Associated with each social class in a society is a differential degree of access to status and prestige, and the ability to pass both on to one's children.

Social classes are not cut-and-dried categories. It can be difficult to define the boundaries and differentiate among members of social classes. In fact, few social scientists now consider social or economic class as the only means for describing stratification or inequality in a society. Many would argue that stratification and inequality expressed along ethnic and gender lines are equally important (Smith, 1984). Even though sociologists have identified in American society a number of dimensions of social class membership (power, job prestige, wealth, education, family position, and ethnicity), these variables do not correlate neatly.

An Italian-American building contractor may have a great deal of money and considerable power in local politics but less prestige than a middle-income college professor with a similar background. The daughter of the same contractor may enter a low-paying clerical job while her brother goes into a prestigious law firm. The professor's children may find employment in a trade such as carpentry more to their liking than a profession. Thus such categories as "upper class," "middle class," and "working class" tell us only a little about American society. But at the same time, popular perceptions of such distinctions can be important: individuals spread along a very broad spectrum of occupation, income, and education regard themselves as middle class. Despite the ambiguous nature of class membership, social class is useful as a means of describing some dimensions of social identity and the relative position (real or perceived) of individuals in a stratified society.

Economic Class. Closely related to social class is **economic class**, a grouping that is defined by the economic position of its members in relation to the means of production in the society—the wealth and relative economic control they may exercise. Again there is the presumption that in societies marked by economic class distinctions, each class tends to replicate or perpetuate itself. Thus in a society that includes a class of landless farmers, one would expect most of the children of this group to remain in the same condition. People who form a distinctive economic grouping may or may not also form a social class. In general, social standing, political power, and economic position are closely interrelated.

Economic class is also an analytic construct, but it is perhaps somewhat easier to delineate with

In urban centers, members of different social classes and ethnic groups often find themselves in close proximity, as in this park in La Paz, Bolivia. Proximity, however, does not always mean that people from different backgrounds will mix.

(Ulrike Welsch)

precision than the concept of social class. The concept of economic class is used by the anthropologist or sociologist to describe the way people fit into an economic system. The approach most commonly taken is to see how people relate to the organization of production. Do they sell their labor? Do they control primary resources? Do they control capital and the labor of others? Those who occupy a similar position in the productive system often share political interests—either in maintaining or in changing the economic system. But it may be difficult for members of such economic classes to organize themselves, particularly if they already lack political power. Moreover, it is often the case that people do not clearly perceive their own economic interests.

Perceptions of Class and Class Interest. Most Americans think of themselves as middle class as long they work for a living and do not depend on welfare or inherited money. This distinction among work, wealth, and welfare is very important in shaping one's identity in America, but it obscures important differences; is a corporate executive earning $1,000,000 a year really in the same class

with a housekeeper earning $12,000? (Light & Keller, 1994, p. 218). One sociological analysis of American class structure summarizes it this way (Calhoun, Light, & Keller, 1994, p. 218):

1. The upper class: owners of a great deal of property and of old, established families.

2. The corporate class: individuals with great bureaucratic authority in major corporations; very high salaries and high prestige, moderate amounts of property.

3. The middle class: individuals with high to middle incomes and occupations that give them some prestige; divided into upper-middle- (lesser corporate managers, doctors, lawyers) and lower-middle-class (office workers and salespeople).

4. The working class: consists of people with little or no property, whose jobs give them middle to low incomes and little prestige. The working class is further divided into the skilled and unskilled.

5. The lower class includes those individuals with no property, often unemployed, and no prestige—that is, the poor.

While these and similar pictures of the class structure in America may be more insightful than the popular tendency to lump everyone who is employed into the middle class, it very difficult to define precisely. Much depends on perception. What is meant by "old family," for example? What constitutes "prestige," and how can it be gained or lost? How does wealth relate to prestige? Also, all of these categories are transient. Changes in the stage of life would affect class membership in this scheme. What is not in doubt is that class in the United States is closely tied to economics.

It is doubtful that the various classes of a single society do, in fact, have truly separate value systems. Some Americans who oppose spending public money on improving education and job opportunities for the poor have argued that it is not inequality of opportunity that defeats the poor in the schools and in the job market, but rather a lack of initiative and of a strong work ethic. The evidence, however, is otherwise. Often what may appear to be lack of initiative is actually a realistic appraisal of the chances of success, given the opportunities available. Also, economically deprived people may place a premium on sharing and reciprocity as a survival technique. As a consequence it becomes very difficult for any individual family or person to accumulate enough resources to make drastic changes in lifestyle.

Behind these vaguely differentiated stereotypes, some attitudes cut across class lines. In the United States, for example, materialism and an interest in job security are not the preserve of any one class. Furthermore, any tendency for the so-called upper class to vote the same way or express similar interests is deeply rooted in economic self-interest rather than simply an expression of a value system. More significant than any value system is whether perceptions of social or economic class are translated into social action.

Some societies and some classes are probably more class-conscious than others. Not surprisingly, members of the American upper class find their networks and associations, derived in part from participation in select schools, clubs, and the like, useful in promoting their economic advantages. This advantage is certainly reflected in a self-conscious identification with others who have similar values, backgrounds, and economic interests. But class consciousness can vary with political cur-

rents. Political parties associated with working-class or minority interests draw heavily for support on people whose economic interests are at some remove from those of people who make their living by physical labor.

Caste-stratified Societies

Although social classes may perpetuate themselves, a family can change its class membership, sometimes in a relatively short time, sometimes over the course of generations. **Castes,** on the other hand, resemble a series of ranked ethnic groupings, each closed and each defined by its relative position. Membership in a caste is fixed at birth and usually is unchangeable. An Indian boy born into the Brahman (priestly) caste will always be a member of that caste, whether or not he ever performs a ritual. One must marry endogamously within the caste, and all of one's descendants will be members of the same caste despite changes in wealth, education, or class.

CASE STUDY:

Caste in India

INDIA IS OFTEN CITED AS THE CLASSIC EXAMPLE of a caste society. It should be noted, however, that caste observances are illegal in modern India, where all citizens are presumed to be equal under the law. Nevertheless, de facto caste organization and social distinctions made on this basis are evident in many ways and are often the subjects of bitter social commentary in Indian newspapers, novels, and films.

According to Hindu belief, humankind is divided into four basic categories: Brahmans (priests), Kshatriya (warriors and rulers), Vaishya (tradesmen), and Shudra (servants). The rest of the Hindu community, regarded as outside the overall religious hierarchy, was, until recently, called Harijans (untouchable). These five macro-groups are further subdivided into about 3,000 subcastes: the goldsmiths, the blacksmiths, the potters, the water carriers, the barbers, the shoemakers, the oil pressers, the washermen, and so on. The term often

The lives of many in class or caste-stratified societies are largely spent "on the outside, looking in" in the sense that the resources and rewards of others are visible but unobtainable. This Indian woman, a Harijan, engages in work thought to be "polluting" by other castes.

(The Image Works)

Each jati has its own occupational role and its own status, ranging from the Brahmans at the very top of the hierarchy to the Harijans, who were considered spiritually unclean and whose occupations traditionally reflected this belief. They served society in the most menial of jobs or engaged in activities such as leather working, which were thought to be "polluting." Often such a group is forced to live at the periphery of the community.

In keeping with Hindu belief, the various levels of status are perceived as degrees of ritual purity. Every general category must guard itself against pollution from intimate contact with members of lower categories (Mayer, 1968). The degree of pollution depends on the caste distance between the people involved. Theoretically, anyone who eats with or has sexual intercourse with a member of a lower spiritual category has been polluted and must undergo purification. The code is not simple for the people who follow it closely, but many care little for strict adherence to it.

Discussions of the Indian caste system often focus on these religious rules. But underlying the religious rules is an extremely pragmatic economic system, based on the familiar principle of the "haves" benefiting from the labor of the "have-nots." In most Indian villages the resident jatis are joined in a complex network of rights and obligations, whereby each individual has a predetermined task and a predetermined reward. Ultimately, of course, those who receive the most services are the landowners (often of high caste); in return, they provide those who work the land with a plot on which to build a house and with a yearly allowance of grain. The grain the landowners do not distribute to the other castes is sold. Thus the lower castes may eat, but the higher castes profit. In sum, the religious code serves as a justification for an economic system that is extremely beneficial to the top castes. ◗

used for these occupational subcastes is **jati.** The system of castes, or jatis, has to be understood as it functions in a particular locality, as the organization varies. In Gopalpur village in southern India, Alan Beals (1962) identified about 15 jatis comprising 113 households. The larger region of which Gopalpur is a part has about 50 jatis. Each jati is associated with definite economic, social, and ceremonial roles. While members of the castes of higher rank, such as the Brahmans, tend to be landowners, some are not. Many of the richest villagers are members of middle-ranked castes, and anyone of any caste can be poor.

Castelike Systems. Some theorists claim that India is not only the classic example of a caste society, it is the *only* example—that the caste system has been defined on the model of India and no other society has a comparably rigid system. According to other social scientists, however, caste systems (or at least castelike systems) exist in Polynesia, South Africa,

Japan, Guatemala, and the Arabian Peninsula as well as in India. Indeed, it has been argued that African-Americans in the southern United States formed a caste (Berreman, 1972).

South Africa, until 1994, was an extreme example of a castelike system: blacks were disadvantaged not only by a social position ascribed at birth by reason of their ancestry, but by the laws that prohibited marriage between races and forbade blacks to reside in white towns, or to use the same bathrooms, drinking fountains, and beaches as whites. While the laws have changed and there is a new African-led government in place, the effects of this castelike system are readily apparent. In 1995, Africans still own only 13 percent of the land; the rest is owned primarily by whites. Access to education, employment, and other opportunities is similarly shared unequally among Africans, Coloureds (of mixed ancestry, in South African terms), Indians, and whites.

One thing that characterizes caste distinction, in India and elsewhere, is that the boundaries separating stratified groups are reinforced by ideology: in India by the notion of spiritual cleanliness, in South Africa and even in North America by the notion of racial superiority. Certain minorities (not all, by any means) are subordinated socially, politically, and economically in countries as diverse as Israel, the United States, Rwanda, the Russian Confederation, New Zealand, Japan, and England—to name only a few.

Recently an educational controversy has again raised the issue of caste or castelike social categories in the United States. Educators have long been troubled by the fact that there is a gap of approximately fifteen percentile points between the IQ scores of African-Americans and whites in America. The extent of the gap varies from decade to decade, but it has been observed for the last seventy years (Goleman, 1988, April 10). In a very controversial book, *The Bell Curve: Intelligence and Class Structure in American Life* (1994), psychologists Richard Herrnstein and Charles Murray argue that cognitive ability as measured by IQ scores is genetically inherited and that races vary in their genetic endowment in this regard. They maintain that African-Americans' scores are consistently lower than whites' and that the gap is increasing; the possible result being a large, cognitively disadvantaged underclass. While the main thesis of this book regarding heredity and IQ is hotly disputed, most do accept that the differences in scores exist. Obviously the gap does not apply to all African-Americans, and the scores of those who go on to attend university are virtually indistinguishable from those of whites. The gap is based on the averages of millions of test scores, and there are African-Americans among the highest 1 percent and whites among the very lowest scores. Nevertheless, the gap is significant because IQ scores are good predictors of academic success. The IQ gap has been attributed to everything from the home life of the individuals tested to their heredity. Anthropologists and many other scientists have long believed that the tests themselves are culturally biased and that they reflect the socioeconomic status of the people who devise them. New studies confirm this suspicion. Herrnstein and Murray's book, inadvertently, does support the theory that stratification in the United States is more like a caste system than a class system and that this can be reflected in such things as test scores.

This theory posits that African-Americans and some other minorities—Mexican-Americans, American Indians, native Hawaiians—are in a castelike position similar to that of minority castes elsewhere in the world, such as the Harijan of India and the Maoris of New Zealand. The IQ test scores of these children, too, are approximately ten points lower than those of other children in their countries. John Ogbu, a Nigerian-born anthropologist, contends that this gap is found wherever castelike divisions exist in society (cited in Goleman, 1988, April 10, p. 23). The divisions need not be based on race, but may be based on religion, tribal identity, or ethnicity. Such gaps in IQ scores reflecting caste lines are found in many countries.

Among the social concomitants of belonging to a castelike minority are pervasive prejudice, lack of political and economic power, and the fact of being raised with a very limited set of expectations. Children reared in such an environment of discrimination and poverty have very little prospect of desirable employment and do not see education as making much of a difference. Further, they may have been underweight when born and nutritionally deprived as infants, which can cause retardation.

When members of a subordinate caste move to a country where they do not face discrimination, their IQ scores rise dramatically. George DeVos, an anthropologist, has studied the IQ scores of a Japanese minority caste, the Burakumi, who were traditionally thought to be "unclean" because they worked as tanners. In Japan, their test scores reflected their disadvantaged social and economic position; the gap between the scores of Burakumi and Japanese children was similar to the gap between the scores of African-Americans and whites in the United States. But Burakumi children whose families migrated to the United States achieved scores identical to those of other Japanese-American children (five to eleven points higher than average white scores) (Goleman, 1988, April 10, p. 24).

Slavery

Slavery, until recently, was widespread on every continent and is, in one form or another, not unknown today. While we tend to think of slavery as having been abolished through enlightened legislation, a more important cause was the Industrial Revolution. With industrialization came the need for an educated, skilled work force. Still, slavery has persisted in the twentieth century in the slave labor camps of Nazi Germany and in the gulags of the Soviet Union. A slave is an individual who does not own his or her own labor. In general, slaves can be thought of as belonging to an extremely disadvantaged economic class. The serfs of Czarist Russia prior to 1868 had a status not unlike slaves; they were bound to their masters and to their places of birth and had little control over their own labor. In the instance where people are slaves from birth, with few chances of being granted freedom, they would constitute a caste, as in the days of slavery in the United States. In the American system of slavery, slaves had no rights to marry nor to possess their children. In order to rationalize this brutal practice, an ideology evolved that stressed alleged African inferiority, further emphasizing the castelike nature of Southern society. The legacy of this belief still troubles this country.

Ethnicity, Nationalism, and Conflict

We have discussed ethnicity in terms of social identity, how it may be adapted or changed, and how it can be used for purposes of internal stratification. There is a related dimension to ethnicity, and

that is how people utilize their sense of ethnic identity to mobilize for political action. This is very closely related to **nationalism**, which is the underlying ideology legitimizing most of the world's contemporary states.

While we take the idea of "nation" or "nation state" for granted as the basis for the world political order, the idea of nations is relatively recent. Until World War I, most of the world's peoples lived in multilingual and multicultural empires or kingdoms. Now most live in states that view themselves as having a strong primary, or national, identity with a particular ethnic group. The United States is something of an exception in that the Constitution, legal tradition, and popular feeling recognize that the nation is comprised of people of diverse origins and religions. Many countries, in spite of internal diversity, espouse ideologies proclaiming an ancient unity between a land and its rightful inhabitants, thus forming a nation. The obvious problem with extreme nationalism is that in almost every instance there are competitors for the nation's territory, and within every state there are populations who are marginalized by nationalist ideology. For example, Palestinians are marginalized in Israel, Kurds in Turkey, Turks in Greece and Bulgaria, Albanians in Serbia, Moslems and Sikhs in India—to name a few.

The ideology of nationalism and the nation-state has a vital territorial component, even if, as is usually the case, the actual realization of these territorial limits is perceived as falling short of historical claims. Anderson (1991) devotes considerable attention to the importance of the fact that the nation is seen as having clear, albeit often contested, territorial expression. Sovereignty, threats to sovereignty, or the lamented lack of sovereignty are the daily fare of nationalist discussions.

However, ethnic constructions, following the pioneering formulation of Fredrik Barth (1969), need have no territorial component nor need they be concerned with the perennial problem of nationalism: reconciling who is and who is not included. Ethnic boundaries are, as Barth notes, rooted in individual self-ascription as well as ascription by others (1969), and so are contextual and malleable. Thus, in at least one important respect, it may be inaccurate to speak of ancient ethnic animosities and primordial ethnic hatreds, as, sadly, is so often the case with respect to the Balkans, the Middle East, and Africa.

The effects of nationalism. These refugees were forced from their homes in Bulgaria by a violent anti-Moslem campaign in the 1980s.

(John Reardon/Woodfin Camp & Associates)

Nationalism and Ethnic Conflict

Daniel Moynihan has written that there are

> . . . only eight states on earth today which both existed before 1914 and have not had their form of government changed by violence since then. These are the United Kingdom, four present or former members of the [British] Commonwealth, the United States, Sweden and Switzerland. Of the remaining 170 or so contemporary states, some are too recently created to have known much recent turmoil, but for the greater number that have, far the most frequent factor involved has been ethnic conflict. [1993, pp. 10–11]

Throughout Eastern Europe, the republics of the former U.S.S.R., much of Africa, and South Asia one issue dominates political discussion: the specter of nationalism, politicized ethnicity, and conflict. The bloody aftermath of the dissolution of Yugoslavia into the states of Serbia, Croatia, Bosnia, Slovenia, and Macedonia, together with the war in Bosnia (not to mention the 1994 slaughter in Rwanda of half a million people) give a special poignancy to the problem of ethnic minorities of many countries. These events also raise basic anthropological questions. Is internecine strife inevitable? Can local and national political structures peacefully accommodate ethnic and cultural diversity?

While there can be no definitive answers, we can learn from the past. Ethnic politics should not be equated with ancient, intractable animosities, even though parties to conflicts often try to justify their actions in these terms. In the 1994 Rwandan massacres, the numerically dominant Hutu leaders rationalized their actions by referring to Tutsi oppression in the past—ignoring the fact that both ethnic groups also had a long history of intermarriage and communal peace. Rather, the idiom of ethnicity, like appeals to "nation" or "tribe," becomes operative in specific contexts or environments. What gives shape and continuity to political behavior might be called ideological or moral models, and these often draw on notions that are strikingly similar in tribal, ethnic, and national expressions. They draw upon ties of emotion rooted in beliefs about morality, kinship, family, and history; and they are expressed in recognizable codes and symbols, including language and religion.

Nationalism, like ethnicity, is a persistent social and political force bringing together people for many different purposes, and doing so in the context of many different, competing, or alternative principles of alignment. Benedict Anderson (1991) has described the nation as an "imagined political community" in which a demonstrably shallow history is asserted by members of dominant classes or aspiring elites to have great antiquity; despite apparent linguistic, ethnic, and religious diversity this community is imagined in an idiom of unity and kinship. And as the nation-state is imagined as a shared referent or social identity, ethnic communities likewise are constructed from shared myths, perceived histories, and selectively utilized common experience. In Anderson's view, newspapers and popular literature play key roles in forging this sense of identity.

Politicized Ethnicity as a Response to the State

Vaclav Havel has said that a measure of a state is how it treats its minorities. We might add that how a state treats its minorities is likely to affect its continued existence. There is a close relationship between the uses of nationalistic ideology to justify state politics and ethnic mobilization. Just as nationalism, when enshrined as state ideology, proclaims the eternal unity of a land and a people, assertion of a distinct ethnicity can be a potent response by those whose perceived interests and identities are threatened by this same formulation of nationalism. However, this distinct and shared ethnic identity is often as manufactured as the national identity, but it can have potent mobilizing potential.

Thus, ethnicity must be considered within specific political environments. While we can easily find instances where inter-ethnic conflict occurs in the absence of strong state control, the "genie in the bottle" model, wherein politicized ethnicity suddenly erupts when controls are relaxed, is not particularly helpful for understanding any case. It is, of course, true that appeals to history and assertions of a community rooted in primordial ties are crucial in forging a sense of shared ethnic identity, just as they are vital to "imagining" the nation. Nevertheless this need not imply that the political importance of ethnicity need be continual and forceful, lying just below the surface waiting to emerge when a powerful center weakens. In fact, it often obscures the fact that strong central government control, particularly where accompanied by single-party rule, very often establishes the preconditions for the emergence of politicized ethnicity.

"Nation-building" typically involves processes of centralizing power and authority as well as the creation of modes of political discourse that exclude or marginalize some minorities. But even the fairly heavy-handed imposition of limits to linguistic, religious, and cultural expression need not generate ethnically organized political responses. Quite apart from overt coercion, which may increase the costs of responding, it is not easy for dispersed minorities to come to visualize themselves as a unified community with common interests.

However, forced assimilation that leaves no realistic hope of participating in the nation-state simply fuels the political importance of ethnicity. As noted by Bell (1975) and Horowitz (1985), among others, violent efforts at suppressing or denigrating the symbols and codes of national minorities will likely strengthen minority opposition. This was certainly the case in Bulgaria, as we shall see in the following case study. Often, in a centralized political environment or in the aftermath of a collapsing regime, ethnicity (in the absence of alternative political institutions) becomes a vehicle of last resort for expressing local interests. It is not so much that ethnicity (as a political force) is dormant or suppressed; rather, in some political environments it is not particularly relevant.

Similarly, the economic context influences the appeal of ethnicity. When national-level economic processes are organized around centrally controlled institutions, markets, and regulatory agencies, ethnicity as a means of organizing labor and production may lose its importance. On the other hand, if centrally regulated institutions fail or impinge negatively on local interests, assertions of ethnicity may be a way of responding. Closely related to the growth or importance of central economic institutions is the increase in economic specialization—the division of labor becomes more complex and differentiated. The demand economies introduced by the Communists in many countries represent an extreme form of centralizing economic processes and specialization in division of labor. At the same time, due to the inherent inefficiencies of the centralized system, a pervasive informal sector took over many areas of production, including food production, building, entertainment, and numerous services. One would expect ethnicity to appear as an important organizing principle in the informal sector: ethnicity can form the basis for building trust, forming clandestine networks, and controlling resources. Thus, ethnicity and the growth of the informal sector should be closely linked.

Finally, resources—their nature, abundance, and distribution—affect the nature of ethnic competition and potential for conflict. That is, how the economy performs, how members of society benefit, and how ethnic groups perceive their rewards relative to others both within and outside the country are important.

CASE STUDY:

What's in a Name: Bulgaria's Program of Rebirth

WHILE THE WORLD'S ATTENTION FOCUSED ON the drama of East Berliners being shot crossing the Wall, twice as many Bulgarians were killed while attempting to flee to Greece or Turkey. While in 1989 the world's attention was riveted by the attempts of East Germans to escape westward, in Bulgaria twice as many ethnic Turks were either deported or forced to leave their homeland. Between May and August of that year, over 320,000 Bulgarian Turks either emigrated or were summarily deported to Turkey; in the months prior to May, thousands more, including at least 5,400 Communist Party members, had been deported to Western countries, primarily Austria (Eminov, 1990).

This exodus marked the culmination of a program of forcible ethnic assimilation or expulsion in the name of a monolithic Slavic Bulgarian national identity that had continued intermittently since the creation of Bulgaria in 1878. The primary targets of "ethnic cleansing" were Turkish-speaking Moslems, Bulgarian Moslems, and Gypsies or Roma. Comprising 10 percent of the population, all have lived in Bulgaria for hundreds of years: the Turkish speakers remain from the 500 years of Ottoman Turkish rule in the Balkans, the Bulgarian Moslems are of the substantial local population that converted to Islam, and the Roma entered the region in the Middle Ages. From the outset, Bulgarian nationalism has had to confront a difficult reality. From 1878 until today, the creation of a Christian-Slavic national culture has involved the incorporation or suppression of considerable ethnic, linguistic, and religious diversity.

Around 1971, forced assimilation, referred to as the "Process of Rebirth," became official Party policy, although it is hard to date the implementation of this policy precisely. There is scant documentation of a formal policy decision, nor is there any legislation to this effect (Petkov & Fotev,

The leader of a Turkish civil rights party in Bulgaria stands by the bombed-out ruins of his office, a victim of ethnic strife.
(Daniel Bates)

1990). One can only speculate why this policy was adopted at this time. Bulgarian intellectuals suggest that the regime felt it necessary to secure a broader appeal among the masses by playing the nationalist card. Initially, this was weakly implemented. Beginning with rural areas in fall, 1984, Turkish speakers (including smaller numbers of Gypsies) who had not already done so, were compelled to take Bulgarian names. At the same time, Islamic religious practice and education were curtailed and the public use of the Turkish language prohibited. A campaign in the media, including the publication of purported archaeological and physical anthropological investigations, revealed "evidence" in the form of physical remains, burial customs, icons, articles of dress, etc., proving that all Bulgarians were of one common racial stock and that minorities were simply the product of quite recent forced conversion by the Ottomans. Bulgarian Moslems were depicted in the media as grateful for being allowed to assume Slavic names.

The legal instrument for the name change program was in the form of a petition to the courts signed by the individual, or by a parent on behalf of a minor child. Petitions were characteristically administered in rural areas by teams of bureaucrats, accompanied by police or militia, moving from village to village in a targeted region; in urban areas, the program was carried out in the workplace, or among pensioners when they were to paid. Over

815,000 names were changed. Generally, there was no pretext of voluntary compliance. The teams of bureaucrats would have the requisite forms prepared; if the individual wished to choose a Slavic name, he or she could do so, but in some instances would be required to choose again if the selected name was later seen to have close similarities to Islamic ones or had some political significance. The new names selected by individuals tended to bear maximum phonemic, syllabic, or lexical affinity with the original Turkic-Arabic name (Konstantinov, 1992, p. 78). If the individual did not cooperate, names would be arbitrarily assigned and the individual forced to sign the petition. Furthermore, all documents containing the old names had to be altered: identity cards, housing records, deeds, death certificates, grave markers, etc.—in short, anything that gave evidence of the existence of a minority population was eliminated. The name change measures were enforced at gunpoint, or by withholding pay, pensions, housing, health services, and ultimately by imprisonment and/or exile.

The 1984–85 program of forced assimilation, through its drastic intervention at the individual, psychological level, heightened Turkish and Moslem self-awareness and reemphasized the importance of kinship and communal ties. This brought both religious and linguistic distinctions into sharper relief, since these were the only remaining tangible symbols of cultural identity. To a great extent, the Moslem population had accepted socialist ideology and goals, but now the government and Communist Party lost their legitimacy (as they did, too, among Bulgarian intellectuals). The campaign created a national consensus among Moslems of all backgrounds that they had no future in a socialist Bulgaria. It was at this juncture that Bulgarian Moslems and others began to identify themselves with the larger Turkish community, and, where they could, to study Turkish (Konstantinov, Gulbrand, & Igla, 1991). The strength of this newly created sense of unity became evident in the massive protests of 1989, culminating in the exodus of refugees. Subsequent to the collapse of Communism in Bulgaria, ethnic Turks have formed a political party, participate peacefully in national politics and have representatives in parliament, showing that short of genocide, even the most oppressive ethnic policies can be reversed. Contemporary Bulgaria is, in many respects, an example showing that ethnic diversity can be accommodated within a strongly nationalistic society. The rights of minorities to use their own languages, practice their religious beliefs and, importantly, pass on their traditions to their children have been recognized. ▶

Ethnic Terrorism

Collective identity and organization using the idiom of ethnicity require a perceived interest in common as well as an emotional bond (Bell, 1975, p. 169). Terror and oppression can supply this. Mischa Glenny's (1992) insightful account of the origins of the conflicts in the former Yugoslavia vividly demonstrates how, beneath the swirl of changing loyalties and alignments, individual underemployed military officers, warlords, and would-be leaders use the rhetoric of ethnic rivalries to attract followers and gain power. Then they use terrorism and fear to promote their interests, using perceived ethnic rivalries as their justification.

The same can be said for Rwanda: ethnic terrorism was initiated by then government leaders in order to consolidate their power, which was threatened by an agreement to bring opposition leaders into government. Leaders who engage in terrorist acts sometimes achieve or maintain power they might otherwise not have. In Liberia, it is widely reported that terror in the form of ritual killings, cannibalism, and torture is often used systematically by one group to shock villagers of another tribe and force them to abandon their homes, an act of "ethnic cleansing" (Goldberg, 1995, p. 38). This was the case also in Croatia and Bosnia, where rape, murder, and torture were used to achieve the expulsion of targeted peoples (Denich, 1994, p. 370 ff). Furthermore, political leaders use terror to recruit followers: once atrocities have been carried out, even those opposed to such acts fear retribution and join the conflict.

Whether the ethnnic conflicts arise in response to a repressive national ideology or as a result of warring factions in a weakened state, it is clear that while ethnic identity can be an effective rallying cry, it is rarely the root cause of a conflict. Specific conflicts, on examination, have very specific causes that have little to do with ethnicity. However much the rhetoric of kinship, community, and culture is evoked, a look to the past will almost invariably reveal quite different patterns of alignment and notions of community boundaries.

In Liberia, Rwanda, and Burundi millions of people have been killed or made stateless by ethnic conflict. These soldiers belong to one of many competing militias in Liberia.

(AP/Wide World Photos)

Summary

THIS CHAPTER HAS DEALT WITH THE INTERRELATED topics of race, ethnicity, and nationalism. Very frequently these social constructs do more than simply serve as a frame of reference for individuals—they often structure access to resources and political participation and thereby underlie social stratification. Within societies, people constitute themselves in an array of groups, each having a distinctive identity and claim on its members. From household to nation, these identities and claims are reflected in a pervasive "we-they" dichotomy. Societies at all levels of technology place a heavy emphasis on their uniqueness vis-à-vis outsiders; xenophobia (the fear of foreigners) is a global phenomenon.

Personal social identity is formed in the crucible of family life as the growing child experiences the behavior, attitudes, and values of those around it, especially parents, older siblings, grandparents, etc. Even very small aggregates of people tend to arrange themselves in groups set apart from the rest in a collective identity for some purposes.

All societies are formed by the integration of smaller groups or subsets of the whole, whether the smaller entities are households, lineages, political parties, labor unions, or other groups. The great nineteenth-century French sociologist Émile Durkheim (1964) referred to this process as the social division of labor. One form of society is built up of similar parts; for example, societies in which all of the social units are comparable (households, lineages, or other descent groups). Every member of the society (of the same sex and age category) belongs to the same sorts of social groups as does every other member. This form of organization, which exhibits mechanical solidarity, is exemplified by the egalitarian social organization of the Ariaal of Kenya.

The second form of social organization is more complex: society is built up from dissimilar, specialized social groupings. No individual can participate in all of them but each participates in at least some. Durkheim characterized this sort of society as exhibiting organic solidarity because it resembles the structure of a living organism, constructed from numerous but specialized parts, each with a separate function.

The way we classify people greatly influences the way we behave toward them and the way we expect them to behave. A social category is composed of all people who share certain culturally identified characteristics. We are also using a system of categories when we refer to people according to their age, sex (or, more accurately, gender), and family status—not to mention such categories as social class, race, and ethnicity. In other words, social categories often establish boundaries to our personal networks. Social categories are not groups or even networks, but such distinctions can and do supply the basis for the formation of groups and influence access to resources and power.

Some criteria that define social categories are universal; others are not. Gender identity is a universal, although the social ramifications of gender have only recently come to be intensively studied. Gender distinctions are often reflected in how children are socialized, how work is organized and rewarded, and in access to political power and control over resources. In the case of politically more complex societies that bring together local populations of different ancestral or historical antecedents, race and ethnicity are particularly important criteria. Of the two, race has various and contradictory meanings; many social scientists prefer not to use the term at all, using the term "ethnicity" instead.

The term "race" has different meanings when used as a biological concept as opposed to a social one. A biological race is a population sharing a distinctive genetic makeup derived from a common gene pool; that is, a biological subgrouping of a species. The visual means for categorizing such as race is in terms of its phenotypic characteristics; that is, the physiological manifestations of genetic differences: skin color, eye color, hair form, etc. The main problem lies in the fact that it is hard to agree on what "distinctive" means, and, importantly, most genetic variation within a species is not apparent except at the molecular level—hence of little use. Since every individual differs genetically from all others, what constitutes a biological race is arbitrary. Given the arbitrary nature of this biological classification, it is entirely unwarranted to relate such groupings to any aspect of social or learned behavior. Learned behavior is not inherited; it is acquired, and thus is not a characteristic of biological race.

When race is used to describe social or cultural groupings we might term this usage "social race," and most social scientists discourage this usage. Racial categories such as white, black, African-American, etc. do not refer to biological groupings; after all, most African-Americans, for example, carry a significant portion of their genes from white ancestors. Whites, in turn, have received their genes from very diverse ancestral gene pools. What appear to be phenotypic or physical indicators of distinctive ancestry are, in practice, simply clues to social identity—and often incorrect ones.

Closely related to social constructions of race is the practice using these criteria for invidious comparisons or distinctions. Racism is the acting on the belief that races are biologically unequal in terms of their ability to acquire culture; or, more broadly, behaving as though races have unique behavioral propensities and can be ranked. Use of racist appellations can be part of ideologies that maintain social and economic inequality.

A more useful way of describing social identity is in terms of ethnicity since this term, in current usage, has no biological connotations. Ethnicity refers to a social or group identity that the individual ascribes to himself or herself and that is also accepted by others. Ethnicity is a basis for categories that are rooted in socially perceived differences in origin, language, and/or religion. In many respects, ethnicity resembles descent ideology: it stresses one's origins or descent as part of one's social identity and is usually ascribed at birth. References to race, as in racial equality or racial discrimination, are in fact usually references to ethnicity. Because ethnic categories are culturally defined, they can be manipulated and changed. The definition of an individual's ethnicity can change with his or her situation.

When ethnic differences are expressed in economic deprivation or monopoly of a resource, they do not generally promote harmonious relations. Relations between members of different ethnic groupings within a nation-state are frequently characterized by conflict. Even societies that pride themselves on democratic access to political power, such as the United States and Great Britain, are not immune to such conflict. A society in which extensive subpopulations are accorded differential treatment is said to be stratified.

A common, if deplorable, feature of polyethnic societies is the use of ethnic categories to restrict access to resources or full participation in political decision making. If racial or ethnic groupings are ranked in a society, it is often referred to as *stratified*. This process can be seen most clearly when members of the dominant group in a society discriminate against other ethnic groups.

In this sense, the groupings formed in stratified societies perpetuate inequality, and such inequality has little to do with the personal strengths or weaknesses of individuals. We can understand this phenomenon better if we concentrate on three concepts that describe stratification: class, caste, and slavery. Most modern state societies, including our own, can be viewed as stratified to some degree along lines of social and economic class. The term "social class" is used to describe people who have generally similar educational and social histories, job opportunities, and social standing. Related to social class is economic class, a group that is defined by the economic position of its members in relation to the means of production in the society—the wealth and relative economic control they may exercise. Again there is the presumption that in societies marked by economic class distinctions, each class tends to replicate or perpetuate itself.

Although social classes may perpetuate themselves, a family can change its class membership. Castes, on the other hand, resemble a series of ranked ethnic groupings, each closed and each defined by its relative position. Membership in a caste is fixed at birth and usually is unchangeable. An Indian boy born into the Brahman (priestly) caste will always be a member of that caste, whether or not he ever performs a ritual. One must marry endogamously within the caste, and all of one's descendants will be members of the same caste despite changes in wealth, education, and class.

Slavery, until recently, was widespread on every continent and is, in one form or another, not unknown today. A slave is an individual who does not own his or her own labor and as such can thought of as belonging to an economic class. When people are slaves from birth, with few chances for manumission (being granted freedom), slaves would constitute a caste, as in the days of slavery in the United States.

Ethnicity is more than passive social identity; all over the world we see people mobilized for political action along ethnic lines, and most of today's conflicts have ethnic expressions. This is very closely related to nationalism, which is the underlying ideology legitimizing most of the world's contemporary states.

Ethnic politics should not be equated with ancient, intractable animosities, even though parties to conflicts often try to justify their actions in these terms. What gives shape and continuity to political behavior might be called ideological or moral models, and these often draw on notions that are strikingly similar in tribal, ethnic, and national expressions. These models are based on ties of emotion rooted in beliefs about morality, kinship, family, and history; and they are expressed in recognizable codes and symbols, including language and religion. Nationalism, like ethnicity, is a persistent social and political force bringing together people for many different purposes, and doing so in the context of many different, competing, or alternative principles of alignment. Benedict Anderson (1991) has described the nation as an "imagined political community."

There is a close relationship between the uses of nationalistic ideology to justify state politics and ethnic political mobilization. Just as nationalism, when enshrined as state ideology, proclaims the eternal unity of a land and a people, assertion of a distinct ethnicity can be a potent response by those whose perceived interests and identities are threatened by this same formulation of nationalism.

Key Terms

biological race	nationalism
caste	organic solidarity
economic class	phenotype
ethnicity	racism
gender hierarchies	slave
genotype	social category
jati	social class
mechanical solidarity	social division of labor

Suggested Readings

Chen-Shui, H. (1992). *Chinatown no more: Taiwan immigrants in contemporary New York*. Anthropology of Contemporary Issues, Ithaca and London: Cornell University Press. Chen's ethnography, from the perspective of an observer as well as a participant, gives an informative view of a Taiwanese community in Flushing/Queens, their ethnic relations, and their adaptation to American society.

Gill, L. (1994). *Precarious dependencies: Gender, class and domestic class in Bolivia*. New York: Columbia University Press. A discussion of gender, ethnicity, and changing power relations through a look at female Bolivian domestic duty over a period of sixty years.

Gordon, R. J. (1992). *The Bushman myth: The making of a Namibian underclass*. (Conflict and Change Series), S. Whiteford & W. Derman (Eds.). Boulder and Oxford: Westview Press. An interesting ethnohistorical work examining colonialism in Namibia. Articles show how "Bushmen," speaking different languages, having different histories and physical characteristics, have been lumped into one ethnic group and how studies have failed to focus on those Bushmen who have essentially become serfs.

Hill, H. & Jones, J. E., Jr. (Eds.). (1993). *Race in America: The struggle for equality*. Madison: University of Wisconsin Press. An impressive collection of essays dealing with race relations in the U.S., giving a historical perspective as well as the present status and possibilities for the future that is confronting American society.

Peshkin, A. (1991). *The color of strangers, the color of friends: The play of ethnicity in school and community*. Chicago: University of Chicago Press. A detailed ethnography, including student and teacher accounts of interaction in a multicultural public high school.

Sider, G. M. (1993). Lumbee Indian histories: Race, ethnicity and Indian identity in the southern United States. In *Culture and class in anthropology and history*, vol. 2. Cambridge and New York: Cambridge University Press. This book gives an interesting analysis of how Indians have fitted into the broader U.S. political economy as well as offering a controversial analysis of Indian cultural history.

Van der Veer, P. (1994). *Religious nationalism: Hindus and Muslims in India*. Berkeley: University of California Press. An interdisciplinary study of religion and politics in India, showing how Indian religious identity has been shaped.

Yoshino, K. (1995). *Cultural nationalism in contemporary Japan*. New York: Routledge. By examining how ideas of cultural uniqueness are formed in Japan, this book also tests general theories of ethnicity and nationalism.

Concepts of Economic Behavior

Diversity in the Organization of
Economies

Regulating Access to Resources
   Property Rights
   Ownership versus Use Landholding
      Systems
   Private Ownership and Commercial
      Farming
   *State of the Peoples: The Ecology of a
   Peasant Revolt*
   Case Study: Where the Dove Calls
   The Control of Capital Goods

Production
   The Organization of Production
   Productive Strategies
   Labor, Gender, and Productivity in
      the Household
   *Case Study: The Productive Labor of
   Gainj Women*

The Exchange of Resources
   Mechanisms of Exchange
   Case Study: The Kula Ring
   The Organization of Exchange
   *Gender Issues: Money Makes
   Us Relatives*

Economic Experimentation and
Adaptation
   *Human Ecology:
   Over the Mountains
   Are Mountains*

Summary
Key Terms
Suggested Readings

Chapter 10

Economics:
Resources, Production, and Exchange

conomics is a means of studying some of the material aspects of adaptation. Economics, in its simplest definition, is the study of the way people use certain means—time, money, or even social skills—to obtain desired resources. In this broad sense, all societies have an economy and virtually every human activity has economic implications. The Ariaal man in Kenya who gives a member of his age grade a cow, accepts no payment, but knows that he has gained future rights in his friend's herd, has engaged in an economic transaction with the expectation of a delayed return on his investment. He has also secured his perishable capital by moving it away from his main herd. The New York City stockbroker, buying and selling shares in unseen companies all over the world, is engaging in very similar economic transactions of a less personalized nature.

A society's *economic system* may be defined as the ideas and institutions that people draw upon and the behaviors in which they engage in order to secure resources to satisfy their needs and desires. An economic system, then, has the basic components of ideas, patterns of behavior, and special-purpose institutions.

Anthropology contributes to the study of economics by offering a perspective that looks beyond impersonalized, monetarized transactions to the culturally varied and often emotionally charged means by which people acquire critical resources. The anthropological approach stresses the cultural or social context in which people operate and the importance of social or kinship relationships in the shaping of economic behavior. To the Western economist, the fact that a man may sell his car to his brother-in-law for less money than a stranger would pay is of little consequence in terms of the millions of cars sold each year. But when one deals with a relatively small population, as anthropologists frequently do, transactions involving relatives or socially close individuals are the norm, not the exception. And, as we shall see, social relationships in every society affect what we might think of as straightforward material exchanges.

Whether economic activities occur at the level of the household or on a global scale all involve three basic processes:

1. **Regulation of access to resources**—control over the use of land, water, and raw materials.
2. **Production**—the conversion of natural resources to usable forms.
3. **Exchange**—the distribution of goods and services among the members of the society.

A population's strategy for securing and using a resource is generally based on some assurance of continued access to the resource. Thus, access to resources and the rights by which individuals and groups hold resources is the first process. The second is the nature and organization of production. Resources are rarely used exactly as they are found in nature; they are transformed through processes of production. Finally, goods, services, or resources are, by necessity, exchanged or redistributed by various means among individuals. Despite intersocietal variations, these processes occur in all cultures and will be the focus of discussion in much of this chapter. However, before exploring these processes, we must first understand some basic economic concepts.

Concepts of Economic Behavior

The study of economic processes lies at the heart of social science research and has generated considerable controversy. At the end of the eighteenth century, Adam Smith, the founder of the discipline of economics, posed a question fundamental to the social sciences: How is it that the independent actions of people made without reference to one another result in orderly patterns or processes? Why does not chaos reign as people pursue their separate interests? The answer, Adam Smith suggests, is that if people have free will and if they act rationally, chaos will not erupt because people will be making similar decisions under similar circumstances; the result will be orderly patterns. In a society with a "perfect market" (a purely hypothetical possibility, as we shall explain shortly), it is expected that prices of goods will follow orderly patterns directly related to supply and demand as a consequence of many choices made by many people acting rationally to maximize gains and minimize costs. A central concept in this approach is that of **scarce resources**: people inevitably have many more wants than they have resources to satisfy them. Therefore they must make **rational economic decisions**, weighing the available alternatives and deciding which will benefit them the most at the least cost. In short, classical economic theory views individual rational behavior as the driving force behind all economic dealings.

This assumption of individual free will and rational, self-interested decision making is not universally accepted. Social scientists of the nineteenth century, including Karl Marx and Émile Durkheim, argued that society imposes its own rationality on people and that social and economic institutions perpetuate themselves regardless of the needs of the individuals concerned. The economy is seen as the process by which a society is provisioned, each society using its own (and sometimes unique) institutions. This view does not assume individual rationality and choice; instead, one looks to the way institutions, whether explicitly economic or not, serve the material needs of society. Different societies, it is argued, may have quite different economic structures, and individuals will behave in ways that the classical assumptions cannot predict.

Proponents of this view note that most economic theory is rooted in industrial capitalism, and its basic concepts—capital goods, surplus, the profit motive, the allocation of scarce resources—are abstractions developed in the effort to study that system. They suggest that these concepts are not very useful in efforts to study the economic systems of people who are not involved in market or capitalist economies. This school of economic anthropology is called **substantivism**. According to the substantivists, analyzing nonindustrial societies according to the concepts of Western economics is misleading: it would wrongly attribute motivations, such as the profit motive, to these people. Substantivists propose to develop theories that will enable them to understand economic processes as the maintenance of an entire social or cultural order. Individual decision making and choice, which are of primary concern in classical economic theory, are of secondary concern in substantivist studies.

Other anthropologists, drawing on mainstream economic theory in the tradition of Adam Smith as well as upon contemporary models of risk minimization and game theory, argue that if the concepts of formal economic theory are broadened, they can serve as analytic tools for the study of economic systems quite unlike those of market-structured societies. This approach is sometimes called **formalism**. The fact that individuals in a nonmarket society do not pursue profits in an immediate material sense, the formalists argue, does not mean that the concept of profit is irrelevant to their behavior. In the broadest sense, profit is the maximizing of something scarce or limited, which need not be money or even a material possession. If in their economic transactions people are looking for profit in terms of prestige or establishing a social network, they are seeking to maximize some perceived advantage. People everywhere, formalists argue, direct their behavior toward maximizing scarce ends; that is, toward benefiting themselves, however this benefit may be measured.

As Harold Schneider (1974) has noted, in many African societies cattle are capital goods, savings, and consumer goods all in one. They are capital goods in the sense that they produce calves, milk, and manure; savings in the sense that they are a means of keeping and accumulating wealth; and consumer goods in that ultimately they are eaten

and their hides used. They are also, as we have seen with the Ariaal, a primary social institution in many instances. These observations suggest to Schneider and others that there is a universality to human economic behavior. Studies in this vein stress individual variation and diversity in the making of choices, entrepreneurship, individual strategies, and their attendant costs and benefits.

This is not to say that people are assumed to operate on the basis of what is immediately gainful or gratifying. Herbert Simon, for example, suggests that rationality in economic decision making is not necessarily getting the most for the least, but simply the "selection of preferred behavior alternatives in terms of some system of values whereby the consequences of behavior can be evaluated" (1966, pp. 75–76). Thus if the desire for prestige or the need for good relationships with kin is considered more important than immediate material gain, one might rationally ignore material profits and seek to obtain only what one needs, giving away the rest or perhaps even ostentatiously wasting it.

For example, Lesotho pastoralists whose major source of income is from work as migrant laborers in South African mines prefer to convert their cash into cattle rather than vice versa (Ferguson in Barfield, 1993, p. 52). In fact, they are buying so many cattle that Lesotho, traditionally a cattle-producing region, has become a net importer of cattle. Nor do these pastoralists regard the cattle as merely insurance against disaster, for they refuse to sell them during periods of drought even when it is obvious that many will die. Only owning cattle can make a man both rich and respectable. By investing in cattle, men who are away from home for long periods can maintain their social networks and at the same time demonstrate that no matter how long their absence, they will eventually return.

As the economist Kenneth Boulding (1961) has pointed out, even in market economies people do not reevaluate their economic practices in terms of profitability every day. Rather, they tend to keep doing what they have been doing in the past unless they have some reason for dissatisfaction. According to Boulding, this practice—and not the effort to maximize short-term advantage—is the essence of economic rationality.

Finally, the rationality of economic decisions must be considered in relation to the situation of the person making the decision. As Scott Cook has pointed out, "tribesmen and peasants do not always choose the best or least costly alternative [that] is possible under the circumstances" (1966, p. 844). Such choices may seem irrational to outside observers, but only because they are unaware of the specific situation. In many respects this resembles the evolutionary paradigm (Chapter 3), which looks at how individuals make decisions and pursue strategies in terms of the often competing demands thrown at them by the environment: to pursue game at the expense of foraging, to pursue high-value food but at individual risk to life and limb (Smith & Winterhalter, 1992, p. 53). Individuals must continually balance such competing rewards and potential risks; they rarely go simply for the greatest possible reward, but choose a mixed result that weighs gains against costs and risks. Once circumstances are taken into account, seemingly poor economic decisions may appear more logical. Economic anthropologists believe that people in nonliterate societies are as rational in their economic behavior as are people in complex industrial societies, and that if they appear irrational, the fault lies either in an ethnocentric definition of rationality or in the observer's ignorance of the circumstances.

As we have seen in our discussion of the difficulties currently faced by Ariaal pastoralists in Kenya, governments tend to view traditional pastoralism as viable only if the object is to produce for a market by culling the maximum number of cattle for slaughter (Barfield, 1993). What governments regard as wastage—that is, keeping cattle long after it would be profitable to sell them—makes perfect sense to pastoralists since the cattle simultaneously serve so many different needs, from providing subsistence to meeting social obligations and as insurance against disaster. Especially where national economies cannot guarantee that in times of scarcity needed goods will be available for purchase with the money derived from the sale of cattle, the social advantages of lending cattle to bond friends can far outweigh the economic advantages of selling them (Barfield, 1993, p. 52). And it is far from clear that as pastoralists become increasingly integrated into the cash economy, they will eventually treat cattle-raising strictly as a way to make money.

Diversity in the Organization of Economies

In the actual measures it employs, Western economic theory assumes the existence of specialized economic institutions that exist purely for the sake of mobilizing resources. It assumes further that these institutions will be "subspecialized"—that is, each will control a separate aspect of economic life. In our own society, these assumptions are reasonably valid. We have stores for buying and selling, banks for lending and storing money, and so forth. And these institutions are, for the most part, exclusively economic. But in nonindustrial or nonmarket societies, we often find not only that many economic functions have been lumped together in one institution, but also that this institution serves many purposes other than economic ones. In many societies, for example, the household is the unit of production and the center of economic life as well as the focal point of religious activities, politics, kin organization, socialization, and numerous other functions, all intermingled. The economic institutions of people living in nonmarket societies are embedded in the social structure, so that it is almost impossible to separate what is economic from what is not.

Even when we consider market-structured economies, the economic institutions within them may be very different. If we need money for a major expense, we borrow it from a bank and then pay it back gradually. In many other societies, this function may be performed by rotating credit associations, rather like our credit unions. These are groups of perhaps ten individuals who meet regularly and contribute a fixed amount of their earnings to the group's "pot." At established intervals, the pot is turned over to one of the members for his or her exclusive use. A new pot is then accumulated and it is turned over to another member.

In Cameroon, West Africa, just such an informal credit system, the **tontine**, exists side by side with the banks. The classical tontine is a financial arrangement in which participants contribute an equal amount and the entire sum goes to the one who survives the others. In the Cameroon variant, participants contribute an agreed-upon sum each month and then periodically loan it to one of the members. A recent innovation in Cameroon is the interest-bearing tontine: members not only borrow but receive interest on their contributions (Brooke, 1987). Variants of tontines are found throughout the world and are vital means by which people pool resources so that members of the group can buy consumer items, make home improvements, or even get the capital to open a business. Tontines work because of social pressure; people who might default on a bank loan will rarely let their friends down. Should they do so, they not only would face social disgrace but could never join another tontine. As James Brooke notes (1987), tontines are built on trust, and their participants generally are people of the same neighborhood and ethnic background.

In Bali, Indonesia, according to J. Stephen Lansing (1991), an elaborate network of temples dedicated to water goddesses is controlled by priests who regulate and coordinate the irrigation of fields belonging to thousands of farmers. In the 1970s in an effort to modernize farming the government encouraged farmers to irrigate their fields according to whatever schedule they judged would increase their rice production. As a consequence, fields were irrigated according to individual farmers' timetables and unexpectedly this provoked an ecological crisis that resulted in a massive decline in overall yields. When farmers planted and irrigated on their own schedules, pests that were formerly controlled by the coordinated flooding dictated by the temples simply moved from field to field. Coordinated irrigation turned out to be a vital means of crop cycling and pest control. In this case we see a traditional religious institution playing a critical role in resource management. Stephen Lansing, an anthropologist, was instrumental in making government planners aware of the value of this supposedly non-economic and anachronistic cultural system.

Even when the economic institutions of two societies superficially resemble each other, they may in fact be organized very differently. Every country has markets today, yet markets are by no means uniform everywhere. In some places people of neighboring villages who specialize in certain kinds of production regularly congregate in a central market town to exchange their surpluses for necessities produced by other villages—potters buy baskets, basketmakers buy rice, and so forth. In such markets the **interlocking specializations** keep the producers in a state of mutual interdependence; the potters, for example, must continue making pots in order to procure the baskets they need. In other markets, ties are looser. Producers may haggle with one another, and if they do not like the proposed deal, they can go elsewhere; there is no sense of inescapable dependence.

Markets may also vary in the degree to which non-economic dealings are combined with economic ones. Buyers and sellers in the Grain Exchange in Chicago are there only to buy and sell. But in peasant societies, farmers come to market not only to exchange their goods but also to perform a variety of other functions: to see the doctor, to have their children baptized, to arrange marriages for their older children, to vote, to attend meetings, and of course to socialize with relatives and friends (Cook, 1966). This social exchange, not to mention the acquisition of critical information and political news, is inseparable from the actual marketing processes.

Regulating Access to Resources

In order to secure resources, a group must have some assurance of continued access to an area where resources are located. They can do so by establishing a territory and restricting its use to members of the group. People define and regulate access to productive resources in a variety of ways; the way chosen depends on the nature of the resources and the means available to control and use them. In many respects, this aspect of economic behavior overlaps what is usually thought of as political organization.

Property Rights

Most agricultural and industrial societies maintain clear-cut rules that define rights to productive land and other resources. Among most hunting-and-gathering societies, an individual's rights to use resources are virtually unrestricted. Hunters and gatherers such as the Eskimo and the Dobe !Kung must be able to move according to the seasonal availability of resources; otherwise, they might starve when normal fluctuations in climate depleted the local water supply or altered the distribution of wild animals or plants. The more uncertain or mobile the food supply, the greater the need for flexible boundaries and collective rights of access.

The extent to which people define and defend a territory also depends on the gains versus the costs of maintaining exclusive rights. A group that stakes out and defends its own territory retains the resource supply in that territory. But to guard a territory requires time and energy that might be spent in other activities. It also involves risk; one can be killed defending a boundary. Finally, reliance on a restricted area for resources may be disadvantageous, as it would be for hunter-gatherers. To the degree that costs outweigh the gains, territoriality will be relaxed. To the degree that the gains outweigh the costs, territoriality will be strictly observed. Thus while hunters and gatherers have territories to which groups lay primary claim and stake out possession of strategic resources such as wells or rich stands of vegetable foods, they do not necessarily defend the boundaries as vigorously as farmers defend their fields (Dyson-Hudson & Smith, 1978). Generally, permission is readily granted to outsiders to visit wells or traverse territories.

The gains-cost formula is well illustrated by the pastoral Pokot of East Africa, a population closely resembling the Ariaal (Chapter 6). The Pokot's sorghum fields are critical to their survival and they are relatively easy to defend, for they are small and located near the people's houses. The fields are carefully guarded against both intruding animals and human thieves. The pastureland on which the Pokot graze their cattle is almost impossible to defend, and it would be unwise to try to defend it. It covers too large an area, and the water resources and the quality of grass vary seasonally in any one area. A well-defended patch of brown grass with dry water holes would benefit no one. The Pokot therefore exercise far less control over grazing land than over fields and farmland.

Maintaining control over a territory, whether loosely or strictly, is only the first step in regulating access to resources. Every society has principles that govern who may use which resources and under what circumstances. One important principle observed in our own society is that of private ownership of property, or **freehold**. Americans regard land, water, minerals, machinery, and all types of productive resources as things that someone can own. Owners, whether individuals or corporations, decide who has access to their resources and when. They may exploit them in any way they wish; they may also rent or sell them.

Of course, even capitalist economies recognize that the concept of private property has limits. Systems that provide essential resources, such as transportation and electricity, are often considered public utilities and are heavily regulated, sometimes even owned outright by the government. Zoning laws further define actual use of private property. And social constraints may restrict the way one disposes of it. Few urban neighborhoods in the United States allow one to keep chickens in the backyard, although not too long ago this practice was widespread. At the same time, effective ownership may depend on active use: in many European and American cities, squatters have taken over buildings that the owners have left unoccupied. In many less-developed countries, entire sections of major cities are given over to illegal shantytowns formed by rural settlers who simply erect rough dwellings on vacant land, without municipal approval or title to the land. In Turkey, for example, such settlements are called *gecekondu*, or "built in the night." Taking advantage of a customary law that prohibits the destruction of one's

This collective farm in Bulgaria collapsed along with the Communist regime in 1990. It has proved very difficult for collectivized farmers to take up private farming; they lack most equipment formerly supplied by the state.

(Daniel Bates)

domicile, poor people rapidly put up a house and dare the authorities to evict them.

In many nonindustrial societies, groups rather than individuals control the land and other productive resources, along with the equipment necessary for production. The individual gains rights to these resources only by virtue of affiliation with a group. We can see this form of **corporate ownership** best by looking at the way such groups control land.

Ownership versus Use Landholding Systems

In traditional societies that do not recognize individual ownership of land, the kin group or the community at large either is the landholder, or at least has a great deal to say about who uses what resources. Individuals or households may have the right to use these resources for limited periods, but they do not own them—they can neither buy nor sell the land they farm. Such kin-group or community landholding rights are often termed "corporate" rights, as we noted in Chapter 8.

Thus while people in most industrial countries acquire land and the resources on it through inheritance, purchase, or rental, people in most non-state societies gain their right to land as a birthright or through marriage to a member of a landowning group. As a member of a band, for example, a Dobe Ju/'hoansi (!Kung) man or woman automatically has the right to hunt and collect wild foods within the area used by that band. The !Kung say it does not matter who owns the land itself, since one cannot eat the ground. Rather, each band collectively holds the right to exploit specific water resources and patches of wild plant foods (Marshall, 1965). With few exceptions, pastoral peoples follow the same rule. Grazing lands are generally treated as a communal asset, open to all members of the tribe, or at least to all members of the large and cooperating kin groups that typically migrate and settle together.

Horticulturists, on the other hand, are generally concerned with allocating rights to use specific plots, for they invest a great deal of time and labor in these plots. Like hunter-gatherers and pastoralists, they acquire rights to land by virtue of group membership, but in order to retain the right to a particular plot, one must actively use it. Among the

A contemporary Turkmen landowner. Each year he employs dozens of migrant workers on his cotton fields.

(Daniel Bates)

Tiv of Nigeria, for example, the head of the household is allowed to cultivate any unused piece of land within a territory belonging to his lineage. He may lay claim to as much land as his household can handle. So long as the household actively works these fields and keeps them clear, the members are entitled to their exclusive use. When fields revert to fallow, however, rights lapse and the land becomes part of the public domain, to be claimed by other families in the lineage. Nevertheless, a Tiv man always retains the right to some land—if not to one particular field, then to another—simply because he is a member of a certain kin group (Bohannan, 1960). In other horticultural societies, rights of use may be acquired simply through residence in the village or through the performance of some social obligation, but again the land must be cultivated if those rights are to remain in force.

As with hunter-gatherers and pastoralists, collective as opposed to private ownership of land may be critical to a horticultural group's way of making a living. Consider the Western Pueblo, discussed in Chapter 8, who must plant their crops in a variety of settings in order to ensure that some will survive. Each clan owns some land in several microenvironments—some on the gully floor, some at the base of the hill, and so forth. If these properties were owned by individuals rather than by the clan, and were therefore subject to sale, the actions of one or two individuals could upset the entire group's intricate pattern of land use.

Private Ownership and Commercial Farming

In areas that were ruled by European colonial powers, European systems of private ownership usually replaced traditional land-use systems. As a result, the economic system became more impersonal and less tied to a larger system of social relationships. Sometimes already-existing discrepancies between the property rights of men and women were amplified. Very often, even in horticultural and pastoral societies, property rights differ by gender; even the egalitarian Dobe !Kung recognize different rights to possession for men and women. When the colonial powers imposed the concept of private property as a means of controlling productive resources, they usually allocated ownership to men rather than to all individuals (Etienne & Leacock, 1988). Among the Buganda of Central Africa, for example, chiefs traditionally allotted portions of their estates to tenant farmers. These grants could be revoked at any time. Once the British took control of this region, they passed a law enabling tenants to do as they liked with their land grants, even pass them on to their heirs without the chief's permission. The aim was to protect tenant farmers from exploitation—and, in the process, to bring them more thoroughly under colonial control through land registration and systematic taxation. As a result, in Uganda land is now individually owned.

By different routes the movement toward private land rights has taken place in many other societies. Private ownership allows a certain freedom for individuals to make a living by using their land for their own exclusive benefit. This freedom, however, significantly alters an individual's ties to the group, along with the psychological and social advantages it once afforded. Under a system of corporate rights, since ownership is collective, the individual has a sense of place—a knowledge of belonging, in perpetuity, to this group and this piece of land. Under private ownership, land is transferable and it may well belong to someone other than those who work on it. Individuals who must sell their labor because they do not own the land they farm may come to be commodities themselves, with few economic rights in, and limited benefit from, what is being produced.

Not infrequently, rural people rise up in open rebellion or revolution in order to assert their perceived rights to land or better conditions. The Chinese Revolution, the Mexican Revolution, and the Cuban Revolution were essentially agrarian movements, although led by urban educated intellectuals. At the present, there is a similar peasant rebellion underway in Mexico, as described in the State of the Peoples box, *The Ecology of a Peasant Revolt*, on page 281.

Of course private ownership is not the only European model to have been transferred or adopted elsewhere. Various forms of collective farming, essentially products of European socialist or utopian philosophy, are found throughout Eastern Europe, South America, Asia, and Africa, as we have seen in the case study on collective farming in China in Chapter 7. One common denominator of these systems is that they are usually imposed on peasant farmers by outsiders, so that in some respects they contain the most oppressive aspects of absentee landlordism: the people who farm have a limited say in the actual management of their work and must sell their crops at prices set by impersonal agencies.

CASE STUDY:

Where the Dove Calls

THERE IS LITTLE THAT IS OF GREATER IMPORTANCE to farmers than access to land and water. What follows is a description of the complex ways in which land can be held in even a small community and the logic that underlies what seems to be a strange combination of private and public or communal resources. Cucurpe, whose name, according to the Opata Indians, means "where the dove calls," is a farming community in northwestern Mexico studied by Thomas Sheridan. He writes:

> To those of us who have grown up in the modern cities of Mexico or the United States, a place like Cucurpe seems idyllic, offering us a vision of a distant agrarian past. But if we go beyond that vision, we see that life in Cucurpe is predicated on

struggle, not pastoral harmony: struggle to raise crops when the rains won't come or when floods wash away the topsoil; struggle to keep cattle from turning into emaciated ghosts; struggle to prevent neighbors from diverting your irrigation water or fencing your pasture or stealing your land. [1988, p. xv]

The modern community of Cucurpe is, as it has been since the arrival of the Spanish, caught up in conflict between corporate and private land tenure. It is one of the more than 22,000 corporate farming communities in Mexico where 70 percent of Mexico's farm population live (Sheridan, 1988, p. 198). "Corporate" here means that some village resources are legally owned by the community as whole; in this case, about half the land and most water rights. This conflict over access to land is complicated: it involves fending off the private ranchers, who are ever-ready to intrude on the grazing lands of Cucurpe. The conflict is also internal: between those who have land and communal rights, those with some land and no communal rights, and those without land at all, but who seek it.

Even though the community is described as corporate, this does not means that there is economic equality or even that all have equal access to resources. Communal lands are interspersed with private holdings, the owners of which also can claim rights to corporate lands. Wealth distinctions are extreme. People view these distinctions of wealth in terms of three groupings. *Los ricos,* "the rich," produce entirely for the market, not for domestic consumption, employ labor, use mechanized technology such as pumps and tractors and own considerable land and cattle. The wealthiest ten households own over half of all private land in the community and have little interest in preserving any communal rights; generally they would prefer to privatize all resources. *La gente ordenada* or "middle class," about 60 percent of the households, are generally self-sufficient peasant-farmers utilizing both some private land (*milpa*) and running cattle on the commons, or corporate lands. They work their own fields and do not employ labor. Their interests in the corporate resources are very strong, as they rely on free grazing for their cattle and free water for their fields. *Los pobres* or "the poor," about 18 percent of the families, own no more than five or six cat-

tle, little or no land, and must work for others to make ends meet. Many of los pobres feel that they should be given community-owned land to develop and farm and thus find themselves in competition with the others who view these claims as threatening to their own interests. However extreme these differences may appear, within the community care is taken to minimize them socially. The wealthy do not flaunt their wealth, and all take pains to avoid conspicuous consumption within Cucurpe itself.

This is an extremely arid region where water is a critical resource. There are three major forms of land use, largely distinguished by the availability of water. *Milpa* are fields created laboriously by clearing stones and brush, leveling them by hand, and then bringing in water via canals from one of the drainage systems. They are usually privately owned or treated as though they were private even if technically the title is with community. *Temporales* are fields carved out of the margins of water courses. They are not irrigated, but absorb sufficient runoff water in good years to raise squash and vegetables; they are also treated as though they were private. *Agostadero,* or grazing land, is communal and members can use it at will if they are not restrained by some community decision. These three forms of land use allow people to pursue a diversity of strategies, depending on whether they emphasize raising cattle for market, cash crops, subsistence crops, or some mix of these and wage labor. For those who would specialize in ranching, something to which most aspire, a privately owned spread of less than 1,000 hectares would be an unreliable economic base. Any family without outside sources of income—as some have from jobs on ranches or remittances from relatives in America—will require access to at least two of the three major zones of land use; no one can make a living by just committing to only one. Here lies the root of both conflict and cooperation.

Politics are heated and unrelenting, reflecting the inequitable division of resources. Ranchers cut fences and are confronted by armed youths from the village, delegations of the poor petition for land, others complain about inequitable use of pastures, those with milpas come together to resist the claims of those without. But usually these conflicts are played out in nonviolent ways: in the courts, town meetings and ever-changing coalitions.

As this suggests, the community "is not an expression of peasant communal solidarity" (Sheridan, 1988, p. 189). Households plot, compete, and only sometimes cooperate. Sheridan's analysis indicates a predictable order underlying the ever-present disputing and alliance-making—what he terms the "political ecology" of land use. Agostadero, or rangeland, is a resource that individuals cannot own and defend alone—unless they happen to be extremely wealthy. Members of the community can best get access to this by working together in defending their rights, keeping outsiders off, and convincing the government of their rights. The land itself is not very valuable in small aggregates, but when taken as a whole it is worth maintaining as a corporate or common grazing area. Thus, while the rich try to use their influence to gain control of common grazing, or even to steal it, most of the others in the community will respond cooperatively to defend it—even where it is necessary to suppress old antagonisms.

Another resource held corporately is surface water: while rich families can drill wells and run pumps, most must use surface water diverted to the fields by canals and dams. This cannot be done by families acting alone; they must cooperate or not gain access. Here the "middle class" of peasantry gets little support from either the rich or the poor: both, one way or another, would like to get access to milpas and temporales. All small land-owning families assist in building and maintaining these canals, and each has a right to a specific amount of water for the household's milpa, or leveled field. They guard this right jealously and pass their fields on to their sons and daughters, even though technically some of the land is really corporate property. Families invest great effort in building their fields and planting them, and resist any attempt by the landless to have them redistributed. For middle-class peasants, the milpa is the key to survival; even though they make more money from cattle, they can rely on the milpa for food.

Thus, the ranchers and the wealthy continually spar with those who defend the corporate rights of the community; those with fields contend with those without, while those without strive to get the community to grant them land on which to farm. Both the landless and the small holders unite (or partially unite) to defend the grazing areas from

In Chiapas province of Mexico, conflict over land rights has developed into an armed struggle.
(AP Wide World Photos)

the rich, but even in this there are bitter divisions: some of the farmers own many cattle, while others only a few. Everyone knows that the grazing is being damaged by overstocking, but since it is common land there is little regulation. Thus the owners of only a few cattle feel that they are victimized by those who own many. Still, "Cucurpe is not a battle ground between collectivism and free enterprise. On the contrary, most Cucurpenos want to be as independent as possible—to run their own cattle, farm their own fields" (Sheridan, 1988, p. 146). Most peasant villages, upon close examination, are likely to show similar sentiments and similar divisions. ◗

The Control of Capital Goods

In addition to a system for allocating land, all peoples must have some way of establishing and coordinating rights to tools, storage of equipment, means of transportation, and other capital goods. In our own society, most capital goods (factories, machinery, tools, trucks, and warehouses) are privately owned. In socialist countries, many capital goods are owned by the state and access is regulated bureaucratically. In peasant farming societies, whatever the form of landownership, major implements and other agricultural inputs are often

State of the Peoples

The Ecology of a Peasant Revolt

ON NEW YEAR'S EVE, 1994, writes a distinguished scholar of Latin America, 800 members of the Zapatista National Liberation Party blocked the Pan American highway, seized two gas stations belonging the Mexican government and declared war on the ruling party—all only hours after the ratification of the North American Free Trade Agreement (NAFTA) (Nash, nd). The fact that Mexico and its powerful northern neighbor were now linked in trade gave the local people a platform from which to air grievances that the ruling party had long suppressed. The rebellion has continued through 1995, with little sign of abating.

Who are the participants? If you ask the government, they are outside agitators, either from foreign revolutionary groups or radical elements within the Roman Catholic Church. However, observers, including anthropologists such as June Nash, report that they are from indigenous groups, speaking the Mayan languages of the region. The rebellion, after centuries of rule by non-Mayans, is a powerful testimony to the extraordinary retention of distinctive ethnic cultures in Chiapas (Nash, nd, p. 2). She attributes the persistence of coherent systems of Mayan beliefs and practices, which made this rebellion possible, to both internal resources and external pressure exercised by the dominant group.

What has stimulated these people to express themselves so forcibly at this juncture in Mexican history? Anthropologist James Nations suggests that this is an "ecological revolution" (1994, pp. 31-33). It is about who controls the land and for what purpose. Since the colonial era, the Mayan highlands have been a source of products extracted for the benefit of outsiders: its dams supply 30 percent of Mexico's surface waters and a third of its hydroelectric power; it has much of the nation's petroleum reserves. But the state is last in terms of households with electricity and its once-massive forest cover is being rapidly cut and the land converted to pasture for beef cattle. The Zapatista revolt took place in a region where the three zones come together: the Tzotzil Mayan highland forests, an area of foothills now cleared for cattle, and a lowland tropical forest, which is itself rapidly being cleared.

In the colonial era, as the forest was cut back, much land was converted to hacienda production for the benefit of Spanish landlords. Mayan peasants were relocated to work on the haciendas. In the 1950s and 1960s, with agrarian reform, thousands of Mayan families were released from debt peonage and moved into forested lands, to establish homesteads on state-owned forestland where timber had been cleared. Soon these were followed by wealthier outsiders who bought up or otherwise acquired their plots and consolidated them into cattle ranches, forcing the farmers out. By 1981, 80 percent of the cleared lands had been turned into privately owned cattle ranches, many of them fenced and patrolled. Not only were indigenous farmers increasingly desperate for crop land, turning to forest lands of the Montes Azules Biosphere Reserve, but ethnically different local Mayan populations were in competition.

In 1989, the government dismantled its coffee price control system, which meant that many coffee bean growers were forced into bankruptcy; the 1994 NAFTA agreement was seen as the last straw by many. The remaining cash crop was corn and with NAFTA, cheap American corn would destroy their market. The indigenous people came to feel that they would soon be without a market for their crops and without land to grow them on. Chiapas farmers faced some hard choices. They could move to the already crowded urban centers, they could perhaps work as hired hands on cattle ranches, or they could rebel. As Nations writes, it is not surprising they have chosen rebellion. Their goal is to reclaim land for farming by getting it back from the cattle ranchers.

owned by individuals—even by those who may only work the land as sharecroppers. Animals in pastoral societies are almost always owned by individuals or by households, but, as we noted, individuals may have shares in animals herded by others or have expectations of being given livestock held by others.

Among hunters and gatherers, a person may be said to own a weapon or a tool, but ownership need not imply an exclusive right to the item. A hunter who makes a spear thrower or a bear trap may own the implement only in the sense that he has first right of use; when he is not using the tool, others may lay claim to it. Since hunters work together closely and survival depends on sharing, tools and weapons are often lent and exchanged freely. It may be that proprietary rights usually become more fixed and formalized where productive goods are more complex and difficult to make or acquire.

Production

Manufacturing is largely a specialized activity in most agricultural societies, and it becomes even more specialized as industrialization increases. In agricultural societies, the specialist who makes plows or pottery is the owner and operator of the production equipment: the forge, potter's wheel, kiln, or whatever materials and instruments he or she uses. The maker sees the product through from start to finish and owns it until it is sold. In industrial societies, however, the relationship of workers to their tools and their products is far less intimate. The factory workers who make tractors and combines will probably never use any of the farm machinery they produce. They are involved only in a specific and limited portion of the production process, and they own neither the product (unless they choose to buy it from the company) nor the factory and manufacturing equipment. They are simply selling their labor to a business at a rate set by the workings of the market system. Labor becomes a salable commodity like any other. **Alienation**—the fragmentation or separation of individuals' relations to their work, the things they produce, and the resources with which they produce them—is one possible consequence of industrial specialization and private enterprise.

When we consider cross-cultural variation in production, we need to consider two major aspects of production: how production is organized and what productive strategies are used.

The Organization of Production

In every society, production is an organized process. That is, it is handled by specific productive units—groups of people organized to do certain jobs. The nature of those productive units varies widely from society to society. In our own society, the basic producing unit is the business firm, be it an individually owned gas station, a farm, or a giant oil corporation with thousands of shareholders. Households in our society, for example, are typically consuming rather than producing units. As a consequence, production is usually far removed from the domestic economy. People who live in vastly different domestic circumstances may be working side by side on the same assembly line or in the same office. Productive tasks are divided up in complex and specialized ways. Rarely does one worker see an item produced from start to finish, and rarely is production based on local resources alone. Even on the family-owned and -operated farm, fuel, equipment, hybrid seeds, fertilizers—not to mention electricity and water for irrigation—are "imported."

In most nonindustrial societies, the basic producing unit is the household or domestic group. When technology is relatively simple, all the skills and many of the resources needed for production can be found in a single household, specialized along gender lines. In most horticultural societies, such as the Yanomamö, the members of a household will have among them the knowledge and abilities required to plant and tend their gardens, to hunt, to fashion hoes, spades, digging sticks, and other cultivating tools, to make clothing, ornaments, pots, baskets, and other implements and utensils. If a task is too large to be handled efficiently by a single household, the additional effort will simply be supplied by kin or friends. For the Trobriand Islanders, for example, the construction of a canoe is a village event; dozens of friends and kin cooperate in this large-scale project, which is also marked by ritual and feasting (Malinowski, 1922/1961). Nevertheless, most aspects of production are located in the household, which is also the

Workers in a South African shellfish processing factory on the Indian Ocean. Most workers are former farmers.
(George Bates)

main unit for organizing consumption. The organization of economic production and consumption primarily in the household is often referred to as the **domestic mode of production**.

Sometimes the risk of loss or damage dictates that a task be handled jointly by more than one household. Among the herders of East Africa, as we have noted earlier, a family will often herd cattle belonging to friends and kin along with their own, which has the efffect of minimizing the risk that any one household's entire stock will be destroyed if disease strikes.

Productive Strategies

In many societies, as we have noted, the productive unit serves many purposes other than just production. When a Temang farm family gather together their kin and friends to harvest their fields, the resulting productive unit is largely the same group with which they share their religious, political, social, and other activities. In the United States, farming is still a family business in many instances, and the organization of labor draws heavily on the household (Salamon, 1992). Production in nonindustrial societies affects and is affected by noneconomic matters, whereas industrial production is performed by people pursuing economic ends, largely to the exclusion of social considerations, as we saw in Chapter 7.

In addition to productive units, an economy must develop **productive strategies**—methods for converting natural or already processed resources into usable products. Productive strategies involve at least three major elements: resources, labor, and capital. Any one of these three elements can be varied in accordance with the needs of the society. Intensity of labor can be increased or decreased; capital can be saved, borrowed, or invested; the use of natural resources can be adjusted by a switch from one available alternative to another, as from a tobacco crop to corn. In industrial societies, the critical variable in a productive strategy is usually capital.

In traditional agrarian societies, the most important variable is often labor. In industrializing countries today, however, a characteristic of agriculture is a rapid increase in the importance of capital in relation to labor. Louise Lennihan (1988), who worked with Hausa farmers in northern Nigeria, notes that agriculture may appear to be carried on as it has been for generations—one still sees farmers in the fields with their hoes—but the social facts have been transformed by the increased presence of capital in agricultural production. Now the field a farmer hoes may not be his own, and if it is his own, it may be neglected because he is forced by circumstances to work for wages. Agriculture has come to require commercial fertilizer, hybrid seeds, and insecticides. Many farms and fields are owned by people who have made money in nonagricultural pursuits and wish to reinvest it.

Strong parallels to these observations on domestic production in nonindustrialized economies can be seen in industrializing countries. Egypt is a case in point. Agriculture is dramatically changing with industrialization, but the household still remains the primary unit of rural production and consumption. In one village in Upper Egypt, Nicholas Hopkins (1983) found considerable variation in the way households deployed their labor, the pattern chosen being determined largely by both the family's size and the amount of land to which they had access. Richer farmers had tractors, and did not work the land directly themselves. Poorer families sent their male members elsewhere to work for wages or to work as laborers in the fields of neighboring farmers. Though here the intensity of work is based less on the ratio of household workers to consumers than on ownership of land, the household remains the main vehicle for organizing the work force. Cultural ideals as to the work that is appropriate for men and for women also condition the household's strategy. Only in a family that has no other choice do women work in the fields in Egypt.

In manipulating productive strategies, a household almost always has choices. Such specialized pastoralists as ranchers, dairy farmers, and even nomadic pastoralists such as the Yörük of southeastern Turkey, for example, are dependent on **exchange**—trading or selling their products in order to acquire the means to purchase what they need to sustain themselves and to accumulate capital for expansion or against future need. Therefore they are extremely vulnerable to fluctuations in the relative values or prices of animal, agricultural, and industrial products. If the price of wheat goes up or the price of milk or meat goes down—or if both fluctuations occur simultaneously—even owners of large herds may find themselves in severe financial straits. They may consume less of their animal

products in order to have more to trade, or they may increase the productivity of their herd by investing more labor or capital in it, or they may join with other families under a single leader, the more prosperous members of the group helping the needier. All of these strategies are relatively cheap responses in that they can easily be abandoned without great loss. Another alternative, considerably more costly, is selling the herd and trying to make a living by some other means—perhaps buying a farm, hiring out as an agricultural worker, or taking up urban employment.

Labor, Gender, and Productivity in the Household

Anthropologists have paid considerable attention to the role of labor in different productive systems. Marshall Sahlins, drawing on the formulation of an early Soviet economist named Chayanov, has stated the relationship of labor to productive strategy as follows: intensity of labor in a system of domestic production for domestic use varies inversely with the relative working capacity of the producing unit (Sahlins, 1972, p. 91). In other words, since people in a household work for what they need in a domestic mode of production, the more mouths they have to feed in relation to the number of people capable of producing food, the harder they must work. If a household is composed primarily of very young and very old people, for example, the few adults in their prime productive years will have to work quite intensively to supply the group's needs. At the same time, what people need depends on what they think they need, and thus if the opportunity to acquire and accumulate things is very limited, rational people do not work very hard. Conversely, if a household has many productive members and few dependent ones, its producers will find themselves in the enviable position of having much time to devote to leisure, unless they have access to some means of saving or investment (Durrenberger, 1984, p. 20).

All things being equal, the more consumers each worker in a household has to support, the harder he or she has to work. Since the very young and the elderly consume more than they produce, households with a large proportion of such individuals must bear a heavy burden. Michael Dove (1984) found this idea borne out when he investi-

Members of the Ariaal warrior age grade work together to repair a well in a highland cattle camp.

(Elliot Fratkin)

gated the household economy of the Kantu of West Kalimantan, Indonesia. A large extended household is a cultural ideal among the Kantu horticulturists, but social reality falls short of the ideal. Of the thirty households Dove studied, thirteen were nuclear. The nuclear households were smaller than the others, and, most importantly, the ratio of workers to consumers was proportionately lower. Using various measures of productivity, Dove found that households with adverse worker-consumer ratios did in fact intensify their labor output proportionately. Some of them had to hire labor to make up for their own deficiencies. In fact, the organization of labor was a major problem faced by all households. Some had to sell their labor to make ends meet and others had to hire labor. The demographic measures of workers available to support consumers is a good predictor of labor deployment and the amount of work people have to do.

The Productive Work of Women. A key factor determining the productivity of a household is the relationship between household demographic and gender characteristics and the way labor is deployed. As a traditional agrarian society makes the transition to a market economy, the gender-based division of labor in the household often changes. If men go away to work for wages, women must as-sume male responsibilities at home. If women are drawn into the wage labor force, this change will similarly have domestic consequences for men. Usually substantial time elapses before men come to assume some share of domestic tasks. The overall configuration of society affects the gender division of labor, so it is inevitable that a major economic transformation, such as a shift to industrialized production, brings changes in the lives of men and women.

On the modern American farm, women play a role even more central than before, even though farm women always worked very hard. Since many men are employed off the farm in order to secure a reliable income apart from farming, women increasingly drive heavy equipment and engage in tasks that were formerly thought to be men's work (Salamon, 1992). Still, it is the Midwestern custom for women to refer to their labor as "helping out"; what the men do is "real work." Despite this attitude, women are doing productive work and, even though it is unpaid, it is critical to the success of the farm within the market economy. Patricia Johnson (1988) found the same dynamic in her study of Gainj women. Even though these women have been portrayed primarily as wives and mothers—that is, reproducers rather than producers—Johnson's research revealed that the commercial success of the household's coffee production was directly related to women's labor.

CASE STUDY:

The Productive Labor of Gainj Women

THE GAINJ LIVE IN THE RUGGED AND FORESTED Takwi Valley, on the northern edge of the central highlands of Papua New Guinea. Their settlements are widely dispersed and there are no large aggregations of people that could be described as villages. The Gainj remain to a large degree subsistence slash-and-burn horticulturists, growing mixed gardens of sweet potatoes, taro, yams, bananas, sugar cane, a variety of leafy greens, and some introduced plants such as corn and pumpkin. They raise a few pigs and chickens, more for their ceremonial value than for consumption. Hunting is so sporadic that it contributes little to a household's diet. The Gainj men are responsible for the initial clearing and fencing of garden plots. Women are responsible for secondary clearing, burning, and planting. They also cultivate, harvest, carry, process, and cook garden produce. Since 1963, a large percentage of the men have worked as wage laborers for coastal copra (coconut) plantations, usually on two-year contracts.

Coffee was first introduced as a cash crop in 1973, and the manner of its introduction followed a pattern identified by Esther Boserup (1970, p. 53 ff.) in other parts of the developing world: regardless of the traditional division of labor in subsistence activity, cash crops and the technology that accompanies them tend to be introduced to men by men. Despite the clear identification of women with gardening, the male agricultural extension officer provided coffee seedlings and information about their cultivation, processing, and sale only to Gainj men. The men then established a new division of labor for this new garden product: men plant the coffee trees and sell the final product; all the remaining labor—cultivation, harvesting, processing, and much of the local transportation—falls to the women. Since the Gainj accord ownership of trees and their fruit to the person who plants them, and since men plant the coffee seedlings, the profits

from coffee sales go exclusively to the men. "These profits are spent on investment in all-male business cooperatives, education (almost exclusively male), air travel by men to the provincial capital, and consumer goods," despite the fact that women do most of the work (Johnson, 1988, p. 111).

Taking as the unit of study the conjugal family household (that is, a household that has a male head and at least one of his wives), Johnson compared data gathered in 1978 and again in 1983 to analyze the effects of five variables on success in coffee-growing: (1) age of male household head, (2) migration experience of male household head, (3) number of resident wives per household, (4) number of other women between the ages of twenty and sixty per household, and (5) number of dependents per household.

She discovered that migration experience had no significant effect on coffee-growing, as measured by the number of coffee gardens a household cultivated: clearly one did not have to go out of the community to learn how to grow coffee. Age was marginally significant in that the younger male household heads, no longer able to achieve status in the traditional manner (by exhibiting prowess as a leader in warfare) tended to follow the cash-cropping path to glory and worked hard to increase their coffee crop. The number of wives per household had a significant positive effect on success in coffee production: the more wives a man had, the more gardens he could manage. But the greatest effect on coffee production was produced by women other than wives of the household head: his unmarried daughters and sisters, the wives of sons who shared the household, and widows who chose to attach themselves to the household. This finding is explained in part by the fact that few of these women have to deal with the demands of children.

Johnson analyzed the effects of the number of dependents per household in terms of "dependency ratio"; that is, the ratio of nonworking dependents to female producers (both wives and other adult women). She found that the more successful households (three or more coffee gardens) significantly decreased their dependency ratios between 1978 and 1983, while the less successful households (fewer than three coffee gardens) had increased them. The decrease in the dependency ratio is "entirely attributable to an increase in the number of producers" (1988, p. 117). Johnson points out that in all cases the producers are women other than the household head's wives. Between 1978 and 1983, she found, the number of such women declined in the less-successful households and increased in the successful ones.

Those households considered in 1983 to be successful in producing coffee as a cash crop were the same households that in 1978 had had more dependents and fewer adult women other than wives of the household head. Johnson postulates that it was the pressure of the high dependency ratios that had motivated their move into cash-cropping. But by 1983 these households had drastically altered their structure by adding women to lower their dependency ratios. Where did these women come from?

Fifty-four percent were young women who had not yet married. A mere 14 percent were women of marriageable age who had been brought into the household. The remaining 32 percent were widows who had joined the household. Most of the widows were close friends of the women already in the household and were related to the male head in such a way (either genealogical or classificatory) as to preclude their ever becoming his wives.

Johnson notes that both the retention of marriageable women and the admission of widows carries a cost to the household. The family that delays in arranging a marriage for a daughter forgoes, at least temporarily, the bridewealth that her marriage would bring, as well as the marriage ties that it would create. Widows more often than not bring dependent children with them; in fact, because widows with children are the least likely to remarry, they are the most likely to be available for incorporation into another household.

Widows currently seem to be making their decisions on the basis of strong sentimental ties with women of a particular household. At the time of this study, women had not yet made serious demands on men for compensation for their labor, and any material benefits they may acquire (clothing, pots, purchased foods) do not seem to weigh heavily in widows' decisions to ally themselves with a particular household. If women do come to demand some material compensation for their labor, same-sex affective ties may then become less important and the costs of such demands will have to be included in consideration of a household's economic success.

Johnson assumes that the addition of productive women enabled a household to increase its coffee production. But even if she were wrong—if, that is, it was the success of households with multiple coffee gardens that led widows to join them—the conclusion that there is a dynamic relationship between the number of female hands at work and the number of coffee gardens would not be affected. Johnson warns that ethnographers should recognize not only that women's unpaid domestic work is productive, but also that in many areas of the developing world women are "crucially involved in commercial, nondomestic production, in labor that must by any standard be recognized as productive" (1988, p. 120). ▶

Variations in the Intensity of Labor. Households in preindustrial societies vary the intensity of their labor by modifying one of several factors, all of which are governed to some extent by cultural norms. First there is the speed and efficiency with which a person works; the amount of work he or she accomplishes in a given period of time. This amount is often referred to as output per worker-hour, or level of **productivity**. The members of every society have a general notion of what the average person's productivity should be in a particular task. Productivity is, of course, greatly influenced by the kinds of tools people have at their disposal. A person with a tractor can obviously furrow a field more quickly than a person with an ox and a wooden plow. But even when they use similar equipment, people in different societies define the acceptable level of productivity in different ways.

Another factor that influences intensity of labor is the **productive life span,** the period bounded by the culturally established ages at which a person ideally enters and retires from the work force. The Bushong of Africa, for instance, define the productive years as those between the ages of twenty and sixty; the neighboring Lele regard the twenty years between the ages of thirty and fifty as an appropriate working life (Douglas, 1962). Throughout Eastern Europe, the formerly Socialist regimes established 55 as the age of retirement for men and 50 for women; as a consequence, these countries now have very large populations of people dependent on government pensions. Since the collapse of

Communism, pensions are a very serious burden for these countries.

There is also the concept of **workday** or work-week—the culturally established number of hours that a person ideally spends at work each day or each week. Clocks, calendars, and schedules establish temporal control within modern states, determining to a great extent who does what, and when (Rutz, 1992, p. 5). Industrial and postindustrial economies make great demands on the individual's time; long work days are the norm. Members of many hunting-and-gathering bands consider it normal to work three to five hours a day; in most other preindustrial societies, underproduction—that is, the practice of working fewer hours a day than are available for work—is also the rule. People in such societies attach a good deal of value to leisure and to the fulfillment of social obligations, and little value to the accumulation of food they can neither eat nor store and goods they do not need.

The concepts of productivity, productive life span, and workday, although culturally defined, are often redefined by individuals and households as they adjust to their own particular circumstances. We know in our own society, for instance, that some people ignore cultural guidelines in regard to the normal length of a workday and take on two eight-hour jobs, one in the daytime and one at night. Their reason may be the need to make ends meet or the wish to accumulate a large savings account rapidly. The same is true in preindustrial societies. A Lele household that found itself particularly short of members in the culturally defined productive years might well assign tasks to members under thirty or over fifty. A survey of a sample of any large set of households would doubtless find significant variation in the ages of the youngest and oldest working members of each domestic group. Such variation reflects adjustment to individual circumstances. Households adjust the intensity of labor, the sexual division of labor, the working age, and working hours to meet their particular requirements.

As we mentioned earlier, intensity of labor is also affected by factors other than material need. Sahlins (1972) found, for instance, that among the Kapauku of New Guinea some households produced more than would be expected on the basis of their numbers, while others produced far less than their sizes seemed to warrant. The Kapauku

have a form of political organization with well-established leaders known as "big men." These leaders and their families tend to be overproducers, while their followers and their followers' families tend to be underproducers. The big men maintain their authority primarily through conspicuous and carefully calculated generosity toward their followers. In the end, all receive enough to fulfill their individual needs. Among the Kapauku, therefore, political and economic decisions are very closely related.

The Exchange of Resources

Some resources are kept and consumed by the producers, while the rest enter the society's network of exchange. Exchange, a basic part of any economic system, allows people to dispose of their unneeded surpluses and to acquire necessities from other people's unneeded surpluses. At the same time exchange serves as social cement. Indeed, some anthropologists have argued that regardless of what is exchanged, the very act of exchange is the primary bond that holds societies together.

Mechanisms of Exchange

The three mechanisms that characterize the various systems of economic exchange in human society—reciprocity, redistribution, and markets—broadly reflect the evolution of economic exchange in the course of human cultural history. **Reciprocity**, or mutual giving and taking between people who are bound by social ties and obligations, is universal (and also important among nonhuman species). **Redistribution**, or reallocation of a society's wealth by means of obligatory payments or services, is a more recent phenomenon associated with specialized political institutions. **Market exchange**, or the trading of goods and services through a common medium of value—money—arrived only with the advent of state societies.

People in most societies use all three mechanisms, as we do, but vary considerably in the mechanism they rely on most and the kinds of transactions they enter into by means of each mechanism. In agrarian and industrial societies, the majority of economic exchanges are conducted in highly specialized marketplaces. But in other

!Kung men return from a hunt with game, all of which will be shared in camp according to rules that take into account who killed the game, sex, relationship to the hunter, and need.

(Anthony Bannister/ABPL)

economies (now quite rare), the market serves only a peripheral function; reciprocity and redistribution predominate. Where the market mechanism is nonexistent or is used only for certain goods, exchange is conducted through reciprocity alone or through a combination of reciprocity and redistribution.

Reciprocity. Reciprocity may play a more important role in nonindustrial societies than in industrial societies. While systematic reciprocity is important everywhere, in nonindustrialized settings gifts are given more often, in greater quantity, and to more people. The obligation to reciprocate is stronger; most important, reciprocity plays a fundamental part in the actual production process, as it is likely to involve strategic productive resources—such as the giving or loaning of cattle in East Africa (Barfield, 1993, p. 52).

Reciprocity does not always take place in the atmosphere of casual benevolence associated with our familial and neighborly exchanges of favors. Anthropologists have identified three forms of reciprocity, each involving a distinctive degree of intimacy between giver and taker (and hence a dis-

tinctive measure of formality and goodwill): generalized, balanced, and negative reciprocity.

Household members, other relatives, and friends usually engage in **generalized reciprocity**—informal gift giving for which no accounts are kept and no immediate or specific returns are expected (Sahlins, 1965). Household members routinely provide services for one another with no calculation of expected return; a mother does not record for future use the cost of the breakfast cereal she feeds her children. Wage earners in households usually pool all or most of their earnings and share in their expenditures without close regard to who may be getting the most out of each transaction. Even the most casual form of reciprocity, however, operates with the implicit understanding that goods and services exchanged are to be balanced in the long run. Household members assume that they can rely on long-term mutual support; neighbors who help out assume that when they need help, others will come to their assistance. So in one important respect reciprocity is a form of storage or warehousing: you give goods or services to someone else and ultimately, even without close calculation, receive something comparable. This is particularly useful when the goods are perishable and cannot otherwise be stored for future use.

Generalized reciprocity historically was the characteristic form of exchange among hunting-and-gathering peoples and was essential to their adaptation. The Dobe Ju/'hoansi or !Kung, as we have seen (Chapter 4), have no means of preserving meat, so they exchange access to meat by sharing. When a hunter kills a sizable animal, he keeps only a small share for his family. The rest he distributes among his hunting companions, who share their portions with their kinsmen, who in turn share with other kinsmen. Tomorrow or next week, the favor will be returned. The result is that despite constantly shifting and uncertain resources, everyone eats (Marshall, 1965).

Of course, this is not to say that individual self-interest is lost sight of in these transactions. Melvin Konner, who worked many years with the !Kung, recalled that one respected man in the group approached him with the leg of an antelope he had killed and asked that the anthropologist keep it for him so he could consume it later (1983, p. 375). It was clear that one reason why members of this group shared widely was that they had limited means of storage, and that it was physically very difficult to keep one's relatives and neighbors from eating one's food or using one's other possessions.

Somewhat more formal than generalized reciprocity is **balanced reciprocity**, gift-giving that clearly carries the obligation of an eventual and roughly equal return. This form of reciprocity normally takes place between more distantly related individuals, friends of roughly equal social or economic status, or formal trading partners. The expectation is explicit: what is given must be balanced by a return of something comparable. As with generalized reciprocity, what is returned may be quite different from what is received, and the return gift or favor may be given later.

Many pastoral and agricultural societies have labor-exchange systems based on balanced reciprocity. At planting and harvest time, when the work load is too great for one household, neighboring households or kin groups take turns working one another's fields. The participants in such systems keep fairly close mental accounts of their debits and credits. A person who does not reciprocate within an appropriate time and with the same measure of labor or an equivalent gift will meet with severe social disapproval and future lack of cooperation.

The distinction between balanced and generalized reciprocity is not always clear; indeed, reciprocity or gift-giving may be manipulated to advantage by individuals. The **potlatch** among many Native American groups of the Northwest Coast and the "pig feasts" of Melanesia are ceremonies in which wealth is given away in competitive efforts to gain prestige and public influence. In Melanesia, men host expensive feasts; dozens of pigs may be slaughtered and much other food consumed or taken away. The status a host gains is roughly proportionate to the extent of his feast compared with others. Today, the term "potlatch" has acquired the more general meaning of competitive feasting and ostentatious display of largesse, such as seen in an extravagant wedding party. Among the Northwest Coast groups, the potlatch given by a chief involved his giving away blankets, copper, and canoes, not to mention great quantities of food. The potlatch is a form of balanced reciprocity, albeit delayed, because the host has, over the years, received presents of the sort he is now giving away. It is competitive because the giver gains prestige or status if he can outdo other hosts. This form of feasting and gift-giving is more than simply individual exchange and social strategizing; it can be a major way in which goods are exchanged among communities.

CASE STUDY:

The Kula Ring

SOMEWHAT SIMILAR BUT RATHER MORE COMPLEX is the ceremonial exchange system that links a large number of islands, the Trobriands, off the east coast of New Guinea. The Trobriand Islanders are a matrilineally organized horticultural society inhabiting a large number of islands—some of which depend on trade for food. The **kula ring,** described originally by Malinowski, is a highly complex system for trading two varieties of shell ornaments: the white armbands called *nwal* and the red shell necklaces called *soulava.* Paralleling the ceremonial trade, which is governed by the rules of reciprocity, items of essential goods are also traded, but these transactions operate according to a completely different set of rules: those that apply to market exchange. Ornaments are never traded for food, or other essential goods, nor are essential goods used to buy ornaments. They occupy different spheres of exchange.

A Trobriand Islander who possesses a group of kula ornaments has the option of making a trading expedition to another island. After deciding to make the trip, the islander must abide by the strict rules governing trade. The islander can only offer the valued kula ornaments to one of his lifelong trading partners with whom there exists a relationship of trust. Trading partners are located on all of the islands where trade takes place. An old chief may have as many as one hundred partners to the north and an equal number to the south, while a young commoner might have only a handful of partners. In addition, the kula ornaments must travel through the islands in a special direction: the red shell necklaces move in a clockwise direction; the white shell armbands move counterclockwise. Thus, the kula ornaments continually move around the chain of islands, passing from one partner to another. The objects do not remain in any individual's hands for much more than a year.

Every part of the expedition is steeped in custom and ceremony. Now, travel is by modern transport, but formerly canoes would be overhauled and elaborate preparations made for the trip. The individual trader always goes with a party from his community. Once the trade party arrives, trade partners go through an elaborate exchange of kula ornaments, following the principle of balanced reciprocity. When one partner gives an ornament as a ceremonial gift, he can expect to eventually receive a roughly equal gift. At the same time as the ritual exchange, the trade partners begin exchanging utilitarian items that may actually be vital to the individuals involved. The kula ceremonial exchange provides a kind of "social cement"; the existence of trading partners throughout the islands helps to maintain lines of cultural and political communication. It is also a means by which men, in accumulating partners and ornaments, gain prestige and political influence.

While the kula ring has received the most attention, Trobriand women have their own exchange system based on balanced reciprocity (Weiner, 1976). Following a death, women from

Trobriand Islanders set out for a kula exchange in traditional attire worn for the occasion. This ceremony has retained its importance.
(Andre Singer/The Hutchison Library)

nearby hamlets bring gifts of food to the people in mourning. Women associated with the deceased prepare bundles of banana leaves and weave fiber skirts to give in return. Husbands assist in this accumulation necessary for the final, major mortuary ceremony (which is held by the women). Much like a pig feast or a potlatch, each senior woman in mourning tries to distribute as many bundles and skirts as possible, perhaps over a thousand bundles and dozens of skirts. This is balanced reciprocity because the givers have in the past received comparable gifts as well as food and other services. Women can gain socially from this competitive gift-giving, just as do men. ❱

Exchanges between enemies or strangers are generally impersonal transactions, with each side trying to get the better end of the bargain. Such exchanges, classified as **negative reciprocity,** involve an effort to get something for nothing or for as little as possible. They can range from unfriendly haggling to outright theft. The Mbuti Pygmies, for example, find it expedient to exchange meat and their own labor for the produce and metal of their horticultural neighbors, but these exchanges are marked by a good deal of mutual antagonism. The villagers use threats and bribes in an effort to get as much from the Mbuti Pygmies as they can, while the Pygmies do their best to work as little as possible (Turnbull, 1965). If negative reciprocity is to be truly reciprocal, the two parties must outwit each other by turns.

Redistribution. Redistribution of goods or labor occurs where payments of goods, currency, or services are made to some central agency (a king, a chief, a religious leader, the state), which subsequently reallocates some of these resources in the form of community services, emergency help, or special rewards. Alternatively, the payments may be used to support public institutions and infrastructures, whether political or religious.

In the United States, the federal income tax is supposed to function as this sort of redistribution mechanism. In nonmonetary societies, tribal chiefs typically redistribute unused land, hunting sites, and food surpluses to members of their tribes. This system has several advantages. It may help to guarantee adequate subsistence to all members of a society in the face of variation in the local availability of resources. It is a means of collecting some resources and storing them against future needs. In some respects, simple forms of redistribution resemble balanced reciprocity; the main difference is that very often the people who give are not necessarily going to receive anything back, or if they do, it may not be comparable to what they gave up.

William Abruzzi (1993) describes how the Mormons colonized the valleys of Utah in the nineteenth century. Each household was required to tithe to the church and to contribute labor to the community; when the Mormons experienced devastating floods or poor harvests, the church used these resources to support them through the crisis—or, if a community failed, to help people settle elsewhere. Redistribution may also support specialists who serve the interests of the community—warriors, priests, artisans, and so forth. One social consequence of redistributive exchange is that it enhances the prestige, power, and authority of the person or agency responsible for collecting and controlling it. Whereas reciprocity is usually found between social equals, redistribution is based on the power of leaders over their subjects and is common in societies with marked political and social hierarchies (Sahlins, 1965).

Market Exchange. Unlike reciprocity and redistribution, market exchange is a commercial transaction largely removed from social considerations. Goods and services may be traded (bartered) directly, but they are usually bought and sold through a standard medium of exchange: money. Beyond the requirement to pay the agreed amount and to deliver the goods or services paid for, the parties usually are under no social obligation to each other—they have no ties based on kinship, friendship, or political affiliation. Relative values of goods and services reflect supply and demand, and participants in a market economy have means of learning prevailing values—they can compare offerings by shopping, walking around a marketplace, or reading a newspaper. The seller can sell the product or service to anyone who offers the best return; the buyer can shop around for the best bargain. Not all market exchanges need be impersonal. People often establish long-term relationships with those with whom they trade. Yörük nomads, for example, usually do all their town shopping with merchants with whom they have a long-standing tie of friendship and, not incidentally, good credit. In almost any market setting, some individuals play the role of middleman or broker, expediting the flow of information among buyers and sellers and, in many instances, personalizing, and thus facilitating, transactions.

Just as market behavior can be quite diverse, so the importance of market exchange in a society can vary widely. A West African farmer, for example, may meet most of her family's subsistence needs through her own productive activities. If she happens to have a small surplus, she may sell some of the extra crops in the marketplace and use the profit to buy a manufactured item or to pay taxes. The range of consumer goods sold in these peripheral market systems is usually quite limited; land, labor, and capital resources change hands only through reciprocity and redistribution. The economies of most industrial nations, by contrast, are based largely on market exchange. A vast commercial network, linking millions of individuals

This market near Nyeri, central Kenya, is open two days a week and hundreds of vendors, mostly women, come to sell produce and craft items.
(Daniel Bates)

The collapse of Communism and state-dominated redistributive systems has led to informal markets springing up, such as this one in Hungary.
(Daniel Bates)

and business firms, allocates not only an enormous array of consumer products but also land, labor, and capital resources.

The Organization of Exchange

All three forms of exchange—reciprocity, redistribution, and market exchange—operate together to some degree in all contemporary societies, but certain rules determine to which particular goods each mechanism of exchange applies, and in what situations. Anthropologists describe this differentiation as the operation of **spheres of exchange**. Among the Siane of New Guinea, for example, luxury goods (tobacco, salt, nuts, oil) circulate in a free-market setting, but subsistence items are distributed through reciprocity (Nash, 1966). In the Trobriands, as we have just seen, ceremonial objects are exchanged according to the principle of reciprocity; subsistence items, through purchase and barter. The islanders keep these two spheres of exchange entirely separate: one can never sell a ceremonial armband for yams or a canoe. In every society, many transactions of household members are

kept distinct from those with outsiders; a wife does not pay her husband to wash her car, nor does a husband pay his wife for her care when he is ill. But the distinction can become blurred as, for example, when one borrows money from a relative and pays interest or employs one's child to make repairs on the family dwelling. In most societies, sex is not considered a market commodity, but prostitution is nevertheless common; people everywhere find opportunities and strategies for such **conversion**—the use of a sphere of exchange for a transaction with which it is not generally associated.

Just as some rules dictate which mechanisms of exchange are appropriate, other rules govern the terms on which a given exchange is transacted. Supply and demand, of course, influence price, but other factors are also involved. Among the Kapauku of New Guinea, for example, the kinship relationship between traders and their relative statuses can affect the terms of the deal (Pospisil, 1963). And in our own society, although we are fond of saying that business is business and a person always sells to the highest bidder, we may know of relatives and friends who could sell us items at cost rather than at retail prices. It also may transpire that market transactions are phrased and conceptualized in the idiom of kinship and reciprocity—in effect, disguising what may be an exploitative relationship, as we see in the Gender Issues box, *Money Makes Us Relatives,* on page 294.

Gender Issues

Money Makes Us Relatives:
Women's Labor and Ideals of Social Relations

DURING TWO YEARS OF FIELD-work (1986–1988), Jenny White (1994) studied a number of families who had migrated from rural areas of Turkey to live in poor, working-class neighborhoods of Istanbul and who are now engaged in small-scale production. Women play a central role in producing knitted, stitched, and embroidered clothing and decorative items, either at home or on a piecework basis in family atelier workshops. Many of the goods produced in this fashion are exported to Europe, the Middle East, and the United States, where they are sold at prices astronomically higher than the cost of their production. They are also sold through middlemen to tourists, as well as directly to friends and neighbors.

Both the women who work at home or take in piecework and the organizers of their labor (gen-erally men) regard this work as a part of traditional female domestic activities rather than as productive labor. "For the working-class women of Istanbul, labor, along with honor and childbearing, is a central defining theme of their lives" (White,1994, p. 7). Since the women insist that this labor is not "work," they do not keep track of the time they spend on it; a piece of sewing or knitting is taken up and put down throughout the day by different adult women and unmarried girls, the piecework becoming integrated into their other activities. "Both piecework and the family atelier are particularly suited to the organization of women's labor . . . since the women are able to reconcile earning additional income with traditional role constraints that discourage [them] from leaving the home, making contact with strangers, and taking over the male role of provider" (White, 1994, p. 109). In this view, "work" or a "job" is a public-sector activity unsuited to women and to be engaged in only as a last resort.

In a recent survey, it was found that 64 percent of women spent between four and seven hours a day doing paid work, mostly piecework knitting. One of the women White visited, Şengül, a Koran teacher, owns a knitting machine and produces clothing to sell to friends and neighbors. But when White pressed her as to why she was doing this knitting, she became uncomfortable and insisted that she did not do a lot of it, taking orders only from friends and working only in spare moments between housework, taking care of the children, and entertaining relatives and neighbors. She did not see herself as "belonging to a category of people who

Economic Experimentation and Adaptation

Like all aspects of adaptation, strategies of production and exchange are never static. By experimenting with new approaches or by being forced to deviate from traditional ones, people inevitably discover new methods that may eventually alter their economic organization.

The human capacity to cope with new situations is seen to good advantage in the phenomenon of **entrepreneurship**—economic innovation and risk-taking. In their efforts to solve some pressing economic problem, some people, even in socialist states, manage to gain a personal advantage and ul-timately effect a change in the larger economic system. Gerald Creed, one of the few anthropologists to have carried out extensive fieldwork on a collective farm, found that Bulgarian villagers were extremely talented in integrating the formal, state-owned socialist sectors of the economy into their own, private entreprenuerial activities (1994). While they were only allowed small, 1.3 acre personal plots to farm for their personal needs, they made use of collective farm equipment to cultivate and harvest crops grown on these plots, and they used collective farm grain to produce livestock for private sale and home use. Further, they took the skills acquired in their state-controlled jobs and sold their labor and crafts on the informal but perdo regular work, sell to strangers, and rely on the money earned in this way" (White, 1994, p. 113), although clearly her income from this labor contributed significantly to the family budget. When asked how many sweaters she made in a month, she replied, "Last month . . . I had guests from the village so I couldn't do very many. About fifteen I guess . . ." (p. 114). Since she had previously estimated that it takes her two days to make a sweater, this meant she worked every day, a fact about which she seemed embarrassed.

In most working-class neighborhoods, there are also ateliers run by families that give out piecework to women in the neighborhood. This arrangement allows the women to work at home and to see their labor as part of their roles as women, family members, and neighbors. Women doing piecework will generally do so in the company of other women, thus making the work part of other social activities that bring them together. Hatice and her husband, Osman, run an atelier in the squatter district of Yenikent, specializing in clothes made from scraps of fine leather sewn together by crocheted panels. They have three daughters, who help out in the atelier, and one seven-year-old son. The family members prepare the leather and yarn and then give them to neighborhood women with instructions for assembly. Osman keeps a book that lists what each women takes and what she brings back.

These women are generally from the neighborhood, although some are from nearby neighborhoods. Murat, a neighbor who runs his own atelier, says, "They are stranger women but they are [the ones who have been made kin through money]" (White, 1994, p. 119). Osman and Hatice do not differentiate between donated labor (such as that of Güllü, their eldest daughter's best friend, who punches holes in the leather and takes the outfits home to assemble them, without pay) and the paid labor of the neighborhood women. "In their view, the women are kin (*akraba*) by virtue of their participation in the exchange of labor for money, providing of course that this is done . . . as collective reciprocal assistance with no expectation of return" (p. 120). Just as this relationship, while clearly a commercial transaction, is euphemized as a kin relationship, so Güllü's donated work is explained in kinship terms: she is Emine's "sister." Kin relations are based on "participation in a web of reciprocal obligations and indebtedness," so in this situation money becomes "a thing or a service . . . which can be freely given, just as labor is freely given. . . . Labor, whether paid or unpaid, is seen as part of the obligations for mutual assistance that is required for group membership" (pp. 120–121).

The idea that women's labor, either at home or in the ateliers, is not "work" allows women to contribute financially to their families while remaining within their traditionally perceived roles in the family and neighborhood. The undervaluing of women's labor is also is one of the major factors keeping production costs low and profits high for distributors, middlemen, merchants, and exporters.

vasive black market. Even state-subsidized, inexpensive bread was bought in large quantities to fatten privately owned pigs.

Patricia Vondal (1987) describes the efforts of some small farmers in Borneo to break out of their poverty and obtain consumer goods by investing in ducks. Ducks could be sold on the regional market to satisfy an increasing need for low-cost meat in the cities. But to take advantage of this possibility, innovating farmers had to risk their land and homes to make the initial investment in the novel enterprise. Cages and other structures had to be built, bran and poultry feed either produced in quantity or purchased, and market outlets secured—all of which required capital and risk. Some duck farmers failed; others reaped the rewards of the successful innovator.

Lucie Saunders and an Egyptian colleague, Sohair Mehenna (1986), who worked together in a village in the Nile Delta, had good data on the economy and social life of this community spanning several generations. They found that certain families were consistently involved in risk-taking through entrepreneurial innovation. At the end of the nineteenth century, when the transport system was rapidly improving and cotton was the dominant cash crop, one individual used proceeds from successful village shops to consolidate a modest estate on irrigated land. In the postrevolutionary era, land reform and new laws governing farm labor limited

Human Ecology
Over the Mountains Are Mountains

"OVER THE MOUNTAINS ARE mountains" is a Korean proverb, taken as the title for a book by Clark Sorensen, which suggests that as soon as you overcome one crisis, another one looms (1988, p. 3). His study is aptly named and examines how Korean villagers responded to the rapid industrialization of Korea in recent years. He uses data collected in two field investigations of the same village carried out six years apart, as well as historical sources, and focuses on household and family structure. He finds that traditional family structure can be instrumental in shaping how a society responds to change. This need not mean a massive shift in family and household values and organization, as is often assumed. Rather, the accommodations can involve considerable social continuity even as families are being drawn into the larger world and coming to rely on mechanization and on conveniences such as electricity, TVs, and telephones.

In 1976 Sorensen went to Sangongni, a fairly poor rural community, for the first time; he wanted to study a relatively stable, isolated, and undisturbed village in order to study its social organization in terms of ecological adaptation (Sorensen, 1988, p. 37). He collected genealogical, demographic, and agricultural data, noting that agricultural technology was rapidly changing: "Vinyl greenhouses were used to sprout rice seedlings. Composite fertilizer was used in the fields. There were even a few motor tillers and power sprayers that had been introduced into the village in 1975" (p. 37). Nevertheless, the overall impression was of tradition and stability; there were a number of well-organized patrilineages. Household organization appeared to adhere to traditional rules of patrilocality and primogeniture with the eldest son and his wife gradually assuming the duties and rights of the household head and mistress

(p. 39). The household still was the mainstay of rural production and the means by which labor was organized.

By the end of his first year of fieldwork, Sorensen found that his first impression of stability was questionable. People were speaking of Japanese quotas on silk cocoons and world export patterns, inflation and labor shortages, rising prices for land and agricultural inputs, some discussed migrating to the city, and everyone talked of the impending electricification of the village that would enable them to watch television. He then realized how closely the village was integrated into the world economy and began to see the scale and importance of national politics, the market economy, and off-farm migration. It was not, he concluded, realistic to try to view the community in terms of a small system narrowly adapted to its immediate environment.

Sangongni exhibits many of

the profits from farming. Members of the same family, who had been innovators a generation earlier, sought out new activities. Most recently the grandsons were experimenting with the introduction of chickens. They purchased foreign stock, acquired the necessary equipment, and built hatcheries. As their profits mounted from the sale of poultry to Cairo families, others emulated their operations and a new industry was founded.

Whether or not the efforts of entrepreneurs reflect a conscious strategy, they inevitably have important consequences. First, entrepreneurs most commonly engage in activities that take them over the boundary between traditional and modern economic organization. They recognize the potential of market exchange, for example, and bring the products of new factories or imported goods into the countryside to compete with traditional handicrafts and to create new needs. Second, while an entrepreneurial effort may originate with an individual, it rarely succeeds unless others join and support the new enterprise (Barth, 1963). And finally, these entrepreneurial actions typically lead to fundamental changes in the systems of production and distribution. Farmers may begin to produce more cash crops; they—or their children—may choose to work in the factory rather than the fields. These changes, in turn, will begin to transform gender re-the common responses of a peasant community in an industrializing society. Handicrafts are now almost totally absent, people have acquired urban tastes, and all participate in the national market economy. There has been a massive migration to the cities, where many become wage laborers, and a general decrease in family size as sons and daughters move away to seek employment off the farm. Farm size, too, has increased in response to market pressures. But even after twenty years of rapid development, land ownership has not become seriously concentrated (Sorensen, 1988, p. 11). What has happened is that while there has been a gradual increase in farm size, the now-close integration of town and country means that rural wages are almost as high as urban ones. As a consequence, farmers invest in modern technology and adopt new techniques that they employ themselves on quite small holdings. The shortage of rural labor does not favor the large farm.

Sorensen's second period of fieldwork in 1983 helped to highlight the nature of change and continuity in an industrial environment. Farm size increased from 1.14 hectares to 1.33 hectares, agricultural wages had more than doubled since 1977, there were more than a dozen motor tillers (but also a serious shortage of labor), household size decreased slightly, and at least thirteen families had left for the city (Sorensen, 1988, pp. 42, 88–89). But, contrary to what is often predicted, those who left usually had found good jobs and improved their standards of living. Those who remained in the village also fared well. While not everyone had equal success, no impoverished class of rural worker had emerged. Virtually every household in the village was self-sufficient even though it was integrated into the market economy. Rather than a massive change in social structure, Sorensen found that even with mechanization, demographic shifts and the new economy, the household remained the basic unit of production and consumption. The successful industrialization of Korea has added, however, a new dimension to decision making within households: now, in addition to the usual decisions concerning crops to plant and ways to use the land, members have to estimate the rates of return on capital and labor in market terms (p. 206). Should one farm, or take up factory work? Is it better to rent one's land out to others and seek urban employment, or will hiring farm workers be more profitable? Should one sell one's land and open a business, or not? Thus, "industrialization provides rich and poor alike with choices" (p. 206). Family labor thus remains central to successful agriculture, much as it has in many parts of Europe and the United States. In many ways, this has reinforced family ties rather than eroded them. As for those who could not make a go of farming in a market-centered economy, many have moved to cities where they have invested the proceeds from the sale of their land in small businesses or have secured good jobs in the industrial sector. They do not, however, cut themselves off from their rural kin, but continue to visit, sometimes still keeping houses and fields in the village.

lations, social and family structures, and eventually the whole society. A study in Korea illustrates this as we see in the Human Ecology box, *Over the Mountains Are Mountains*, above.

But no matter how they are introduced, innovations are not always successful. People may experiment a good deal before arriving at an idea, technique, or product that proves more effective or socially beneficial than the old method. Changes can be relatively easy to effect in one situation but not in another. Or they may quite simply be inappropriate for a particular society or at a particular time.

Today in India, for example, the rush toward large-scale heavy industry that characterized efforts at development after independence in 1947 has largely stopped, because the consequences often have been the opposite of what was desired and expected. The country simply could not compete with already industrialized nations. Now the development emphasis is on privately owned, light, high-technology industry, but the results are as yet unclear. One thing is clear, however: instead of experiencing large-scale reorganization and better distribution of wealth, the country is seeing an accentuation of the traditional dichotomy between rich and poor. A populous nation such as India does not always benefit from labor-saving innovations and mass-production techniques.

Summary

A SOCIETY'S ECONOMIC SYSTEM CONSISTS OF IDEAS, behaviors, and institutions. Basic to classical economic theory is the idea of scarce resources. As people inevitably have more wants than they have resources to satisfy them, they must make rational economic decisions, weighing alternatives and deciding which will benefit them most at the least cost. Many social scientists have argued that social and economic institutions perpetuate themselves regardless of the needs of individuals. The economic view of anthropology sees the economy as the process by which a society is provisioned by its own institutions. One school of thought, substantivism, seeks to explain economic processes as the maintenance of an entire cultural order rather than the workings of individual decision makers. Another, formalism, argues that formal economic theory can be broadened to be made applicable to any economic system. Recent investigators have found that the rationality of an economic decision cannot be judged without an awareness of the circumstances surrounding it, and that in some societies markets serve non-economic as well as economic functions.

In order to explain and compare the economic systems of different societies, anthropologists investigate three economic domains: regulation of access to resources, the production process, and the exchange of goods and services.

Strategies for securing natural resources are devised to ensure access to resource-rich land. Agricultural and industrial societies generally maintain clear-cut territorial boundaries that restrict the use of land to certain groups. Hunters and gatherers, however, require greater flexibility to account for seasonal variation in the availability of resources. Typically, the more uncertain or mobile the food supply, the greater the need for flexible boundaries. The extent to which a territory is defended depends on the gains versus the costs of maintaining exclusive rights to a parcel of land.

Industrial societies observe the concept of private ownership of property, or freehold, emphasizing individual control of resources for individual benefit. This concept is alien to the majority of horticultural, pastoral, and hunting-and-gathering societies, in which the individual gains rights to resources only by virtue of affiliation with a group that controls them (corporate ownership). In these societies, individuals have the right to use the community's resources but they do not own them. As more and more societies are affected by industrialization, however, the practice of private ownership is replacing traditional land-use systems; economic systems are becoming less tied to the general system of social relationships. One outcome is alienation, the fragmentation of individuals' relations to their work, the things they produce, and the resources with which they produce them.

Producing usable goods is as important a part of survival as acquiring resources. In studying cross-cultural variation in production, one must consider how production is organized and what the productive strategies are. In industrial societies, the production unit is the business firm, whose function is strictly economic. In nonindustrial societies, the basic production unit is often the household, or domestic group. Nearly all the skills needed for production can be found in a single household; additional effort is supplied by kin and friends. In these societies that employ the domestic mode of production, productive activities are linked to many noneconomic functions. Like collective ownership of resources, this type of domestic production has declined with the spread of industrialism.

Productive strategies combine three elements: natural resources, labor, and capital. In industrial societies, the critical variable in a productive strategy is usually capital; in nonindustrial societies, labor decisions are generally most important. The more mouths people have to feed in relation to the number of workers in the household, the harder they must work. Factors that influence the intensity of labor include people's concepts of productivity (the amount of work a person accomplishes in a given amount of time), productive life span (the period bounded by the culturally established ages at which a person enters and leaves the labor force), and workday (the culturally established number of hours that a person ideally spends at work each day). These culturally defined concepts are often redefined by individuals and households as they adjust to their circumstances.

After goods are produced, those that are not kept or consumed by the producer enter the society's network of exchange. There are three major exchange mechanisms: reciprocity, redistribution, and market exchange. Reciprocity, which plays a much greater role in nonindustrial societies than in our own, involves giving and taking without the exchange of money, between people who are bound by certain social ties and obligations. Three forms of reciprocity involve different degrees of intimacy between giver and taker: generalized reciprocity, balanced reciprocity, and negative reciprocity. Redistribution involves obligatory payments of goods, currency, or services to a central agency, which then reallocates some portion of them. Market exchange is the trading of goods and services through a common medium of value, a transaction removed from social considerations. Most societies use all three forms of exchange, but each society has rules that determine the spheres of exchange that apply to particular goods and situations. But these distinctions are often blurred; people everywhere find opportunities for conversion of a sphere of exchange to a transaction of a sort not usually associated with it.

A degree of economic experimentation and variation is usually necessary for survival. When we study entrepreneurship, or economic innovation and risk-taking, it is clear that in every society the economy is part of the overall system of social organization; one aspect cannot be changed without provoking changes in the others. The needs and values of a particular society at a particular time may determine the course of economic change.

Key Terms

alienation	potlatch
balanced reciprocity	production
conversion	productive life span
corporate ownership	productive strategies
domestic mode of production	productivity
economic system	rational economic decisions
entrepreneurship	reciprocity
exchange	redistribution
formalism	regulation of access to resources
freehold	scarce resources
generalized reciprocity	spheres of exchange
interlocking specializations	substantivism
kula ring	tontine
market exchange	workday
negative reciprocity	

Suggested Readings

Bennett, J. W. & Bowen, J. R. (Eds.). (1988). *Production and economy: Anthropological studies and critiques of development*. In *Monographs in Economic Anthropology* (no. 5). Lantham, MD: University Press of America. Original essays that explore anthropology and development through numerous case studies from different regions.

Bernal, V. (1991). *Cultivating workers: Peasants and capitalism in a Sudanese village*. New York: Columbia University Press. A study based on the political economy of a village on the Blue Nile Irrigation Scheme in Sudan and how it is linked to broad national and international economic systems.

Heyman, J. McC. (1991). *Life and labor on the border: Working people of northeastern Sonora, Mexico, 1886–1986*. Tucson: University of Arizona Press. This book focuses on the life of working-class Mexicans along the U.S. and Mexican border with an insightful view of women's changing economic roles.

Kung, L. (1994). *Factory women in Taiwan*. New York: Columbia University Press. A study dealing with first-generation working women and how work affects their roles and relationships.

Leacock, E. & Safa, H. I. (Eds.). (1988). *Women's work: Development and the division of labor*. South Hadley, MA: Bergin & Garvey (paperback edition). Examines development and modernization in terms of changing rewards and costs for women.

Nash, J. & Safa, H. I. (1985). *Women and change in Latin America*. South Hadley, MA: Bergin & Garvey. A collection of accounts that document the effects on women of the economic crisis in Latin America and the survival strategies they are employing, such as migration, industrial occupations, and mobilization through various forms of collective action.

Schneider, H. K. (1989). *Economic man: The anthropology of economics*. Salem, WI: Sheffield Publishing. A now-classic investigation of how culture affects resource allocation and how scarcity and conflicting needs determine how people cope with uncertainty.

White, J. B. (1994). *Money makes us relatives: Women's labor in urban Turkey*. Austin: University of Texas Press. This book explores the interrelationship between gender, class, and labor in Turkey, based on two years of research documenting the undervalued and underpayed situation of women's work in a rural immigrant community.

White, S. (1992). *Arguing with the crocodile: Gender and class in Bangladesh*. London and New Jersey: Zed Books Ltd. This study looks at the impact of socioeconomic development, including foreign aid, on Bangladesh and the interrelationship between gender and class.

The Political Process
  The Politics of Making Decisions
  Access to the Political Process
  *Gender Issues: Women, Men,
  and Power*
  Power and Authority
  *Case Study: Varieties of Leadership
  among the Turkmen*

The Ecology of Political Behavior
  Access to Resources: Cooperation and
    Competition
  *Case Study: "Scramble Competition"
  among the Pathans of Pakistan*

Evolution of Political Organization
  Bands and Tribes
  Chiefdoms
  States
  *Contemporary Issues: Responding to
  Oppression: Las Madres de Plaza
  de Mayo*

The Politics of Social Control
  Rules and Behavior
  Informal Means of Social Control
  Formal Means of Social Control
  *Using Anthropology: The Politics of
  Time in Ceausescu's Romania*
  Law and Tribes in the Twentieth
    Century

**Political Relations
Among Societies**
  Mechanisms of Peace
  Armed Conflict

Summary

Key Terms

Suggested Readings

Chapter 11

Politics, Social Control, and Political Organization

Politics, from an anthropological perspective, closely resembles economics in that virtually every social activity can be seen as having political implications. In every society there are scarce or limited rewards for which people compete, rules that govern this competition, and procedures for mitigating conflicts that arise among individuals and groups. *Politics* is the process by which decisions are made, rules for group behavior established, competition for positions of leadership regulated, and the disruptive effects of disputes minimized. More succinctly, politics is the process of "who gets what, when, and how" (Lewellen, 1992). Political organization is the larger context in which political processes occur.

Politics is a universal aspect of all human relations. Even very small groups such as families and households can be considered arenas of political behavior. Political scientists tend to focus on state-level institutions, national parties, state policy, and international diplomacy.

By contrast, anthropologists tend to focus on individual communities and relatively small-scale political systems. For example, Victoria Burbank has closely observed and described the role of women as political actors in Aboriginal Australian societies, with an emphasis on how aggression is related to gender roles (Burbank, 1994). Also, anthropologists focus on the political implications of ideas or behaviors that are not often thought of as "political." For example, Henry Rutz looks at the politics of time; that is, in Rutz's words "time is power," and who controls it is an arena for competition everywhere (Rutz, 1992, p.14). This chapter will discuss local-level politics, social control, and the varieties of political organization, and how they may have arisen.

The Political Process

At the bottom of all political competition lies disagreement—conflicting ideas about individual interests and community life. The specific issues involved can be almost anything individuals or groups consider important; anything that is worth competing for. In all these cases, the decisions that are eventually reached will benefit some people or groups more than others, in spite of any lofty rhetoric to the contrary. But there is wide variation from society to society in the kinds of decisions people attempt to influence, and in the nature of the rewards.

The Politics of Making Decisions

Among hunting-and-gathering peoples, for example, political competition might arise over disagreements about where to search for game, marriage arrangements, food sharing, when to move camp, where a new camp should be located, or any other matter relating to the entire group. The resolution of these disagreements involves politics, even though the process may not seem very competitive by our own standards. A decision affecting the community has to be made, and often one group's or one individual's desires or needs prevail over those of others.

Almost all of the societies we have described in the chapters on hunters and gatherers, horticulturists, and pastoralists make their decisions in fluid, personal, and informal ways. Ariaal men spend a good part of each day in small groups discussing current events and, in effect, making group or **consensual decisions**. A consensus is a solution or de-

cision that everyone is willing to accept—there are no obvious losers. Arriving at decisions by consensus is time-consuming, but it tends to keep the group united. This method is also used by the Dobe !Kung people and the Yanomamö. Even where, as with the Bedouin of Arabia and the Hopi of the American Southwest, there are more formally designated leaders and even hereditary lines of succession, most day-to-day decisions are made in the context of informal discussion and debate.

Consensual decision making is particularly effective where group cohesion is important, but it can also lead to surprising results. Consider a hypothetical, but realistic case, where a small group decides to eat out together in a restaurant. The majority prefer to go to an Italian restaurant while the minority strongly prefers a local French bistro: the consensual decision might well be to end up at a Thai establishment. Even though it was no one's first choice, it was acceptable to all. A democratic vote would have led to a result that some, at least, would have found objectionable. A dictator, of course, could impose the minority's preference on the majority, but at the risk of a confrontation. While we think of consensual decision making as limited, it can be important even at the highest levels of government. The British Prime Minister, John Major, it is widely said, was no one's first choice to succeed Margaret Thatcher but he was broadly acceptable to his party's leadership and therefore was tapped for the job. When American presidential candidates were selected by party leaders, the process was essentially consensual.

There are obvious limitations of scale to consensus politics. Also, it is possible to arrive at consensus judgments, which, while socially acceptable, prove disastrous due to the fact that participants may have unequal knowledge or expertise. Corporations, government organizations, and the military have clear rules about who makes decisions and who has to be consulted, and then the decisions are implemented through the actions of lower-level leaders. The advantages of a "chain of command" system whereby decisions made at the top, by whatever means, are that it can coordinate the activities of huge numbers of people and bring expertise to bear on the issues involved. Moreover, centralized decision making can enforce codes of behavior that facilitate cooperative group life on a very large scale: systems of policing, laws, and in-

Market women attend a political rally in Accra, Ghana. Women play a major role in the marketing system and have considerable political influence.

(The Hutchison Library)

numerable codes and regulations all create environments in which individuals, completely willingly or not, work with others to some common end. The disadvantages of centralized decision making and a strong chain of command are equally apparent: despotism, war, mass murder, and environmental destruction, to name a few. We will return to some of these issues later.

Access to the Political Process

As well as the norms governing how people may participate in political competition, every society also has both formal and informal rules governing who may participate. In politics, the formal rules are usually the legal or institutionalized ones; the informal codes arise from everyday behavior. While the results of political competition may affect every member of a society, it does not necessarily follow that everyone in the community is equally involved in the political process. All societies impose certain formal qualifications for participation in different areas of politics. Group membership is the most basic of these formal qualifications; age and gender restrictions are also common, with women often underrepresented or excluded from the formal political decision-making process. Even in the egalitarian society of the Va-

natinai, studied by Maria Lepowsky, contact with male-dominated societies has led to the dominance of men in political affairs that extend beyond the boundaries of Vanatinai. (See the Gender Issues box, *Women, Men, and Power,* pages 304–305.)

But exclusion from the formal decision-making process does not necessarily imply lack of political influence. As anyone familiar with the American political system knows, formal offices and positions of authority do not tell the whole story about who actually holds power. Frequently, informal channels of access to decision making are open to those who cannot or do not hold recognized positions of authority. In the United States, lobbies for powerful interest groups have no formal place in Congress: in practice, they strongly influence elected lawmakers. Women may exercise power in societies that formally restrict their access to political office. This is often accomplished by the influence that they can exert on their husbands, brothers, and sons. Among the Iroquois, men held the dominant political positions, but women selected the officeholders. Thus we must not confuse norms defining formal participation in the political process with the actual exercise of influence and power. The two may be quite different.

The number of criteria restricting access to political roles increases as societies become more

Gender Issues

Women, Men, and Power

MARIA LEPOWSKY CONDUCTED fieldwork on Vanatinai, a small, remote island southeast of New Guinea, from 1977 to 1979, and subsequently returned twice, in 1981 and in 1987. The matrilineal society she describes in her book, *Fruit of the Motherland* (1993), is a startling contrast not only to many of the surrounding Melanesian cultures, but to most cultures throughout the world. On Vanatinai there are no ideologies of male superiority and female inferiority; "[T]here is considerable overlap between the roles and activities of women and men, and the actions of both sexes are considered equally valuable. Men have no formal authority or powers of coercion over women except for the physical violence that both sexes abhor and that is rare in the extreme." Social rules emphasize the personal autonomy of each individual, and the low population density (about 2,300 people) probably contributes to this ethic of respect for the individual, since in the event of a serious conflict either party has the option of moving to another hamlet. However, both the high value placed on giving to others, and the fear of arousing anger or jealously in a sorcerer or witch serves as means for regulating individual behavior.

Lepowsky finds the most striking evidence that Vanatinai is a sexually egalitarian society in the fact that there are both "big women" and "big men." In Melanesian societies, which generally lack chiefs or other forms of stratified political power, big men are the main form of authority. Va-

natinai society offers every adult, regardless of sex, the opportunity to acquire personal prestige and influence over others. The principal arena for acquiring prestige and influence centers on the elaborate ceremonial exchange and mortuary ritual complex.

> Both men and women give and receive ceremonial valuables, foodstuffs, goods made by women such as clay cooking pots, sleeping mats, and coconut-leaf skirts, and goods made by men such as carved hardwood bowls and lime spatulas. They exchange with partners of both sexes. . . . Women and men alike host the mortuary feasts held intermittently for years after each death, giving and receiving enormous quantities of customary wealth (pp. viii–ix).

Both men and women can choose to host and make contributions to mortuary feasts over the minimum expected of everyone, and can accumulate ceremonial valuables and other goods both to distribute in acts of public generosity and to honor obligations to exchange partners. These people are known as *giagia*—givers.

Women also participate in other activities that earn prestige, such as ritual expertise and the production of garden surpluses. They inherit land and use rights over forest and reef areas as well as pigs, household goods, and valuables equally with men, and retain control of the land and valuables they inherit or possess. Both men and women work in the gardens and tend pigs and control the fruits of their labors, but it is the women

of a hamlet who decide if there is a sufficient surplus of garden produce in a particular year to exchange with outsiders for other goods or to use to host a major commemorative feast. The postmarital residence pattern is bilocal, so that both partners participate in the important decisions of their natal group and neither loses the right to matrilineal resources.

While Lepowsky characterizes Vanatinai society as egalitarian, she emphasizes that this does not mean that there are no differences among individuals on the island. "Some islanders hold more rights to land, food trees, and reef areas than others, and some inherit more ceremonial valuables, pigs, and potential exchange partners from maternal kin or fathers. Some have more kin and more affines who can potentially offer aid, while others are disadvantaged in accruing prestige by chronic poor health" (p. 39).

Of course, Vanatinai society, like any other in the world, is not static but evolves through cultural innovations and reinterpretations. While this is true over time, for small-scale non-Western societies, contact with Europeans is invariably a crucial challenge to their cultures. Vanatinai was first sighted by Europeans in 1606, but its remoteness and dangerous barrier reefs ensured its isolation for about another two hundred years. However, by the mid-nineteenth century European traders and fishermen began to have regular contacts with the islanders. These early contacts were unregulated by any government, and there were many instances of local women being kidnapped and local people being terrorized. Oral tradition on Vanatinai records a marked increase in inter-island warfare prior to the British extending colonial control over the region in 1888,[1] although people on Vanatinai say there were inter-island raids as late as the 1920s. During World War II there were episodes of violence. Mission influence in the region, which had begun in 1891, increased greatly after World War I, although a significant minority of older people on Vanatinai do not adhere to any Western religion and many Christians continue to retain their indigenous religious beliefs.

Papua New Guinea became independent in 1975, and Vanatinai became part of Milne Bay Province, with the right to elect representatives to the provincial assembly and a member to the national parliament. In 1979, in response to representations from the Vanatinai and neighboring Saisai peoples that they felt neglected by the government and wanted aid posts and government schools, the Yeleyamba council was formed, with its chamber located on Vanatinai.

How have these changes affected women's lives and relations between men and women on Vanatinai? "[The] people say that the central position of women in island life is *taubwaragha*, which means both 'ancient' and 'the way of the ancestors'" (Lepowsky, 1993, p. 72).

By the 1870s, a pattern of Europeans trading with island men (and dealing with island women only when they wanted sex, either forcible or consensual) had been set that persisted through the colonial era. Since the early 1950s under the Australian colonial government and, after 1975, the national government of Papua New Guinea, elected local government council members from Vanatinai have all been male. Lepowsky reports that "[w]omen who were nominated, by men, on an occasion I witnessed in 1978 withdrew their names in embarrassment. I was told that this was because they do not speak English" (Lepowsky, 1993, p. 76). The other two official languages, Pidgin and Motu, are rarely spoken on the island. Not only have hardly any women left the island to seek employment or schooling, but many officials are from parts of the country that have a strong ideology of male dominance and consequently expect to deal with Vanatinai men. In addition, older men who have had no schooling and have never worked for wages off the island are also uneasy about dealing with government officials, so the local government council members are almost entirely men in their early twenties to their early forties. This means that the new form of political authority (election to local, regional, or national bodies) is effectively open only to younger men, thus disenfranchising virtually all women and male elders, even those who are *giagia*.

There is probably no Melanesian society where wealth distribution is the only route to becoming a big man; another way is prowess in warfare. In Vanatinai the (now extinct) role of *asiara*—an exemplary and legendary warrior—was available only to men, (notably younger men), although women were not excluded from councils of war or diplomacy or even the battlefield. The suppression of warfare has given more equality of opportunity to women to achieve prestige through other traditional means. For example, they no longer need male escorts when sailing on inter-island trade and exchange trips. However, election to local government has opened another route to prestige for younger men. Local council members often perceive themselves to be in direct competition with the *giagia*. Having left the island to work for wages, they tend to possess few pigs or ceremonial valuables and do not participate in traditional exchanges, and many have been active in trying to regulate the number of pigs that can be owned by a household and to limit opportunities for exchange visits between islanders.

Lepowsky concludes that while externally imposed systems of political, legal, and religious authority have clearly meant a certain loss of autonomy for every islander, "the principle of respect for individual autonomy remains extremely strong in Vanatinai culture, and this principle continues to underlie egalitarian social relations—including gender equality" (1993, pp. 79–80). The availability of education on Vanatinai has dramatically increased in recent years, and parents are sending both their daughters and sons to school. "The numbers of women who will seek education or employment off-island and then return home will therefore probably also increase in the near future" (p. 80). And there is no reason to believe that women will not begin to participate in politics on a local level and perhaps eventually on a national level as well.

[1] Lepowski postulates that this may have been due to a rise in population and the increased availability of rifles brought in by white traders.

complex. In state societies, not only group membership, age, and gender, but also ethnicity, religion, caste, wealth, and education may circumscribe political participation, as shown in Chapter 9. These criteria can be embedded in formal rules as well as in informal practices. In our own society, gender, ethnicity, and wealth are not a basis for formal restrictions to political access, yet women and members of some ethnic minorities are still not proportionately represented among officeholders and those with political influence. Political access in societies such as our own is hierarchically organized. While the right to vote has given most minority groups access at one level of participation, the higher levels—the domain of the ruling elite—are still less broadly accessible.

As the level of social complexity increases, so do the number and scope of objectives that unite and potentially divide people. In our society, overt political competition is focused on access to public office and such issues as what portion of income and personal property should be taxed, where a new housing project or nuclear power plant should be built (or not built), and what kind of arms or trade agreement should be reached with a foreign nation. Parties to the competition typically mobilize impressive support to bolster their positions and apply all sorts of legal and, on occasion, illegal pressure in an effort to turn the decision in their favor.

Power and Authority

Naturally, restrictions on access to political influence affect the determination of leadership. Certain criteria for leadership may be highly idiosyncratic; individuals might be able to influence others because they possess charisma or because they have persistently demonstrated wisdom or good fortune.

Leadership can also be established by success in mobilizing organizational support. The general rules because he has the support of the army; candidates are elected to office because they can mobilize the greatest numbers of voters. Often these two kinds of leadership criteria work together. In Melanesia, status and prestige are accorded to certain individuals known as "big men." A big man has typically demonstrated certain personal qualities, such as bravery or speech-making ability, that make him worthy of admiration. But these qualities alone will never accord him the status of big

man. He must also have a following, which can be acquired only through exceptional, habitual, and calculated generosity. Such generosity, in turn, is largely based on the skillful manipulation of food production or trade relations with others.

In discussing political leadership, it is useful to distinguish between **power**, the ability to exert influence because one's directives are backed by sanctions of one sort or another (the ultimate negative sanction being the use of physical force), and **authority**, the ability to exert influence simply because of one's personal prestige or the status of one's office (Fried, 1967). Among the Dobe Ju/'hoansi or !Kung, for example, certain individuals may acquire authority but not power. They can affect the behavior of others because their opinions for one reason or another are respected, but they cannot effectively impose threats or sanctions of any kind. In Melanesia, a "big man" has a somewhat more clearly defined political position, but again his authority rests ultimately on his persuasive abilities. In state societies, however, officials can exercise both power and authority. They can force citizens to behave in certain ways through the use of sanctions backed by armed force. Authority may be ascribed or achieved; that is, it may be based on ancestry or other ascribed qualities such as divinity or holiness, or it may be achieved by military success, electoral success, demonstrated moral worth, or some other factor.

CASE STUDY:

Varieties of Leadership Among the Turkmen

THERE ARE THREE DISTINCT FORMS OF LEADERSHIP among the pastoral and agricultural Yomut and Göklan Turkmen tribes of north-central Iran.[1] These illustrate the complex ways in which different modes of decision making and different sources of political influence can coexist in the same general population. Among the largely nomadic pastoral groups occupying the arid steppes along the

[1] Based on fieldwork in Iran, 1974–75, with William Irons, and upon a number of writings by William Irons.

*Two Turkmen leaders: the one on the left is known for his religious scholarship
and probity; the other is influential because of his great wealth and the number of
families he employs.*
(Daniel Bates)

Atrek River marking the border with the new Republic of Turkmenia, subsistence is based on a mix-
ture of animal husbandry and small-scale agriculture where sufficient ground water permits.
Population densities are low, and patrilineally related families live together on territories that are
held to belong to their lineages, dwelling in black
felt yurts clustered in village-like communities
called *obas*. These range in size from two to ten
yurts. Leadership is consensual among household
heads, with a smaller group of senior males called
aq sakal, or "grey beards," having the greatest say
in communal matters. Households who wish to
join another oba must secure the agreement both
of the households of the oba they are leaving and
of the one they wish to join. This is because grazing rights are viewed as the common property of
the descent group. In short, most decisions regarding the use of resources and residence are made by

consensus among male heads of households. The
main exception to this pattern historically has been
in times of war, when for purposes of conducting
raids, for example, a temporary military leader
would be selected who was given the authority to
issue directives.

Among the Yomut and Göklan communities
living along the better-watered Gorgan River,
where both irrigated and rainfall agriculture is
practiced, leadership and political decision making
are more centralized. Households also dwell on
lands associated with major lineages in large villages, which often contain over eighty households.
Villages are invariably divided into named neighborhoods, each closely associated with families
closely related in the patrilineal line. Land is
owned and worked as the private property of the
household, although it may be rented out or accessed through sharecropping. The neighborhood,

Teahouses or coffee shops in Turkey are important venues for socializing and are often the location for intense political discussion.

(Ed Kashi)

inasmuch as it has anything to decide, is a highly consensual grouping, but significant decision making is located elsewhere. One leader whose importance varies widely from village to village is the *kathoda,* or mayor, who represents the village in official governmental matters and in turn brings state authority to bear on village life: tax collection, military conscription, road repair, school repairs, and the like. These individuals may be elected or not, but always hold office with the approval of the Iranian government. Their authority depends on the degree of respect and esteem accorded the state by the people, together with what they bring to the office in their person. Some are respected and trusted; others are seen as flunkies of the government and ignored as much as possible. Their power, of course, derives from the government's ability to bring police or soldiers into the village to enforce orders.

In addition to the kathodas, there are a number of regional leaders who have great influence, usually over many villages. One type of leader, who holds no formal office but who is known by the honorific title *khan,* is similar to the "big man" of Melanesia. He (it is always a male) is someone who has acquired great influence, and hence power,

through his wealth and ability to control the activities of the many households who depend on him for credit, employment, or as sharecroppers. The house of a major khan is readily recognizable from its size; it is usually a multistoried dwelling surrounded by a high wall, with numerous expensive vehicles parked in the yard, and is topped by a roof displaying significant evidence of the electronic age. The younger khans are not khans because they have inherited the title or acquired it, but because they inherited the lands that yield the power. The older generation of khans acquired their lands and influence through their close relations with the state during a period when the government was trying to develop agriculture and was granting private title to fields. Many khans were able to have formerly corporate, communal lands registered in their names. Some are known for their rapacity; others have earned community respect through treating their dependents fairly, dispensing acts of charity and hospitality. Thus, these men have a degree of authority or legitimacy as well as the power that stems from great wealth and government contacts.

Another major source of political influence and decision making rests with individuals who often have little wealth but significant authority as religious teachers and mediators of renown. The most significant of these are called *akhunds,* and they are highly regarded as men of learning. The best-known akhunds have large followings. Groups of akhunds meet regularly and, although they have no coercive power, their pronouncements can and do influence temporal events. In some respects, their moral authority serves to check the activities of the khans.

A final element in the local political environment are individuals belonging to a number of small sacred or holy lineages, called *ewlad* (descendants), because of their putative descent from one of the first four caliphs or successors to the Prophet Mohammed. Certain ewlad men serve as mediators in disputes, since they are considered neutral and it is a major sin to assault their person. Accordingly, they can intervene in feuds and in property disputes without being drawn into conflict themselves. ◗

Power and authority need not always accompany each other. If there is a common denominator to local-level politics, it surely must be the complexity of factional alignments and, for the observer at least, the bewildering shifts in the centers of power and decision making. At the heart of this lies a factor that is hard for the outsider to comprehend: the ability of certain individuals to mobilize supporters and allies, and to translate personal qualities of charisma and sociality into political influence.

The Ecology of Political Behavior

There are many ways in which politics determines how humans interact with their environments, and also many environmental factors that affect the political process. Many anthropologists consider most human ecological studies to really be analyses of **political ecology**, since the main determinants for how resources are accessed and distributed are political. This might also be called the "political economy" approach, since it considers the ways in which politics and economics intersect (Peet & Watts, 1994). The previous discussion of leadership in Iran makes this obvious; politics rewards some more than others. Among the Turk-

men, wealthy and influential men occasionally hire teams of large tractors and set them to plowing arid and only partially arable public lands that the rest of the community uses for grazing. They then seed the new fields and, if they are lucky with the rains, make a handsome profit on the resultant wheat crops (that are guarded by their hired help); the soils, however, quickly erode and common pastures are lost to both farming and grazing.

Access to Resources: Cooperation and Competition

There are important environmental factors that can render a highly personalized and flexible system of local-level politics advantageous at every level of political complexity. These highly personalized local political activities, in turn, affect the development and stability of supra-local forms of political organization and institutions. Local populations, even individuals, by necessity cultivate and maintain multiple political and social ties with each other that allow them to cope with uncertainties of all sorts. Until very recently in the West, and still in many parts of the world, local populations were dependent on local food resources. At the same time, as we have noted in Chapter 7, the potential for agriculture or other forms of food procurement is highly variable, with sharp contrasts between highly productive and marginal areas.

Even within regions, members of particular societies are often differentiated in terms of access to critical resources and their place in the system of production. There is inevitably a great deal of exchange of food items, labor, and other services both within communities and among them—virtually no local population is completely self-sufficient. Pastoral farmers and herding households exchange continually, the pastoral Yörük sell their animal products in markets, the Pygmies of the Ituri Forest in Zaire trade forest products for grain with their Bantu farming neighbors, and so forth. In the settlement of the arid reaches of the Little Colorado River, as we saw with Abruzzi's study of Mormon colonization, the political ties of each community to the central church hierarchy were critical to survival; local communities were supported during lean or disastrous years (1992).

The nature of resources affect political behavior. Competition for resources will arise only where those resources (such as fields or irrigation works) have a high intrinsic value and are in a clearly bounded area. In Swat, Pakistan, as we will see in the following case study, culturally different neighboring populations make it difficult for landowners to expand into areas that are not already owned by Pathan households; the fields over which they contend are highly productive and worth defending. Hunters and gatherers, on the contrary, may occupy lands where resources are not concentrated; thus, land ownership or control is not a major source of competition.

Environmental uncertainty is another factor encouraging individuals and groups to maintain a multiplicity of political associations. Most communities periodically face conditions of drought, crop and animal epidemics, disease, and the like that necessitate seeking help from others—even from those with which relations may be strained or hostile. For example, observers of social life in the Middle East have been struck by the great amount of time and energy individuals spend socializing and politicking (Bates & Rassam, 1983, p. 242). Whether it be the ubiquitous teahouses of rural Turkey, Iraq, and Iran; the village guesthouses of Syria; or the urban coffee shops of Egypt; clusters of men and women meet (usually separately) on an almost daily basis to reaffirm existing ties, to forge new ones, and to keep an eye on the activities of others. Farming and pastoralism in these regions is carried out in an environment that demands close attention to ever-shifting political winds in addition to changing market conditions.

The result of this variability and interdependence is that people are unevenly distributed, with prosperous communities frequently abutting poorer ones; households and groups are simultaneously faced with the need to compete and to cooperate. Peasants and pastoralists may fight for the same well; upstream villagers may fight with downstream neighbors over water rights: communities, neighbors, and even relatives may find themselves in competition even as they rely on each other for help and the exchange of goods. Individuals try to maintain as wide a range of contacts as possible and are continually prepared to shift alliances as interests dictate. Since the most important predator or competitor any local population might face is its neighbors, politics is an integral part of the environmental setting.

CASE STUDY:

"Scramble Competition" among the Pathans of Pakistan

THE PATHANS OF SWAT, PAKISTAN, ARE IN MANY respects like the Turkmen. They have important leaders who achieve their positions by competitive economic, military, and social activities carried out over a long period of time (Barth, 1959; Boone, 1992). Here population densities are high, positions of authority are formalized, and power is centralized in them. There are many reasons why this is so, although the lines of causality are not entirely clear. For example, with the development of irrigation agriculture, some communities and some regions emerge as especially favored, grow rapidly, and expand at the expense of others. Certainly, the extension of political control, via warfare or otherwise, entails the development of mechanisms for enforcing orders over a large area.

Like the Turkmen khans, whose power is based on their economic wealth, the large landowners among the Pathans also assume leadership roles. However, unlike the khans, who acquired their lands from the state, the Pathans landowners compete for power and authority, each vying to increase his wealth at the expense of competitors. In what James Boone calls "scramble competition," would-be leaders "scramble" for clients—tenants and warriors who will remain loyal and perhaps aid in extending their leader's power and reputation (Boone, 1992, p. 326). First, the landowner builds his economic resources by encroaching on the land of his neighbors, farming it, and staking claim to the property. If he is successful, this strategy leads to increased wealth, which is used to attract more followers to work his land and defend his holdings. Essential in this are the great feasts and other forms of display and hospitality he sponsors and which, in turn, contribute to his reputation as a powerful leader.

But there are limits to the ability of any one leader to completely dominate the valley. What emerges is often a balance of power due to the fact that each leader also runs the risk that his followers might defect if a competitor offers better terms. In a sense, there are two scrambles going on: one for followers among large landowners and the second, among followers or tenants to secure the most hospitality and best rewards for their labor and support (Boone, 1992, p. 326). Even though this competition is carried out largely (but not entirely) in the social arena, it results in certain men acquiring great influence over others. Such a person has the ability to give away food in time of need, mobilize public opinion, and generally shape public policy. They can also mobilize armed retainers when needed. But since there are always rivals waiting for their own opportunity for advancement, the leaders have to be careful not to alienate their followers. ◗

Evolution of Political Organization

Political activity occurs within the context of a larger social framework. Procedures for making decisions and defining authority follow certain patterns, that can be seen as recurring in similarly constituted societal settings.

Essentially, political organization varies broadly along two dimensions. The first is the degree to which political roles and institutions are specialized or differentiated from other roles and institutions. For example, a society may have political offices such as king, chief, judge, or legislator—statuses vested, in varying degrees, with power and authority. A king, for example, might have absolute power of life or death over his subjects, while a judge, however powerful, will have more restricted powers. The more specialized or differentiated a society's political organization, the more formal is its structure—that is, focused on institutions dedicated more or less exclusively to running the political system. The second dimension concerns the degree to which power and authority are centralized as opposed to divided among the members of a society. Where political power is highly centralized, there will likely be a hierarchy of decision-making offices and access to the political process may be restricted to members of certain classes or ranks.

It is generally believed that from the beginnings of human society, until about 10,000 years ago, most groups were organized as relatively egalitarian societies. Over the last ten thousand or so years, human society has moved toward greater specialization of roles and institutions, including political institutions. Positions of influence and authority become more centralized and increasingly restricted to a relatively small subset of the larger population; centralized decision making and bureaucracies are involved in more and more aspects of peoples' lives. Very often these emerging bureaucracies are exclusively male, a fact that may further solidify gender hierarchies.

The development of political centralization is thus fairly recent. It probably began long after the Neolithic revolution in food production (the changeover from hunting and gathering wild food to the domestication of plants and animals), which took place around 10,000 years ago. This is not to say that a shift from food collection to cultivation in itself required increased political complexity, but the effects of this shift on the way people lived acted as selective pressures for greater political and social integration. With food production, human populations became larger and denser and were sustained through much more economic specialization than before. Also, vital resources had to be protected from external threats and competition. In conflicts between groups, the one that is best organized and best consolidated will have an advantage (Carniero, 1981).

In general, as population size increases within political entities, the volume of information that has to be processed, the number of decisions made, and the number of possible communication problems generated are all so great that some political division of labor is essential. Groups that can develop an administrative hierarchy gain an advantage in coping with the problems facing them. Even the nomadic and fiercely independent Turkmen submit to the orders of leaders in time of war. Nevertheless, while the chief, khan, or big man in a small community can talk to everyone on a one-to-one basis, for a fairly large regional population (subsumed as one political system) this is not practical.

By delegating authority, leaders extend their control and in so doing create a form of bureaucratic hierarchy. This bureaucratic hierarchy can coordinate the activities of many workers, fighters, and food producers. In groups without administrative hierarchies, there are fairly narrow limits as to how many people can be coordinated without resorting to dividing the population into subgroups, each with its own leader or spokesperson (Johnson, 1983).

While external threats or competition may have been a factor in the rise of centralized political systems, economic factors appear to be most important. Warfare does not generally need a permanent agency of coordination, as we saw with the Yanomamö, but an increasingly specialized economy does. Once that agency exists in the economic realm, extension of its planning capabilities into other areas such as warfare would be logical and would undoubtedly prove advantageous.

Bands and Tribes

Nomadic hunter-gatherers are characteristically organized as egalitarian societies, although this is not a necessary outcome of a hunting-and-gathering procurement strategy. Groups of hunters and gatherers in areas of rich food supplies may well have a political organization similar to that of ranked or stratified sedentary agricultural communities. The relative abundance of the food supply affects the size and social complexity of local groups (Price, 1981; Earle, 1991).

The simplest form of egalitarian political organization, following Service (1971) is sometimes referred to as the *band*—a loosely integrated population sharing a sense of common identity but few specialized institutions. To recapitulate points raised in Chapter 4, the Dobe Ju/'hoansi or !Kung people and the Inuits or Eskimo are illustrative. In such societies, political life is largely one dimension of social life. Until recently, there were no specialized political roles; that is, no political leaders with designated authority. Economic exchange is effected through reciprocity, with no individual having disproportionate control over or access to resources. Some degree of competition for influence may arise over day-to-day problems such as decisions to hunt or move to new camps, but it is resolved in give-and-take discussions involving all members of the group. Within !Kung bands, the headman has no power and only limited authority. He is essentially a symbol of the group, and as such is given certain ceremonial prerogatives, such as walking at the head of the line when the band moves. But the position carries no rewards of power and riches, and the headman hunts, works, and shares his food like all others in the band (Marshall, 1960).

Although we term such societies "egalitarian," the term has to be used cautiously. Not everyone is equal on closer inspection. First, as we have noted, many positions of respect are reserved for males; in fact, many are reserved for only a few successful older males. Speth, in a recent survey of the literature on hunting-and-gathering groups, finds that women are frequently less well-nourished than are males—particularly male hunters (1988). Most currently studied hunter-gatherers occupy lands that sustain only very low population densities and require frequent movement. Much of the egalitarian nature of hunters and gatherers is probably a product of technological difficulties of food production, storage, and security. Unless you can safely store something of value, accumulation for personal ends is difficult. Since political power often rests ultimately on economic clout, as we saw in the preceding section, an inability to accumulate material resources precludes individuals from gaining great power. From the archaeological evidence it is clear that in areas of abundant, predictable resources, we find far more complex societies than in marginal zones.

The band is not the only political expression of egalitarian society; many societies that are organized tribally are comparatively open with regard to access to the political process. The term *tribe*, as discussed in Chapter 8, is often used to describe an organization similar to that of the band, but coordinating the activities of more people—perhaps even a number of villages or small communities. The tribe is a descent- and kinship-based grouping in which subgroups are clearly linked to one another, with the potential of uniting for common defense or warfare. Nevertheless, tribal societies need have no specialized political roles, no authoritative leaders, no permanent centers of administration, and no formal mechanisms of coercion. Like the band, the tribe is egalitarian inasmuch as everyone within certain age and sex categories has access to status and prestige. And again, as with bands, we have to be careful of the term egalitarian: the Yanomamö men might be regarded as roughly equals in the political arena, but women are decidedly disadvantaged.

Chiefdoms

The term *egalitarian*, as we have noted, has to be used cautiously but still it is possible to see organizational differences between what we have termed egalitarian systems and political systems in which power is significantly concentrated in the hands of a few and where specialized political institutions maintain social order. Such systems are sometimes referred to as being "ranked." Ranked societies are those in which valued positions of status are somehow limited (Fried, 1967, p. 109). This is, of course, a far broader category than is egalitarian society, as it encompasses systems ranging from very minimal differentiation to extreme forms of stratification.

An intermediate expression of ranking is exemplified by what is often referred to as *chiefdoms*. A chiefdom is distinguished by the presence of a permanent central political agency to coordinate the activities of multi-community political units. From an evolutionary perspective, chiefdoms mark a major stage in political development. As Carniero puts it, "They represent the first transcending of local autonomy in human history" (1981, p. 37). With chiefdoms, we see political decisions occurring at two levels: that of the chief or senior leader, and at the local level, as subordinates carry out commands.

Although the upper ranks may be composed of a large number of people, at its core is the office of chief. While there is great variability among chiefdoms, all are characterized by profound inequality (Service, 1971, p. 140). The paramount leader or chief occupies a hereditary position and typically has great powers over subordinates. Often, as in Polynesia, chiefs had supernatural qualities and were distinguished from other high-ranking individuals by elaborate dress, expensive residences, and, upon death, special burial ceremonies. The archaeological record shows that often chiefs were buried with wives and retainers to serve them in the afterlife (Feinman & Neitzel, 1984).

The office of chief is a specialized political position with well-defined areas of authority. Hawaiian chiefs, for example, were considered the owners of the resources their people used and had the right to call on their labor and collect a portion of their crops. These chiefs accumulated great storehouses filled with goods of all sorts: food, tools, clothing, and so on. Chiefs would use the surplus to support lavish community feasts or to subsidize large-scale construction projects such as irrigation works, all of which would enhance both their status and their potential for accumulating ever-larger funds (Earle, 1991). While most see the redistribu-

Kwakuitl chiefs assumed great power and prestige.
(William Heick)

tive activities of chiefs as important, it is not clear whether this is the source of their power or the outcome of their having it (Carniero, 1981). In many respects, chiefs act like tribute-takers, even though they may provide a service to the society at large by giving back some of what they collect.

Chiefs can deploy labor, give commands, and ask others to do things that they themselves might never do. Their authority is backed by sanctions of one kind or another. In most Polynesian chiefdoms, religious status is probably the chief's most compelling tool of persuasion. Chiefs are believed to be richly infused with a supernatural force known as *mana*, which sanctifies their right to office and otherwise protects their persons. Invested with this kind of strong spiritual power, chiefs are able to enforce their authority by threats of curses or other spiritual sanctions (Sahlins, 1963).

In chiefdoms, a person acquires rank through heredity—being the eldest son of a chief or his sister's eldest son. Sometimes, however, kinship ties are complex and overlapping, enabling more than one person to lay claim to the position of chief. Kinship and ancestry are often the basis of many status positions other than that of chief. The chief's closest kin may form something of a noble lineage. In many cases, a hierarchy develops in which those kin closest to the chief have a higher status than more distant relations. On Tahiti, for example, the population was basically divided into three grades of people (with levels of rank within each grade): the immediate family of the paramount chiefs; those of a lesser, intermediate lineage; and the commoners. The nobles of a chiefdom may exercise various levels of authority and possess prestige and influence, but they are still more like a hierarchy among kin than a bureaucratic administration of the type that exists in state societies.

The fact that chiefs rule through bureaucracies largely comprised of relatives may, according to Eric Wolf, be the reason why chiefs are often quite eager to collaborate with outsiders, even to the detriment of their people (Wolf, 1982, p. 96). Wherever European colonialists went, they usually found local chiefs willing to collaborate in the exploitation of their own people. The reason for this, Wolf suggests, is that by acquiring European allies, money, and guns the chiefs free themselves from the limits imposed by having to rule through relatives. They gain what they hope is an independent source of power.

States

The most complex and centralized of political systems are states. A **state** is essentially a complex of institutions that organize power on a supra-kinship basis. This does not mean that all power in such societies is preempted by the state. Kinship networks that possess limited authority not only usually coexist with states, but may be fundamental to the political process. In ancient Greece, until approximately 800 B.C. the population could be characterized as being organized along the lines of chiefdoms, with chiefs on occasion forming alliances for war but rarely recognizing any superior political order (Ferguson, 1992). But around 800 B.C., a new polity emerged: the *polis*, or city state, whose peoples were not defined by kinship and ties to chiefs but by residence within a territory with its own codes of law and governance. Still, the ties of

tribe (*phylai*) and clan (*gens*) and allegiance to chiefs were not abandoned, only weakened (1992, p. 192). By definition, it is the state that holds ultimate power. Acts of coercion or violence not legitimized by the state are punishable by law. To maintain internal order and regulate relations with other populations, the state maintains mechanisms of coercive control: a police force, militia, army, arsenals, and so on.

Perhaps the most useful way to describe the state is in terms of the organization of lines of authority and decision making (Wright & Johnson, 1975). States have at least three levels in their chain of command or hierarchy, as opposed to the two levels associated with chiefdoms. A chief gives orders either directly to his followers, or through one intermediary, such as a clan leader. In a state, orders routinely flow through a complex chain of command involving several distinct stages. Thus, decisions made by rulers or administrators are often implemented by a bureaucratic organization far removed from the upper level of government. Decisions regarding even very basic elements of production, such as land and water rights, may be made by administrators who have little direct relationship to the community. Stalin, for example, ordered the construction of canals, which by 1995 had effectively destroyed the Sea of Aral; the government of China is preparing to dam the Yangtze River beginning in 1997, thus implementing the world's largest hydroelectric project. The millions of people affected in both instances were not consulted.

State-level political organization is associated with large populations, substantial segments of which live in towns and cities. The rise of the Greek city-states, just noted, was closely associated with population increase and a rise in agricultural productivity. The complex of communities that comprise a state is supported by intensive agriculture, relatively well-developed communications systems, markets, and extensive economic specialization that allows for the production of large surpluses, although these are not equally distributed among the population. In fact, state societies are usually stratified: access to factors of production—such as land or capital—is restricted in many cases to an elite group or economic class. Control of resources is a key to political power, and wealth and political power tend to be self-perpetuating.

The vast extent of social, economic, and political activities in a state requires a centralized system of administration. At the hub of the system are those with the greatest power. This group creates laws and formulates the overall political strategy of leadership. It often utilizes a bureaucracy to carry out directives. Even where a single ruler has absolute power, a hierarchically organized bureaucracy is needed to implement policies at the local level. In fact, the leaders are dependent to a large extent on information given them by subordinates. The organization of states is closely tied to the need to assimilate and control the flow of information. Even ancient states, such as those of Egypt and Mesopotamia, maintained elaborate records and archives.

In state-organized societies, the working of politics is most evident in the working of **bureaucracy**—the formal system of specialists whose tasks are to ensure that rules are obeyed, penalties are imposed on those who deviate, and that taxes and revenues reach their approved destinations. This may reflect such formal distinctions as are found among the judicial system, the civil service, the legislative system, and the executive or ruling cadre. Such a formal political system may overshadow the way the political process operates at the local or informal level, but the fact remains that the political process is rooted in the daily decisions and actions of individuals. And in every society, local-level politics is intensely personalized and extremely fluid.

Nothing illustrates this more vividly than politics in the formerly socialist countries of East Europe: within just a few years of the overthrow of communism, parties formed around reformed ex-Communists have been voted back into the offices they once held by dint of force. That such a turnabout could happen was unthinkable in 1990. For example, in the last Bulgarian elections in 1995, voters rejected the democratic opposition parties and elected a parliament dominated by the Bulgarian Socialist Party, running as a minimally reformed Communist Party and even using the same slogans. Why vote Communist after years of brutal totalitarian rule, many ask. Even much-persecuted minorities have done so for the same reasons as the rest of the population. Grinding poverty, unemployment, and the costs of inflation have led individuals to seek the "best deal" even if it is at the sacrifice of earlier beliefs (see Bates, 1994, 1995, for a discussion). Those offering the "best deal" are the still-powerful officials from the old order who dispense patronage, jobs, pensions, and welfare payments. The old socialist order carried centralization to an extreme: the Central Committee of the Party, and even a small subgroup within the committee, directed the activities of regional Party organizations, the police, military, and industrial organizations, etc. Even though this was structured as a rigid, centralized hierarchy, local Party officials interacted with one another on the basis of friendship, reciprocity, and mutual support, thus forming closely knit groups of power brokers. When democracy arrived, they could easily adapt since they were long accustomed to wheeling and dealing; it is no accident that in most formerly Socialist states, the ones who have benefited the most from private enterprise and even the ballot box have been newly reformed Communists.

Evolution of the State. No single factor was solely responsible for the emergence of state society in different parts of the world, but a complex of interrelated factors probably contributed to its evolution. One might speculate that more efficient methods of food production (such as irrigation or greater specialization), coupled with social changes (such as village and town settlements, higher population density, the development of trade networks and centers of redistribution) provided important stimuli to the production of economic surpluses. These surpluses could be used to support large numbers of people not directly engaged in food production. Dominant groups assumed control over much of food production and the task of mobilizing surpluses. Of course, this chain of events did not proceed at the same rate in all communities. Those communities that controlled land highly suitable for agricultural intensification were able to produce more and monopolize access to strategic resources. Eventually, they came to control food production over large areas, thus becoming important centers of redistribution that were able to wage war on weaker groups. As outlying groups fell under their control, these powerful communities gradually became the centers of economic, political, and religious life, as well as of technological, artistic, and scientific innovations. These developments, in turn, would reinforce the advantages of the dominant societies over their neighbors.

It is not necessary to assume that all processes of state formation or even the expansion of existing states need be based on simple coercion and the use of force to drag unwilling populations into the fold of centralized administration. David Nugent has pointed to a number of instances where local populations actively work toward the goal of having their loosely organized region incorporated into an existing state (1994). The expansion of the United States illustrates this process, as does the expansion of other systems. Nugent cites the development of Peru as a recent example, where, since 1930, the process of nation-building has involved local communities in the rugged north-central region actively striving to be incorporated within the state structure. In part this was self-interest, as the people thought they would benefit from stronger government, but also it involved what Nugent describes as the "moral community" ideology (p. 357). Members of local communities viewed themselves as deserving of being a part of the nation-state of Peru and called for state intervention to regulate their affairs; it is only recently that this feeling has been reversed. Today, there are increasing calls for regional autonomy in the face of what is now perceived as too much intervention in local life.

However hard it may be to unravel, it is clear that various economic and social pressures are central to political evolution. A complex interaction between population growth, intensification of production, nucleation of settlements, specialization of production, stratification, and more widespread exchange relationships, all of which require more centralized authority, underlies state formation processes. But the presence of these pressures will not always lead a society to a greater level integration or complexity. Some groups may resolve resource and other problems they encounter by moving or limiting their own growth rather than by centralizing. Similarly, some societies might revert to less-integrated forms. Chiefdoms threatened by outside armies, for instance, might at first unite, only to break apart and return to a tribal way of life should the external force be too strong. Even for our own society, it is possible to envision conditions that would cause the state system to fragment, just as established states have so often done in the past. It is easy to find forces at work within any state-organized society that can potentially pull it apart. Competing ethnic, economic, and regional interests, as we noted in Chapter 9, can be important centrifugal forces, as is obvious in the highly centralized former states of Czechoslovakia, Yugoslavia, and the U.S.S.R. Since 1991, these three states have divided into twenty-three new states, and the number will probably increase. One factor that is often seen, in addition to whatever ethnic or economic problems may be occurring, is that of legitimacy. No polity can long endure if people come to view it as lacking a legitimate or moral basis.

The Moral Basis of State Authority. Although coercive power is essential to state control, the state also exercises its authority and power through ideology. In any state system, there is a moral basis that establishes its **legitimacy**—the right of the state to govern. The legitimizing ideology of the state may be secular, as in most contemporary nation-states; religious, as in some of the Islamic states; or focused on the legitimacy of a particular ruling dynasty, as is the case in traditional monarchies. Whatever the source, the notion of legitimacy is a powerful force, and few regimes survive long if their people view them as lacking the moral authority to govern. Thus, in state societies a great deal of attention is paid to maintaining the symbols of authority, be they the ceremonial stools of West African kings, great shrines and monuments, or national constitutions preserved in archives.

When new states or radically different national governments are brought into being, a great deal of attention is devoted to legitimizing the new establishment. In Iran, following the Shah's overthrow in 1979, the moral basis of the new government was its claim to conform to the precepts of Islam and Islamic law: accordingly, much attention was paid to passing new legislation to bring family codes into accordance with Islamic law by prohibiting alcoholic beverages and enforcing female dress codes (Fisher, 1980, p. 232 ff). One might think that a more pressing problem would have been the reorganizing of the bureaucracy, but first priority was given to establishing the moral basis to rule.

This is not a Third World phenomenon: we see it in U.S. history, clearly spelled out in the Constitution and Declaration of Independence, not to mention symbolized by building a brand-new capital city named after a major hero of the revolution. Simon Schama, a historian, interprets much of Dutch art of the sixteenth and seventeenth centuries as having political significance: it expresses the cultural unity and political legitimacy of the principalities that had fought for their independence from Spain (Schama, 1987). Here art was used to help create a political culture and to validate a newly-formed confederation: The Netherlands.

The notion of politics as having a moral basis can provide the rationale for oppositional politics. The civil rights movement in the United States is a case in point. Martin Luther King, Jr., became a national hero by focusing on human rights abuses that clearly violated widespread perceptions of how every citizen should be treated under the law. Nelson Mandela is viewed by South Africans of all races as a man who speaks for justice; his towering authority and broad popular acceptance led to a major transfer of power and a dismantling of apartheid with far less violence than could have occurred had civil war broken out. In Argentina, during a period of brutal military rule, a small organization of previously powerless women served as the vehicle for major political change by raising basic moral issues, as we see in the Contemporary Issues box, *Responding to Oppression: Las Madres de Plaza de Mayo* (pages 318–319).

The Politics of Social Control

Political competition, whether heated or muted in tenor, is rarely a free-for-all; there are always conventions or norms governing how people can and cannot compete. Rules of conduct allow some types of political activity and prohibit others. Clearly, some kind of rules are necessary; they allow us to predict with relative accuracy what other people will do in a given situation and how they will respond to our behavior. Yet, as we well know, rules are not necessarily followed nor are all of a society's rules made to protect the self-interest of its members. Thus the potential for conflict is fundamental to all political processes, and when conflict becomes intense enough, it may erupt into violence or rebellion. However, certain features that are present in all societies serve to restrain violence and

disruption while conflicting interests are being resolved, thus preventing the political process from dissolving into chaos.

One such factor is the multiplicity of competing social demands for an individual's or group's loyalty. This is inherent in any social order, for individuals and groups are socially interrelated in complex ways. Thus, opponents in one area may well be allies in another. Brothers who are at odds may well unite to face the threat of an outsider; households might be in hostile competition for land, but still belong to the same church and have relatives in common. Such cross-cutting ties tend to discourage wholehearted enmity and reduce the potential for violence.

But cross-cutting ties may also limit the possibility for unity when important matters requiring solidarity arise. Consequently, although they are a deterrent to violence, such ties may also be sources of instability. In the idealized tribal segmentary political structure, ties of descent override all others as a principle of mobilizing people for action. But such unity may be very difficult to achieve. In reality, the local descent group is composed of individuals who are related in numerous ways and are involved in continually shifting alliances. Even if unity, say for warfare, is achieved, it is frequently short-lived. The result is a very dynamic political system in which violence is limited but long-term stability is highly elusive. In Arabia, before the establishment of strong, centralized rule over the Bedouin tribes of the interior, raiding for camels was a regular occurrence. Any particular tribal group would be usually engaged in warfare with one neighbor, allied with a second, and in a state of neutrality with yet another; what changed regularly were allies and enemies—not unlike the situation with the Yanomamö.

Conventions designed to keep political competition within reasonable bounds are also built into the formal structures of most political systems. The electoral laws (not to mention the criminal codes) of the United States serve this end. Of course, political prescriptions cannot spell out exact behaviors for every situation. There is almost always room for individual interpretation and choice. "Thou shall not kill," for example, may sound quite unambiguous. Yet some individuals subscribe to the interpretation "Thou shall not kill, except during wars or when acting on behalf of the state." Others may find

Contemporary Issues
Responding to Oppression:
Las Madres de Plaza de Mayo

THERE ARE OCCASIONS WHEN apparently passive and powerless individuals in a society galvanize themselves in rebellion against authority. What combination of circumstances and motivations provokes active opposition to oppression, and what circumstances determine the success or failure of these small-scale revolutions? Let us look at an example that began in 1977 and in 1995 still has relevance in Argentine politics: the movement of Las Madres de Plaza de Mayo—the mothers of the disappeared in Argentina.

Marysa Navarro (1989) describes a situation in which a group of mothers, mostly housewives, transformed themselves into political activists and ultimately into the symbol of resistance to military dictatorship. In March 1976, Argentine President Isabel Perón was deposed by a military coup that placed power in the hands of a junta composed of the commanders-in-chief of the army, the navy, and the air force. One of the first acts of this junta was to declare war on subversion, a war that was waged on two levels: conventional confrontations with guerrilla forces either in the cities or the countryside, and more ominously, a clan-destine campaign of terror carried out by right-wing death squads under the control of the armed forces. The junta never officially acknowledged responsibility for either the existence or the activities of these squads. Tens of thousands of "subversives" (a term used to encompass guerrillas, Marxists of varying persuasions, liberals, reform-minded Catholics and Jews, as well as anyone suspected even remotely of sympathizing with them) were arrested, some formally. Many others were brutally abducted—from their homes, on the street, even at school. All were held incommunicado in inhuman conditions, grotesquely tortured, and since they were never charged, they were never brought to trial. Some were released after several years, but others were never released and they became known as *desaparecidos*, "the disappeared." Most of the desaparecidos were young people between the ages of twenty and thirty.

According to Navarro, "the existence of a parallel but hidden . . . structure of repression, that carried out actions not acknowledged by the government and for which it did not take responsibility" meant that "all legal resources for redress available under normal circumstances [were] . . . either shut or controlled by the armed forces" (1989, pp. 31–32). Even the Catholic Church never clearly disassociated itself from the junta. Gradually this void was filled by human rights organizations, although the junta did all it could to repress them.

Las Madres de Plaza de Mayo first appeared in April 1977, when a group of fourteen women who had met in various public offices while attempting to obtain information about their children decided to meet in the Plaza de Mayo (the main square in downtown Buenos Aires) to publicize their plight. By June 1977, the group had grown to 100 and had established a weekly ritual of marching silently around the square. Given the circumstances, this innocuous act was "an extraordinary act of defiance that no human rights group or political organization had dared to undertake" (1989, pp. 31–32). By 1982, Las Madres had a membership of 2,500. The junta did not at first recognize the political nature of the women's actions, and the fact that it ignored them gave them crucial time in which to strengthen and build the

killing justifiable only in cases of self-defense; still others to defend personal property or even family honor. Social rules set broad guidelines for much of our behavior, but individual decision making is inevitable, and with it comes variation in how the rules are actually followed—or not followed.

Rules and Behavior

Rules of behavior, whether coded as law or simply the outcome of community sentiment and collective expectation, govern life in all societies and structure interpersonal and intergroup relations.

The mothers and grand-mothers of missing political prisoners in Argentina continue to demonstrate in order to secure information on the fate of the missing and punishment for those responsible for their disappearance.

(Enrique Shore/Woodfin Camp & Associates)

movement. However, at the end of 1978 the Junta started a vicious campaign of harassment, which by 1980 forced Las Madres to cease their marches in the Plaza, and to meet in churches instead.

According to Navarro, what distinguished Las Madres from other human rights groups was their militancy, which was rooted in the devastating impact of the disappearance of their children. Their socialization as wives and mothers forced them to act. Further, not only did they have more time than men to search for their missing children, but because they were older mothers they could move about Buenos Aires without too much fear for their safety. "In a society that glorified mother-hood . . . they were implicitly ex-cluded from the different groups defined as 'subversives'" (1989, pp. 31–32). They were politically invisible. Since those abducted by the junta were between twenty and thirty years old, this created a crit-ical mass of women who, despite class and other differences, had one thing in common. And as most of them lacked any kind of politi-cal experience, they were not con-strained by any previous ideolo-gies and were free to use new symbols and attempt previously untried actions. In the terrorist state created by the junta, moth-erhood protected them and al-lowed them freedom and power not accessible to traditional polit-ical actors.

Ultimately, the actions of Las Madres contributed to the fall of the military and the transition to civilian rule in October 1983. Members of the movement con-tinue to be active in other ways in-volving human rights abuses. In 1995, a former officer gave dra-matic evidence of how he had par-ticipated with many others in dis-posing of students by throwing them, still alive, from high-flying planes over the Atlantic (Sims, 1995). Las Madres renewed their organized protests once again, now seeking punishment for their lost children's killers.

Taken collectively, the sorts of rules we usually see as moral, righteous, honorable, or just are those that limit individual behavior in ways that enhance the well-being of others or that confer group bene-fits (Pojman, 1995). For example, feeding one's child is normal; taking in an orphan is moral; de-fending one's house is acceptable but unremark-able; fighting for community, tribe, or country, however, is honorable. Some rules describe the ap-propriate retribution due one who trangresses. Other rules may simply set limits to how far one may go before committing to transgression. The

Ten Commandments, for example, not only guide behavior but do so in terms of supernatural sanctions. The net effect of behavioral rules is to make possible the benefits of group life: sharing, cooperative defense, mutual aid of all sorts (Irons, 1995).

At the same time, deviance from social rules and laws is part of the fabric of daily life. Individuals are bound to differ in the ways they think, feel, and act, so it is not surprising that people deviate from social expectations. When an infraction is not considered damaging to anyone else (such as scanty or bizarre dress), it is often tolerated, and eventually it may be considered acceptable. More serious infractions may or may not be tolerated. Every society labels certain acts as deviant, such as theft, incest, and murder. When an infraction is considered serious enough, a society's response can be extremely severe.

Considering the variability of human behavior, we might well ask why people do not deviate more often than they do, and how they are induced to follow the rules even when such obedience runs counter to apparent self-interest. Much of the answer lies in social control. Social control restructures individual self-interest by providing a framework of rewards and penalties or sanctions that channel behavior (Irons, 1995). Individuals who lie, cheat, or steal, for example, not only face specific penalties but, if they persist, may lose entirely the support they need from others to live in the community. Every society has its own means, **formal sanctions** and **informal sanctions**, of dealing with deviance. Formal sanctions are those rewards or penalties that are institutionalized or officially instigated; informal sanctions are those that are largely due to the reactions of others or are part of the social milieu. Obviously, there are instances where the distinction is blurred; is the blood feud or vengeance killing an institutional (formal) sanction or not? It depends on the context. In societies that also have written, codified laws governing murder and its penalties, a revenge killing would be seen as an informal (and illegal) sanction; in other societies, such as the Bedouin or Turkmen, vengeance killings are required of kinsmen in specific relationships to the victim. An individual who fails to attempt revenge will himself be punished. Still, the distinction is useful in conceptualizing how behavior is constrained, particularly in the absence of an institutionalized legal system.

Informal Means of Social Control

The most obvious means of social control are often the formal or institutionalized ones. In our society, police forces, courts, reformatories, and prisons deal with those who step too far out of line, but the average citizen seldom feels the full force of these agencies of social control. For most people, a society's informal means of control are sufficient to ensure a reasonable amount of conformity to the rules.

Social Pressure. When people venture over the boundaries of their society's rules, *social pressure* often brings them back into line. Such pressure can be very subtle or very blunt; regardless of form, it can be a highly successful means of social control. Social pressure can channel even political and economic action. During the civil rights movement in the United States in the 1950s and 1960s, social pressure helped mobilize black and white activists—many of whom were recruited to the movement from colleges and universities where justice and civil rights were major intellectual concerns. On the other hand, social pressure in the white communities was a primary means of continuing segregation even in the face of legal penalties and black opposition. For a period of time in the 1960s, after the repeal of formal segregation laws, small-town southern shopkeepers or restaurant owners who desegregated would be subject to community disapproval or boycotts. Terrorist groups such as the Ku Klux Klan, who organized rallies and cross-burnings, also contributed to an atmosphere that perpetuated racism even after the repeal of racist legislation. Social control does not, unfortunately, only structure just behavior; it can set and perpetuate norms that many regard as odious.

Often *satire* and *gossip* are powerful social pressures. People everywhere dislike being publicly ridiculed or having their misdeeds broadcast to others. In the Arab village of Kufr al Ma in Jordan, satire has been honed to a sharp edge in an elaborate system of nicknaming (Antoun, 1968). The system is organized in such a way as to indicate the degree of dissatisfaction caused by the violation of social expectations. The hierarchy of terms begins with neutral occupational names, proceeds to slightly ironic names based on personal habits, and culminates in distinctly pejorative names based on physical or social defects. The villagers most often criticize slander and backbiting, behaviors that are expressly condemned in Koranic verses and traditions. The satirical use of such epithets as Gossiper or Busybody thus serves to humiliate a person who has violated an important social rule. The Yörük of Turkey do almost exactly the same but take great care never to use the derogatory nickname in the presence of the offender or his or her relatives. They achieve the same result, since everyone knows that with unacceptable behavior they will acquire an unfortunate label.

David Gilmore, who studied a small town in Andalusia, Spain, found much the same situation and came to the conclusion that it was not the laws of the Spanish state that enforced conformity; rather, it was a moral structure enforced by gossip, name-calling, and backbiting (Gilmore, 1987, p. 28; 1994, pp. 353–365). People in this small town were intensely interested in one another's activities, envious of those who were able to suddenly better their economic lot, and quick to aggressively attack through gossip and slander those who violated the social status quo.

Even poetry and carnival songs work to express social norms and to mock those who transgress or exceed their perceived station in society (Gilmore, 1994, p. 357). The *mayetes* are independent, small farmers who are sometimes regarded with envy by landless workers, and seen to be too eager to gain at the expenses of others, as this poem sung at carnival expresses (1994, p. 358):

So this year they're paying
mayetes to grow sugar beets
instead of cotton.
If you're a mayete,
you can get the dough,
just lie and say you're needy.
This is a scandal and a disgrace,
and anyone who wants to collect
this whore's money
can just ask Manuel "la Quilina"
who's been scooping it up
for days now.

Social pressure can also take the form of informal *shunning* and *ostracism*, or ignoring and excluding offenders. Being ignored is generally a painful experience, and even the threat of it can of-ten be an effective means of social control. Among traditional peoples living outside of state systems, such the Inuit or !Kung, ostracism could be tantamount to a death sentence as one cannot survive alone. In close-knit religious communities in the United States, ostracism is sometimes a very powerful means of punishing one who has violated a moral code.

A widespread means of social pressure is rooted in beliefs about the supernatural. Moral codes expressed in religious terms are familiar to all of us. Not so familiar today, but quite common in the past, is the condemnation of individuals viewed as threatening to a community's interest as heretics or witches. In medieval Europe and in colonial America, individuals thought to be practicing witchcraft were driven from their communities or executed. Their real crime was to have aroused the fears and hostility of their neighbors by behaving differently from others of their sex and age group.

Vengeance and the Blood Feud. Informal social pressure can also be brought to bear in the form of threatened vengeance. **Vengeance** is an extreme response to assault or similar crimes against one's person and is common in tribal societies. In a sense it is a formal mechanism of control in that the response is both highly predictable and is considered appropriate among members of the society. But it differs from other formal legal sanctions in that it is embedded in the structure of kinship relations rather than administered by an impersonal authority outside the family (Boehm, 1984). Not infrequently, a vengeance homicide invokes its own response—another killing—and a blood feud ensues. While it might seem that such feuds are logically interminable in that each assault or killing requires a response, in actuality a score is kept and at some juncture pacification is mediated (Boehm, 1984, pp. 234–236).

A blood feud pits kin groups or families against each other, with revenge as the principal motive. A typical blood feud starts when a member of one family is murdered or assaulted. The victim's relatives then seek to avenge the crime, attempting to kill the murderer or one of his close relatives. This pattern occurs, for example, among the Yörük of southern Turkey (described in Chapter 6). When a person is killed, close patrilineal male relatives feel a strong obligation to seek revenge on the aggressor's patrilineal relatives (excluding the women and children). Even if the state arrests and punishes a murderer, the victim's relatives will still try to avenge the killing. Only then is it possible to arrange peace between the families. But this peace is an uneasy one, and one murder may result in a series of killings. The sense of mutual obligation arising from kinship is so strong that a man killed in the course of aggression toward another will usually be avenged by his relatives, even though they would agree that he had been wrong. At the same time, this strongly felt sense of mutual responsibility encourages people to control the behavior of their relatives and to avoid confrontations in the first place.

Following the collapse of communism in Albania in 1991, much of the power of the central government to administer remote mountain communities also disappeared. This did not mean that lawlessness reigned; what occurred was that traditional, largely uncodified, informal clan law, the Kanun or "law" of Lek Dukagjin, came into play. This ancient set of oral traditions specifies punishments for a wide range of crimes and also legitimizes vengeance in cases of homicide, making clear who is an appropriate target and who is not. Passed down for centuries, it is interpreted by community or clan elders.

Formal Means of Social Control

No society functions with only informal means of social control. Sooner or later in the course of daily life, conflicts or disputes between individuals will erupt or acts will be committed that are viewed as threatening to the entire community. Such events are the inevitable result of human beings living together. Of course, the extent of conflict varies, but in most societies conflicts and disputes are a normal part of everyday existence. And when such problems arise, most societies have established some kind of formalized action to resolve the dispute before it becomes too heated or to deter the offender before he or she disrupts the fabric of social life.

Of course not all social control can be viewed in terms of either the individual's or the population's well-being. One unfortunate but long-established fact is that in very diverse political systems relatively small numbers of individuals, often referred to as the elite or ruling class, come to dominate the political process. In such systems, social control is more directed to maintaining power than simply expediting cooperative social relations. While the formal legal system may serve this function, with jural codes forbidding assembly, free speech, and opposition, there are important (but less obvious) ways to achieve the same ends, as Katerine Verdery shows in her analysis of "the politics of time" in totalitarian Romania. The Romanian case is clearly very similar to other dictatorial regimes. (See the Contemporary Issues box, *The Politics of Time in Ceaușescu's Romania*, page 323.)

Law and the Legal Process. Laws and the legal process implementing them are the most formal means of social control. As we noted earlier in the chapter, a **law** is a rule of social conduct enforced by sanctions administered by a particular source of legitimate power (Fried, 1968). It serves the important function of resolving potential conflict as well as minimizing the degree of actual conflict. Without this formal means of social control, disputes or retaliation for wrongs committed could become very costly, even for those not directly concerned. Still, laws and the legal process usually benefit or penalize some individuals in a society more than others. Thus, while laws may structure behavior, resolve disagreement, and penalize wrongdoers, they also may engender further inequality and conflict.

In nonliterate societies, the legal tradition is oral rather than codified. In many ways these noncodified systems of social control—or law—appear to resemble codified systems, but there are some very important differences. The law administered by codified legal systems may be much further removed from the desires and needs of particular segments of the society. In fact, the general public may be ignorant of most of the actual body of law. This gulf between individuals and the legal apparatus gives considerable power to those who interpret, administer, and enforce laws and adjudicate disputes.

Between the extremes of informal customary practices and codified bureaucratic legal systems lies a broad range of forms, procedures, or quasilegal mechanisms for settling disputes and regulating conflicting interests. All societies have methods

Using Anthropology

The Politics of Time in Ceauşescu's Romania

ANTHROPOLOGISTS HAVE LONG noted that the nature of time differs in different cultures. Katerine Verdery demonstrates how time is used by regimes for political purposes by exploring the situation in Romania before the violent overthrow of the Communist Party leader Nicolae Ceauşescu in December, 1989 (Verdery, 1992, pp. 37–61).

Even though conceptions of time may vary, there is one constant: the human body in a given setting can only accomplish so much in a day (p. 37). By imposing time-consuming activities on people and by maintaining a system of distribution of consumer items which demanded hours of waiting in queues, the Communist Party reinforced its control over a population that resented its rule. One mechanism for this is what Verdery calls "marking time" or a "time tax": making individuals expend time they would otherwise use for other purposes.

One obvious example is the "immobilization of bodies in food lines"; the state-controlled redistributive system created economically unnecessary shortages (p. 45). All but the elite had to wait hours every day to purchase essentials such as potatoes, meat, eggs, flour, bread, and the like, even though the same goods were being exported. Bus and train tickets were deliberately not sold in advance, thus requiring travellers to line up for hours before depar-

ture; fuel for automobiles was rationed and, even for productive enterprises such as collective farms and factories, was delivered on an unreliable basis that caused much wasted time. Queues or shortage-induced "time taxes" added hours to the work day. While some of this might have been simply due to faulty scheduling in a highly centralized police state, Verdery and others see a more sinister purpose in it. It broke down resistance; created a docile population in which, to survive, each individual would have to break the rules and thus be vulnerable to police action; and it simply destroyed any threat of initiatives from the bottom that would threaten the control of the regime.

One villager who commuted daily by train to a factory job told Verdery that on some days he would hang around the factory doing very little, while on other days he would commute two hours just to be sent home due to insufficient electricity (p. 41). When he was forced to work overtime, for which he was not paid, he would compensate by skipping out of work to help his mother in her garden whenever he could—thus attempting to recoup time taken by the state. Poor scheduling of fuel for farms also meant that more time was needed to accomplish production goals, further restricting the personal time available to individuals. Another form of "time tax" was the many hours

that were devoted to official rituals: workers and bureaucrats would frequently be forced to assemble for hours to listen to Party speeches, greet visiting officials, and celebrate ceremonial occasions established to commemorate dates or events in Party history.

One effect of all this was to break down individual initiative, even self-esteem. One informant reported that, having heard that broken eggs were to be sold without requiring a ration card, she queued up with a jar for three hours to feed her hungry son (p. 55). In the end, she was given one egg, then after pleading, a second by the reluctant clerk.

Time was expropriated or marked in another manner. Traditional religious holidays and ritual occasions were replaced by new ones following a different calendar sequence. Many new holidays, including "week ends" or days of rest, were made to fall in different parts of a week or month; which days were to be rest days varied from year to year, breaking the traditional rhythm of work and rest and further occupying peoples' time. "Being immobilized for some meager return, during which time one could not do anything else one might find rewarding, was the ultimate experience of impotence. It created the power sought by the regime, as people were prevented from experiencing themselves as efficacious" (p. 55).

of mediation or adjudication and modes of settlement or redress.

Methods of Adjudication. In our own society, the trial before a judge and jury is a method of **adjudication,** or deciding a case. Two parties who contest the interpretation and application of laws in particular situations are handed a decision by a jury and a judge. Some method of adjudication is found in every society. Typically, such methods involve some sort of hearing conducted according to accepted procedures. The final settlement can be reached in any one of several ways. Disputants may, for instance, seek a solution through negotiation, which may or may not be mediated by an impartial third party; or they may state their case in the presence of an adjudicator, whose job it is to hand down a decision. There are numerous variations on these basic themes, which in a very general sense can be termed both "social" and "legal," within and among societies.

What distinguishes **mediation** from adjudication is that the desired outcome is as much social harmony as simple justice. The parties to a conflict end up with a result that they can accept. Mediation requires the intervention of a party or institution that has the respect of all concerned.

The Kpelle of central Liberia utilize both formal and informal social proceedings. Formal or legal adjudication takes place in a court where procedures are basically coercive and authoritarian. Because of its somewhat harsh tone, the court is not suited for disputes in which reconciliation is of primary importance. For this, the informal meetings, or "moots," are better suited. These proceedings take place in a home, where the complainants sit among a group of their kin and interested neighbors and before a mediator. Unlike the rigid structure of the courtroom, the structure of the moot is relatively loose, with people mixing freely and both sides being able to state their cases fully and question each other and anyone else present. After all the evidence has been given, the group as a whole determines who is in the right. The proceedings then close with the guilty party making a public apology and giving token gifts to the wronged party and the winner reciprocating with small gifts of acceptance (Gibbs, 1963).

Among the Nuer cattle herders and farmers of the Sudan, if disputes break out among members of the same lineage, the parties are expected to turn to their oldest living common ancestor for mediation; among most Middle Eastern tribes, they would turn to the formally recognized leader of their descent group; among the Yanomamö, they would likely seek out the headman or possibly the shaman. The Nuer also have special chiefs, called "Leopard Skin Chiefs," who use supernatural sanctions to arbitrate feuds and other conflicts within groups. In Lebanon, villagers often employ mediation or "wasta" in disputes; the mediators are often men who are recognized for their impartiality or honesty (Bates & Rassam, 1983, p. 245).

It is important to realize that the informal and formal means of social control described above are never completely effective. They do serve to reduce deviance, but they do not eradicate it. It is also important to realize that the social rules underlying mechanisms of social control are not necessarily agreed upon by all members of a society. Finally, we should note that the mechanisms of social control do not affect all people equally. Particularly in highly stratified societies, laws and methods of adjudication may be used by the rich and powerful to maintain their position. This has been said about some of our own mechanisms of social control—as when our laws and legal procedures work to the disadvantage of the poor and sometimes women.

Law and Tribes in the Twentieth Century

With the spread of colonialism in the late nineteenth and early twentieth centuries (earlier in the Americas), many local populations were integrated into complex, codified legal systems that were generally based on European models. British administrators who encountered established legal systems quite different from their own avoided imposing English law in its entirety on local peoples. Rather, local law or custom was modified to suit the purpose of the new rulers. Often this change was rationalized as a progressive move, such as granting women greater legal standing. However, the revisions imposed and the new laws enacted generally served the interests of the colonial power and its local allies.

These systems have usually remained even after the populations gained their independence. For example, in Africa today the legal systems of every

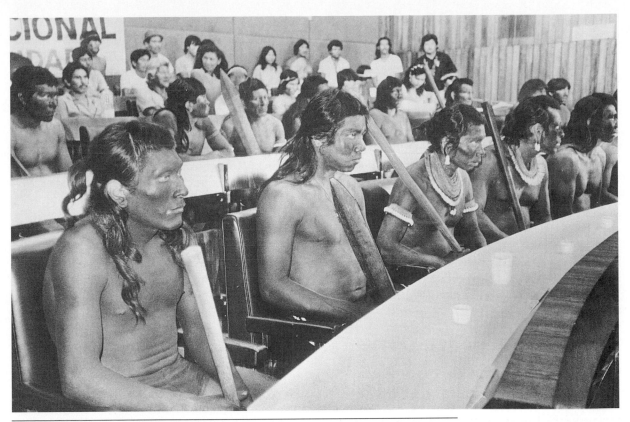

Kayapo Indian leaders attend a 1988 meeting of the Constitutional Assembly in Belem, Brazil. The assembly was voting at that time on the rights the central government would grant to the Indians.

(Marlise Simon/*NYT Pictures*)

country are based on various European codes. And except in very limited spheres, Native Americans are governed by the U.S. legal codes, which in turn evolved primarily from English common law.

Such integration of local systems into national (and, from the local community's point of view, alien) systems has created a number of problems. In a bureaucratic, complex, and highly centralized legal system, access to the courts, to redress, to protection of legal rights, involves working through a series of intermediaries—lawyers, prosecutors, judges, and so forth. These legal intricacies tend to be intimidating and discouraging.

On every continent, when Europeans encountered peoples whose economies were based on foraging or where access to resources was open to the entire local population, they treated land as untitled. That was the legal device by which it could be appropriated without consultation and people re-

moved from it; they had no inherent rights to it (Wilmsen, 1989, pp. 2–3). This is not restricted to Europeans; today in Botswana, substantial portions of tribal communal land are being converted to private ranches. In Brazil, as we saw in Chapter 5, the lands of indigenous peoples in the Amazon are not clearly titled; other than lands that fall within vaguely demarcated areas, they are basically open to outsiders to clear and settle (Rabben, 1993).

In addition to using an alien legal code regarding property rights to gain land, these centralized systems of law were often introduced with the explicit purpose of transforming the political and economic basis of the colonized society. This transformation benefited the colonial power by making the local population more malleable, and their elite dependent on the colonial regime (Wolf, 1983).

A case in point is that of Bunyoro, a kingdom in western Uganda colonized by the British, who introduced a land tenure act that registered all land as freehold. Bunyoro society had been a feudal society, with all land nominally owned by the king, who had allocated plots to the people who actually worked it. It might seem that giving land title to individuals would promote equal access to land. But, because the British gave land title to a group of nobility who had formerly had rights to manage land tracts on behalf of the Bunyoro king, the new system actually created a landed aristocracy. Whereas previously these notables did not own the land and had to maintain good relations with those who worked it, now they became the landowners, and their former tenants became workers, with no right to communal use of the fields. The new land tenure system weakened the power of the Bunyoro king, but it also decreased the traditional access rights of many of the people who farmed the land (Middleton, 1960).

Political Relations Among Societies

Strategies and methods for dealing with outside groups are important aspects of every society's political system. Many of these strategies are peaceful: intergroup law, mediation, and diplomacy are common ways of regulating relations and resolving conflicts and disputes between societies. But inevitably some conflicts will be more difficult to settle peacefully than others, and many of these will ultimately reach the point of violence.

Mechanisms of Peace

Relations with other populations are often the most critical aspect of a group's environment—sometimes its most important resource—so it is not surprising that societies have created mechanisms to regulate intergroup exchange peacefully.

Among certain New Guinea tribes, ritual feasts are commonly held to appease the ghosts of ancestors. These events are used as occasions to entertain neighboring groups and thereby establish more lasting alliances. Often the relationships strengthened at these ritual feasts are further cemented through marriages (Rappaport, 1967). In North Africa and the Middle East, where inter-

group conflict has been common in some areas, religion also serves as a means of mediating disputes. In some places, certain lineages or lines of descent have come to be recognized as sacred or holy. Removed from the threat of attack because of their presumed sanctity (injuring such a person is a serious offense), these individuals have been free to play an important role in mediating disputes among warring groups. Among the Turkmen of northeast Iran, as described earlier, lineages comprised of such holy individuals actually occupy land between competing tribes (Irons, 1975).

Among the Bedouin of the Arabian Peninsula, elaborate rules regulating hospitality to members of other groups and protection of travelers all facilitate intergroup communication. Such communication is particularly important among nomadic pastoralists living in a harsh and often unpredictable environment, where knowledge of rainfall and conditions of pasturage in different areas is critical to survival. Bedouin etiquette requires heads of households to give three days of hospitality—a place to sleep, food, entertainment—to anyone who enters their tents. If the visitor happens to be an enemy, the rule still holds; in addition, the guests must be given a head start out of camp when they leave. The Bedouin also have rules protecting travelers from attack. As long as travelers are accompanied by the proper guides, it is considered wrong to harm them. Traveling merchants are also protected under tribal rules. If a raid occurs while a merchant is camped there, the raiders are required to make restitution. Despite conflict among groups, these rules ensure a constant flow of information.

Armed Conflict

Of course, not all political relations between societies are peaceful. Anthropologists have found that armed conflict occurs in all types of societies, regardless of their level of political organization. In less-complex societies, such conflicts are typically tied to specific perceived transgressions, while wars waged by the state are often justified by broad political and religious ideologies. Nevertheless, the frequency of warfare, when defined simply as combat between separate territorial groups, is apparently no greater among states than among bands. This is not to say that all band societies make war

The rifles of these Korean soldiers (top) are far more sophisticated and destructive than the bows and arrows of the Pygmy tribe in Zaire (bottom). However, since less-centralized groups have much smaller populations than organized states, their traditional weaponry can cause equally high casualty rates.

(Top: David Burnett/Stock, Boston Inc.; Bottom: E. E. Kingsley/Anthrophoto)

against neighboring groups. But the majority of bands do engage in some form of armed conflict that can generally be classified as warfare. We can surmise, therefore, that warfare has existed for many thousands of years—probably long before the development of political organizations more complex than the band.

Two anthropologists, Carol and Melvin Ember note that while warfare is a human universal, the frequency of warfare varies; what seems to predict a high frequency of warfare cross-culturally is a combination of factors (1992, pp. 242–267). Fear appears to be a common factor: fear of nature and fear of others. Fear of nature is the result of frequent natural disasters leading to resource scarcity, while fear of others arises from how children are socialized to view other people (p. 256). Access to vital resources is also recognized as a key impetus to wage war against a neighbor (Ferguson, 1984). Andrew Vayda (1976) has argued that warfare between horticultural societies is frequently precipitated by population pressures on scarce land resources. Vayda suggests that warfare can provide a mechanism for establishing a balance between available resources and human population, although this is only one of a number of possible solutions.

Land is not the only resource over which armed conflict can arise. Among certain Bedouin tribes of northern Arabia, mentioned previously, camels

Kurdish Pesh Merga training new recruits in North Iraq. Armed conflict takes many forms; here informal militias are based largely on clan or tribal affiliation.

(Ed Kashi)

were the object of armed raids and counter-raids. The camel was a strategic resource for the Bedouin; the foundation of their traditional economy. First, camels were a reasonably stable source of food, providing milk (a dietary mainstay) and occasionally meat; second, the camel was an effective means of transportation in a desert environment, allowing the Bedouin to reach areas inaccessible to sheep or goat herders and to migrate long distances; finally, camels were valuable commodities for trading. Male camels and old or barren females could be exchanged in oasis town markets for such valuable items as grain, cloth, domestic utensils, or weapons. Because the camel was so central to the Bedouin way of life, there was constant pressure on tribal sections to increase the size of their herds. This was particularly vital since a single female camel could yield only a small amount of milk a day. Relatively large numbers of animals had to be kept merely to meet subsistence needs.

It is impossible to increase the size of a herd quickly through breeding, for camels reproduce and mature at a very slow rate. Consequently, raiding proved an efficient way of replenishing a declining herd as a safeguard against future losses to

drought, disease, accident, or theft. Elaborate rules governed raids between Bedouin tribes, all of whom were thought to be related to one another, however distantly. These rules ensured that no group that was the target of a raid would be completely routed; only camels (particularly adult females) were taken, and enough camels would always be left for the victims to reach their nearest kin for aid. In this way camel-raiding served as a mechanism for distributing a valuable and scarce resource among different groups spread over a large area (Sweet, 1965). It was a costly but apparently effective way for each local group or tribal section to alleviate, at least temporarily, scarcity of a vital resource. And, as is often the case with warfare, each raid or act of armed aggression set the stage for a response in kind.

Evidence indicates that the relative casualty rate for combatants in warfare is no higher among states than among less-centralized political organizations, even though state societies clearly have more highly specialized and complex military establishments and more sophisticated weapons. In band societies, people usually fight with spears, clubs, or bows and arrows, and often both sides to a conflict will withdraw if they incur any serious injuries. But since the total populations of bands are so small, only a few deaths can result in a significant overall casualty rate. Among the Murgin of Australia, 28 percent of all male deaths have been attributed to combat. The Yanomamö have similarly high casualties. Among Western nations during this century, in contrast, less than 1 percent of all male deaths have occurred because of warfare (Livingstone, 1968). These figures do not apply to specific countries considered individually, such as Germany or the former U.S.S.R., where mortality due to warfare has been much higher.

What does seem to distinguish modern warfare, and even warfare in the earlier state-level societies, is the impact on noncombatants. Today the effects of war are felt by every member of society, even if the actual fighting is distant. And, of course, modern technology, including elaborate systems of communication, draws more and more people into particular conflicts and increases the costs in lives and resources associated with warfare. At the end of the twentieth century, warfare continues to plague world politics, its devastation unabated by the end of the Cold War.

Summary

THE STUDY OF POLITICS IS CONCERNED WITH WHO benefits in any competition for power and rewards. In a given society, particular rules govern political competition and leadership: who has access to the political process, how leadership is determined, and what mechanisms keep political competition within reasonable bounds.

At the bottom of all political competition lies disagreement about how issues affecting individual interests and community life should be decided. Societies vary in the kinds of decisions that are regarded as important, in the intensity of political competition, and in the kinds of rewards that are distributed. Generally, as the level of social complexity increases, so do the number and scope of political objectives as well as the use of force to achieve political ends.

In all societies, access to political power is limited by both formal and informal means, with the number of such restrictions increasing as societies become more complex. Political leadership may be established either through a person's idiosyncratic qualities or through the ability to mobilize organizational support, or because of a combination of the two. In discussing political leadership, one should distinguish between power (the ability to exert influence because a person's directives are backed by such negative sanctions as the use of force) and authority (the ability to exert influence because of personal prestige or status).

When political conflict becomes intense, certain mechanisms in all societies act to restrain violence and disruption. One such mechanism is the multiplicity of competing demands for a person's or group's loyalty. Other mechanisms may be built into the formal political structure, such as positions that command the authority to mediate issues.

Rules, or standards for proper political behavior, vary widely among societies, but every society has rules governing behavior and the means of enforcing them. Rules give social relationships order and a certain amount of predictability—essential to the functioning of society. Social rules establish broad guidelines for behavior, but individual interpretation and decision making produce variations in how the rules are actually followed or flouted.

Individual behavior can vary or deviate from social rules. Some deviations from prescribed behavior are tolerated more than others. Deviant behavior and the exclusive pursuit of self-interest are modified by a system of social control that channels behavior through rewards and sanctions. Every society has evolved mechanisms for dealing with deviance. These mechanisms of social control have been broadly classified as formal and informal.

Social pressure—including satire, gossip, shunning, ostracism, and moral sanctions based on beliefs about the supernatural—is applied when infractions of the rules do occur. Vengeance or threatened vengeance is a form of social control embedded in the structure of kinship relations. In the case of blood feuds, violence often erupts.

No society functions with only informal mechanisms of control. The conflicts that are an inevitable part of social life often need to be resolved through formal, institutionalized channels. Formal mechanisms help resolve disputes before they become violent, or they deter an offender before the fabric of social life is disrupted.

Law is the most formal mechanism of control. Laws help structure behavior, resolve disagreements, and penalize wrongdoers, but they may also engender conflict since they tend to benefit or penalize certain individuals more than others in a society. The elements of the legal process are widespread, though they vary widely from one society to another. In our own and other industrialized societies, the legal process is highly developed. Laws are codified (systematically recorded and preserved) and interpreted by specialists like judges and lawyers. In technologically simpler societies, the legal tradition is largely oral and more directly related to the day-to-day concerns of the people.

Methods of adjudication are means of arriving at a decision in a dispute. Typically, such methods involve some sort of a hearing that is conducted according to accepted procedures. Settlement may be achieved through negotiation or through an adjudicator who makes a decision. Methods of adjudication may be formal or informal. An informal procedure involves mediation between parties and usually reaches compromise decisions. Formal procedures often take place in an established court, but formal and informal procedures may be used simultaneously.

Neither the formal nor the informal mechanisms of social control are entirely effective; they reduce, but do not eradicate, deviance. In highly stratified societies, these mechanisms are often used by the elite to maintain their position. Legal inequality is particularly pronounced in cases where colonized tribal societies had centralized and codified legal systems based on European models imposed upon them. The centralized legal system has had the effect of heightening the discrepancy in power between the rural class and the central bureaucracy.

Although variations of individual political systems exist, four general organizational patterns have been identified: bands, tribes, chiefdoms, and states. The band is the least complex and probably the oldest form of political organization; it may be defined as a small group of individuals with a fluid membership. No overriding political institutions act to unite several bands into a larger polity, and no specialized political roles exist. In effect, political life is an integral part of all social relations.

The tribe is similar to the band in that it is egalitarian, economic exchange is via reciprocity, and the group has no specialized political roles, no authoritarian leaders, no centralized administration, and no formalized mechanisms of coercion. However, the tribe possesses mechanisms for mobilizing pan-tribal sodalities that integrate all its local segments for the purpose of participation in religious ceremonies or the settlement of disputes. However, the major role of pan-tribal institutions often is to create a unified force capable of dealing with other groups in competition for resources. Bands and tribes are considered egalitarian in that most political positions are available on the basis of ability, although actual equality may be tempered by gender differences and extreme status differences based on age.

The chiefdom, among nonegalitarian political systems, is distinguished from the tribe by the existence of a central agency, headed by the chief, that coordinates economic, religious, and social activities. Another common feature of the chiefdom is greater specialization in the means of production, which allows for the production of surpluses and for support of a larger population. The office of chief is a specialized political position, with well-defined areas of authority backed by sanctions of one kind or another. In chiefdoms, positions of status and authority are not accessible to everyone, even though major resources may be commonly held.

The state is the most complex and centralized of political systems. It may be defined as a hierarchical complex of institutions that organize power on a supra-kinship basis. The state also gains its authority through ideology, which legitimizes the state's right to rule. State-level political organization is associated with densely populated, largely urban units that are supported by intensive agriculture, sophisticated technology, markets, and a high degree of productive, ad-

ministrative, and economic specialization. Control over the means of production, trade, and the surpluses thus created are not equally distributed: state systems are socially and economically stratified. It is generally believed most human groups were organized as bands until about 10,000 years ago. Since then, political society has moved toward stratification, greater role specialization, and centralization of authority and bureaucracy.

All societies must deal with outside groups. Different mechanisms have been developed to regulate intergroup exchange and to minimize conflict. The most obvious of these are intergroup laws, mediation, and diplomacy, but other more subtle mechanisms are also operative. Among these are religion; certain people are designated as sacred and thus removed from the threat of attack, allowing them to act as mediators among warring groups. Another mechanism is etiquette and hospitality, which may protect certain groups and provide for the exchange of information despite conflict.

Despite these mechanisms, warfare is a universal phenomenon. For the most part people use warfare to deal with a threatening problem, often one relating to scant resources and/or population pressures. In this case, war acts as a mechanism for redistributing resources by establishing a balance between available resources and population.

Key Terms

adjudication	legitimacy
authority	mediation
bureaucracy	political ecology
consensual decisions	politics
formal sanctions	power
informal sanctions	state
law	vengeance

Suggested Readings

Atkinson-Monnig, J. & Errington, S. (Eds.). (1990). *Power and difference: Gender in island Southeast Asia.* Stanford: Stanford University Press. A compilation of essays, with a wide ethnographic range that discuss gender systems and power in southeast Asia.

Benedict, R. & O. A. (1990). *Language and power: Exploring political cultures in Indonesia.* Ithaca, NY: Cornell University Press. Written over a period of 25 years, this collection of papers meticulously examines the interrelationship of language and literature, political ideas, and culture in modern Java.

Boehm, C. (1984). *Blood revenge: The anthropology of feuding in Montenegro and other tribal societies.* Lawrence: University Press of Kansas. An account using ethnographic materials from Yugoslavia and Albania that details the functioning of blood feuds as a mechanism of social control.

Ferguson, B. R. (Ed.). (1984). *Warfare, culture, and environment.* Orlando, FL: Academic Press. A collection of eleven original essays on the anthropology of war. All focus on the need to understand the material circumstances involved in order to understand the nature of war itself.

Gilmore, D. D. (1987). *Aggression and community: Paradoxes of Andalusian culture.* New Haven, CT: Yale University Press. Traditionally aggression has been viewed as maladaptive and disruptive in small-group dynamics. Based on field research in rural Andalusia, the author argues for the usefulness of limited aggression in promoting social cohesion.

Rutz, H. J. (Ed.). (1992). *The politics of time.* American Ethnological Society Monograph Series, No. 4. The focus of this collection is time; different cultural constructions of time, as well as the notion that control of time shapes power relations.

Wedel, J. R. (Ed.). (1992). *The unplanned society: Poland during and after communism.* New York: Columbia University Press. This collection concentrates on informal activity and informal institutions (rather than formal economic and political institutions) that shape the organization of Polish society.

Williams, B. (Ed.). (1991). *The politics of culture.* Washington D.C. and London: Smithsonian Institution Press. A series of articles, covering a wide range of topics that illustrate the interconnection between politics, cultural meaning, and material culture.

Wilmsen, E. N. (Ed.). (1989). *We are here: Politics of aboriginal land tenure.* Berkeley: University of California Press. This volume confronts the issue of the relation of foragers to land and seeks to promote an understanding of land claims by aboriginal people.

Defining Religion
 Religion as Ideology
 Religion and "The Sacred"

Belief Systems
 Animism and Animatism
 Theism
 Belief Systems and Social Organization
 Human Ecology: The Production of Protestants in Guatemala
 Belief Systems and Social Boundaries

Ritual
 Rites of Passage
 Rites of Intensification
 Gender Issues: Honoring the Dead
 The Organization of Ritual

Religion and Resource Management
 Case Study: The Maring "Plant the Rumbim"

Psychological and Sociopolitical Functions of Religion
 Religion and Individual Coping
 Social Integration
 Using Anthropology: Religion and the Spread of Disease
 Reduction of Conflict
 Promotion of Social Control
 Case Study: The Vodoun Church of Haiti
 Validation of Change:
  Revitalization
 Case Study: Cargo Cults
 Case Study: Islamic Revolution

Summary
Key Terms
Suggested Readings

Chapter 12

Religious Belief and Ritual

Humans weave intricate intellectual webs of faith and imagination that relate them to the universe and to each other, and that express basic premises linking event to event, past to present. Religious beliefs, cosmologies, myths, and rituals are basic to our perceptions of time and space, our views of our own behavior and that of others, and our conceptions of the world as it is and as it should be. Religion is a human universal—perhaps one of the key distinguishing features of our species and undoubtedly as ancient as human language.

Through religion, people are led to accept propositions about activities and events remote from any experience or sensation. No society would survive if people did not accept some things they cannot prove. It is not simply a matter of taking on faith what earlier generations have verified for themselves, but rather of accepting abstract principles about what is ultimately unknowable. This ability is important in a number of activities with an ideological base, from politics to aesthetics.

Many contemporary psychologists and linguists see this ability to accept the unknowable as a product of the evolution of the human brain and its specific structures for processing information (Pinker, 1994). Just as it is thought that the brain is biologically adapted for the rapid acquisition of human language (including complex grammar), it is predisposed to accept other information—even including ideas that cannot be directly verified. James Alcock has termed the human brain "the belief engine," and writes, "Our brains and nervous systems constitute a belief-generating machine, a system that evolved to assure not truth, logic and reason, but survival" (1995, p. 14). Most learning, he argues, takes place nearly automatically. In particular, we always explain things in terms of cause and effect, even if we have to infer causality where none exists. We are born, in effect, to think magically as a survival mechanism. If, for example, we are walking in the woods, hear a rustling sound, and see a snake-like object on the ground, we immediately activate the fear response. Only later do we assess the validity of that initial impression. Moreover, for the same survival reasons, individuals are predisposed to accept that certain classes of events are not to be subjected to reason; we are taught by our parents to trust the experiences of others (Alcock, 1995, p. 16).

We may never fully know just how and why the human brain evolved in the way it did, but clearly one consequence of its evolution is the universal need to explain the world and our place in it. Religion rests on a bedrock of belief that, while ever-changing, need not conform to observation or experience. It is a cosmology accepted on faith and can, and often does, guide behavior from family relationships to political movements.

Defining Religion

Anthropologists are concerned with understanding how religious ideology or ritual behavior relates to larger cultural patterns and to the social, political, and economic processes in a society. Some anthropologists broadly define **religion** as any system of beliefs in supernatural forces, symbols, and rituals that serve to make life meaningful and intelligible. Conspicuously absent from this definition is any mention of religious leaders, gods, or places of worship.

If the Mbuti Pygmies of the Ituri forest in Central Africa are plagued by sickness or poor hunting and if every practical remedy has failed, a festival known as *molimo* is held to awaken the forest to their plight and to restore balance and harmony to their world. For about a month, all the adult men gather nightly to sing and "rejoice" the forest. No specific invocations are made for better hunting or an end to sickness. The purpose of the festival is simply to express through song the Mbuti's trust in the forest as the benevolent provider of all good things. Having done so, the Mbuti say that whatever happens must be the will of the forest and therefore it is good. This feeling is clearly expressed in the Mbuti creed: "The Forest is Mother and Father, because it gives us all the things we need . . . food, clothing, shelter, warmth . . . and affection. We are the children of the forest. When it dies, we die" (Turnbull, 1965, p. 312). The Pygmies' belief in the forest, the molimo ceremony, and the creed of the forest constitute the elements of a religion: a model of the world for its participants. No church or temple has been erected; the molimo is not led by a priest or other intercessor with the supernatural. In fact, the supernatural itself does not exist for the Mbuti as it does in Western tradition. Not only is there no intangible, otherworldly power known as a god, but the object of the worship is exactly that which is most natural and tangible in the Pygmies' life: the forest environment.

Thus, religion cannot be defined in terms of what is worshipped, believed in, or the form of worship. In general terms, all religions have two common characteristics: they include a recognition of the *supernatural* or sacred, and they express (whether or not in specific terms) an ideology that orders the world.

Religion as Ideology

Clifford Geertz (1966) maintains that religion is essentially an ideology, or a system of very potent symbols that have a powerful emotional appeal and can provide a rationale for human existence. It is a means by which the individual facing the unknown or pain and suffering can explain events through divine intervention.

Religious ideology provides a framework that allows an individual to understand his or her place in the universe. Here, religion expresses itself in myths. The myths of the book of Genesis, for instance, describe in symbolic terms the creation of the world and people's place within it. Myths about

In Zaire, these young Lese and Efe women are undergoing a ceremony marking their translation to adulthood.
(RichardWrangham/ Anthrophoto)

dying, too, use a variety of images—such as passing between jaws, or entering a mountain that has no visible entrance, or crossing over a bridge that has been filed to a razor-sharp point—to describe a journey that the body cannot make, but the spirit can (Eliade, 1975, pp. 349–350). Such myths put complex ideas into a framework that people can relate to from their own experience. Typically, the myths that are of greatest importance to a culture are the ones people refer to as sacred. These are myths that occur in holy books or scriptures, or tales told by a shaman, for example, and are, as Geertz (1966) has noted, highly charged symbols.

Claude Lévi-Strauss and other anthropologists have argued that the symbolic expressions embodied in myths are arranged in a common pattern. The typical structure of myths and legends juxtaposes three sets of symbolic elements: those that define a value, a desirable object, or a course of action; those that define its antithesis; and a mediating set of values that resolve the conflict between the two. Thus myths may be symbolic formulas for the resolution of conflicts of values and moral quandaries within a society. According to Lévi-Strauss (1955), myths have an internal logic of their own, unrelated to the real world; since they are highly abstract models that are open to a variety of interpretations, they permit people considerable leeway in defining their positions in the real world. Often a wide variety of myths take the same

form; what distinguishes them is how the theme is expressed. Ancient Greek myths, in this view, have themes strikingly similar to the Oedipus complex as understood by Freud—the story of a son who kills his father and becomes his mother's lover (Leach, 1970, p. 82).

A myth, writes Lévi-Strauss (1988), has an authority that cannot be denied. "It arises from the depth of time, setting before us a magnifying mirror that reflects, in the massive form of concrete images, certain mechanisms by which the exercise of thought is ruled" (p. 28). Thus, in Lévi-Strauss' view, myths can be deciphered as various systems of codes, including sexual, zoological, and cosmological ones.

Religion and "The Sacred"

The sociologist Émile Durkheim (1961) argued that the essence of religion is not a specific set of beliefs, attitudes, or practices, but a broader, more universal phenomenon: the expression of a community's moral values and collective beliefs, whatever they may be. He maintained that each society distinguishes between the **sacred** (the sphere of extraordinary phenomena associated with awesome supernatural forces) and the **profane** (the sphere of the ordinary and routine; the natural, everyday world). Religious beliefs express what a society considers sacred. These values may be represented symbolically by a cross, a star, a statue, a rock, an animal, a tree, or any object that a society selects; this symbol becomes the focus of collective ceremonies (communion, dances, feasts, and so on) that serve to unite believers into a single moral community.

It has been pointed out, however, that few societies make a clear distinction between the sacred and the profane or the natural and the supernatural. For the Mbuti, the forest is not an awesome, mysterious entity that exists on a different level of reality. It is an ever-present factor that shapes every aspect of their lives and must be related to in concrete, practical terms. Thus, while a supernatural dimension is common to all religions, the categories of "sacred" and "profane" or "natural" and "supernatural" are analytic constructs and do not always reflect distinctions that people actually make in a consistent fashion. In the United States, as in many other countries, symbols that at first appear to be devoid of religious meaning can take on near-sacred significance—the flag, for instance. Often we hear the term "desecration" used when the national flag is altered or damaged; strictly speaking, only something that is sacred can be desecrated. In countries that have what might be called "national" religions, (e.g., Israel, Japan, Iran, Greece, Armenia, Russia, Serbia, and Bulgaria), religion and the sacred blend closely with concepts of nation, homeland, and nationalism. Under communist rule in the former U.S.S.R., Lenin and the personal items he used in his life came to acquire near-sacred qualities.

In fact, upon examination, we find that the distinction between the natural and the supernatural is not very clear at all. On the one hand, the natural world is the center of many religions (like that of the Mbuti Pygmies); on the other, the supernatural often plays a routine role in secular affairs. A case in point is the practice of **divination**, in which an element of nature—the configuration of tea leaves, the movement of a water witching stick, or the side on which a flipped coin lands—acts as a sign to provide supernatural information to the diviner. **Witchcraft** is another practice that is as likely to involve the profane as it is the sacred. It has been defined as an "individual's use of religious ritual to control, exploit, or injure unsuspecting, or at least uncooperating, other persons" (Wallace, 1966, p. 144). While we associate the practice with bizarre tales of evil spells, witchcraft is not necessarily either furtive or even socially unacceptable, as we shall see in our discussion of the Vodoun church of Haiti. Many cultures regularly attribute illness, including psychological ailments, to spirit possession (the supposed control of a person's behavior by a supernatural spirit that has entered the body). Is a line drawn between the natural and the supernatural? For some religions, the answer is clearly not at all. For others, a sharp boundary is the essence of belief, and the dialogue concerning the boundary may be the essence of the faith in question.

Belief Systems

Animism and Animatism

The nineteenth-century anthropologist E. B. Tylor (1871) was one of the first to try to understand and systematically explain the phenomenon of religion. Tylor asserted that the foundation of all religion is the idea of a soul, a spiritual essence that differs from the tangible, physical body and becomes active during trances and dreams. When a person dies, the soul leaves the body. This concept of a soul, according to Tylor, developed from a curiosity and concern about the difference between living and dying, waking and dreaming. He called this belief in a personal supernatural force **animism** and suggested that it was the first stage in the evolution of religion, which then passed through a belief in many gods, culminating in a belief system focusing on one god.

R. R. Marrett, a contemporary of Tylor, maintained that **animatism**, or a belief in an impersonal supernatural force, preceded animism. Animatism can be seen among the people of Melanesia, who attribute extraordinary events, unusual prowess, and both good luck and misfortune to *mana*, an invisible force that exists in the universe. This force may reside in people, places, or objects, both animate and inanimate. It can be harnessed for good or evil and is easily transmitted by touch. An unusually shaped stone found in an especially productive garden, an exceptionally swift boat, a particularly skillful leader, may all be said to possess mana.

While animatism as a complete belief system is rare today, there are many people who believe that sacred or holy forces come to reside in certain objects and places. Many people in the Near East, for example, believe a person may acquire *baraka*, or holiness, by touching the clothes worn by a holy man or the ground on which he has walked, or by visiting Mecca. Roman Catholics in many parts of the world attribute healing powers to saints' relics, holy water, and places where miracles are said to have occured (such as Lourdes). When certain objects, such as the saints' relics, come to possess special qualities, they are referred to as **totems**. While they are frequently religious in nature, totems also can be taken as emblems of social groups such as clans or tribes, fraternities, and even nations.

Another widespread belief that may have its roots in the earliest forms of religion is the idea that sacredness, some other spiritual attribute, or divine ordinance makes certain actions prohibited, or **taboo**. We have already discussed the incest taboo in Chapter 8. Other widespread taboos include prohibited foods (pork for Muslims and Jews, cattle for Hindus, and totemic animals for most groups who have them). Another taboo mentioned earlier is for a Muslim to strike an individual descended from the Prophet's immediate successors. Totemism is not a type of religion so much as a manifestation of religion. In some important respects, it is found in almost every faith, as are taboos. The Christian Bible can be regarded as totemic, along with many other items in different branches of Christianity; the Torah and Koran are regarded similarly. They are also taboo objects to be handled only by believers and referred to in ways that do not desecrate them.

Theism

In many parts of the world, religion centers on one or more gods of extrahuman origin. Such a pattern of belief is called **theism**. Dahomeans in Africa, for example, worshipped a pantheon of Great Gods, each involved in Creation, each responsible for some part of nature, each endowed with a human or animal form and a strong personality. Like humans, Dahomean Great Gods occupied themselves with sex, war, economic endeavors, and mischief. Their intervention in life on earth was largely unpredictable (Wallace, 1966, pp. 93–94). Similar forms of **polytheism** (a belief in many gods) flourished in the Inca, Maya, and Aztec cultures of Latin America and in east Asian kingdoms, as well as in central African kingdoms, Greece, and Rome.

Judaism, Christianity, and Islam, all of which arose in the Middle East, recognize only one supreme God, who created the universe and all that is in it, watches over human affairs, occasionally sends messengers to earth, and works in mysterious ways. But **monotheism** (strictly, belief in one god) is relative, since all three of these belief systems deify their saints and prophets to some extent and all have made room at various points in their histories for other supernatural beings or forces: angels, demons, and witches, and of course the devil.

Belief Systems and Social Organization

It has been suggested that these patterns of religious belief are related to the way society is organized. Religious belief systems seem to reflect basic characteristics of the social order in which they appear. Durkheim held that when people worship their objects of veneration, they are actually reaffirming their own society and its social order; true or not, there is obviously a relationship between religious belief and the larger society. As social organization became more centralized and stratified, so did the conception of the supernatural. While this relationship between stratification and a hierarchy of divine beings is not absolute, those religions in which there is a belief in a "high god" or superior divine force ruling lesser ones is far more likely to be found in societies with a clear hierarchy or stratification (Swanson, 1960, p. 62).

At a more general level, Marx argued much as did Durkheim, that religion always reflects the dominant class in class societies. It worked to maintain the power and position of the ruling elite, however constituted. Thus, in feudal Europe, the Catholic Church was closely allied with the nobility and preached that the temporal order was divinely ordained. Following the industrial revolution and the rise of capitalism, Marx wrote, organized religion supported the ruling class by obscuring the interests of the working classes—diverting attention from conditions of exploitation, stressing humility, and promising rewards in the hereafter. Max Weber, a leading German sociologist of the nineteenth century, stressed the role that the Protestant Reformation had in preparing Europe for the advent of capitalism. It did so, he

Human Ecology

The Production of Protestants in Guatemala

IN HIS CLASSIC STUDY, *THE Protestant Ethic and the Spirit of Capitalism*, Max Weber postulated that the individualistic values of Protestantism encouraged the rise of modern European capitalism and entrepreneurship. Though most social scientists today consider Weber's generalizations too sweeping, Sheldon Annis (1988) finds in Guatemala something close to Weber's "Protestant ethic"—an emphasis on individual salvation that justifies self-interested economic activity, in contrast to the traditional focus on the community. In Guatemala, however, this emphasis is the result of economic change rather than the force that drives it. In recent years, a tide of evangelical Protestantism has swept through Latin America, long a bastion of Catholicism. Annis found that by 1987 well over 20 percent of Guatemalans had been converted to Protestantism, and some enthusiasts were predicting that the country would be half Protestant in the 1990s.

What has caused Protestantism to flourish in an overwhelmingly Catholic country? And what are the underlying dynamics of the competition between Catholicism and Protestantism? Annis argues that the key to religious behavior is rooted in economic production. Annis bases his argument on an analysis of the ideology of the traditional milpa economy—an ideology of egalitarianism and communalism that is central to Indian culture. What he describes as "milpa logic" evolved as an expression of the Indians' place in Guatemalan colonial society; they occupied a separate and unequal sphere in which economic subordination was offset by a limited cultural autonomy (1988, p. 105). And milpa logic is Catholic. As the milpa economy is gradually breaking down, "undramatically, Protestantism makes its entry at the frayed edges, where stable systems of economic production, culture, and social relations are beginning to come apart" (p. 10).

A milpa is a plot of corn interplanted with beans and small quantities of secondary crops. Despite the low rate of return, almost all highland Indian families grow corn as their first crop. Planting a milpa in fact optimized resources in a very particular way. First, corn is remarkably hardy and will survive misuse, neglect, and drought; and when eaten with beans and some fresh vegetables, it makes a nutritionally sound diet. Second, the milpa makes use of household resources that may be abundant but otherwise unusable—dawn weeding hours, after-school hours, waste water, and so forth. Third, it reinforces the family and household unit as the basis of social organization by optimizing the resources of the family—a grandmother's knowledge of herbs and her availability for weeding, for example. Fourth, because milpa horticulture is built upon the principle of optimizing inputs rather than maximizing outputs, it works against the accumulation of capital. The milpa's product is consumed by the family or traded within the village. Because of this system's fundamentally anti-entrepreneurial character, it reinforces the egalitarian nature of the village—a central characteristic of Indian society (Annis, 1988, pp. 37–38).

The cultural stability of the milpa system has been disrupted during this century by population pressure, with its resultant increase in landlessness and environmental deterioration; by military repres-

argued, by equating worldly individual success with divine approval; people came to recognize individual accomplishment even at the expense of the community.

Since religious beliefs and expressions are related to the social organization of society, religion and religious practice regularly change as society does. The Protestant Reformation is one example of a major religious transformation that reflected changes in the European economy. In the Human Ecology box, *The Production of Protestants in Guatemala,* above, we can see how widespread conversion to Protestantism reflects similar changes in the Guatemalan economy.

The ideas of Durkheim, Marx, and Weber are important in the study of religious belief, but they should be understood in the context of the times when they were propounded. While the connec-

sion; by new technology and development programs; and by expanding primary education. These pressures have led to a skewing of the distribution of wealth within the ostensibly egalitarian Indian community, and this development has undermined the cultural rationale of milpa production (Annis, 1988, p. 75).

In a sense, two different modes of production have developed, each centered on the way in which peasant families choose to handle surplus. Those whom Annis describes as "milpa-promoting" are willing to invest their surplus in symbolic acts that celebrate and reinforce communalism. By doing so they not only tie themselves to a stable and coherent cultural system, but they are restrained from purchasing significant power or prestige outside the community. The Catholic Church has historically been very active in promoting pan-community activities and associations, all of which call upon the villagers to spend a good part of their family income above household needs. As Annis notes, people say that "it is expensive to be a Catholic." Even poor Catholic families spend as much as a quarter of their combined income on ceremonial events (1988, pp. 93–94).

In the mode of production associated with Protestantism, families either have no surplus (they are dispossessed peasants) or choose to invest in expanding their economic opportunities. They turn their backs on communal values to reach for a different set of rewards that confer personal prestige, family well-being, or spiritual gratification (Annis, 1988, p. 75). By investing in consumer goods, trucks and buses, and cash crops, they explicitly reject the ideology of the milpa.

The Protestant message provides an ideological rationalization for personal gain. And in general, Annis found that Protestants were better prepared and far more motivated than Catholics to pursue lifestyles that would either lift them out of poverty or protect hard-won financial gain. Despite the fact that Catholics own 1.41 times as much land and rent twice as much, Protestants have higher disposable incomes from agriculture—money they can deploy for immediate personal benefit or use to invest in future production. Protestants own better land (as a consequence of frequent buying and selling of plots), plant more intensively, and plant a higher proportion of cash crops than Catholics. The only crop the Catholics produce more intensively than the Protestants is corn—presumably because of their greater reliance on the milpa. A contrast between Catholics and Protestants can be seen also in the matter of textile weaving, a traditional Indian pursuit: for the Catholic women, handweaving is a "kind of celebration of the integrative power of the identity of Indianness . . . for Protestants, handweaving and textile entrepreneurship are a path leading away from Indianness" (Annis, 1988, p. 141). The very fact of their success, whether they started at the bottom or further up the economic scale, reinforces the spiritual choices of the Protestants with a material rationale.

The early Protestant missionaries viewed the Indians as being "spiritually, biologically, and economically enslaved" (Annis, 1988, p. 106), and they viewed the Catholic Church, alcohol, and debt as the instruments of that enslavement. They attacked the culture of the Indians. In the late 1970s and early 1980s, the rate of conversion increased as Protestants found fertile ground for conversions among people who had become marginalized economically by extreme poverty or socially by increased entrepreneurship. The disintegration of the milpa ideology created an atmosphere in which Protestant fundamentalism could flourish.

tion between religion and social organization is still widely accepted, the idea that societies are closely analogous to living organisms and that social features or practices, such as religion, could be best accounted for by showing how they functioned to "maintain the system" is now judged to be too simplistic. A phenomenon as complex and varied as religious belief is unlikely to have a simple explanation.

Belief Systems and Social Boundaries

There is another way in which religion is related to social process: it often defines the outer limits of certain important social relationships. It is obvious how coreligionists constitute a kind of language family or dialect; they, after all, have to communicate with one another while communicating with

Monumental religious architecture does more than shelter the worshipper. It symbolizes the power of those who order it constructed, as with the Sultan Ahmet Mosque built at the height of the Ottoman Empire.

(Roland & Sabrina Michaud/Woodfin Camp & Associates)

the divine. Not so obvious is how religion sets limits or presents obstructions to communication. In polyethnic communities or in complex societies where people from diverse heritages comingle, very often religion is seen as the outer limit of marriage. People from different nationalities or descent lines may interact more closely than they would across the lines of faith. This is not absolute, of course. Intermarriage in the United States among members of all faiths is quite common. Still, there is a general sense that marriage with coreligionists is preferable, and thus religion sets the outer limits to exogamy for many American families of diverse faiths. Among Catholics, Jews, and Muslims this is particularly strongly felt, even though intermarriage is not uncommon. In Bosnia, religion is critical to ethnic identity: Bosnian Moslems speak the same language as their Croatian (Roman Catholic)

and Serbian (Greek Orthodox) neighbors and all are descendants from the same ancestral population. Paradoxically, even though the three groups have intermarried regularly over the years, today they are locked in bitter and bloody intercommunal conflict.

Ritual

It is difficult to distinguish religious beliefs and symbols from religious behavior. In all societies, basic beliefs are embodied in rituals of religious observance (Rappaport, 1979). In simple terms, **ritual** can be defined as behavior (religious or not) that has become highly formalized and stereotyped. In the process, its original function often changes. Viewed objectively, the behavior of the practitioners of some rituals appears to have no direct stimulus; it is a response only to the rite itself, such as kneeling, standing, or sitting during different parts of a Christian church service. In other cases, an individual invents his or her own ritual for a specific purpose: to succeed in an exam by dressing in one's lucky sweater or using the pen that brought an A in previous efforts. It is extremely difficult to consistently differentiate between religious and secular ritual; the distinction often would seem to lie in the mental state of the individual participant. Ostensibly religious rituals, such as those associated with All Saints Day, etc., may be engaged in with bawdy revelry; an atheist's visit to Lenin's Tomb might occasion deep reverence.

Religious ritual often involves the manipulation of symbols, including combining symbols with very different origins. In the modern Catholic-Mayan community of Chamula, for instance, the ritual display of religious symbols reinforces fundamental beliefs and values. The sun symbolizes all that is good and desirable to the people of Chamula. The ritual procession of saints' images in the church runs from the eastern side (where the sun rises) to the western side of the church, and candles are arranged so that the largest and most expensive are nearest the east and the inferior ones are placed in the west (Gossen, 1972). Beliefs, symbols, and rituals are closely interconnected in all religions. Symbols or icons such as pictures, statues, crosses, stars, crescents, and architectural detail in religious buildings (such as the orientation of a mosques so that the direction of prayer is toward Mecca) all convey a message to the believer. Rituals in the form of religious theater act out stories or themes such as Catholic Passion Plays (depicting the life and death of Christ) and Shi'a ritual (reenacting the betrayal, death, and burial of Imam Huseyn). Less explicitly spelled out than such theater-like dramatizations are rituals that encode messages the believer is taught to understand (such as the Catholic or Greek Orthodox mass) but that remain obscure to the uninitiated.

Ritualistic behaviors may appear to produce little benefit for the people who engage in them, but in fact ritual can perform the basic function of reinforcing group solidarity. Genuflecting upon entering and leaving a Roman Catholic church, for example, helps integrate individual behaviors into a group structure, thereby reducing anxiety: one's sense of belonging is reinforced when one acts with the group (although the stated purpose is to acknowledge God's presence). Certain broad categories of ritualistic behaviors, which provide a sense of solidarity, are associated with religions in various parts of the world. These categories include prayer, music, physical exertion, pleading, recitation of codes, taboos, feasts, sacrifice, congregation, inspiration, and the manufacture and use of symbolic objects. A given rite may include one or more of these ritual behaviors.

Robert Frank theorizes that what he calls the "costly-to-fake-principle" may be involved in much ritual, particularly those that require a great deal from the participants (1988, pp. 99–102; in Irons, 1995). What this principle implies is that when an individual meets heavy requirements in funds and in time to observe elaborate, time-consuming rituals, his or her commitment to the group or religious sect is communicated in an emphatic manner. **Ordeals**—painful or humiliating experiences—usually mark a transition between social statuses. By voluntarily paying these costs, the individual demonstrates belief and loyalty. For example, the dangerous practice of "taking up snakes" or handling live rattlesnakes without protection (in the belief that God will provide protection) exacts its price each year from members of some fundamentalist Christian sects in the United States.

William Irons suggests that ritual can be used to induct individuals into groups by forcing them to demonstrate the commitment they are expected to make. Such rituals range from indoctrination into religious knowledge to a number of costly behaviors imposed by society as its "price of admission" (Irons, 1991, 1995). These may be associated with gender roles and adulthood (see also Gilmore, 1990): subincision of young men among the Australian Aborigines or clitoridectomy and infibulation of women in the Sudanic region of Africa. Subincision consists of cutting the underside of the penis and letting it heal with the urethra open, clitoridectomy consists of removing all or part of the clitoris, and infibulation consists of scarifying the vaginal opening so that it heals shut with a tube inserted for drainage. These are examples of extremely costly rituals or ordeals that are largely imposed on members of these societies, but even less onerous rituals may serve similar purposes. Having undergone such rituals, individuals may feel that they have a strong interest in maintaining a commitment to the group—rather like hazing in college fraternities or boot camp in the U.S. Marines.

Another explicit function of ritual is to promote some form of change, be it in the weather, in the fortunes of war, or some other area of concern. The actual effect that occurs may be quite different from the one overtly desired by the group. For instance, there is no evidence that rain or war dances bring rain or victory, or that a healing rite cures a sick child other than psychosomatically. But such rituals may have the effect of bringing about a measure of physiological change in the individuals who participate as tensions and excitement rise, peak, and then subside in the course of the ritual. This group experience also has the effect of reinforcing group solidarity.

Anthropologists identify two major categories of transition rituals, according to the kind of change they are designed to effect: rites of passage and rites of intensification. Because these two categories encompass much of ritual behavior, we will briefly explore each of them.

Rites of Passage

Rituals that mark a person's transition from one set of socially identified circumstances to another are known as **rites of passage**. Birth, puberty, marriage, parenthood, and death are all occasions for such ceremonies. According to Arnold Van Gennep

Xhosa young men celebrate the circumcision rites of their peers in South Africa.

(Strauss & Curtis/Offshoot Stock)

(1960), rites of passage normally include three separate phases: rites of separation, rites of segregation, and rites of integration. In many societies the transition from childhood to adult status, for instance, is marked by an extended ritual that involves first a symbolic end to childhood status, then a period of physical separation from normal community life, and finally, ceremonial reintegration into society as an adult. During this period of transition, the individual is said to be in a **liminal state**—that is, of ambiguous social status. Candidates for officer's rank in the military are in a liminal state while they undergo training, as they are neither in positions of leadership nor are they soldiers. Pilgrims, while undertaking a visit to a sacred shrine, may be in a liminal state until they complete their obligations. More than a million Muslim pilgrims visit Mecca and Medina in Saudi Arabia each year as they fulfill a central obligation of their faith. During the days that they perform the key steps of the pilgrimage, they all wear the same simple white garment, refrain from sexual intercourse, leave their hair uncut, and do not bathe; once the last rite is completed, they move from this liminal state, resume normal activities, and are known as *hajis* for the remainder of their lives.

Among the Nbemdu of Africa, the ritual marking the transition from boyhood to manhood, known as *mukanda*, lasts four months. After a night of feasting, singing, and sexual license, the initiates receive a last meal from their mothers (rites of separation). Then they are marched to another camp known as the "place of dying," where they remain in seclusion under the supervision of a group of male guardians. Here they are circumcised, hazed, harangued, and lectured on the rules of manhood (rites of segregation). Finally, daubed with white clay that signifies rebirth, the initiates are taken back to their families. At first their mothers greet them with songs of mourning, but as each realizes that her son is safe, the laments turn into songs of jubilation. After the novices are washed and given new clothes, each performs the dance of war to signify his new status as an adult (rites of integration). The function of these rites is not merely to celebrate the changes in the life of an individual, but to give public recognition to a new set of roles and relationships in the community (Turner, 1967).

Female circumcision, mentioned elsewhere, is a special case. While analogous to male circumcision in that it marks a transition to adulthood, it is not always celebrated publicly and it does not enhance the individual's status except to make her marriageable. It is often explicitly rationalized by practitioners as a means of controlling female sexuality; in the words of several informants, it "keeps girls 'clean.'" It is widespread in Egypt, Africa, and part of the Arabian Peninsula. While it is not sanctioned or even condoned by either Christian or Islamic doctrine, it is practiced by members of both faiths either overtly or covertly. It is, for example, almost universal among rural Coptic Christians and Moslems in Egypt, as well as among people practicing indigenous religions throughout East and Central Africa. The World Health Organization estimates that about 2,000,000 girls a year are subjected to procedures ranging from excision of the clitoris to having genital walls removed and the vagina stitched shut, to be opened upon marriage (Cairo Population Conference, 1994). Canada is the only country in the world to ban this operation. The effects are to sharply reduce or eliminate female sexual pleasure from intercourse.

Rites of Intensification

Rites of passage are related to individual transitions, but **rites of intensification** are usually directed toward either nature or the society as a whole. Their avowed intent is to reinforce or bolster some natural process essential to survival or to reaffirm the society's commitment to a particular set of values and beliefs.

Many agricultural societies, for example, perform rites of intensification at the coming of spring and the renewal of fertility. Among the Iroquois Indians, ritual celebration was tied to important events in the agricultural cycle of the seasons: the rising sap in the maple trees, ripening strawberries, maturing corn, and finally, the harvest.

Weekly Christian church services are rites of intensification that are intended to reinforce the commitment of the believers. Similarly, the molimo festival of the Pygmies, described at the beginning of this chapter, is a social rite of intensification, its purpose being to strengthen the trust of the community in the will of the forest.

While these categories are useful for analysis, they do not always precisely reflect the actual ritual performance. A rite of passage can be performed as a part of a rite of intensification. A baptism, which is a rite of passage, can occur in a weekly church service, a rite of intensification. Similarly, the nature of a given ritual can change over time. Circumcision in the Judeo-Christian-Moslem tradition, for example, almost certainly began as a rite of passage marking the transition from boyhood to manhood. Among Moslems, it is still practiced in this manner. A boy between the ages of eight and twelve undergoes circumcision in the context of a ceremony that explicitly emphasizes the fact that he is no longer an infant but rather a young adult ready to assume certain responsibilities. Among Jews, circumcision is performed when the boy is eight days old and marks his arrival into the community; no subsequent adult responsibilities are implied. This later transition is marked by a separate ceremony (the bar mitzvah) at puberty. When Christian boys are circumcised, the procedure usually is carried out in a hospital shortly after birth and is associated with no religious symbolism. It is done for putative health reasons, although no medical evidence supports the practice. Other familiar examples of the changing contexts or meanings of ritual can be seen in the incorporation of many pre-Christian rituals into the Christian liturgical calendar: Christmas and Easter are two notable examples, not to mention local practices accommodated by the local church in different countries.

Even mortuary rites can be seen as attempts not only to assuage the grief of individuals but also as efforts to rebuild social relations that have been altered by death. On Vanatinai, a small, remote island in the South Pacific, now part of Papua New Guinea, death is accompanied by a complex array of culturally ordained responses among the survivors. Each deceased person should be honored by a series of increasingly elaborate feasts, a sequence that lasts anywhere from one to twenty-five years. The importance of mortuary rituals mirrors the central place of ancestor spirits in the culture. The spirits of the dead aid and protect their decendants. Exchange and mortuary rituals on Vanatinai also reflect the ideals of gender equivalence and the interdependence both of men and women and of matrilineages (Lepowsky, 1993). The Gender Issues box, *Honoring the Dead*, on page 344, explains these mortuary rituals in more depth.

Gender Issues

Honoring the Dead

MARIA LEPOWSKY (1993) HAS characterized the matrilineal society of Vanatinai as being egalitarian; that is, there are no ideologies of male superiority or of female inferiority. This egalitarianism is reflected in the elaborate mortuary rituals. Mortuary ritual and the hosting of feasts and exchange of valuables that accompany it are the primary avenues to personal power and prestige in the society. On Vanatinai, the deaths of men and women are marked equally by elaborate mourning and feasting, and the burden of mourning obligations is the same for men and women. Women play prominent and public roles in funeral rituals and their exchange obligations are the same as men's. They are expected to obtain and present ceremonial valuables, and both women and men may strive to enhance their reputations as "big men" (*giagia*, literally "givers") by first accumulating these valuables and subsequently giving them away and by hosting or contributing a great deal to feasts.

The sequence of mortuary feasts involves up to hundreds of people from distant communities and islands. All contribute to public, ritualized exchanges among the lineages of the deceased, affines, and the deceased's father. "Burial initiates exchanges of the living and the dead and continues exchanges that took place during the life of the deceased. It is followed within days or weeks by a dramatic feast called *jivia*, in which valuables are exchanged

and the deceased's kin ritually feed the mourning spouse or representatives of the father's lineage" (Lepowsky, 1993, p. 222). A *velaloga* feast two weeks to two months later releases a widow or widower from taboos against leaving the hamlet, bathing, or shaving. Taboos on the house and hamlet of the deceased are removed at the *ghanarakerake*, or "food goes out" feast about six months after the jivia. About a year after the death, there is an optional feast, *vearada*, for those who cried at the burial. And lastly, each death must be honored by the *zagaya*, the final feast and the largest of all, which is held usually after about three years of intensive preparations. After the zagaya, all taboos are lifted from people and places, and the bereaved spouses can again make themselves attractive, court, and remarry.

Women create much of the wealth for these exchanges and certain women are recognized as "food magicians" who are asked by the host of the feast (who may be a man or a woman) to use their skills and knowledge to ensure that he or she is not shamed by running out of food. In addition to garden produce, grown largely by women's labor and under women's supervision, women are responsible for providing other forms of wealth, including decorated coconut-leaf skirts, intricately woven and dyed coconut-leaf baskets, garden baskets, pandanus-leaf sleeping mats, and clay pots. All have roles in the rituals, and have

to be produced in large quantities. Sago starch, long carved sago-stirring paddles, wooden combs, fern-fiber armlets stuffed with valuables and magic herbs, small coconut-leaf pouches, and carved wooden handles used ceremonially to hold valuable greenstone axe blades, are generally generated by male labor but are distributed by both sexes. Pigs are raised by both men and women and contributed by both as individuals.

The relations of power revealed by ceremonial exchange on Vanatinai do not separate men from women. Different forms of wealth are not associated exclusively with one or the other. Strength, wisdom, and generosity are qualities looked for in both men and women. Only those with these qualities will be able to host a successful zagaya feast. The giagia are both male and female, and their power stems from their possession of wealth and their knowledge of magic. They are "fertile and maternal through their growing and feeding of wealth objects and persons . . . " (Lepowsky, 1993, p. 279). Mourning taboos and enforced celibacy also desexualize the widowed spouse, who becomes symbolically identified with the corpse, which reverts to being a child of its matrilineal fathers, male and female. "The corpse evokes maleness through its representation of sorcery and of death itself and femaleness through its representation of the matrilineage that gave birth to it and by bearing fruit" (p. 279).

The Organization of Ritual

In any society, ritual behavior does not occur at random: it is organized and closely structured. Not surprisingly, it is organized in different ways in different societies. It may be individualistic or communal, or operate with the use of ritual specialists.

In individualistic rites, the individual worshipper draws on the powers of the supernatural. A Crow Indian man who wanted to excel in hunting or war, to find a cure, or perhaps to avenge the death of a relative went off alone for four days (four was the Crow's mystic number) to fast, pray, and seek visions. This individualistic seeking usually produced revelations that fitted neatly into Crow traditions. Spirits nearly always appeared on the fourth day, bringing the supplicant a sacred song, describing special ways to dress and medicines to use, and imposing certain taboos (Lowie, 1954, pp. 157–161).

Religious rituals may also be organized communally, with everyone in a particular group or society participating. One person may be assigned a special role—dancer, speechmaker, prayer leader—just for the occasion. People who adopt these temporary roles are not imbued with unusual powers or vested with full-time religious duties.

In most societies, however, people seek help from intermediaries who are specialists in the art of reaching the spirits and gods, men and women who are trained in or have inherited a special vocation that distinguishes them from others. They are seen to be more knowledgeable about the belief system and, more to the point, know how to use this knowledge.

Shamans. One such religious specialist is the **shaman**, a medium of the supernatural who acts as a person in possession of unique curing, divining, or witchcraft capabilities. In addition, chiefdoms and societies organized as states usually, if not inevitably, have a religious-ritual system that is organized in some form of ecclesiastical bureaucracy: specialized mediators with the supernatural who constitute a clergy or a priesthood. With such ecclesiastical organizations, religious practice takes a distinctive form: on the one hand is a religious specialist or priest who performs or directs the ritual, on the other a more or less passive audience or congregation.

Shamans often assume their religious status through visions of contact with a supernatural force. Here an Ariaal diviner sits with his gourd and stones, which he uses to foretell the future.
(Elliot Fratkin)

Shamans assume their religious status through birth (sometimes all the men or women of a particular family become shamans), through visions, through contact with some form of supernatural force, or through what amounts to simple vocational training. The word "shaman" can be traced to the Tungus reindeer herders of eastern Siberia, where part-time religious specialists are consulted for curing and communicating with the spirit world. They are able to transport themselves to the world of the supernatural (however it is conceived) and to act as mouthpieces for spirits, and often have privileged access to knowledge of the future. However, even within Siberia and Central Asia, there is such variability among forms of shamanism that some would question how valid it is to treat it as a universal category (Atkinson, 1992, p. 308).

One of the earliest studies of shamanism examines an Eskimo shaman in Greenland. Yearly, the shaman undertakes a dangerous spiritual voyage to the bottom of the sea to seek out the goddess Sedna, stroke her hair, and listen to her complaints against humans. When the shaman returns, he or she exhorts the living to confess their sins, so that Sedna will release the game for another year and allow success in the hunt (Rasmussen, 1929). On other occasions, shamans may be called on to reveal a witch or thief, to cure illness, or to help people make decisions. In all cases, the rituals are organized around the role of the shaman, who performs his or her services for a fee.

Many shamans have a substantial knowledge of pharmacologically active plants and herbs, which they employ along with healing or other rituals. Thus they may be offering more than what we would term psychological support—they may, in fact, be effecting medical cures (Atkinson, 1992). They also perform magic, perhaps chewing various plant and natural substances that congeal to form "stones" that are extracted from the patient. In an **exorcism** related to the "evil eye" in the Balkans, the exorcist, as shaman, in effect "reads" the nodules formed on a piece of molten lead dropped in cold water to prove that a victim was truly smitten with the affliction in question. Once this was established, the patient was cured by a ritual to remove the curse. On a more negative side, as we shall see, shamans can sometimes use their knowledge of plants and herbs to make effective poisons that add considerable authority to their reputation for supernatural power.

The mainstays of religion in many Eskimo, Native American, and other hunting-and-gathering societies, shamans of one sort or another are found throughout the world. In our society astrologers, mediums, and fortune tellers are essentially shamans, and anthropological studies have suggested that the shaman's techniques do not differ greatly from those of the psychiatrist.

Shamanism can exist very comfortably alongside organized churches, as we see in our own society. For example, astrology has no scientific basis and thus must be considered a form of supernatural belief and ritual, and the people who practice it are

shamans or diviners. It is big business in the industrialized world, where the rich and famous as well as the poor and disenfranchised spend a great deal of money to peer into the future. Even Nancy Reagan, wife of the former president of the United States, is said to have consulted an astrologer to determine auspicious days for the president's appointments and to have used her influence to persuade him to avoid certain activities on inauspicious ones. Human beings seem to have a compelling urge to seek out the future; the obviously vague and ambiguous advice found in newspaper horoscopes is sought by avid readers in even the most advanced societies.

Closely related to shamanism is the idea that people can be influenced or controlled by powerful external forces or entities; that is, possessed by spirits. This belief is widespread through Asia, Africa, the Americas and the circum-Mediterranean region. It is generally, but not exclusively, associated with "ecstatic" or "transporting" religious expression—such as in Pentecostal or fundamentalist Christian practice, mystic cults in Islam and Judaism, and Vodoun in Haiti. The Catholic Church and the Church of England still authorize exorcism rites on occasion (Boddy, 1994, p. 407).

The *zar* cult of the Sudan is a case where women are thought vulnerable to spirit possession (Boddy, 1994, p. 416). Zar spirits are mischievous, social creatures, rather like humans but incorporeal. They especially like to afflict women with fertility problems, and thereby gain access to the material world through rituals of appeasement that involve feasting.

The "evil eye" belief found throughout the Balkans and the Middle East is a form of possession involving two individuals: the individual who is the involuntary host to the malevolent force, or "evil eye"; and the afflicted individual, human or animal, who experiences illness, misfortune, or even death as a result of encountering this force. Handsome children, valued livestock, and owners of fine properties are at risk; in short, anyone or anything that attracts attention or envy. Most often it is the "outsider," or marginal individual, who is thought to possess the evil eye (an involuntary condition). Similarly, it is the socially marginal individual who is the likely victim. Once an affliction is diagnosed, an exorcism must be performed. The exorcism rite may be extremely structured and accompanied by much formal ceremony, as those performed occasionally by the Catholic Church, or it may be extremely informal—much like a visit to the doctor's office. In either case, there is no evidence that anything other than a psychological effect is produced in the victim or his or her family.

Clergy. In our own and many other stratified societies, religion is often administered by a full-time professional clergy. Priests, like shamans, are religious specialists who act as intermediaries between the community and the supernatural. Also like shamans, priests are considered qualified to perform sacred rituals that lay people cannot perform, such as dispensing penance and communion in the Roman Catholic Church. But priests differ from shamans in many important respects. Whereas shamans seek to resolve crises as they occur and usually work in the context of the family group, priests and other qualified members of the clergy more often perform rites for the community as a whole, in a public forum, on a regular, calendrical basis. Whereas shamans are individual entrepreneurs whose influence in a group depends on their ability to perform cures and the like, priests are part of a self-perpetuating organization. The training, sanctioned activities, dress, deportment, and responsibilities of the clergy tend to be much more highly regulated by rules or conventions; these people are members of a church—an ecclesiastical bureaucracy. In many societies, religious and political authority overlap. For example, in some cases the head of the church is also the head of the state. In other societies, political and religious organizations are entirely separate. One thing that distinguishes any member of a clergy is that the individual practitioner is part of a larger, fairly closely organized system involving others who practice the same profession.

Established churches and priesthoods tend to be found in highly complex, stratified societies. While people in complex societies may also practice individualistic or communal rituals, the importance of the established, bureaucratic religion in maintaining social and economic stratification cannot be ignored.

Religion and Resource Management

Religion, in validating a prescribed course of action, may affect the relationship between people and their environment. Many religious beliefs include important environmental information, and ritual observances frequently mark or even trigger events critical to the success of economic production and distribution. For the Waswanipi Cree, a tribe of Canadian Indians, hunting success depends on acting in a responsible manner toward the animals that nourish them. An animal, they say, will not give itself to a hunter unless the hunter fulfills certain moral obligations: limiting the number of animals killed, using all of what he takes, and showing respect for the bodies and souls of the animals by following established procedures for hunting, butchering, and consuming the game. Failure to live up to these responsibilities will anger the animals and bring a hunter bad luck.

According to Harvey Feit (1973), these beliefs and practices are a critical factor in the way the Waswanipi use their environmental resources. Because they live in a subarctic ecosystem in which productivity is low, they have to manage their resources carefully. Waswanipi hunters regulate the harvests of moose and beaver and control the distribution and population levels of these species by using alternative resources such as fish during some years and by occupying a different hunting territory each season. These practices allow the animal populations to expand for several years after each periodic harvest. In effect, Waswanipi religious beliefs and practices actually incorporate a basic ecological principle: people and animals will survive as long as they remain in balance.

The ecological significance of religious beliefs and practices may be unintentional. Among the Naskapi of Labrador, hunting strategies are sometimes regulated by divination. When food supplies are low and Naskapi hunters are uncertain where to find game, they usually consult a shaman, who tells them what direction the hunt should take. He decides the question by holding the scraped shoulder blade of a caribou over hot coals and "reading" the cracks and burned spots that appear in the bone. Thus the hunters select their routes on a random basis—wherever the spots and cracks indicate.

As a result, the game supply is not depleted in particularly successful hunting places and the hunters follow no habitual routes that the animals can learn to avoid.

Some religious beliefs and customs may seem maladaptive on first consideration. For instance, the Hindu prohibition against the killing or eating of cattle appears illogical in a land where hunger is prevalent. But the cattle produce three essential products: fuel and fertilizer (in the form of dung) and traction with which to plow the fields (Harris, 1966). To eat the cattle in times of famine would be rather like an unemployed worker selling the car needed to look for work. In the short run, the car money (or the beef) would come in handy, but in the long run the means of making a living would have been eliminated. Hence the taboo against killing cattle, Marvin Harris argues, is cost-effective, even in an area where hunger and starvation are chronic.

The attitudes toward cattle held by many East African peoples, which are collectively referred to as the "cattle complex," serve a similar function, as we have discussed in Chapter 6. This is to say not that such religious prohibitions or taboos are a necessary component of resource management, only that religious belief and ritual usually encode information and encourage ways of behaving that have environmental impacts (Rappaport, 1979). And as Michael Dove writes in regard to Indonesia (1988, p. 17), "When traditional uses of the environment by peasants are investigated, they are usually found to embody sound principles of utilization and conservation—which are often expressed through the idiom of ritual."

Like religious beliefs, ritual cycles serve important functions in the regulation of the relationship between people and their resources. The Pueblo Indian groups of the American Southwest, for instance, celebrate most major occasions in the life of an individual and all major religious festivals with an exchange of food throughout the community. Given the unpredictable climate, the variable land quality, and the social setting (in which one family may be living in abundance while another faces lean times), these practices ensure that all individuals receive ample food from time to time during the year.

The most important mechanism of redistribution, however, is not via randomly occurring rituals but through time-dependent ones that fall on the same day each year (Ford, 1972). These rituals are most frequent in late winter, when families whose harvests have been lean are most likely to be out of food. On some saints' days, feasts are held and food and clothing may be thrown from the rooftops to the people below. Thus, Pueblo groups have built a welfare system into their ritual celebrations. Richard Ford (1972) suggests that this system depends on surplus and that in the face of real famine, the society would have to turn to other mechanisms that involve feedback from the environment.

In Chapter 10 we mentioned the economic role of Balinese water temples in agriculture. J. Stephen Lansing (1991, 1995) found that a hierarchy of water temples, with their attendant priests and ritual specialists, coordinates a complex system of water catchment and distribution that affects thousands of farmers. Farmers participate in rituals held throughout the year at various temples and, at the same time, discuss water availability, pests, planting schedules, and harvest times. The priests facilitate decisions about cropping patterns by considering the trade-off between two constraints: water sharing and pest control (1995, p. 93). Leaders meet at the main temple and agree on an auspicious time to begin planting. This decision is relayed down through a hierarchy of local water temples where farmers also gather for rituals. If farmers in a watershed area all plant at the same time, they can harvest at the same time and then a very large area will be left fallow until the next planting. This interval, it transpires, is critical for pest control. If all the fields can be either flooded or their grasses burned at the same time, numerous pests are eradicated; if this is not synchronized, rice pests simply move to adjacent fields and adversely affect the following crop. Temple rituals provided the means to synchronize cropping and flooding.

CASE STUDY:

The Maring "Plant the Rumbim"

THE BEST EXAMPLE OF SUCH A REGULATORY RITUAL system can be found among the Maring of highland New Guinea. Roy Rappaport (1967) has demonstrated in a now-classic study that the ritual slaughter of pigs functions as a mechanism for redistributing surplus pigs, providing local populations with a supply of animal protein at critical times and ultimately regulating the territorial distribution of Maring groups.

The Maring are horticulturists of the central highlands, who farm hillside fields and raise semi-domesticated pigs as a primary source of meat. It is the latter that are vital to their diet and potentially in short supply. It is also the case that pigs, if raised in overabundance, threaten the basis for Maring subsistence: they eat essentially the same garden products as the people themselves.

The Maring are inveterate fighters. Neighboring groups often fight sporadically for weeks until one group is driven from its ancestral territory. The victors then perform a ritual called "planting the rumbim." Every man places his hand on the ritual rumbim plant, and the ancestors are addressed as follows:

> We thank you for helping us in the fight and permitting us to remain on our territory. We place our souls in the rumbim as we plant it on our ground. We ask you to care for this rumbim. We will kill pigs for you now, but they are few. In the future, when we have many pigs, we shall again give you pork and uproot the rumbim and stage a kaiko [pig festival]. But until there are sufficient pigs to repay you, the rumbim will remain in the ground. [Rappaport, 1967, pp. 23–24]

This ceremony is accompanied by the ritual slaughter of some pigs. These animals are dedicated to the ancestors, and their meat is distributed among the group's allies in payment for military assistance. A period of truce follows. Until the kaiko is staged and the rumbim is uprooted, the group may not engage in hostilities. The Maring believe that until these rituals are completed, they have not fully paid their debts to their ancestors and allies and therefore will not be given further military aid. Rappaport maintains that by limiting warfare, this taboo on fighting ensures that the regional population level does not become dangerously low.

The dynamics of this system are evident at the local level. Before the rumbim can be uprooted, a tribe must raise a sufficient number of pigs. If a place is good, the Maring say, this process requires

Ritual cycles may mark points in the agricultural round; in fact, they may regulate or coordinate agricultural activities.
(Philip Jones Griffith/Magnum)

only about five years. If a place is bad, however, it sometimes takes ten to twenty years. A bad place is one in which frequent misfortunes require people to kill large numbers of pigs: ritual demands that whenever group members are injured or fall ill, they and their families must be given pork to eat—a practice that ensures the afflicted of high-quality protein at a time when they need it most. Even in a bad place, however, the number of pigs eventually increases. And as the herds become larger, they require more and more food, and Maring women are forced to expend more energy in caring for the pigs. When this situation becomes intolerable and pigs are actually competing with humans for food, the community normally decides that it is time to hold a kaiko. The ceremony begins with the uprooting of the rumbim and generally lasts for most of the year, with many feasts, weddings, and tribal alliances. It concludes with a wholesale sacrifice of pigs and distribution of pork to tribes throughout the region. Once a group has completed this ritual cycle, it is free to begin fighting again and to start a new cycle of territorial shifts, population redistribution, and manipulation of food sources. ▶

Psychological and Sociopolitical Functions of Religion

Religious beliefs and rituals provide more than ways of dealing with resources. They also explain the meaning of life and death. By answering existential questions, religion helps people to cope psychologically and otherwise with the pains and disappointments that inevitably attend every life, answering a need for certainty that their concrete experiences cannot fulfill. Religion does not only operate on a personal level. Following the lead of Émile Durkheim and Max Weber, A. R. Radcliffe-Brown (1952) argued that the main function of religion is to establish, codify, reaffirm, and enforce the fundamental social values that integrate society. Through religious symbols and their manipulation, people are taught not only how to accept certain beliefs but also how to demonstrate those beliefs in socially effective ways. Religion validates the social and moral order through forms of governance, social hierarchies, codes of law customs, and morals. While religion often serves to preserve the status quo, it may also be used to validate social change—as we see in revolutionary movements and religiously-inspired warfare.

Religion and Individual Coping

"Religion," Malinowski observed, "is not born out of speculation and reflection, still less out of illusion or misapprehension, but rather out of the real tragedies of human life, out of the conflict between human plans and realities" (1931, p. 99). Religions reduce anxiety by supplying some answers to the imponderables of human experience: Why do we suffer? Why do we die? Why are we subject to natural disasters? In addition to supplying a system of meaning—a way of thinking about human existence—religion prescribes clear-cut institutional ways of dealing with the often frightening uncertainties of life. The Trobriand Islanders, for example, despite their highly developed skills as navigators and fishermen, perform magico-religious rituals before embarking on a long ocean voyage. They do not bother with such rituals for everyday fishing expeditions, but a long voyage on the open sea in a fragile canoe is a dangerous undertaking, and the rituals help to allay their apprehensions.

A reduction in anxiety is not simply a more peaceful state of mind. A patient's attitude is as important as medical treatment to recovery from many diseases; a lessening of anxiety may strengthen a person's commitment to recovery and tip the balance toward a return to health. In the same way, a crew paralyzed by fear is less likely to complete a dangerous canoe voyage than one that is confident of the protection of providence. The same can be said for warriors, and despite the cynical observation that "God is on the side of the heaviest artillery," every military organization from the tribal to the very modern makes liberal use of adrenalin-arousing ideology and rituals to bolster the resolve to fight.

Social Integration

In addition to the psychological functions of religion, one of the most basic social functions of religion is simply to bring people together periodically and thus to maintain lines of communication and cooperation. Most religious rituals involve groups of people. In the Mbuti Pygmy molimo, in the weekly meetings of Christian and Moslem congregations, even in the awesome ceremonies the Aztecs once performed to appease their gods, people come together. The express purpose of their meeting is to perform some ritual or reaffirm an ideology, but while they are together, a range of social and economic activities may also take place. The haj, or once-in-a-lifetime pilgrimage to Mecca required of all Moslems, brings more than a million believers to one holy place at the same time each year. This huge gathering has political and economic implications. Not only is commerce carried out in the process, but members of different national and political entities make contact, exchange ideas, and reinforce their social and political aspirations. Unfortunately, this regular gathering of people, so common to religions, has also contributed to the spread of disease. (See the Using Anthropology box, *Religion and the Spread of Disease,* page 351 .)

Reduction of Conflict

The potential for tension and strife in social roles and relationships—between kinfolk, spouses, men and women, and rulers and subjects, for example—is inherent in every society. When disputes

Human Ecology
Religion and the Spread of Disease

WHETHER VIRUSES OR LARGER organisms are involved, infectious diseases need big populations in which to thrive, since in a small population either they will wipe out the host population and hence themselves, or the host population will develop immunity so again the disease agents will die. Religious occasions that bring large numbers of people together, especially from diverse places, will tend to foster conditions in which infectious diseases thrive, while aspects of religions that isolate individuals or close boundaries provide barriers to infectious disease. Certain religious practices can also foster genetic and deficiency diseases. For example, among the Amish in the northeastern United States, inbreeding has produced a large proportion of defective traits; children raised on a total vegetarian diet by the Black Hebrew community in Israel suffered growth retardation and a wide range of deficiency diseases (Reynolds & Tanner, 1995).

In 1348 bubonic plague had reached Europe, and it is estimated that the disease killed one third of the population. Initially it was spread by rat fleas, but later it became pneumonic (spread by droplet infection). The plague was thought to have been sent by God in retribution for the wickedness of the people, and since the efforts of some civil authorities to keep travellers away or to quarantine them did not prove effective against the virulent disease, it was almost inevitable that people would support religious explanations and reactions. An extremist group of Protestants, the Flagellants, seeking atonement, toured towns whipping themselves severely before large and appreciative crowds. Since pneumonic plague spreads fast where many people are gathered together, the penitents were in fact spreading the disease widely as they travelled. St. Bridget of Sweden advocated, among other things, celebrating special Masses—again bringing large numbers of people together and increasing the chance of infection. Pope Clement VI ordered a jubilee year in 1350, granting special indulgences to all who made the journey to Rome; "it has been estimated that very large numbers came from all over Europe and later returned home, thus spreading the infection into areas not previously touched" (Reynolds & Tanner, 1995, p. 268). It was not until the seventeenth and eighteenth centuries that it was clearly understood that the plague was spread by contact and appropriate preventive measures were enforced.

Pilgrimages also provide occasions for the spread of disease. The best-known pilgrimage, to Mecca, has often been accompanied by outbreaks of cholera. In 1863, pilgrims carried cholera from India to Mecca, and it is estimated that one third of the 90,000 pilgrims died. The disease was subsequently spread by returning pilgrims to Mesopotamia, Syria, Palestine, and Egypt. A recent minor outbreak occurred in 1974 among some Nigerian pilgrims, in which about 300 died. Air travel has increased the problem; in the past the incubation period of a disease might have passed before the pilgrims reached Mecca, the weaker would have died, and those who did arrive would have been acclimatized to a degree. In India, the major Hindu pilgrimages have also been connected to outbreaks of cholera. Every one of the major religious gatherings on the Ganges between 1879 and 1950 was followed by an outbreak of cholera (Reynolds & Tanner, 1995).

---

arise, religion can serve to structure points of disagreement and then provide a common ground that all the participants can accept as valid for the entire community, whatever the subsequent course of action that is chosen.

Sometimes ritual is used as a way of channeling and controlling conflicts that arise when a person is caught between incompatible social obligations or when the moral norms of the social order as a whole run counter to the interests of particular groups.

Rites of conflict publicly express both the bonds of social unity and the tensions inherent in these bonds. Among the Shilluk of Sudan, the coronation ritual is a rite of conflict that dramatizes the surface struggles between rival settlements of kin groups. At a deeper level, it also represents the conflict ·that arises because a single prince who comes from a particular kin group and settlement is supposed to represent Shilluk unity. Before the new king can take office, competing groups stage a mock battle. One army carries the effigy of Nyikang, the symbol of Shilluk unity; the other army includes the king-elect. The army of the effigy captures the king from his clansmen and takes him to the capital. Here he is placed on the throne and the spirit of Nyikang is said to enter his body. Physically and symbolically separated from his relatives and followers, the new king is placed above sectional loyalties. By confronting the sources of social tensions, such rituals help to promote cooperation and reduce conflict.

Promotion of Social Control

Every religion is a system of ethics that defines right and wrong ways to behave, and prescribes sanctions against wrongdoers. When moral standards of conduct are invested with supernatural authority, their values and prescriptions are made more compelling. The Bible, for instance, describes in graphic detail the severe punishment awaiting one who breaks the Lord's commandments. In other belief systems, misdeeds are thought to provoke the wrath of ancestral spirits. The ancestors may bring misfortune to the person who fails to carry out obligations to the spirits themselves, or to one who engages in antisocial behavior toward close kin.

CASE STUDY:

The Vodoun Church of Haiti

IN THE VODOUN RELIGION OF HAITI, WITH ITS associated secret societies, called *bizango*, we see one way in which religion can promote social control as well as provide a set of beliefs that guides behavior in all aspects of life. The processes by which it does so reveal much more than a simple mechanism for maintaining social order. They lead one to see how the natural world merges with the supernatural, how religion merges with magic, how religion can be the basis for the practice of

medicine, and how a proud people have maintained their identity through the beliefs of their forebears. Vodoun (often called "voodoo") is poorly understood and often associated with very negative connotations. The truth is far less lurid and rather more interesting.

Until 1791 Haiti was a rich colony of France. Its plantations, worked by slaves under conditions that must have been incredibly severe, produced prodigious quantities of sugar. The slaves, imported from West Africa, suffered such high mortality that they were continually replaced by new arrivals; in the last year of French rule, more than 350,000 slaves were imported (Davis, 1988, p. 25). The slaves came from many societies and from many walks of life. Among them were potters and other craftworkers, farmers, hereditary chiefs, warriors, herbalists, sorcerers, and priests. The Haitian revolution of 1791, which abruptly ended direct colonial rule, marked the first successful slave revolt in history and the birth of the world's first black republic. It also ended the plantation system and opened the hinterlands of the country for settlement by newly freed slaves—many only recently brought from their homelands. The Vodoun religion is one aspect of the African heritage that took root in the New World.

Vodoun believers are preponderant among the rural population of Haiti and are found in significant numbers in the urban centers, where the Vodoun Church exists in an uneasy relationship with the Catholic Church. The core of the belief system is that the spirits, *loa,* are multiple expressions of God. The believers recognize Agwe, the sovereign of the sea; Ogoun, the spirit of fire and metallurgical elements; and numerous others; but they also recognize Erzulie, goddess of love; Ghede, the spirit of the dead; and Legba, the spirit of communication among all the spheres. "Vodounists, in fact," writes Wade Davis, "honor hundreds of loa because they so sincerely recognize all life, all material objects and even abstract processes as the sacred expressions of God"(1988, p. 47). God thus stands as the supreme force at the apex of a vast pantheon; but he is distant, and it is with the spirits that one interacts on a daily basis.

Vodoun not only embodies a set of spiritual beliefs but prescribes a way of life. It is a code of ethics, a philosophy, a view of human nature. "As surely as one can refer to a Christian or Buddhist

Vodoun ceremonies summon loa spirits, which then possess one or more of the congregation.
(Steve Winter/Black Star)

society, one may speak of a Vodoun society, and within that world one finds completeness: art and music, education based on the oral transmission of songs and folklore, a complex system of medicine, and a system of justice based on indigenous principles of conduct and morality" (Davis, 1988, p. 43). It cannot be abstracted from the day-to-day lives of the people; the sacred and the profane are one.

Community equilibrium is sought and maintained, and trouble and troublemakers are eschewed with the help of the *houngan* and the *mambo.* As spiritual leaders, the Vodoun priests and priestesses are called upon to interpret a complex set of spiritual concepts and to perform complex rituals. They may direct ceremonies to restore community health, to divine the future, and to protect society against evildoers and sorcerers. However, the *bokor,* a professional sorcerer, is usually used to confront the effects of other sorcerers.

In many ways the antithesis of the priest, the bokor commands an arsenal of spells, potent potions, powders, and supernatural entities. For every force that harms, there is one that heals, and vice versa. The roles of houngan and bokor merge as each needs the other; every religious ceremony requires magic, and magic itself is worthless without knowledge of the loa, or spirits, commanded by the houngan. The bokor may be feared, even despised, but he is an essential member of the community.

It is in this ideological context that the belief in zombies, or the "living dead," has to be understood. The word itself is probably derived from the Congolese *nzambi,* or "spirit of a dead person." It is the interplay between life and death, the forces of good and evil, and their human expressions in priests and sorcerers that makes Vodoun and the fear of zombification such a powerful social force. The bokor, if sufficiently skilled, can do more than cast powerful spells and assume animal form; he is thought to be capable of creating two forms of zombies. One is a spirit of a person, sold to or captured by a bokor, who is doomed to wander the world endlessly. The second is the more familiar "living dead," raised from the grave by the sorcerer and led away as a slave. Zombies are recognizable by their docile natures; glassy, empty eyes; and evident lack of will and emotion. Zombies are not feared; they are viewed as pathetic relics of their former selves. What is feared is zombification. This is why the concept has such force as a means of social control.

Obviously, the people who act as intermediaries between ancestors (or saints or gods) and mortals, such as the mambos, houngans, and bokors of the Vodoun Church and the priests, rabbis, and mullahs of Christianity, Judaism, and Islam, may occupy positions of great power. And while they serve as instruments of social control, it also happens that their tremendous power is sometimes used for worldly rather than religious ends (Boyd and Richerson, 1991). In Haiti, the overthrow of the Duvalier regime was marked by public rage directed at houngans who were tied to the regime through memberships in the semisecret, paramilitary Tonton Macoute, a bizango organization that had served the state. Elsewhere, the mullahs of Iran have effectively run the country since the Shah's ouster in 1979. They employ their power much as would any secular administrator, but on occasion the religious nature of their rule comes into play. Not only have they presided over legislation designed to bring Iran's laws into strict conformity with Islamic teaching, but the late Ayatollah Khomeini, paramount leader, used the call of Islam to mobilize the country for war with Iraq, a war in which Iranians were urged to seek martyrdom for the faith. As many as half a million did just that. ◗

Validation of Change: Revitalization

Religious beliefs and rituals can be vehicles or catalysts for social change. At times strain and tension within a society become so great that conflict and instability can no longer be contained. Religious **revitalization movements**—conscious efforts to build an ideology that will be relevant to changing cultural needs—are often part of the social eruption that follows. As Anthony Wallace has explained: "Societies are not, after all, forever stable; political revolutions and civil wars tear them apart, culture changes turn them over, invasion and acculturation undermine them. Reformative religious movements often occur in disorganized societies; these new religions, far from being conservative, are often radically destructive of existing institutions" (1966, p. 30). The primary if unstated goal of such revitalization movements is to resolve conflict and promote stability by reorganizing society. These movements often serve an important function in the adaptation of a society to external forces that threaten to overwhelm it.

Because anthropologists have often been eyewitnesses to (and sometimes even agents of) the drastic impact of Western culture on other societies, there is a substantial anthropological literature on nativistic revitalization movements. In the late 1880s, for example, the Ghost Dance appeared among the Indians of the western United States. Promoted as a nonpolitical religious vision by an Indian named Wovoka, the Ghost Dance expressed the belief that dead Indian forebears were soon to return on trains to take possession of the technology of the whites, all of whom would be simultaneously exterminated in a great explosion. This vision soon became a rallying cry for many Indian tribes, as the return of their dead ancestors would so increase their strength that they would certainly outnumber the whites. Sioux warriors, in particular, were encouraged to challenge the U.S. Army: they had only to perform the Ghost Dance and wear special shirts, they were assured, to become impervious to bullets. After several years of raids and counterraids, the last remnant of 200 Sioux was killed at Wounded Knee, South Dakota, on December 29, 1890 (Mooney, 1965).

Some belief systems call for nonconfrontational behavior; others call for rebellion. In all instances, however, an unstable and conflict-ridden society uses a combination of old and new symbols to define a new view of the world and its own place in it. This response can be the basis for successful political and cultural resistance to external threats and hostility.

Both Christianity and Islam have their origins in what amount to revitalization movements. Both arose in the context of cultural and social disruption and both developed an ideology that mobilized their followers to construct a utopian social order; to right the wrongs that afflicted the present. Christianity arose among a people defeated by an imperial power—Rome. The subsequent course of the movement was very similar to that of others before and since: a visionary leader, an emphasis on a return to fundamental virtues, bypassing the established religious structure, and triumph in the face of persecution. In fact, persecution and oppression are often essential to the ultimate success of revitalization movements, because they are seen to confirm the righteousness of the members.

Anthony Wallace (1966) analyzed the nature of such movements in North America in his study of the Handsome Lake movement among the Iroquois during the late eighteenth and early nineteenth centuries. In the decade preceding the appearance of this movement, the Iroquois had increasingly suffered from disease, poverty, death, and confinement to reservations as the result of policies pursued by the U.S. government. The prophet Handsome Lake claimed to have received word of a means of resolving these problems in a series of visions. His first visions emphasized the need to return to traditional Iroquois practices, and the symbols he used emphasized traditional religion. A second set of visions revealed proscriptions—against drinking and witchcraft, for example. A third set prescribed radical departures from traditional Iroquois practices. White farming patterns were to be employed, and men, not women, should do the labor. Couples should live in neolocal, not matrilocal extended households. The husband-wife relationship was held to take precedence over the mother-child bond. What had at the outset seemed like an extremely conservative movement ultimately embodied a program for radical societal change. It is precisely because of the richness and the ambiguity of religious symbols that old symbols can be manipulated and recombined to justify what is or what should be, even if the new program differs markedly from currently accepted social practices.

CASE STUDY:

Cargo Cults

PETER WORSLEY (1968) HAS EXAMINED A SIMILAR but rather more recent instance of religious response to the political subjugation of one society by a technologically more advanced one. In Melanesia, the arrival of European colonial administrators, merchants, and missionaries had a dramatic impact on the traditional social order. Worsley shows that the spread of cults announcing the end of the world—cargo cults—was one means by which people adapted to their new circumstances. Members of the cults, such as the John Frumm Cult of the New Hebrides, built airstrips and bamboo towers from which they summoned planes with "microphones" fashioned from tin cans, constructed jetties to receive ships, and worked themselves up to a state of great anticipation. Much like the cults in the United States whose members gather to await the second coming of

Christ or the end of the world, the failure of the prophecy does not usually discourage the believers. Failure is explained as the result of errors in the ritual performances or due to treachery. In Melanesia, the belief in the treachery of white administrators who diverted the awaited cargo became a rallying cry against colonial government. The John Frumm Cult, named after an American serviceman who apparently served in the Pacific during World War II, is just one of many; a Lyndon Johnson Cult arose in 1964 (Lawrence, 1964). The cults all shared certain features: a set of beliefs spread, people began to organize in reference to them, and gradually the beliefs came to acquire an anti-European orientation. Finally they evolved into active forces for political opposition to foreign rule.

"Cargo" is Pidgin English for much-coveted trade goods. The cults of New Guinea and elsewhere start with the belief that when the present world ends, as it shortly will in a terrible cataclysm, all wrongs will be righted and ultimately the riches or cargo of the whites will accrue to the Melanesians. Although the followers are inevitably doomed to disappointment when the prophecy is not fulfilled, they usually persevere in their beliefs, anticipating the arrival of the cargo at any moment. The followers continue to await the millennium, which has been described as "something you go to but never arrive at." The cults help make sense of a changing social order. More pragmatically, they end up being the means by which scattered groups come together and gain the motivation to resist the outsiders. Once resistance is successful, much of the protest nature of the cults is forgotten; many of the independence movements and postindependence labor movements in Melanesia have their origins in cargo cults. ▶

CASE STUDY:

Islamic Revolution

A MORE RECENT REVITALIZATION MOVEMENT IS the Islamic revolution that led to the overthrow of the Iranian monarchy in 1979 and the establishment of a state based on Islamic law. This new state would, its proponents assured the world, restore

Ali Khamenei, a senior cleric and President of the Islamic Republic of Iran. Islamic ideology legitimizes his political power and that of other religious leaders.

(Eslami Radiaison/Gamma Liaison)

the moral order the shah had abandoned. On January 16, 1979, His Imperial Majesty Muhammad Reza Pahlavi, Shah of Shahs, Light of the Ayrans, and not coincidentally a close ally of the United States, ignominiously fled his country, never to return. The Shah's ouster followed several years of increasingly violent confrontations between government police and troops and masses of people united in their opposition to what they saw as a foreign-dominated, corrupt, and immoral regime. Religious leaders provided both the organizational stimulus and, through a radical interpretation of Islamic ideology, the justification for a massive outpouring of people to the streets. The day before the Shah left, crowds estimated at 2 to 4 million filled the streets of Teheran.

In the two decades before the revolution, Iran had experienced very rapid economic and social change. Large numbers of formerly rural families had migrated to urban centers in search of a better life, many with little success. While the country had been transformed economically through urbanization, industrialization, and oil revenues invested in massive development projects, a large segment of the population was bypassed by these

processes. Moreover, the Shah had systematically suppressed most secular forms of opposition in the country; thus the clergy alone were in a favorable position to express popular discontent.

From an economic perspective, the spreading discontent was fueled by a decline in oil revenues, rampant inflation, and a drop in employment. From a sociopolitical point of view, important factors included the alienation of the traditional middle classes and old elites and the partial erosion of the clergy's power and economic base during the "white revolution," or land reform. The traditional merchant classes were losing their edge to an emerging technocratic and Western-trained class. The cities of Iran were swollen with rural settlers who found themselves cut off from the wealth they could see around them. However prosaic the causes, much of the discontent was expressed in moral terms: disgust with a highly visible foreign presence in the country (in 1979, there were more than 20,000 U.S. technicians, businessmen, and military personnel in Iran, and many Europeans besides) and the spread of such non-Islamic customs as the use of alcohol, public displays of ostentatious consumption, and the Western dress adopted by substantial numbers of urban women. The so-called modern aspects of society were seen as immoral and corrupt, and more and more people responded to the call for "purification." As opposition grew, each act of repression by the government fueled the movement. Every person arrested, injured, or killed became a martyr whose fate reinforced the legitimacy of the revolution.

When the revolution was finally successful, its leaders, like those of other successful revolutions,

had to face the mundane job of reconstituting a social order and perpetuating their rule. Many of the clergy, formerly operating in the streets as revolutionary leaders, became parliamentarians, government officials, militia leaders, and administrators. Now, sixteen years after the revolution, the clerics are finding it increasingly difficult to justify their continued rule in the face of widespread disillusionment and discontent. ◗

Summary

THERE IS NO SOCIETY IN WHICH RELIGION DOES NOT play an important role. Religion and cosmology encode not only a model of the world but also a model for the world—a plan of what it should be like. Thus religion can, and often does, guide economic and political behavior. A functional definition of religion must encompass the wide variety of religious beliefs and practices that we find in human society, but in general we can say that all religions include a dimension of the supernatural and express an ideology. Some anthropologists have defined religion as any system of beliefs, symbols, and rituals that serve to make existence meaningful and intelligible.

As ideology, religion has a powerful emotional appeal, particularly in the use of symbols, and it provides a rationale for human existence. Lévi-Strauss has argued that myths are symbolic formulas for the resolution of conflicts of values and moral quandaries within a society.

The sociologist Émile Durkheim posited that religion is each community's way of expressing its moral values and collective beliefs. He suggested that each society distinguishes between the sacred (the world of supernatural forces) and the profane (the everyday, natural world). Religious beliefs, according to Durkheim, embody the sacred.

Actually the distinction between the natural and the supernatural is not always clear. The natural world is central to some religions; in others, supernatural forces play an important role in secular life, as in the case of divination, witchcraft, and spirit possession.

A belief system is inherent in every religion. The nineteenth-century anthropologist E. B. Tylor thought that all religion was based on the idea of a soul, or a

personal supernatural force that is distinct from the physical body. He called the belief in the soul "animism" and argued that early people assigned a soul to all living things. Others felt that animatism, the belief in an impersonal supernatural force, preceded animism. Beliefs in totems and taboos derive from the beliefs that the sacred can reside in certain objects and that sacredness makes certain actions prohibited.

Some religions conceive of supernatural beings, either of human origin (as in the case of ghosts and spirits) or of extrahuman origin (as in the case of a god or gods). The latter pattern of belief is called "theism." Religions characterized by polytheism, or the belief in many gods, often portray gods as having human emotions and preoccupations. Monotheism is a belief in one supreme god. In many monotheistic religions, however, lesser figures, both supernatural and human, are deified.

Studies of the relationship between religion and social organization have found that beliefs reflect the basic characteristics of the social order: as societies become more highly stratified, so do their religious concepts.

All peoples embody their basic religious beliefs in rituals—highly formalized and stereotyped behaviors that frequently involve the manipulation of symbols. Religious ritual performs two basic functions: it reinforces group solidarity and brings about change (as in the release of tensions in the course of a ritual). The two major categories of ritual identified by anthropologists are rites of passage and rites of intensification. By celebrating such events as birth, puberty, and marriage, rites of passage note an individual's transition from one social circumstance to another. Rites of intensification are practiced to bolster a life-giving natural process or to emphasize the society's commitment to a set of values or beliefs.

Religion is organized in different ways in different societies. Some use highly individualistic rites, in which the worshiper relies on himself or herself to draw on powers of the supernatural. Other societies organize their rituals communally, and assign special roles to people on a one-time basis. In most societies, people seek help from individuals with special abilities to mediate between the community and the supernatural. In many nonindustrialized societies, a shaman, or medium of the supernatural, performs ritual services, usually for a fee. Shamans are found in every society; the term includes curers, fortune tellers, astrologers, and diviners. Politically centralized societies usually have a professional, bureaucratized clergy to perform religious functions on a calendrical basis for the entire community.

Religion can serve to maintain a balance between people and their environment. The practice of many religious customs regulates the way a society views and uses its resources. Religious practices also adapt to changes in the environment. The relationship between ritual and ecology, anthropologists have discovered, is a dynamic one.

Religions serve society as means of explaining existential questions, helping the individual to cope with life crises, and validating social or political systems (or future ones). Religious beliefs and rituals tend to validate the status quo and maintain social stability. They act to provide a set of shared values that integrates society, they provide mechanisms for reducing conflict, and they promote social control. This can be seen very clearly in the analysis of the Vodoun religion.

Religion may also validate social change. In some cases, religious symbols are manipulated and recombined to validate a new social order. This is evident in the cargo cults of Melanesia. Religious revitalization movements such as the Islamic Revolution, which may arise in response to a disorganized social system, incorporate new goals and symbols to fill changing needs.

Key Terms

animatism

animism

divination

exorcism

liminal state

monotheism

ordeals

polytheism

profane

religion

revitalization movements

rites of intensification

rites of passage

ritual

sacred

shaman

taboo

theism

totems

witchcraft

Suggested Readings

Bremen-van, J. & Martinez, D. P. (Eds.). (1995). *Ceremony and ritual in Japan: Religious practices in an industrialized society*. New York: Routledge. These essays discuss the incorporation of a wide range of traditional religious and ritual practices into industrialized Japanese society.

Brown-McCarthy, K. (1991). *Mama Lola: A vodou priestess in Brooklyn*. Berkeley: University of California Press. An intimate ethnographic work, clarifying misconceptions about vodou; it is very valuable for those interested in vodou and, by extension, Haiti.

Davis, W. (1988). *Passage of darkness: The ethnobiology of the Haitian zombie*. Chapel Hill: University of North Carolina Press. Anthropological investigation and ethnobotanical research are used in this study to taxonomically identify the plant and animal ingredients of a folk toxin that had long been rumored to play a part in the process of zombification. The ethnographic context of zombification is also examined.

Gaffney, P. D. (1994). *The prophet's pulpit*. Berkeley: University of California Press. Based on in-depth research in Egypt, this book describes the preaching of religious leaders and how it spreads the message of Islam.

Geertz, A. W. (1994). *The invention of prophecy: Continuity and meaning in Hopi Indian religion*. Berkeley: University of California Press. An important contribution to the clarification of the often misrepresented Hopi religion and culture through researching the role of prophesy in that belief system.

Herdt, G. (1987). *The Sambia: Ritual and gender in New Guinea*. New York: Holt, Rinehart and Winston. A detailed ethnographic report of long-term institutionalized homosexuality as ritualized preparation and training for warrior status, political participation, and warfare.

Lansing, J. Stephen. (1991). *Priests and programmers: Technologies of power in the engineered landscape of Bali*. Princeton, NJ: Princeton University Press. A unique analysis of an ancient system of water temples in Bali that coordinates planting, harvesting, and irrigation of the fields of thousands of farmers. Lansing shows the history of this complex system and shows why the Dutch colonial as well as contemporary Indonesian authorities completely overlooked the practical role of the temples.

Parkin, D. (1991). *Sacred void: Spatial images of work and ritual among the Giriama of Kenya*. Cambridge Studies in Social and Cultural Anthropology, No. 80. Cambridge: Cambridge University Press.

Rappaport, R. (1979). *Ecology, meaning and religion*. Berkeley, CA: North Atlantic Books. A collection of essays that relate religious consciousness to the naturalistic assumptions of ecological and evolutionary theory.

Taylor, C. (1994). *The black churches of Brooklyn*. New York: Columbia University Press. This work illustrates the importance of the church for an African-American community in a Brooklyn neighborhood as a way to ease the difficulties of life.

Worsley, P. (1968). *The trumpet shall sound: A study of "cargo" cults in Melanesia*. (2nd ed.). New York: Schocken. This detailed and now-classic account of the rise of large numbers of millenarian cults in Melanesia attempts to define the conditions under which cargo cults occur.

Beyond Industrialism
    Organization of the Postindustrial
        World
    Global Communications, Global
        Culture, and the Emergence
        of "Cyberculture"
    The Ecological Consequences of
        Postindustrialism
    *Using Anthropology: Imaging
    Resource Depletion*
    *State of the Peoples: The Abuse
    of Environmental Rights in
    South Africa*
    *Case Study: The Anatomy of the
    SOB Disaster*

Medical Anthropology
    Case Study: AIDS in Brazil

Development Anthropology
    Case Study: The Vicos Project
    Environmental and Ecological Factors
        in Development
    Social Ties
    Managing Social Change
    Impact Assessment and Evaluation
    Case Study: Sahel Visions
    The Ethics of Development Work

Summary
Key Terms
Suggested Readings

Chapter 13

Anthropology for the Twenty-First Century

While there is no way to predict the future, sometimes the present offers reliable clues to the shape of things to come. We know, for example, that we will rely increasingly on advanced electronics, high-speed communications, DNA-based computers, and genetically engineered food sources as we see these trends developing at present. Moreover, many products of late twentieth-century society are so much a part of our everyday lives that it is difficult to imagine living without them. Even those of us who have lived and worked in what have been called "less-developed" societies have found that few populations have not come to integrate the products of advanced technology into their ways of life. People as remote from us as the Ariaal farmers and herders of Kenya learn of national events from their portable radios and television sets. Not only are modern firearms and aluminum pots and pans part of everyday life in the Amazon basin, so are items that only a few years ago would have been called high-tech: miniature cassette players and video recorders. Lapp reindeer herders go about their business on snowmobiles equipped with mobile phones, and the camel has been long replaced in the Middle East by Japanese-made trucks.

Even without venturing beyond our own society we can see immediate costs and benefits of life in our **postindustrial society.** It has been designated "postindustrial" because its dominant technology has shifted from heavy industry (steel mills, locomotives, automobiles) to electronics and biochemistry, which make possible nearly instant global communications, space travel, and genetic engineering—not to mention the ever-present potential of nuclear catastrophe.

Among the benefits afforded by industrial and postindustrial society, we count advances in the medical sciences. The CAT scan (computer-aided tomography, a way of enhancing X-ray images of the body) was an exotic diagnostic instrument in the 1970s, available only at a few hospitals and at great expense; CAT scans are now routinely available. Computing power that twenty years ago existed only in research facilities is now lodged in automobiles and home appliances. Another benefit of industrial and postindustrial society is the enormous growth in public and private educational facilities. More than ever before, knowledge is power. Access to training is an essential component of survival in the modern world. Money, power, and social standing are all now coming to be linked as firmly to what you know as to whom you know: young persons looking for jobs in technological fields cannot rely solely on their family and friends, the conventional support networks of the past.

But industrial society imposes equally obvious costs. Pollution from industrial sites in the Midwest of the United States ends up as acid rain in the Northeast and Canada. Controversy over nuclear waste dumps rages wherever sites are proposed. Polluted waters off our coasts have disastrous effects on marine life. The much-discussed greenhouse effect and the lowering of the ozone level in the upper atmosphere are clear and present dangers—even though no one can say with confidence just what the consequences will be. One thing seems to be certain, however: industrial pollution, together with the effects of the massive loss of rain forests in the tropics, are causing global temperatures to rise.

Another and different kind of cost is the high level of stress and anxiety that seems to be built into the special socioeconomic system associated with industrial and postindustrial systems—irregular alternations between boom and bust can have devastating psychological consequences for large segments of our urban and suburban communities.

Finally, the postindustrial world is a world on the move; from farms to cities, and from one country to the next, always searching for a way to escape the poverty that only seems to grow more pervasive throughout the world. The surge of people seeking entry into Europe and North America is tremendous. In China, a country with 900 million peasants, people are abandoning the land; over 200 new cities have sprouted up since the 1980s and people are flocking to them in order to find jobs that pay better than farming (Tyler, 1995, p. 4). Not only does this exacerbate China's loss of farm lands to urbanization, but even the diminishing farm lands are increasingly underutilized. A Chinese farmer working a one-acre plot, larger than average, explained to an American, "Look, I work on four *mou* of land year in and year out, from dawn to dusk, but after taxes and providing for our own needs, I make $20.00 a year. You can make that much in a day. No matter how much it costs to get there, or how hard the work is, America is still better than this" (Kwong, 1994, p. 425). This simple statement expresses the motivation that underlies the decision of millions to move each year; the knowledge of better conditions elsewhere.

Beyond Industrialism

The technological and social transformation we call *industrialism* started on a small scale and was restricted to certain forms of production in a few countries, but it did not remain limited for long. In a relatively short period peoples all over the world were affected by it. Today we have moved into yet another era in the organization of production and integration of peoples. This has been termed variously the communications era, the age of the computer, and the high-tech age. The labels are not important. What is interesting from an anthropological perspective is that the processes of change appear to occur at an increasingly rapid rate.

The organization of commerce and industry is changing. The historian David Noble (1984) describes this transformation as the triumph of "numerical control" in industry. Following World War II, there was a great advance in the development of servomechanical and electronic controls capable of running complex precision tools. This development, Noble suggests, opened up the possibility of moving the effective control of manufacturing from the shop floor to the main office. The outcome is a lessening of blue-collar power in industry and further centralization of control in productive organizations. This thesis is interesting, though in some instances the same technology has broken up large industries into smaller components—another outcome of high-speed communications. Certainly it is clear that job opportunities for production-line workers are rapidly decreasing while new ones open up for people who have skills appropriate to the new technologies. The long-term significance of these changes will be profound; not only are entire segments of the populations of already-industrialized nations marginalized, but the peoples of many countries lacking an educational infrastructure will not participate fully in the economies of the future.

The "modernization" model associated with the economist Walter Rostow (1960) postulated that development was an evolutionary stage through which all countries pass; it has long since been proven wrong by experience. Today, about one billion people live in absolute poverty; many more not far above it (Wilson, 1993, p. 27). In many countries, there are large groups of people who have not only remained impoverished, but their living standards have declined relative to others. The people of East Pakistan, however poor they were in the 1960s, enjoyed life chances roughly comparable to the peoples of rural China, Thailand, Malaysia, and Korea. Today, the rural population of Bangladesh, as it is now known, is untouched by the prosperity that has transformed at least some of the other nations of the region. But they are not alone in the world; the peoples of the Philippines, Cambodia, Vietnam, Sudan, Central Africa, and parts of South and Central America have also seen their living conditions remain extremely low or even fall further.

It is not that some populations or nations are being left out; quite the contrary, the rural and urban poor of many agrarian countries are closely integrated into the world economic and political system, but at its peripheries (see Figure 13–1). That is, they have little control over the resources to which they have access, profit little from what they sell in a market characterized by worldwide competition, and generally are without vote or voice in their own countries. This, in many respects, reflects a process of incorporation of peoples around the globe that began long before anthropology was a discipline: the expansion of European power and economic influence far beyond that continent (Wolf, 1982). Much of the present unequal distribution of the benefits of the postindustrial era, together with attendant environmental degradation as people desperately try to make a living, "is not a problem of the relationship of people with their habitats, but of relationships *among* peoples competing for access to productive resources" (Horowitz, 1994, p. 8).

As the world's population grows, so will the competition for productive resources. The world's population doubled within the last 50 years to 5.5 billion; it is expected to double again in the next 50 years (Wilson, 1993, p. 24). Nigeria, one country whose citizens, like China's, often opt to move, has a population of over 100 million, which is expected to reach 216 million by 2010 (Wilson, 1993, p. 26). "The awful truth remains that a large part of humanity will suffer no matter what is done" (p. 27).

Organization of the Postindustrial World

In 1974, Richard J. Barnet and Ronald E. Muller wrote a book on a phenomenon closely related to the organization of production in the postindustrial era: the growth of multinational corporations. Twenty years later, their ideas have increased relevance. They suggest that the degree to which international corporations have taken over functions once performed by governments and succeeded where governments have failed in creating a "global organization for administering this planet" is difficult to comprehend. This is not to suggest that corporations have consciously evolved into multinationals in order to dominate the world. They simply make use of the communications and transport technology available to compete in the world marketplace. The sheer size and complexity of their operations, however, have made them a force unto themselves.

Figure 13–1 The gross domestic product (GDP) per region and per capita in high-income and less-developed regions of the world, for 1990 and projected for 2030 shows that income distribution will remain extremely skewed in favor of the already developed countries.

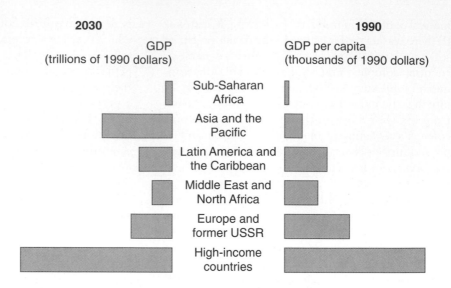

Even in 1974, the operating budgets of about five hundred giant multinational corporations exceeded those of most nation-states. In the 1980s, the operating budgets of global corporations grew at over twice the rate of the GNP of the United States and other advanced industrial nations, and this has continued through the 1990s. This fiscal expansion is based on what has been called the corporations' "global reach"—today they know no boundaries. The European Union and the 1995 North American Free Trade Agreement (NAFTA) are regional arrangements that facilitate the global organization of production, exchange, and consumption.

Through expansion and diversification, global enterprises insulate themselves from many political and market pressures. High-speed communications permit a multinational corporation to control everything from raw materials to final distribution. It may, for example, buy raw materials from a subsidiary company at less than the actual market price in order to avoid taxes, or it may sell to another foreign division at inflated prices in order to transfer income out of a country. Price-fixing cannot really be controlled under such circumstances. Further, and of greater social consequence, a giant corporation can easily shift operations to areas of low labor cost. Such a move can be catastrophic for the workers the corporation leaves behind. The very fact that a corporation operates on a global scale places it beyond the reach of national governments. Regulatory agencies lack the informa-

tion and in many cases the jurisdiction to investigate global enterprises. Corporations plan centrally and act globally, and nation-states do not.

A more subtle problem, which underlies Barnet and Muller's analysis, is the instability that such global interdependence implies. India's ability to feed its people depends on modern farming, which in turn requires reliance on chemical pesticides, fertilizers, fuel, and machinery. All of these inputs are globally interconnected. Local disasters can now have immediate global repercussions, be it the 1995 Kobe earthquake in Japan, the nuclear fires of Chernobyl in the Ukraine, Arctic pollution, or acid rain in the United States and Canada. There is an obvious good side to interdependence in that global trade and communications even out some disparities—the goods of the industrial states are widely available, people can move great distances to seek out a livelihood, the effects of famine and natural disasters can be mitigated. But it also puts all of us at the mercy of events in distant places. The Kobe earthquake was followed shortly by the bankruptcy of England's oldest investment bank, Baring and Sons, with branches all over the world. The bank's traders had invested heavily in Japanese stocks, betting on anticipated short-term rises, when they were hit by a sudden decline in share prices caused by the earthquake. The 1995 collapse of the Mexican peso had immediate effects in other countries; suddenly, factories in the United States had to cut production as Mexican consumers could

A major problem throughout the world is the increasing gulf between those with resources and those without, as seen here in Calcutta.

(Jehangir Gazdar/Woodfin Camp & Associates)

no longer afford to purchase foreign goods, and stock market investors around the world experienced losses due to the heavy involvement of mutual funds in the Mexican market. As the United States tried to prop up the currency of its new partner in NAFTA, the dollar itself fell to an all-time low against other major currencies. Interdependence and vulnerability are two sides of the same process.

Global Communications, Global Culture, and the Emergence of "Cyberculture"

One of the key features of our interdependent world is the global communications network. Satellite communications, global television networks, fax machines, the Internet, and improved international phone service have contributed to an information revolution. The 1990 Tiananmen Square demonstrators were in communication by telephone and fax machine with people all over the world and, apart from physically removing them, there was nothing their government could do to prevent this. The organizers of the coup attempt in August 1991, which, when it failed, ended the U.S.S.R.'s existence as a state, had not anticipated how decentralized communications had become in that country. As resistance spread, anti-Communist groups all over the country were able to coordinate

their actions and attract worldwide attention using computer links, faxes, and the telephone.

In China and Iran, to name two countries where the authorities feel they need to control the media to retain power, millions of families now have their own satellite dishes and receive news and other programming over which the government has no control. However strongly these governments may rail against Western culture, this is what their people are getting on CNN and hundreds of other channels.

In Bulgaria during the 1980s, for example, very little direct contact with the foreign press, movies, and television was allowed. Nevertheless, dissident groups kept in close touch with the outside world via videotapes, faxes, and the telephone. Even though the countryside in some regions was dotted with radio-TV jamming towers, they were largely ineffectual against new technology. This two-way communication was instrumental in bringing world opinion to bear on a government that had previously acted as though it were in isolation. This was an important factor in rallying individuals to oppose the government, and even members of the Communist Party realized that they could not rule without legitimacy, including world acceptability. When the Communist regime fell in 1990, the borders opened, and along with newspapers, international magazines, and serious movies, came an avalanche of pornography, cultist religious literature, and advertisements for phony investment schemes. Most would find the contents of a great deal of this newly available "information" deplorable or, as with Bevis and Butthead cartoons presently on local TV, simply without any merit.

In the 1990s, for better or for worse, Bulgaria is participating in a globally shaped media culture, as is virtually every country. The good aspects of this are obvious: free communications are critical to maintaining Bulgaria's shaky movement toward democracy and economic recovery. The negative aspects are not just visible in the extreme cases of pornography and the like, but in a diminishment of regional cultural heterogeneity. Just as world material culture is becoming more homogeneous, so is expressive culture—the arts, dress, and even social conventions.

Closely linked to new developments in computer, information, and biological technology is what some have termed **cyberculture** (Escobar, 1994, p. 211). The term comes from "cybernetics" or systems theory, and refers to the emerging importance of computer-mediated communication, including global networks such as Internet, Bitnet, and more specialized computer networks such as Peacenet and Econet. These link a large variety of electronic bulletin boards, conference systems, and data bases, which in turn bring together millions of users. This is fundamentally different from telephonic or television communication: entire groups of individuals can interact with one another in what are called "on-line communities" or "virtual communities" (p. 219). Academics coauthor papers with distant colleagues; groups are formed to play team games; business executives meet to plot strategy. What makes this a form of culture is that a learned, shared code of behavior and specialized language has emerged that does not conform to existing national and cultural frontiers. As Walker puts it, "When you are interacting with a computer you are not conversing with another person. You are exploring another world" (1990, p. 443, cited in Escobar, 1994, p. 219).

Global communications, internationalized media products, and patterns of trade and production have led to increasing conformity in consumption and basic patterns of life. With only limited exceptions, people with similar access to resources in particular regions come to live much the same way in spite of historical differences in religion, ethnicity, and language. In an earlier era these differences would have been vividly expressed in cultural insignia; in dress, ceremony, and life style. Also, the vast majority of the world's population is directly or indirectly involved in wage labor or commercial production. This, too, tends to shape patterns of life in roughly similar ways for those involved in the same sort of production. A Turkish coal miner and an English coal miner will lead lives dominated by the tempo of the industry—in both instances, increasingly stressful as mining declines in importance. In addition to the development of broadly shared patterns of life, we see broadly shared expectations and aspirations. Increasingly, one's wants or needs are not defined by local culture or tradition, but in terms of goods and services that are part of what might be called the **global culture**: while folk medicine persists and has its place, people also expect modern treatment as well; they seek education for their children, electricity, sanitation, and consumer goods of all sorts.

The Ecological Consequences of Postindustrialism

Not only is cultural diversity yielding to a global culture, diverse habitats are also being brought into a measure of global conformity. Amazonian and Malaysian forests are converted to pastures or farms; African bush and Chinese forests are cleared for farming; farm lands in China, North America, Egypt, and elsewhere are paved over to accommodate urban expansion and industry. There are few stands of native European forest left; farmlands, highways, and planted or managed forests have replaced them. Tropical rainforests, containing about one half of the earth's species, have declined to about one half of their prehistoric area and continue to be cleared at the rate of 2 percent a year—an amount of land equal to the size of Florida (Wilson, 1993, p. 29). Thus, as technology spreads over the globe, humans increase their energy consumption with too little attention paid to the inevitable result: resource depletion.

Energy Consumption and Resource Depletion. Since World War II, per-capita energy consumption throughout the world has risen at an ever-increasing rate. However, while technology requires a higher energy consumption, it also helps to make energy sources such as low-cost fossil fuel, nuclear

Deforestation threatens most of the remaining rainforests; the Amazon is being significantly reduced each year as settlers move in. This development is in Jarib, Amazon region, Brazil.

(Martin Rogers/Stock, Boston Inc.)

energy, and solar energy widely available. A recurring political issue is the need for more cheap and readily accessible energy sources. The 1990 Gulf War was fought in order to retain European and North American access to oil; energy prices in the United States are lower than almost anywhere else in the world. On every continent, we see the material effects of abundant energy harnessed to advanced technology: millions of people routinely commute long distances to work and move from country to country, homes are filled with appliances, items from around the world are available in neighborhood stores from Albania to Zambia. In the case of Albania, for example, since the collapse of communism in 1991, it is difficult to find anything but foreign products in shops; in most of Africa, this has long been the norm.

The availability of cheap energy and high rates of consumption has stimulated the mass use of numerous items that only a few years ago would be considered luxuries, if they were imagined at all. Thirty-five years ago few homes or workplaces in the United States were air-conditioned; today most are. Even the poorest individual in almost any country has access to vehicular transportation, uses facilities that run on electricity, and consumes imported goods. In short, the material culture of the world is rapidly becoming homogeneous.

The energy that pulses through human society affects where and how people live, the material goods available to them, and their relations with their physical environment. Cheap energy allows huge cities to emerge because they are sustained by foods grown in distant fields and by water from distant reservoirs. Because energy is cheap, people are consuming the world's resources at a phenomenal rate; it has been estimated, for example, that tropical forests that once covered great portions of South America and Southeast Asia will be gone by the year 2000.

Sussman et al. (1994) have studied deforestation in Madagascar and have found that rainforest probably covered 11.2 million hectares of the east coast at the time of colonization, approximately 1500–2000 years ago. By 1950, 7.5 million hectares remained, and by 1985 only 3.8 million hectares remained—50 percent less than in 1950, and only 34 percent of the original forest. They found that deforestation is directly related to population growth and the slope of the land, with the greatest amount of deforestation occurring in the more densely populated areas and on the lower slopes. Sussman et al. predict that thirty-five years from now, at current rates, only 38 percent of the forest remaining in 1985 will still exist; that is, only 12.5 percent of the original extent—a mere 1.4 million hectares, and this will be fragmented into many small parcels.

Using Anthropology
Imaging Resource Depletion

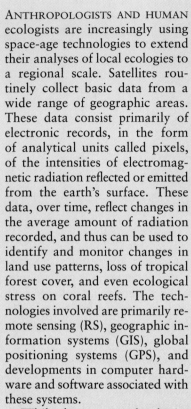

ANTHROPOLOGISTS AND HUMAN ecologists are increasingly using space-age technologies to extend their analyses of local ecologies to a regional scale. Satellites routinely collect basic data from a wide range of geographic areas. These data consist primarily of electronic records, in the form of analytical units called pixels, of the intensities of electromagnetic radiation reflected or emitted from the earth's surface. These data, over time, reflect changes in the average amount of radiation recorded, and thus can be used to identify and monitor changes in land use patterns, loss of tropical forest cover, and even ecological stress on coral reefs. The technologies involved are primarily remote sensing (RS), geographic information systems (GIS), global positioning systems (GPS), and developments in computer hardware and software associated with these systems.

While these new technologies allow for a regional view of land use not easily obtainable from ethnographic or archaeological research on the ground, many of the patterns revealed by the analysis of these data are creations of human decision making and historical events. Satellites cannot interpret what is observed nor explain changes. Consequently, all researchers emphasize the importance of understanding land use from the perspective of the people who manage the land; this is known as "people truthing." In addition, sound ethnographic information on demographic trends and land use practices is a safeguard against erroneous or exaggerated claims made on the basis of remotely sensed data; this is known as "ground truthing."

Stoffle et al. (1994) conducted a study of the coastal waters and coral reefs on the north coast of the Dominican Republic, in the area around Buen Hombre. This is a community of approximately 900 residents, living much as did the indigenous Indian people at the time Columbus first sighted the coast in the late fifteenth century. Stoffle et al. argue that were the pressures on this coastal marine ecosystem derived only from the people of Buen Hombre and similar villages along the coast, the human population could exist in sustainable balance with the ecosystem. However, this is not the case, and the future of the ecosystem is in doubt. Fishermen report lower fish catches and smaller fish sizes over the past generation; a dive shop operator from a nearby international resort hotel reports having to take tourists to new reefs because the ones close to the hotel have died during the past five years; fishermen from distant towns are beginning to fish in the area's coastal waters with illegal large nets, and the local fishermen say that the manatee have disappeared from the areas where these nets are used; and similar coral reefs to both the west and east have been characterized as "dead."

Stoffle et al., an interdisciplinary team of cultural anthropologists, remote sensing scientists, and a marine ecologist, used satellite imagery to identify changes in small areas of the coastal marine ecosystem of Buen Hombre, including the coral reef. Even though their study showed that the coastal waters and coral reefs on the north coast are still in good condition, they did find ecologically significant changes associated with changes from dark to light, indicating losses of highly productive coral, seagrass, and mangrove. By comparing the satellite imagery with marine and ethnographic data, they found these changes (from 1985 to 1989) were closely related to fish-

Even though a number of reserves established in the 1920s and 1930s remain relatively untouched, they appear to be protected by their remoteness and inaccessibility rather than by conservation efforts. So it is likely that as population and economic pressures increase, these areas will become vulnerable to deforestation. Conservation efforts to slow deforestation and prevent the fragmentation of areas of forest need to be concentrated at the fronts of deforestation and must involve cooperation between conservationists and local people to develop sustainable use of lands that have already been cleared. Once areas of intense deforestation have been identified by remote sensing, Sussman et al. argue that basic ethnographic research needs to be done to place this deforestation in the actual social, economic, and poing, tourism, and land use practices. They concluded that if global warming is affecting this ecosystem, its effects are still masked by the effects of these more predominant stresses. They further concluded that there are differences in the types of impacts on the ecosystem being made by the local people, who have a sense of ownership and an intergenerational commitment to its resources, and those being made by outsiders, such as urban fishermen and tourists. "Given the opportunity, local inhabitants seek to preserve the long-term productivity of the coastal environment, even at the expense of current harvest" (1994, p. 375).

While the satellite data provided a comprehensive technique for studying changes in this coastal marine ecosystem, Stoffle et al. were also able to use them to transfer information about these changes to policy makers at the village, regional, and national levels. Satellite images of the north coast reef system were shown to villagers and national government officials at two meetings in Buen Hombre, and the local fishermen were immediately able to identify familiar locations and point to named fishing spots. The images, supplemented with ethnographic and marine ecological data, were instrumental in persuading government officials that measures were needed to protect the coral

reef and secure the rights and interests of the local community. This is not an isolated case. Bernard Neitschmann (1995), a cultural geographer, has assisted the Miskito people of Nicaragua to map and inventory the extensive Miskito Reefs in the Caribbean in order to protect their traditional fishing grounds. A well-designed map can convey a great deal of information and can be sent to international organizations to document claims.

In fact, all over the world indigenous peoples are using maps to rename and reclaim their lands. Renaming is important because names are symbols and instruments of power, and maps are documents of possession. In Sarawak, where indigenous forest lands are under threat, simply possessing a map can get a Penan arrested (Poole, 1995, p. 1). Geomatics (satellite imagery) can be useful when it amplifies local capabilities to respond to external pressures. For example, 470 Menkragnoti Kayapo in Brazil have regained control over 4,400,000 hectares and use satellite imagery to defend and monitor this land, a small percentage of what they had earlier lost. Maps based on geomatic sources are useful to reinforce claims, to show what has been demarcated, and to demonstrate incursions (Poole, 1995). Neitschmann puts it succinctly: "More indigenous terri-

tory can be reclaimed and defended by maps than by guns." (1995, p. 37).

The studies cited here stress the interdisciplinary nature of research utilizing satellite data, and the importance of "on the ground" research in the analysis and interpretation of the images. Francis Conant (1994) makes four predictions about the impact these space-age technologies will have on the discipline of anthropology:

1. Remote sensing and allied technologies will generate more fieldwork, not less, for anthropologists and others.

2. The services of anthropologists will become indispensable in the interpretation of satellite products, especially as these relate to non-Western cultural practices.

3. As a consequence of the foregoing, basic training in remote sensing and allied methodologies (in particular, GIS) will become a regular offering in undergraduate and graduate programs in anthropology.

4. These new technologies will be used increasingly in a retrospective mode to study past adaptations as well as ongoing or contemporary ecological processes (p. 406).

litical context, after which scientists, in conjunction with the local people, can begin to develop alternative, sustainable land use practices. Susmann, who used satellite-based remote sensing to reveal the extent of the deforestation, believes that remote sensing can also be used to monitor the progress of these projects and their effectiveness in slowing deforestation. The Using Anthropology box, *Imaging Re-*

source Depletion (pages 368–369), explores this imaging technology in more depth and shows how it can be used to evaluate the health of a coastal marine ecosystem in the Dominican Republic.

A giant new dam has been completed in the middle of the Brazilian rainforest. When it is in operation, it will flood more than 600 square miles of forest in order to produce electricity for the city

As demonstrated on this polluted beach in North Yemen, the handling of human waste products is a global concern and one that will affect our ability to sustain ourselves in the future.
(Michael Jennes/Robert Harding Picture Library)

of Manaus, on the banks of the Amazon. Manaus's population has recently swollen to over a million inhabitants—many of whom come to the Amazon to escape intolerable conditions elsewhere. Similar projects are underway throughout the Third World as governments respond to the need to feed ever-growing populations. Once such resources as the rain forests are gone, they cannot be reestablished; most of what we consume is nonrenewable.

Although development planners, economists, and politicians usually see the supply of energy as a factor limiting growth and development, and hence favor huge hydroelectric and other projects, this is short-sighted. What is more important is **sustainable energy**, energy recovery that does not damage the environment, and manageable energy. Energy experts predict that Central Africa will run out of precious wood—a major energy source for cooking among the very poor—before it runs out of food although the two are closely related. Fossil fuels are a nonrenewable resource and, although inexpensive relative to long-term abundance, are being depleted. Hydroelectric projects that flood vast areas of cropland, or potential cropland, as in China and Amazonia, are also counterproductive since, as we discussed in Chapter 7, maintaining

extant farms is extremely important. Finally, energy management—control over its downstream impact—is as important as simply securing it.

Pollution and Toxic Waste. Quite apart from how we will cope with the depletion of our resources there is the even more urgent problem of how we will dispose of the toxic by-products of what we have already consumed. Unfortunately, this is not usually viewed as an energy-related issue except with regard to nuclear energy. The use of any energy source has consequences, whether they are higher population levels, consumption of nonrenewable resources, habitat destruction, or environmental impacts such as global warming, water shortages, deforestation, or waste disposal. All industrialized countries are faced with the unanswered question of what to do with nuclear and other radioactive wastes. With the breakup of the Soviet Union and the economic chaos in its successor states, there is great uncertainty as to the security and safety of vast quantities of spent nuclear material. The nuclear energy program of every country was developed for political reasons far in advance of any solution to the problem of disposing of highly toxic by-products. However serious,

In the Philippines, a family living in a slum on Manila's Smokey Mountain. The "mountain" is a garbage dump.
(Michael Macintyre/The Hutchison Library)

nuclear waste is probably less critical than chemical waste in general, generated by massive deployment of cheap energy sources to build the infrastructure of the postindustrial world. There is still no easy and safe way to dispose of highly toxic chemicals such as PCBs, dioxin, etc., which are necessary ingredients in constructing our telecommunications systems, plastics industries, and so on.

Less apparent, but still very important to our future, the world's oceans are under siege. In 1995, it was found that as a result of global warming, the temperature of the Pacific Ocean off the coast of California and Mexico had increased by one degree fahrenheit over the mean recorded temperature since records were first kept. As a consequence, plankton, temperature-sensitive microorganisms, have declined approximately 40 percent. Since plankton are fundamental to the marine food chain, this is likely to be reflected very soon in declining fish catches in this once-rich fishing region.

In the Pacific and Atlantic vast amounts of human waste, toxic and nontoxic, threaten marine life as never before. The same crisis threatens the Caribbean and Mediterranean: the fishing industries of these areas are experiencing severely declining catches. In 1987, the American National Academy of Sciences reported that each year the world's fishing fleets dump 350 million pounds of plastic debris in the world's oceans. It is thought that over 30 percent of the world's fish have ingested bits of plastic that can interfere with their digestion. In 1995 much of the American North Atlantic fishing fleet stayed in port.

The problem of pollution and waste disposal is not, of course, restricted to the oceans. Over half of the solid landfill areas available to American cities in 1980 are now full. Each year the United States produces more than 20 million tons of plastics, most of which require more than five hundred years to degrade fully. Every country has petrochemical plants churning out polyethylene and other plastics. Megacities in the Third World face enormous problems; Mexico City generates 10,000 tons of waste a day, most of which is left in giant piles exposed to wind and rain. Manila has at least ten huge open dumps (Cunningham & Saigo, 1995, p. 501). Thousands of people live and work on one called "Smokey Mountain" because of its constant smoldering fires; they make a living sorting out edible and reusable items. Archaeologists of the future may find this global accumulation a treasure trove, but meanwhile the time is rapidly approaching when our wastes will over-

State of the Peoples

The Abuse of Environmental Rights in South Africa

RAPID URBANIZATION COMBINED with apartheid in South Africa has brought significant health and safety hazards to millions. In the years leading to the final collapse of white political rule, the attention of the world was often transfixed by pictures of incredible urban squalor as the backdrop to scenes of violent resistance in the townships, as urban areas designated for nonwhite settlement were called. Anthropologist Ben Wisner describes and analyzes these hazards and how they may be now corrected through what he terms "two optics: environmental rights, which are human rights to healthful environment and a sustainable livelihood, and community participation" (1995).

From 1948 to 1993, urban policy in South Africa was to control nonwhite access to and residence in cities; a policy that generated constant conflict with African, Coloured, and Asian communities. This system of racial separation distorted relations with nature in a profound way (p. 3). It created overcrowding and led people to engage in dangerous and environmentally unsound practices simply to satisfy their basic needs for shelter, water, sanitation, cooking fuel, and income. Urban waterways were polluted, housing densely packed, open space rare, trees cut down, and the air polluted by the smoke of thousands of coal braziers used for cooking and heating. Personal security was bad as well; the density of houses (often rudimentary, since their owners had been forcibly relocated more than once) resulted in poorly aligned lanes with attendant injuries to pedestrians, especially children, from passing vehicles. Moreover, emergency vehicles were too large to penetrate the narrow lanes (p. 4). Unexpectedly, the collapse of apartheid in April 1994 brought new problems to the townships as a "tidal wave of immigrants from the countryside began to reappropriate urban space from which they or their parents had been removed by apartheid" (p. 5). By restricting nonwhites, some 87 percent of the population, to only 13 percent of the land, the apartheid system clearly violated the rights of millions to health and livelihood (p. 5).

Now the new government must deal with the legacy of the past policies if it is to have legitimacy. In 1993, the population of South Africa was estimated at 40 million; urban growth rates were as high as 5 percent in the late 1980s and the city-dwelling population grew from 8.5 million in 1985 to 14 million in 1993 (p. 6). Not only are these communities congested, with poor sanitation and drainage, but many were deliberately situated near areas of heavy industry where air and water pollution threaten environmental health and safety.

South Africa now suffers the consequences of apartheid, but the pattern of risk and vulnerability to hazards of urban populations in South Africa is not unique. As Wisner shows, within the past few decades there has

---

whelm us. As illustrated in the State of the Peoples box, *The Abuse of Environmental Rights in South Africa* (pages 372–373), this is particularly imminent in ghettos around the world, where overcrowding and poverty exacerbate the problems of pollution and waste, seriously threatening the environmental rights of the individuals living there.

Toxic Accidents. We accept the fact that modern life demands that we continually submit to new risks; any day a major industrial accident might occur. We rely on technology that we do not understand, and we have little say in its deployment and regulation. Chronic technological disasters, as Eric Wolf has argued, are revealing events because "the arrangements of society become most visible when they are challenged by crisis" (1990).

Within one month in 1989, there were four oil spills causing significant environmental damage: the Exxon *Valdez,* in Alaska; off Rhode Island; in

been a worldwide growth of mega-cities. "These urban regions—whether Cairo, São Paulo, Manila, Los Angeles, or Greater Johannesburg—share a number of morphological, socio-economic, political and environmental characteristics" (p. 8). They have spread over very large areas, absorbing preexisting settlements, and have diverse economic patterns ranging from high-tech to the "parallel economies" of the homeless and street populations. Politically, mega-cities are fragmented into hundreds of jurisdictions; environmentally, they import water and energy from long distances, and they produce "mega" quantities of waste (p. 9). Polarization of wealth means that the poor tend to bear the costs of concentration. In Los Angeles, Wisner reports, the Hispanic population lives in the zone of highest air pollution, and it is their housing stock that is at greatest risk in earthquakes; in Alexandra township in Johannesburg, the population density is 688 people per hectare, while in predominantly white areas the average density is only about 40 (p. 9). Distinct hazards, ranging from the social (crime, homelessness), the geophysical (flood, fires, earthquakes, etc.), and the technological (in-

dustrial explosions, pollution) to the biological (HIV infection, rates of cancer, water-borne diseases, etc.) intersect in complex ways to produce what Wisner calls "'cascades' of secondary and tertiary hazards" (p. 10). For example, a flood in Alexandra township washed drums of toxic chemicals into residential areas. Vulnerability to these hazards is not evenly distributed by class, ethnicity, age, and gender (p. 10). "So numerous are the risks and so great the number of people exposed to them in a township like Alexandra, that South Africa has given rise to a new term: the 'situational disaster'" (p. 18).

The question facing the new South Africa is how can these environmental conditions be alleviated and disasters such as Bhopal and Love Canal (near Buffalo, New York) be avoided. Ben Wisner does not presume to have the answers, but drawing on his expertise as an anthropologist and human ecologist he suggests how to approach them.

First, local knowledge must be central to the program of reconstruction. People know of many of the hazards and are willing to take initiatives if they are consulted. Under apartheid, they were not consulted. Only local people

can closely monitor actions taken and subsequent results. While "top down" aid may be essential, if it is administered without consultation, as all too often happens when people are relocated after a disaster, their vulnerability is increased, not decreased.

Second, citizen-based, nongovernmental institutions have to be maintained and strengthened. In Alexandra, for example, church-based groups have been very active. Popular participation is vital to continued monitoring and improvement. Such participation helps to achieve a number of important goals at once: disaster prevention, disaster mitigation once a problem has occurred, and recovery.

Third, planning should be holistic, not a piecemeal response to disasters. Thus social, geophysical, and biological hazards all have to be addressed. This will involve a very large investment in urban infrastructure improvements, combined with technical assistance in reconstruction and monitoring. Environmental health will ultimately "depend on community groups sensitized to their rights and ability to call for and participate in hazard assessment . . . " (p. 22).

the Delaware River; and in the Houston shipping canal. The *Valdez* spill alone dumped over 11 million gallons of crude oil into a fragile marine environment. In 1993, there was a similar very costly oil spill in the Shetland Islands, UK, which has still to be fully assessed in terms of damage. This later spill, like many others, created great uncertainty among the affected populations because of misleading and confused reports offered by the government agencies concerned (Button, 1995). These

cases are not cited as an indictment of modern life, but to illustrate the problems of sustaining it; they are, in Roy Rappaport's words, part of "the anthropology of trouble" (1993).

What distinguishes these disasters from other environmental calamities such as the spread of the desert in the African Sahel or the burning of the Amazon, writes Lee Clarke, is that *organizations* have played primary roles both in causing the problems and in seeking solutions (1989, p. 2).

These are tragedies over which the victims have no control and for protection must necessarily rely on organizations: state and federal governmental agencies, international agencies, and myriad private and public ones. These are a form of disaster for which our previous adaptations have not prepared us. Lee Clarke (1989) gives us the anatomy of one such disaster, not a major one by global standards, but serious enough to have all of the elements to illustrate how organizations we must rely on handle their responsibilities.

CASE STUDY:

The Anatomy of the SOB Disaster

THE BINGHAMTON STATE OFFICE BUILDING, OR SOB as it is locally known, has eighteen stories, the tallest building in town, and it incorporates most modern technologies, including advanced fire protection systems. One fire prevention system automatically opens doors on the roof; another involves the use of a solution of 65 percent polychlorinated biphenyls (PCBs) and 35 percent chlorinated benzenes to cool the SOB's electrical transformers, located in the basement (Clarke, 1989, p. 5). PCBs have now been banned because they cause cancer, liver ailments, and other diseases; moreover, they can combine with other elements and produce the deadly toxin dioxin. Still, PCBs remain in wide use in transformers and electrical capacitors built before the ban.

"At 5:33 A.M. on February 5, 1981, a switch gear (which functions much as a fuse box or circuit breaker does) in the SOB's mechanical room failed, causing an electrical arc that lasted twenty to thirty minutes. The heat in the room rose to an estimated 2000 degrees Fahrenheit, causing a ceramic bushing on one of the two nearby transformers to crack. About 180 gallons of the transformer's PCB-containing coolant were released by the accident" (Clarke, 1989, p. 6). The coolant was vaporized by the intense heat and the vaporized PCBs mixed with a dense soot caused by burning electrical insulation. The automatic fire doors worked perfectly; unfortunately, as soon as they opened, the

eighteen-story building turned instantly into a gigantic chimney, with the draft sucking the PBC-contaminated soot up throughout the building and out to downtown Binghamton (p. 7). Interestingly, had the building been privately owned, this would not have happened; as a state building, it was exempted from codes that prohibit air shafts reaching directly into mechanical rooms. Every room, every desk, file, and closet, was filled with highly toxic soot, as were airways between walls and ceilings. Moreover, the soot contained significant quantities of deadly dioxin. The question is not just how something like this could happen, but how did federal, state, and local organizations respond: "How 'tragic choices' are assessed and ameliorated" (p. 11).

The morning after the fire, media personnel, politicians, and state and country officials convened on the scene. It was immediately apparent that highly toxic substances were involved and, given the publicity that Love Canal had already generated, it was clear that the fire was potentially a major environmental, health, and political problem. In the absence of any single chain of command, federal, state, and local politicians, health workers, and department heads all offered separate and usually conflicting assessments of the problem and its solution. Since the SOB was managed by the state's Office of General Services (OGS), this department was involved from the start; since PCBs are considered an oil product, the state Department of Transportation (DOT) was called in; followed by appeals to a veritable alphabet soup of federal agencies, including the Small Business Administration (because of the multi-million-dollar losses suffered by local businesses), OSHA (because of hazards faced by workers), NIOSH (because of long-term health threats), and the EPA (because of environmental impacts). After some initial uncertainty while the DOT (the only agency with experience with PCBs) decided it lacked jurisdiction since the oil spill was indoors rather than outdoors, OGS, under high-level political pressure, ordered an immediate cleanup and sent in teams of janitors and security guards (Clarke, 1989, p. 31).

In some respects, the cleanup was a disaster itself; workers often worked without face masks, some used toilets in the SOB (flushing toxins into the city's sewer system), some took home contaminated food, cigarettes, money, lottery tickets, and items from offices, and left contaminated work clothes in neighboring buildings; as a result, over five hundred people were directly or indirectly exposed to toxic soot (Clarke, 1989, p. 15). Within a month after the fire, lawsuits totalling over a billion dollars had been filed against the state, many occasioned by the botched cleanup (p. 16). One could, Clarke writes, attribute OGS's decision to attempt a rushed clean up with janitors (not trained chemical personnel) to a callous attitude toward the health of its workers in an effort to respond to political orders (p. 22). Actually, OGS officials acted in a manner that would have been appropriate in 99 percent of the circumstances they usually faced following a fire in a state building; unfortunately, this was the exceptional case—as disasters so often are. The lesson is that organizations, by their conservative nature, are rarely prepared to handle exceptional circumstances. There was no single person or office sufficiently in charge to define the problem; in the absence of a well-defined objective, OGS simply did what it was designed to do: it "cleaned" the SOB.

Once the seriousness of the problem became apparent, the bureaucratic behavior changed. Initially agencies hurried to the scene and announced various plans and assessments; following the discovery that the SOB problem was not to go away soon, the scurrying was in the other direction: one agency after another found what Clarke terms "exiting mechanisms"—that is, they declined active responsibility (Clarke, 1989, p. 57). This once again left the SOB problem in the hands of OGS and local health authorities in Binghamton. In the second phase, the clean-up was redone with greater inputs from specialized consultants from the chemical industry, with less publicity, and under the aegis of one agency. Today, in 1995, after spending many millions of dollars, the state of New York declares that the building now only contains an "acceptable" level of contaminants.

Far from a rational, precise, scientific endeavor, risk assessment is really a haphazard result of the colliding and colluding of competing and complementary organizational interests. However precisely a risk may be measured (for example, that of getting cancer from ingesting PCBs), it is the outcome of assumptions based on bad or missing data and compromises among competing interests. Even

The eighteen-story state office building in Binghamton, N.Y. (known not so affectionately as SOB) was contaminated with PCB and dioxin as a result of an electrical fire that damaged a transformer. The building remained sealed from the public from February 5, 1981, while officials searched for a safe way to clean it. After many millions of dollars were spent, the building was reopened in late 1994.

(UPI/Bettman Archives)

with regard to the Binghamton SOB, a relatively small disaster, opinions still differ as to acceptable risk. One is that there is no established level at which dioxin is acceptable—it is too deadly. The evaluation of state officials is that the building is finally "acceptably clean." The opinion of those who would have to spend forty hours a week in it, is that the risk is too great. Also, most risk assessments, as with the SOB, are made after the fact—once the disaster has occurred.

The poor management and chaos following this accident are not unusual and often occurs in what Clarke has identified as the first phase of a disaster involving a potential risk to the environment and people in the surrounding area. He calls the first phase, "the inter-organizational garbage can," and it is characterized by a multitude of competing lines of authority, no clear definition of the problem, and a lack of political accountability on the part of decision makers (1989, p. 168). At the time when rational decision making is the most crucial, it is virtually nonexistent. Decisions occur in a chaotic swirl of competing organizational interests. The assessment of the risk to the public as a result of the accident is based on bad or missing information and confusion among the agencies involved.

In phase two (which, in Binghamton, followed the first by nine months), after the bungled first phase has barely managed to contain the damage (much less accurately assess the risk), "the action set" arrives to deal with the victims of the accident. All but one or two governmental organizations pull out or are forced out of the problem area, groups of semi-independent nongovernmental organizations establish a division of labor representing victims (for example, unions, health workers, merchants, environmental activists), and one organization takes official responsibility for directing operations and announcing formal risk assessments—here the OGS (Clarke, 1989, p. 171). It is clear from Clarke's analysis that what is needed, if we are to control the damage that results from toxic accidents, is a more coordinated, efficient, and informed approach to disasters of this nature. They will continue to happen, no matter how many safeguards are put in place to prevent them. So some organization should be prepared to respond with appropriate action when they do. ◗

Can We Adapt? In Chapter 3 we discussed "resilience," or the amount of change or impact that an ecological system might be able to sustain before becoming unrecognizably altered. Biodiversity is thought to be the key to resilience. The exponential growth of human population and technology continually erodes the resilience of our biosphere. One source of this threat is through mass extinctions of species in every part of the world. As one noted naturalist and evolutionary biologist, E. O. Wilson, writes:

> With people everywhere seeking a better quality of life, the search for resources is expanding even faster than the population. The demand is being met by an increase in scientific knowledge, which doubles every 10 to 15 years. It is accelerated further by a parallel rise in environment-devouring technology. Because Earth is finite in many resources that determine the quality of life—includ-ing arable soil, nutrients, fresh water and space for natural ecosystems—doubling of consumption at constant time intervals can bring disaster with shocking suddenness. Even when a nonrenewable resource is only half used, it is still only one interval away from the end. [1993, pp. 26–27; see also 1994]

What is to be done? There is no easy solution; as Wilson notes, while scientists may have the ability and political will to control the nonliving components of the biosphere (the ozone layer and carbon cycles), they have no ability to micro-manage natural ecosystems. They are simply too complex. The only real solutions are population limits and habitat preservation—both very difficult to achieve for political reasons.

Postindustrialism is a recent development and it remains to be seen how humans will adapt to its consequences. As history has shown, an increase in energy sources creates as many problems as it solves. The impending advent of superconductors—materials that can transmit electricity with no loss to resistance—will make available even more usable energy. If we merely use this energy to support more people and to speed up consumption, the results are quite likely to be disastrous for the environment.

The problem is that change is coming so rapidly that it may outrun our ability to respond appropriately, especially with regard to natural resources. We must keep in mind that individual behavior is basic to adaptation; people generally alter their behavior to serve their self-interest as they see it. What is in the interest of elites and corporations may not be appropriate for long-range conservation of the world's resources and habitats. In earlier eras of human adaptation, people were severely constrained by their technology and by their limited access to sources of energy. By and large, people had to deal directly with the environmental consequences of their activities. Farmers who allowed their fields to erode might face hunger. Now, many decisions that affect the environment are made by people far removed from the consequences. The manager of the factory whose sulfuric wastes contaminate a water supply distant from the head office may receive a bonus for efficiency. Perhaps we shall have to devise ways to reward those who, in the words of the ecologist René Dubos, "act locally but think globally."

Medical Anthropology

Medical anthropology has its roots in the ethnographic study of ritual and religion as well as the study of physical anthropology, but has gone on to flourish as a subfield in its own right (Johnson & Sargent, 1990). Most graduate programs offer courses in medical anthropology and students from other disciplines such as nursing, medicine, public health, and demography are prominent in them. Increasingly, medical anthropology is an interdisciplinary endeavor. In the final analysis, all medicine is an exercise in applied anthropology; that is, "action for human beings" (Romanucci-Ross, Moerman, & Tancredi, 1991, p. x). Medical anthropology brings together the two main themes in the health sciences: the biomedical and the behavioral sciences.

The biomedical approach tells us that, for example, tuberculosis is caused by *Mycobacterium tuberculosis*, whereas the behavioral sciences tells us that it is caused by poverty and malnutrition. The concept of "culture" brings these paradigms together in the field of medical anthropology (Romanucci-Ross et al., 1991). Culture, as we have seen throughout this book, is how people organize their lives with systems of knowledge, belief, and action. Culture structures the diseases to which people are subject and determines how they will be perceived and confronted. Diseases are always experienced by people as mediated by their culture.

Some modern biomedical scientists may question what there is to learn from the bizarre practices of the past and of other cultures. This feeling may be due to the fact that from an anthropological perspective, European medicine in the premodern era was a special case—it was based in one of the least healthy societies in human history (Romanucci-Ross et al., p. xi). Europe's population was subject to dozens of new and deadly diseases as a consequence of rapid population growth in conjunction with the widespread and close contact with domesticated animals (giving rise to zoonotic infection and adaptation to a human host). "This 'one-two punch' of domestication and urbanization created conditions for the evolution and communication of infectious disease organisms on a scale unprecedented in human history, well beyond the abilities of the best-intentioned physician to control or prevent" (p. xi). And, we might add, the

Medical anthropologists learn much from traditional healers such as this Dobe !Kung woman. A knowledge of indigenous medical practice is important when attempting to deliver modern medical services.

(Irven DeVore/Anthrophoto)

attempts of the best-intentioned give pause for thought before recommending their further application: bleedings and drastic purges, bat's blood, bear feces, and frog sperm, and extensive septic surgery on unanesthetized patients.

By contrast, in 1480, paleopathological evidence indicates that Native Americans were very healthy and had life expectancies longer than Europeans. Almost all diseases transmitted from one continent to another went outward from Europe; in the Americas, they were the main reasons for the estimated 90-percent drop in Native American population levels between 1490 and 1890 (Romanucci-Ross et al., 1991, p. xii). Native Americans, and non-Western peoples in general, were extremely inventive in using the pharmacopeia at hand, however limited, and, more important, in manipulating the social and human dimensions of medicine. Today, mainstream medicine has learned to treat the patient, not just the disease, and this requires attention to the cultural environment. We see this in how the AIDS epidemic is being confronted.

CASE STUDY:

AIDS in Brazil

IN BRAZIL—A COUNTRY THAT DOCUMENTED ITS first case of AIDS in 1983 and that in 1995 has an estimated 300,000 to 500,000 carriers of the HIV virus and 49,300 cases of AIDS—anthropologists who had formerly been working in unrelated areas have turned their attention to the epidemic. Nancy Flowers, who has worked among Amazonian populations, is concerned with two issues: the potential of the disease to spread from urban areas to rural ones, thus putting far more people at risk; and the effect AIDS will have on indigenous populations of the Amazon, such people as the Yanomamö, who have already suffered much from introduced diseases (Flowers, 1988). These complex questions have no simple answers. Some rural areas seem to be at considerable risk, as members of the poorest segments of urban society migrate to the frontiers in search of work in mining, logging, cattle-raising, and trucking. The cultural isolation and marital endogamy of the Amazonian Indians is thought to afford them some protection against sexually transmitted diseases, but should such a disease enter a small, relatively closed population, it would spread rapidly. Prostitutes have followed the young men to the frontiers. The AIDS virus may easily spread along the same route.

Richard Parker's primary interest was Rio de Janeiro's famous carnival, but he found the sexual symbolism and activities associated with the festival shifting his attention to sexual practices and attitudes in urban Brazil. When the AIDS epidemic appeared, his understanding of Brazilian sexual culture led him to suggest that models and predictions based on the experience of the United States may not be relevant to Brazil (Parker, 1987, pp. 164–166). Others have suggested the same for

Africa, where AIDS is also a very serious health problem (Conant, 1988). There the disease is spreading rapidly among heterosexuals. In Brazil, the disease first appeared among urban, middle-class male homosexuals, as in the United States. But in Brazil it is much more likely to spread throughout the population, because bisexual behavior in men is condoned there, particularly if they maintain their masculine gender identity. Further, the Brazilians' emphasis on a bride's virginity encourages unmarried women to engage in anal sex in order to avoid vaginal penetration, and anal sex is known to be a major mode of transmission among both heterosexuals and homosexuals. Clearly Parker's work is sensitive and potentially controversial. Whatever the outcome of such studies, they are undertaken in the belief that anthropology has insights of immediate value to offer. ▸

Development Anthropology

Development anthropology is closely related to medical anthropology as a major area within applied anthropology; in fact, a major concern within development work is human health and nutrition. Anthropologists have identified themselves as "development anthropologists" for only about twenty years, largely as a result of a U.S. congressional mandate that tied all foreign aid to a commitment to study its impacts on equity and the poor. Even though the discipline had from its beginnings been concerned with the theoretical issues of cultural and economic change, from the 1970s onward it became engaged in the practical problems of alleviating poverty, environmental degradation, disease, malnutrition, gender inequity, and ethnic conflict.

Following Michael Horowitz (1994), who is himself a leading practitioner, some of the main contributions development anthropologists have made include:

1. Providing a critical understanding of the nature of development. This has included showing that indigenous expertise cannot be ignored, that forced resettlement of populations is costly and rarely results in improving standards of living, that "top down" planning usually only benefits those at the top, and that local communities are rarely homogeneous and should

be carefully studied to determine who really benefits and who does not.

2. Showing the importance of long-term research. Typical development projects bring experts through for extremely brief periods of time; "rapid rural appraisal" say some, "rural development tourism" say others. Anthropologists at the World Bank and elsewhere have successfully argued for long-term social research in a number of regions. This has led to important recommendations, as with a project in the Middle Senegal river valley where the anthropologists demonstrated the need to augment the flood of a hydropower dam for the benefit of downstream ecosystems and smallholder productivity (Horowitz, 1994, p. 6).

3. Increased sensitivity to environmental issues and the need for an alliance between anthropologists, social scientists, and biophysical ecologists. Environmental sustainability requires a social component since both poverty and resource abuse are caused or exacerbated by similar policies seeking short-term returns on investments.

The Vicos project, while a successful experiment in development, could not be carried out by anthropologists today. It involved too much direct intervention in the lives of the participants.
(Courtesy of the Vicos project)

CASE STUDY:

The Vicos Project

THE VICOS PROJECT, ONE OF THE BEST EXAMPLES of a positive change, was initiated by a group of Cornell University anthropologists in Vicos, Peru, in the 1950s. Vicos was a farm, or hacienda, purchased by a charitable society. At the time of the Cornell project, a patrón could rent the hacienda for a period of five to ten years. Traditionally the patrón reserved the best land for his own use and sublet less-profitable plots to Indian tenants. Each tenant family paid its rent by sending one adult to work the patrón's land for three days a week; the peasants also provided cooks, grooms, servants, watchmen, and the like. For the most part, the vicosinos were illiterate subsistence farmers who lacked modern skills, health care, social respect, and any hope of participating in decisions that affected their lives.

In a year when the potato crop failed, however, Vicos was put up for rent. In January 1952, Cor-

nell University signed a five-year lease on Vicos. The goals of the Cornell anthropologists were to give the vicosinos the right to self-determination by gradual diffusion of power, to raise the standard of living by increasing productivity and sharing the wealth, to introduce modern agricultural techniques and medical care, to bring Indians into the modern world by schooling and other means, and to raise their status among their neighbors.

The Cornell anthropologists proceeded on the assumptions that innovations in areas where people felt most deprived would be most readily accepted, and that an integrated approach to the introduction of innovations would last longer and produce less conflict than would a piecemeal approach (Holmberg, 1958). They began by paying the vicosinos back wages (a symbolic gesture, for the pay amounted to three cents a week) and asking volunteers to perform services the Indians had long been forced to provide without pay. In the first year, the new patróns introduced modern seeds, fertilizers, and agricultural techniques, and plowed the profits from their cash crop back into the hacienda. Between 1952 and 1957, productivity rose from $100 to $400–600 per acre. All residents shared in the profits from the bottomlands, and all learned modern techniques for farming their own land. They built a health clinic and school with a capacity of 400 students (the old school accommodated 10 to 15 students).

Initially the Cornell administrators did not attempt to alter the traditional hierarchy among overseers and workers. However, the weekly meetings at which previous patróns had distributed work assignments were now used to explain innovations, discuss goals and plans, draw vicosinos into the decision-making process, and give residents news of the outside world. By 1957, a council of ten elected delegates had taken over the management of the community's affairs. Younger men committed to improvement rather than to tradition had largely replaced the elders in positions of village authority.

In addition, Cornell sought to regularize relations with the local authorities and to create numerous occasions on which vicosinos could meet neighboring mestizos (people of mixed Spanish and Indian blood) on an equal footing. By 1957, mestizos were turning to the peones they had once regarded as unworthy of the slightest respect for advice on agricultural techniques.

Despite strong resistance from the local elite, the Indians were able to purchase Vicos—and their independence—in July 1962. Since then, the Peruvian government has initiated five similar programs on other haciendas, in some cases with vicosinos acting as advisers. In almost all respects, then, the project was a success. Cornell took power (something anthropologists have rarely had the opportunity or inclination to do) in order to restore power to the Indians, with the deliberate intention of changing their way of life. Many of the innovations tested in this project have been adopted elsewhere, and no other project has ever been subjected to the scrutiny that this one has. Some people, however, have debated whether the Cornell approach was ethical. ◗

Environmental and Ecological Factors in Development

A development project may have a profound effect on the ecological system, as we have just noted. Large dams, for example, almost always have a legacy of large-scale environmental damage such as destruction of habitat, downstream pollution, increased salinity of the soil as a result of a rise in the water table, increased risk of flooding and erosion, and even, many people argue, an increase in the risk of earthquakes (Goldsmith & Hildyard, 1984). But innovations need not be so massive as a huge irrigation scheme or a giant dam to have significant effects on ecological systems. The introduction of shotguns, for example, has dramatically reduced the numbers of many game species used by the Yanomamö, not to mention the human toll (Chagnon, 1993). A new strain of rice introduced in Nepal increased yields as much as 200 percent, but because the rice grew on short, tough stalks that produced little fodder for cattle and required threshing machinery that was not available locally, the innovation was not without serious costs. The more intensive cultivation has led to loss of topsoil from erosion, and an increased dependence on firewood instead of straw for fuel has resulted in deforestation and increased risk of downstream flooding. Everywhere we see the effects of fertilizers, pesticides, and herbicides in contaminated water sources. Environmental costs must figure in any evaluation of the effectiveness of a proposed innovation.

Social Ties

Development may have unintended consequences for social relations as well. If these consequences are negative, they must be included among the costs of planned change. Attempts to introduce improved clothes-washing facilities, for instance, may cause women to lose the opportunity to meet and exchange information with their neighbors at a community washing place. Changes in cattle management, as with the Dinka of Sudan, may deprive elders of their special status as camp group leaders (Lako, 1988). The building of modern high-rise apartment houses to replace slum housing may have negative social consequences by breaking down established social networks, patterns of social control, and even pride of residence. Of course, an innovation may have an even more significant impact on traditional social ties, as when a traditionally subordinate group is placed in an economically competitive position with a traditional elite. This was the case in Syria, where the French, during the mandate period before World War II, recruited members of the small Aloui sect to the army and police forces. They now rule the country.

Managing Social Change

Any country faces problems when it sets out to manage social change and tries to anticipate the costs. The anthropologist can help at the community level, where detailed knowledge can mean the difference between success and failure. Anthropologists' respect for indigenous solutions and ways of doing things can also make a difference. All too often planners work from the top down, with little interest in or respect for traditional, time-proven methods. Indigenous solutions in the areas of land use and food production are almost always critical to the long-term success of a new strategy. As Della McMillan found in her study of the land-use project in the Sahel (discussed in the case study on pages 382–386), the effectiveness of any development plan is dependent on the involvement of the people who are the intended beneficiaries of the project.

Much of the present crisis in food production is attributable to the fact that the growth rates of the populations of many countries in the tropics have outstripped their ability to feed themselves. But most of the techniques that are being imported by such countries are based on farming methods first developed in temperate climates. In the Amazon region, large development schemes involving the clearing of forests, introduction of new food crops, and mechanization have had very poor economic results. Most cleared land in the Brazilian Amazon is used for cattle ranching; 85 percent of recently cleared land is now altogether unproductive because of soil degradation (Posey, Frecchone, Eddins, & DaSilva, 1984, p. 95). Tropical soils are generally thin and subject to rapid erosion and breakdown of nutrients once the protective cover of the rain forest is removed. As a consequence, intensification of agriculture or other uses of once-forested land often result in less rather than more food. Many people who have worked in tropical agricultural systems think the way out of this dilemma is to pay more attention to developing more productive farming based on plants and techniques that are already locally established.

Impact Assessment and Evaluation

Since 1973, anthropologists have become increasingly involved in new areas of work. In that year, Congress passed legislation mandating a variety of **impact assessments** to be carried out when federal funds are to be used in large-scale projects, both at home and abroad. Also, development projects are required to be directed toward benefiting the "poorest of the poor" and ensuring growth with equity (see Horowitz, 1994). A variety of state and national environmental protection acts require evaluations of the impact of government-supported projects on biological, geological, social, historical, and cultural resources. An agency that proposes to undertake a potentially disruptive project must prepare an impact statement that identifies any adverse consequences, direct or indirect, that the project will have. These consequences must be taken into account at the earliest possible stage of planning. If the impacts are judged to be damaging, procedures must be designed to alleviate the problem. Anthropologists, like other social scientists, have been drawn into planning and development work that was formerly the almost exclusive domain of engineers and economists.

Extensive fieldwork is a beginning point for such studies. In the case of highway projects, for example, planners identify several alternative corridors in which the highway might be built. Archaeologists then attempt to determine how many important sites would be destroyed by construction in the various corridors. Cultural anthropologists assess the impacts on existing communities. Recommendations concerning the desirability of particular alternatives or modifications that will alleviate problems are based on such studies.

George Appell, who has worked on development projects in Indonesia, offers a set of principles that, in somewhat abridged form, aptly summarize the sorts of negative impacts that planned change occasions and that have to be weighed against possible benefits (Appell, 1988, p. 272):

Every act of development necessarily involves an act of destruction.

Any new activity introduced is likely to displace an indigenous activity.

Each act of change has the potential to cause physiological, nutritional, psychological, and/or behavioral impairment among some segment of the subject population.

Modernization can erode indigenous mechanisms for coping with social stress, such as regulating conflict and solving family problems.

To this list we might add one more caution:

> The costs and benefits of any innovation or
> planned changed are not going to be
> distributed equally throughout the
> population; some people will benefit and some
> will lose. What has to be kept in mind is
> whether the distribution of costs and benefits
> is fair or desirable.

The ultimate cost-benefit outcome of any development project or effort to effect some form of desired social change can be influenced by many factors. Some of the most important are environmental and ecological factors, traditional values and beliefs, and social ties.

CASE STUDY:

Sahel Visions

DEVELOPMENT INVOLVES MANY ACTORS WITH many different visions. What implications does this have for the design of foreign development assistance and for anthropological research?

This case study describes the first attempt by a West African government to develop a comprehensive land-use plan for its river basins covered by the Onchocerciasis (meaning "river blindness") Control Program (OCP) (Figure 13–2). The government agency charged with the coordination of this plan was the Volta Valley Authority (or AVV) of Burkina Faso (McMillan, 1995).

River blindness control was one of the great development visions to emerge from the 1968–1974 drought in West Africa. The disease river blindness (onchocerciasis) is spread through the bites of female black flies that breed in fast-running water; the disease is caused by threadlike worms that inhabit the subcutaneous tissues of the skin. In its advanced stages, the disease causes serious skin ailments, eye damage, and blindness. In 1974, nearly 700,000 million square kilometers with a population of 10 million were affected in the original seven-country control zone (Figure 13–2). In 1986, the control program was expanded to cover 1.3. million square kilometers, including additional areas of Benin, Ghana, Mali, and Togo, and parts of

Guinea, Guinea-Bissau, Sierra Leone, and Senegal (Figure 13–2).

In 1974, the high incidence of onchocerciasis was considered to be the major reason that large areas of river basin in the Sudano-Sahelian areas of West Africa remained sparsely inhabited despite high population pressure in surrounding zones. Foreign donors like the U.S. Agency for International Development (USAID) and the United Nations Development Program (UNDP) thought that by controlling river blindness, they could create vast new settlement opportunities for impoverished farmers and pastoralists from the areas worst hit by the drought. They also reasoned that the anticipated increase in rainfed and irrigated crop production would reduce trade imbalances, raise rural living standards in the areas being resettled, and minimize the threat of future famines. One attraction of the project for foreign donors was that once disease abatement was underway, they could report success to their headquarters in faraway capitals like Bonn, Riyadh, and Washington.

For Burkina Faso (then known as Upper Volta), the control program appeared to offer an unprecedented opportunity to resettle one-tenth of the country's population on more productive land and at the same time to triple cotton production. To implement this vision, the Burkinabè government created a centralized program of planned settlement and development that restricted the amount of land that individual households could farm and required settlers to adopt a prescribed package for intensive agriculture and new democratic institutions designed to encourage sustainable cropping.

In 1977, Della McMillan, then a second-year graduate student in anthropology, arrived to study the effects of resettlement on villagers who moved from three traditional villages near Kaya to a group of AVV planned settlements that were located in the river basins. She returned to study the home village and the immigrants living in the AVV project villages as part of her doctoral dissertation research (1978–1980), and again in 1983, 1988, and 1989–1990, making her involvement in this project unique for its length. (It is her 1995 book from which this case is drawn.) When she showed up at the compound of the chief of the traditional village that had lost the largest number of immigrants to the project, she did not know how closely her career was to be bound up with the Sahel, the

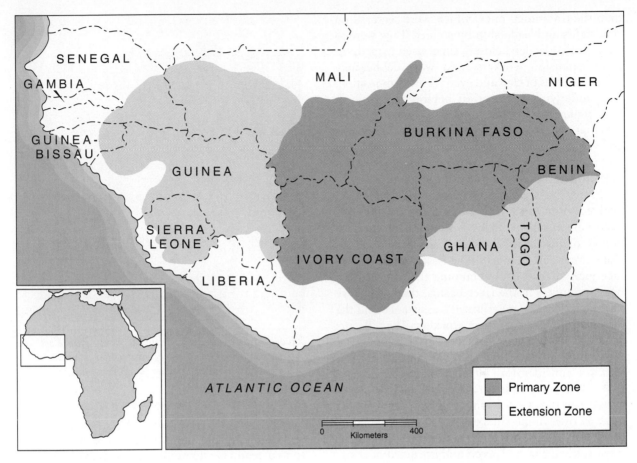

Figure 13–2 The Sahel

OCP, and the AVV. Accepting the invitation of the chief or *naba,* she constructed a small house attached to his court, signifying to the populace that she was under his protection. McMillan's vision was to compare the agricultural production patterns and income patterns of farmers remaining in the traditional homelands with those of the settlers who were just beginning to filter into the AVV-sponsored settlements. This form of research is often termed a baseline study, as it can provide a base for later comparison. The chief, in turn, envisioned that the presence of a foreign anthropologist would attract government and donor money to his region, where farming was a precarious venture.

The development theories that guided foreign donor funding and government planning in the AVV changed dramatically in the two decades that followed the start of control in 1974. Initially (1974–1981), the AVV planned settlement project was managed from the top down and focused on the design and implementation of a project program for intensive farming that could be closely monitored by extension service personnel. Once a site was considered to be suitable for planned settlement (based on aerial photos and soil and water surveys), the AVV was responsible for the creation of all basic infrastructure including roads, wells, schools, and health facilities, as well as the design and implementation of extension programs to promote intensive farming. In return for the right to cultivate a 10–20 hectare project farm, the settlers were to use high-yield seeds and fertilizers, follow a strict crop rotation, practice monoculture rather than polyculture (see Chapter 5), and apply insecticides. The labor potential of each household was evaluated, and land was awarded on the basis of family labor supply—families with more adults getting more land. The new villages were to be organized differently than the traditional ones, which were centered on clan rights and leadership by a chief. They were to have elected leaders, closely supervised by government extension workers, and were deliberately mixed in terms of clan and even ethnic composition. The underlying assumption behind the project's land tenure, settlement, and government policies was that once removed from their traditional norms and values, the settlers would be freer to experiment and adopt more modern, environmentally sustainable crop and livestock production practices.

McMillan soon found that as the settlements evolved, both the social and economic results began to diverge from the project model. In short, the people themselves had other visions and these visions grew and changed. The first settlers had to face many hardships in claiming their new fields; being strangers in the river basins, they were very dependent on the government's assistance and the leadership of the extension workers. The villagers shared labor and cooperated in house building and numerous activities critical to community survival without consideration of clan or ethnic distinctions. While the first sorghum harvest was poor, the cotton did well, and the settlers could report back to their home villages that things were going well. The first years, in fact, went very well, and most settlements prospered and attracted new settlers, often relatives of the initial families.

One divergence from the planners' model was that money was not being reinvested in intensive farming. Instead of respecting the project policy of cultivating a restricted area intensively, most farmers cleared additional land outside the 10–20 hectare farms that they were authorized to farm. In addition, they invested in more animals, trade, and crafts, and in education for their children. In sum, over time, the settlers' selective nonparticipation in the proposed system of intensive farming led them to abandon the proposed system of monoculture and rotation in favor of a more diversified system of crop, livestock, and nonagricultural employment. The communities came also to increasingly reflect the social realities of kinship and ethnicity; de facto leaders emerged who led by drawing on these ties. None of these deviations from the donor's vision or the government's vision meant that the project failed; it was simply not meeting its original policy goals. In particular, farmers were not producing the quantities of cash crops originally desired. One major problem turned out to be the labor supply. Cot-

River blindness is a major health hazard in West Africa that has been largely controlled in recent years. Here a young boy leads a blind man so that he can work in his field.

(D. Deriaz/The World Health Organization)

ton's demand for labor inputs is such that even low-yielding cereal crops produce more per human investment of labor. In addition, the cotton production required commercial fertilizers that would have to be paid for even if the crop failed.

When McMillan returned in December 1988, she saw how dramatically things had changed in the preceding five years. Especially important, almost all the households who had emerged as highly successful had re-immigrated to a new town that was adjacent to the country's first hydroelectric dam. This new town was located more than 250 kilometers away from the AVV-sponsored settlements where the settlers had lived for periods ranging from eleven to thirteen years. Here again, the settlers' response demonstrated not only their resilience and creativity, but their determination to diversify their subsistence bases. In contrast to the isolated river basins where the AVV planned settlements were located, the new town offered opportunities to set up shops, find employment, and educate their children, while still farming.

In sum, the AVV planned settlement project did succeed in raising incomes; its failures were in not

A mother attends to her child while cooking a meal in a Mossi village in Burkina Faso. The lives and roles of women are greatly affected by development efforts such as World Bank projects.

(Ron Gilling/Panos Pictures, London)

increasing export crops to the level desired and in the partial adoption of the desired modern farming techniques. In addition, the high costs of developing the planned settlements restricted the number of settlers that could be relocated, so the problem of overcrowding in traditional farming areas was only slightly alleviated. The doors of the AVV closed finally in 1989, but the settlements and their farmers remain.

What are some of the main lessons McMillan draws from her long involvement with the settlers living in the AVV-sponsored settlements? One of the most basic lessons is that people, consciously or not, are interested in building diversity into their resource base in order to avoid dependency on any one natural resource or income stream. The settlers living in the AVV project villages were vividly aware of how dependent the extension workers and the project were on foreign donor countries and organizations. Moreover, they knew better than the anthropologists and the project managers just how fickle these organizations can be, and did not wish to become dependent on their support. McMillan suggests that policy guidelines to promote more diversified social and economic systems should be built into any future planning for resettlement and regional development in the valleys.

Second, planners usually think of rural labor as being abundant—usually overabundant. From the perspective of the settler households living in areas with short-term supplies of "new" land, like the river basins covered by this project, labor is in short supply and is a limiting factor in intensifying farming.

Third, where settlement is envisioned, it should not be planned from the top down, but allowed to develop spontaneously with appropriate direction and assistance. That is, settlers should be largely self-selected and self-organized, but directed and assisted to help avoid economic and ecological problems that often plague completely spontaneous settlement: destruction of forest covers, soil erosion, land tenure disputes, etc. In particular, she points to the paradox arising from donor schedules and the needs of the people involved in the program. Donors usually want prompt results that they can showcase, and they are willing (sometimes required) to spend large amounts of money in relatively short periods of time. Sometimes they are investing money much more rapidly than can be usefully absorbed in the project. Many times, it is in the final stages of a project that good investment opportunities become clear, but as with the AVV, little money is available at that point. For example, the AVV administration tried to establish several market towns but was unsuccessful; when a major market did spring up without any government assistance, there were few funds left to assist its growth.

Finally, she points to the absolute necessity of reconciling the many different visions that ultimately shape the outcome of a development project—including those of foreign donors and the national government, as well as the local beneficiary households. ◗

The Ethics of Development Work

Ethical issues are a major concern in anthropological development work, from the time anthropologists make their initial decisions as to where and how they will do fieldwork through their final evaluations of the effects of their projects. The effort of McMillan and her coworkers is exemplary in making anthropological expertise serve the needs of people who require assistance. In some respects, it combines the traditional role of anthropological advocacy, discussed in Chapter 1 with the role of the modern, socially responsible scientist, as we saw in the Using Anthropology box on pages 368–369. The Vicos project is another example of anthropologists truly helping in development efforts. It was one of the first opportunities for anthropologists to act as policy makers, not just as theorists or advisers and go-betweens.

Some anthropologists consider it unethical to interfere so directly in other people's lives. Arturo Escobar, for example, has argued that development projects increase the incorporation of indigenous peoples into the larger economy, hence marginalizing them, and that anthropological assistance on development projects adds legitimacy to this process (1991). The assumption seems to be that participating in national economies is "bad" and that individuals affected by development projects

have numerous options. Neither seem valid points. Further, if anthropologists were not involved, would the same people be less marginalized, less dependent? While the Vicos project is unique in the degree of involvement of anthropologists in the lives of the people, it is not unique in that the anthropologists and social scientists made a positive contribution. As Horowitz reports, World Bank projects where anthropologists and other social scientists are involved show a 15-percent higher rate of return of investment than comparable projects where they are not (1994). McMillan's study (1995) shows why this occurs; anthropologists not only accumulate factual data, they bring together experience from other areas. McMillan, in studying settlement, drew heavily on previous work by other anthropologists in Africa and Asia on resettlement. The Vicos project is another example.

While ethical issues may appear to be more sharply focused in development work, they are present in all kinds of anthropological research. Taking a thoughtful and balanced approach to these issues is essential—even more so when the lives of people are affected. The key question may be, "Is it ethical for anthropologists not to put their expertise to practical use?" Whether involved in an advocacy role, development projects, or just disseminating their knowledge and expertise to others, anthropologists in the next century need to make their voices heard. In concluding his statement of the theme for the 1995 AAA meeting, James Peacock states that anthropologists should be involved in "shaping the world as it moves beyond 1999 to the next millenium. Let us—the most interdisciplinary of disciplines—look beyond immediate debates and projects to demonstrate resoundingly and creatively the understanding and guidance we can bring this new—or once-again *renewed*—world" (1995).

Summary

Change is constant in all societies, despite a marked human tendency to maintain the status quo. Anthropologists focus on a variety of aspects of social change, but common to all approaches is some measure of costs and benefits, success and failure.

The problems facing today's world—food shortages, rapid population growth, depletion of resources, pollution, and the difficulty of adapting to rapid and continuous change—are many and complex.

Today we have moved into yet another era in the

organization of production and integration of peoples. This has been termed variously the communications era, the age of the computer, and the high-tech age. The organization of commerce and industry is changing. The historian David Noble (1984) describes this transformation as the triumph of "numerical control" in industry. It has removed control from the factory to the central office; it has also allowed for decentralized production. The long-term significance of these changes will be profound; not only are entire segments of the populations of already-industrialized nations marginalized, but the peoples of many countries lacking an educational infrastructure will not participate fully in the economies of the future.

Much of the present unequal distribution of the benefits of the postindustrial era, together with attendant environmental degradation as people desperately try to make a living, is not a problem of the relationship of people with their habitats, but of relationships *among* peoples competing for access to productive resources.

Since World War II, per-capita energy consumption throughout the world has risen at an ever-increasing rate. New technology makes low-cost fossil fuel, nuclear energy, and solar energy widely available. The energy that pulses through human society affects where and how people live, the material goods available to them, and their relations with their physical environment. Cheap energy allows huge cities to emerge because they are sustained by foods grown in distant fields and by water from faraway reservoirs. Because energy is cheap, people are consuming the world's resources at a phenomenal rate.

Energy management, or control over its downstream impacts, is as important as simply securing it. Quite apart from how we will cope with the depletion of our resources, there is even the more urgent problem of how we will dispose of the toxic by-products of what we have already consumed.

Global communications and the emergence of "cyberculture" has also transformed culture. Satellite communications, global television networks, fax machines, and cellular telephones have, within the last decade, become part of world culture. People of all countries are participating in a globally shaped media culture. The good aspects of this are obvious: free communications are critical to maintaining democracy, human rights, and economic exchange. The negative aspects are not just visible in the extreme case of pornography and the like, but in a diminishing of regional cultural heterogeneity. Just as world material culture is becoming more homogeneous, so is expressive culture—the arts, dress, and even social conventions.

Closely linked to new developments in computer, information, and biological technology is what some have termed "cyberculture." The term comes from "cybernetics," or systems theory, and refers to the emerging importance of computer-mediated communication, including global networks such as the Internet.

Anthropologists have become increasingly interested in analyzing the relationship between general trends and innovations on the one hand and development on the other. In the process of assessing the impact of change on society, some of them become personally involved in efforts to bring about change.

Medical anthropology brings together the two main themes in the health sciences: biomedicine and the behavioral sciences. Culture structures the diseases to which people are subject and determines how they will be perceived and confronted. Diseases are always experienced by people as mediated by their culture.

Development anthropology is closely related to medical anthropology as major areas within applied anthropology; in fact, a major concern within development work is human health and nutrition. Anthropologists have identified themselves as "development anthropologists" for only about twenty years but have made numerous contributions: providing a critical understanding of the nature of development, including showing that indigenous expertise cannot be ignored; showing the importance of long-term research; increased sensitivity to environmental issues, and the need for an alliance between anthropologists, social scientists, and biophysical ecologists.

Applied anthropologists may work to analyze problems in order to draw lessons for future policy (as in the case of the Sahelian drought analysis) or they may get involved in actually implementing (or preventing) change (as in the Vicos project). Recently anthropologists have been called upon to develop impact statements that evaluate the effects of large-scale projects on cultural resources.

Some principles regarding development work have emerged. Every act of development necessarily involves an act of destruction. Any new activity introduced is likely to displace an indigenous activity. Each act of change has the potential to cause physiological, nutritional, psychological, and/or behavioral impairment among some segment of the subject population. Modernization can erode indigenous mechanisms for coping with social stress, such as regulating conflict and solving family problems. And finally, the costs and benefits of any innovation or planned changed are not going to be distributed equally throughout the population; some people will benefit and some will lose. What has to be kept in mind is whether the distribution of costs and benefits is fair or desirable.

Ethical issues are a major concern in development work as well as other areas of anthropology. Many feel that anthropologists should use their expertise to facilitate the planning and modification of development projects so that they will provide the most benefit to the people they are designed to help. Others attribute the marginalization of indigenous groups to development and believe that any participation in development projects legitimizes that process. In the end, though, the breadth and depth of the expertise that anthropologists can provide should equip them to play a dominant role in shaping the world in the next century.

Key Terms

cyberculture

development anthropology

global culture

impact assessment

medical anthropology

postindustrial society

sustainable energy

Suggested Readings

Bodley, J. H. (1985). *Anthropology and contemporary human problems.* Palo Alto, CA: Mayfield. An examination of resource depletion, hunger and starvation, and other problems of our industrialized world. The author reexamines tribal cultures and compares their solutions with those of our society.

Chambers, E. (1985). *Applied anthropology: A practical guide.* Englewood Cliffs, NJ: Prentice-Hall. A synthesis of the field of applied anthropology that reviews the ways in which the profession has adapted to new career opportunities, the ethical concerns associated with applied work, and the training of applied anthropologists.

Davis, S. H. (1977). *Victims of the miracle: Development and the Indians of Brazil.* New York: Cambridge University Press. This book documents the effects of Brazil's program of development on indigenous populations that have often suffered in the name of economic progress.

Finkler, Kaja. (1994). *Spiritualist healers in Mexico: Successes and failures of alternative therapeutics.* Salem, WI: Sheffield Publishing Company. Finkler provides a rich and detailed account of alternative healing systems in a rural Mexican setting. Through a systematic approach she meticulously documents client complaints, the therapeutic process, and the outcome of nonbiomedical healing treatment. This is a valuable contribution to medical anthropology as well as international health.

Grillo, R. & Rew, A. (Eds.). (1985). *Social anthropology and development policy.* New York: Tavistock Publica-
tions. A collection of papers that examines the role of the anthropologist in different political contexts, the contribution to be made by anthropologists to policy, and what working in the applied field might mean for anthropologists and those who hire them.

Johnson, T. M. & Sargent, C. F. (Eds.). (1990). *Medical anthropology: Contemporary theory and method.* New York, Westport, and London: Praeger.

McElroy, A. & Townsend, Patricia K. (1989). *Medical anthropology in ecological perspective* (2nd ed.). Boulder, San Francisco, and London: Westview Press. Through an ecological perspective this text introduces the study of medical anthropology and the expansion of research in this field in the last ten years. It emphasizes the increasing importance of biocultural approaches to contemporary health problems. Included are updated case studies on health problems such as sickle cell anemia, health problems of refugees, and strategies for developing health care.

McMillan, D. E. (1995). *Sahel visions: Planned settlement and river blindness control in Burkina Faso.* Tucson and London: University of Arizona Press. McMillan's study examines a period of fifteen years in which a development plan was implemented in order to relieve population pressure, increase food production, improve health conditions, and establish communities in areas afflicted with onchocerciasis (river blindness) in Burkina Faso in West Africa. An insightful study on land settlement and human development concerns.

Miller, M. S., Project Director (with the Cultural Survival staff). (1993). *State of the peoples: A global human rights report on societies in danger.* Boston: Beacon Press. This text provides us with contemporary and well-researched data on critical issues such as human rights, endangered societies, and resources for action. A valuable contribution that presents innovative solutions.

Newson, L. A. (1988). *Indian survival in colonial Nicaragua.* Norman, OK: University of Oklahoma Press. A detailed description of the colonial experiences of Indians in Nicaragua that focuses on the cultural and demographic factors that have resulted in different rates of survival for indigenous populations.

Romanucci-Ross, L., Moerman, Daniel E., & Tancredi, Laurence R. (Eds.). (1991). *The anthropology of medicine: From culture to method,* (2nd ed.). New York: Bergin & Garvey. The latest edition of a classic text, this volume is an introduction to the field of medical anthropology and pays increased attention to various topics ranging from aging to creativity in illness. The authors approach the subject from a cultural and medical anthropologist's perspective. This book also provides comprehensive reference work on Western and non-Western medicine.

Glossary

acculturation Cultural change that occurs in response to extended first-hand contacts between two or more previously autonomous groups.

adaptation The process by which organisms or populations of organisms make biological or behavioral adjustments that facilitate their survival and reproductive success in their environment.

adjudication Formal or administrative systems for the resolution of conflict.

administrative system A twentieth-century system of ownership in which land is owned and managed by the state; found in China, the former Soviet Union, and some parts of Africa and Latin America.

affinal kin Persons related by marriage.

age grade A group of people of the same sex and approximately the same age who share a set of duties and privileges.

age set A named grouping of individuals of approximately the same age; as with age grades, predominantely found in East Africa.

alienation The fragmentation of individuals' relations to their work, the things they produce, and the resources with which they produce them.

ambilineal descent A descent ideology based on ties traced through either the paternal or the maternal line.

ambilocality Residence of a married couple with or near the kin of either husband or wife, as they choose.

animal husbandry The breeding, care, and use of herd animals such as sheep, goats, camels, cattle, and yaks.

animatism Belief in an impersonal supernatural force.

animism Belief in a soul, a spiritual essence that differs from the tangible, physical body.

archaeology The study of the relationship between material culture and behavior; investigations of the ways of life of earlier peoples and of the processes by which their ways of life changed.

authority The ability to exert influence because of one's personal prestige or the status of one's office.

avunculocal residence Residence of a married couple with or near a brother of the husband's mother, who is usually a senior member of his matrilineage.

balanced reciprocity Gift giving that clearly carries the obligation of an eventual and roughly equal return.

band A loosely integrated population sharing a sense of common identity but few specialized institutions.

bifurcation A basis of kin classification that distinguishes the mother's side of the family from the father's side.

bilateral descent A descent ideology in which individuals define themselves as being at the center of a group of kin composed more or less equally of kin from both paternal and maternal lines.

biolocal residence Regular alternation of a married couple's residence between the household or vicinity of the wife's kin and of the husband's kin.

biological (physical) anthropology The study of the human species, past and present, as a biological phenomenon.

biological race A genetically distinct population within a species.

biological species A group of interbreeding populations that is reproductively isolated from other such groups.

Blue Revolution Modern aquaculture, producing fish, shellfish, and other products.

bride price Payment made by a man to the family from whom he takes a daughter in marriage.

bride service Service rendered by a man as payment to a family from whom he takes a daughter in marriage.

bridewealth Property given by the family of the groom to the family of the bride to compensate them for the loss of their daughter's service.

bureaucracy Institutionalized political administration, usually hierarchically organized.

call system A repertoire of sounds, each of which is produced in response to a particular situation.

carrying capacity The point at or below which a population tends to stabilize.

caste A social category in which membership is fixed at birth and usually unchangeable.

cattle complex An East African socioeconomic system in which cattle represent social status as well as wealth.

centralization Concentration of political and economic decisions in the hands of a few individuals or institutions.

chiefdom A society distinguished by the presence of a permanent central political agency to coordinate the activities of multicommunity political units.

clan A group that claims but cannot trace precisely their descent from a common ancestor.

closed corporate community A community that strongly emphasizes community identity and discourages outsiders from settling there by restricting land use to village members and prohibiting the sale or lease of property to outsiders.

cognates Words so similar from one language to the next as to suggest that both are variants of a single ancestral prototype.

collateral relatives People to whom one is related through a connecting person.

commune Collective ownership of land or other factors in production, ostensibly for members to share proceeds and expenses.

conjugal relationship The relationship between spouses.

consanguineal kin Persons related by birth.

consensual decisions Arriving at decisions that the entire group can accept.

conversion The use of a sphere of exchange for a transaction with which it is not generally associated.

co-resident household People living together, sharing expenses and consumption.

corporate ownership Control of land and other productive resources by a group rather than by individuals.

corporateness The sharing of specific rights by group members.

corvée Unpaid labor in lieu of taxation, usually on road construction and maintenance.

creole A pidgin language that has evolved into a fully developed language, with a complete array of grammatical distinctions and a large vocabulary.

cross cousins Mother's brothers' children and father's sisters' children.

cross-cultural research (holocultural research) A method that uses a global sample of societies in order to test hypotheses.

cultural anthropology The study of specific contemporary human cultures (ethnography), and of the underlying patterns of human culture in general (ethnology).

cultural ecology An approach to the study of cultural diversity that requires the simultaneous investigation of technology, culture, and the physical environment.

cultural evolution The idea that human culture has been transformed by regular and cumulative changes in learned behavior.

cultural materialism The theory, espoused by Marvin Harris, that ideas, values, and religious beliefs are the means or products of adaptation to environmental conditions ("material constraints").

cultural relativism The ability to view the beliefs and customs of other peoples within the context of their culture rather than one's own.

culture area A region in which several groups have similar culture complexes.

culture of poverty A self-perpetuating complex of escapism, impulse gratification, despair, and resignation; an adaptation and reaction of the poor to their marginal position in a class-stratified, highly individuated, capitalistic society.

culture A system of shared beliefs, values, customs, behaviors, and artifacts that the members of a society use to cope with one another and with their world and that are transmitted from generation to generation through learning.

cyberculture The emergent worldwide system of communication via computers.

demographic transition A rapid increase in a society's population with the onset of industrialization, followed by a leveling off of the growth rate due to reduced fertility.

descent group A group of consanguineal kin united by presumed lineal descent from a common ancestor.

descent ideology The concept of kinship as a basis of unambiguous membership in a group and possibly of property rights and political obligations.

descent relationship The ties between mother and child and between father and child.

development anthropology Employment of anthropological theory and findings to have a practical and ameliorating effect on the lives of people.

diachronic studies Use of descriptive data from one society or population that has been studied at many points in time.

dialect A distinctive speech community within a language.

differentiation Organization in separate units for various activities and purposes.

diffusion The spread of an aspect of culture from the society in which it originated by migration or imitation.

divination A practice in which an element of nature acts as a sign to provide supernatural information to the diviner.

domestic cycle The changes in household organization that result from a series of demographic events.

domestic herds Animals maintained for domestic consumption.

domestic mode of production The organization of economic production and consumption primarily in the household.

domestication The process by which people try to control the reproductive rates of animals and plants by ordering the environment in such a way as to favor certain species.

dowry Payment made by the bride's family to the groom or to the groom's family.

early cultural evolutionists Early cultural anthropologists who held to the basic premise that cultures progress through a sequence of evolutionary stages.

ecology The study of the interplay between organisms (or the populations to which they belong) and their environment.

economic class A group that is defined by the economic position of its members in relation to the means of production in the society—the wealth and relative economic control they may command.

economic stratification The segmentation of society along lines of access to resources.

economic system The ideas and institutions that people drawn upon and the behaviors in which they engage in order to secure resources to satisfy their needs and desires.

ecosystem The cycle of matter and energy that includes all living things and links them to the nonliving.

ecosystem equilibrium A balance among the components of an ecosystem.

ego An individual selected as the point of reference in describing a kinship or genealogical system.

empiricism Reliance on observable and quantifiable data.

enculturation Becoming proficient in the cultural codes of one's society.

endogamy Marriage within a particular group with which one is identified.

entrepreneurship Economic innovation and risk-taking.

ethnicity A basis for social categories that are rooted in socially perceived differences in national origin, language, and/or religion.

ethnocentrism The tendency to judge the customs of other societies by the standards of one's own.

ethnographic present Describes the point in time at which a society or culture is frozen when ethnographic data collected in the field are published in a report.

ethnography Gathering information on contemporary cultures through fieldwork or first-hand study.

ethnology Uncovering general patterns and "rules" that govern social behavior.

evolution The process by which small but cumulative changes in a species can, over time, lead to its transformation; may be divided into two categories: physical evolution (adaptive changes in biological makeup) and cultural evolution (adaptive changes in thought and behavior).

evolutionary ecology The study of living organisms within the context of their total environment, with the aim of discovering how they have adapted.

exchange The distribution of goods and services among members of a society.

exogamy Marriage outside a particular group with which one is identified.

exorcism Ritual intended to remove or placate spirits thought to be associated with people, places, or things.

extended family household A multiple-family unit incorporating adults of two or more generations.

extensive agriculture Farming using limited sources of nonhuman energy.

fallow time The time required for soils to regain nutrients following planting; industrial farming has greatly shortened this time leading to increased production.

family household A household formed on the basis of kinship and marriage.

fictive kin Persons such as godparents, *compadres*, "blood brothers," and old family friends whom children call "aunt" and "uncle."

fieldwork The first-hand observation of human societies.

formalism A school of economic anthropology that argues that if the concepts of formal economic theory are broadened, they can serve as analytic tools for the study of any economic system.

formal sanctions Prescribed penalties for behavior defined as inappropriate.

fossils The naturally mineralized remains of earlier forms of plant and animal life.

fraternal polyandry Marriage of one woman with a set of brothers.

freehold Private ownership of property.

free morphemes Morphemes that are complete words when standing alone.

functionalism The theory that all elements of a culture are functional in that they serve to satisfy culturally defined needs of the people in that society or requirements of the society as a whole.

gender A cultural construct consisting of the set of distinguishable characteristics associated with each sex.

generalized reciprocity Informal gift giving for which no accounts are kept and no immediate or specific return is expected.

genotype The genetic makeup of an individual or of specific genetically defined traits.

global culture Due to recent developments in communication and transportation, people all over the world are coming to share similar aspirations, cultural codes, and patterns of consumption.

grammar The formal structure of a language, comprising phonology, morphology, and syntax.

Green Revolution Use of recently developed new genetic strains of major food crops, which has transformed agriculture since the 1970s.

habitat The specific area where a species lives.

headmen Leaders in tribal- or band-organized societies, usually informally selected with limited formal coercive power.

historical particularism An anthropological approach characterized by the collection of detailed ethnographic data.

holism The philosophical view that no complex entity can be considered to be only the sum of its parts; as a principle of anthropology, the assumption that any given aspect of human life is to be studied with an eye to its relation to other aspects of human life.

Homo sapiens sapiens The human species.

horizontal migration A nomadic pattern characterized by regular movement over a large area in search of grass.

horticulture A simple form of agriculture based on the working of small plots of land without draft animals, plows, or irrigation; also called *extensive agriculture*.

household A domestic residential group whose members live together in intimate contact, rear children, share the proceeds of labor and other resources held in common, and in general cooperate on a day-to-day basis.

hypothesis A statement that stipulates a relationship between a phenomenon for which the researcher seeks to account and one or more other phenomena.

impact assessment Measuring the social, economic, or cultural impacts of development efforts.

incest taboo The feeling or belief that sexual contact with certain relatives is divinely or supernaturally prohibited.

independent family household A single-family unit that resides by itself, apart from relatives or adults of other generations.

industrial agriculture Farming using large inputs of fossil fuel and industrial technology.

informal sanctions Penalties for inappropriate behavior imposed on offenders in the course of everyday social life.

institutions A society's recurrent patterns of activity, such as religion, art, a kinship system, law, and family life.

intensification An increase in the product derived from a unit of land or labor.

intensive agriculture A form of agriculture that involves the use of draft animals or tractors, plows, and often some form of irrigation.

jati Occupational categories or groupings within the Indian caste system.

joint family household A complex family unit formed through polygyny or polyandry or through the decision of married siblings to live together in the absence of their parents.

juncture The linkage or separation of syllables by pauses.

kin terminology The terms that systematically designate distinctions between relations of different categories.

kindred A collection of bilateral kin.

Kula Ring Ceremonial exchange among trading partners in the Trobriand Islands.

law A rule of social conduct enforced by sanctions administered by a particular source of legitimate power.

legitimacy The right to rule on the basis of recognized principles.

levirate A social custom under which a man has both the right to marry his dead brother's widow and the obligation to provide for her.

liminal state Refers to the ambiguous status or position of an individual moving from one socially defined state to another.

lineage A unilineal descent group composed of people who trace their genealogies through specified links to a common ancestor.

lineal relatives Direct ascendants and descendants.

lingua franca Any language used as a common tongue by people who do not speak one another's native language.

linguistic anthropology A subdivision of anthropology that is concerned primarily with unwritten languages (both prehistoric and modern), with variation within languages, and with the social uses of language; traditionally divided into three branches: *descriptive linguistics*, the systematic study of the way language is constructed and used; *historical linguistics*, the study of the origin of language in general and of the evolution of the languages people speak today; and *sociolinguistics*, the study of the relationship between language and social relations.

low-energy budget An adaptive strategy by which a minimum of energy is used to extract sufficient resources from the environment for survival.

market exchange Trading goods and services through a common medium of value.

Marxist anthropology The study of internal sources of social change, with a focus on a society's distinctive set of elements and contradictions.

material culture The technology and all material artifacts of a society; used primarily by archaeologists.

matriclan A group that claims but cannot trace their descent through the female line from a common female ancestor.

matrifocal Centered on the mother; said of a family situation common to the urban poor worldwide in which the woman and her relationships with her children and her female kin form the core of family life.

matrifocal family household A family unit based solely on the bond between a mother and her children.

matrilateral Relatives on the mother's side in a genealogy or kinship system.

matrilineage A lineage whose members trace their genealogies through specified female links to a common female ancestor.

matrilineal descent Descent traced through the female line.

matrilineal descent group A unilineal descent group in which membership is inherited through the maternal line.

matrilocal residence Residence of a married couple with or near the wife's kin.

mechanical solidarity The unity of a society formed of social units that are comparable (Durkheim).

mechanization The replacement of human and animal labor by mechanical devices.

mediation Intervention by an outside party in a dispute.

medical anthropology Specialization within anthropology focusing on medical knowledge and practice; often related to practical efforts in health care delivery.

moiety One of the two subdivisions of a society with a dual organizational structure.

monogamy An exclusive union of one man and one woman.

monotheism Belief in one god.

morphemes The smallest units of speech that convey meaning.

morphology The system by which speech units are combined to form meaningful words.

multilineal evolutionism An anthropological approach that focuses on the development of individual cultures or populations without insisting that all follow the same evolutionary pattern.

nationalism The feeling or belief that a people and land are inherently linked, and using this belief to legitimize a particular state or nation.

natural selection The process whereby members of a species who have more surviving offspring than others pass their traits on to the next generation, whereas the less favored do not do so to the same degree.

negative reciprocity An exchange between enemies or strangers in which each side tries to get the better end of the bargain.

neolithic revolution Refers to the development of agriculture and consequent cultural changes that occurred at different times and places in the Old and New Worlds.

neolocal residence Residence of a married couple in a new household established apart from both the husband's and the wife's kin.

niche The environmental requirements and tolerances of a species; sometimes seen as a species' "profession" or what it does to survive.

nomadic pastoralism The strategy of moving the herds that are one's livelihood from pasture to pasture as the seasons and circumstances require.

nonunilineal descent A way of looking at kinship in which descent may be traced through either parent or through both.

nuclear family household An independent family unit formed by a monogamous union.

nucleation The tendency of populations to cluster in settlements of increasing size and density.

organic solidarity The unity of a society formed of dissimilar, specialized groupings, each having a restricted function (Durkheim).

paleontologists Experts on animal life of the distant past.

parallel cousins Mother's sisters' children and father's brothers' children.

participant observation Actual participation in a culture by an investigator, who seeks to gain social acceptance in the society as a means to acquire understanding of her or his observations.

pastoralism A form of social organization based on herding.

patriclan A group that claims but cannot trace their descent through the male line from a common male ancestor.

patrilineage A lineage whose members trace their genealogies through specified male links to a common male ancestor.

patrilineal descent Descent traced through the male line.

patrilineal descent group A unilineal descent group in which membership is inherited through the paternal line.

patrilocal residence Residence of a married couple with or near the husband's kin.

patron-client relationship A mutually obligatory arrangement between an individual who has authority, social status, wealth, or some other personal resource (the "patron") and another person who benefits from his or her support or influence (the "client").

peasants Farmers who lack control over the means of their production—the land, the other resources, the capital they need to grow their crops, and the labor they contribute to the process.

phenotype The physical expression of a genotype in a specific environment.

phoneme A class of sounds that differ slightly from one another but that may be substituted for one another without any change of meaning.

phonology The sound system of a language.

pidgin A language based on a simplified grammar and lexicon taken from one or more fully developed languages.

political ecology Focuses on the ecological consequences of the distribution of power.

politics The process by which a community's decisions are made, rules for group behavior are established, competition for positions of leadership is regulated, and the disruptive effects of disputes are minimized.

polyandry Marriage between one woman and two or more men simultaneously.

polyculture Closely associated with horticulture, the planting of many species or strains of plants in close proximity.

polygamy Plural marriage.

polygyny Marriage between one man and two or more women simultaneously.

polytheism Belief in many gods.

postpartum taboo Supernaturally justified sanctions on certain activities following a birth.

power The ability to exert influence because one's directives are backed by negative sanctions of some sort.

primates A grouping of mammals that includes humans, apes, and New and Old World monkeys.

primatology The study of living nonhuman primates.

production The conversion of natural resources to usable forms.

productive life span The period bounded by the culturally established ages at which a person ideally enters and retires from the work force.

productivity The amount of work a person accomplishes in a given period of time.

profane The sphere of the ordinary and routine; the everyday, natural world.

racism Acting upon the belief that different races have different capacities for culture.

random sample A sample in which each individual in a population has the same chance of being selected as any other.

rational economic decisions Weighing available alternatives and calculating which will provide the most benefit at the least cost.

reciprocity Mutual giving and taking between people who are often bound by social ties and obligations.

redistribution Reallocation of a society's wealth by means of obligatory payments or services.

regulation of access to resources Control over the use of land, water, and raw materials.

resilience The ability of an ecosystem to undergo change while still maintaining its basic elements or relationships.

revitalization movements Conscious efforts to build an ideology that will be relevant to changing cultural needs.

rites of intensification Rituals intended either to bolster a natural process necessary to survival or to reaffirm the society's commitment to a particular set of values and beliefs.

rites of passage Rituals that mark a person's transition from one set of socially identified circumstances to another.

ritual Behavior that has become highly formalized and stereotyped.

role A set of behavioral expectations appropriate to an individual's social position.

sacred The sphere of extraordinary phenomena associated with awesome supernatural forces.

sampling bias The tendency of a sample to exclude some members of the sampling universe and overrepresent others.

sampling universe The largest entity to be described, of which the sample is a part.

scarce resources A central concept of Western economics that assumes that people have more wants than they have resources to satisfy them.

scientific theory A statement that postulates ordered relationships among natural phenomena.

sedentary pastoralism Animal husbandry that does not involve mobility.

sedentism The practice of establishing a permanent, year-round settlement.

segmentary lineage A descent group in which minimal lineages are encompassed as segments of minor lineages, minor lineages as segments of major lineages, and so on.

serial monogamy An exclusive union followed by divorce and remarriage, perhaps many times.

shaman A medium of the supernatural who acts as a person in possession of unique curing, divining, or witchcraft capabilities.

sharecropping Working land owned by others for a share of the yield.

slash-and-burn agriculture A method of farming, also called *swidden agriculture,* by which fields are cleared, trees and brush are burned, and the soil, fertilized by the ash, is then planted.

slavery A practice that permits some people within a society to own other persons and to claim the right to their labor.

social category A category composed of all people who share certain culturally identified characteristics.

social class A category of people who have generally similar educational histories, job opportunities, and social standing and who are conscious of their membership in a social group that is ranked in relation to others and is replicated over generations.

social control A framework of rewards and sanctions that channel behavior.

social division of labor The process by which a society is formed by the integration of its smaller groups or subsets.

socialization The process by which a person acquires the technical skills of his or her society, the knowledge of the kinds of behavior that are understood and acceptable in that society, and the attitudes and vlaues that make conformity with social rules personally meaningful, even gratifying; also termed *enculturation.*

social racc Defining a population using both cultural and phenotypic criteria.

sociolinguistics The study of the interrelationship of social variables and language.

sororate A social custom under which a widower has the right to marry one of his deceased wife's sisters, and her kin are obliged to provide him with a new wife.

specialization The limited range of activities in which a single individual is likely to be engaged.

specialized pastoralism The adaptive strategy of exclusive reliance on animal husbandry.

speech community A socially distinct group that develops a dialect; a variety of language that diverges from the national language in vocabulary, pronunciation, and grammar.

spheres of exchange The modes of exchange—reciprocity, redistribution, and market exchange—that apply to particular goods or in particular situations.

spirit possession The supposed control of a person's behavior by a supernatural spirit that has entered the body.

stability The ability of an ecosystem to return to equilibrium after disturbances.

state A complex of institutions that transcend kinship in the organization of power.

status A position in a pattern of reciprocal behavior.

stratification The division of a society into groups that have varying degrees of access to resources and power.

stratified sample A sample obtained by the process of dividing a population into categories representing distinctive characteristics and then selecting a random sample from each category.

stratified society A society in which extensive subpopulations are accorded differential treatment.

structural functionalism The theory that the central function of the various aspects of a society is to maintain the social structure—the society's pattern of social relations and institutions.

subsistence agriculture Farming directed to domestic consumption with limited nonhuman energy sources.

substantivism A school of economic anthropology that seeks to understand economic processes as the maintenance of an entire cultural order.

syntax The arrangement of words into meaningful utterances.

taboo A supernaturally justified prohibition on certain activities.

terms of address The terms by which people refer to their kin when they speak about them in the third person.

theism Belief in one or more gods of extrahuman origin.

time allocation A method of collecting data by making observations according to a systematic schedule.

tontine A group of people who agree to collect and pool funds, and then use the pot in an agreed-upon order.

totem A plant or animal whose name is adopted by a clan and that holds a special significance for its members, usually related to their mythical ancestry.

transhumance Seasonal movement of livestock between upland and lowland pastures.

tribe A descent- and kinship-based group in which subgroups are clearly linked to one another, with the potential of uniting a large number of local groups for common defense or warfare.

unilineal descent A way of reckoning kin in which membership is inherited only through either the paternal or the maternal line, as the society dictates.

unilineal evolution A pattern of cultural progress through a sequence of evolutionary stages; the basic premise of the early cultural evolutionists.

vengeance A form of social control arising from shared responsibility and the idea that each offense will be met with comparable and automatic retaliation.

water table The level of water under the earth.

witchcraft Use of religious ritual to control, exploit, or injure unsuspecting, or at least uncooperating, other persons.

workday The culturally established number of hours that a person ideally spends at work each day.

References

Aberle, D. F., Bronfenbrenner, U., Hess, E. H., Miller, D.R., Schneider, D. H., Spuhler, J. N. (1963). The incest taboo and the mating patterns of animals. *American Anthropologist, 65,* 253-265.

Abramson, A. (1987). Beyond the Samoan controversy in anthropology: A history of sexuality in the eastern interior of Fiji. In P. Caplan (Ed.), *The cultural construction of sexuality* (pp. 193-216). New York: Tavistock.

Abruzzi, W. (1987). Ecological stability and community diversity during Mormon colonization of the Little Colorado River Basin. *Human Ecology, 15,* 317-338.

————. (1993). *Dam that river! Ecology and Mormon settlement in the Little Colorado River basin.* New York: Penn State University Press.

Abu Lughod, L. (1988). *Veiled sentiments.* Berkeley: University of California Press.

————. (1993). *Writing women's worlds: Bedouin stories.* Berkeley: University of California Press.

Abu-Rabia, A. (1994). *The Negev Bedouin and livestock rearing: Social, economic and political aspects.* Providence, RI: Berg Publishers.

Adams, J. W., & Kasakoff, A. B. (1976). Factors underlying endogamous group size. In C. Smith (Ed.), *Regional analysis: Social systems* (Vol. 2, pp. 149-172). New York: Academic Press.

Adams, R. M. (1966). *The evolution of urban society: Early Mesopotamia and prehispanic Mexico.* Chicago: Aldine.

Agrawal, A. (1994). Mobility and control among nomadic shepherds: The case of the Raikas II. *Human Ecology, 22,* 131-144.

Alcock, J. (1995). The belief engine. *Skeptical Inquirer, 19*(3), 14-18.

Anderson, B. (1991). *Imagined communities.* London: Verso.

Angeloni, E. (Ed.). (1994). *Annual editions: Anthropology 94-95* (17th rev. ed.). Guilford, CT: Dushkin Publishing.

Angier, N. (1995, January 3). Heredity's more than genes, new theory proposes. *New York Times,* pp. B13, B22.

Annis, S. (1988). *God and production in a Guatemalan town.* Austin: University of Texas Press.

Antoun, R. T. (1968). On the significance of names in an Arab village. *Ethnology, 7,* 158-170.

Appell, G. N. (1988). Casting social change. In M. R. Dove (Ed.), *The real and imagined role of culture in development: Case studies from Indonesia* (pp. 271-284). Boulder, CO: Westview.

Armelagos, G. (1987). Biocultural aspects of food choice. In M. Harris & E. B. Ross (Eds.), *Food and evolution: Towards a theory of human food habits* (pp. 565-578). Philadelphia: Temple University Press.

Atkinson, J. M. (1992). Shamanism today. *Annual Review of Anthropology, 21,* 307-330.

Bailey, R. C., & Peacock, N. R. (1990). Efe Pygmies of Northeast Zaire: Subsistence strategies in the Ituri Forest. In I. DeGarine & G. A. Harrison (Eds.), *Uncertainty in the food supply.* New York: Cambridge University Press.

Balee, W. (1994). *Footprints of the forest: Ka'apor ethnobotany-historical ecology of plant utilization by an Amazonian people.* New York: Columbia University Press.

Balikci, A. (1970). *The Netsilik Eskimo.* New York: Natural History Press.

Barfield, T. J. (1993). *The nomadic alternative.* Englewood Cliffs, NJ: Prentice Hall.

Barnet, R. J., & Muller, R. E. (1974). *Global reach: The power of the multinational corporations.* New York: Simon & Schuster.

Barry, H., III, Child, I. L., & Bacon, M. K. (1959). Relation of child training to subsistence economy. *American Anthropologist, 61,* 51-63.

Barry, J. W. (1965). *A study of Temne and Eskimo visual perception: Preliminary report.* (Psychology Laboratory Report No. 28). Edinburgh: University of Edinburgh

Barth, F. (1959). Political leadership among Swat Pathans. *Monographs on Social Anthropology, 19,* London School of Economics.

——. (1961). *The nomads of south Persia: The Basseri tribe of the Kamseh confederacy*. New York: Humanities Press.

——. (1963). *Role of the entrepreneur in social change in Northern Norway*. Bergen: Norwegian Universities Press.

——. (1966). The problem of comparison. *Royal Anthropological Institute* (Occasional Paper No. 23, pp. 22-23).

——. (1969). *Ethnic groups and boundaries: The social organization of cultural difference*. Boston: Little, Brown.

——. (1981). *Process and form in social life*. London: Routledge & Kegan Paul.

Bates, D. G. (1973). *Nomads and farmers: The Yörük of Southeastern Turkey*. (University of Michigan Museum of Anthropology Monograph, p. 52). Ann Arbor: University of Michigan Press.

——. (1974). Normative and alternative systems of marriage among the Yörük of Southeastern Turkey. *Anthropological Quarterly, 47*, 270-287.

——. (1994). What's in a name? Minorities, identity and politics in Bulgaria. *Identities, 1*(2-3), 201-225.

Bates, D. G., & Lees, S. H. (1977). The role of exchange in production specialization. *American Anthropologist, 79*, 824-841.

——. (1979). The myth of population regulation. In N. A. Chagnon & W. Irons (Eds.), *Evolutionary biology and human social behavior: An anthropological perspective* (pp. 273-289). North Scituate, MA: Duxbury Press.

Bates, D. G., & Plog, F. (1990) *Cultural anthropology* (3rd ed.). New York: McGraw-Hill.

Bates, D. G., & Rassam, A. (1983). *Peoples and cultures of the Middle East*. Englewood Cliffs, NJ: Prentice Hall.

Beals, A. R. (1962). *Gopalpur: A south Indian village*. New York: Holt, Rinehart & Winston.

Beattie, J. (1964). *Other cultures*. New York: Free Press.

Beck, L. (1986). *The Qashqa'i of Iran*. New Haven, CT: Yale University Press.

——. (1991). *Nomad: A year in the life of a Qashqa'i tribesman in Iran*. Berkeley and Los Angeles: University of California Press.

Beckerman, S. (1983). Does the swidden ape the forest? *Human Ecology, 11*, 1-12.

Bell, D. (1975). Ethnicity and social change. In N. Glazer & D. P. Moynihan (Eds.), *Ethnicity*. Cambridge, MA: Harvard University Press.

Benedict, R. (1959). *Patterns of culture*. New York: New American Library. (First published 1934.)

Bentley, G. (1985). Hunter-gatherer energetics and fertility: A reassessment of !Kung San. *Human Ecology, 13*, 79-110.

Berleant-Schiller, R., & Shanklin, E. (Eds.). (1983). *The keeping of animals*. Totowa, NJ: Allenheld, Osmun.

Bernard, H. R. (1988). *Research methods in cultural anthropology*. Beverly Hills, CA: Sage.

——. (1994). *Research methods in anthropology: Qualitative and quantitative approaches* (2nd ed.). Thousand Oaks, CA: Sage.

Berreby, D. (1995, April 9). Unabsolute truths: Clifford Geertz. *New York Times Magazine*, pp. 44-47.

Berreman, G. D. (1972). Race, caste, and other invidious distinctions in social stratification. *Race, 13*, 500-536. London: Institute of Race Relations.

Bettinger, R. L. (1987). Archaeological approaches to hunter-gatherers. *Annual Review of Anthropology, 16*, 121-142.

Binford, L. R. (1968). Post-Pleistocene adaptations. In S. R. Binford & L. R. Binford (Eds.), *New perspectives in archaeology*. Chicago: Aldine.

——. (1983). *Working at Archaeology*. New York: Academic Press.

——. (1989). Ancestral lifeways: The faunal record. In A. Podolefski & P. J. Brown (Eds.), *Applying anthropology: An introductory reader*. Mountain View, CA: Mayfield Press.

Bird, G., & Melville, K. (1994). *Families and intimate relationships*. New York: McGraw-Hill.

Blackwood, E. (1984). Sexuality and gender in certain Native American tribes: The case of cross-gender females. *Signs, 10*, 27-42.

Blanton, R. E. (1994). *Houses and households: A comparative study*. New York: Plenum.

Bloomfield, L. (1965). Language history. In H. Hoijer (Ed.), *Language*. New York: Holt, Rinehart & Winston.

Board of Education of the City of New York, Division of Bilingual Education. (1994). *Facts and figures*.

Boas, F. (1940). *Race, language and culture*. New York: Macmillan.

——. (1966). *The limitations of the comparative method of anthropology*. New York: Free Press. (First published 1896.)

Boddy, J. P. (1988). Spirits and selves in Northern Sudan: The cultural therapeutics of possession and trance. *American Ethnologist, 15*, 2-27.

——. (1994). *Aman: The story of a Somali girl*. New York: Pantheon.

Boehm, C. (1984). *Blood revenge: The anthropology of feuding in Montenegro and other tribal societies*. Lawrence: University Press of Kansas.

Bogen, J. E. (1969). The other side of the brain: An oppositional mind. *Bulletin of the Los Angeles Neurological Societies, 34*, 135-162.

Bohannan, P. (1960). Africa's land. *Centennial Review, 4*, 439-449.

——. 1965. The Tiv of Nigeria. In J. L. Gibbs, Jr. (Ed.), *Peoples of Africa*. New York: Holt, Rinehart & Winston.

Bongarts, J. (1988). Modeling the demographic impact of AIDS in Africa. In R. Kulstad (Ed.), *AIDS 1988: American Association for the Advancement of Science Symposia Papers* (pp. 85-94). Washington, DC: AAAS.

Boone, J. (1992). Competition, conflict and development of social hierarchies. In E. R. Smith & B. Winterhalter (Eds.),

Evolutionary ecology and human behavior (pp. 301-338). Hawthorne, NY: Aldine de Grutyer.

Borofsky, R. (Ed.). (1994). *Assessing cultural anthropology.* New York: McGraw-Hill.

Boserup, E. (1970). *Women's role in economic development.* Chicago: Aldine.

Boster, J. (1983). A comparison of the diversity of Jivaroan gardens with that of the tropical forest. *Human Ecology, 11,* 47-68.

Bott, E. (1957). *Family and Social Networks.* London: Tavistock.

Boulding, K. (1961). *Economic analysis* (4th ed.). New York: Harper & Row.

Bourguignon, E., & Greenbaum, L. (1973). *Diversity and homogeneity.* New Haven, CT: HRAF Press.

Bowen, E. S. (1964). *Return to laughter: An anthropological novel.* New York: Doubleday/American Museum of Natural History.

Bowlby, J. (1969). Attachment. *Attachment and loss series* (Vol. 1). New York: Basic Books.

Boyd, R., & Richerson, P. J. (1985). *Culture and the evolutionary process.* Chicago: University of Chicago Press.

———. (1991). Punishment allows the evolution of cooperation (or anything else) in sizable groups. *Ethology and Sociobiology, 13,* 171-196

Brace, C., Brace, M. L., & Leonard, W. R. (1989). Reflections on the face of Japan: A multivariate craniofacial and odontometric perspective. *American Journal of Physical Anthropology, 78,* 93-114.

Bradburd, D. (1980). Never give a shepherd an even break: Class and labor among the Komanchi of Kerman, Iran. *American Ethnologist, 7,* 604-620.

———. (1984). The rules and the game: The practice of Komanchi marriage. *American Ethnologist, 11,* 738-754.

———. (1990). *Ambiguous relations: Kin, class and conflict among Komachi pastoralists.* Washington, DC: Smithsonian Institution Press.

Brandes, S. (1980). *Metaphors of masculinity: Sex and status in Andalusian folklore.* Philadelphia: University of Pennsylvania Press.

Bray, F. (1994). *The rice economies: Technology and development in Asian societies.* Berkeley and Los Angeles: University of California Press.

Briggs, J. L. (1970). *Never in anger: Portrait of an Eskimo family.* Cambridge, MA: Harvard University Press.

Brondizio, E., Moran, E., Mausel, P., & Wu, Y. (1994). Land use change in the Amazon estuary: Patterns of Caboclo settlement and landscape management. *Human Ecology, 22*(3), 243-248.

Brooke, J. (1987, November 30). Informal capitalism grows in Cameroon. *New York Times,* p. 8.

Brown, D. (1991). *Human universals.* New York: McGraw-Hill.

Browne, M. W. (1994, October 16). What is intelligence? And who has it? *New York Times Book Review,* pp. 3ff.

Buchler, I., & Selby, H. A. (1968). *Kinship and social organization: An introduction to theory and method.* New York: Macmillan.

Burbank, V. K. (1994). *Fighting women: Anger and aggression in Aboriginal Australia.* Berkeley and Los Angeles: University of California Press.

Burch, E. S., Jr. (1994). North Alaskan Eskimos: A changing way of life. In M. Ember, C. Ember, & D. Levinson (Eds.), *Portraits of a culture* (pp. 1-36). Englewood Cliffs, NJ: Prentice Hall.

———. (1994). The future of hunter-gatherer research. In E. S. Burch, Jr. & L. J. Ellanna (Eds.), *Key issues in hunter-gatherer research* (pp. 441-455). Providence, RI: Berg Publishers.

Burch, E. S., Jr., & Ellanna, L. J. (Eds.) (1994). *Key issues in hunter-gatherer research.* Providence, RI: Berg Publishers.

———. (1994). Introduction. In E. S. Burch, Jr. & L. J. Ellanna (Eds.), *Key issues in hunter-gatherer research.* Providence, RI: Berg Publishers.

Burling, R. (1970). *Man's many voices: Language in its cultural context.* New York: Holt, Rinehart & Winston.

———. (1974). *The passage of power.* New York: Academic Press.

Button, G. (1995). What you don't know can't hurt you: The right to know and the Shetland oil spill. *Human Ecology, 23,* 31.

Cairo Population Conference. (1994, September 11). *New York Times,* p. 10.

Calhoun, C., Light, D., & Keller, S. (1994). *Sociology* (6th ed.). New York: McGraw-Hill.

Campbell, B. K. (1995). *Human ecology* (2nd ed.). Hawthorne, NY: Aldine de Gruyter.

Cane, S. (1987). Australian Aboriginal subsistence in the Western Desert. *Human Ecology 15,* 391-434.

Cann, R. L. (1988). DNA and human origins. *Annual Review of Anthropology* (Vol. 17, pp. 127-143). Palo Alto, CA: Annual Reviews.

Caplan, P. (Ed.). (1987). *The cultural construction of sexuality.* New York: Tavistock.

Carneiro, R. L. (1981). The chiefdom: Precursor to the state. In G. D. Jones & R. R. Kautz (Eds.), *The Transition to Statehood in the New World* (pp. 37-77). New York: Cambridge University Press.

Carrington, J. F. (1949). *Talking drums of Africa.* London: Carey Kingsgate Press.

———. (1971). The talking drums of Africa. *Scientific American, 255,* 90-94.

Cashdan, E. (1992). Spatial organization and habitat use. In E.A. Smith & B. Winterhalter (Eds.), *Evolutionary ecology and human behavior.* New York: Walter de Gruyter.

Cavalli-Sforza, P., & Piazza, A. (1994). *The history and geography of human genes.* Princeton, NJ: Princeton University Press.

Chagnon, N. A. (1967). Yanomamî social organization and warfare. In M. Fried, M. Harris, & R. Murphy (Eds.), *War: The anthropology of armed conflict and aggression.* New York: Natural History Press.

———. (1983) *Yanomamö: The fierce people* (3rd ed.). New York: Holt, Rinehart & Winston.

———. (1992). *Yanomamö: The last days of Eden.* San Diego: Harcourt Brace Jovanovich.

———. (1993, October 23). Covering up the Yanomamö massacre. *New York Times,* Op. Ed.

———. (1995). L'Ethnologie du déshonneur: Brief response to Lizot. *American Ethnologist, 22*(1), 187-189.

Chagnon, N. A. & Hames, R. (1979). Protein deficiency and tribal warfare in Amazonia: New Data. *Science, 203* (4383), 10-15.

Chagnon, N. A., & Irons, W. (Eds.). (1979). *Evolutionary biology and human social behavior: An anthropological perspective.* North Scituate, MA: Duxbury Press.

Chagnon, N. A., & Melancon, T. (1983). Epidemics in a tribal population. In *The impact of contact: Two Yanomamö cases,* Report No. 11 (pp. 53-75). Cambridge, MA: Cultural Survival International.

Chance, N. A. (1990). *The Inupiat and Arctic Alaska: An ethnography of development.* Fort Worth, TX: Harcourt Brace College.

Cheal, D. (1993). Changing household financial strategies: Canadian couples today. *Human Ecology, 21*(2), 197-213.

Chibnik, M. (Ed.). (1987). *Farm work and fieldwork: American agriculture in anthropological perspective.* Ithaca, NY: Cornell University Press.

Chira, S. (1995). Struggling to find stability when divorce is a pattern. *New York Times,* pp. 1, 42.

Chomsky, N. (1972). *Language and mind.* New York: Harcourt Brace Jovanovich.

Clark, K., & Uhl, C. (1987). Farming, fishing, and fire in the history of the upper Rio Negro region of Venezuela. *Human Ecology, 15,* 1-26.

Clarke, K. B. (1993). Racial progress & retreat: A personal memoir. In H. Hill & J. E. Jones (Eds.), *Race in America: The struggle for equality* (pp. 3-18). Madison: University of Wisconsin Press.

Clarke, L. (1989). *Acceptable risk? Making decisions in a toxic environment.* Berkeley and Los Angeles: University of California Press.

Colchester, M. (1985). *The health and survival of the Venezuelan Yanomamö* (IGWA Document No. 53). Cambridge, MA: Cultural Survival International.

Cole, J. B. (Ed.). (1988). *Anthropology for the nineties: Introductory readings.* New York: Free Press.

Collier, J., Jr. (1967). *Visual anthropology: Photography as a research method.* New York: Holt, Rinehart & Winston.

Collins, W. T. (1974). An analysis of the Memphis garbage strike of 1968. *Public Affairs Forum, 3,* 1-6. Memphis State University.

Colson, E. (1954). Ancestral spirits and social structure among the plateau Tonga. *International Archives of Ethnography, 1,* 21-68.

Conant, F. P. (1965). Korok: A variable unit of physical and social space among the Pokot of East Africa. *American Anthropologist, 67,* 429-434.

———. (1982). Thorns paired sharply recurved: Cultural controls and rangeland quality in East Africa. In B. Spooner & H. Mann (Eds.), *Anthropology and desertification: Dryland ecology in social perspective* (pp. 111-122). London: Academic Press.

———. (1984). Remote sensing, discovery, and generalizations in human ecology. In E. Moran (Ed.), *The ecosystem concept in anthropology.* Boulder, CO: Westview Press.

———. (1988). Social Consequences of AIDS: Implications for East Africa and the Eastern United States. In R. Kulstad (Ed.), *AIDS 1988: American Association for the Advancement of Science Symposia Papers* (pp. 147-156). Washington, DC: AAAS.

———. (1994). Human ecology and space age technology: Some predictions. *Human Ecology, 22*(3), 405-413.

Cook, S. (1966). The obsolete anti-market mentality: A critique of the substantive approach to economic anthropology. *American Anthropologist, 68,* 323-345.

Coughenour, M. B., Ellis, J. E., Swift, D. M., Coppock, D. L., Galvin, K., McCabe, J. T., & Hart, T. C. (1985). Energy extraction and use in a nomadic pastoral ecosystem. *Science, 230,* 619-625.

Coult, A. D., & Habenstein, R. W. (1965). *Gross tabulations of Murdock's world ethnographic sample.* Columbia: University of Missouri Press.

Cowell, A. (1994, September 11). Cairo parley hits anew on migrants. *New York Times,* p. 10.

Craige, B. J. (Ed.). (1988). *Literature, language and politics.* Athens: University of Georgia Press.

Creed, G. W. (1994). Bulgaria: Anthropological corrections to cold war stereotypes. In M. Ember, C. Ember, & D. Levinson (Eds.), *Portraits of culture.* Englewood Cliffs, NJ: Prentice Hall.

Cronk, L. (1991). Human behavioral ecology. *Annual Review of Anthropology, 20,* 25-53.

Cunningham, W. P., & Saigo, B. W. (1995). *Environmental science, a global concern.* Dubuque, IA: William C Brown.

Curran, J. W., Jaffe, H. W., Hardy, A. M., Morgan, W. M., Selik, R. M., & Dondero, T. J. (1988). Epidemiology of AIDS and HIV infection in the United States. In R. Kulstad (Ed.), *AIDS 1988: American Association for the Advancement of Science Symposia Papers* (pp. 19-34). Washington, DC: AAAS.

Cyriax, R. J. (1939). *Sir John Franklin's last Arctic expedition.* London: Methuen.

Dalton, G. (1962). Traditional production in primitive African economies. *Quarterly Journal of Economics, 76,* 360-378.

———. (1972). Peasantries in anthropology and history. *Current Anthropology, 13*, 385-415.

D'Andrade, R. G. (1973). Cultural constructions of reality. In L. Nader & T. W. Maretski (Eds.), *Cultural illness and health: Essays in human adaptation*. Washington, DC: American Anthropological Association.

D'Aquili, E. (1972). *The biopsychological determinants of culture*. McCaleb Modulein Anthropology. Reading, MA: Addison-Wesley.

Davis, W. (1988). *Passage of darkness: The ethnobiology of the Haitian Zombie*. Chapel Hill: University of North Carolina Press.

———. (1993). Death of a people. Logging in the Penan homeland. *Cultural Survival Quarterly, 17*(3), 15-20.

Dawson, J. L. M. (1967). Cultural and psychological influences upon spatial perceptual processes in West Africa. *International Journal of Psychology, 2*, 115-128, 171-185.

Denevan, W., Treacy, J., Alcorn, J., Paddoch, C., Denslow, J., & Paitan, S. (1984). Indigenous agroforestry in the Peruvian Amazon: Bora Indian management of swidden fallows. *Interciencia, 9*, 346-357.

Denich, B. (1994). Dismembering Yugoslavia: Nationalist ideologies and the symbolic revival of genocide. *American Ethnologist, 21*(2), 367-390.

Dennett, D. C. (1994). *Darwin's dangerous idea: Evolution and the meaning of life*. New York: Simon & Schuster.

Diamond, J. (1994). Race without color. *Discover, 15*(11), 82-91.

Dietz, T. (1987). *Pastoralists in dire straits*. Netherlands Geographical Studies (No. 49). Amsterdam: University of Amsterdam, Institute for Social Geography.

Divale, W., & Harris, M. (1978). The male supremacist complex: Discovery of a cultural invention. *American Anthropologist, 80*, 668-671.

Dore, R. P. (1994). *Shinohata: A portrait of a Japanese village*. Berkeley and Los Angeles: University of California Press.

Douglas, M. (1962). The Lele resistance to change. In E. E. LeClair, Jr., & H. K. Schneider (Eds.), *Economic anthropology: Readings in theory and analysis*. New York: Holt, Rinehart & Winston.

Dove, M. R. (1984). The Chayanov slope in a Swidden society: Household demography and extensive agriculture in Western Kalimantan. In P. Durrenburger (Ed.), *Chayanov, peasants, and economic anthropology* (pp. 97-132). Orlando, FL: Academic Press.

———. (1988). Introduction. In M. R. Dove (Ed.), *The real and imagined role of culture in development: Case studies from Indonesia* (pp. 1-37). Honolulu: University of Hawaii Press.

Downs, J. F. (1965). The social consequences of a dry well. *American Anthropologist, 67*, 1387-1417.

Dozier, E. P. (1970). *The Pueblo Indians of North America*. New York: Holt, Rinehart & Winston.

Draper, P. (1976). Social and economic constraints on child life among the !Kung. In R. B. Lee & I. DeVore (Eds.), *Kalahari hunter-gatherers* (pp. 199-217). Cambridge, MA: Harvard University Press.

Duben, A. (1986). The significance of family and kinship in urban Turkey. In C. Kağitçibaşi (Ed.), *Sex roles, family and community in Turkey*. Indiana University Turkish Studies No. 3. Bloomington: Indiana University Press.

Duranti, A. (1994). *From grammar to politics: Linguistic anthropology in a Western Samoan village*. Berkeley and Los Angeles: University of California Press.

Durham, E. (1987). *High Albania*. Boston: Beacon.

Durham, W. H. (1991). *Coevolution: Genes, Culture, and Human Diversity*. Stanford, CA: Stanford University Press.

Durkheim, E. (1961). *The elementary forms of the religious life*. New York: Collier. (First published 1912.)

———. (1964). *The division of labor in society*. New York: Free Press.

Durrenberger, P. (Ed.). (1984). *Chayanov, Peasants, and Economic Anthropology*. Orlando, FL: Academic Press.

Dyson-Hudson, N., & Dyson-Hudson, R. (1982). The structure of East African herds and the future of East African herders. *Development and Change, 13*, 213-238.

Dyson-Hudson, R. (1988). Ecology of nomadic Turkana pastoralists: A discussion. In E. Whitehead, C. Hutchinson, B. Timmerman, & R. Varady (Eds.), *Arid lands: Today and tomorrow* (pp. 701-703). Boulder, CO: Westview.

Dyson-Hudson, R., & Little, M. A. (Eds.). (1983). *Rethinking human adaptation: Cultural and biological models*. Boulder, CO: Westview.

Dyson-Hudson, R., & Smith, E. A. (1978). Human territoriality. *American Anthropologist, 80*, 21-42.

Earle, T. (Ed.). (1991). *Chiefdoms: Power, economy and ideology*. Cambridge: Cambridge University Press.

Eder, J. F. (1988). Batak foraging camps today: A window to the history of a hunting-gathering economy. *Human Ecology, 16*, 35-57.

Edgerton, R. B. (1971). *The individual in cultural adaptation: A study of four East African peoples*. Berkeley and Los Angeles: University of California Press.

Eggan, F. (1950). *Social organization of the Western Pueblo*. Chicago: University of Chicago Press.

Ehrlich, P., & Ehrlich, A. H. (1972). *Population, resources, environment: Issues in human ecology* (2nd ed.). San Francisco: Freeman.

Eicher, M. (1988). *Nonsexist research methods: A practical guide*. London: Allen & Unwin.

Eliade, M. (1975). In W. C. Beane & W. G. (Eds.), *Myths, rites, symbols: A Mircea Eliade reader* (Vol. 2). New York: Harper & Row.

Ember, C. R. (1978). Myths about hunter-gatherers. *Ethnology, 17*(4), 439-448.

———. (1983). The relative decline in woman's contribution to agriculture with intensification. *American Anthropologist, 85*, 285-304.

———. (1992). Resource unpredictability, mistrust & war. *Journal of Conflict Resolution, 36*(2), 242-262.

Ember, C. R., & Ember, M. (1992). Peace between participatory polities: A cross-cultural test of the "democracies rarely fight each other" hypothesis. *World Politics, 44*(4), 573-599.

Ember, C. R., Ember, M. & Pasternak, B. (1974). On the development of unilineal descent. *Journal of Anthropological Research, 30,* 69-94.

Ember, M., & Ember, C. R. (1971). The conditions favoring matrilocal versus patrilocal residence. *American Anthropologist, 73,* 571-594.

Ember, M., Ember, C., & Levinson, D. (Eds.). (1994). *Portraits of culture.* Englewood Cliffs, NJ: Prentice Hall.

Eminov, A. (1990). There are no Turks in Bulgaria: Rewriting history by administrative fiat. In K. Karpat (Ed.), *The Turks of Bulgaria: The History, Culture and Political Fate of a Minority.* Istanbul: Isis Press.

Engels, F. (1972). In E. B. Leacock (Ed.), *The origin of the family, private property, and the state.* New York: International Publishers. (First published 1884.)

Escobar, A. (1991). Anthropology and the development encounter: The making and marketing of development anthropology. *American Ethnologist, 18*(4), 658-682.

———. (1994). Welcome to "Cyberia." *Current Anthropology 18*(3). 38–45.

Estioko-Griffin, A., & Griffin, P. B. (1981). Woman the hunter: The Agta. In F. Dahlberg (Ed.), *Woman the Gatherer* (pp. 121-151). New Haven, CT: Yale University Press.

Etienne, M., & Leacock, E. (Eds.). (1988). *Women and colonization: Anthropological perspectives.* South Hadley, MA: Bergin & Garvey.

Evans-Pritchard, E. E. (1940). *The Nuer: A description of the modes of livelihood and political institutions of a Nilotic people.* Oxford: Clarendon Press.

Fagan, B. M. (1992). *People of the Earth: An introduction to world prehistory* (7th ed.). New York: HarperCollins College.

Farb, P. (1974). *Word play: What happens when people talk.* New York: Knopf.

Farley, R. (1993). The common destiny of blacks and whites: Observations about social and economic status of the race. In H. Hill & J. E. Jones (Eds.), *Race in America: The struggle for equality* (pp. 197-233). Madison: University of Wisconsin Press.

Fay, R. E., Turner, C. F., Klassen, A. D, & Gagnon, J. H. (1989). Prevalence and patterns of same-gender sexual contact among men. *Science, 243,* 338-348.

Feder, B. J. (1994, March 7). Big decisions before spring planting. *New York Times,* p. D1.

Feinberg, R. (1988). Margaret Mead and Samoa: Coming of age in fact and fiction. *American Anthropologist, 90,* 656-663.

Feinman, G., & Nicholas, P. (1992). Prehispanic interregional interaction in southern Mexico: The Valley of Oaxaca and the Ejutla Valley. In E. M. Schortman & P. A. Urban (Eds.), *Resources, power, and interregional interaction* (pp. 77-114). New York: Plenum.

Feinmen, G. & Neitzel, J. (1984). Too many types: An overview of sedentary prestate societies in the Americas. *Advances in Archaeological Methods and Theory, 7,* 39-102. Orlando, FL: Academic Press.

Feit, H. A. (1973). The ethno-ecology of the Waswanipi Cree; or how hunters can manage their resources. In B. Cox (Ed.), *Cultural ecology: Readings on the Canadian native peoples.* Toronto: McClelland & Stewart.

———. (1994). The enduring pursuit: Land, time and social relationships in anthropological models of hunter-gatherers and in Subarctic hunters' images. In E. S. Burch, Jr. & L. J. Ellanna (Eds.), *Key issues in Hunter-gatherer research* (pp. 421-439). Providence, RI: Berg Publishers.

Ferguson, B. R. (Ed.). (1984). *Warfare, culture, and environment.* New York: Academic Press.

———. (1992). Tribal warfare. *Scientific American, 256*(1), 108-113

———. (1995). A reputation for war. *Natural History, 104*(4).

———. (1995). *Yanomamö warfare: A political history.* Santa Fe, NM: SAR Press.

Ferraro, G. P. (1990). *The cultural dimension of international business.* Englewood Cliffs, NJ: Prentice Hall.

Fischer, J. L. (1958). Social influences on the choice of a linguistic variant. *Word, 14,* 47-56.

Fisher, H. E. (1987). The four-year itch: Do divorce patterns reflect our evolutionary heritage? *Natural History, 10,* 22-33.

Fisher, M. (1980). *Iran: From religious dispute to revolution.* Cambridge, MA: Harvard University Press.

Flinn, M. (1986). Correlates of reproductive success in a Caribbean village. *Human Ecology, 14,* 225-245.

Flowers, N. M. (1988). The Spread of AIDS in rural Brazil. In R. Kulstad (Ed.), *AIDS 1988: American Association for the Advancement of Science Symposia Papers* (pp. 159-168). Washington, DC: AAAS.

Flowers, N., Gross, D., Ritter, M., & Werner, D. (1975). Protein capture and cultural development in the Amazon. *American Anthropologist, 3,* 526-549.

———. (1982). Variation in Swidden practices in four central Brazilian Indian Societies. *Human Ecology, 10,* 203-217.

Ford, R. I. (1972). An ecological perspective on the Eastern Pueblos. In A. Ortiz (Ed.), *New Perspectives on the Pueblos.* Albuquerque: University of New Mexico Press.

Foster, B. (1974). Ethnicity and commerce. *American Ethnologist, 1,* 437-448.

Foster, B., & Seidman, S. (1982). Urban structures derived from collections of overlapping subsets. *Urban Anthropology, 11,* 171-182.

Foster, G. M. (1969). *Applied Anthropology.* Boston: Little, Brown.

Fox, R. (1994). Evil wrought in the name of good. *Anthropology Newsletter* (March), 2.

———. (1994). *The challenge of anthropology: Old encounters and new excursions*. New Brunswick, NJ: Transaction Publishers.

Frank, A. G. (1969). *Capitalism and underdevelopment in Latin America*. New York: Monthly Review Press.

Frank, R. H. (1988). *Passion within reason: The strategic role of the emotions*. New York: Norton.

Fratkin, E. (1991a). *Surviving drought and development: Ariaal pastoralists of Northern Kenya*. Boulder, CO: Westview Press.

———. (1991b). Surviving drought and development. Ariaal pastoralists of Kenya. *Human Ecology, 23*(3).

Fratkin, E., Galvin, K., & Roth, E. A. (1994). *African pastoralist systems: An integrated approach*. Boulder, CO: L. Reinner Publishers.

Frayer, D. W., Wolpoff, M. H., Thorne, A. G., & Pope, G. G. (1994). Getting it straight. *American Anthropologist, 96*(2), 424-438.

Frayser, S. (1985). *Varieties of sexual experience*. New Haven, CT: HRAF Press.

Frazer, J. (1959). *The new golden bough* (Abr. ed.). New York: Criterion. (First published 1900.)

Freeman, D. (1983). *Margaret Mead and Samoa: The making and unmaking of an anthropological myth*. Cambridge, MA: Harvard University Press.

Freeman, J. D. (1961). On the concept of the Kindred. *Journal of the Royal Anthropological Institute, 91*, 192-220.

Freeman, M. M. R. (1971). A social and ecological analysis of systematic female infanticide among the Netsilik Eskimo. *American Anthropologist, 73*, 1011-1019.

Freilich, M. (1971). *Meaning of culture: A reader in cultural anthropology*. Lexington, MA: Xerox College.

Fricke, T. (1994). *Himalayan households*. New York: Columbia University Press.

Fried, M. (1967). *The evolution of political society: An essay in political anthropology*. New York: Random House.

Fromkin, V., & Rodman, R. (1988). *An introduction to linguistics* (4th ed.). New York: Holt, Rinehart & Winston.

Gailey, C. W. (1987). *Kinship to kingship: Gender hierarchy and state formation in the Tongan Islands*. Austin: University of Texas Press.

Galvin, K. A. (1988). Nutritional status as an indicator of impending food stress. *Disasters, 12*, 147-156.

Gardner, A., & Gardner, B. (1969). Teaching sign language to a chimpanzee. *Science, 165*, 664-672.

Geertz, C. (1966). Religion as a cultural System. In M. Banton (Ed.), *Anthropological approaches to the study of religion*. New York: Praeger.

———. (1969). Two types of ecosystems. In A. P. Vayda (Ed.), *Environment and cultural behavior*. New York: Natural History Press.

Giampietro, M., Bukkens, S. F., & Pimientel, D. (1993). Labor productivity: A biophysical definition and assessment. *Human Ecology, 21*, 229-260.

Gibbs, J. L., Jr. (1963). The Kpelle Moot. *Africa, 33*, 1-10.

Gilmore, D. D. (1987). *Aggression and community: Paradoxes of Andalusian culture*. New Haven, CT: Yale University Press.

———. (1990). *Manhood in the making: The cultural construction of masculinity*. New Haven, CT: Yale University Press.

———. (1991). Subjectivity and subjugation: Fieldwork in the stratified community. *Human Organization, 50*, 215-224.

———. (1994). The "mayete" as object and stereotype in Andalusian proletarian poetry. *Ethnology, 33*(4), 353-365.

Gladwin, C., & Butler, J. (1982). Gardening: A survival strategy for the small, part-time Florida farm. *Proceedings Florida State Horticultural Society, 95*, 264-268.

Glenny, M. (1992). *The fall of Yugoslavia: The third Balkan war*. London: Penguin.

Gluckman, M. (1965). *Politics, law, and ritual in tribal society*. Chicago: Aldine.

Goldberg, J. (1995, January 22). A war without purpose in a community without identity. *New York Times Magazine*, pp. 36-39.

Goldschmidt, W. (1947). *As you saw*. New York: Harcourt, Brace.

———. (1971). *Exploring the ways of mankind*. New York: Holt, Rinehart & Winston.

Goldsmith, E., & Hildyard, N. (1984). *The social and environmental effects of large dams*. San Francisco: Sierra Club.

Goleman, D. (1988, August 13). Sex roles reign powerful as ever in the emotions. *New York Times*, pp. C1-C2.

———. (1988, April 10). An emerging theory on Blacks' IQ scores. *New York Times*, Education Supplement, pp. 22-24.

Good, K. (1995). The Yanomamö keep on trekking. *Natural History, 104*(4).

Goodall, J. Van L. (1971). *In the shadow of man*. Boston: Houghton Mifflin.

Goodenough, W. H. (1955). A problem in Malayo-Polynesian social organization. *American Anthropologist, 57*, 71-83.

———. (1970). *Description and comparison in cultural anthropology*. Chicago: Aldine.

Gorkin, M. (1993). *Days of honey, days of onion: The story of a Palestinian family in Israel*. Berkeley and Los Angeles: University of California Press.

Gorman, E. M. (1989). The AIDS epidemic in San Francisco: Epidemiological and anthropological perspectives. In A. Podolefsky & P. J. Brown (Eds.), *Applying anthropology* (pp. 192-201). Mountain View, CA: Mayfield Press.

Gorman, P. (1994). A people at risk. In E. Angeloni (Ed.),

Annual editions: Anthropology. Guilford, CT: Dushkin Publishers.

Gossen, G. H. (1972). Temporal and spatial equivalents in Chamula ritual symbolism. In W. A. Lessa & E. S. Vogt, *Reader in comparative religion: An anthropological approach.* New York: Harper & Row.

Gottesfeld Johnson, L. M. (1994). Aboriginal burning for vegetation management in Northwest British Columbia. *Human Ecology, 22,* 171-188.

Gough, E. K. (1959). The Nayars and the definition of marriage. *Journal of the Royal Anthropological Institute, 89,* 23-34.

———. (1971). Nuer kinship: A Reexamination. In T. O. Beidelman (Ed.), *The translation of culture* (pp. 79-122). London: Tavistock.

Gould, J. L., & Marler, P. (1987). Learning by instinct. *Scientific American, 256,* 74-85.

Gould, S. J. (1986). Cardboard Darwinism: This view of life. *Natural History, 95,* 14-21.

———. (1989). Tires to sandals: This view of life. *Natural History 98,* 8-16.

———. (1994, October 20). So near and yet so far. *New York Review of Books,* pp. 229-260.

Graves, T. D. (1970). The personal adjustment of Navajo Indian migrants to Denver, Colorado. *American Anthropologist, 72,* 35-54.

Greenberg, J. (1993). *Language in America.* Palo Alto, CA: Stanford University Press.

Gregor, T. (1985). *Anxious pleasures: The sexual lives of an Amazonian people.* Chicago: University of Chicago Press.

———. (1988). *Culture, people, nature: An introduction to general anthropology* (5th ed.). New York: Harper & Row.

Grigg, D. B. (1974). *The agricultural systems of the world: An evolutionary approach.* Cambridge: Cambridge University Press.

Gross, D. R. (1983). Village movement in relation to resources in Amazonia. In R. B. Hames & W. T. Vickers (Eds.), *Adaptive responses of Native Amazonians* (pp. 429-499). New York: Academic Press.

———. (1984). Time allocation: A tool for the study of cultural behavior. *Annual Review of Anthropology, 13,* 519-558.

Gross, D. R., & Underwood, B. A. (1971). Technological change and caloric costs: Sisal agriculture in Northeastern Brazil. *American Anthropologist, 73,* 725-740.

Hackenberg, R. (1962). Economic alternatives in arid lands: A case study of the Pima and Papago Indians. *Ethnology, 1,* 186-195.

Hames, R. (1983). Monoculture, polyculture, and polyvariety in tropical forest Swidden cultivation. *Human Ecology, 11,* 13-34.

Hammel, H. A. (1994). Meeting the Minotaur. *Anthropology Newsletter, 36*(4).

Harris, M. (1966). The cultural ecology of India's sacred cattle. *Current Anthropology, 7,* 51-66.

———. (1974). *Patterns of race in the Americas.* New York: Norton.

———. (1984). A cultural materialist theory of band and village warfare: The Yanomamö test. In B. R. Ferguson (Ed.), *Warfare, culture, and environment* (pp. 111-140). New York: Academic Press.

———. (1985). *Good to eat: Riddles of food and culture.* New York: Simon & Schuster.

———. (1987). Comment on Vayda's review of good to eat: Riddles of food and culture. *Human Ecology, 15,* 511-518.

———. (1988). *Culture, people, nature: An introduction to general anthropology* (5th ed.). New York: Harper & Row.

Hart, T. D., & Hart, J. A. (1986). The ecological basis of hunter-gatherer subsistence in African rain forests: The Mbuti of Eastern Zaire. *Human Ecology, 14,* 29-57.

Hart, C. W., & Pilling, A. R. (1960). *The Tiwi of North Australia.* New York: Holt, Rinehart & Winston.

Hayden, B. (1994). Competition, labor and complex hunter-gatherers. In E. S. Burch, Jr. & L. J. Ellanna (Eds.), *Key issues in hunter-gatherer research* (pp. 223-239). Providence, RI: Berg Publishers.

Headland, T. (1987). The wild yam question: How well could independent hunter-gatherers live in a tropical forest ecosystem? *Human Ecology, 15,* 463-492.

Hemming, J. (Ed.). (1985). *Change in the Amazon Basin: Vol. 2: Man's impact on forests and rivers.* Manchester, Eng.: Manchester University Press.

Herdt, G. (1987). AIDS and anthropology. *Anthropology Today, 3,* 1-3.

Hernstein, R. J., & Murray, C. (1994). *The bell curve: Intelligence and class structure in American life.* New York: Free Press.

Herskovits, M. (1924). A preliminary consideration of the cultural areas of Africa. *American Anthropologist, 26,* 50-63.

Hertzberg, H. T. E. (1989). Engineering anthropology: Past, present, and potential. In A. Podolefsky & P. J. Brown (Eds.), *Applying anthropology: An introductory reader.* Mountain View, CA: Mayfield Press.

Hiatt, L. R. (1980). Polyandry in Sri Lanka: A test case for parental investment. *Man, 15,* 583-598.

Hill, K., Hawkes, K., Hurtado, M., & Kaplan, H. (1984). Seasonal variance in the diet of the Ache hunter-gatherers in eastern Paraguay. *Human Ecology, 12,* 101-136.

Hockett, C. F., & Ascher, R. (1964). The human revolution. *Current Anthropology, 5,* 135-168.

Hoebel, E. A. (1954). *The law of primitive man.* Cambridge, MA: Harvard University Press.

Hoijer, H. (1954). The Sapir-Whorf hypothesis. In H. Hoijer (Ed.), *Language in culture* (No. 79). Washington, DC: American Anthropological Association.

Holling, C. S. (1973). Resilience and stability of ecological systems. *Annual Review of Ecology and Systematics, 4,* 1-23.

Holmberg, A. (1958). Research and development approach to the study of change. *Human Organization, 17,* 12-16.

Holmes, R. (1984). Non-dietary modifiers of nutritional status in tropical forest populations of Venezuela. *Interciencia* 9, 386-391.

———. (1985). Nutritional status and cultural change in Venezuela's Amazon Territory. In J. Heming (Ed.), *Change in the Amazon Basin: Vol. 2. Man's impact on forests and rivers.* Manchester Eng.: Manchester University Press.

Hopkins, N. (1983). The social impact of mechanization. In A. Richards & P. L. Martin (Eds.), *Migration, mechanization, and agricultural labor markets in Egypt* (pp. 181-197). Boulder, CO: Westview Press.

Horgan, J. (1988). The violent Yanomomö: Science and citizen. *Scientific American, 255,* 17-18.

Horowitz, D. (1985). *Ethnic groups in conflict.* Berkeley and Los Angeles: University of California Press.

Horowitz, M. (1988). Anthropology and the new development agenda. In Bulletin of the Institute for Development Anthropology, *Development Anthropology Network, 6,* 1-4.

———. (1994). Development anthropology in the mid-1990s. *Development Anthropology Newsletter, 12*(1, 2), 1-14.

Howell, N. (1976). *Normal selection rates of the demographic patterns of the !Kung San.* Paper presented at the 1976 meeting of the American Anthropological Association, Washington, DC.

———. (1979). *Demography of the Dobe !Kung.* New York: Academic Press.

Hughes, A. L. (1988). *Evolution and human kinship.* New York: Oxford University Press.

Hultkrantz, A. (1994). Religion and ecology of Northern Eurasian/Siberian peoples. In T. Irimoto & T. Yamada (Eds.), *Circumpolar religion and ecology* (pp. 347-374). Tokyo: University of Tokyo Press.

Humphries, S. (1993). The intensification of traditional agriculture among Yucatec Maya farmers: Facing up to the dilemma of livelihood sustainability. *Human Ecology, 21,* 87-102.

Hurd, J. P. (Ed.). (In press) *The significance of evolutionary biology for research on human altruism.* Lewiston, NY: Edwin Mellen Press.

Ingold, T. (1980). *Hunters, pastoralists, and ranchers.* Cambridge: Cambridge University Press.

Irons, W. (1975). The Yomut Turkmen: A study of social organization among a Central Asian Turkic-speaking population. Anthropological Papers (No. 58). Ann Arbor: University of Michigan, Museum of Anthropology.

———. (1979). Natural selection, adaptation and human social behavior. Chagnon, N.A. & Irons, W. G. (Eds.) 1979. *Evolution, Biology and Human Social Behavior.* North Scituat, MA. Duxsbury Press.

———. (1991). How did morality evolve? *Zygon: Journal of Religion and Science, 26,* 49-89.

———. (1995). Morality as an evolved adaptation. In James P. Hurd (Ed.), *The Biology of Morality.* Lewiston, NY: Edwin Mellen Press.

Jablonka, E., & Avital, E. (1995, January 3). Heredity's more than genes, new theory proposes. *New York Times,* pp. B13ff.

Johnson, G. A. (1983). Decision-making organization and pastoral nomad camp size. *Human Ecology, 11,* 175-200.

Johnson, P. L. (1988). Women and development: A highland New Guinea example. *Human Ecology, 16,* 105-122.

Johnson, T. M., & Sargent, C. F. (Eds.). (1990). *Medical anthropology: Contemporary theory and method.* New York: Praeger.

Jolly, C. J., & White, R. (1995). *Physical anthropology* (5th ed.). New York: McGraw-Hill.

Jorgenson, J. (1971) Indians and the Metropolis. In J. O. Waddell & O. M. Watson (Eds.), *The American Indian in urban society.* Boston: Little, Brown.

Katz, S. H., Hediger, M. L., & Valleroy, L. A. (1974). Traditional maize processing in the new world. *Science, 17,* 765-773.

Keesing, R. M. (1975). *Kin groups and social structure.* New York: Holt, Rinehart & Winston.

Kelly, R. (1985). *The Nuer conquest.* Ann Arbor: University of Michigan Press.

Kemp, W. B. (1971). The flow of energy in a hunting society. *Scientific American, 225,* 104-115.

Khaldun, I. (1958). Franz Rosenthal (Trans.), *The Muqaddimah: An introduction to history* (Vol. 1). London: Kegan Paul. (Original work published in 1377 A. D.)

Kili, S. (1991). *Modernity and tradition: Dilemmas concerning women's rights in Turkey.* Paper presented at the annual meeting of the International Society of Political Psychology, Helsinki.

Kimball, J. C. (1984). *The Arabs 1984-85: An atlas and almanac.* Washington, DC: The American Educational Trust.

Kirch, P. V. (1994). *The wet and the dry: Irrigation and agricultural intensification.* Chicago: University of Chicago Press.

Kirkby, A. V. (1973). *The use of land and water resources in the past and present, Valley of Oaxaca, Mexico.* Ann Arbor: Museum of Anthropology, University of Michigan.

Konner, M. (1983). *The tangled web.* New York: Harper & Row.

———. (1988, August 14). Body and mind: The aggressors. *New York Times Magazine,* pp. 33-34.

Konstantinov, Y. (1992). "Nation-state" and "minority" types of discourse problems of communication between the majority and Islamic minorities in contemporary Bulgaria. *Innovation in Social Science Research, 5*(3), 75-89.

Konstantinov, Y., Gulbrand, A., & Igla, B. (1991). Names of the Bulgarian Pomaks. *Nordlyd, 17,* 8-118.

Koop, C. E. (1988). Foreword: Current issues in AIDS. In R. Kulstad (Ed.), *AIDS 1988: American Association for the Advancement of Science Symposia Papers* (pp. vii-viii). Washington, DC: AAAS.

Kopytoff, I. (1977). Matrilineality, residence, and residential zone. *American Ethnology, 4,* 539-558.

Korte, C., & Milgram, S. (1970). Acquaintance networks between racial groups: Application of the small world method. *Journal of Personality and Social Psychology, 15*, 101-108.

Kramer, M. (1987). *Three farms: Making milk, meat, and money from the American soil.* Cambridge, MA: Harvard University Press.

Kroeber, A. L., & Kluckhohn, C. (1952). *Culture: A critical review of concepts and definitions.* New York: Knopf.

Kwong, P. (1994, October 17). China's human traffickers. *The Nation*, pp. 422-425.

Labov, W. (1964). Phonological correlates of social stratifications. *American Anthropologist, 66* (Special Issue, Pt. 2), 164-176.

Laderman, C. (1983). *Wives and midwives: Childbirth and nutrition in rural Malaysia.* Berkeley and Los Angeles: University of California Press.

Lako, G. T. (1988). The impact of the Jonglei scheme on the economy of the Dinka. In J. H. Bodley (Ed.), *Tribal peoples and development issues: A global overview.* Palo Alto, CA: Mayfield Press.

Lansing, S. J. (1991). *Priests and programmers: Technologies of power in the engineered landscape of Bali.* Princeton, NJ: Princeton University Press.

———. (1995). The Balinese. In G. Spindler & L. Spindler (Eds.), *Case studies in cultural anthropology.* Fort Worth, TX: Harcourt Brace College.

Lardy, N. R. (1985). State intervention and peasant opportunities. In W. L. Parish (Ed.), *Chinese rural development: The great transformation* (pp. 33-56). Armonk, NY: M. E. Sharpe.

Laswell, H. (1936). *Politics: Who gets what, when, and how.* New York: McGraw-Hill.

Lawrence, P. (1964). *The road belong Cargo: A study of the Cargo movement in the Southern Madang District, New Guinea.* Manchester, Eng.: University of Manchester Press.

Leach, E. R. (1954). *Political systems of highland Burma.* New York: Humanities Press.

———. (1965). *Political systems of highland Burma.* Boston: Beacon Press.

———. (1982). *Social anthropology.* Glasgow: Fontana Paperbacks.

Leaf, M. J. (1972). *Information and behavior in a Sikh village: Social organization reconsidered.* Berkeley and Los Angeles: University of California Press.

Leavitt, G. C. (1989). The disappearance of the incest taboo. *American Anthropologist, 91*, 116-131.

Lee, R. B. (1968). What hunters do for a living, or, how to make out on scarce resources. In R. B. Lee & I. DeVore (Eds.), *Man the hunter.* Chicago: Aldine.

———. (1969). !Kung Bushmen subsistence: An input-output analysis. In A. P. Vayda (Ed.), *Environment and cultural behavior.* New York: Natural History Press.

———. (1979). *The !Kung San.* Cambridge: Cambridge University Press.

———. (1993). *The Dobe Ju/'hoansi.* Fort Worth, TX: Harcourt Brace College.

Lee, R. B., & DeVore, I. (Eds.). (1968). *Man the hunter.* Chicago: Aldine.

———. (1976). *Kalahari hunter-gatherers: Studies of the !Kung-San and their neighbors.* Cambridge, MA: Harvard University Press.

Lees, S. H. (1994). Irrigation and society. *Journal of Archeological Research, 2*(4), 361-378.

Lennihan, L. (1988). Wages of change: The unseen transformation in Northern Nigeria. *Human Organization 18*(3), 45–56.

Lepowsky, M. (1994). *Fruit of the motherland: Gender in an egalitarian society.* New York: Columbia University Press.

Leslie, P. W., & Fry, P. H. (1989). Extreme seasonality of births among nomadic Turkana pastoralists. *American Journal of Physical Anthropology 16*(2), 126–135.

Leslie, P. W., Fry, P. H., Galvin, K., & McCabe, J. T. (1988). Biological, behavioral, and ecological influences on fertility in Turkana pastoralists. In E. Whitehead & C. Hutchinson (Eds.), *Arid lands: Today and tomorrow* (pp. 705-726). Boulder, CO: Westview.

Lessa, W. A., & Vogt, E. Z. (1962). *Reader in comparative religion: An anthropological approach* (2nd ed). New York: Harper & Row.

Levi-Strauss, C. (1943). The social use of kinship terms among Brazilian Indians. *American Anthropologist, 45*, 398-409.

———. (1955). The structural study of myth. *Journal of American Folklore, 67*, 428-444.

———. (1969). *The raw and the cooked.* J. and D. Weightman (Trans.). New York: Harper Torch Book.

———. (1988). *The jealous potter.* Benedicte Chorier (Trans). Chicago: University of Chicago Press.

Levine, N. E. (1988). *The dynamics of polyandry: Kinship, domesticity, and population on the Tibetan border.* Chicago: University of Chicago Press.

Levinson, D., & Malone, M. J. (1980). *Toward explaining human culture.* New Haven, CT: HRAF Press.

Lewellen, T. C. (1992). *Political anthropology: An introduction* (2nd ed.). Westport, CT: Bergin & Garvey.

Lewis, H. T., & Ferguson, T. A. (1988). Yards, corridors, and mosaics: How to burn a boreal forest. *Human Ecology, 16*, 57-78.

Lewis, O. (1959). *Five families.* New York: Basic Books.

———. (1960). *Tepoztlán: A village in Mexico.* New York: Holt, Rinehart & Winston.

———. (1961). *The children of Sánchez.* New York: Random House.

———. (1966). *La vida: Puerto Rican family in the culture of poverty—San Juan and New York.* New York: Random House.

Lewis, P. (1993, November 10). Stoked by ethnic conflict: Refugee numbers swell. *New York Times*, p. A6.

Lewis, R. L. (1987). *Black coal miners in America: Race, class, and community conflict, 1790-1980*. Lexington: University Press of Kentucky.

Lieberman, P., & Crelin, E. (1971). On the speech of Neanderthal. *Linguistic Inquiry, 2*, 203-222.

Lightfoot, D. (1993). The cultural ecology of Puebloan Pebble-Mulch gardens. *Human Ecology, 21*(2), 115-144.

Lincoln, B. (1981). *Emerging from the chrysalis: Rituals of women's initiation*. New York: Oxford University Press.

Linton, R. (1937). One hundred percent American. *The American Mercury, 40*, 427-429. Reprinted in J. P. Spradley & M. A. Rynkiewich (Eds.), *The Nacerima* (pp. 405-406). Boston: Little, Brown.

Little, M. A. (1988). Introduction to the symposium: The Ecology of the nomadic Turkana pastoralists. In E. E. Whitehead, C. F. Hutchinson, B. N. Timmerman, & R. G. Vardy (Eds.), *Arid Lands today and tomorrow: Proceedings of an international research and development conference* (pp. 696-734). Boulder, CO: Westview Press.

Little, M. A., Dyson-Hudson, R., Ellis, J. E., Galvin, K. A., Leslie, P. W., & Swift, D. M. (1990). Ecosystem approaches in human biology: Their history & a case study of the South Turkana Ecosystem project. In E. F. Moran (Ed.), *The ecosystem approach in anthropology: From concept to practice* (pp. 389-434). Ann Arbor: University of Michigan Press.

Little, M. A., Galvin, K., & Leslie, P. W. (1988). Health and energy requirements of nomadic Turkana pastoralists. In I. deGarine & G. A. Harrison (Eds.), *Coping with uncertainty in food supply* (pp. 288-315). Oxford: Oxford University Press.

Livingstone, F. B. (1968). The effects of warfare on the biology of the human species. In M. Fried, M. Harris, & R. Murphy, *War: The anthropology of armed conflict and aggression*. New York: Natural History Press.

Lizot, J. (1994). On warfare: An answer to N. A. Chagnon. *American Ethnologist, 21*, 841-858.

Lorenz, K. (1965). *Evolution and modification of behavior*. Chicago: University of Chicago Press.

Lowie, R. H. (1954). *Indians of the Plains*. New York: McGraw-Hill.

Mageo, J. M. (1992). Male transvestism and cultural change in Samoa. *American Ethnologist, 19*, 443-459.

Magnarella, P. (1993). *Human materialism: A model of sociocultural systems and a strategy for analysis*. Gainesville: University of Florida Press.

Mahdi, M. (1971). *Ibn Khaldun's philosophy of history*. Chicago: University of Chicago Press.

Mair, L. (1965). *Introduction to social anthropology*. New York: Oxford University Press.

Malinowski, B. (1927). *Sex and repression in savage society*. London: Routledge & Kegan Paul.

———. (1931). Culture. In *Encyclopedia of the social sciences* (Vol. 4). New York: Macmillan.

———. (1954). *Magic, science, and religion and other essays*. Garden City, NY: Anchor/Doubleday.

———. (1961). *Argonauts of the Western Pacific*. New York: Dutton. (First published 1922.)

Manners, R. (1956). Tabara: Subculture of a tobacco and mixed crop municipality. In J. Steward (Ed.), *The people of Puerto Rico*. Urbana: University of Illinois Press.

Marett, R. R. (1909). *The threshold of religion*. London: Methuen.

Marks, J. (1994). Black, white, other. *Natural History, 103*, 32-35.

———. (1995). *Human biodiversity: Genes, race and history*. Hawthorne, NY: Aldine de Gruyter.

Marshall, L. (1960). !Kung Bushman bands. *Africa, 30*, 325-354.

———. (1961). Sharing, talking, and giving: Relief of social tensions among !Kung Bushmen. *Africa, 31*, 233-249.

———. (1965). The !Kung Bushman of the Kalahari Desert. In J. L.Gibbs, Jr. (Ed.), *Peoples of Africa*. New York: Holt, Rinehart & Winston.

Maybury-Lewis, D. (1992). *Millennium: Tribal wisdom and the modern world*. New York: Viking Penguin.

Mayer, A. C. (1968). The Indian caste system. *International Encyclopedia of the Social Sciences, 2*, 339-344.

Mayr, E. (1963). *Animal species and evolution*. Cambridge, MA: Harvard University Press.

McMillan, D. E. (1995). *Sahel visions: Planned settlement and river blindness control in Burkina Faso*. Tucson: University of Arizona Press.

McGovern, T., Bigelow, G., Amorosi, T. & Russell, D. (1988). Northern islands, human error, and environmental degradation. *Human Ecology, 18*, 225-270.

McGovern, T. H. (1980). Cows, harp seals, and churchbells: Adaptation and extinction on Norse Greenland. *Human Ecology, 8*, 245-276.

Mead, M. (1935). *Sex and temperament in three primitive societies*. New York: William Morrow.

———. (1949). *Male and female*. New York: Morrow.

———. (1956). *New lives for old: Cultural transformation—Manus, 1928-1953*. New York: Morrow.

———. (1971). *Coming of age in Samoa*. New York: Morrow. (First published 1928.)

———. (1975). *Blackberry winter*. New York: Random House.

Meggars, B. J. (1971). *Amazonia: Man and culture in a counterfeit paradise*. Chicago: Aldine.

Meggitt, M. J. (1964). Male-female relationship in the highlands of Australian New Guinea. *American Anthropologist, 66* (Special Issue, Pt. 2), 204-224.

Micklin, P. P. (1988). Desiccation of the Aral Sea: A water management disaster in the Soviet Union. *Science, 241*(1), 170-171, 175.

Middleton, J. (1960). *Lugbara religion: Ritual and authority among an East African people*. London: Oxford University Press.

Milan, F. (1970). The demography of an Alaskan Eskimo village. *Arctic Anthropology, 71*, 26-43.

Mills, C. W. (1959). *The power elite*. New York: Oxford University Press.

Milton, K. (1985). Ecological foundations for subsistence strategies among the Mbuti Pygmies. *Human Ecology, 13*, 71-78.

Mintz, S. W. (1986). *Sweetness and power: The place of sugar in modern history*. Harmondsworth, Eng.: Penguin.

Moghadam, V. (1993). *Modernizing women: Gender and social change in the Middle East*. Boulder, CO: Lynne Rienner.

Mooney, J. (1965). *The ghost dance religion and the Sioux outbreak of 1890*. Chicago: University of Chicago Press. (First published 1896.)

Mooney, K. A. (1978). The effect of rank and wealth on exchange among the Coast Salish. *Ethnology, 17*, 391-406.

Moore, O. K. (1957). Divination—A new perspective. *American Anthropologist, 59*, 69-74.

Moorehead, A. (1963). *Cooper's creek*. New York: Harper & Row.

Moran, E. F. (1990). Ecosystem ecology in biology and anthropology: A critical assessment. In E. F. Moran (Ed.), *The ecosystem approach in anthropology: From concept to practice* (pp. 3-40). Ann Arbor: University of Michigan Press.

———. (1990). Levels of analysis & analytical level shifting: Examples from Amazonian ecosystem research. In E. F. Moran (Ed.), *The ecosystem approach in anthropology: From concept to practice* (pp. 279-308). Ann Arbor: University of Michigan Press.

———. (1993). Deforestation and land use in the Brazilian Amazon. *Human Ecology, 21*, 1-21.

Morgan, L. H. (1963). *Ancient society*. New York: World. (First published 1877)

Morren, G. E. B., & Hyndam, D. C. (1987). The Taro monoculture of Central New Guinea. *Human Ecology, 15*, 301-315.

Moynihan, D. P. (1993). *Pandaemonium: Ethnicity in international politics*. New York: Oxford University Press.

Munson, H., Jr. (1988). *Islam and revolution in the Middle East*. New Haven, CT: Yale University Press.

Murdock, G. P. (1949). *Social Structure*. New York: Macmillan.

———. (1967). *The Ethnographic Atlas*. Pittsburgh, PA: University of Pittsburgh Press.

Murphy, R. F. (1986). *Cultural and social anthropology: An overture* (2nd ed.). Englewood Cliffs, NJ: Prentice Hall.

Murphy, Y., & Murphy, R. F. (1985). *Women of the forest* (2nd ed.). New York: Columbia University Press.

Nadel, S. F. (1935). Nupe state and community. *Africa, 8*, 257-303.

Nader, L. (Ed.). (1965). The ethnology of law. *American Anthropologist, 67* (Special Issue, Pt. 2).

Nash. J. (n.d.). The revindication of indigenous identity: Mayan responses to state intervention in Mexico. Unpublished paper.

Nash, M. (1966). *Primitive and peasant economic systems*. San Francisco: Chandler.

Nations, J. D. (1994). Zapatism and nationalism. *Cultural Survival Quarterly, 18*(1), 31-33.

Navarro, M. (1989). The personal is political: Las madres de la Plaza de Mayo. In S. Eckstein (Ed.), *Protest and resistance: Latin American experience*. Berkeley and Los Angeles: University of California Press.

Newson, L. A. (1988). *Indian survival in colonial Nicaragua*. Norman: University of Oklahoma Press.

Nietschmann, B. (1995). Defending the Miskito Reefs with maps & GPS. *Cultural Survival Quarterly* (Winter), 34-37.

Nimkoff, M. F., & Middleton, R. (1960). Types of family and types of economy. *American Journal of Sociology, 66*, 215-225.

Noble, D. (1984). *The forces of production*. New York: Knopf.

Nugent, D. (1994). Building the state, making the nation: The bases and limits of state centralization in "Modern Peru." *American Ethnologist, 96*, 333-369.

Obbo, C. (1988). Is AIDS just another disease? In R. Kulstad (Ed.), *AIDS 1988: American Association for the Advancement of Science Symposia Papers* (pp. 191-198). Washington, DC: AAAS.

O'Brien, D. (1984). Women never hunt: The portrayal of women in Melanesian ethnography. In D. O'Brien & S. Tiffany (Eds.), *Rethinking women's roles: Perspectives from the Pacific*. Berkeley and Los Angeles: University of California Press.

Odum, H. T. (1971). *Environment, power, and society*. New York: Wiley-Interscience.

———. (1992). *Energy and Public Policy*. New York: Wiley-Interscience.

Oliver, D. L. (1955). *A Solomon Island society: Kinship and leadership among the Siuai of Bougainville*. Cambridge, MA: Harvard University Press.

Ortner, S. B. (1989). *High religion: A cultural and political history of Sherpa Buddhism*. Princeton, NJ: Princeton University Press.

Otterbein, K. F. (1970). *The evolution of war: A cross-cultural study*. New Haven, CT: HRAF Press.

Parish, W. L. (1985). Introduction: Historical background and current issues. In W. L. Parish (Ed.), *Chinese Rural Development: The great transformation* (pp. 3-32). Armonk, NY: M.E. Sharpe.

Parker, R. G. (1987). Acquired immunodeficiency syndrome in urban Brazil. *Medical Anthropology Quarterly, 1*, 155-175.

———. (1988). Sexual culture and AIDS education in urban Brazil. In R. Kulstad (Ed.), *AIDS 1988: American Association for the Advancement of Science Symposia Papers* (pp. 169-174). Washington, DC: AAAS.

Parker, S. (1976). The precultural basis of the incest taboo: Toward a biosocial theory. *American Anthropologist, 78,* 285-301.

Pasternak, B. (1972). *Kinship and community in two Chinese villages.* Stanford, CA: Stanford University Press.

———. (1976). *Introduction to kinship and social organization.* Englewood Cliffs, NJ: Prentice Hall.

———. (1978). Seasons of birth and marriage in two Chinese localities. *Human Ecology, 6,* 299-324.

———. (1983). *Guests in the dragon: Social demography of a Chinese District, 1895-1946.* New York: Columbia University Press.

———. (1985). On the causes and consequences of uxorilocal marriage in China. In S. Hanley & A. Wolf (Eds.), *Family and population in East Asian history* (pp. 310-335). Stanford, CA: Stanford University Press.

Pasternak, B., & Wang Ching (1985). Breastfeeding decline in urban China: An exploratory study. *Human Ecology, 13,* 433-465.

Pasternak, B., & Salaff, J. (1993). *Cowboys and Cultivators: The Chinese of Inner Mongolia.* Boulder, CO: Westview.

Peacock, J. (1995). Claiming common ground. *Anthropology Newsletter, 36*(4), 1, 3.

Peacock, N. (1984). The Mbuti of Northeast Zaire: Women and subsistence exchange. *Cultural Survival Quarterly, 8,* 15-17.

Peet, R., & Watts, M. (1994). Introduction: Development theory & environmentalism in an age of market triumphalism. *Economic Geography, 69*(3), 227-253.

Pehrson, R. (1957). *The bilateral network of social relations in Kön Kämä Lapp District.* Bloomington: Indiana University Press.

Perlmutter, D. (1986). No nearer to the soul. *Natural Language and Linguistic Theory, 4,* 515-523.

Petkov, K., & Fotev, G. (1990). *Ethnic conflict in Bulgaria, 1989: Sociological archive.* (In Bulgarian with English summary.) Sofia: Profizdat.

Piaget, J. (1954). *The construction of reality in the child.* New York: Basic Books.

Pianka, E. R. (1974). *Evolutionary biology.* New York: Harper & Row.

Pinker, S. (1994). *The language instinct: How the mind creates language.* New York: HarperCollins.

Poggie, J. J., DeWalt, B. R., & Dressler, W. W. (1992). *Anthropological research: Process and application.* Albany: State University of New York Press.

Pojman, L. P. (1995). *Ethics: Discovering right and wrong.* Belmont, CA: Wadsworth.

Poole, P. (1995). Geomatics: Who needs it? *Cultural Survival Quarterly, 18*(4), 1.

Popkin, S. (1979). *The Rational Peasant.* Berkeley and Los Angeles: University of California Press.

Posey, D. (1983). Indigenous ecological knowledge and development. In E. Moran (Ed.), *The dilemma of Amazonian development* (pp. 225-257). Boulder, CO: Westview Press.

———. (1984). Ethnoecology as applied anthropology in Amazonian development. *Human Organization, 43,* 95-107.

Pospisil, L. J. (1963). *The Kapauku Papuans of West New Guinea.* New York: Holt, Rinehart & Winston.

Powdermaker, H. (1966). *Stranger and friend: The way of an anthropologist.* New York: Norton.

Price, D. (1981). Complexity in non-complex societies. In S. E. van der Leeuw (Ed.), *Archaeological approaches to the study of complex society* (pp. 57-97). Amsterdam: University of Amsterdam's Albert van Giffen Institute for Prehistory.

Putterman, L. (1981). Is a democratic collective agriculture possible? *Journal of Development Economics, 9,* 375-403.

Rabben, L. (1993). Demarcation and then what? *Cultural Survival Quarterly, 17*(2), 12-14.

Radcliffe-Brown, A. R. (1952). *Structure and functions in primitive society.* New York: Free Press.

Rapoport, A. (1981). "Realism" and "relevance" in gaming simulations. *Human Ecology, 9,* 137-150.

Rappaport, R. A. (1967). Ritual regulation of environmental relations among a New Guinea people. *Ethnology, 6,* 17-30.

———. (1968). *Pigs for the ancestors: Ritual in the ecology of a New Guinea people.* New Haven, CT: Yale University Press.

———. (1979). *Ecology, meaning, and religion.* Berkeley, CA: North Atlantic Books.

———. (1993). The anthropology of trouble. *American Anthropologist, 95,* 295-303.

Rasmussen, K. (1929). *Report of the fifth Thule expedition, 1921-1924* (Vol. 7, No. 1). *Intellectual Culture of the Iglulik Eskimos.* Copenhagen: Glydendalske Boghandel.

Redman, C. L. (1978). *The rise of civilization: From early farmers to urban society in the ancient Middle East.* San Francisco: Freeman.

Rensberger, B. (1989). Racial odyssey. In A. Podelefski & P. J. Brown (Eds.), *Applying anthropology: An introductory reader.* Mountain View, CA: Mayfield Press.

Reyna, S. P. (1993). Literary anthropology and the case against science. *Man, 29*(3), 555-581.

Reynolds, V., & Tanner, R. (1995). *The social ecology of religion.* Oxford: Oxford University Press.

Riegelhaupt, J. (1967). Saloio women: An analysis of informal and formal political and economic roles of Portuguese peasant women. *Anthropology Quarterly, 40,* 109-126.

Rigdon, S. M. (1988). *The culture facade: Art, science, and politics in the work of Oscar Lewis.* Urbana: University of Illinois Press.

Rindos, D. (1980). Symbiosis, instability, and the origins and spread of agriculture. *Current Anthropology, 21,* 751-765.

Rogers, E. M. (1962). *Diffusion of innovations*. New York: Free Press.

Rogers, E. M., & Shoemaker, F. F. (1971). *Communication of innovations: A cross-cultural approach*. New York: Free Press.

Romaine, S. (1994). *Language in society: An introduction to sociolinguistics*. New York: Oxford University Press.

Romanucci-Ross, L., Moerman, D. E., & Tancredi, L. R. (Eds.). (1991). *The anthropology of medicine: From culture to method* (2nd ed). Westport, CT: Bergin & Garvey.

Roosevelt, A. (1987). The evolution of human subsistence. In M. Harris and E. B. Ross (Eds.), *Food and evolution: Towards a theory of human food habits* (pp. 565-578). Philadelphia: Temple University Press.

Rostow, W. (1960). *The stages of economic growth: A Non-Communist manifesto*. Cambridge: Cambridge University Press.

Rubin, J., Flowers, N., & Gross, D. R. (1986). The adaptive dimensions of leisure time. *American Anthropologist, 13*, 524-536.

Rushforth, S., & Upham, S. (1993). *A Hopi social history*. Austin: University of Texas Press.

Rumbaugh, S. S., & Lewis, R. (1994). *The ape at the brink of the human mind*. New York: Wiley.

Rutz, H. J. (Ed.). (1992). The politics of time. *American Ethnographic Society Monograph Series*, no. 4.

Safa, H. I. (1974). *The urban poor of Puerto Rico: A study in development and inequality*. New York: Holt, Rinehart & Winston.

Saffirio, J., & Hammer, R. (1983). The forest and the highway. In *The impact of contact: Two Yanomamö case studies*. (Report No.11), pp. 3-48. Cambridge, MA: Cultural Survival.

Sahlins, M. D. (1961). The segmentary lineage: An organization of predatory expansion. *American Anthropologist, 63*, 332-345.

———. (1963). Poor man, rich man, big man, chief: Political types in Melanesia and Polynesia. *Comparative Studies in Society and History, 5*, 285-303.

———. (1965). On the sociology of primitive exchange. In *The relevance of models for social anthropology*. Association of Social Anthropologist (Monograph No. 1). New York: Praeger.

———. (1968). *Tribesmen*. Englewood Cliffs, NJ: Prentice Hall.

———. (1972). *Stone Age economics*. Chicago: Aldine.

Salamon, S. (1992). *Prairie patrimony: Family, farming and community in the Midwest*. Chapel Hill: University of North Carolina Press.

Salzman, P. C. (1971). Movement and resource extraction among pastoral nomads: The case of the Shah Nawazi Baluch. *Anthropological Quarterly, 44*, 185-197.

———. (1980). *When nomads settle: Processes of adaptation and response*. New York: Praeger.

Sanjek, R. (1977). Cognitive maps of the ethnic domain in urban Ghana: Reflections on variability and change. *American Ethnologist, 4*, 603-622.

Sankoff, G. (1972). *A quantitative paradigm for the study of communicative competence*. Paper prepared for the Conference on the Ethnography of Speaking, Austin, Texas, April 20-23.

Sapir, E. (1921). *Language: An introduction to the study of speech*. New York: Harcourt Brace and World.

———. (1929). The status of linguistics as a science. *Language, 5*, 207-214.

Sargent, C., & Harris, M. (1992). Gender ideology, child rearing, and child health in Jamaica. *American Ethnologist, 19*, 523-537.

Saunders, L., & Mehenna, S. (1986). Village entrepreneurs: An Egyptian case. *Ethnology, 25*, 75-88.

Schama, S. (1987). *An embarrassment of riches*. New York: Knopf.

Scheper-Hughes, N. (1979). The Margaret Mead controversy: Culture, biology, and anthropological inquiry. *Human Organization, 43*, 443-454.

Schick, K. D., & Toth, N. (1993). *Making silent stones speak: Human evolution and the dawn of technology*. New York: Simon & Schuster.

Schneider, B. E. (1988). Gender and AIDS. In R. Kulstad (Ed.), *AIDS 1988: American Association for the Advancement of Science Symposia Papers* (pp. 97-106). Washington, DC: AAAS.

Schneider, D. M., & Gough, K. (Eds.). (1961). *Matrilineal kinship*. Berkeley and Los Angeles: University of California Press.

Schneider, H. K. (1970). *The Wahi Wanyaturu: Economics in an African society*. Viking Fund Publications in Anthropology (No.48). Chicago: Aldine.

———. (1974). *Economic man: The anthropology of economics*. New York: Free Press.

Schoepf, B. G., wa Nkera, R., Ntsomo, P., Engundu, W., & Schoepf, C. (1988). AIDS, women, and society in Central Africa. In R. Kulstad (Ed.), *AIDS 1988: American Association for the Advancement of Science Symposia Papers* (pp. 175-182). Washington, DC: AAAS.

Schrire, C. (1984). Wild surmises in savage thoughts. In C. Schrire (Ed.), *Past and present in hunter-gatherer societies*. Orlando, FL: Academic Press.

Scott, J. C. (1976). *The moral economy of the peasant*. New Haven, CT: Yale University Press.

Service, E. R. (1971). *Primitive social organization: An evolutionary perspective* (2nd ed). New York: Random House.

Sheets, P. (1989). Dawn of a new Stone Age. In A. Podolefsky & P. J. Brown (Eds.), *Applying anthropology: An introductory reader*. Mountain View, CA: Mayfield Press.

Shepher, J. (1983). *Incest: A biosocial view*. New York: Academic Press.

Sheridan, T. E. (1988). *Where the dove calls: The political ecology of a peasant corporate community in Northwestern Mexico*. Tucson: University of Arizona Press.

Shreeve, J. (1994). Terms of estrangement. *Discover, 15*(11), 56-63.

Sidel, R. (1986). *Women and children lost*. New York: Viking-Penguin.

Simon, H. A. (1966). *Models of man: Social and rational; Mathematical essays on rational human behavior in a social setting*. New York: Wiley.

Sims, C. (1995, March 25). Argentina to issue new list of missing in "Dirty War." *New York Times*, p. 4.

Slobodkin, L. B. (1968). Toward a predictive theory of evolution. In R. C. Lewontin (Ed.), *Population biology and evolution*. Syracuse, NY: Syracuse University Press.

Smil, V. (1984). *The bad earth*. Armonk, NY: M. E. Sharpe.

———. (1994, May 30). A land stretching to support its people. *Herald Tribune* (international ed.), p. 8.

Smith, A. (1994). For all those who were Indian in a former life. *Cultural Survival Quarterly* (Winter), 70-72.

Smith, E. A., & Winterhalder, B. (Eds.). (1992). *Evolutionary ecology and human behavior*. New York: Aldine de Gruyter.

Smith, R. (1984). Social class. In *Annual review of anthropology* (pp. 467-494). Palo Alto, CA: Annual Reviews.

Soffer, O., Vandiver, P., & Klima, B. (1995). Paleolithic ceramics and clay objects from Pavlov I. Paper presented to Society for American Anthropology, May 4, Minneapolis.

Sorensen, C. W. (1988). *Over the mountains are mountains: Korean peasant households and their adaptation to rapid industrialization*. Seattle: University of Washington Press.

Southwold, M. (1965). The Ganda of Uganda. In J. L. Gibbs, Jr.(Ed.), *Peoples of Africa*. New York: Holt, Rinehart & Winston.

Spears, A. K. (1991). Teaching race, racism and ideology. *Transforming Anthropology*, 2, 16-18.

Spence, J. (1988). *The question of Hu*. New York: Knopf.

Speth, J. D. (1988). *Seasonality, resource stress, and food sharing in egalitarian foraging societies*. Paper presented at the Symposium Coping with Seasonal Constraints, 86th Annual Meeting of the American Anthropological Association, Chicago, 1987.

Spiro, M. (1992). Cultural relativism and the future of anthropology. In G. Marcus (Ed.), *Rereading cultural anthropology*. Durham, NC: Duke University Press.

Spiro, M. E. (1952). Ghosts, Ifaluk, and teleological functionalism. *American Anthropologist, 54*, 495-503.

Stacey, J. (1991). *Brave new families: Stories of domestic upheaval in late twentieth century America*. New York: Basic Books.

Stephan, C. W., & Stephan, W. C. (1985). *Two social psychologies*. Homewood, IL: Dorsey Press.

Stevens, W. K. (1994, January 18). Threat of encroaching deserts may be more myth than fact. *New York Times*, pp. C1-C10.

Steward, J. (1953). Evolution and process. In A. L. Kroeber (Ed.), *Anthropology today*. Chicago: University of Chicago Press.

———. (1972). *Theory of culture change: The methodology of multilinear evolution*. Urbana: University of Illinois Press.

Stoffle, R. W., Halmo, D. B., Wagner, T. W., & Luczkovich, J. L. (1994). Reefs from space: Satellite imagery, marine ecology, and ethnography in the Dominican Republic. *Human Ecology, 22*(3), 355-378.

Stone, P. M., Stone G. D., & Netting, R. M. C. (1995). The sexual division of labor in Kofyar agriculture. *American Ethnologist, 22*(1), 165-186.

Stringer, C. & Bauer, G. (1994). Methods, misreading and bias. *American Anthropologist, 96*(2), 416-424.

Stringer, C., & Gamble, C. (1994). *In search of the Neanderthals: Solving the puzzle of human origins*. London: Thames & Hudson.

Sturtevant, W. C., & Damas, D. (Eds.). *1984 Handbook of North American Indians, Vol. 5: Arctic*. Washington, DC: Smithsonian Institution.

Susser, I. (1986). Work and reproduction: Sociologic context. *Occupational Medicine: State of the Art Reviews, 1*, 517-530.

———. (1989). Gender in the anthropology of the United States. In S. Morgan (Ed.), *Gender and anthropology: Critical reviews for research and teaching* (pp. 343-358). Washington, DC: American Anthropological Association.

Sussman, R. W., Green, G. M., & Sussman, L. K. (1994). Satellite imagery, human ecology, anthropology, and deforestation in Madagascar. *Human Ecology, 22*(3), 333-354.

Swanson, G. E. (1960). *The birth of the gods: The origin of primitive beliefs*. Ann Arbor: University of Michigan Press.

Sweet, L. E. (1965). Camel pastoralism in North Arabia and the minimal camping unit. In A. Leeds & A. P. Vayda (Eds.), *Man, culture, and animals: The role of animals in human ecological adjustment* (Publication No. 78). Washington, DC: American Association for the Advancement of Science.

Swift, J. (1974). The future of Tuareg pastoral nomadism in the Malian Sahel. Paper presented at the SSRC Symposium on the Future of Traditional Societies.

Tainter, J. (1988). *The collapse of civilization*. Cambridge: Cambridge University Press.

Tannen, D. (1994). *Talking from 9 to 5: How women's and men's conversational styles affect who gets heard, who gets credit, and what work gets done*. New York: Morrow.

Tapper, R. (1979). *Pasture and politics*. London: Academic Press.

Tekeli, S. (Ed.). (1994). *Women in modern Turkish society*. London: Zed Books.

Thomas, D. H. (1986). *Refiguring anthropology*. Prospect Heights, IL: Waveland Press.

Thompson, L. (1950). *Culture in crisis: A study of the Hopi Indians*. New York: Harper & Row.

Thompson, L., & Joseph, A. (1947). *The Hopi way*. Chicago: University of Chicago Press.

Tierney, J., Wright, L., & Springen, K. (1988, January 11). The search for Adam and Eve. *Newsweek*.

Trevathan, W. R. (1987). *Human birth: An evolutionary perspective*. Hawthorne, NY: Aldine.

Tsiang, H. (1884). S. Bell (trans.), *Buddhist records of the Western world* (Vol. 1). London: Trubner. Reprinted in and cited from C. Coon (Ed.), *A reader in general anthropology* (pp. 452-463). New York: Holt, 1948.

Turnbull, C. (1961). *The forest people*. New York: Simon & Schuster.

————. (1965). The Mbuti Pygmies of the Congo. In J. L. Gibbs, Jr. (Ed.), *Peoples of Africa*. New York: Holt, Rinehart & Winston.

Turner, V. W. (1967). *The forest of symbols: Aspects of Ndembu ritual*. Ithaca, NY: Cornell University Press.

Tyler, P. E. (1994, March 27). Nature and economic boom devouring China's farmland. *New York Times*, pp. A1-A8.

————. (1995, April 10). On the farms, China could be sowing disaster. *New York Times*, p. A4.

Tyler, S. (1987). *The unspeakable: Discourse, dialogue, and rhetoric in the postmodern world*. Madison: University of Wisconsin Press.

Tylor, E. B. (1871). *Primitive culture: Researches into the development of mythology, philosophy, religion, language, art, and custom* (2 vols., 2nd ed.). London: John Murray.

USAID. (1982). Sudan: The Rahad irrigation project. Impact Evaluation Report No. 31. Washington, DC.

U.S. Public Health Service. (1986). *The Coolfont Report. Public Health Report 101*.

Van Gennep, A. (1960). *The rites of passage*. Chicago: University of Chicago Press.

Vayda, A. P. (1974). Warfare in an ecological perspective. *Annual Review of Ecology and Systematics, 5*, 183-193.

————. (1976). *Warfare in ecological perspective*. New York: Plenum.

————. (1987). Explaining what people eat: A review article. *Human Ecology, 15*, 493-510.

Verdery, K. (1992). The etatization of time in Ceausescu's Romania. In H. J. Ruts (Ed.) *The politics of time* (pp. 37-61). *American Ethnological Society Monograph Series, No. 4*. Washington, DC: American Anthropological Association.

Vondal, P. J. (1987). Intensification through diversified resource use: The human ecology of a successful agricultural industry in Indonesian Borneo. *Human Ecology, 15*, 27-52.

Wallace, A. F. C. (1966). *Religion: An anthropological view*. New York: Random House.

————. (1970). *The death and rebirth of the Seneca*. New York: Knopf.

Washabaugh, W. (1986). *Five fingers for survival*. Ann Arbor, MI: Karoma.

Weiner, A. B. (1976). *Women of value, men of renown: New perspectives in Trobriand exchange*. Austin: University of Texas Press.

————. (1988). *The Trobrianders of Papua New Guinea*. New York: Holt, Rinehart & Winston.

————. (1992). *Inalienable possessions*. Berkeley and Los Angeles: University of California Press.

Weisman, S. (1988, January 29). Where births are kept down and aren't. *New York Times*, p. 4.

Wells, M. (1987). Sharecropping in the United States: A political economy perspective. In M. Chibnik (Ed.), *Farm work and fieldwork: American agriculture in anthropological perspective* (pp. 211-243). Ithaca, NY: Cornell University Press.

Werner, D., Flowers, N., Ritter, M., & Gross, G, (1979). Subsistence productivity and hunting effort in native South America. *Human Ecology, 7*, 303-315.

Westermarck, E. A. (1922). *The history of human marriage* (3 vols.). New York: Allerton. (First published 1889.)

Weston, K. (1991). *Families we chose: Lesbians, gays, kinship*. New York: Columbia University Press.

White, J. (1994). *Money makes us relatives: Women's labor in urban Turkey*. Austin: University of Texas Press.

White, L. (1949). *The Science of culture*. New York: Farrar, Straus & Cudahy.

Whiteley, P. M. (1985). Unpacking Hopi clans: Another vintage model out of Africa. *Journal of Anthropological Research, 41*, 359-374.

————. (1988). *Deliberate acts: Changing Hopi culture through the Oraibi Split*. Tucson: University of Arizona Press.

Whiting, B. B. (Ed.). (1963). *Six cultures: Studies of child bearing*. New York: Wiley.

Whiting, B. B., & Whiting, J. W. (1973). Methods for observing and recording behavior. In R. Naroll & R. Cohen (Eds.), *A handbook of method in cultural anthropology*. New York: Columbia University Press.

————. (1974). *Children of six cultures: A psycho-cultural analysis*. Cambridge, MA: Harvard University Press.

Whiting, J. W., & Child, I. L. (1953). *Child training and personality: A cross-cultural study*. New Haven, CT: Yale University Press.

Whorf, B. L. (1956). The relation of habitual thought and behavior to language. In *Language, thought, and reality: Selected writings of Benjamin Lee Whorf*. Cambridge, MA: MIT Press.

Wikan, U. (1992). Beyond the words: The power of resonance. *American Ethnologist, 19*, 460-482.

Wilcox, S., Wilbers, S. (1987). The case for academic acceptance of American sign language. *Chronicle of Higher Education, 33*, 1.

Wilk, R. R. (1991). *Household ecology: Economic change and domestic life among the Kekchi Maya of Belize*. Tucson: University of Arizona Press.

Wilkie, D., & Curran, B. (1993). Historical trends in forager and farmer exchange in the Ituri rain forest of Northeastern Zaire. *Human Ecology, 21*, 389-417.

Williams, T. R. (1967). *Field methods in the study of culture*. New York: Holt, Rinehart & Winston.

Williams, W. L. (1986). *The spirit and the flesh: Sexual diversity in American Indian culture*. Boston: Beacon.

Wilmsen, E. N. (1989a). *Land filled with flies: A political economy of the Kalahari*. Chicago: University of Chicago Press.

———. (1989b). *We are here: Politics of Aboriginal land tenure*. Berkeley and Los Angeles: University of California Press.

Wilson, A., Ochman, H., & Prager, M. E. (1987). Molecular time scale for evolution. *Trends in Genetics, 3*, 241-247.

Wilson, E. O. (1993, May 30). Is humanity suicidal? *New York Times Magazine*, pp. 24ff.

Wisner, B. The reconstruction of environmental rights in South Africa. *Human Ecology, 23*(3).

Wolf, E. R. (1966). *Peasants*. Englewood Cliffs, NJ: Prentice Hall.

———. (1982). *Europe and the people without history*. Berkeley and Los Angeles: University of California Press.

———. (1990). Facing power: Old insights, new questions. *American Anthropologist, 92*, 586-596.

———. (1994). Demonization of anthropologist in the Amazon. *Anthropology Newsletter* (March), 2.

Woods, C. M., & Graves, T. D. (1973). *The process of medical change in a highland Guatemalan town*. Los Angeles: Latin American Center, University of California.

Worsley, P. (1968). *The trumpet shall sound: A study of cargo cults in Melanesia*. New York: Schocken.

Wright, H. T., & Johnson, G. A. (1975). Population, exchange, and early state formation in Southwestern Iran. *American Anthropologist, 77*, 267-289.

Wright, R. (1994). *The moral animal*. New York: Pantheon.

Yellen, J. E., & Lee, R. B. (1976). The Dobe-/Du/da environment: Background to a hunting and gathering way of life. In R. B. Lee (Ed.), *Kalahari hunter-gatherers*. Cambridge, MA: Harvard University Press.

Zentella, A. C. (1988). Language politics in the USA: The English only movement. In *Literature, language and politics* (pp. 39-53). Athens: University of Georgia Press.

Index

the Aborigines of Australia, 102, 302
Abramson, Allen, 42
Abruzzi, William, 68, 292
Abu-Lughod, Lila, 15
Abu-Rabia, Aref, 164
acculturation
    defined, 136
    among Yanomamö, 136
the Ache of Paraguay, 98
acid rain, 364. *See also* pollution.
adaptation, 70
    and culture, 35–36, 81–82
    and selection, 63–64
    of species, 70–71
    of Vikings to Atlantic settlements, 82–83
    of Yörük, 168–169
    to change, 376
    to environmental problems, 75–79
    to other groups, 79–81
"adaptive plasticity" of trait, 65
adjudication, methods of, 324
administration of state, 315–316
administrative system, 187
adultery, 133–134, 144
affinal kin, 211
African human origins, 62–63
age grades, defined, 43, 162
age roles, learning, 42–43
age sets, 162
Agrawal, Arun, 156
agribusiness, 199
agricultural energy use, 124–125
agriculture
    and pastoralism, 142–143
    and resource control, 123
    industrial, 74, 182–187
the Agta of the Philippines, 98
AIDS, 9, 10–11, 12–13, 378
the Ainu of Hokkaido (Japan), 62, 99
Alaska Federation of Natives, 117

Alaska, post-Cold War, 117
"Albanian virgins," 41
Alcock, James, 334
alienation, defined, 282
the Aloui sect (Syria), 380
Amazon acculturation, 79, 136–137. *See also* Kayapo; Mundurcu; Yanomamö.
Amazon deforestation (Brazil), 80. *See also* rainforest destruction; Yanomamö.
Amazon gold rush (1985), 137
ambilineal descent, 220–221
ambilocality, 232
American Anthropological Association (AAA), 13
    and AIDS, 73
American Indian languages, 51
American National Academy of Sciences, 371
American Sign Language (ASL), 44, 45, 48, 49
Anasazi Pueblo Indians, 78
Ancient Society (Morgan), 16
the Andaman Islanders of India, 99
Anderson, Benedict, 263, 264, 269
animal traction for plowing, 139, 177
animatism, 336
animism, 336
Annis, Sheldon, 338–339
anthropology, defined, 5, 8
anxiety reduction rituals, 19
apartheid, 261, 372–373
ape language, 44–45
Appell, George, 381
the Ariaal of Kenya, 43, 78, 156, 157, 158, 160–165, 223–224, 226
    division of labor among, 242
    economy of, 273, 274
Arabic language, 51
Aral Sea, drying of, 84
arboriculture, 177
archaeology, 6
arctic ecosystem, 111. *See also* Inuit, Vikings.
Atomic Energy Commission, 117

Atrek River, 307
Aum Shinrikyo, 242
Australian Central Desert foods, 94
the Australopiths, 74
authority, defined, 306
Avital, Eytan, 38
avunculocal residence, 232

the Baggara of the Sudan, 251
balanced reciprocity, 290
Balinese irrigation control, 275, 348
bands, defined, 312
bands (foraging groups), 98–99
the Bantu of Zaire, 96, 124
barbarism stage (Morgan), 16
bar mitzvah, 343
Barnet, Richard J., 363
Barth, Frederik, 72, 251, 262
the Basarwa of Africa, 92, 103
the Batak of the Philippines, 92, 100–102
Bates, Daniel, 168
Batuta, Ibn, 176
Beals, Alan, 260
beaver skin market, 97
the Bedouin of Arabia, 150, 152, 153, 156, 157, 225, 317
    conflict among, 327–328
    pastoralism of, 164
    peace mechanisms of, 326
the Bedouin of Egypt, 15
behavior
    and biology, 37–38
    and learning, 5, 37–38
    and material culture, 6
behavioral "inheritance," 64–65
belief systems, 336–337
    and social boundaries, 339
    organization of, 337–339
The Bell Curve: Intelligence and Class Structure in American Life (Herrnstein and Murray), 261
Benedict, Ruth, 17
berdache, 40–41
bilateral descent, 221–222
bilingualism, and U.S. politics, 54–55
bilocal residence, 232
Binford, Lewis, 63
biological anthropology, defined, 6
biological inheritance, 64
biological race, 249
biological variability, 126
bisexuality in Brazil, 378
Bitnet, 366
Black English dialect, 54
Black Power movement, 210
Blackwood, Evelyn, 41
blood, as food, 77
blood feud, 321
the Blue Revolution, 185
Boas, Franz, 17
bondage to the land, 140
Boone, James, 310

the Boran of Kenya, 161
Borneo entrepreneurship, 295
Boserup, Esther, 286–287
Bosnia, 264, 266
Bosnian massacres, 263
Bosnian Muslims, 340
Boulding, Kenneth, 273
Bourguiba, Habib, 246
Brace, C. Loring, 62, 249
Bradburd, Ann, 23
Bradburd, Daniel, 23, 156
Bray, Francesca, 176–177, 185
Brazilian peasant migration, 194
the Brazilian sertao, 186
bride kidnapping, 226–227
bride price, 226–227
bride service, 106, 133–134, 226
bridewealth, 163, 215, 226
Briggs, Jean, 113
British Sign Language, 48
Brooke, James, 275
Buddhism, 141
Buddhist lamas, 142
the Buganda of Central Africa, 278
Bulgarian ethnicity, 263
Bulgarian Moslems, language, 56
Bulgarian Socialist Party, 315
bullying in schools, 39
the Bunyoro of Uganda, 325–326
Burakumi (Japan) caste, 262
Burbank, Victoria, 301
bureaucracy, 315
Burke and Wills expedition (Australia), 102
Burkinabà government, 382
Burkina Faso (Upper Volta), 382
Burundi, 11, 178
the Bushong of Africa, 287

call system, as language source, 43
Cameroon (West Africa) tontine, 274
camp groups and household organization, 153–154
camp herds, among pastoralists, 168
Cann, Rebecca, 62
capital goods, control of, 280–281
capitalist mode of production and society, 21
cargo cults, 255
caribou as food, 112
carrying capacity of an environment, 75
cash crops, 186
castelike stratification, 260–261
caste stratification, 259
Catholic Church, 337, 338–339
Catholic-Mayan religious ritual, 340
Catholic Passion Plays, 341
cattle complex, 348
Cavalli-Sforza, Luigi, 249
Ceausescu, Nikolae, 323
centralization, 187–189
    in cultural change, 84
ceremonial chambers (kivas), 216

Chagnon, Napoleon, 26, 129–137, 210
Chance, Norman, 117
change
    and internal conflict, 21
    resilience in, 376, 381
    See also adaptation.
Charles, Prince, of Great Britain, 138
Cheal, David, 224
Cherifati-Merabtine, Doria, 246
Chernobyl nuclear fires, 364
chewar, first haircut (Nepal), 144
Chiapas, Mexico, uprising, 194, 281
Chicanos in California, 193
chiefdoms, 312–314
Chinese communes, 188–189
Chinese immigrant labor, 192
Chinese peasantry, 194
Chinese urbanization, 362
Ching, Wang, 183
Chomsky, [Noam], 71
Christianity, in Nepal, 145
Christian missionaries in Kenya, 164
Christian ritual, 340, 341
chronic famine, 176
the Chumash Indians, 99
circumcision, 71, 343. *See also* clitoridectomy.
city expansion, 189–191
civilization stage (Morgan), 16
clan law, 322
clans, 218
    among the Hopi, 216
    among the Temang, 141, 144
Clarke, Lee, 373, 374
classical economic theory, 272
classification of kin, 211
class interests, 258
class, perceptions of, 258
class stratification, 170, 191, 256–257
    and sisal, 187
Clement VI, Pope, 351
clergy, 347
clitoridectomy, 341, 343
    among Ariaal, 162
clothing and cold (Inuit), 112
clown cult (Hopi), 217
club fights, among Yanomamö, 134–135
coffee as cash crop, 286–287
cognates, 50
collateral relatives, 212
collectivization, 187–189
    and land use, 277
Collins, Thomas, 255
Collor, president of Brazil, 137
Coming of Age in Samoa (Mead), 18
commercial farming, 278
communal marriage, 16
communes, defined, 187
    in China, 188–189
communication
    among humans. *See* language.

among other animals, 44–45
communication technology and Inuit, 116
communism, 187–189
Communist Party in Bulgaria, 265–266, 365–366
communist peasantry, 195
Communist Revolution of 1949 (China), 188
competition for resources, 309
complexity and stability, 86
computing power, 362
Conant, Francis, 369
conflict reduction and religion, 350–351
conjugal relationship, 233
consanguineal kin, 211
consensual decisions, 302
conservationism and pastoralism, 165
cooperation
    and horticulture, 128–129
    for resources, 309–310
Cook, Scott, 274
conversion (exchange) of resources, 293–294
coping, and religion, 350
co-resident households, 154–155
Corn Dance, 217
cousin marriage, 229
cowboys of Mongolia, 154–155
Craige, B. J., 55
Crapanzano, Vincent, 9
creation myth, 334
Creed, Gerald, 294
Creole language, 52
Croatia, 264, 266, 340
cross cousins, 212
cross-gender roles, 40–41. *See also* berdache.
Crow Indian vision quest, 345
Cucurpe, Mexico, 278–280
cultural adaptation, 70–71
cultural anthropology, 7–8
cultural centrism, 8–9
cultural change, long-term, 83–86
cultural complexity and stability, 86
cultural contact, 51
cultural ecology, 20
cultural evolution, 15–16
cultural functionalism, 21
cultural materialism, 21
cultural patterns, 7–8
cultural relativism, 8
cultural resilience and complexity, 86
"cultural success," 65
culture, defined, 5, 33, 34–36
"cyberculture," 365–366

dams and environmental damage, 370, 380
data analysis, 27–28
data collection in field, 22–27
Darwin, Charles, 4–5, 63–64
Davis, Wade, 93, 352
decision-making processes, 72, 302–306
    among Raika pastoralists, 156
    among the Pokot, 214–215

deforestation, 78–81, 93
de Magalhaes de Gandávo, Pedro, 40–41
demographic transition, defined, 182
demography
    of Inuit, 113
    of Ju/'hoansi, 108
depression, 39
descent groups, 213–214
descent ideology, 213
development anthropology, 378–379
development, managing, 381
desertification and pastoralism, 165
De Vos, George, 261–262
dialectical materialism, 21
dialects, 48–49
the Dinka of Sudan, 380
dioxin, 374
"the disappeared," 318–319
diversification, 150
diversity
    in humans, 4
    in livestock, 160–161
division of labor and gender, 97–98
divination, 336
divorce, 223, 225
DNA and evolution study, 62–63
Dobe Basarwa. See Dobe !Kung.
the Dobe !Kung Ju/'hoansi of the Kalahari, 61–62, 92, 94,
        96, 102, 104–105, 109–110, 228, 277, 290, 312
the Dobe Ju/'hoansi. See Dobe !Kung.
Dobe (San) people. See Dobe !Kung.
domestic cycle, 233
    of Timling, 143
domestic herds, 160
domestic mode of production, 282–283
domestic settlements of Ariaal, 161
Dominican Republic coral reefs, 368–369
Dore, Ronald, 195
Dove, Michael, 284–285, 348
dowry, 227. See also bridewealth.
dual-career families, 224
Dubos, Renc, 376
dueling songs (Eskimo), 98
Durkheim, Émile, 16, 19, 242, 272, 337, 350
Dust Bowl era, 194
the Dyak of Borneo, 93
Dyak-Penan region (Borneo), 93
dying, myths of, 335

East Africa, 157
eastern Europe, retirement age in, 287–288
ecology
    and postindustrialism, 366
    of politics, 309–311
    See also environment and adaptation.
Econet, 366
economic anthropology, 273
economic behavior concepts, 252–274
economic class, defined, 275
economic organization diversity, 274–275

economics and politics, 312
economic specialization, interlocking, 275
economic stratification, defined, 170
ecosystems
    defined, 67
    and human impact on, 69
ecstatic cults, 346
Eder, James, 100–102
edible seeds, table of, 95
the Efe of Zaire, 79
"egalitarian" societies, 312
ego kin, 212
Egyptian entrepreneurship, 295–296
Egyptian feminism, 247
Egyptian household labor, 284
Egyptian peasantry, 194
El Haddad, Taher, 246
El Salvador birth rate, 182
elopement among Yörük, 226–227
Ember, Carol, 228, 327
Ember, Melvin, 327
empiricism, 14–15
enculturation, 37
endogamy, 230
energy consumption, 366–368
energy organization, 93–97, 151
energy use
    among Baffin Island Inuit, 114
    in Timling, Nepal, 143
    of agriculture, 124–125
    of Inuit, 112–113
Engels, Friedrich, 16
entrepreneurship, 201, 294–297
environmental resilience, 181
environmental change, 181
environmental destruction
    in Amazon, 80
    in South Africa, 372–373
environmental uncertainty, 310
environment and adaptation, 70–72, 160
epidemics after acculturation, 137
Escobar, Arturo, 386
Eskimo dueling songs, 98
Eskimo earning, 37
Eskimo foods, 94
Eskimo people. See Inuit.
Eskimo shamanism, 346
Eskimo trade items, 96
ethics of development work, 386
Ethiopia, 78
"ethnic cleansing," 263
ethnic conflict, 281
ethnicity
    defined, 250–257
    as response to state, 266
ethnic massacres, 263–266
ethnocentrism, defined, 9
Ethnographic Atlas, 92
the ethnographic present, 92
ethnography, defined, 7–8

ethnology, defined, 7, 8
European anthropology, 4
European Community, 191
European Union, 364
Evans-Pritchard, E. E., 153
"evil eye," 346–347
evolution
    and human culture, 64
    cultural, 16
    focus in anthropology, 4
    of family, 16
    of social behavior, 64–65
    of state, 315–316
    unilineal, 16
evolutionary ecology, defined, 62
exchange of resources, 272, 284, 288–294
exogamy, 229–230
exorcism, 346
extended family households, 233–235
    and extensive agriculture, 124–125
    in Timling, 143
Exxon *Valdez* spill, 372–375

fallow time, 180. *See also* swidden plots.
family
    farms, 200–202
    evolution of, 16
    households, 233–236
    planning, 133
farming and land ownership, 278
farm workers, as machine parts, 199
fax machines, 365
Feit, Harvey, 347
female infanticide, 113, 133–134, 209
female circumcision, 9, 10. *See also* clitoridectomy.
female genital mutilation, 9, 10
female speech patterns, 53–54
femininity, 40–42
feminist Muslims, 246–247
Ferguson, Brian, 136
fertility and population
    among Dobe Ju/'hoansi, 108–109
    among Nepalese, 144
fertility of soil, 176
fertilization and food, 78–79
feuds, among Yanomamö, 133
fictive kinship, 211
field log, 25
fieldwork, 22–27
Fisher, Helene, 225
Flinn, Mark, 5
Flowers, Nancy, 25, 26
food supply and adaptation, 71, 73–74
forage conversion to energy, 151
foraging, 73
    groups, organization of, 97–98
    patterns and settlement, 105
forced assimilation of ethnics, 263
forecasting the future, 361–385
formalism (in economic theory), 273

formal sanctions, 320
fossil fuels, 184
fossil record and evolution, 5
Frank, Robert, 341
Franklin, Sir John, 102
Fratkin, Elliot, 158, 165
freehold ownership of property, 276
freeholders vs. peasantry, 140
Freeman, Derek, 42
Freilich, Morris, 35
French Sign Language, 48
Freud, Sigmund, 15–16, 229
Fricke, Thomas, 140, 144–145
Front Islamique de Salut (FIS), 246
Fry, Peggy, 77
the Fuel Age, 178
functionalism, 18–20. *See also* structural functionalism.
the Fur of the Sudan, 251

Gaelic language revival, 56
the Gainj of New Guinea, 286–287
Galvin, Kathleen, 77
Gardner, Alan and Beatrice, 44
Geertz, Clifford, 12, 15, 334
gender
    and productivity, 284–288
    and property rights, 278
    and wealth, 344
    hierarchies, 245
    issues, 28
"gender-egalitarian" society, 3–4
gender roles, 36–37, 244–248
    among Ariaal, 162–163
    and language, 53
    in Inner Mongolia, 155
    in mortuary rites, 344
    learning, 40
generalized reciprocity, 280–290
genetics and natural selection, 64
genital mutilation, 9, 10
genotype, defined, 249
geographic information systems, 368
German language in United States, 55
ghost dance, 354
Gilmore, David, 34, 41–42, 321
givers (*giagia*) of New Guinea, 305
Glenny, Mischa, 266
globalization, 9, 365, 366
    and AIDS, 10–11
global positioning systems, 368
global specialization, 186
the Göklan Turkmen, 306–309
Goldschmidt, Walter, 197
Gopalpur (India), 260
Gorkin, Michael, 253, 255
Gorman, E. Michael, 10
gossip, 320–321
Gould, Stephen Jay, 63
grammar, 47
grazing rights, 279–280

the Great Wall of China, 154
Greenberg, Joseph, 51
the Green Revolution, 185, 186
Gregor, Thomas, 41
Grimm, Jakob and Wilhelm, 50
Gross, Daniel, 24
group marriage, 223
grower class, 199
Guatemalan Protestants, 338–339
Guinier, Lani, 249
Gujarat, 156
guns, use of, 115

habitat (species), 69
the Hadza of Tanzania, 108
the Haj, 342, 350
Hammer, Raymond, 137
Han Chinese in Mongolia, 154–155
Handsome Lake (prophet), 355
Harris, Marvin, 21, 155, 348
Hart, Teresa and John, 5
headman, defined, 132
Hebrew language revival, 56
Herrnstein, Richard, 261
Herskovits, Melville, 157
heterosexual AIDS transmission, 10, 378
hierarchical tribal organization, 155–156
hijab dress code, 246
Hindu caste beliefs, 259–260
historical particularism, 17
HIV carriers, 11. See also AIDS.
holism, in anthropology, 8
Homo sapiens sapiens, 4
homosexual culture and AIDS, 10
homosexual family, 212
the Hopi of Arizona, 40, 208, 216–217, 218, 219
    marriage, 223
    spirits (Katchina), 217
Hopkins, Nicholas, 284
horizontal migration, 152
Horowitz, Michael, 12
horticultural communities, 129
horticultural cultivation, 125–126
horticulture, 124
household labor
    and gender, 284–287
    in Egypt, 284
household production and gender, 286–287
households
    among Ariaal, 162
    as productive unit, 282–283
Hudson Bay Netsilik Eskimo, 111–113
human adaptation to change, 69–70
human nature as cultural artifact, 18
human ecosystems, 66–70
human evolution, 62–63
human labor as energy, 179
"human materialism," 21
human rights and cultural relativism, 9
hunting and subsistence farming, 132
hunting territory warfare, 135

hydroelectric projects, 370
Hyndman, David, 126, 127
hypothesis, defined, 14

Ibn-Khaldun, 4, 242
the Ibo of Nigeria, 252
impact assessment and evaluation, 381–382
incest taboo, 229
independent households, 233
inequality
    and pastoralism, 156–157
    and social conflict, 21
India
    Andaman Islanders of, 99
    castes in, 259–260
    development in, 297
    Raika people of, 156
Ingold, Tim, 151
industrial agriculture, 74, 182–187
industrial organization changes, 362
industrialization and underdevelopment, 21
industrialization, costs and benefits of, 362
informal sanctions, 320
infibulation, 341
Inner Mongolia, 154–155
innovation, 36
institutions of society, defined, 18–19
integration of culture, 35. See also holism.
intelligence gap in diverse societies, 261–262
intensive vs. extensive agriculture, 74, 124–125,
        175–178, 182
intensification in cultural change, 83, 183–185
internal social conflict, 70
Internet, 366
intrakibbutz marriage, 229
invention, 36
invisibility, achieving, 28
the Inuit (Eskimo), 92, 110–116, 117
Inupiat Inuit, 116, 117
Iran-Iraq War (1980s), 168
irrigation, 78–79, 177, 181, 188
Irish potato famine, 125
iron tools among the Dobe, 105
Irons, William G., 65, 151, 341
Iroquois tribe, 16, 355
Islam and Algerian uprising, 194
Islamic dietary rules, 21
Islamic marriage, 223
Islamic revolution (1979), 355–357
Israel, founding war, 253
Istanbul kinship, 211
Ituri Forest, Zaire, 5, 79

Jalonka, Eva, 38
Jamaica, 7
Japanese Ainu, 62, 99
Japanese peasantry, 195–197
John Frumm Cult, 355
Johnson, Gregory, 154
Johnson, Patricia, 285
joint family household, 236

Judaic dietary roles, 21
Ju/'hoansi. *See* Dobe.
jungle farming, 130–132. *See also* swidden plots.

Kalahari Desert ecosystem, 75. *See also* Dobe; Mbuti
    Pygmies.
the Kantu of West Kalimantan, Indonesia, 285
Kaobää, Yanomamö headman, 132, 133
Katchina societies (Hopi), 217
Kathmandu, 140, 141
the Kayapo of Brazil, 137, 138, 325, 369
the Kapauku of New Guinea, 288, 293
the Kekchi of Belize, 234
Kemalist feminism, 247
Kemp, William, 114
Kenya, 76. *See also* Ariaal; Boran; Rendille.
Khaldun, Ibn, 4, 242
Khan, leader among Turkmen, 308
Khomeini, Ayatollah, 354
kibbutzism (Israeli), 223
kidnapping and elopement, 226
Kili, Suna, 247
kindred, defined, 221
King, Jr., Martin Luther, 317
Kinsey Institute, 40
kinship
    among horticultural societies, 129
    defined, 208
    fictive, 211
    ideologies, 208
    systems, 208, 210
    terms and behavior, 208–209
the Kipsigis of Africa, 223
Kobe earthquake 1995, 364
Kofyar farmers of Nigeria, 234
Koko (gorilla), 44, 45
the Komanchi of Iran, 23, 156
Konner, Melvin, 290
Korean entrepreneurship, 296–297
Korr, Kenya, 165
the Kpelle of Central Liberia, 324
Kramer, Mark, 199
Kufr Qara, Palestine, 253
kula ring (Trobriand Islands), 290–291
the !Kung of Botswana, 61–62, 106, 302. *See also* Dobe.
Kurdish language, 55
Kurdish Liberation Movement, 55
Kwakiutl Indians, 17, 99
Kwong, Peter, 191, 192

labor
    and gender, 245–246
    in household, 284–286
    intensity, 287–288
    social division of, 242
    unpaid, women's, 286–287
lactase enzyme groupings, 249
Laderman, Carol, 8
land
    access, 193

    and ethnic survival, 254
    development in Wasco, California, 197–199
    ownership systems, 276–278
    reform in Chiapas, 281
land rights
    of Kayapo, 137–138
    of Yanomamö, 137–138
land use systems, 276–278
    and religion, 338–339
language
    and nationalism, 55–57
    and transmission of culture, 34
    as call system, 43
    as source of culture, 46–47
    discrete, 48
    human origin of, 46
    roots of, 43–44
    structure of, 47
Lansing, Stephen, 275
Lapp reindeer herders, 153
Las Madres de Plaza de Mayo, 318–319
law, defined, 322
Leach, E. R., 129
leadership and power, 306
learning
    age roles, 42–43
    and biology, 38–40
    as human distinguishing characteristic, 70
    behavior, 37
Lee, Richard B., 24, 103
*The Legal Rights of the Egyptian Woman in Theory and
    Practice,* 247
legal systems, 323–326
legitimacy, 316
leisure among Dobe, 108
Lek Dukagjin, 322
the Lele of Africa, 287, 288
Lengesen, Lugi, 165
Lennihan, Louise, 283
Lepowsky, Maria, 3, 303–305, 344
the Lese of Zaire, 79
Leslie, Paul, 77
Lesotho pastoralists, 273
levirate fatherhood, 163, 228
Lévi-Strauss, Claude, 210, 335
Liberian ethnic terrorism, 266
lifestyles, knowledge of other, 362
liminal state, 342
*The Limitations of the Comparative Method of
    Anthropology* (Boas), 17
lineage, defined, 218
lineages for peace, 326
lineal relatives, 212
lingua franca, 51
linguistic anthropology, defined, 6–7
linguistic borrowing, 51
Lizot, Jacques, 138
low energy budget of foragers, 96
Lyndon Johnson Cult, 355

the Maasai of Kenya, 158, 159
Manarella, 21
Malinowski, Bronislaw, 18–19, 23, 290, 350
malnutrition
    and available foods, 76
    mortality, 190
Mandarin dialect, 154
Mandela, Nelson, 317
the Maring of highland New Guinea, 348–349
marital rules, 228–233. *See also* marriage.
market economy and pastoralism, 166–167
market exchange, 288, 292–293
Marks, Jonathan, 248, 250
Marrett, R. R., 336
marriage, 16, 221–223, 224
    among the Pokot, 215
    and division of labor, 228
    as exchange, 225–227
    economics, 222, 224
Marsabit, 158
masculinity, 40–42
material culture and behavior, 6
matriclans, 218
matrifocal family household, 233
matrilateral, 212
matrilineal descent, 215, 216–217
matrilocal residence, 232
Marx, Karl, 16, 21, 272, 337
Marxist anthropology, 20–21
Mayan-Catholic religious ritual, 340
Mayan peasantry, 281
Mbuti Pygmies, 5, 93, 94, 96, 124–125, 292, 334, 336, 350
McMillan, Della, 12, 381, 382–385
Mead, Margaret, 18, 42
means of production, ownership of, 280–282
meat as delicacy (Dobe), 107
mechanization, 184–185
mechanical solidarity of society, 242
mediation, 324
medical anthropology, 377–378
Mehenna, Sohair, 295
Melanesian Pidgin English (Tok Pisin), 52
Memphis garbage strike, 256
menarche in Nepal, 144
Mendel, Gregor, 64
the Menkragnoti Kayapo in Brazil, 369. *See also* Kayapo.
Merlin, Francesca, 7
Mernissi, Fatima, 246
Mesoamerican society, 178
metallurgical technology, 184
Mexican peso collapse (1995), 364–365
McGovern, Thomas, 82
midwestern farm communities, 201–202
midwife practices, 8
migrant workers, 189–190
migration
    and knowledge, 362
    patterns, 152
milk brothers and sisters, 211

Milne Bay Province, 305
milpa economy in Guatemala, 338–339
mining in Amazon, 137
minority ethnic politics, 263–264. *See also* ethnicity.
the Miskito Indians of Nicaragua, 96, 97, 369
Miwok Indian moieties, 218
mobile food gathering, 98
    and foraging patterns, 105
    and seasonal resources, 115
modernization, impact on Inuit, 114–115
Moghadan, Valentine, 247
the Mongols of Central Asia, 154–155, 156
monoculture, 125–126
monogamous marriage, 16, 223, 230–231
monotheism, 337
the Mons of Thailand, 252
monsoons, in Nepal, 142
Montes Azules Biosphere Reserve, 281
"moots," 324
moral basis of state authority, 316
Moran, Emilio, 80–81
Morgan, Lewis Henry, 15, 16
Mormon
    church, 177
    colonization of Utah, 309
    ecosystem, 68–69
morphology of language, 47
Morren, George, 126, 127
mortality and war, 136
mortuary rites in New Guinea, 343, 344
Moslems in eastern Europe, 56, 264–266. *See also* Bosnia, Croatia.
the Mountain Ok people of New Guinea, 126
Moynihan, Daniel, 263
mukanda rite of passage, 342
Muller, Ronald E., 363
multilineal evolutionism, 20
multinational corporations, 363–365
the Mundurucu of the Amazon, 244
the Murgin of Australia, 328
Murphy, Robert, 193
Murray, Charles, 261
Muslim gender roles, 246–247. *See also* Moslems; Turkmen.
Myobacterium tuberculosis, 377

N!ai: The Story of a !Kung Woman, 110
name systems, and ethnicity, 265–266
Namibian independence, 110
Nash, June, 281
the Naskapi of Labrador, 347
nationalism
    defined, 262
    and ethnic conflict, 262
National Union of Tunisian Women, 246
Nations, James, 281
natural science paradigm, 14
natural selection, 5, 63
Navajo divorce, 223
Navarro, Marysa, 318–319

the Nayar of Kerala (India), 223, 233
the Nbemdu of Africa, 342
Ndeto Mountain camps, 159, 161
Neanderthal cerebral cortex, 46
negative reciprocity, 291–292
Negev shepherdesses, 164
neighborhoods
    among the Tamang, 142
    of the Polit, 214–215
Neitschmann, Bernard, 369
Neolithic Revolution, 84
neolocal residence, 232
Nepal. *See* Tamang of Nepal, 141.
Nepalese development, 380
Netsilik Eskimos, 102, 111–112
New Guinea
    language in, 48
    mortuary rites, 344
    peace in, 326
new-wave feminism (in Turkey), 247
New Woman Group (Egypt), 247
niche (species), 69
Noble, David, 362
nomadic societies, 153–155. *See also* pastoralism.
nonhuman communication, 44–45
nonunilineal descent groups, 213, 220–221
norms, of a society, 19
North American Free Trade Agreement (NAFTA), 281,
    364, 365
nucleation in cultural change, 85
the Nuer of the Sudan, 153, 218, 223, 324
Nugent, David, 316
the Nyae Nyae of Africa, 109

Obbo, Christine, 10
objectivity in anthropology, 9–10, 12
occupational subcastes, 260
Odum, Howard, 178
Ogbu, John, 261
Office of Management and Budget (OMB), 250
Ojibwa Indian, 218
the Ok of New Guinea, 126–127
Olweus, Dan, 39, 40
Onchocerciasis Control Program (OCP), 382–384
On the Origin of Species (Darwin), 4–5, 63
Opata Indians (Mexico), 278–280
organic solidarity of society, 242
The Origin of the Family, Private Property and the State
    (Engels), 16
ostracism, 114, 321–322
ototeman, or relative (Ojibwa), 218
Ottoman ethnic empire, 263
Our Woman in the Shari'a and in Society (El Haddad),
    246
Pahlavi, Muhammad Reza, 356
Pakistan, competition in, 310–311
Palawan Island, 100
Palestine ethnic survival, 254
Palestine Liberation Organization (PLO), 253
Papua New Guinea, 3, 7, 305. *See also* New Guinea.

parallel cousins, 212
participant observation, 23, 24
Pasternak, Burton, 26, 154, 183
pastoral households, 154
pastoralism, 74
    development of, 150–151
    in East Africa, 151
    specialized, 150
pastoral labor pooling, 283
pastoral land use, 277
the Pathans of Pakistan, 310
Patterns of Culture (Benedict), 17–18
Patterson, Penny, 44, 45
patriclans, 218
patrilatcrality, 212
patrilineal descent, 132, 141, 213–214
patrilocal residence in Timling, 143
PCBs (polychlorinated biphenyls), 374–375
peace, mechanisms of, 326
Peacenet, 366
Peacock, James, 386
peasantry, 139–140, 191–192, 280
peasant uprisings, 193, 194, 195
pebble mulching, 78
Pella Bay Inuit, 116
Penan Homeland (Borneo), 93
Perimetral Norte Highway, 137
Perón, Isabel, 318
personality of a society, 17–18
pharmacologically active plants, 346
phenotype, defined, 249
phonology, 47
physical anthropology, 5, 6
physical health and behavior, 39
physiology and limits on behavior, 39
pidgin, 52
pig feast exchange system, 290, 349
the Pokot of Kenya, 162, 214, 276
political alliances among Yanomamö, 135–136
political ecology, 78, 309–311
political organization, evolution of, 311–312
political process, access to, 303–306
politics of social control, 317
pollution, 362, 370–376
polyandry, 231, 236
polychlorinated biphenyls (PCBs), 374–375
polyculture, 125, 126
polyethnic societies, 252–254
polygamy, 231
polygyny, 236
polytheism, 337
population control, 109
population–food ratio (Inuit), 113
population–resource ratio among Dobe Ju/'hoansi, 108
postindustrial society, 362
postpartum taboo (Yanomamö), 133
potlatch exchange system, 290
power and authority, 306
power transmission systems, 184
poverty and class, 187, 191

primatology, 6
Principles of Professional Anthropology, 13
private land ownership, 278
procurement patterns, evolution of, 74–75
production (economic), 272
    organization of, 282–283
    per acre, 139
    productive strategies, 283–284
productive life span, 287
productive strategies, 283
productivity
    and gender, 284–286
    measurement of, 286–287
the profane, 335–336
prolactin and nurturing, 40
prostitutes, 11
protein resources, 135
The Protestant Ethic and the Spirit of Capitalism
        (Weber), 338
Protestantism in Guatemala, 338–339
Proto-Germanic language, 50, 52
Proto-Indo-European language, 50
public domain, 276–278
Pueblo peoples, 177, 215, 216, 217, 235, 348. See also
        Hopi.
purdah, 8

quality of life, among Dobe, 107
the Quashqai of Iran, 80, 156

Rabben, Linda, 138
race and ethnicity, 248–256
    in Accra, Ghana, 251
Radcliffe-Brown, Alfred Reginald, 19, 350
the Raikas of Western India, 156
rainfall in Kalahari, 103–104
Rahad irrigation project (Sudan), 188
rainforest
    agriculture, 124–125. See also Yanomamö.
    destruction, 366–370
Rajistan, 156
random sample, 27
Rassam, Amal, 28
rational economic decisions, 272
reciprocity, 288
    among foragers, 97
    among the Dobe Ju/'hansi, 106–107
    balanced, 290
    generalized, 289
    negative, 291–292
refugee camps, 190
Reinisch, June, 40
religion
    and disease spread, 351
    and land use, 338–339
    and resource management, 347–348
    as ideology, 334–335
    defined, 334
religion, functions of, 350–357
religious belief systems, 336–340

religious lineages (Turkmen), 309
religious ordeals, 341
remote sensing, 368–369
the Rendille of Kenya, 158, 159, 161, 162, 163
reproduction and wealth, 5–6
Republic of Botswana, 61–62. See also Dobe; !Kung.
Republic of Turkmenia, 307. See also Turkmen.
resilience
    and change, 102–103
    and stability of culture, 86
    in ecosystems, 67
resource
    access, 272, 275–282, 309–310
    depletion, 366–368
    fluctuation, 77
    recognition, 76
    redistribution, 288, 292
revitalization movements, 354
Reyna, Steven, 12
rigor, in anthropology, 12
"ring species," 64
rites
    of intensification, 343–345
    of passage, 43, 341–343
ritual
    defined, 340
    in religion, 340–347
    organization of, 345
    to reduce anxiety, 19
river blindness control, 382–384
Roman Catholic clergy, 347
Rostow, Walter, 363
Rumbaugh, Sue Savage, 44
rural starvation, 190
Russian peasantry, 194
Rutz, Henry, 302
Rwandan, ethnic terrorism, 263, 266
Rwandan fertility rate, 182

"the sacred," 334, 335–336
Safa, Helen, 40
Saffirio, John, 137
Sahelian famines, 125–126
Sahlins, Marshall, 109, 284, 288
the Saisai of New Guinea, 305
Salaff, Janet, 154–155
Salamon, Sonya, 200–202
salinization of soils, 181. See also irrigation.
the Samburu of Kenya, 158, 159, 161, 162, 163
same-sex marriage, 222
Samoa, 7
Samoan adolescence, 18, 42
sampling bias, 27
sampling universe, 27
Samurai warrior class, 62
Sanjek, Roger, 251
San Joaquin Valley agribusiness, 199
Sankoff, Gillian, 48
the San of the Kalahari Desert, 24, 85
Sarawak (Borneo), 93

Sarney, President, of Brazil, 137
satellite dishes, 365
satire and social control, 320–321
Saunders, Lucie, 295
savagery stage (Morgan), 16
Schama, Simon, 317
schizophrenia, 39
Schneider, Harold, 273
science in anthropology, 9–10
scientific theory, defined, 13, 14, 15
scramble competition, 310–311
seals as food, 112
seasonal change and swidden farming, 132
seasonality
    of food, 77, 101, 105
    of resources, 111–112, 115
seasonal migrations, 111–112
seasonal nomadism, 165
sedentary foraging, 99
sedentary pastoralism, 151
sedentism, 123, 126
segmentary lineages, 218
Semitic languages, 50–51
Sengül, 294
Serbians, 340
serial monogamy, 231
settlement patterns
    among foragers, 98–101
    among the Dobe, 105
    among the Inuit, 115
sex of researchers, and fieldwork, 27
sex ratio among Yanomamö, 133
sexuality
    and marriage in Nepal, 144–145
    in adolescence, Samoa, 42
sexual practices, and AIDS, 10–11
shabono villages, 132
shamanism, 345–346
shamans
    defined, 345
    in Nepal (bompos), 142
Shan dialect (Thai), 53
sharecropping, 140, 193
shared land use, 277
Shari'a, 246
sharing, 97. See also collectivizations; exchange of
    resources.
Sheridan, Thomas, 278–280
the Sherpa of Nepal, 141
Shi'a ritual, 341
the Shilluk of Sudan, 351–352
Shinohata, Japan, 195–197
Shoshone Indians, 77–78
shunning, 321–322
the Siane of New Guinea, 293
sibling marriage, 229
SIDA, 11. See AIDS.
sign language, 47–48
Simon, Herbert, 273
sisal culture in Brazil, 186–187

slash-and-burn agriculture, 125. See also swidden plots.
slavery, 262
Slobodkin, Lawrence S., 72
Smith, Adam, 272
snakeheads (Chinese immigrant procurers), 192
snowmobiles, 115, 116
social anthropology. See cultural anthropology.
social category, defined, 243
social change
    managing, 381
    sources of, 21
social class, defined, 257. See also class stratification.
social control
    among foragers, 98
    and religion, 352–354
    formal, 322–326
    informal, 320–322
social division of labor, 242–244
social integration and religion, 350
socialization
    defined, 37
    in adulthood, 43
    to violence, 134–135
social organization
    among foragers, 97–98
    among nomadic pastoralists, 153
    and horticulture, 128
    of Ariaal, 167–168
social practices of Dobe people, 105
social pressure, 320–321
social reciprocity, 97
social relations
    among the Inuit, 113–114
    and specialization, 186
social race, 250
social status, in sociolinguistics, 52–53
social structure, and norms, 19
society, defined, 19
sociobiology, 65
sociolinguistics, defined, 7, 52
Sorenson, Clark, 296, 297
the sororate, 228
South African treatment of Dobe, 103, 110
South African environmental rights, 372
South Turkana Ecosystem Project, 76
Soviet collectivization model, 188
specialization, 150, 185–186
    as danger, 8
    in cultural change, 83–89
    in pastoralism, 150
speciation, 64
speech community (dialects), defined, 54
speech patterns, female, 53–54
Spencer, Herbert, 15
spheres of exchange, 293
spiritual leaders (Turkmen), 309
Spiro, Milford, 14
squatter's rights, 276
stability and change, 102
stability of environment, 67, 181

state
    defined, 314
    evolution of, 315
    organization, 314–317
State University of New York (SUNY) at Binghamton, 76
status and pastoralism, 156–157
St. Bridget of Sweden, 351
stem family in Nepal, 144
Steward, Julian, 20
stock camp of Ariaal, 161
Sting, 138
stratification, 191
    among Yörük, 169–170
    and land ownership, 278–280
    by class, 256–257
    by race and ethnicity, 252
    caste, 259–260
    in cultural change, 84
    in India, 191
    in Wasco, California, 198–199
stratified sample, defined, 28
structural functionalism, 19. *See also* functionalism.
subincision (Aboriginal), 341
subsistence agriculture, 73–74, 122
    among Yanomamö, 129–137
substantivism, 273
Sudanese irrigation, 188
the Suku of Zaire, 232
the supernatural, 334
sustainable energy, 370
Swat, Pakistan, 310
swidden plots, 124–125, 132
syntax, 47

taboos, 337
Taher El Haddad Club, 246
Tainter, Joseph, 85
Taiwan, 26
the Tamang of Timling, Nepal, 129, 137, 140–145, 162, 223, 283
taro monoculture, 126–127
technology and environmental monitoring, 81
terms of address, 210
terms of reference, 210
testosterone and aggression, 39
the Thai of Thailand, 252
theism, defined, 337
theory and fieldwork, 23
Tiananmen Square demonstrations, 365
Tikopia (South Pacific), 230
time allocation, 24
Timling village of Nepal, 140–145
the Tiv of Nigeria, 218, 226, 277
the Tiwi of Australia, 85
tontine credit system, 274
Tonton Macoute, 354
totems, 218, 337
toxic disasters, 372, 374–376
toxic waste, 370–376
TransAmazon Highway and deforestation, 80

transhumance, 152, 165
transport, 367
    among Inuit, 112–113, 115
    and food, 78–79
travel and anthropology, 4
trekkers, in Nepal, 145
tribal hierarchies, 155–156
tribe, defined, 218
tribes and bands, 312
Trinidad, 5
Trobriand Islanders, 18–19, 225, 282, 293, 350
    kula rings among, 290–291
    marriage among, 223
the Tungus of Siberia, 345
Tunisian Association of Women Democrats, 246
the Tupinamba Brazilians, 41
the Turkana of Kenya, 76–77, 161, 162
Turkish entrepreneurship, 295
Turkish feminism, 247
Turkish language, 55
Turkish migrant laborers, 189–190, 252, 294
Turkish minority in Bulgaria, 263
the Turkmen of Iran, 151, 152, 326
Tylor, E. B., 229, 336
Tylor, Edward, 15, 16
Tyler, Steven, 12

Uganda, AIDS epidemic, 10–11
the Uktu of Hudson Bay, 113
underdevelopment, causes of, 21
unilineal descent groups, 213, 218–219
unilineal evolution, 16
United Nations Conference on Population in Cairo, 183
United Nations Development Program (UNDP), 382
United Nations Food and Agriculture Organization (FAO), 185
United States Agency for International Development (US AID), 382
untouchable castes, 259–260, 262
urbanization, 190
    of rural society, 197

the Vanatinai of New Guinea, 3, 303–305, 343, 344
Van Gennep, Arnold, 341
Vayda, Andrew, 327
vehicles, 367. *See also* transport.
vengeance, 321–322
Verdery, Katherine, 322
Vicos (Peru) project, 379, 386
Vikings in North Atlantic, 82–83
village social structure, Tamang, 142
violence, Yanomamö, 133–135
visiting, importance of to Dobe, 106
Volta Valley Authority (AVV) of Burkina Faso, 382–385
Vondal, Patricia, 295
Voudoon Church of Haiti, 336, 352

Wallace, Anthony, 354
warfare, 326–327
    among the Yanomamö, 133–135

and political organization, 312
warriors of Ariaal, 162
Wasco, California, 197–199
Washoe (chimpanzee), 44
the Waswanipi Cree Indians, 347
water and culture, in Kalahari, 75
waterlogged soils, 181. *See also* irrigation.
water management, 177
water table and pastoral adaptation, 150
wealth and pastoralism, 156–157
wealth and reproduction, 5–6
Weber, Max, 16, 337, 338, 350
Weinrich, Max, 50
Wells, Miriam, 193
Welsh language revived, 56
Weston, Kath, 212
Western hemisphere use of fire, 94
the Western Pueblo peoples, 277–278. *See also* Pueblo
    peoples.
White, Jenny, 211, 294, 295
White, Leslie, 20, 178
Wilk, Richard, 234
Williams, Walter, 41
Wilson, E. O., 65, 376
Wisner, Ben, 372
witchcraft, 336
Wolf, Eric, 194, 314
Women's Commission of the General Union of Tunisian
    Workers, 246
women's unpaid work, 286–287
wood fuel shortages, 179
World Bank, 12
    forecasts, 179

development strategy, 379
World Health Organization (WHO), 343
Worldwatch reports, 181
workday, defined, 288
Wovoka, 354

the Yakinankarate of Madagascar, 54
the Yanomamö of the Amazon, 9, 26–27, 37, 129–137,
    177, 209, 214, 219, 243, 244, 302, 324, 378, 380
    agriculture, 125
    fallow period, 180
    kinship, 132, 209–210
the Yayoi of Japan, 62
yeoman approach, 201
Yiddish language, 52
Yomut Turkmen (Iran), 37, 65, 66, 306–309
Yörük of Turkey, 157, 165–171, 209, 225, 226, 235, 251,
    321
    egalitarianism of, 165
    gender roles of, 145
    households among, 152, 284
Yugoslavia, dissolution of, 263

Zaire, 5
Zapatista revolt, 281
zar cult of the Sudan, 346
Zedong, Mao, 194
"Zero Grazing" (AIDS) campaign, 10–11
the Zhengs, 192
zombies, 353
Zuñi Indians, 17, 18